The Adolescent – A BOOK

OF READINGS *edited by*

JEROME M. SEIDMAN
MONTCLAIR STATE COLLEGE

Revised Edition

HOLT, RINEHART AND WINSTON, INC., New York

Preface to the Revised Edition

Almost a decade has passed since the selections for the first edition were compiled. In the intervening years much important work in adolescent psychology has been carried on: new areas of investigation have been opened, improved methods of research have been explored, new understandings gained. Hence the primary purpose for undertaking this revision is to provide interesting and useful examples of these new developments.

This new edition, like the first, is designed to be used either as a basic textbook or in conjunction with another text. It has the same structure as the first edition and the chapters are comparable as is the organization of the material. However, this edition is substantially changed from that published in 1953: thirty-nine of the seventy-two selections are new to this volume and all but five of the new selections have been published since 1955.

I am grateful to the authors and publishers of the selections for their kind permission to reprint them; specific acknowledgment is made with each reading. I wish to express warm appreciation to many colleagues and students who evaluated the selections in the first edition and suggested articles for this volume. Special thanks are extended to: Millie Almy, John J. DeBoer, Mitchell Dreese, Jerome D. Frank, Eugene L. Gaier, Susan W. Gray, Dale B. Harris, A. H. Maslow, Phoebe L. Overstreet, Frederic T. Schlamp, and Lois M. Stolz. I also wish to thank Margaret B. Turner and Ann E. Wilson for their proofreading. It is with particular pleasure that I acknowledge the help of my children, Robert and Alan, in the preparation of the index. Finally, for sharing in every stage of the development of this book, I am indebted to my wife, Cindy.

J. M. S.

Montclair, New Jersey
April 1960

Preface to the First Edition

This book aims to provide students in courses in adolescent development with a selection of the original contributions of specialists who have created or expanded the knowledge of the field. The topics and organization follow closely those of the most widely used textbooks. The authors included are those repeatedly cited in the texts; here, however, their contributions are presented in original form, with minimal abridgments. The book lends itself, therefore, to use as a basic textbook by those instructors who prefer having their students read original materials, and who, through their lectures and class discussions, elaborate and integrate the reading materials. On the other hand, when used with a text, this book eliminates the necessity of compiling lists of assignments for outside readings and simplifies the student's task of fulfilling these assignments—especially where library facilities are limited or course enrollments very large.

Many persons have helped make this book possible. For cooperation in my search for authoritative and readable material, I especially wish to thank Gordon W. Allport, Louise Bates Ames, John E. Anderson, Jessie M. Bierman, Glenn M. Blair, Peter Blos, Milton L. Blum, Charlotte Buhler, Kenneth B. Clark, Evelyn M. Duvall, Albert Ellis, E. Franklin Frazier, Karl C. Garrison, H. Harry Giles, A. Irving Hallowell, Dale B. Harris, Hugh Hartshorne, Robert J. Havighurst, Robert Hoppock, Elizabeth B. Hurlock, Wilson H. Ivins, Harold E. Jones, Lester A. Kirkendall, Clifford Kirkpatrick, Abraham E. Knepler, Wilbert J. McKeachie, Anne McKillop, A. H. Maslow, Max Meenes, Maude A. Merrill, Delbert C. Miller, Ralph H. Ojemann, Willard C. Olson, Benjamin Pasamanick, Harold B. Pepinsky, Louis E. Raths, Morton A. Seidenfeld, Ruth Strang, Harold C. Stuart, Percival M. Symonds, Hilda Taba, Florence M. Teagarden, Herbert Thelen, Charlotte Towle.

I am deeply grateful to the authors and publishers for permission to reprint the materials selected; specific acknowledgment is made in the headnote preceding each selection. I wish to thank Professor Theodore M. Newcomb for helping with problems of organization and content, and Professor Herbert Edwards for editorial assistance. I also wish to thank Charles E. Hilt, Myra D. Kimball, Marian H. Knapp, Hugh C. Lord, Earl H. Ramsay, and George R. Shaw for their very able proofreading. Finally, for sharing in virtually every stage of the planning and development of this book, I am greatly indebted to my wife, Cindy Seidman.

JEROME M. SEIDMAN

Orono, Maine
September 1953

Contents

Chapter Fourteen · The Adolescent in the Community

Part Five ▪ Interests, Attitudes, and Ideals

Chapter Fifteen · Interests

Chapter Sixteen · Religious Beliefs

Chapter Seventeen · Ideals and Values

Part One

....

ADOLESCENCE:
A PERIOD OF TRANSITION

Chapter One
THE CULTURE AND THE ADOLESCENT

Chapter Two
THE ADOLESCENT IN MODERN AMERICAN SOCIETY

Chapter Three
ADOLESCENTS WITH PROBLEMS

The Culture and the Adolescent

1

ADOLESCENCE THE HOPI WAY

by Laura Thompson and Alice Joseph

The behavior of adolescents is in large measure—if not predominantly —a product of society and its culture. To what extent do societies shape the behavior of their young people? In this brief excerpt from their book, Laura Thompson of McMurry, Hamstra, and Company and Alice Joseph of New York City show how Hopi Indian adolescent boys and girls living in northern Arizona learn their sex roles. By contrast, the selection provides a basis for understanding how our culture defines our own behavior. [From *The Hopi Way*, Chicago: University of Chicago Press, 1944, pp. 55-64. Reprinted by permission of the authors and the University of Chicago Press.]

The ceremonial initiation of the child into the *kachina* cult marks the second great crisis in his life cycle, the transition from Childhood to Youth. This first initiation . . . takes place every four years in February as a part of the Powamu or "Bean Dance," which is designed especially to speed the early stages of development and is marked by the forced growth of beans and corn in the *kivas* and their distribution to the young children by masked *kachinas*. As the birth rites introduced the child to his father, the Sun, and inaugurated a series of life-long, mutual obligations and privileges between himself and his father's clanspeople, so the *kachina* initiation introduces him to his ancestors, the *kachinas,* and sets up a pattern of regular, correlative obligations by which the *kachinas* give rain and thus food and other essentials to human welfare in exchange for prescribed ritual behavior. It also marks his adoption into another clan, namely that of the man and his sister who become his godfather and godfather's sister and sponsor him in his ceremonial career. Henceforth the child is considered to be related to these ceremonial kin and their clansmen and phratry members, as he is related to his father's clan, and with similar reciprocal obligations and privileges.

The child's godfather and aunt are chosen by the child's parents with regard to their ritual affiliations,[1] for a boy is expected in due course to join the secret societies to which his godfather belongs[2] and a girl those of her ceremonial aunt. Moreover, on Third Mesa the affiliation of the godfather in the *kachina* cult—whether with the Kachina Society in which the novices are whipped, or with the Powamu Society in which they are not—determines whether or not the child must go through the whipping ordeal.

Informants say that a "bad" boy is usually given a Kachina Society godfather and hence the initiation serves as a sanction for behavior in the case of the boys at least. It may be less potent in the case of the girls since, even if whipped, they are allowed to remain clothed and are dealt with much less severely than the boys.

The whipping rite (Eggan, 1933; Titiev, 1944, Chap. 9),* symbolizes the Hopi child training pattern. In it the Mother of the Kachinas, represented by a masked female figure, holds a large supply of yucca switches while the Whipper Kachinas, represented by masked male figures, apply them to the nude boy (or clothed girl) supported and shielded by his godfather and his godfather's sister. Both the boy and his godfather stand on a large sand painting which represents the Kachina Mother and the Whipper Kachinas, while a segmented line drawn from the *Kiva si'papu* southeastward shows the road of life with its four phases. Afterwards the Mother Kachina steps on to the sand painting and is whipped by the Whippers and then the Whippers whip each other.

This ceremony, in which the Mother Kachina may be interpreted

[1] The godfather and aunt are selected from a clan which is not affiliated with either the child's phratry or that of his father (Titiev, 1944, Chap. 1).*

[2] Apparently a boy may also join any society whose chief priest or priestess belongs to his own clan (Eggan, 1933, p. 68).

* For complete citation of references in parentheses, see bibliography at end of book.

from one point of view as symbolizing the mother, the Whipper Kachinas the maternal uncles, the godfather as the father, and the godaunt as the father's sister, illustrates dramatically the complementary functions of the maternal and paternal kin in steering the child along the road of life. It emphasizes especially the role of the Hopi mother as the source of order and control in the child's life, that of her brothers as her active partners in maintaining discipline, and that of the father and his sister as the child's supporters. It also shows the difference between the treatment of boys and girls. And finally, through the discipliners' castigating of one another, it shows that the adult pattern of social control is not one in which one group, namely the adult matrilineal kin, originate action and another group, namely the children, terminate it, but one in which each adult individual is expected to exercise a certain amount of control over the others. From now on the censorship of the group, i.e., public opinion, will gradually replace, to a considerable extent at least, the maternal household group as the principal negative sanction of the child's behavior. On the other hand, the positive role of his paternal kin in motivating his behavior will remain the same.

During the *kachina* initiation the child learns that the supernatural beings whom he has known from infancy as bringers of gifts and rain and also as dispensers of punishment, are really only people he knows dressed up to impersonate them, but he also learns of the *kachinas'* key role in the scheme of things and his own part in the cosmic exchange for the mutual welfare of all. His godfather gives him a new name and from now on he may participate in the *kachina* rites and gradually assume his share of responsibility for the great annual cycle of ceremonies which gives significance and zest to Hopi life. He has acquired a certain status in the tribe as a whole and may return to the Underworld when he dies (Eggan, 1933, p. 67).

Some time after his first initiation the boy is expected to join one or more secret societies usually those of his godfather, and the girl is expected to join those of her ceremonial aunt (Titiev, 1944, Chap. 2). Each of these has its own secret initiation which represents a variation on the general "rebirth" ceremonial pattern, the neophyte observing part of the ritual as well as certain tabus, having his head washed and receiving a new name (Eggan, 1933, p. 68). This means a gradual expansion of ties, responsibilities and creative activities especially for the boy since it opens the definitely male world of the *kiva* to him and a new field of esoteric knowledge. It also gives him a well defined place in the ceremonial organization of the village which tends to compensate for his position in the household group, to build up his self confidence, and to steer him toward the adult male role.

At about the age of eight the boy is expected to kill his first game, usually a rabbit, according to the rules of the chase, and consequently to acquire a "hunt" father and to be formally initiated as a hunter (Beaglehole, 1936, pp. 14-15; Parsons, 1925, p. 24).

With these changes in status, the boy is expected to increase the observance of certain "strength" building practices which were begun in childhood, including bathing in the spring before dawn, drinking "medicine water" (Parsons, 1925, p. 16), and long distance running. This Hopi ideal, taught him by his father, his grandfather and the village elders, is no longer practiced quite so rigorously as in the past when the boy was preparing to be a warrior and hunter of big game. It should be remembered that "strength" to the Hopi means strength of mind or will as well as of body (Kennard, 1937, p. 493), and the boy was and still is expected also to be happy, and to cultivate a "good heart" and the ability to concentrate in behalf of the common weal. This point is clarified by the following advice from a Hopi father to his son:

My child, tomorrow morning you will go for a bath. Just as the sun comes out you will pray (na'wakna) that your life shall be good. Then the sun will come out and give you good life. And you shall live happily. Here you happily will work for me and I'll eat those good things. With them I will grow strong. I shall continue to live well, I won't be sick. Going on (my road) I shall always be happy. And these people having something to live by will think (only) of continuing their good lives. And having made the good life for them, don't ever be mean (angry). Whoever is not mean will live long. Whoever is mean will surely die. Therefore anyone who is happy always sings. And so go take your bath. If you do that you will be strong, and your mothers and fathers (clouds, kachinas, the dead) will be happy when you work for them. They will be parents to your plants. One who lives thinking this way has a peaceful (hopi) life and is always happy (Kennard, 1937, p. 493).

The economic responsibilities of the boy during these years increase gradually. Whereas formerly his chores consisted mainly of helping his female relatives with water and fuel hauling, now he frequently accompanies his male relatives, particularly his father and grandfather, to the fields and sheep camps where his work changes with his growing skill from guarding the orchards and fields to helping with planting, harvesting and herding, and finally, at about the age of 14, to being able to take charge of his own herd (if he has one) and his mother's fields. In the winter months, when farm work is slack and the men gather in the *kivas*, he also learns the Hopi men's crafts—carding, spinning, and finally weaving, moccasin making and other handwork—to the accompaniment of story and song. The learning of all these skills contributes to his understanding of the Hopi Way, which is systematically taught him in *kiva* and camp. During long, quiet days and nights away from the distractions of the household, he is expected to master the secrets of his clan and society rituals and to learn the tribal lore.

The initiated boys form their own play groups from which the uninitiated as well as peers of the opposite sex, are usually excluded. These groups are spontaneous and unrestricted as to clan or other affiliations, as are all Hopi play groups. Most of the youths' play occurs in the late afternoon and evening after the day's work is done (Dennis, 1940, p. 49). Besides imported games such as basketball, which is very popular, the boys play a number of organized Hopi games, many of which are seasonal and competitive. An analysis of these reveals that rivalry is expressed between teams rather than individuals and in the form of running, throwing, shooting with arrows or darts, and striking or whipping balls or tops—activities which, according to Hopi ideology, have magical efficacy. Moreover, each activity occurs at the season of the year when it is part of the ceremonial pattern used as an aid in the fertilization and growth of crops. For example, the archery game (Dennis, 1940, pp. 59-60), in which two teams chosen alternately by leaders take turns shooting arrows at a rolling hoop, and which has to be won three times before the final victory is assured, is played only after the Niman ceremony in July, when bows and arrows are given as presents by the *kachinas* and is associated with the bringing of rain and speeding of maturation. Shinny (Dennis, 1940, p. 53), in which each team tries to make its own goal by striking a ball with a club, is played only after the Powamu in February when shinny balls and clubs are distributed, and is associated with the whipping or purification rites designed to aid the early stages of growth.

Besides providing a socially approved outlet for aggression, and the display of skill and initiative, the boys' games afford an opportunity for the expression of peer preferences. They also channelize sport into a pattern of give-and-take or reciprocity between two teams, neither of which can expect to win the goal (Dennis, 1940, p. 53) easily even with a high degree of skill and teamwork. Moreover, the interest is centered not so much on winning as on the actual playing of the game for its own sake, and even in the case of imported games such as baseball, there is little or no interest in the score.

Compared with the boys, the girls have few organized games and these are mainly non-seasonal. The girls rarely compete through opposing teams except in races such as the ceremonial Basket Race, but seem rather to follow either the big-girl-little-girl set-up of the girls' play groups or the cooperative pattern of the women's household groups. The former is illustrated by the Pursuit Game (Dennis, 1940, p. 64) and the latter by the Grinding Party (Dennis, 1940, p. 58). In the Pursuit Game the leader chases the other players along a complicated and twisted path marked in sand from the outside of the play area to the center, while any girl who steps off the path must drop out of the game. Here the guidance role of the mother and the difficult and centripetal life course of the Hopi girl are faithfully portrayed. On the other hand, at the Grinding Party, a group of girls grind together for several days, each girl working each day for a different relative who reciprocates by supplying her with corn. This takes place before the Niman ceremony and serves not only as a social occasion but also as a means of accomplishing necessary work in a pleasant manner.

. . . Hopi girls' play groups . . . provide an opportunity for the expression of verbal aggression in the form of mutual critcism and through this of the development on the part of the individual of an objective attitude toward her own and others' work, as well as for the expression of a sort of reciprocal praise pattern by which praise of another's efforts or disparagement of one's own calls for a compliment in return.

All these activities and learning processes are quite apart from the school experience which, although usually beginning in the Indian Service Day School at about the age of six and continuing until the age of 12 to 16, occupies only a small percentage of the child's time until, as is frequently the case in the communities studied, he leaves home at the secondary level to go to boarding school, either on or off the Reservation. When a boy is ready for boarding school, at about the age of 14, he is expected to have mastered the main adult male skills, especially farming (Watson and Pijoan, 1943, p. 33), as well as part of his share of the ceremonial. . . .

Although school attendance is not compulsory, it is urged by many of the village leaders and most Hopi boys and girls go to school for a period of from six to ten years. Regularity of attendance differs among families and villages, children in the more acculturated groups having the highest attendance records. When school

interferes too greatly with ceremonial or economic activities, however, the children are likely to drop out for two or three days. To
overcome this difficulty, last year the principal of the Polacca Day
School persuaded the First Mesa leaders to hold some of their cere-
monials on weekends, rather than during the week, and since this
time, he reports, regularity of attendance has increased.

In school the children are expected to acquire, first and foremost,
a speaking knowledge of the English language and also certain tools
of the White culture such as the three R's, together with a
knowledge of White ways which will be of use to them in their
future life on the Reservation. There is little interest among the
parents in many aspects of White culture included in the curriculum, and even some active opposition to such subjects as arts
and crafts, which many parents consider to be within the teaching
sphere of the clan and ceremonial groups. There is also some objection to the fact that school is coeducational, according to the
American pattern.

On the whole, the school experience to most Hopi stands out as
something unique and somewhat detached from the main stream of
their life careers. This seems to be true in spite of the fact that the
Indian Service administrators have succeeded, especially in the two
communities studied, in building up day schools which are definitely
progressive and, judged according to modern standards of pedagogi-
cal theory and practice, superior to most rural or even urban White
schools in the United States. They have spent a great deal of effort
in seeking, in accordance with the new Indian Service policy, to develop and establish a curriculum which ties in with the interests and
needs of the Hopi child and contributes creatively to his personality
development. Our study of the Hopi society and world view, however, has already revealed some of the problems which would probably baffle even the most liberal-minded and creative educators in
trying to put this policy into practice. As the study progresses, the
problems of the White school in Hopiland will become clearer.

To the little boy the early school experience, beginning just at
the time when he is allowed to accompany the men to the fields and
range during the period of expansion of mobility and interest from
the female to the male world, has the effect of curbing a newly developing freedom by drawing him into another restricted and largely
female-dominated situation (Birdwhistell, 1944, pp. 40-43). On the
other hand, for the little girl, who by the age of six is already carrying a considerable burden of work which limits her mobility and
play time, the school, in freeing her from childcare and housework

for part of the day and giving her time to associate with her peers, has a liberating effect. In spite of the fact that outside of school hours she is expected to continue her nursemaid duties and to start learning to grind, cook and tend the household fire (Dennis, 1940, p. 84), her work is still comparatively light, and the early school years are for her a period of greater freedom than she has had before or will have again for many years, if ever.

This period, however, does not last long. When the girl is about ten years old, an age formerly marked by a pre-puberty ceremony in which she ground corn for one day in the house of her paternal grandmother and had her hair done up for the first time (Beaglehole and Beaglehole, 1935, p. 44), her home duties increase and gradually she loses her freedom of mobility in the village and most of her leisure (Dennis, 1940, pp. 84-85). Now she begins to assume her share of the laborious daily grinding and of the complicated Hopi cookery, which occupy much of the adult woman's attention in Hopiland. By the 15th year, that is, about the time when some Hopi girls leave home to go to boarding school, she is expected to have mastered the preparation of the most difficult Hopi dishes and to have started, at least, to learn the craft techniques of the women, namely pottery making, basketry and plaquework, depending on her mesa affiliations.

From her 12th year until marriage, which may occur as early as the 17th year (Dennis, 1940, p. 85) for either sex, a Hopi girl is not supposed to go out unless chaperoned by an older woman, although this prohibition is being relaxed somewhat now in some Hopi families, and soon after the onset of the menses she is expected, in some of the more conservative families, including many on First Mesa, to go through an adolescence rite somewhat like the pre-puberty ceremony but distinguished by its greater complexity and by a four day grinding ordeal (Beaglehole and Beaglehole, 1935, p. 45; Stephen, 1936, pp. xxviii, 139-143; Parsons, 1939, p. 58). During this period she is shaded from the sun "like a baby," she eats no meat or salt and she uses a special body scratcher. On the fifth day her hair is washed and she receives a new name and wears her paternal aunt's clothes. Formerly, at this time, she assumed the squash blossom hair dress which she wore until marriage, but [now] this custom is rarely observed; most Hopi girls wear their hair cut short according to the American mode.

The girl usually begins to be courted at about this time or a little later. She is expected to encourage the attentions of an eligible young man of good character whom she favors in various socially

approved ways, e.g., by presenting him with a gift of specially prepared food on certain occasions such as a Rabbit Dance, Bean
Dance or "Spinach" Gathering (Titiev, 1944, Chaps. 3 and 10),
and she is expected to discourage the attentions of all married men,
widowers and divorcés, and also all men and boys who are considered to be lazy or "bad" or who either belong to her own clan and
phratry or her father's and who fall thereby within the Hopi incest
tabu. Ideally the girl, but not the boy, is supposed to remain chaste
both before and after marriage, but actually, although irregularities
on the part of a girl are penalized by gossip, scolding and even
whipping in some cases, apparently a considerable amount of covert
premarital sex experimentation on the part of both sexes occurs and
is expected, the boy seeking the girl out in her home after her family has retired (Titiev, 1944, Chap. 3; Beaglehole and Beaglehole,
1935, p. 62) and reciprocating her favors with gifts, with the expectation that if she becomes pregnant and wishes to marry him he may
be required to marry her. On the other hand, a young man may
also visit widows, divorcées and married women (though more
rarely), with whom he will not be in danger of becoming involved.
For the first marriage of a Hopi of either sex is expected to be (and
usually is) with a person who has never been married before (Beaglehole, 1935), since the wedding garments of the bride and the
wedding plaque of the groom, necessary according to Hopi ideology
for a safe passage to the Underworld after death (Beaglehole and
Beaglehole, 1935, p. 46), may be acquired only in connection with
the elaborate rites of a first marriage. It is believed that those who
violate this tabu will be punished by having to carry a heavily
loaded basket on the journey to the house of the dead (Titiev,
1944, Chap. 3).

Thus by the time a young Hopi, whether boy or girl, is 15 or 16,
besides having attained physical maturity, he is expected to have
mastered the technical skills and to have gained the self control and
sophistication of the Hopi Way so that he will have completed the
requirements of the Youth phase of life's journey and be prepared
to take on the full responsibilities of adulthood.

FROM YOUTH TO ADULTHOOD

The transition from Youth to Adulthood is marked not by a single crisis as is the passage from Childhood to Youth, but by a series
of crises involving adolescence and marriage ceremonies for both

sexes and also, for the girls, rites which accompany the birth of the first child. The girls' puberty rites take place some time before the corresponding adolescence ceremonies for the boys, which are expected to occur between the age of 15 and 20 years and usually precede marriage.

Practically all Hopi youths go through this second initiation. The ceremony takes the form of an introduction into one of four tribal secret societies, . . . conducting the annual Wuwuchim (Grown Man) ceremony, of which it is periodically a part, and it is a prerequisite to membership in the tribewide Soyal Society which controls the supremely important Winter Solstice ceremony. Hence it is frequently referred to as the tribal initiation (Stephen, 1936, pp. 957-992; Parson, 1939, p. 866).

Each of the four societies has a different role in the ceremonial system, [two] being closely associated with war, hunting and death, and [two] with fertility. Each has its "home" in the Underworld whence its members are believed to repair after this life. A young man is expected to join the society to which his godfather (who sponsors him as he did at the first or *kachina* initiation) belongs and thus to establish his position in the Underworld.

The boys' adolescent rite is one of the most complicated of all Hopi ceremonies, and no outsider has witnessed its most esoteric parts. In connection with the annual "New Fire" ceremony, it seems to emphasize the death and rebirth motif of Hopi ideology on not only an individual but also a cosmic scale, the youth apparently actually undergoing a realistically dramatized death and introduction to the spirits of the dead. He is then born again (Titiev, 1944, Chap. 10), delivered by the Dawn Woman (a major deity), a concept linked with that of Emergence from the Sipapu, and he receives a new name and is aided symbolically by his godfather to grow up to full, vigorous manhood.

With the second initiation the youth is expected suddenly to become a man, with the responsibilities and privileges of manhood, to eschew quarreling and petty fights and to follow assiduously the Hopi Way. (It should be noted that no such injunction is placed on the girl in connection with her adolescent rite). He may now take part in dangerous missions on behalf of the group, such as the salt and trading expeditions which formerly reestablished contact with the Underworld (Titiev, 1937, p. 244) and in the crucial Winter Solstice rites.

In the past his career in defensive warfare began at this time and, with the taking of his first scalp, he underwent another initiation of the "rebirth" type, marking his acquisition of warrior status (Bea-glehole and Beaglehole, 1935, pp. 23-24). It is interesting to note that the "prayer" or "wish" for the warrior neophyte was that he would be rich, "happy with women," successful in war, and free from evil spirits and witchcraft; that he would live a long life; and that there would be rain, fertility and happiness.

By the time a young person of either sex is about 20 years old he is expected to marry, although many young men and also some girls marry at a later age, and a few men do not marry at all. Bache-lors . . . over 30 are rare in Hopiland, and spinisters are unknown (Titiev, 1944, Chap. 3; Beaglehole, 1935, p. 50). In this matrilineal, matrilocal society, where adult males outnumber adult females, it is said that some men cannot get spouses on account of "defec-tive speech or singular appearance" (Titiev, 1944, Chap. 3).

Although young people are advised by their parents, uncles and clan heads to select mates who are industrious, thrifty, reliable, and even-tempered, and who belong to families of some means and good repute, there is no compulsion regarding the choice. The selection of a spouse, within the limits imposed by the incest tabu and the "basket carrier" tabu is left to the individual, each sex being free to accept or reject the advances of the other, and the girl as well as the young man having socially accepted and formalized patterns of behavior by which she may make known her preference or propose marriage.

A Hopi wedding is an important ceremonial, economic and social occasion, lasting several weeks or even months and involving most of the members of the inter-marrying clans, as well as practically all the villagers and usually individuals from other villages. It centers in the correlative exchange of bridal garments, supplied by the groom's relatives and made by the men of the village, for food and plaques supplied by the bride's relatives and prepared to a considerable ex-tent by the bride. As has been noted, the bridal garments and plaques are believed to be necessary to the bride and groom re-spectively for safe passage to the Underworld, and their significance emphasizes the preparatory nature of the wedding rites in respect to the phases of life cycle that are to come, particularly after death. The magical function especially of the wedding garments renders their acquisition through the prescribed long and arduous rites indis-pensable to a Hopi woman. And it is mainly for this reason that most Hopi are married for the first time according to the Hopi Way, even though they may also go through a civil ceremony as well (Beaglehole, 1935, p. 47; Parsons, 1925, pp. 21-22). Moreover since only one wedding outfit is needed per person, an individual goes through the Hopi marriage rites only once, regardless of how many times he may wed.

The actual marriage rites are initiated by the bride's four-day grinding ordeal which takes place in the household of the groom's mother. During this time a mock attack is made on the bride and the groom's parents by the groom's paternal aunts who, by means of water-pouring and mud-throwing, formally express their "anger" over the "loss" of their "sweetheart" (Titiev, 1944, Chap. 3; Parsons, 1925, pp. 34, 71). On the fourth day the heads of the bridal pair are washed in one basin by their mothers, the couple prays to the Sun and henceforth they may sleep together. However, the bride remains in her mother-in-law's house, doing the major part of the cooking, until the long process of spinning, carding and weaving her nuptial costume has been completed and then, clad in her new garments, she returns to her mother's house. A final exchange of food gifts between the intermarrying families concludes the ceremony and the groom, bringing a share of his father's property, including part of his herd if he has one (Titiev, 1944, Chap. 2), takes up residence in his mother-in-law's household, and assumes the difficult role of a Hopi son-in-law. Since he now begins to work the clan lands of his wife and to contribute most if not all the yield to her household rather than that of his mother, the bride's household gains economically by the marriage while the groom's suffers a corresponding loss (Titiev, 1944, Chap. 3).

Before or soon after the wedding rites have been completed the bride is expected to become pregnant, although it is not uncommon for a girl to bear a child before marriage. During pregnancy both parents are expected to observe certain tabus, and continence during gestation is apparently the ideal (Titiev, 1944, Chap. 2). Although the marriage rites prepare a woman properly for the afterlife and raise her status in the clan and the village, it is with the birth of a child, especially a girl, that she fulfills the aim toward which her whole existence is oriented, namely the perpetuation of life—the life of the clan. As has been noted, children are welcomed into the Hopi household and a family increases a woman's prestige. The central importance among the Hopi of the female function of child-bearing and the perpetuation of life is stressed in every phase of the culture.

Although matrilocal residence is still the rule (Beaglehole, 1935, pp. 45-46), there is a tendency in Hopiland today for a young man to build his wife a house of her own after the birth of two or three children.[3] But whether or not the couple establish a separate residence, the ties of a daughter with her mother, sisters, and clansmen remain paramount throughout life and those with her husband and his relatives, secondary. If the union endures, however, a man tends to identify himself more and more with his wife's household, fulfilling at the same time his ceremonial and economic responsibilities toward his ancestral household and clan.

Notwithstanding the fact that the wife's position in the home is socially and economically much more stable and emotionally more secure than that of her husband, the relationship between spouses tends to be an equalitarian one, with the emphasis on individual freedom within the limits of the Hopi Way, which is so characteristic of Hopi interpersonal relations. Hopi spouses rarely make decisions for each other and, if marital obligations be fulfilled, each tends to allow the other to follow his inclinations, even in such vital matters as religion. Hence, it sometimes happens that the wife, but not the husband, officially becomes a Christian or (less frequently) vice versa.

Moreover, either spouse is free to terminate the relationship at will, the wife by putting her husband's personal possessions outside the door of her home, the husband by moving to his mother's or sister's house or that of another woman. In spite of the comparative lack of restrictions and social censorship in regard to divorce, it is interesting to note that apparently about two-thirds of the first marriages in Hopiland are stable, the remaining third being characterized by one or more divorces, most frequently occasioned by extra-marital relationships on the part of one or the other partner (Beaglehole, 1935, pp. 45-46). Opportunities for such relationships occur especially when a man is away from home at sheep or field camp and when he is sleeping in the *kiva* during his wife's 30 to 40 day confinement or during a ceremony when participants are supposed to observe a period of ritual continence varying in length from 13 to 20 days (F. Eggan, personal communication).

In the case of divorce, each party retains his property, the young children remaining with the mother, and the older ones, although free to follow either parent, usually staying also. Since a woman with her house, clan lands and clan backing is not necessarily dependent on her husband so far as her material welfare is concerned, divorce does not disrupt the household organization.

---

[3] The wife helps in building the house and is considered to be the owner. Upon her death it is inherited by her female heirs (Titiev, 1944, Chap. 2).

Divorce is often followed by remarriage but frequent divorce and remarriage on the part of either sex results in a loss of respect in the community, social censorship being somewhat more tolerant in the case of a man than a woman.

·············· 2 ··············

A COMPARISON OF SOCIAL ATTITUDES AMONG

AMERICAN AND GERMAN YOUTH

by Donald V. McGranahan

To what extent do the social attitudes of adolescents differ from one society to another? This is the question that Donald V. McGranahan, a special adviser at the United Nations, attempts to answer. In the selection that follows he presents the results of a study he made in the United States and Germany directly after the fall of the Nazi regime. [From *Journal of Abnormal and Social Psychology,* 1946, *41,* 245-257. Reprinted by permission of the author and the American Psychological Association, Inc. Some of the footnotes have been omitted.]

The psychological study of nations is handicapped by the lack of any systematic frame of reference. To determine the extent to which an individual is neurotic or submissive or aggressive, we can compare his behavior with the norm of his group, by means of standardized tests and observational methods, and note the degree of deviation. There are as yet, however, no international norms in psychology by which to judge the attitudes and traits of character of the people of an entire nation. Nor are there good prospects for such norms in the near future. Under these circumstances, comparable data from at least one's own country can provide a valuable point of reference. Without some empirical guide of this type, the psychologist who studies foreign character is apt to fall easy victim to the emotional forces that pervade this field, his interpretations of his research data serving only to confirm his prejudices and preconceived ideas.

The following study is to be considered a limited experiment in this field of comparative national psychology. It represents an attempt to obtain comparable data on certain broad moral and social aspects of personality among German and American youth, without dwelling on the more obvious political differences.

METHODS AND PROCEDURES

The data were obtained through anonymous questionnaires, a procedure that has been found useful in getting German youth to overcome their anxiety about expressing personal opinions. Even so, it must be realized that certain of the differences found would probably be greater if the German tests were not given under the circumstances of U.S. occupation, since German youth have a strong propensity to conform to what they consider to be the official creed of their new rulers. In the case of all German questions and nearly all American questions used, the form was headed by the statement: "We are interested to learn what young people your age are thinking. No one of you will be asked for your name. You have an opportunity to express your opinion freely and without restraint." The only background information requested was age, sex, religion, and father's occupation. Brief instructions were given on how to fill out the form.

In a number of questions, a conflict of values was set up. We can assume that both American and German youth will approve of patriotism, obedience, justice to individuals, and the like. It is in the relative status of such values that the chief differences presumably lie.

In the United States, the questionnaire was given in November, 1945, to 1600 high-school students between the ages of 14 and 18 in the following places: Malden, Massachusetts; Lowell, Massachusetts; Concord, Massachusetts; Brooklyn, New York; Toledo, Ohio; and Oak Park, a suburb of Chicago. The data for each city were separately analyzed. In addition, a stratified sample was obtained by selecting 200 cases at random so as to fulfill the following requirements: Jewish—7 per cent, Catholic—28 per cent, Protestant et al. —65 per cent; boys—50 per cent, girls—50 per cent; upper economic level—20 per cent, middle economic level—50 per cent, lower economic level—30 per cent (roughly judged by father's occupation). The youth were also equally divided with respect to lower and higher age groups within the range. This sample, considered to be fairly representative of urban and suburban youth in eastern and middle western U.S.A., will be used in most comparisons with the German youth, although certain other data will also be called in.

The German sample that plays the largest role in the study was a group of 191 youth, aged 14-18, from the town of Bad Homburg. Their names were taken at random from the food-rationing cards, and they were summoned through the Burgomeister to take the test in late November, 1945. Bad Homburg is a fairly well-to-do town just outside Frankfurt, once a favorite resort place. The youth indicated that their fathers were mostly skilled artisans, merchants and tradesmen, and "civil servants." Since Bad Homburg probably corresponds more closely to Oak Park, a well-to-do suburb of Chicago, than to any of the other U.S. towns or cities, the Oak Park data (163 cases) will also be used for comparison. The Bad Homburg sample contained 94 boys and 97 girls; 106 Protestants ("evangelisch"), 78 Catholics, and 7 miscellaneous (1 Jew). The age distribution was slightly weighted in the 16- and 17-year groups, and weak in 18-year-olds. Official Nazi records indicate that, in terms of party membership, Bad Homburg was a normal town. In attitude questions that have been asked both in Bad Homburg and in other German communities, the distribution of answers has been remarkably uniform. For example, in the question as to whether Germany needs a strong new "Fuehrer" in order to recover, 74 per cent of the boys and 90 per cent of the girls agreed in Bad Homburg, as compared with 73 per cent of the boys and 88 per cent of the girls in Offenbach, a considerably more industrial suburb of Frankfurt on the other side of town. However, it is obvious that Bad Homburg youth cannot be considered representative of youth in all areas and all types of community in Germany today.

The Bad Homburg youth were broken down into three groups for further comparison: a "Nazi" group, an "anti-Nazi" group, and a middle group. This was done by dividing the youth on the basis of answers to two questions that have been tested and found useful in differentiating *political* Nazis from *political* anti-Nazis: "Do you believe that National Socialism was a bad idea, or a good idea badly carried out?" "Was Hitler a bad person, or a good person who had bad advisers?" The anti-Nazis were defined as those who chose the first alternative in both questions, or took one first alternative and did not answer the other question. The Nazis were defined as those who favored the second alternatives. The middle group consisted of those who checked the two questions inconsistently. It must be realized that this procedure, which brought forth 55 anti-Nazis, 81 Nazis, and 55 middle cases, is a purely arbitrary way of chopping up a continuum. By more rigorous or less rigorous criteria, the size of the categories could be changed. German youth today do not divide easily into Nazis and anti-Nazis, but are in great majority confused, holding both pro-Nazi and anti-Nazi views, in one or another proportion. The pure type who whole-heartedly defends or whole-heartedly rejects all of National Socialism is rare.

The anti-Nazi group, so defined, contained 27 boys, 28 girls; 23 Protestants, 30 Catholics. The Nazi group contained 36 boys, 45 girls; 53 Protestants, 26 Catholics. The tendency for boys and Catholics to be somewhat more anti-Nazi than girls and Protestants has been found in other attitude studies in German towns.

Samples of German youth from Friedberg and Offenbach have also been used to a slight extent in this report. Studies of the attitudes of these groups have already been reported (McGranahan and Janowitz, 1946). For lack of available data, Friedberg and Offenbach youth have not been divided into Nazis and anti-Nazis.

Among other difficulties of procedure, the matter of translation presented a considerable problem. Bilingual experts, it has been found, rarely agree on the exact translation from English into German of attitude questions. The more basic difficulty lies in the fact that so frequently there is no exact German equivalent of the English meaning ("fair play," "bully," "tolerance," etc.). Even where there appears to be a simple German equivalent, as in "crime"—"Verbrechen," it may be argued that the German phrase has a context of meaning, a connotation derived from German life, that sets it off from the English phrase. Since it is well known that an apparently small difference of meaning may have a considerable effect on the results of an opinion poll or attitude test, one may ask whether it is theoretically feasible and possible to make a comparative attitude study by means of a translated questionnaire. The difficulties should be acknowledged, but they are not prohibitory. Culturally conditioned differences in meaning hold for objects and acts, as well as words, and are involved in all comparative psychological analysis. It is felt that if words can be found in German and English that are simple, direct, and conventional references, denoting the same type of objective fact or situation, then inevitable differences in connotative meaning should not be too great a cause for concern. Judging from written-in comments, most of the difficulties in wording in this study arose from ambiguities that appeared equally in the English and the German form—a result of the fact that it was not possible to do careful pre-testing of the majority of the questions.

THE STATE AND THE INDIVIDUAL

According to Gertrude Stein, the most important thing to teach Germans is disobedience. More prosaically stated, the German is noted for his unquestioning obedience to authority, his failure to exercise individual responsibility and act on the basis of independent moral judgment. In questions where individualistic action is opposed to the authority and dignity of the state, German youth differ in a way consistent with this view, although a number of the more sophisticated ones were undoubtedly cognizant of the "American" answer.

QUESTION 1

"DO YOU THINK THE AMERICAN (GERMAN) SOLDIER WHO REFUSED, DURING THE WAR, TO OBEY AN ORDER TO SHOOT AN INNOCENT PRISONER WAS JUSTIFIED?"

Percentages

	Yes	No	N.A.
U. S. Sample	68	29	3
Oak Park	84	14	2
Bad Homburg Sample	50	44	6
Bad Homburg anti-Nazis	56	35	9
Bad Homburg Nazis	46	50	4

QUESTION 2

"SHOULD PEOPLE WHO UNJUSTLY CRITICIZE THE GOVERNMENT OF A COUNTRY BE THROWN IN JAIL?"

Percentages

	Yes	No	N.A.
U. S. Sample	22	77	1
Oak Park	21	78	1
Bad Homburg Sample	36	57	7
Bad Homburg anti-Nazis	24	67	9
Bad Homburg Nazis	46	53	1

German philosophy was succinctly expressed by several boys who wrote in the comment, "Befehl ist Befehl," in answer to the first question. In both questions, the anti-Nazis are closer to the American norm than the Nazis. Note, however, that in these results, as well as in the results of other questions in this study, "Fascist" and "democratic" attitudes appear by no means perfectly correlated with Fascist and democratic political loyalties. One may ponder the fact that such a sizable element of American youth, as well as many German anti-Nazis, are disposed toward throwing a person in jail for the sin of making an unjust criticism of the government.

The following data suggest that the American-German difference in attitude toward authority is not peculiar to matters of state authority, but applies to the simplest types of social relation.

QUESTION 3

"WHICH OF THESE BOYS IN YOUR OPINION IS THE WORSE? (a) THE BOY WHO TYRANNIZES AND BEATS UP SMALLER CHILDREN. (b) THE BOY WHO DISOBEYS HIS SUPERIORS"

Percentages

	(a)	(b)	N.A. or "Equal"
U. S. Sample	68	29	3
Oak Park	85	13	2
Bad Homburg Sample	41	30	29
Bad Homburg anti-Nazis	49	22	29
Bad Homburg Nazis	30	42	28

A large number of German youth found it impossible to make a decision in this question and answered "equal." [1]

With submissiveness to state authority usually goes the attitude that the state is wise beyond individuals, understands what is "good for the masses," and should accordingly exercise strict control over the press and other media of information. (Captured directives from the German Propaganda Ministry have revealed that the Nazis carried propaganda control to a more severe degree than

[1] It should be noted that in this question, the Oak Park high-school students chose the first alternative 17 per cent more often than the "U.S. Sample." In several other questions, also, the Oak Park children, and to a somewhat lesser extent the Malden high-school children, differ from the Germans considerably more than do the children in the overall sample. The children in the poorer high schools in Lowell, Brooklyn, and Toledo tend to diverge from the U. S. sample in the direction of the Germans. The economic and educational backgrounds of the parents may be a partial reason for these differences, and also the fact that the poorer groups contain a larger proportion of immigrant stock which may carry the influence of continental tradition, particularly in matters of personal and family relations.

had even been imagined.) While Germans today have had good reason to question the ultimate wisdom of the state and the value of
intellectual regimentation, the youth are still hesitant about
granting newspapers independence and democratic freedom of expression. They also feel that the common man is stupid and incapable of thinking for himself.

QUESTION 4

"IN YOUR OPINION SHOULD NEWSPAPERS WRITE (a) WHAT THEY WISH, OR
(b) ONLY WHAT IS FOR THE GOOD OF THE PEOPLE?"

Percentages

	(a)	(b)	N.A.
U. S. Sample	65	33	2
Oak Park	81	17	2
Bad Homburg Sample	51	43	6
Bad Homburg anti-Nazis	64	29	7
Bad Homburg Nazis	35	63	2

QUESTION 5

"THE AVERAGE MAN IS STUPID AND EASILY MISLED BY PROPAGANDA"

Percentages

	Agree	Disagree	N.A.
U. S. Sample	54	45	1
Offenbach Sample	86	11	3
(N=256)			

As indicated by comments in Question 4, a number of American
youth, as well as some anti-Nazis, favored the second alternative because they could not allow that anti-democratic newspapers
should have the democratic privilege to publish what they wish.

In Question 5, Americans occasionally remarked that the common man was easily misled by propaganda, but not stupid, a distinction the Germans did not make. Average German young people
appear to have a remarkably uniform contempt for the mental capacity of the average person. Such lack of faith in their fellow coun-
trymen is doubtless one of the reasons why many Germans have misgivings about the possibilities of democracy in their country, and
feel that Germany needs a strong new Fuehrer. The many anti-
Nazis who take such a position say that this time they want a "good
Fuehrer."

The Hitler regime gained notoriety for its arbitrary and brutal treatment of individuals. Foreign observers express the view that Germans in general have a sadistic tendency and personally approve of such action by the state. Adult anti-Nazis, on the other hand, attribute sadism only to the Nazi leadership, and maintain that the average German is a humane, considerate person who does not approve of brutality, although he may not take action against it because of his habits of obedience.[2] Two questions were included in an attempt to deal with this issue.

QUESTION 6

"DO YOU THINK IT RIGHT TO MAKE ONE PERSON SUFFER IN A MEDICAL EXPERIMENT IF THE RESULTS WILL BENEFIT THE WHOLE NATION?"

Percentages

	Yes	No	N.A.
U. S. Sample	60	38	2
Oak Park	59	40	1
Bad Homburg Sample	49	42	9
Bad Homburg anti-Nazis	27	60	13
Bad Homburg Nazis	59	37	4

QUESTION 7

"DO YOU BELIEVE THAT A CRIMINAL WHO REFUSES TO GIVE THE NAMES OF HIS ACCOMPLICES SHOULD BE BEATEN UNTIL HE CONFESSES?"

Percentages

	Yes	No	N.A.
U. S. Sample	8	87	5
Oak Park	6	94	0
Bad Homburg Sample	15	78	7
Bad Homburg anti-Nazis	24	69	7
Bad Homburg Nazis	11	89	0

The data do not indicate any significant difference in "humanitarian" feelings between the Germans and the Americans on these questions. The largest differences are actually between the German

[2] These observations are based on a study made by the author on a group of 30 selected and confirmed adult anti-Nazis. Questioned on the average German's "worst characteristic," they agreed almost unanimously that it was his extreme obedience and "susceptibility to influence." Qualities of brutality, cruelty, over-bearingness and the like were associated only with the Nazi leaders, and special groups like the SS. The German's obedience and susceptibility to influence were used to explain, (a) why he fell victim to a brutal Fascist regime in the past, and (b) why he could not be democratic in the future.

Nazis and anti-Nazis, with the Nazis in both cases being closer to the American figures. However, certain complications unfortunately entered into these questions to give the results a dubious value. In Question 6, a number of youth, both German and American, commented that the medical experimentation was justified only if the subject voluntarily submitted himself to it. The question was thus ambiguous in both languages, some subjects interpreting it in the sense of heroic self-sacrifice, and others considering it to refer to cold-blooded practices such as those carried out in German concentration camps against the victim's will (the ambiguity centered about the word "make"). In Question 7, the complication lay in the fact that in Germany today the word "criminal" is being most widely used to refer to "Nazi criminals," with whom the more Nazi-minded youth might be expected to have considerable sympathy.[3] Another factor in German answers to Question 7, indicated by spontaneous comment, was the belief that confessing accomplices violated the code of "Kameraderie."

ATTITUDES TOWARD FAMILY AUTHORITY

According to a plausible genetic view, German submissiveness to authority in general is derived in good part from childhood training in family life under an authoritarian, dictatorial father. The following data suggest large differences in German and American attitudes regarding family authority.

QUESTION 8

"DO YOU THINK A BOY IS JUSTIFIED IN RUNNING AWAY FROM HOME IF HIS FATHER IS CRUEL AND BRUTAL?"

	Yes	No	N.A.
U. S. Sample	68	30	2
Oak Park	80	19	1
Bad Homburg Sample	45	50	5
Bad Homburg anti-Nazis	27	67	6
Bad Homburg Nazis	51	48	1

[3] It should be noted that in Question 3, which sets up a conflict between obedience to authority and humanitarian, fair-play attitudes, and which does not involve the complications apparent in Questions 6 and 7, there is a clear trend on the part of the Germans, and specifically of the Nazi youth, to favor obedience considerably more than the Americans do.

QUESTION 9

"DO OLDER BROTHERS HAVE THE RIGHT TO GIVE ORDERS TO YOUNGER BROTHERS
AND OBTAIN OBEDIENCE WITH FORCE?"

Percentages

	Yes	No	N.A.
U. S. Sample	9	90	1
Oak Park	8	90	2
Bad Homburg Sample	23	72	5
Bad Homburg anti-Nazis	22	76	2
Bad Homburg Nazis	25	74	1

QUESTION 10

"DO YOU BELIEVE THAT THE OLDER AMERICAN (GERMAN) GENERATION UNDER-
STANDS THE PRESENT-DAY PROBLEMS OF AMERICAN (GERMAN) YOUTH?"

Percentages

	Yes	No	N.A.
U. S. Sample	31	67	2
Friedberg Sample (N=135)	53	34	13

The Nazi youth are much closer to the American pattern than the anti-Nazis on the issue of running away from home (Question 8), although the overall American-German differences are clear. There is evidence from other sources that older Germans are less pro-Nazi than younger ones, and that Naziism among German youth implied a certain amount of conflict between state (party) authority and family authority. Becoming a Nazi meant, if not open rebellion, at least a certain independence of attitude toward the family, because the youth transferred his primary loyalty—and obedience—to the state. The majority of young anti-Nazis, on the other hand, in all probability derived their anti-Naziism from their families, who succeeded in maintaining authority over the children, in opposition to state authority. The Catholic youth appear to have been particularly embroiled in this conflict between two sets of value and authority. While the numbers are small, breakdown into religious groups does suggest that the young Catholic Nazis stand at the very opposite extreme from the Catholic anti-Nazis on Question 8, with less difference between Protestant Nazis and anti-Nazis.

The fact that a favorable attitude toward family authority appears positively associated with anti-Naziism among the German youth does not exclude the likely possibility that many adult Germans rejected National Socialism for the very reason that they had unusually liberal, non-authoritarian backgrounds, and found the extreme authoritarianism of the Nazis repugnant. Various other factors presumably contributed to adult anti-Naziism, including personal grudges, old-line political party affiliations, and labor union sympathies.

NUMBERS IN ANSWER TO QUESTION 8

	Yes	No	N.A.
Catholic Nazis	15	10	1
Catholic anti-Nazis	5	25	0
Protestant Nazis	24	27	2
Protestant anti-Nazis	9	13	1

HEROES OF AMERICAN AND GERMAN YOUTH

The type of man a youth chooses to admire provides a clue to his values. The German and American youth were asked to indicate whom they considered to be "the greatest man in the history of the world." (The German data in this case are from Friedberg and Offenbach; the American data are from a group of 986 high-school students from the east coast, midwest and west coast, polled in September, 1945.) If we contrast the ten most frequently mentioned names in both groups, comprising more than 90 per cent of the total references in each case, significant differences emerge.

QUESTION 11

"WHO IS THE GREATEST MAN IN WORLD HISTORY?"

FIRST TEN CHOICES

American Youth (N=986)		German Youth (N=391)	
Name	No. of References	Name	No. of References
F. D. Roosevelt	336	Roosevelt	63
Lincoln	227	Bismarck	50
Christ	157	Frederick the Great	49
Washington	98	Hitler	19
Columbus	24	Eisenhower	14
MacArthur	23	Stalin	14
Edison	23	Charlemagne	8
Caesar	18	Truman	8
Ben Franklin	12	Caesar	6
Eisenhower	11	{ Alex. the Great	3
		{ Napoleon	3

All the individuals in the above German list are symbols of great political or military power, rulers of states or armies or both. Of the first American ten, four men are distinguished for contributions to history that did not involve the wielding of great military or political power (Christ, Columbus, Edison, Franklin). In their current subservience to American authority, the German youth have curiously rated Eisenhower and Truman higher than have the American youth. (In a similar test done on a small group of German children in the French zone by French officials, Eisenhower and Truman did not appear, and Roosevelt dropped in popularity, leaving Bismarck and Frederick the Great to head the list. No Frenchman figured high.)

In terms of total votes, 26 per cent of the Americans chose non-political and non-military figures, as opposed to only 3 per cent of the Germans. The less-frequently mentioned individuals in the American list were: Mme. Curie, G. W. Carver, Pasteur, Truman, Churchill, Napoleon, Adam, Theodore Roosevelt, Jefferson, Henry Ford, "atomic bomb discoverer," Mark Twain, Plato, Shakespeare, Al Smith, J. D. Rockefeller, Stonewall Jackson, Louis XII. In the German list, the additional names were: Christ, Columbus, Galileo, Bach, Churchill, "Founder of the 2nd Reich," Goethe, "the Great Elector," Heinrich VI, Karl V, Leo XII, Otto the Great, "the Pope," Theodoric, General Steuben. About half the names mentioned by Americans, and one fourth the German names, were writers, scientists, religious figures, business men, inventors, explorers, etc.

German admiration for power and authority, evidenced above, is presumably an important psychological element in the well-known German tendency toward political and social organizations in which, as in the feudal system, each individual has a superior toward whom he is submissive, and inferiors over whom he can wield power. In psychoanalytic terms, the German seeks to be a father and a son, but not a brother.

IDEAS OF CRIME

As a means of testing relative moral values, the American and German youth were asked what they thought was the "worst crime" a boy could commit [Question 12]. The American answers were first broken down into categories, and the categories then applied to the German data. It was not possible to have the same person classify both sets of data, so that certain discrepancies in classification may well have crept in, especially with the categories of "dishonesty" and "cruelty," although in general the answers fell easily into the categories indicated. However, approximately one-fourth of the German youth did not venture to answer the question. For this reason the number of useful German cases in the breakdowns is quite small, and the percentages should be regarded only as rough indications of rank order.

QUESTION 12

"WHAT IN YOUR OPINION IS THE WORST CRIME A BOY CAN COMMIT?"

Percentages

Crime	U.S. Sample	Bad Homburg Sample	Anti-Nazis	Nazis
1. Murder	38.5	13	18	7
2. Dishonesty and Dishonor	15.5	20	15	21
Cheating, stealing, lying, cowardice, dishonorable action, loss of honor or character				
3. Disobedience	12.5	7	9	5
Breaking law, disrespect to parents				
4. Sex Crimes	12	..	..	..
Rape, incest, adultery				
5. Assault and Cruelty	6.5	6	10	6
Hurting people, torture, unfair treatment of innocent, injustice				
6. Treason	4	20	2	32
To country, people, or leadership "Fahnenflucht"				
7. Miscellaneous	4	9	13	6
"Immorality," not repenting sin, shirking duty, supporting Nazis, committing a crime, acting against God's commands, etc.				
8. No answer	7	25	33	23
	100	100	100	100

Inspection of the data reveals that, for the American youth, the worst type of crime is crime of violence against another person—murder, rape, and assault. For the German, it is crime against the state, together with what might be called "crime of character"—dishonesty, dishonor, cowardice. "Rape," frequently mentioned by American youth, was listed by no German as the major crime. (The vaguely sexual word, "immorality"—"Sittlichkeitsvergehen," used by several Americans and Germans, has been classified under "Miscellaneous.") "Cowardice," on the other hand, appears to be in no sense a serious crime for the Americans, as it is for the Germans. A number of Germans felt that the worst thing a boy could do was to "besmirch his honor" ("seine Ehre beschmutzen" "seine Ritterlichkeit in den Schmutz zu treten"), or "lose his character," while the American children, in the category of "dishonesty and dishonor," spoke more of the simple and overt sins of cheating, lying, and stealing. The German conception of cruelty and injustice was more legalistic than the American ("condemning an innocent person," etc.), but, unlike the Americans, the Germans did not think in terms of "torture" as such. Several of the German references falling under the category of "assault" expressed admonition against "shooting at an American." A few of the non-Nazi youth said that the worst sin was "supporting the Nazis," "getting worked up by a false regime into war," "being a war volunteer." It should be noted that a large difference exists between the Nazi and anti-Nazi attitudes toward treason. The fact that, contrary to what one might expect, the Germans did not rank "disobedience" higher than the Americans may be explained by their emphasis on treason, which is an extreme form of disobedience toward the state. It is interesting to note that the one Jewish boy in the sample, while indicating strongly anti-Nazi views in a political sense, selected "Fahnenflucht" as the worst crime.

* * *

IDEAS OF NATIONAL SUPERIORITY

The superiority of Germans and all things German was a favorite Nazi idea, promoted by all the devices of propaganda. Although the majority of German youth no longer profess loyalty to the cause and leadership of National Socialism and have witnessed a compelling demonstration of power on the part of other peoples, feelings of German superiority linger on, apparently confined now to moral and cultural pre-eminence. (From the time when the tide of battle changed, Germans have clung to the supposition that their spiritual superiority was overcome only by the brute force of materiel.)

The German youth clearly display a greater degree of nationality prejudice, with the understandable exception that they do not venture to express superiority over the Americans [Question 13]. It should be recognized, of course, that the American youth are not exponents of the democratic theory by an overwhelming majority. Question 13 was not given at Bad Homburg and data are not available to break down the German replies into Nazi and anti-Nazi.

QUESTION 13

"IN YOUR OPINION ARE THE AMERICANS (GERMANS) AS A PEOPLE BETTER THAN:

Percentages

	U. S. Sample			Friedberg and Offenbach		
	Yes	No	N.A.	Yes	No	N.A.
"The Italians?"	43	56	1	70	20	10
"The Russians?"	37	63	0	64	25	11
"The Poles?"	38	52	0	71	18	11
"The French?"	40	60	0	57	29	14
"The Germans?"	41	59	0			
"The Americans?"				27	52	21

However, another question was given [Question 14], the results of which indicate that Nazi youth differ markedly from the anti-Nazis on matters of nationality prejudice.

QUESTION 14

"DO YOU CONSIDER IT RIGHT FOR A GERMAN MAN TO MARRY A POLE?"

Percentages

	Yes	No	N.A.
Bad Homburg Sample	34	63	3
Bad Homburg anti-Nazis	53	45	2
Bad Homburg Nazis	20	80	0

SEX DIFFERENCES

It has already been observed that, in attitude studies in Germany, girls have been found to be consistently more Nazi in their orientation than boys. A larger proportion of girls appear in the "Nazi" category of the Bad Homburg sample, and sex breakdowns on the various questions for which data are available indicate that, with few exceptions, the girls are more distinctly "German" in their answers than the boys; differences average around 10 per cent. Small sex differences also appear in the American answers to the questions that have been discussed, ranging between 5 and 10 per cent for approximately half the questions. Here there is also a clear trend: the girls are more "American," farther from the Germans, than the boys. Thus, the American girls and the German girls stand at the opposite extremes on such questions as whether the child who tyrannizes is worse than the child who disobeys and whether a soldier should refuse a command to shoot an innocent prisoner; while the American boys and German boys stand closer together in their attitudes.

Further evidence is required to confirm this apparent pattern of sex differences. Further investigation in other western countries is also needed to test the hypothesis indicated—that women characteristically express and preserve typical national values more than do men.

SUMMARY

1. Attitude questions, designed to probe broad social and ethical aspects of personality, were given to samples of American and German youth. Differences emerged that are consistent, in general, with other known information about American and German behavior.

2. In questions that set up a conflict between obedience to authority—state or other—and independent decision and action, the German youth favored obedience distinctly more than did the Americans. The Germans appeared to have very little faith in "the common man."

3. While Germans and Americans differed widely in attitude toward rebellion against paternal authority, the German Nazi youth were closer to the American pattern on this particular item than were the German anti-Nazis. Young Nazis apparently substituted state authority for family authority, in the process of their political conversion, while young anti-Nazis opposed the state, not because they rebelled against authoritarianism as such, but because they remained under the influence of family authority that was in conflict with the state.

4. The German youth revealed considerably more admiration than did the Americans for men of great power in world history, individuals who controlled the lives and destinies of other men by virtue of supreme military or political status.

5. Basic differences in ethical values appeared. The American youth viewed crime primarily as a matter of personal violence against other individuals, while for the Germans it was primarily a matter of disloyalty to the state and dishonor in one's own character. Correspondingly, the Americans placed relatively greater emphasis upon teaching children to be considerate of others, while the Germans stressed the importance of developing a sense of patriotism and an honorable character in children.

6. In spite of defeat, the German youth appear to have maintained a stronger attitude of national superiority over other peoples than is held by American youth.

7. Differences in attitude between Americans and Germans, and between political Nazis and political anti-Nazis, are clear in the majority of the questions. However, young Americans, as well as a number of young German anti-Nazis can always be found who take typically Fascist views with regard to state authority, national superiority, and the like. Correspondingly, a few young Nazis can be found who reveal typically democratic social attitudes.

8. In both countries, the data on sex differences suggest that it is the girls who tend more to reflect the typical national pattern, while the boys tend to deviate from it.

CHAPTER TWO

The Adolescent in Modern

American Society

3

THE FIELD THEORY APPROACH

TO ADOLESCENCE

by Kurt Lewin

Various theories have been suggested to explain the behavior of adolescents. In the following excerpt from an article, Kurt Lewin (1890-1947), the distinguished social psychologist, presents the gist of his field theory of social behavior as it applies to adolescence. [From "Field Theory and Experiment in Social Psychology," *American Journal of Sociology*, 1939, *44*, 868-897. Reprinted by permission of the University of Chicago Press. One figure and some of the footnotes have been omitted.]

The field-theoretical approach is intended to be a practical vehicle of research. As is true with any tool, its characteristics can be understood fully only by the use of it in actual research. Therefore, instead of stating general methodological principles *in abstractum*, I prefer to discuss, as an illustration, the problem of adolescence. . . . The purpose . . . is not the proving of certain facts or theories (which might or might not be fully correct) but to survey certain major aspects of the field-theoretical approach as applicable to social psychology. . . .

We have chosen the problem of adolescence because the changes in behavior which are supposed to be characteristic for this period seem, at first sight, to give excellent backing to a biological view in sociology. Obviously, adolescence has something to do with sexual hormones and with certain periods of bodily growth. The more recent treatments of the problem of adolescence, however, seem to emphasize its social aspect. They point particularly to the fact that the behavior typical of this age is rather different in different societies (Cole, 1936; Reuter, 1937). Considerable argumentation has been advanced for and against both views.

However, it does not help much to argue whether adolescence is a biological or psychological effect. It does not help much either to try to describe, on a statistical basis, to what degree this problem is biological or psychological in nature. Even if an answer could be found, it would be of as little value as, for instance, the determining of the degree to which heredity and environment affect intelligence. We still would not have gained any insight into the way in which bodily and social factors are working together and against each other, integrating the concrete behavior of the adolescent. It would seem to be more fruitful to start with an analysis of the setting in a concrete case. This case should be chosen not so much according to the frequency of occurrence as according to the amount of insight it offers into a constellation which is typical at least for a part of the setting in question.

In regard to the problem of adolescence, it might be helpful to refer first to cases which show the so-called "typical" difficulties of adolescent behavior. A field-theoretical analysis of such a situation should give some hints as to what conditions would increase or decrease these symptoms.

The period of adolescence can be said to be a period of transition. It seems to imply, at least under certain circumstances, a more rapid or deeper shift than the period before. After the rather important changes around the age of three years, often a more stable situation has arisen. Maybe minor crises have come up; but particularly in cases where the adolescence is characterized by special disturbances, a relatively quiet or stable time might have preceded it. If one tries to characterize the nature of the transition, one can point to several aspects.

a. One can view adolescence as a change in group-belongingness. The individual has been considered by himself and by others as a child. Now he does not wish to be treated as such. He is ready to separate himself from things childish and to try seriously to enter adult life in manners and in outlook on occupation, as on life in general. Any change in belongingness from one group to another is of great importance for the behavior of the person; the more central for the person this belonging is, the more important is the change. A shift in group-belongingness is a "social locomotion," that is, it changes the position of the person concerned.

It is a simple fact, but still not sufficiently recognized in psychology and sociology, that the behavior of a person depends above all upon his momentary position. Often, the world looks very different before and after an event which changes the region in which a person is located. That is the reason why, for instance, a *fait accompli* is so feared in politics. A change in position, for instance, the locomotion from one group to another, changes not only the momentary surroundings of a person but more or less the total setting: what has been a neighboring region, easily accessible from the previous position, might now be farther away or no longer accessible at all. On the other hand, different regions are now neighbors, and new ones may be accessible. The shift into the group of the adults, for instance, makes possible certain activities which previously were forbidden but which are now socially permitted. The individual might attend certain parties, have access to certain activities. On the other hand, certain taboos exist for the adults that do not exist for the child (Figure 1, *a* and *b*).

b. The change from the group of children to that of the adults is a shift to a more or less unknown position. Psychologically, it is equivalent to entering an unknown region, comparable to coming into a new town. Experiments in the field of learning, for example, give some kind of picture of the fundamental differences between a situation which is familiar to an individual and that which is unfamiliar. The unfamiliar can be represented psychologically as a cognitively unstructured region. This means that that region is not differentiated into clearly distinguishable parts. It is not clear therefore where a certain action will lead and in what direction one has to move to approach a certain goal. This lack of clearness of the direction in the field is one of the major reasons for the typical "uncertainty of behavior" to be found in unknown surroundings. Studies on social pressure and on ascendant and submissive behavior (Jack, 1934) clearly indicate that an individual in an unfamiliar surrounding is less ready to put up a fight or to show ascendant behavior. An unfamiliar surrounding is dynamically equivalent to a soft ground. Or, to be more specific, the lack of a cognitively clear structure is likely to make every action a conflicting one. The individual, not knowing whether the action will lead him closer or farther away from his goal, is necessarily uncertain as to whether or not he should carry it out.

The child's development naturally leads to an opening up of new unknown regions. Periods of transition are characterized by more

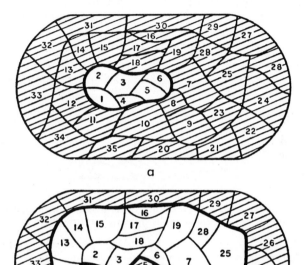

a

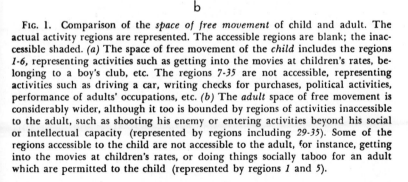

b

Fig. 1. Comparison of the *space of free movement* of child and adult. The actual activity regions are represented. The accessible regions are blank; the inaccessible shaded. (a) The space of free movement of the *child* includes the regions *1-6,* representing activities such as getting into the movies at children's rates, belonging to a boy's club, etc. The regions *7-35* are not accessible, representing activities such as driving a car, writing checks for purchases, political activities, performance of adults' occupations, etc. (b) The *adult* space of free movement is considerably wider, although it too is bounded by regions of activities inaccessible to the adult, such as shooting his enemy or entering activities beyond his social or intellectual capacity (represented by regions including *29-35*). Some of the regions accessible to the child are not accessible to the adult, for instance, getting into the movies at children's rates, or doing things socially taboo for an adult which are permitted to the child (represented by regions *1* and *5*).

than the usual impact of such new regions. Entering a new social group can mean something very similar to being thrown into a cognitively unstructured field, being forced to stand on unfirm ground and not knowing whether the "right thing" is being done. The uncertain character of the adolescent's behavior and his conflicts can partly be explained by the lack of cognitive clarity concerning the adult's world which he is going to enter (Figure 2). It follows that this uncertainty is greater the more the individual has previously been kept out of the adult world and has been kept in the dark about it.

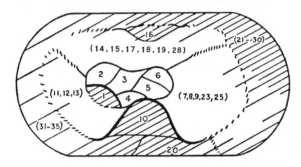

FIG. 2. The *space of free movement* of the *adolescent* as it appears to him. The space of free movement is greatly increased, including many regions which previously have not been accessible to the child, such as freedom to smoke, returning home late, driving a car (regions *7-9, 11-13, . . .*). Certain regions accessible to the adult are clearly not accessible to the adolescent, such as voting (represented by regions *10* and *16*). Certain regions accessible to the child have already become inaccessible, such as getting into the movies at children's rates, or behaving on too childish a level (region *1*). The boundaries of these newly acquired portions of the space of free movement are only vaguely determined and in themselves generally less clearly and sharply differentiated than for an adult. In such cases the life space of the adolescent seems to be full of possibilities and at the same time of uncertainties.

c. One region particularly close and important to the individual is his own body. Psychologically one's own body can be treated in some respects in the same way as one's environment. Generally the individual "knows" his body sufficiently. That means he knows what he can expect from it and how it will react under given circumstances. The time of sexual maturity brings with it changes which make the individual sometimes disturbed by his own body. More or less strange and new body experiences arise and make this part of the life space, which is so close and vital to the individual, strange and unknown. In this case the change does not mean merely the usual uncertainties of a new and strange environment; but, in addition, a region which previously appeared to be well known and reliable becomes now unknown and unreliable. This change necessarily shakes the belief of the individual in the stability of the ground on which he stands and perhaps even in the stability of the world at large. Since the region of the body happens to be very important and central for anyone, this doubting might be rather fundamental. It might lead, on the one hand, to increased uncertainty of behavior and to conflicts; on the other, to the aggressiveness of some of the adolescent reactions.

Such explanation would be in line with the findings of L. B. Murphy (1937) that insecure situations lead both to highly aggressive and highly sensitive behavior. The disastrous effect which the breakdown of a previously firm ground might have is dramatically illustrated by foster-children, who discover at a late age the true facts concerning their parentage. The trauma of such a collapse of a social ground sometimes permanently destroys their belief in the world.

d. The "radicalism" which makes some adolescents flock to extreme "left" or "right" political parties and be extreme in many judgments has to deal also with a second factor. A period of radical change is naturally a period of greater plasticity. The very fact that a person is in the state of moving from one region A to a new region B, and is therefore cut loose from the region A but not yet firmly established in the region B, puts him in a less stable position and makes him, as any object in *statu nascendi,* more formative.

The psychological environment has to be regarded functionally as a part of one interdependent field, the life space, the other part of which is the person. This fundamental fact is the keynote of the field-theoretical approach. In psychology it has become, in various forms, more and more recognized and can be expressed simply by the formula: Behavior = Function of person and environment = function of life space $(B = F [P,E] = F [L Sp])$. The instability of the psychological environment leads, in some respects, therefore, to greater instability of the person. "Being established" means having a well-defined position and definite relations to the many regions of a highly differentiated life space: under such circumstances any major change means a great number of steps and a shift of interrelation. In an unestablished, new situation the field is not very much differentiated, and whatever differentation has occurred is not very firm. The shift of position of the individual from one region to another, which in the less differentiated field might be merely one step (Figure 2), would have to be considered a major change (equivalent to many steps) in a more differentiated field (Figure 1, *b*). Similarly, what in reality is a not very great and easily made shift in cognitive structure of the ideological field of the adolescent, which contains relatively few regions, appears to be a radical shift to the adult, with his highly differentiated cognitive field. The difference in cognitive differentiation is probably one of the reasons why adolescents easily go to extremes.

e. The widening of the life space into unknown regions concerns not only geographical surroundings (interest in traveling, hiking, etc.) and social surroundings (more inclusive social groups like political or occupational ones) but also the time dimension of the life space. Persons of all ages are influenced by the manner in which they see the future, that is, by their expectations, fears, and hopes.

The scope of time ahead which influences present behavior, and is therefore to be regarded as a part of the present life space, increases during development. This change in time perspective is one of the most fundamental facts of development. Adolescence seems to be a period of particularly deep change in respect to time perspective.

The change can be partly described as a shift in scope. Instead of days, weeks, or months, now years ahead are considered in certain goals. Even more important is the way in which these future events influence present behavior. The ideas of a child of six or eight in regard to his occupation as an adult are not likely to be based on sufficient knowledge of the factors which might help or interfere with the realization of these ideas. They might be based on relatively narrow but definite expectations or might have a dream—or playlike character. In other words, "ideal goals" and "real goals" for the distant future are not much distinguished, and this future has more the fluid character of the level of irreality.

In adolescence a definite differentiation in regard to the time perspective is likely to occur. Within those parts of the life space which represent the future, levels of reality and irreality are gradually being differentiated. That which is dreamed of or wished for (level of irreality in the future) becomes separated from what is expected (level of reality in the future). Vague ideas have to be replaced by more or less definite decisions in regard to preparation for future occupation. In other words, one has to "plan": to structure the time perspective in a way which is in line both with one's own ideal goals or values and with those realities which must be taken into account for a realistic structuring of the plane of expectation.

This task is characteristic for all kinds of planning. The situation of the adolescent in this respect is particular only in that he has to form the time perspective in regard to a field which is especially great and unknown. What he learns from books and adult counsel about what an individual might accomplish is full of contradiction. the adults praise the hero who has realized what seemed to be impossible, and at the same time preach the moral of "standing with both feet on the ground."

In another respect the adolescent finds the adults (the group he is to enter) full of contradiction. A variety of conflicting religious, political, and occupational values is obviously powerful within that group. A child may fail to bring to adolescence a well-established framework of values, or he may have thrown the values of his childhood away. In either case the structure of his adolescent time perspective will be unstable and undetermined, owing to the uncertainty of not only what can be done (which we have discussed previously) but also what should be done. The uncertain character of the ideals and values keeps the adolescent in a state of conflict and tension which is the greater the more central these problems are. The wish to structure these fields in a definite way (and in this manner to solve the conflict) seems to be one of the reasons behind the readiness of the adolescent to follow anyone who offers a definite pattern of values.

f. The transition from childhood to adulthood may be a rather sudden shift (for instance, in some of the primitive societies), or it may occur gradually in a setting where children and adults are not sharply separated groups. In case of the so-called "adolescence difficulties," however, a third state of affairs is often prevalent: children and adults constitute clearly defined groups; the adolescent does not wish to belong any longer to the children's group and, at the same time, knows that he is not really accepted in the adult group. In this case he has a position similar to what is called in sociology the "marginal man."

The marginal man is a person who stands on the boundary (Figure 3, *b*) between two groups, A and B. He does not belong to either of them, or at least he is not certain about his belongingness. Not infrequently this situation occurs for members of an underprivileged minority group, particularly for the more privileged members within this group. There is a strong tendency for the members of the underprivileged minority group to cut loose and to try to enter the majority group (Lewin, 1948, Chap. II). If the person is partly successful in establishing relationships with the privileged group without being fully accepted, he becomes a marginal man, belonging to both groups but not fully to either of them. The fact of being located in a social "no man's land" can be observed in very different types of minority groups—for instance, racial groups or the hard-of-hearing, which is a marginal group between the deaf and the normal group.

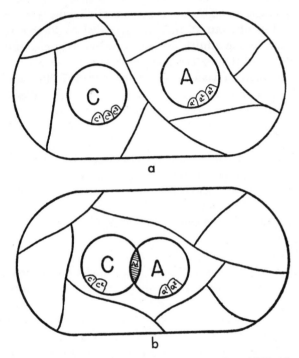

Fig. 3. The adolescent as a *marginal man*. (a) During *childhood* and *adulthood* the "adults" *(A)* and "children" *(C)* are viewed as relatively separated groups, the individual child *(c¹, c²)* and the individual adult *(a¹, a²)* being sure of their belonging to their respective groups. (b) The *adolescent* belonging to a group *(Ad)* which can be viewed as an overlapping region of the children's *(C)* and the adults' *(A)* group belonging to both of them, or as standing between them, not belonging to either one.

Characteristic symptoms of behavior of the marginal man are emotional instability and sensitivity. They tend to unbalanced behavior, to either boisterousness or shyness, exhibiting too much tension, and a frequent shift between extremes of contradictory behavior. The marginal man shows a typical aversion to the less privileged members of his own group. This can be noted in the hostile attitude of some subgroups of the Negroes or other races against members of their own race, and the hard-of-hearing against the deaf.

To some extent behavior symptomatic for the marginal man can be found in the adolescent. He too is oversensitive, easily shifted from one extreme to the other, and particularly sensitive to the shortcomings of his younger fellows. Indeed, his position is sociologically the same as that of the marginal man; he does not wish to belong any longer to a group which is, after all, less privileged than the group of adults: but at the same time he knows that he is not fully accepted by the adults. The similarities between the position of the members of the underprivileged minority and the adolescent, and between their behavior, seem to me so great that one might characterize the behavior of the marginal members of the minority group as that of permanent adolescence.

We might sum up our discussion of the adolescent in the following manner:

a. The basic fact concerning the general situation of the adolescent can be represented as the position of a person during locomotion from one region to another. This includes (1) the widening of the life space (geographically, socially, and in time perspective), and (2) the cognitively unstructured character of the new situation.

b. Somewhat more specifically, the adolescent has a social position "between" the adult and the child, similar to a marginal member of an underprivileged minority group.

c. There are still more specific factors involved in adolescence, such as the new experiences with one's own body, which can be represented as the baffling change of a central region of the established life space.

From this representation one can derive conceptually:

I. The adolescent's shyness, sensitivity, and aggressiveness, owing to unclearness and instability of ground (follows from *a, b,* and *c*).

II. A more or less permanent conflict between the various attitudes, values, ideologies, and styles of living (follows from *b*).

III. Emotional tension resulting from these conflicts (follows from *a, b,* and *c*).

IV. Readiness to take extreme attitudes and actions and to shift his position radically (follows from *a, b,* and *c*).

V. The "adolescent behavior" should appear only if the structure and dynamics of the field are such as represented by *a, b,* and *c*. The degree and particular type of behavior should depend upon the degree of realization of this structure and upon the strength of the conflicting forces. Above all, the degree of difference and of separation between adults and children which is characteristic for a particular culture is important; also, the extent to which the particular adolescent finds himself in the position of a marginal man. According to field theory, actual behavior depends upon every part of the field. It follows that the degree of instability of the adolescent should be greatly influenced also by such factors as general stability or instability of the particular individual.

·· *4* ··

ADOLESCENCE AND THE SOCIAL STRUCTURE

by Kingsley Davis

Every society has its own set of behavior standards. In complex societies such as ours the number of standards is ever increasing and more and more of them tend to shift in emphasis and to be contradictory. This may result in additional stresses and strains upon the people. In the article that follows Kingsley Davis, of the University of California (Berkeley) describes the lag between physical and social development during adolescence and some of the contradictory and confusing demands made by American society on adolescents. [From *Annals of the American Academy of Political and Social Science,* 1944, *236,* 8-16. Reprinted by permission of the author and the American Academy of Political and Social Science.]

Whether recognized as a separate status or not, the adolescent period seemingly has one outstanding peculiarity—namely, that it is a time when the individual is attaining physical maturity without necessarily attaining social maturity. In terms of growth, strength, fecundity, and mental capacity, full maturity tends to be attained only a short time after puberty; but socially the adolescent still has a long way to go, in most cases, before full status is reached.

This tendency for the adolescent to be more mature physically than socially is most pronounced in settled and traditionalized, and also modern, societies, but it is a condition that is to some extent inherent in the nature of all human society. Evolving through uncounted millennia, culture has developed a complexity of principle and a fullness of content that require a long time for the individual to master. At the same time it has made possible a type of social organization in which power and advantage are dependent on social position, knowledge, experience, and reputation, rather than brute strength or innate cunning. In so far as these things have anything to do with age, they are more likely to come with middle age, or even old age, than with adolescence. There has grown up, therefore, a situation in which the adolescent, despite his physical equality with or even superiority to the older person, is nevertheless placed in a socially subordinate position. The result is a sort of disharmony which, in times of social disorganization, *sometimes* expresses itself in conflict between the generations.

If mental and physical maturity came between 30 and 35 years of age, instead of between 15 and 20, there would be a much longer period of youthful plasticity during which an enormously enhanced amount of culture could be absorbed. As it is, especially in modern society, the individual must keep on learning after his capacity to do so has already begun to decline. Even though his mental *capacity* has reached its peak during adolescence, his acquired knowledge, judgment, insight, and self-reliance are generally far from their peak.

The great extension of the average length of life in modern times, while it has afforded more scope and rationale to post-adolescent learning, has not lengthened the adolescent period itself. Instead, it has prolonged the duration of adulthood, and has consequently made adolescence a smaller fraction of the average life span.

Also helping to make the complex heritage of modern culture possible is specialization. Each individual is not required to learn the entire culture, but only that part of it which concerns him. The mechanism, however, like the extension of the length of life, has its limitations, as one can readily see by imagining a society with no general language but merely a separate language for every occupational group.

Societies of course differ as to how freely they permit young people to accumulate knowledge and experience. Frequently in order to transmit first the ideal elements of the culture, the elders select the cultural content that is given to children and protect them from contrary experiences. To the extent that this happens, it postpones social maturity to some stage beyond adolescence. In modern society, because of this protectiveness as well as other factors, even middle-aged people are commonly accused of being emotionally immature.

In addition to the increasing complexity of culture and the consequent length of time required for socialization, social evolution has progressed to the point where power does not ordinarily depend on physical prowess. Even an army, which presumably depends par excellence on physical skill and strength, is controlled by elderly generals and colonels. The adolescent, despite his achievements in battles, sports, and tests, has long been forced to defer to older persons whose biological capacities are less than his. The latter, by virtue of having held a position early in life, are able, in a stable society, to continue to hold it later in life, and by virtue of it to acquire other positions of even greater influence. Furthermore, because of the endlessness of the educational process, they are in a way better qualified for responsible positions. Their qualification, however, is a socially acquired and not a biologically maturing qualification. It is based on knowledge and experience, both necessary for successful political and administrative decisions.

Thus in a sense (the physical sense) the community does not utilize its great men until they are already past their prime; but in another sense (the social sense) it utilizes them at the peak of their greatness—in what one might call their administrative or sociological maturity. The principle of seniority, therefore, is no accident, no empty form. The charge is frequently made that the old hang onto their positions as vested interests, and that this is the explanation of the subordination of youth to age (Mead, 1935, pp. 77-78). That older persons seek to hold what power they have is generally true, but their desire does not explain the fact that they *can* do so. They are able to hold their power because they have a kind of superiority—a superiority developed and buttressed by an organized society, but a superiority nonetheless.

If our hypothesis is true, then adolescence is ordinarily the time when the lag of social development behind physical development first becomes pronounced. As society grows more complex the lag becomes greater, and adolescence, as socially defined, extends farther into organic adulthood.

MAJOR POINTS OF ARTICULATION

Sociologically, it is necessary to get behind the kaleidoscopic array of customs in different societies and to examine the alternative principles which *any* human society, as a functional and structural system, has at its disposal in utilizing the adolescent generation. Between the adolescent stratum and the rest of the social structure there are numerous points of articulation where alternative principles may be employed. Indeed, anyone unfamiliar with the anthropological literature is likely to be surprised at the number of junctures in which adolescence must somehow be handled but in which the mode of handling is open to several divergent possibilities. In what follows, only four such points of articulation will be discussed, viz.: occupational placement, reproductive control, authoritarian organization, and cultural acquisition. These correspond to four major foci of institutional organization, namely: the economic, the familial, the political, and the educational. In each case the alternative employed by any given society depends primarily on that society's total structure.

Occupational Placement

Since every society involves some specialization of function, an important matter is the selection of individuals for various occupations. This selection may be made by ascription or by choice. If by choice, it can be made at any time, but if much training is required, it needs to be made by the time of adolescence at the latest, because this period represents the last stage of rapid learning. The earlier the choice is made, the more intensive can be the training. On the other hand, the later it is made, the more it may rest on a true evaluation of personal talent and preference.

It is probably no accident, therefore, that the most complex societies (i.e., modern Occidental ones) on the whole defer the final decision until adolescence and provide most of the specialized training during that period. Less complex societies, such as that of classical India, may decide the matter at birth and provide what training is necessary during the entire childhood. In simpler societies the division of labor may be so slight that the question, except perhaps as regards the positions of chief and shaman, may be unimportant. In a complex but changing society the decision as to occupation tends to be deferred until late adolescence or early adulthood, because occupational possibilities are altering so fast that decisions made earlier may be subsequently rendered inadvisable; yet it is precisely in such a society that an elaborate training, and hence an early decision, are necessary.

The handling of occupational placement plays a significant role in determining the status of the adolescent. If in a simple and stable society the occupation is ascribed or chosen early in life, if the training extends through childhood or is relatively simple in character, adolescence does not stand out occupationally as a period of any particular importance. By the time he reaches adolescence the individual may in fact be practicing his occupation, and may be looked upon in this regard as an adult. If on the other hand the society is complex and changing, adolescence tends to become a time of difficult choosing and intensive training, and hence to acquire a pronounced importance as a socially recognized, eventful period of life. If there is a gradation within each occupation, the adolescent generally starts at the bottom rung. This tends to give him a distinct subordinate status. If the element of competition is introduced, it acts as an individualizing force that makes of adolescence a period of strain and perhaps of deprivation, at the same time that it raises the level of general achievement.

Reproductive Control

In its determination of the adolescent status, every society must somehow recognize the fact that the reproductive capacity first appears at the inception of adolescence. One crucial question is whether the adolescent shall be permitted to gratify his sexual desires through normal heterosexual intercourse or whether such gratification must be postponed. A second is whether the gratification, if permitted, shall be in marriage or in premarital relations; and if the latter, whether the illegitimate children shall be killed, disposed of to relatives, or kept by the girl. Finally, there is the question of whether marital choice is free or is controlled by others, and whether marriage establishes a separate household or merely an extension of the parental menage.

Among most peoples of the world, at least until recently, there was some variation of a recurrent pattern. Either marriage occurred shortly after puberty or premarital intercourse prevailed. The choice of a marital partner was generally in the hands of parents or kinsmen, though the right of veto, in theory at least, supposedly belonged to the parties to the marriage. Wedlock did not usually imply a separate household, and did not convey full emancipation from the parents. Although there were countless variations on this generalized pattern, the underlying theme was extremely widespread. Its main characteristic was that it gave a sexual and reproductive function to the adolescent but carefully controlled the exercise of this function.

By way of contrast, American society is unusual, though not entirely unique, in the following ways: It maintains the ideal of premarital chastity in the face of a long period of postponement of marriage after puberty. In connection with this, it upholds the freedom of marital choice and fosters competition and the doctrine of *caveat emptor* in courtship. Finally, it emphasizes the independence and separateness of the wedded couple. As a consequence, the adolescent period becomes one of considerable strain. The young person is permitted to associate closely with the opposite sex but is put on his honor to remain virtuous, is supposed to choose his own mate independently but is in many ways still under the authority of the parents, and is forced to compete for love in a rating and dating system that interferes and gets entangled with his fortunes in that other competitive system, the occupational. The strains are somewhat different for boys and for girls (Parsons, 1942), but only as two different sides of the same situation.

Authoritarian Organization

Whereas American youth think that getting a job and getting married entitle them to independence, the case is quite different in many other societies. In old India, Ireland, China, and Japan, for example, the authority of the parent tended to continue until death. The end of adolescence did not mean a significant change in authority, and hence the adolescent phase, for that reason at least, did not stand apart as a separate period. In addition, there was little conflict over authority, not only because complete emancipation did not occur, but also because such emancipation as did occur developed by well-grooved, mutually accepted, publicly ritualized steps.

In modern society, by contrast, the child is supposed to become completely emancipated from the parental power, but the exact time, manner, and cause of such emancipation remain uncertain, a subject of dispute, recrimination, and remorse. The individual may become a full-fledged wage earner as early as childhood or as late as adulthood. Marriage is often postponed so long that there tends to arise a distinction between the adolescent and the unmarried adult. Neither employment nor matrimony, therefore, may be accepted as a standard criterion of emancipation. There is no such standard criterion. Each family must virtually settle the matter for itself as a result of private interaction. This in spite of the fact that the emancipation, once it does come, is relatively more complete than in most societies.

In Peter Blos's book, *The Adolescent Personality* (1941), one of the three major goals of adolescence is claimed to be "emancipation from the family." Achieving this goal is viewed as a long and hard psychic struggle. Yet in most societies it either comes in the normal course of affairs or never comes at all. Among us, it comes as a struggle because the adolescent needs the protection of his family at the same time that he rebels against its authority, because he dreads to leave the glamorous irresponsibility of youth for the humdrum cares of adulthood, and because he has no standardized steps by which emancipation can be automatically and publicly achieved.

In relation to older persons outside his family, the adolescent, if he has a separate status at all, usually has a subordinate one, because of the sociological reasons for the seniority principle already discussed. The adolescent boy is most likely to be accorded full adult status in simple, mobile, warlike societies, where physical prowess is emphasized as a societal necessity. Even so, it is only during the latter part of the adolescent period, say between the ages of 18 and 22, that he achieves virtual parity. The Comanche culture, for example, prior to the coming of the whites placed considerable emphasis on youth but the older men nevertheless retained a superiority in magic which partially compensated them for their loss of prestige due to physical decline (Linton, 1936, pp. 120-121).

In our society, even apart from the family, the adolescent finds an absence of definitely recognized, consistent patterns of authority. Because of the compartmentalization of the culture he is defined at times as an adult, at other times as a child. Furthermore, he is subjected to a confusing array of competing authorities, of which the school is the principal but not the happiest one.

Cultural Acquisition

In most social systems the child acquires the rudiments of the culture informally. Any definite instruction by parents or elders is of short duration and limited scope. Only the highly civilized societies possess specialized educational establishments professionally staffed and forming a separate phase of life, and even they until recently reserved these establishments primarily for the upper social ranks (as in most of Latin America today).

For inculcating modern culture, the universal and specialized school system is a necessity. Its concentrated and abstract curriculum, professional staff, physical separateness, and internal organization all give a rapid and systematic grounding in the principles of the civilization, and remarkably facilitate the educational process. But by virtue of the very qualities that make it efficient in teaching abstractions, it tends to divorce itself from the facts and experiences of everyday life. For years the pupil is drilled in principles, on the assumption that he will subsequently apply them in actual life. His childhood is thus treated as the preparation for life, not as real life itself.

The difficulty, of course, is that not everything can be taught in school. The person often emerges with a hoard of abstract knowledge, but with little knowledge of the concrete situations he must negotiate in order to get along. The harder he studies, the more unfit he becomes for ordinary day-to-day existence. Above all, there is such a long interval between learning and application that the incentive to learn often flags and must be bolstered by an amazing system of planned competition and artificial rewards.

Out of ennui and practical necessity the average pupil finally begins to participate in a more vivid world, the world of youth culture. This, in its adolescent phase, is characterized by irresponsibility, "having a good time," athletics, sex attraction, and the repudiation of adult control (Parsons, 1942, pp. 606-608). One reason it takes this form is that it is "denied status by society at large, and is regarded primarily as a destructive and undesirable, a foolish and queer expression of the impulses of young people" (Blos, 1941, p. 254). It has, in other words, no avowed function in the institutional structure, but is interstitial, officially purposeless (Thrasher, 1927), a phenomenon seldom found in other societies.

No wonder the cry of unreality is raised against the school system, and reforms are proposed which have in view the reintegration of education and life. Some of the reforms, however, have missed the point. They have overlooked the efficiency of systematic instruction and have attempted to make education "grow out of real life situations" (Berkson, 1943, Chap. 8), not realizing that since modern culture rests on abstract knowledge, to confine all instruction to the applied and the concrete would soon produce stagnation.

The root of the difficulty apparently lies in the fact that while the young person is going to school he is doing little else of a responsible and productive nature. Therefore, the remedy is, perhaps, to give him an essential function in the world outside of school—i.e., to let him work—and to relate his schooling to this function. He could then receive his reward not solely in terms of grades, diplomas, honors, and degrees, but also in terms of wages and things accomplished. Thus the learning of principles would be attached to actual situations, not by the radical method of reducing all learning to a clumsy empiricism and thereby bankrupting the culture, but by making the young person a citizen who produces to the limit of his natural and acquired capacities.

The objection that a thorough grounding in basic principles leaves little time for participation in economic and political activity is valid. But there are three directions in which this obstacle may be overcome: first, the invention of new educational technology; second, the elimination of irrelevancies from the curriculum; and third, the overhauling of the incentive mechanism. New educational technology, such as the recent methods of improving reading habits, may make possible the absorption of the same amount of knowledge in a much shorter time. As to irrelevancies in the curriculum, it seems clear that they are there because the purpose of schooling, both for the society and for the individual, is not clear. One way of eliminating them would be to define more clearly the fundamentals in our culture and thus reduce the number and the variety of "liberal arts" subjects. An additional way would be to eliminate applied subjects, such as manual training and shorthand, except in so far as they relate to the pupil's known vocation. This would require specialization earlier in the school career than is now in fashion, and would have the disadvantage of requiring the choice of an occupation when the individual is still young and hence incapable of choosing wisely; although under a planned economy, vocational guidance by experts would be required in any case. Early specialization would allow the school work to be tied to actual life, because the child would enter the first stages of his occupation while already going to school. This, in turn, would help to solve the incentive problem. If a child were already launched on the first stages of his occupation, if his school subjects had specific application to his job, so that his wages, advancement, and so forth, depended on them, he would be more disposed to study.

5

ADOLESCENCE IN OUR SOCIETY

by Harold E. Jones

The relationship between physical growth and acceptance by peers and self-acceptance has long been recognized. For more than twenty-five years Harold E. Jones of the University of California (Berkeley) has studied a group of children whose physical growth and development and social behavior has been measured periodically. Here he summarizes the results of some of the studies showing how various physical changes affect social behavior, and how adolescents must adapt to their groups in order to maintain their status. [From "Anniversary Papers of the Community Service Society of New York," *The Family in a Democratic Society,* New York: Columbia University Press, 1949, pp. 70-82. Reprinted by permission of the author and Columbia University Press.]

The period of adolescence is sometimes referred to as a flowering and fulfillment, sometimes as a calamity. Taken literally, adolescence is the process of becoming adult, growing into maturity. But the term has gained other, less favorable meanings. These are implied when we speak of adolescent "stress and strain," "growing pains," "teen-age troubles," "the silly phase," and other phenomena to which we attach the adjective "adolescent," sometimes in a resigned mood and sometimes in exasperation.

Many persons have raised the question of whether this process of growing up is naturally and inevitably a difficult one, or whether its painfulness is in some sense a disease of society, and therefore remediable through appropriate social changes. The answer to this question has varied widely according to the preoccupations of the person answering it. The biological answer stresses changes in hormone secretions, changes in the rate of skeletal growth, and temporary imbalances in body structure and function. It is these imbalances, we are told, which are the immediate source of adolescent maladjustment. The sociological and anthropological answer, on the other hand, stresses the conditions and demands of the culture in which the child is growing up. It is pointed out that the same processes of biological maturing that place a child in jeopardy in one culture may offer no special problems in another culture. Each of these answers is a partial one. Adolescence is not necessarily a period of acute disturbance. When disturbance occurs, the determining agencies lie in multiple form both in the organism and in society; we cannot hope to achieve understanding or control if we look at merely one of these two groups of factors.

It may be appropriate to begin this discussion with some account of the physical aspects of adolescence and of the developmental processes which set off this period so clearly from earlier childhood.

First, we know that at about eight or nine years of age on an average, in girls, and some two years later in boys, a change occurs in the rate of physical growth (Shuttleworth, 1939). In the preceding years, ever since early childhood, growth has occurred at a fairly even and steady pace; growth in height, for example, involves gains of about 4 per cent per year during these childhood years. But now, near the end of childhood, growth becomes slower; there is often a pause which marks the transition point between the slow, gradual development of childhood and the accelerated, more irregular growth changes of adolescence. It is as though the organism needed a little time in which to consolidate childhood gains, to muster resources, and to get ready for the abrupt transformations that are now to take place. This is a figurative way of putting it, but it does appear that we have during this period an interval in which the growth controls of childhood are fading and the adolescent growth factors are not yet fully ready to function.

In some respects, the problems of adolescence bear a resemblance to the problems of infancy, so that adolescence is sometimes called a second infancy. Physiologically, this may in a way be justified, in view of the fact that infants show an instability in many physiological processes, and gradually win a greater degree of equilibrium. With the beginning of the puberal cycle we have a renewal of unstable conditions. Basal metabolism, for example, may show marked fluctuations at this time (Shock, 1943).

In an adult such metabolic changes could readily be a matter of some concern; in an adolescent they are physiological in the sense that they are very commonly and perhaps normally shown in the process of adjusting to the new phase of more rapid growth and to new conditions in the internal environment. At the same time, changes are also occurring in other basal functions. Among girls, for example, in the three years just preceding the menarche the average pulse rate increases and then decreases; the systolic blood pressure increases and then levels off (Shock, 1944).

It is not surprising that the adjustments in bodily processes should not always be smooth and orderly. The adolescent awkwardness, which we sometimes observe at the level of motor skills, may have its parallel in a kind of physiological awkwardness. The transition to a changed body economy may be difficult, and there may be further difficulties because of an interacting relationship with social and psychological transitions.

In a standard work on pediatrics the author observes that "the age of puberty is attended with many dangers to health. The changes in the organs are sudden. The heart grows larger, the blood vessels narrower. . . . At this time particularly mental disorders may develop and hereditary defects appear. Anemic conditions arise and may be followed by constitutional diseases. . . ." (Diven, 1923, p. 192.) Such statements may cause unnecessary alarm and over-emphasize the health hazards of adolescence, and yet it is true that the morbidity rate increases during the 'teens, and you have only to enter any classroom of adolescent youngsters to observe in posture, skin color, and, particularly, in skin conditions such as acne, abundant evidence of defects in the smooth course of adolescent maturing. Growth discrepancies also occur in the proportionate development of legs, arms, and trunk and in the deposition of fat. The timing of growth for different parts of the body may vary in different individuals, resulting in cases of poorly synchronized and markedly disproportionate development (Stolz and Stolz, 1944).

Psychoanalysts have emphasized another way in which adolescence is like a second infancy, in that it involves a recurrence, in their terms, of infantile sexual impulses. The increased sexual drives of adolescence are countered by inhibitions; the adolescent may be afraid of these drives in the genital form in which they now appear, and may regress to more familiar infantile forms of sexuality. Fenichel (1945, p. 111) points out that adolescence is often marked by contradictory psychological expressions: "Egoism and altruism, pettiness and generosity, sociability and loneliness, cheerfulness and sadness, silly jocularity and over-seriousness, intense loves and sudden abandonment of these loves, submission and rebellion, materialism and idealism, rudeness and tender consideration—all are typical." These contradictions as cited by Fenichel are related to the fact that in adolescence there appear side by side or following one another "genital heterosexual impulses, all kinds of infantile sexual behavior, and attitudes of extreme asceticism, which not only try to repress all sexuality but everything pleasant as well" (Fenichel, 1945, pp. 110-111). The intensification of the sexual impulses at puberty, and the resulting conflicts, mark the end of the relatively peaceful latency period. Fenichel expresses the view that all the mental phenomena characteristic of puberty may be regarded as reactions to these disturbances, and as attempts to re-establish the equilibrium of the latency period, and he adds that "in a society that treated infantile sexuality differently puberty, too, would assume a different course" (Fenichel, 1945, p. 111).

In commenting upon this interpretation we may return again to our earlier statement that the difficulties of adolescence have a

multiple origin and cannot be interpreted solely in terms of psychological, or cultural, or biological agencies. The student of child
development is aware of many factors, by no means evidently related to sexual dilemmas or the Oedipus complex, which emerge
at puberty to bedevil and perplex the child, his parents, and his
teachers. Some of these factors have already been mentioned in connection with disturbances in physiological functions and in physical growth. Since adolescence is a period of increased susceptibility
to psychosomatic disorders, no doubt a certain proportion of
these cases of physiological disturbance trace more or less directly
to the child's psychosexual development. A psychosomatic origin
may also be found for some instances of disturbed physical growth.
But we should not be too confident that all or even a majority of
the physiological and physical anomalies which occur in adolescence
have a primarily psychological source. The child's reaction to these
apparent anomalies, the extent to which he tolerates them or is
deeply worried by them, is a psychological matter, but their source
and incidence seem quite as likely to depend upon intrinsic factors
in the biological growth pattern as upon factors in the family situation or in the child's personality structure.

It is difficult to discuss the physical aspects of adolescence without reference to the factor of timing, and to differences in the age
at which the puberal growth cycle begins. Let us consider first the
facts as to the timing of puberty, and then the bearing of these facts
upon adolescent problems. We shall see that it is of the first importance to know not merely what bodily changes are brought about
by puberal growth, but also when these changes are induced.

In the case of girls, the most commonly used landmark for recording individual differences in puberal maturing is the menarche
or the time of first menstruation. This occurs, of course, relatively
late in the puberal growth cycle: a little more than a year after the
adolescent growth spurt has reached its peak, and a little more than
three years after the beginning of the growth spurt (Shuttleworth,
1937).

In our California sample the menarche coincides, on the average,
with the beginning of the teen age, falling at thirteen years and one
month. In some Eastern studies a somewhat later age has been indicated, nearer thirteen and a half or even fourteen. The question
has been asked whether this difference is due to the stimulation of
being near Hollywood, or whether it is an example of earlier maturing in a milder climate. The latter may be a factor, but we
should point out the error in the popular idea that adolescence

comes earliest in the Tropics. Adolescence is probably earliest in the Temperate Zone, and arrives somewhat later as we go north into the colder regions or south into tropical countries. For example, in a recent study in South America (Arrieta, 1932), the average age of menarche directly under the equator, both in the mountains and in coastal areas, and for different ethnic groups, was found to be retarded almost a full year as compared with our California records.

We cannot be sure, however, that this is related to climate in any direct way rather than to general socio-economic conditions and conditions of health. Unfavorable living standards apparently tend to retard the beginning of adolescence; recent observers of child development in war-stricken areas of Europe have been impressed by this fact. A related finding may be the tendency for American children in the same social groups to mature earlier in this generation than was true fifty or a hundred years ago (Mills, 1939). This is probably an illustration of the complex, biosocial nature of adolescence; for while earlier maturing may be attributable to gains in health and nutrition, these, in turn, rest upon social trends.

There is an implication here which may be worth noting. One effect of civilized living has been to extend the term of social adolescence, by delaying the time at which young people can begin to earn their own living. As society becomes more complex, educational demands increase, and more years must be devoted to preparation for adult life. One effect of this has been, of course, to delay the age of marriage and to lengthen the period of sexual postponements or compromises. But social adolescence is also being lengthened at the other end, by pushing the time of maturing down to an earlier age. It is probably safe to say that the period of social adolescence is now from two to three times as long as was the case in America several generations ago. Thus the improved conditions for healthy physical growth, which our society has gradually achieved, tend to make more difficult some of the adolescent problems of mental hygiene, because of the much greater length of time during which these problems must be faced.

Our chief purpose, however, is not to discuss the average age of maturing of various groups, but the great diversity within any group. In any normal sampling of schoolgirls we may expect to find some who reach the menarche at eleven years of age or even a little earlier; and some who are delayed until sixteen or even a little later. In terms of physical growth changes, some girls in a normal sample show the beginning of rapid puberal growth as early as nine years of age and others not until after twelve or thirteen. These extreme differences are not without important after effects. The early-maturing girl who reaches her peak of growth at eleven or even earlier also reaches an early limit of growth. By thirteen she has attained nearly her adult stature, and this adult stature is short (Bayley, 1943). The adolescent growth period is more or less abruptly brought to an end, epiphyses at the growing ends of the bones are closed, and no further increase in height is possible. If you plot the growth curves of early- and of late-maturing girls, you will find that the former are taller in childhood, even at six or seven years of age; they gain in relative height until the age of twelve, when they may be as much as four inches taller than the late-maturing, but by fifteen they are definitely in a shorter-than-average classification.

At the University of California we conducted a series of studies to determine the relationship of these early changes to problems of adjustment. In general, it appears that the very early-maturing girl, at least in an urban culture, is in many respects in a disadvantageous position. In one of our studies, . . . we selected two groups of early- and late-maturing girls, on the basis of skeletal maturity as read from X rays. These were not clinical deviates nor cases of endocrine pathology, but merely the physically most precocious 20 percent and the physically most retarded 20 percent in a normal sample of girls from a public school. The two groups were similar in intelligence, in socio-economic status, in racial background, and in their childhood health records. When we compared them, however, with regard to various social traits, as noted by careful observers in a long series of records, we found that the early-maturing were below the average in prestige, sociability, and leadership; below the average in popularity; below the average in cheerfulness, poise, and expressiveness. In the opinion of their classmates, as judged from a reputation test, they were considered to be rather submissive, withdrawn, and lacking in assurance.

These deficiencies in social attitudes and behavior may indeed be interpretable in terms of deeper layers of personality, but before seeking a more recondite explanation we may point out certain obvious and external ways in which the early-maturing girl is handicapped. The first thing to note is that she finds that she has become physically very conspicuous, at a time when conspicuousness is not valued. She finds herself embarrassingly tall and heavy; she is embarrassed by a greater breast development than seems to her to be normal; she is handicapped when she attempts to participate in the active playground games which are still within the interests of her classmates—for in the case of girls, sexual maturing, although it brings greater strength, often leads to a decreased skill in physical activities involving running and jumping.

The early-maturing girl quite naturally has interests in boys and in social usages and activities more mature than those of her chronological age group. But the males of her own age are unreceptive, for while she is physiologically a year or two out of step with the girls in her class, she is three or four years out of step with the boys —a vast and terrifying degree of developmental distance.

Sometimes the early-maturing girl manages to escape into an older age group, and to associate with other adolescents in her neighborhood who are nearer her own physiological level. In doing this, however, she may encounter other problems that are even more serious. Some of these may be involved in the attitudes of her parents, who are scarcely prepared for this sudden jump into young womanhood. They may feel that she is not yet old enough to go to parties or to have "dates"; they may demand that she continue to dress and act like other eleven- or twelve-year-olds. In this they may have some slight justification; for, unfortunately, a physical growth spurt does not carry with it any corresponding spurt in mental growth, and the physiologically mature youngster may not have the judgment nor mental level which go with longer living. So she is caught in this dilemma: if she remains in her own age group she is frustrated and ill at ease; if she moves into an older group she may fall under parental restrictions and, in any event, may lack the social maturity necessary to make a good adjustment among others of greater experience. To a considerable extent these difficulties are due to the age-grade system of our public schools, which make a physiologically deviate child conspicuous among her classmates. This would be less likely to occur in a small modern school which can make flexible provisions for individuals or, indeed, in the old-time district school, in which the grades are mixed in a single room. A completely heterogeneous grouping, as in the latter instance, may have disadvantages from a teaching standpoint, but for both early- and late-maturing children it may carry great advantages from a social standpoint.

In the case of girls, however, the late-maturing appear to need no special aids or compensations, unless their growth lag is so great as to imply a pathological condition. In the study mentioned above, the girls who were late-maturing were not only superior to the early-maturing but also superior to the average in a great number of the characteristics included in our social observation schedules. They were significantly higher than the early-maturing in traits related to personal appearance and attractiveness, in expressiveness and activity, in buoyance, poise, and cheerfulness, and also in sociability, leadership, and prestige. We are here, of course, speaking of each group taken as a whole; individual cases can be found which do not by any means conform to these generalizations.

Several points may be noted in explaining the apparently better status of so many of the late-maturing girls. The first is a physical advantage. Because of lateness in sexual maturing and in the closing of the epiphyses at the growing points of the bones, she has a long time in which to grow. Her growth is less sudden, less abrupt, than in the early-maturing, seldom reaches as great a velocity at the peak of growth, and involves fewer hazards of physiological imbalance and physical disproportion. The longer period of growth affects particularly the legs, and the late-maturing girl is therefore long-legged, and tends to conform closely to our American standards of beauty of figure, which in the present code of commercial advertising must always be long-legged and usually a bit hypofeminine.

Moreover, in this slower process of adolescence, the parents and the girl herself have a longer time in which to get used to the new interests, new impulses, and new requirements as to behavior. One further point is probably rather important. The late-maturing girl is more nearly in step with the boys in her age group than is the case with the early- or average-maturing girl. The two-year lag in the average maturity patterns of boys as compared with girls is reduced or eliminated among those girls who mature late, and their interests in mixed social activities, when they emerge, are more immediately satisfied.

If now we consider what adolescence may mean to the early- or the late-maturing boy, we find results quite the reverse of those reported for girls. The early-maturing boy enters adolescence at a time when girls in his age group are appreciative of male acquaintances who no longer insist upon being children. He also acquires traits of strength and athletic ability which give him prestige with his own sex. He is likely to be nearer the Apollonian build than the boys who mature later. He wins friends and influences people through the mere fact of physiological precocity, and through the physical dominance which follows (Jones, 1949b).

This is, of course, not without its hazards. The hazard lies partly in discrepancies in different aspects of growth, and discrepancies between what a boy is prepared to do and what his parents and other adults expect and demand of him. The boy who at thirteen is as tall as an adult may be assigned tasks beyond his years. His teacher chooses him for positions of responsibility. The athletic coach grooms him for the first team. His parents expect him to carry a larger share of the family burdens. A thirteen-year-old may not be ready for all this. Muscular development tends to lag somewhat behind skeletal development, and although he is strong, the early-maturing boy is not so strong as he looks. These new demands fall upon him at a time when he is already carrying a heavy load of adjustment to a changed physical structure, a new body image, and new interests and impulses. Nevertheless, in spite of these handicaps, and his very rapid rate of physical change, the early-maturing boy may readily find more advantages than disadvantages in his position. Moreover, unlike the physically precocious girl, his growth is not arrested at an early age; he reaches an average height as an adult, and somewhat better than average strength and general physical ability.

On the other hand, the boy who matures late, like the girl who matures early, is out of step with all the others in his age group. At fifteen or even sixteen he may still be a little boy, ignored by other boys and girls alike, and unable to compete effectively in playground games. In my book *Development in Adolescence* (Jones, 1943), I have presented an example of such a case, a boy who developed many subjective inferiorities in connection with his retarded maturing, and whose compensation took the form of an ineffective social striving. Many of our late-maturing boys adjust by withdrawing from competition, becoming submissive and self-effacing. Others may take a more positive line of action; these are the active small boys, noisy, aggressive, and attention-getting. When at long last the late-maturing boy attains his growth spurt he is likely to reach normal height, but he may be slow to recover from the psychological scars of the period when he was a deviate. Such boys can be helped by giving them a prediction of their adult height and of the time when they may expect to enter the puberal phase of rapid growth. On the basis of Bayley's (1946) work, we can now make this prediction, from skeletal X rays, with a fair degree of accuracy. The boy's pressing but often unasked question, "Am I normal?" can usually be answered in the affirmative. He can be more patient in waiting for nature to take its course, if he understands that his difficulty is merely one of timing and not of basic deficiency.

We have mentioned the sex difference in puberal maturing, which inducts girls into adolescence a year or two earlier, on the average, than boys. Another sex difference has been pointed out from one of our other studies by Dr. Caroline Tryon (1944, p. 234). Achieving manhood or womanhood in our society

is a long, complex, and often confusing learning task. . . . For the most part boys and girls work at these tasks in a stumbling, groping fashion, blindly reaching for the next step without much or any adult assistance. Many lose their way. It seems probable that our adult failure to give assistance derives as much from ignorance about this developmental process as it does from the extensive taboos on sex which characterize our culture.

One of the aspects of this developmental process is that, at least in an urban American culture, girls appear to have a greater problem than boys in adjusting to changing social requirements. In the adolescent culture itself girls encounter many changes in the conception as to what constitutes desirable behavior, changes and even reversals in the value system and in the relative ranking of traits which are important for popularity and prestige. Perhaps the principal single change which we have found in our California group is that at the beginning of adolescence the group standards for conduct among girls emphasize a quiet, demure, rather lady-like demeanor. By the age of fifteen this has altered, and we find that the girls who are now most popular in their set are active, talkative, and marked by a kind of "aggressive good fellowship." These traits, which may in part be adaptations to the hesitant and immature social approaches of boys, must again undergo considerable change in the later years of adolescence, if a girl is to maintain her status in the group. Dr. Tryon points out that boys, by comparison, seem to have a somewhat more consistent set of criteria to meet in developing their sex roles during this growth period.

*   *   *

CHAPTER THREE

Adolescents with Problems

6

OUT-OF-SCHOOL YOUTH TELL THEIR STORY

by Howard M. Bell

Although many of our personal and social problems differ from those of other people, the problems we experience during certain periods of our lives are somewhat similar to those experienced by persons during the same periods. The problems of children are different from those of adults; similarly, the problems of adolescents differ from those of children and adults. What are some of the problems confronting American youth? During the depression years of the 1930's, a study was made of more than thirteen thousand youths sixteen to twenty-four years of age, most of whom were out of school. A part of the study dealt with the problems of these young people and what they thought were the problems of youth in general. In this brief excerpt, Howard M. Bell, the director of the study, presents the results of this part of the study and the conclusions to be drawn from it. [From *Youth Tell Their Story*, Washington, D. C.: American Council on Education, 1938, pp. 249-255. Reprinted by permission of the American Council on Education.]

Toward the close of the interview, each youth was asked to express himself freely on what he considered his most perplexing personal problem. Then, as a final question, he was asked, in a leisurely and informal way, whether or not he believed that there was such a thing as a "youth problem."

A comparison of the responses to these two questions (Table 1) reveals a fact that we have already pointed out—that youth, like so many adults, are impelled to interpret general problems in the light of their personal experiences. Although there were a few differences in the responses to these two questions, it is clear that, as a general rule, a young person believes that the basic problem confronting all youth is essentially the same as the problem which he personally has to face.

TABLE 1

YOUTH'S MOST PERPLEXING PERSONAL PROBLEMS COMPARED WITH THEIR OPINIONS ON WHAT CONSTITUTES THE YOUTH PROBLEM

YOUTH'S OWN PROBLEM		YOUTH PROBLEM IN GENERAL	
Type of problem	*Percentage of youth*	*Type of problem*	*Percentage of youth*
Economic security	66.6	*Economic security*	57.7
Education, vocational choice	13.1	Conduct or morals	11.1
Home	9.0	*Educational, vocational choice*	10.6
Personality adjustment	3.2	*Home*	7.1
Social relations with opposite sex	2.6	Recreation	4.9
Other	5.5	Other	8.6
Total	100.0	*Total*	100.0
Number of youth stating problem	9,414	Number of youth stating problem	8,111

Perhaps it should first be recorded that only one-fourth of the youth believed that there was *no* youth problem, while less than a third reported that they had no "perplexing personal problem" of their own. Of the youth who specified the nature of these problems, substantially more than half named some economic problem as the one that was giving them the greatest personal concern, as well as the one which they considered the basic problem of youth in general.

It is significant that the factors which usually operate to color attitudes and opinions seem to have had little effect upon a youth's interpretation of what constitutes the youth problem. Table 2 reveals that, for most of the basic groups, the differences of opinion are almost negligible.

Whether one considers these interpretations of the general youth problem from the standpoint of sex, race, age, relief status, or parentage, one discovers but slight differences in the frequency of the various responses. While 58 per cent of the white youth considered the problem of their generation as essentially economic, 53 per cent of the Negro youth shared the same point of view. While 59 per cent of the youth from relief families defined the general youth problem as basically a matter of dollars and cents, 58 per cent of the youth from nonrelief families were of the same opinion. A comparable similarity appears in the frequency with which youth characterized the general problem as moral, educational, domestic, or recreational.

TABLE 2

OPINIONS OF YOUNG PEOPLE ON WHAT CONSTITUTES THE YOUTH PROBLEM

Classification of youth	Percentage of each group						
All youth stating	Eco-nomic	Conduct or morals	Education	Home	Recreation	Other	Percentage base
problem	57.7	11.1	10.6	7.1	4.9	8.6	8,111
Male: single	59.5	11.6	11.3	4.8	4.9	7.9	3,692
married	62.8	9.7	9.4	6.3	3.1	8.7	524
Female: single	54.7	9.9	12.1	7.9	5.4	10.0	2,663
married	56.1	12.7	5.8	12.5	5.0	7.9	1,232
White	58.3	10.9	10.5	7.1	4.7	8.5	7,160
Negro	52.9	12.3	10.6	7.0	6.5	10.7	951
16-year-olds	53.5	10.4	13.1	7.6	7.9	7.5	820
20-year-olds	58.6	10.1	10.3	7.4	4.0	9.6	1,009
24-year-olds	60.8	11.2	8.1	8.3	4.1	7.5	957
Relief	59.4	12.7	7.8	8.0	4.2	7.9	887
Nonrelief	57.5	10.9	11.0	6.9	5.0	8.7	7,183
Native parentage	57.1	11.3	10.8	7.5	4.3	9.0	5,916
Foreign-born parentage	63.4	9.1	9.3	5.3	6.6	6.3	1,219

Considering the implications of a good deal of the data previously submitted, this belief that the nature of the youth problem is basically economic should surprise no one. It will be remembered, for example, that 54 per cent of the out-of-school youth had left school for economic reasons. The median weekly wage for all workers was under $13. Large numbers were found to be vocationally maladjusted, and about one out of every five was totally unemployed. It is hardly surprising therefore that young people regard their own personal problems, as well as the basic problem of all youth, as essentially a matter of bread and butter.

Although there is a clear-cut tendency on the part of young people to emphasize the lack of economic security as the most serious problem confronting their generation, it can hardly be assumed that there is a monotonous uniformity in either their interpretations of the problem or the suggestions they offer for its possible solution. On no question did we get such a wealth of varied and colorful comments. Our space will permit the presentation of only a fraction of their spontaneous expressions of opinion.

"We can't get a job like other people used to before." Solution: "The government should pass some kind of law."

"Young people worry about where the next meal is coming from."

"Getting jobs is the main problem. Employers want experienced people, and I don't see how you can get experience if they won't give you a job."

"No work . . . no money . . . no good education . . . no good times . . . these are the problems that young people have to face."

"The problem is how to get married on $15 a week."

"The main thing in any young person's mind is getting a job he likes. Financial security . . . there must be some answer, but it's way over my head. If so-called brain trusters can't do anything, I can't suggest anything."

"It used to be you could get a job anywhere, but now you can't hardly buy one."

"They [young people] have a feeling of defeatism because of the depression. Buck them up! Make them feel the country is not neglecting them."

"The general problem is economic—the problem of finding a suitable permanent job. The so-called moral problems are the result of the failure of the older generation to guard their own conduct and to teach children how to live."

"There is nothing to do when you get out of school. There should be shorter hours and give more people a chance to work."

"The problem is one of having a fair chance—the possibility of getting somewhere. I feel very strongly about young people who are clever and yet who will be stunted by economic conditions. By the time you are twenty-two, you are no longer young. The youth of America will have to wake up and organize themselves. Other people won't help if youth does nothing for itself . . . here I've been saying things I've never said out loud before. I enjoyed it."

"A fellow wants to have a good time and have a little spending money. You go crazy if you hang around the same block with nothing to do. Work is the only solution. How you get it, I don't know."

According to about 10 per cent of the youth, the basic problem that faces their generation is not economic, but moral.

"Some are too wise in sexual matters. They are doing things they will be sorry for. Drinking is one reason for this. They won't be frightened or won't learn until they get into a scrape."

"Young people smoke and drink too much just because they think it is smart."

"Sex education is a big problem in the life of any youth, and I think such education should begin as soon as the child is old enough to understand."

"Boys and girls are wild these days. They get that way from following older people."

"Girls worry too much about love."

"Social relations with opposite sex is the main problem. If you love a girl and she don't love you, it's awful."

"The trouble with most boys is that they try to act like the gangsters they see in the movies."

Another 10 per cent believed that the problem was essentially a matter of education.

"Young people worry most about what their futures are going to be." Solution: "An adequate system of personal vocational guidance in the schools."

"They ought to have a course in school on how to go about getting a job. One ought to know how to approach an employer, how to ask for a job, and where to look for it."

"The government should continue its help so that those who can't afford higher education could get it free."

"When youth want to quit school, let them quit and don't force them to go. It drives me nuts to sit in school when you are not learning anything."

"Everybody should have a chance to take a college education. The more education you get, the better you are able to face life."

"Young people stop school too soon because parents can't afford to keep them there. A provision should be made to allow them to go through at least high school."

"Educational programs are too full of frills. Young people are not trained; they are merely put through school."

"Those who do not appreciate it have a chance of education, but those who really need it cannot get it."

And others:

"Youth is in a muddle. Out of school too young; they don't know what they want to do or why. They are in the midst of a great social and economic change."

"Young people very restless because economic conditions are making the future uncertain. Most of them aren't free to marry and establish a home because they have no financial security. They feel that life is somewhat futile and that there is no use in struggling for anything, as no one knows what the future holds."

"Young people having a tough time getting jobs. Those that they get don't pay well enough to enable them to get married or to do other things they want to do. There are more people than there are jobs. Many elderly people who aren't able to work have to keep on working anyhow, as they have nothing to fall back on. Meanwhile, the young people who are idle are getting into trouble because they have nothing to do."

"Young people have had to do a great deal of thinking for and about themselves, so if older people would make a greater effort to consider and respect their opinions and ideas, instead of robbing them of self-confidence and killing ambition by constantly reminding them that they are 'too young' to know what they are talking about or too young for real responsibility, youth would be far better off than they are today."

"If people would either let young people alone or actually do something for them instead of just talking about it, youth might have a chance."

*   *   *

SUMMARY

As youth themselves see it, the "youth problem" is largely a matter of economic security. In many respects, their conception of the basic problems that confront their generation has been reflected in the conclusions that have been set down in various sections of this report.

It seems to us, as apparently it seems to them, that the most pressing problems, involving the need for the most vigorous social action, fall into three general areas:

1. *Employment.* For hundreds of thousands of youth in America, this means getting a job. For as many others, it means a wage that will provide both an acceptable standard of living, and an opportunity to provide for future years.

2. *Education.* For large numbers who have been forced out of school for economic reasons, this means the creation of a less fictitious equality of opportunity, and, for many others who are still in school, it means an educational program that is more clearly in harmony with their interests and needs.

3. *Recreation.* For no less than millions of young people in America, this calls for an awakening, on the part of communities, to the social as well as the personal values of healthful and satisfying recreation, and a determination to develop leisure-time programs that will not only absorb energies that often lead to delinquent behavior, but which will add something valuable to the spiritual stature of those who participate in them.

.... 7 ....

PROBLEMS OF NORMAL COLLEGE STUDENTS
AND THEIR FAMILIES

by Clark W. Heath, M.D., and
Lewise W. Gregory

What are the personal and social problems of normal college students and their families? Clark W. Heath of Harvard University and his collaborator sought answers to this question in their study of Harvard University sophomores who voluntarily participated in a college counseling service. The results of the study are presented in the following article. [From *School and Society*, 1946, *63*, 355-358. Reprinted by permission of the authors and the Society for the Advancement of Education.]

College counseling services as a rule are limited to providing help to students who are in trouble or who voluntarily bring their problems for discussion. Most students, however, have "problems" and would benefit greatly by a broad counseling or consultative program in which they all took part. Of 259 healthy, "normal" students investigated by the Grant Study in 1938-1942, 232 men, or 90 per cent, either raised problems that they wished to discuss or presented problems which the staff recognized as ones that thorough discussions would help to solve. It is of interest to analyze the kinds of situations presented by these young men.

The subjects of the study were [Harvard University] sophomores from the classes entering in 1937, 1938, 1939, and 1940. Their participation in the research was voluntary. They were chosen in general for good health, satisfactory academic status, and overtly good social adjustment, as evidenced by the medical records and reports from the deans. In respect to socioeconomic conditions, race or creed, and pre-school training, they represented a fair cross section of the college population. The investigations consisted of the co-operative observations of a physician, several psychiatrists, a physiologist, an anthropologist, a psychologist, and a social case-worker (who interviewed practically all the families as well as the young men themselves) (Wells, 1944; Heath et al., 1945). All the men were studied by uniform methods, and each was given ample opportunity to discuss any problems that he had.

In arranging the data we asked ourselves the following four questions:

1. How many men sought answers to problems which they proposed themselves, and were glad to talk about when they had the opportunity?
2. How many really needed advice, to help in problems which we recognized ourselves, whether or not they sought our opinion?
3. How many of these had really urgent or acute problems?
4. How many men had parents who raised problems which they were glad to discuss?

Of course, it is a matter of judgment as to what constitutes a "problem" or one which it is felt worth while to try to help a boy solve. In deciding what were "problems" in this sense, we have kept in mind the sorts of things that might come up in a college counseling system. We have omitted aspects of a boy's life which occurred before college or during postgraduate years. We have omitted purely medical or other technical aspects that would not be in the sphere of the counselor. We have included, however, some of the sexual matters which we believe could be adequately handled by a mature lay consultant. We have omitted the many problems occasioned by entrance into the war services. Situations met very objectively with little emotion, without the solicitation of help, and without clear indication that help was needed, were omitted. More "problems" than are here listed would probably occur in the unselected college population, since obviously poorly adjusted students were eliminated in the selection of participants in the Grant Study. In a formal college counseling system, probably more questions of an academic nature would be asked than here. Table I gives the number of men and their families who raised problems.

The important point is that the great majority of students raised questions for which they wanted answers or otherwise presented situations which would benefit from discussion. What sort of students were those who raised no particular issues? There were 27 of these. Eighteen were young men who were judged to have natively good judgment and insight and seemed to be relatively invulnerable, so that one could scarcely see how they could get into real trouble. Six were men who showed sound judgment but possessed rather marked degrees of blandness, conventionality, or lack of feeling or imagination, which would prevent them from reacting unfavorably to most situations. The remaining three men failed to reach really good rapport with the examiners, although an adequate amount of time was devoted to them. Of course, circumstances may have been so even and secure for these men that problems were not occasioned. On the other hand, a more exhaustive inquiry might have revealed deep-seated trouble, but it would be outside the realm of the college consultative service.

Table I

"PROBLEMS" PRESENTED BY 259 GRANT-STUDY PARTICIPANTS

	Number of participants	Percentage
1. Self-offered problems	187	72
2. Problems recognized by the staff	227	88
3. Urgent or acute problems	43	17
4. Problems raised by families	190	73
5. Total number having problems	232	90
6. No definite problems recognized	27	10

The kinds of problems varied greatly according to individual situations. Most of them centered around social or family relationships. Many men revealed multiple interconnected problems such as personality difficulties, adjustment to family and friends, college finances, and career. Others revealed only isolated problems in a setting of very sound personality. Any classification of problems is somewhat artificial. In Table II, however, are illustrated the types of issues raised, grouped according to certain areas which seemed important.

Table II

KINDS OF PROBLEMS RAISED

(Including both self-offered problems and those recognized by the Staff.)

	Number of participants
1. *Social adjustment* (shyness, feelings of inferiority, social sensitivity, making friends, meeting and getting along with girls, immaturity per se, roommates, class dissatisfactions)	113

TABLE II (cont.)

	Number of participants
2. *Adjustments to family*	
a. Parental discord, separation, divorce, remarriage	14
b. Antagonism to parents, reaction to domination or discipline, family criticism, lack of understanding, family relations in general	69
c. Advice concerning physical or mental health of parent	18
d. Adjustment to death of parent	6
3. *Career and life work*	67
4. *Finances in college*	35
5. *Need for discussions centering around subject's personality*	
a. Emotional instability, tenseness, excitability, fears and concerns, "psychoneurotic" symptoms	50
b. Discussions of personality in general, integration of personality, handling of arrogance and egotism	47
c. Need for directions, objectives, purpose, and values	32
d. Mood swings	21
e. Rigidity, "just-so" personality	12
f. Possible mental illness	6
6. *Academic*	
a. Adjustment to Harvard, dissatisfactions with Harvard	20
b. Academic help needed, organization of time and work	14
c. Intellectual lacks for college or career	6
d. Field of concentration (majoring)	3
7. *Sex*	
a. Marriage, love affairs, sex relations	39
b. Problems arising from masturbation	17
c. Need for information concerning homosexuality	3
d. Information about venereal disease	2
8. *Others*	
a. Anti-Semitism, anti-Nazism	8
b. Religious conflict, search for religious belief	8
c. Alcohol	7
d. College scrapes	6
e. General advice needed	6
f. Help in getting job	5
g. Stammering, speech	4
h. Insomnia	3
i. Handwriting	2
j. Extracurricular activities	2
k. Revolt against New England	2
l. Extreme wealth	1

Table III illustrates the kinds of problems which were considered urgent or acute. The largest proportion of these referred to relations with parents. Social adjustment in general was not an urgent problem but was often a matter of immaturity, requiring time and help in self-understanding.

TABLE III

URGENT OR ACUTE PROBLEMS

	Number of participants
1. Active assistance needed for repair of relations with parents	8
2. Mental adjustment, depression, acute panic, need of better understanding of self	7
3. College scrapes	5
4. Mental adjustment, question of mental disease	4
5. Anti-Semitism, anti-Nazism	3
6. Help needed because of death, divorce, separation, or illness of parents	3
7. Sexual	3
8. Relationships with girls, fiancée	3
9. Career choice, training	3
10. Alcoholism	2
11. Financial	1
12. General advice	1
Total	43

The parents of nearly all participants were interviewed informally in the home. Such interviews lasted at least several hours. In the course of them, mothers and fathers were made to feel free to discuss many of their problems. Most of the topics discussed did not necessarily concern the son in college. They often had to do with financial difficulties and general conduct of the relations between parents and their children. In Table IV, only current problems are listed. Those having to do with the years preceding the son's entrance into college or after college are omitted.

COMMENT

In some ways, a broad investigative organization such as the Grant Study offers advantages in reaching students' problems which

TABLE IV

CURRENT PROBLEMS RAISED BY FAMILIES OF PARTICIPANTS

	Number of participants
1. *Financial difficulties at home*	72
2. *Financial help for participant*	6
3. *Concerns about participant*	
a. Conflict with boy's attitude in home	14
b. General adjustment, social attitude, drinking, direction needed, etc.	26
c. Health, physical, or sexual development	11
d. Love affair or marriage	7
e. Career choice	7
f. Academic progress	2
g. Question of changing college	2
4. *Concerns about other children*	
a. Social adjustments	12
b. Stability, marriage, morals, jealousies, etc.	39
c. Discipline in general	6
d. Religious teaching	1
5. *Dissensions between parents, separation, divorce*	19
6. *Other dissensions in family*	6
7. *Health or mental illness of partner*	20
8. *Adjustment to death of partner*	6
9. *Anti-Semitism, anti-Nazism*	4

a college counseling service or dean's office may not have. In the first place, the students were made to feel that they were helping in the investigation by talking about themselves or asking questions, and that they were not encroaching on anyone's time. In the second place, each participant knew that he would be put through certain routine examinations by different observers: the medical examination, the anthropological measurements, the psychometric tests, the psychiatric interviews, etc. In this way he became aware of different fields in the study of man, and his interest in his personal characteristics was aroused. We could observe a certain educational advantage in the system. Thirdly, he could voluntarily choose any one of the various examiners to discuss matters of concern to him. These conditions could be easily duplicated in college counseling if it were assumed that ordered interviewing is important for all students, in fact, if it were made a part of the curriculum and if a certain amount of research were incorporated in the work.

A large share of the problems raised either by the participant or by the staff centered about social and family adjustment. In most instances this was an aspect of immaturity. Great improvement was observed in many of the men as they grew older. The objection can be raised that these problems and many others would take care of themselves with time and the maturing influence of the college environment. In many cases this would be true. It is felt, nevertheless, that a great deal can be done and time saved by helping a young man to gain confidence and to develop a sense of reliance upon his own judgment. His path can be eased and in many instances mistakes avoided.

The manner of handling problems in the Grant Study is one which largely avoids giving direct advice. The procedure used, which we feel is an important technique, has been to open up the "problem" for discussion, taking a fair and unimpassioned viewpoint of all sides and allowing the young man to reach his own decision. Occasionally it is necessary to review certain well-known facts, as would be the case in certain sex problems. By maintaining as good relations as possible with each student, freely offering the facilities of the staff, resistances of the more reserved men would be broken down. Analysis of the effects of the study upon the lives of the men will have to await future appraisal. The group as a whole registered wholehearted approval and appreciation of the work.

As maturation takes place, circumstances change and different sorts of "problems" arise. The data of the Grant Study contain many examples of childhood and adolescent "problems" which could well have been solved by consultative means at that earlier time. A postgraduate follow-up procedure is being employed at present and the participants are still finding uses for the Grant Study services. These young men now range in age from about 22 to 29 years. Most of them are returning from the war and renewing their career interests. There have been many calls for information in the postgraduate years as well as many return visits to the study. In fact, many have married, and the problems associated with a new generation of parents and their children are being called to our attention. One can say that counseling ends only with the lifetime of the person.

One of the most troublesome problems was that of strained relationships with parents. This sometimes necessitated personal discussions with parents themselves. The conclusion is unavoidable that many quite "normal" young men enter college not well prepared for adjusting themselves to college life and that many of them have parents who themselves are poorly prepared to encourage or secure the most favorable atmosphere for higher education. This is not to point criticism at the parents of our subjects, whose support of the work has been most generous, but it is meant as criticism of a widespread complacency existing throughout the structure of our society. In some ways, college advising is a patchwork affair, trying to make the best out of difficult situations that had their origins much earlier in life. Note in Table IV the relatively few families concerned with career choice or academic progress, compared with various social adjustments. Yet, ideally, the type of training for the kind of career should be the primary concern while their sons are in college. It is as though the earlier problems of parents and their children and the various aspects of personal relations had not been solved by the time the boy entered college, so that a good portion of his energies still had to be spent in developing a workable knowledge of how to get on with others.

SUMMARY

1. Two hundred thirty-two out of 259 college men (90 per cent), selected for good health, satisfactory academic status, and overtly good social adjustments, presented problems for solution.

2. One hundred eighty-seven (72 per cent) proposed problems themselves and were glad to talk them over when given the opportunity. Two hundred twenty-seven (88 per cent) were recognized as needing help in problems uncovered by the staff. Forty-three (17 per cent) presented urgent or acute problems. The families of 190 (73 per cent) of these men raised current problems which they were glad to discuss.

3. Although there was considerable individual variation in the type of problems discussed, most of them centered around social and family relationships. Comment is made upon the relatively poor preparation of even "normal" young men for adjusting themselves to college life and the lack of the best encouragement from the family to secure the most favorable atmosphere for higher education.

.... 8 ....

SEX DIFFERENCES IN THE LIFE PROBLEMS AND

INTERESTS OF ADOLESCENTS, 1935 AND 1957

by Dale B. Harris

How do adolescents in 1957 compare with adolescents in 1935 in their personal problems and interests, the latter in terms of what they would like to read about and discuss or hear discussed? To what extent do adolescent boys and girls differ in their life problems and interests? These are the topics investigated in this repeat study by Dale B. Harris of Pennsylvania State University. The list of problems and instructions for ranking are appended to the selection. [From *Child Development*, 1959, *30*, 453-459, with minor additions by Dr. Harris. Reprinted by permission of the author and Society for Research in Child Development.]

This is a study of interests and problems which uses the method of rank order rather than a check list as its research techniques. The items ranked are 15 topics selected from the concerns of adolescents. High school students were asked first to consider the items as personal problems and to construct an order reflecting their own experience with the issues as personal problems. The students then re-ranked the same items in order of interest, considering the topics as things they would like to read about and discuss or hear discussed.

The problems and instructions for ranking were taken verbatim from a study published by Dr. P. M. Symonds (1936a,b). He had selected the issues from young people's own discussions and phrased the issues in terms used by young people themselves. His 1641 students attended junior and senior high schools in Tulsa, Oklahoma, and New York City. The 1165 youth in the present study came from the junior-senior high school in a Minnesota community. Twenty-two years and considerable social, cultural, and economic change separate the circumstances of the two studies. Whether geographic or regional differences also influence the data cannot be said. In both studies, the samples represented in general the socioeconomic distribution of the communities from which they were drawn. The comparability of samples drawn from different geographic areas without close control through a stratification procedure is questionable. But the comparability of samples is also problematical across long time intervals, in which social and cultural changes have occurred, even when stratification by some socioeconomic index has been attempted. Changing conditions may themselves affect the index.

The hypothesis of the present study is taken from Professor Symonds' discussion (1936a): "Change the social and economic structure of society and you immediately change the relative emphasis of these problems and interests."

In a ranking process as in any *system,* change in one feature or aspect may have widespread effects throughout the system. The elements are *relative* to one another. The resulting rank order is not a *scale* of values. Each choice made removes a degree of freedom and relates to the choices already made and those yet to be made. In comparing two orderings of a set of items, a difference in judgments on one item must be reflected in a difference in judgments elsewhere in the system. When problems or interests are ranked, and rankings compared, one can assume that an observed difference may portend a real change in the stimulus value of one of the items ranked. He does not know that there has been a comparable shift throughout the system. The other changes observed may or may not be equivalent, psychologically. And from ranks, one knows nothing at all about shifts of a particular one, or a few, or all the items on a *scale* of values. Which change may be psychologically significant and which may merely reflect the upset in the equilibrium of the system is not automatically apparent.

The ranks accorded a series of stimuli are systematically affected by the order in which the stimuli are first presented. Symonds removed this effect in his study by presenting the items in reverse order to approximately half his subjects. This study used the same procedure. The sample of children was drawn randomly from the available supply to constitute groups of 100 boys and 100 girls at each grade; half of each sex responded to the items in the order Symonds presented them in his report, and the other half responded to a reversed order.

For fifteen items ranked in one experience, a rho value of .535 is required to establish a relationship greater than chance at the 5 per cent level of significance. To interpret differences in rankings accorded items by boys and girls, or changes between two sets of rankings made at different times, one can place more confidence in *mean* ranks of samples than in ranks made by individuals. But the meaning of the magnitude of the differences thus described is still elusive. By building a body of experience with different arrangements of the data one can possibly increase the insight he brings to bear on any one arrangement.

For example, when means of rankings of items considered as problems, established by 100 boys in each grade, 7 through 12, are compared, the average or typical between grade-group rank-order correlation is +.74 (estimated from the W statistic, Kendall [1948]). For the same items considered as interests, the typical between grade-group rank-order correlation is +.78. For girls, the corresponding values are +.70 and +.72. Thus, children's rankings from grade to grade change no more on the average than is suggested by correlation values in the .70's. Putting the data of boys and girls together in each grade, thus increasing reliability through the size of N but also introducing any existing systematic sex differences, the values become +.65 (problems) and +.63 (interests). (Both estimated from Kendall's W.)

Because there are likely to be intrinsic relationships in any set of values ranked by a group of judges, simply because judges from similar backgrounds are not reacting blindly or randomly to meaningful material, it is instructive to examine some typical inter-array correlations estimated from Kendall's W. If we consider the four ranks of mean values accorded by boys and girls in 1935 and 1957 to *problems*, this typical inter-array correlation is +.58. For four arrays of *interests* this value is also +.58. Throwing together the eight arrays of problems and interests, the value becomes +.36. These values provide a pragmatic bench-mark to judge the meaning of the correlation values presented below, which have a theoretical top value of +1.00 and describe a chance relationship as .00.

Taking all boys regardless of grade and similarly combining all girls for purposes of comparison with data obtained on the same items by Symonds in 1935, some interesting observations can be made. Youth showed greater consistency in the ordering of these items, considered first as problems and then as interests, in 1935 than they do at present. This change is true both for boys (+.63 compared with —.23) and for girls (+.66 compared with +.25). Thus in 1957, there is little correspondence between a set of issues considered as problems and the order of interest in the same issues. This was not true in 1935, when there was a noticeable correspondence between the sets of ranks.

But how do young people separated by almost a generation compare in the ordering of their problems and their interests? Boys' rankings of interests across the years are somewhat more consistent

TABLE 1

RANKS ACCORDED ISSUES CONSIDERED AS PROBLEMS BY HIGH SCHOOL
BOYS AND GIRLS IN 1935 AND IN 1957

| | Boys | | | | Girls | | | |
| | 1935 | | 1957 | | 1935 | | 1957 | |
Issue	Mean Rank	Rank	Mean Rank	Rank	Mean Rank	Rank	Mean Rank	Rank
Health	6.7	2	9.1*	12	6.6	2	8.7*	12.5
Love, marriage	10.8	15	9.2*	13.5	11.0	15	8.5*	10
Safety	8.3	8.5	9.2*	13.5	8.8	12	10.0*	14.5
Money	6.2	1	6.3	2	6.8	3	6.5	2
Mental hygiene	8.7	13	8.2	8	8.2	9.5	6.9*	3.5
Study habits	6.8	3	5.0	1	7.4	6	6.3*	1
Recreation	8.3	8.5	10.1	15	8.4	11	10.0*	14.5
Personal and moral qualities	7.1	4	6.6*	3	7.3	4	7.1	5
Home and family relationships	8.2	7	8.4	10	8.2	9.5	7.6	6
Manners	8.5	11.5	7.6*	5	7.4	6	8.6*	11
Personal attractiveness	7.9	6	7.7	6	6.2	1	6.9*	3.5
Daily schedule	9.0	14	8.3*	9	9.4	14	8.7*	12.5
Civic interest	8.5	11.5	7.9*	7	9.0	13	8.4	9
Getting along with other people	8.4	10	8.6	11	7.9	8	8.0	8
Philosophy of life	7.5	5	7.5	4	7.4	6	7.7	7

* Change from 1935 significant at the 1 per cent level.

(+.76) than their rankings of problems then and now (+.47). For girls, there is little difference between relative positions accorded problems and interests over the years (problems, +.50; interests, +.55).

Do boys and girls accord the same order of importance to a set of adolescent problems? In both periods boys and girls rank their problems similarly. In 1935, the similarity of the rank order of the sexes is expressed by a correlation value of +.80. In the 1957 study, the value is +.77. The similarity of boys and girls is as great, on the average, as the similarity of successive grade groups of boys, or of girls. When the items were ranked according to interest in 1935, a value of +.80 expresses the similarity of boys' and girls' judgments. The comparable figure in 1957 is .58.

The changes described above become more interesting when we look at specific ranks in Tables 1 and 2. As problems (Table 1), three items change five ranks or more across time for both boys and girls (health, mental health, manners), three more for boys only (safety, recreation, schedule) and two more for girls only (love and marriage, and study habits). As interests (Table 2), three change for both sexes across time (love and marriage, family relations, manners), and one more for each sex singly (recreation for girls; getting along with others for boys). There are as many sex differences now as in 1935. At that time seven topics significantly differentiated the sexes as problems at the .01 level of certainty.[1] Now eight topics satisfy the .01 level.

Sex differences in interests also are about the same. In 1935 boys and girls rated nine topics quite different. In 1957, ten topics satisfied the .01 level.

Attention to item placements show that a number of topics are relatively high as sources of problems: *Money* is still high as a problem to both boys and girls (ranks 2, and 2, respectively). It is of considerably greater interest to boys than to girls (rank 3 as compared with rank 10).[2] *Health* at rank 2 as a problem in 1935 is no longer seen as such (rank 12), though interest in it is still relatively high, especially among boys. *Study habits* are somewhat more of a prob-

TABLE 2

RANKS ACCORDED ISSUES CONSIDERED AS INTERESTS BY HIGH SCHOOL
BOYS AND GIRLS IN 1935 AND IN 1957

	Boys				Girls			
	1935		1957		1935		1957	
Issue	*Mean Rank*	*Rank*	*Mean Rank*	*Rank*	*Mean Rank*	*Rank*	*Mean Rank*	*Rank*
Health	5.6	2	6.4*	2	6.6	4	7.0	6
Love, marriage	9.3	13	7.7*	8	9.4	12	6.5*	4.5
Safety	7.8	7	8.7*	11	9.2	10	10.2*	14
Money	7.1	3	6.5*	3	8.1	8	8.2	10
Mental hygiene	9.6	14	9.5	13	9.8	13.5	8.0*	9
Study habits	8.7	11	9.4*	12	9.3	11	9.9*	12.5
Recreation	4.9	1	5.6*	1	5.6	2	7.8*	8
Personal and moral qualities	7.7	5.5	7.3*	6	7.6	7	7.1	7
Home and family relationships	8.4	10	7.2*	5	8.3	9	6.4*	2.5
Manners	7.5	4	8.6*	10	6.3	3	8.5*	11
Personal attractiveness	8.1	8	8.0	9	5.4	1	6.0*	1
Daily schedule	10.5	15	10.9	15	10.4	15	11.4*	15
Civic interest	9.0	12	9.6*	14	9.8	13.5	9.9	12.5
Getting along with other people	8.2	9	7.1*	4	7.0	5	6.4*	2.5
Philosophy of life	7.7	5.5	7.4	7	7.3	6	6.5*	4.5

* Change from 1935 significant at the 1 per cent level.

[1] This index of statistical significance refers to the difference between mean ranks, interpreted in terms of the standard errors of these means. It does not refer to shift in rank order.

[2] In 1935 Professor Symonds attributed the high ranks accorded money to the current economic stress. Studies of allowances show that modern youth "never had it so good" from an economic point of view, but inflation and rising standards of living expectancy keep the teen-age group keenly aware of the medium of exchange.

lem now than in 1935, especially for boys, but the topic ranked quite low in interest value in both periods. *Moral qualities* and *philosophy of life* come next in position both as problems and as topics of interest and are of similar relative magnitude in both periods.

Of intermediate concern as problems are the following: Both sexes see *mental health* as somewhat more of a problem to them now than they did in 1935, and for girls it now appears in the top five ranks. It has, likewise, moved up significantly (P = .01) in rank of interest to girls, though it remains low on the boys' list. *Home and family relations* is likewise ranked higher as a problem by girls than by boys now (P = .01). Relative to 1935, boys rank it slightly lower and girls slightly higher as a problem, though in these intermediate positions such shifting is statistically meaningless. Both boys and girls rank this topic higher on the list of interests than they did in 1935, girls very considerably so (rank of 2.5 compared with 9, P = .01). *Manners and courtesy,* up somewhat (P = .01) as a problem for boys as compared with the earlier period, is significantly less a problem for girls now (rank 11 compared with rank 6, P = .01). As a topic of interest it is down sharply for both sexes.

Attractiveness, of intermediate value both as a problem and as an interest for boys in both periods, ranks high in both interest value and as a problem for girls in both periods. Likewise, *getting along with others* was and is of considerable interest to girls and has risen (rank 4 compared to rank 9, P = .01) as a topic of interest to boys. It is of intermediate significance as a problem.

Civic affairs was and is of about median significance as a problem to both boys and girls and is of even less relative importance as a topic of interest.

Of least concern as problems now are the following:

Recreation, of intermediate significance as a problem to both boys and girls in 1935, is negligible now. It was and is number one in interest value to boys but has dropped from second to eighth place for girls (P = .01).

Health, of high significance both as a problem and as a topic of interest to boys and girls in 1935 is now negligible as a problem to either sex. It is now only of intermediate interest to girls, though it remains high on the boys' list.

Safety is of little interest and even less a problem to both boys and girls now than in 1935 (P = .01).

Love and marriage, ranked low as a problem by boys in both periods, has risen to an intermediate rank as a problem for girls. Both sexes now give it an intermediate interest rating, some several ranks higher than twenty-two years ago. The change in both problem and interest values of this topic is statistically significant, highly so for girls.

Daily schedule is of little significance then or now, both to boys and girls, as problem or as interest.

This observation concerning the specific rankings accorded the issues should be made. Both psychologically and statistically, the highest and lowest ranks are most differentiated in any ranking or scaling procedure. The method in this study called for the identification of the first three positions, and then positions 13, 14, and 15. The intermediate positions were assigned last and may, particularly in the ranking of interests, represent a state of psychological indifference or lack of discrimination more than a state of intermediate significance. Should this be the case, the significance attributed by Symonds to the "relatively high" rank of philosophy of life (sixth in fifteen issues) may be modified somewhat. He affirmed (1936a) that "values and goals are craved" by youth and challenged teacher and counselors by the rank accorded this topic. Symonds attributed the high rank of money as a problem to the depression years and observed "it is a pity" that money drops to a much lower rank in interest value. The problem significance of money was not just a function of depression years, it is now clear.

The lack of concern with love and marriage, identified by Professor Symonds as "sex adjustments," puzzled him, and he explained the low ranks by reference to "repression." His own hypothesis concerning social change appears from the present data to be equally plausible. A similar point can be made about mental health as an issue in adolescence. Professor Symonds dismissed the low ranks attributed to this issue in these words: "Mental health likewise is no concern of healthy, growing adolescents. The crest of life is before them. Their failures and thwartings have not yet turned back upon themselves." The changed cultural ethos apparently has made a difference in the significance accorded this issue in the adolescent years.

The shifts noted in the tables and in the brief discussion for the most part confirm what observers of recent social trends have noted. Today, youth marry younger and show an earlier interest in social relations, love, and marriage. Our culture appears to recognize more openly now than two decades ago the sex, love, and marriage problems of young people. Physical health is actually less a problem today, and possibly receives less attention in school and in the popular press, whereas mental health discussions, literature, and posters appear in every newspaper, magazine, and waiting room. An increase in informality and casualness in dress and behavior may reflect itself in the decline in concern with manners.

The student of adolescent behavior will not be surprised at the significance of money as a problem, high interest in recreation, lack of concern with and interest in safety, unconcern over daily schedule and civic affairs, considerable concern over study habits as a problem but lack of interest in the topic, nor will he be surprised by the greater interest of girls than boys in attractiveness, love and marriage, mental health, and philosophy and beliefs; of boys than girls in money, health, and recreation.

If adults wish to "view with alarm," they may regard the adolescent's relative unconcern with safety and hazard, set over against the teen-age driving problem, and the young person's continuing unconcern with civic affairs, set over against the continued increased emphasis on "modern problems," and citizenship in the secondary-school's curriculum theory and effort.

PERSONAL PROBLEMS

1. *Health*—eating, drinking, exercise, posture, sleep and rest, air and temperature, sunlight, clothing, bathing, care of special parts, cleanliness and prevention of disease, excretion and elimination, use of drugs.
2. *Sex adjustments*—love, petting, courtship, marriage.
3. *Safety*—avoiding accidents and injuries.
4. *Money*—earning, spending, saving, etc.
5. *Mental hygiene*—fears, worries, inhibitions, compulsions, feelings of inferiority, fantasies, etc.
6. *Study habits*—skills used in study, methods of work, problem-solving.
7. *Recreation*—sports and games, reading, arts and crafts, fellowship and social activities, hobbies.
8. *Personal and moral qualities*—qualities leading to success, qualities of good citizenship.
9. *Home and family relationships*—living harmoniously with members of the family.
10. *Manners and courtesy*—etiquette.
11. *Personal attractiveness*—personal appearance, voice, clothing.
12. *Daily schedule*—planning twenty-four hours in a day.
13. *Civic interests, attitudes, and responsibilities.*
14. *Getting along with other people.*
15. *Philosophy of life*—personal values, ambitions, ideals, religion.

[The following directions for ranking the items were given to each pupil.]

You are asked to place in the boxes below the numbers of the problems on the accompanying mimeographed sheet, first to indicate the order in which they are *personal problems* to you; and second the order of *interest* to you.

RANKING OF PROBLEMS IN ORDER OF BEING PERSONAL PROBLEMS TO YOU

First enter the numbers of the problems which are 1st, 2d, and 3d in order of being your own *greatest personal problems.* Then skip down and insert the numbers of those which are your *least personal problems*—13th, 14th, and 15th in order. Then come back and fill in the rest in order in groupings of three. When you have finished, check over your rankings to make sure that you have used each number from 1 to 15. Be certain that your ratings represent your best judgment.

Place in the three boxes below in order the numbers of topics which are your *greatest personal problems.*

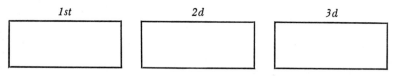

Place in the next three boxes the numbers of the next three in order of being *personal problems* to you.

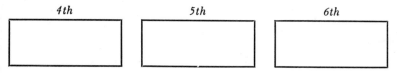

Place in the next boxes the number of the next three in order of being *personal problems* to you.

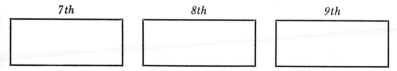

Then the next three in order of being *personal problems.*

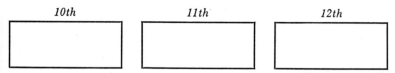

And finally place the number of the three which are your *least personal problems.*

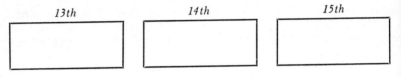

13th   *14th*   *15th*

RANKING OF PROBLEMS IN ORDER OF INTEREST

Rank the problems in order of *interest* to you, the things you would like to *read about* and *discuss* or *hear discussed.* First enter the numbers of the first three in order of interest, then the last three in order of interest, and then fill in the rest. (The rankings for interest were entered in boxes similar in character to those shown for the rankings as problems.)

Part Two

GROWTH AND DEVELOPMENT

CHAPTER FOUR

Physical Growth and Development

9

NORMAL GROWTH AND DEVELOPMENT

DURING ADOLESCENCE

by Harold C. Stuart, M.D.

One step in the direction of understanding oneself and others is to know the facts derived from scientific inquiry. In the selection that follows Harold C. Stuart of Harvard University presents a comprehensive account of the physical changes occurring during adolescence. [From *New England Journal of Medicine*, 1946, *234*, 666-672, 693-700, 732-738. Reprinted by permission of the author and the Massachusetts Medical Society. Abridged and edited by the author and editor.]

It is difficult to select suitable criteria for the beginning and end of adolescence. . . . According to [Webster's] definition [of adolescence as "the state or process of growing up from childhood to manhood or womanhood"], which is the one accepted here, [adolescence] covers a long portion, roughly the second half, of the period of development. Adolescence begins and ends much earlier in girls than in boys and in some persons than in others, and the early and late changes indicative of the period occur gradually and are usually not readily observed. As the early indications of sexual differentiation are considered it will become evident that by certain criteria, as, for example, an appreciably increased excretion of sex hormones, an earlier age of onset can be assigned than would be possible if one were guided by the first appearance of clinical signs of sex differentiation. Adolescence ends when functional reproductive capacity is fully established and the child has thus become an adult. Again, the time of arrival at this state is not easily recognized, and it probably differs widely between persons, but the evidence that will be reviewed suggests that it is near to the ages at which boys and girls are usually considered to have reached manhood or womanhood.

For purposes of presentation in this review, three stages of adolescence will be recognized. These will be referred to as prepubescence, pubescence and postpubescence. The term "pubescence" (or the pubescent period) taken in its literal sense refers to the period of time during which the pubic hair is developing. The various criteria by which these three stages may be recognized . . . will . . . receive attention in various sections of this review.

The adolescent period is one during which profound changes take place in physical, physiologic, mental and emotional development. Since the literature dealing with these changes is voluminous and leads into many diverse fields, it will be necessary to restrict the scope of this report in a number of ways. Attention will be limited to physical growth, . . . principal physiologic changes of interest in clinical medicine, . . . [and] to the individual or group variations that are encountered in apparently normal persons. . . . It will not be possible to deal fully with the studies of fundamental genetics, endocrinology and ecology to see what light they shed on the causes for the changes observed with growth and development during adolescence. The endocrine glands will be considered [only] from the viewpoint of their development and functioning during this period. . . .

LONGITUDINAL STUDIES OF THE GROWTH AND DEVELOPMENT OF NORMAL CHILDREN

Davenport (1926, 1930) and Boas (1932) may be considered to have been pioneers in the movement to arrive at a better understanding of adolescence by repeated observations of adolescents over long periods of time. Davenport (1926, 1930) established the forms of the average curves for growth in height and weight by this method and demonstrated that a so-called "adolescent spurt of growth" is a characteristic phenomenon. He also clarified the differences between the two sexes in the time and magnitude of this occurrence and emphasized the wide individual variability in these respects.

It is of interest to re-read the paper published by Boas (1932) in the light of many of the studies published since that time. He based his conclusions on careful repeated measurements, determination of the age of first menstruation in girls and other data obtained for children attending the Horace Mann School in New York City, some of whom were followed during the succeeding college years. In the article referred to, he reported many findings that have since been substantiated by workers dealing with larger numbers of children, particularly in regard to size and rate of growth in relation to the period of maximum growth and the age at which the menarche occurs. He introduced the question whether his findings did not imply a different tempo of physiologic changes in different persons, a suggestion that has since been clearly demonstrated. Credit will not be repeatedly given to Boas when considering the many aspects of growth and development for which he deserves recognition, because later work offers more adequate reference material, but the article cited should be looked on as a classic in this field.

At the time of the deliberations of the committees of the White House Conference on Child Health and Protection (1932), interest was aroused in adolescence as a neglected and little understood period. The reports of this conference, as well as of one called during this period by the Brush Foundation and Western Reserve University (1930), revealed many gaps in the knowledge regarding this period. Shortly thereafter, with the financial backing of the General Education Board of the Rockefeller Foundation and the support of other foundations as well as of local institutions, a number of research centers were organized with the primary purpose of following children through their entire adolescence. The purpose was usually to study these children from many viewpoints, but with emphasis on comprehensive personal records rather than on mass statistics. These programs are for the most part still under way, and a large number of reports from these centers have already appeared. Collectively, they give a much clearer concept of the normal course of events and the interrelations between them than would otherwise be possible. The studies here reviewed come from many centers, but the following are the principal examples of this movement for organized research into human maturation: the Brush Foundation, Western Reserve University School of Medicine, Cleveland; the Denver Child Research Council, University of Colorado; the Institute of Child Welfare, University of California; the Adolescent Study Unit, School of Medicine and Institute of Human Relations, Yale University; the Harvard Growth Study, Harvard School of Education, the Center for Research in Child Health and Development, Harvard School of Public Health, and the Co-operative Study of School Children, Harvard University.

. . . The major reports [of these studies] have appeared in monographs published by the Society for Research in Child Development, National Research Council, Washington, D. C., and in *Child Development.* . . .

Out of all these extensive studies, reinforced by many special or restricted ones, the substance of only a few can be considered here. Several previous reviews may be consulted by those who wish a more complete bibliography, especially those by Greulich and his associates (1938), and by Shuttleworth (1938), and that by Jones (1944) and a committee of the National Society for the Study of Education.

PHYSICAL GROWTH

In studying the growth of children, curves based on averages for each age have some value in showing general trends, but they must be interpreted guardedly, for they tend to mask characteristic differences among various types of persons. This is particularly important in considering growth during the adolescent years, when such wide differences in progress are encountered between those who mature early and those who mature late. A few general features of growth will be deduced from the composite curves before individual and group differences are discussed.

The following brief statement regarding the rate of growth in height and weight by year of age and by sex is based primarily on a recent report by Simmons (1944). This report gives average figures from repeated measurements taken at the Brush Foundation throughout the adolescent years in a large number of children. The averages obtained from this source may be somewhat advanced for the United States as a whole, since the children enrolled did not represent a true sample of the population but a group representing rather better than average socioeconomic levels. These averages are, however, in close agreement with those obtained for girls by Dearborn and Rothney (1941) from the Harvard Growth Study, by the Ministry of Health of Canada on Toronto school children (Toronto, Canada, 1942) and from other extensive sources in the United States. . . .

Considering only average occurrences, the rate of growth in height—that is, the increment year by year—is continually diminishing from birth to maturity except for a short period that is referred to as the adolescent spurt of growth. The rate of this decrease is rapid during the first two years but diminishes year by year during the preschool period. During the early school years it becomes so slow that the curve of increments appears almost flat. According to Simmons, girls gain in height at an accelerating rate from nine to twelve years, whereas boys do so from eleven to fourteen years. This results in the fact that girls are taller than boys between eleven and thirteen years. From thirteen years in girls and fifteen years in boys the rate of growth in height decelerates rapidly, and after about three years it ceases. According to these yearly averages, the twelfth year in girls and the fourteenth year in boys appear to be those of maximum growth.

*   *   *

The average increments for weight by years show a somewhat different picture. Following the initial infantile spurt of growth, deceleration takes place more rapidly for weight than for height, and the increment each year remains about the same between two and five years, a period during which it is smaller than at any other time before maturity. From five years onward there is a slight but progressive increase in gain each year. This acceleration of gain in weight becomes much more rapid at the time when accelerating growth in height begins, and it terminates at approximately the same time as does that in height, although it tends to be spread over a somewhat longer period. The curves produced by the increments for height and weight for both sexes are reproduced from Simmons's monograph in Figures 1 and 2.

*   *   *

Meredith (1935) for boys and Boynton (1936) for girls give means for eighteen body measurements for each age up to eighteen years, as well as increments for each of these at the successive age intervals. In subsequent publications these authors (Meredith and Boynton, 1937; Meredith, 1939) give further anthropometric norms, and Gray and Ayres (1931) give norms for some of these measurements based on studies of private-school children. Although many other tables of norms based on studies of large groups of children have been published and are useful as standards, the references

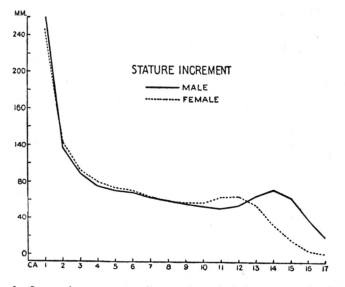

FIG. 1. Stature increment according to chronological age (*reproduced from Simmons [1944] by permission of the author*).

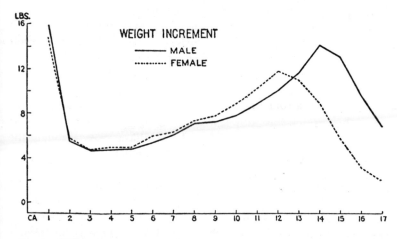

FIG. 2. Weight increment according to chronological age (*reproduced from Simmons [1944] by permission of the author*).

cited are as complete and representative as any available for clinical purposes. In Table 1 a few of the segmental and sex differences that emerge during adolescence are revealed by the ages at which maximum growth occurs in some of the principal measurements for each sex, as given by Meredith and Boynton (1937).

TABLE 1

SEGMENTAL AND SEX DIFFERENCES ACCORDING TO YEAR OF MAXIMUM GROWTH

MEASUREMENT	YEAR OF MAXIMUM GROWTH	
	Boys	Girls
Weight	15	12
Height	14	12
Sitting height	15	12
Shoulder breadth	14	12
Pelvic breadth	—	13
Hip breadth	14	—
Thoracic circumference	14	11

INDIVIDUAL VARIATIONS IN GROWTH

Davenport (1926, 1930) called attention to the marked differences between children of the same age—in the age at which the adolescent acceleration in growth begins and ends and in the magnitude of this spurt of growth. Many studies dealing with these differences have appeared since Davenport's description was published. Shuttleworth (1937) has shown that when the yearly increments of gain in height for different groups of girls selected on the basis of their ages at the time of maximum growth are charted with the years of maximum growth superimposed, the several curves fit remarkably well but differ in their magnitudes. . . . The same applies for the curves of height increments for boys and for those of weight and other dimensions for both sexes. The point of importance to be derived from all these studies is that children pass through the adolescent phase of accelerated growth at widely different chronological ages, but that in all aspects of growth they follow much the same sequence or pattern for any particular measurement regardless of when the adolescent phase is initiated. Thus, when chronological age is ignored and age of either initial growth acceleration or maximum growth is substituted, there is far greater uniformity between children. Certain differences have, however, been recognized between children taking this growth very early and those taking it very late. Children having early occurrence of maximum growth tend to differ from those having late occurrence in the following ways: the maximum increment is greater in amount; the whole cycle is completed in a shorter time; the children are larger before maximum growth but are likely to be more alike or even shorter at the end because growth is completed more quickly; and maximal growth occurs early rather typically in broad-hipped persons and those with relatively short legs—that is, in those with a feminine configuration.

The actual variability in age of maximum growth is suggested by Shuttleworth's (1937) analysis of its occurrence among 174 girls. In 6 cases it occurred between $10\frac{1}{4}$ and $10\frac{3}{4}$ years, and the numbers for each successive six-month age interval were respectively 13, 26, 34, 37, 28, 18, 7 and 5, the last falling between $14\frac{1}{4}$ and $14\frac{3}{4}$ years. In 99 of 174 girls, or more than half, it occurred between $11\frac{3}{4}$ and $13\frac{3}{4}$ years. For boys the distribution was approximately the same but occurred two years later. The stimulus to be advanced or retarded in growth is a general one and affects all dimensions. One may therefore use age of maximum growth, preferably in height, as an indication of the characteristics of a given child in respect to his speed or advancement of growth. . . .

For correlation with other indices of adolescent development, the significant points about physical growth may be summarized as follows. As shown by average occurrences in groups of healthy children in the United States, the change from a decelerating rate of growth in height to an accelerating one, which marks the beginning of the adolescent spurt, occurs during the tenth year in girls and during the thirteenth years in boys. The change from an accelerating to a decelerating rate occurs in the thirteenth year in girls and in the fifteenth year in boys. A change from a slow to a more rapidly accelerating gain in weight occurs at about the same time as the first inflection in height increments, and a change from an accelerating to a decelerating rate occurs at approximately the same time as does that for gain in height. Second, the change from a decelerating to an accelerating rate of growth in height— as in most linear dimensions—represents a characteristic stage in adolescent development, and this can usually be recognized when subjects are measured at regular intervals. It is more readily recognized and is more certainly attributable to a stage of development than is the initial stage of adolescent acceleration in gain in weight. The latter is likelier to be a gradual change from slight acceleration to greater increments and is more irregular. Third, the period during which maximum growth takes place is much more easily recognized than is the beginning of acceleration, because the increase in the rate of gain is usually much greater. One cannot be sure that the maximum has been attained until measures of the first phase of deceleration are at hand, but a study of the amounts of gain period by period makes it possible to conclude that the maximum has probably been reached or that the point of inflection in the curve is about to take place. Other physical characteristics, usually associated with maximum growth, described below, help to identify this period. Lastly, the time interval between onset and termination of adolescent acceleration in growth in height averages three years but is usually much shorter for the individual. When children are divided into groups on the basis of the age at which they attain maximum growth, the duration of the period of acceleration for the separate groups averages about two years. Those maturing early may complete this phase in about a year, and late or slower maturing persons usually take considerably longer. The duration of the accelerating period is somewhat longer for measurements of breadth. On the average, the duration of the period of rapid gain in weight is greater than that of growth in height, owing to the influence of acceleration in other measurements that precede or follow that of height.

GROWTH OF PRINCIPAL TISSUES

The adolescent spurt of growth has a far greater proportional magnitude for weight than for height. This is due in part to a tendency to accumulate larger quantities of fat in the subcutaneous tissue during adolescence, a trend that is more pronounced in girls than in boys. . . . The obesity of adolescence can be looked on in most cases as an exaggeration of a normal tendency, possibly complicated by the particular emotional factors, food habits or lack of activity usual at this time.

The large increase in weight associated with the rapid growth of pubescence is also accounted for in large measure by broadening of the skeleton and increased massiveness of individual bones. . . . This increased stockiness of bones becomes much more marked in boys than girls during the late adolescent years, as exemplified by the differences in the growth of the jaws and facial bones in the two sexes. The muscles are also growing rapidly at this time, and this is again more marked in boys than in girls. This accounts for a considerable part of the gain in weight, although members of both sexes differ greatly in this respect.

* * *

Dimock (1935) has studied the development in boys of physical strength and endurance and in motor abilities, using the Rogers test for physical strength or capacity and the Brace test for motor ability or co-ordination. He finds that strength virtually doubles between twelve and sixteen years, but that the peak of increase takes place after the maximum rate of growth in height and weight and during the years of postpubescence. The tests of motor ability or co-ordination showed continuous moderate improvement, but this improvement was more rapid in the prepubescent and post-pubescent periods than during the period just preceding that of maximum growth. Dimock's findings did not confirm the widely accepted view that a substantial loss of motor control and resulting awkwardness are associated with the period of rapid growth.

In 1940, Espenschade reported the results of motor-performance tests applied periodically to a group of adolescent children being followed at the Institute of Child Welfare, University of California. Because of the extensive observations being made on these children, it was possible to study the relation between motor performance and both physical growth and the evidences of maturity. Six tests of motor performance were used that had been found to be sufficiently reliable, valid and consistent for the purpose of giving evidence concerning co-ordination, strength, speed and accuracy. The mean performance of boys in all tests increased steadily and markedly at each age up to seventeen years, whereas girls failed to improve after fourteen years and in some cases showed a decline thereafter. There were marked individual differences in all tests and in both sexes, but boys on the average surpassed girls in all tests, and this difference increased with age.

This field of study has recently been greatly stimulated by a national realization that an unnecessarily large proportion of American youths are handicapped by faulty development or physical defects at the time when they must begin to assume the responsibilities of adult life. Anyone who has devoted much time to the study of adolescents is familiar with the inactive and generally poorly adjusted youth who eats unwisely and excessively, takes little exercise and in consequence becomes fat and flabby and performs poorly in tests of physical fitness. It is a pertinent question whether lack of regular physical activity and effort during the years in which muscles naturally enlarge and strengthen rapidly may not lead to permanent underdevelopment in this respect. Adequate but controlled use appears to stimulate muscle development and is probably most effective when muscles are developing most actively. Possibly the likes and habits of girls during these years, since girls are less athletic than boys, lead in part to late sex differences in muscularity. It does appear that psychologic problems in adolescence may have much to do with the rounding out of physical development in this respect and that they deserve attention. Shuttleworth has pointed out that, since the individual adolescent usually passes through the period of rapid growth in about two years, with one period of extremely intensive growth, and not in the less intense and more prolonged manner suggested by the average curves, force is added to the argument for greater attention to food and other needs during this period.

SKELETAL OR OSSEOUS DEVELOPMENT

The characteristic picture of the development of the skeleton as seen in roentgenograms of the hand and other areas has been studied in great numbers of children at each age, and standards representing average occurrences have been published. The *Atlas of the Hand* prepared by Todd (1937) [and revised and improved by Greulich and Pyle (1950)] is the most extensive of these and serves as a practical standard for comparing subjects. Flory (1936) has prepared an additional set of standards, and a number of other methods have been suggested. . . .

*   *   *

Most writers have found that the comparable stage of osseous development is attained during adolescence on the average between one and two years later in boys than in girls. . . . Based on x-ray films of the hand, the average girl of nine years is about one year advanced in osseous age over the average boy of that age, and at eleven she is about eighteen months advanced. After twelve years of age she is two years ahead until she has reached osseous maturity in this area. [This sex difference in the age of skeletal maturation is associated with advancement of girls in other pubescent changes.] . . .

Some children are quite irregular in osseous development, and the impression gained from the study of one aspect of the hand or one part of the body may be quite different from that obtained from another. In these cases it is difficult to assign an exact osseous age. With experience, however, it is usually easy to recognize from x-ray films of the hand the children who are either advanced or retarded in osseous age for their chronological age. Variability in this respect is quite as great as that in other aspects of development. . . .

PRIMARY AND SECONDARY SEXUAL CHARACTERISTICS

There is a natural sequence in the manifestations of development of the sex characters, just as one has been shown to exist in the patterns of growth and ossification. This sequence is followed with great consistency, but there are marked differences in the chronological ages at which different milestones are passed, both between the sexes and among members of the same sex. There are also considerable differences in the degree of differentiation or in the magnitude of change in size to which any attribute attains. Hence, there is a wide range of variability in the size or general appearance of the sex characters and the functional state of the sex organs of boys or girls of the same chronological age, particularly between ten and eighteen years of age.

Development of Male Sex Characters

Schonfeld (1943) classifies the testes, the epididymis, the seminal vesicles, the prostate, the genital passages and the penis as primary sexual organs. These are rudimentary structures in infancy and remain so, although growing slowly, until the onset of pubescence. All the secondary sex characters—that is, the pubic, axillary and facial hair and the male quality of voice—make their first appearance at different intervals after the rapid growth of the primary characters has begun, and they reach different stages but usually not complete development during pubescence. Associated with the maturation of these secondary characters and properly considered among them is rapid growth of muscles and bones in certain groups or parts that leads to masculine contours and proportions. These changes also continue well into postpubescence.

According to Schonfeld (1943), the epididymis is relatively large in comparison with the testes before the onset of pubescence, being one third to one quarter the size of that organ. During pubescence and postpubescence the testes grow much more rapidly than the epididymis, so that in the adult the latter are only one ninth the size of the former. The accelerating growth of the testes begins at about eleven years of age but does not become rapid until about fourteen years. It has reached its peak by seventeen years, after which deceleration takes place. Thus, rapid growth of the testes begins at about the time of maximum linear growth and continues until it has ceased. Under eleven years of age the length of the testis is usually between 1.5 and 2.0 cm. and its weight is about 2 gm. By eighteen years of age its length is usually between 3.5 and 5.0 cm. and its weight is about 17 gm.

The penis approximately doubles in both length and girth in association with the enlargement of the testes. The prostate, which is hardly palpable before pubescence, increases rapidly in size and changes markedly in shape and contour during this period. Evidence of prostatic secretion appears fairly soon after the gland begins to enlarge, or between ten and eleven years, but active spermatozoa are not found until considerably later. Motile mature spermatozoa are not usually found until fifteen or sixteen years, although Baldwin (1928) has reported them in morning urine specimens of boys in increasing percentages after thirteen years. . . .

The goal of all changes in the primary sex characters is the capacity to reproduce, and the age at which this capacity is fully developed is by definition the end of adolescence. The appearance of morphologically fully differentiated motile spermatozoa in the semen is usually accepted as evidence of the capacity to reproduce, but this is not necessarily an indication that full sexual maturity has been attained. The evidence concerning the time when this stage is reached in boys is far from adequate, but by inference from that for comparable development in girls, which is considered below, it is after general growth has begun to slow down, if it has not fully ceased. . . .

The range of variability in the time of occurrence of these developmental stages of sexual maturation may be judged from Schonfeld's (1943) study of the growth of the testes. He found that in 80 per cent of the boys in his group, the age of onset of rapid testicular growth was between twelve and sixteen years, and that the range for the termination of this rapid growth was sixteen to twenty years. Thus, excluding the extremely advanced and the extremely retarded boys, there was still four years' difference in the time of occurrence of these changes.

Greulich and his collaborators (1942) made a most detailed study of the successive stages of the development of the principal male secondary sex character, that of adult body hair. . . . In almost all cases the pubic region is the first in which maturing hair is seen, and the developmental changes in its characteristics in this region are spread over a major portion of the period of rapid development of the other sex characters. Hence, the term "pubescence," which derives from this sex character, may properly be used to signify this central and major period of adolescence. The first change to be noted in the pubic region occurs shortly after the accelerating growth of the testes and penis has begun and consists of a denser, longer vellus hair about the base of the penis. Shortly thereafter occasional longer, coarser pigmented straight hairs appear. Still later these become dense, and finally they begin to curl or kink. . . . After pubic hair has been present for some months, but while it is still localized about the base of the penis, mature hair begins to appear in the axillas, first as sparse, long pigmented hairs centrally located but progressing in area, type and density, as in the pubic region.

Facial hair first appears after considerable axillary hair is present, and it progresses in a characteristic manner. It begins laterally on the upper lip, spreading medially, and appears in succession over the upper part of the cheeks, centrally under the lower lip, on the chin and under the maxillas, finally spreading down to the neck and up to the face. Again the progression is from sparse to dense and longer vellus hair appearing like down, then as occasional longer, darker and thicker hairs and finally as dense, coarse adult hairs. At this time in boys the hair line on the forehead may begin to recede on either side, producing the laterally indented configuration of the masculine type, but this change may begin much later and progress gradually into adult life. During these stages longer, coarser pigmented hairs are often developing amid the vellus hair on certain parts of the extremities and about the nipples, but the extensive development of mature hair on the chest and on the extremities comes later and continues well into adult life. The degree of this development varies greatly.

Development of the breasts of boys is variable and only rarely marked, but some changes are seen quite regularly. The usual one is an elevation of the nipples on a slightly full areola. Occasionally a mass of firm, sharply demarcated tissue several centimeters in diameter underlies this areola and gives the appearance of true breast development. This occurs at about the time dense, dark pubic hair is present at the base of the penis and when axillary hair is beginning to appear. This tissue disappears after a variable number of months, depending on its degree of development.

Change of voice is a late manifestation of the pubescent period in boys, but the larynx develops rapidly throughout pubescence, increasing in internal dimensions, with associated changes in the vocal cords. The voice, however, usually does not begin to acquire the deeper tone characteristic of the mature male until the fifteenth year.

Each of the phenomena described passes through several developmental phases covering a considerable period of time, although varying among individuals. Since each phenomenon is initiated at a different time, an early phase of one quite regularly accompanies a later phase of another, and at any one time a characteristic combination of phases is to be expected. Collectively they span the period referred to as pubescence, and some continue to mature throughout postpubescence. The duration of pubescence varies to a certain extent but is rarely less than two years and may be considerably longer. As with growth, so with these manifestations of differentiation, those who begin to mature early tend to pass through this period rapidly, whereas those who mature late tend to progress through it more leisurely. Schonfeld (1943) and Greulich et al. (1942) have both attempted to classify boys into various precisely definable stages of pubescence. For clinical purposes, evidence that a boy has entered this period,—consisting of enlargement of the external genitals and the appearance of downy pubic hair,—that he has ended it—consisting of a deep voice, extensive facial and axillary hair and quite mature pubic hair up to the pubic crest—or that he is in a midstage of these changes seems to be sufficient. The association of these readily observable phenomena with the rapid phase of adolescent growth, with definite stages of osseous development, with rapid increases in the urinary excretion of the 17-ketosteroids and with certain immature functional activities of the sex organs, is the feature that gives them significance. . . .

Development of Female Sex Characters

The evidence relating to the growth of the ovaries is extremely meager. It has been reviewed by Greulich and his associates (1938). As in the case of the testes, this is apparently very slow during the prepubescent period and is most rapid during postpubescence. Scammon (1930) has shown by means of a graph that the characteristic features of the growth of the ovary are extremely slight progress up to eight years of age, moderately rapid and accelerating growth between eight and seventeen years, and extremely rapid enlargement between seventeen and twenty years. According to this graph, the ovary at the time of the menarche has attained only 30 per cent of its ultimate weight. Apparently both the testes and the ovaries follow this pattern of maximum growth after development in most other respects has been substantially completed. If these data are correct, full growth of these organs is not essential for reproductive function. The growth of the uterus, according to Scammon, is that of a straight-line increase from about ten to eighteen years of age, during which time it approximately doubles in length. The uterus also changes considerably in shape and in the proportions of its parts during this period.

The first of the female secondary sex characters to appear is often the rounding out of the hips, but if this attribute is not to be highly developed, the first stage of breast development can be observed earlier. This rounding out of the hips is due in part to broadening of the bony pelvis but more particularly to increased deposition of fat in the subcutaneous tissue of this area. Greulich and Thomas (1944) have studied by means of repeated roentgenograms the developmental changes taking place in the pelves of adolescent girls. They have shown that during the prepubescent period the pelvis grows slowly and symmetrically. During pubescence, however, it not only grows much more rapidly but changes in shape and undergoes considerable remodeling. During this time the pelvis increases more rapidly in width than in depth. . . . This period of rapid growth and fundamental changes in the character of the pelvis usually requires about eighteen months for its accomplishment. The changes described ordinarily begin after the first signs of breast development have appeared, are well along at the time of the menarche and end shortly thereafter. During the postpubescent period there is apparently a slight further growth of the pelvis but not much further change in its shape.

The earliest changes in the appearance of the breasts are usually noticeable before any pubic hair is seen. In the prepubescent period the papilla is small and slightly elevated and the areola is flat. The first stage of pubescent development is characterized by elevation of the surrounding areola, causing embedding of the papilla in a small conical protuberance on a flat chest. This stage, known as the "bud" stage, generally develops in the eleventh year but not infrequently does so in the tenth to twelfth years. The second stage is primarily brought about by an infiltration of fat under and surrounding the areola, referred to as the "primary breast," which causes a further elevation of the areola and further embedding of the nipple. The third stage involves further enlargement of the breast itself with incorporation of the formerly elevated areola, so that only the nipple remains elevated. This is the so-called "secondary" or "mature" breast, but its size at maturity varies widely. The breast is most frequently in the primary stage at the time of the first menstrual period, but it may still be in the bud stage and occasionally has attained the form of the mature breast.

The vaginal changes that occur during the pubescent period have been observed by Pilcher and Tuchewicz (1943). . . . The exact stage at which these changes occur has not been determined, but it is thought that they usually come about at some time after the first stage of breast development, but several months, if not a year or more, before the first menstrual period.

The development of body hair is less extensive in the female than in the male. . . . As in the male, the pubic hair appears first and the axillary hair appears after a considerable interval. . . .

AGE OF OCCURRENCE OF MENARCHE AND MENSES

Many studies of adolescent girls have now been made that include the recording of the age at which the first menstrual period occurred. The average age in the different studies of girls in the United States is about thirteen years, with the range for separate groups between twelve and a half and thirteen and a half years. It appears that this average has become somewhat earlier in recent years and that girls reach the menarche on the average a few months earlier than did their mothers. According to an analysis by Shuttleworth (1938) of data compiled by Mills, representing nine geographical areas of the world, girls in the United States menstruate earlier than do those in any of the other regions—two or more years earlier than do those in some of them.

As concerns the range of variability of the time of the menarche within any one group, this occurs in very few girls more than two years before or two years after the age for the average. Thus, for the United States the range of usual occurrence is between eleven and fifteen years, with about 3 per cent falling below and 3 per cent above these limits. In the main, variations in the time of occurrence of the first menstrual period are closely correlated with variations in other developmental occurrences and may therefore be looked on as due to the speed or advancement of general maturation. The timing of this event occurs quite regularly at or near a particular stage of general development. There is, however, some variability in this respect; that is, girls with extremely early menarches tend to be less mature, and those with extremely late ones more mature in other respects. Greulich et al. (1938) suggest that some of the variability in the age of menarche may be due to the same factors that cause irregularities in the early menstrual cycles themselves. He believes that the menarche should be looked on only as a reflection of a general physiologic state, and that it may occur at somewhat different times or stages of pubescent development in different persons.

Engle and Shelesnyak (1934) have studied the length and regularity of the menstrual intervals during adolescence. Their findings may be summarized as indicating that the menstrual intervals are considerably longer and much more irregular during the first year after the menarche than subsequently. Girls who menstruate before thirteen years have slightly shorter intervals during both the first and subsequent years than do those who first menstruate after fourteen years. [These authors] state that variability in cycles decreases as menstrual age increases, and that menstrual regularity is not usually established until twenty to twenty-four cycles have been passed, or until about two years after the menarche. Seventy-eight of 100 girls in [their] series experienced an interval of more than fifty-seven days, suggesting that menstrual function had been temporarily suppressed or that one period had been missed. In one third of these cases the long cycles were between the first and second periods. . . .

In describing the development of the sex organs in boys and their functional maturation, it was pointed out above that the precise stage of development at which the capacity to reproduce is attained is not known, but there is probably a considerable period during which some motile spermatozoa are present and hence fertilization may take place but during which sterility appears to be the rule. Attempts to determine how soon after the menarche girls can become pregnant are subject to the same difficulties, except that the menarche can be determined exactly. Mills and Ogle (1936) recorded the ages of the menarche and of the first conception in various groups among which promiscuity was frequent from an early age. The lag between the two occurrences was much longer in the girls reaching menarche extremely early than in those reaching it late. Obviously, the former are less likely to be exposed soon after this event than are the latter, but it may also be that the initiation of menstrual cycles does not always occur when reproductive capacity is equally near to attainment. The evidence suggests that conception is extremely unlikely to occur during the first year following the menarche, and that for a period of four to six years it is less likely than after full maturity but does occur with increasing frequency. This period of adolescent or physiologic sterility progressively shortens as the menarche is delayed. Conception can occur very early, but it seldom does so before the age of sixteen, regardless of the age at the menarche.

* * *

INTERRELATIONS BETWEEN GROWTH, OSSEOUS DEVELOPMENT AND SEXUAL MATURATION

In discussing individual variability in growth, it was shown that if chronological age is discarded as the basis for comparing individual children and the time of occurrence of maximum growth is substituted, growth during these years appears to be much more uniform. In like manner if, for comparing children, the age of appearance of one of the sex characters is chosen rather than the chronological age, all persons at this stage are found to be much more alike in other aspects of sexual maturation. As a landmark in this developmental schedule, the menarche in girls is the most definite event that can be selected, much more so than any specific event in the course of maturation in boys. Hence, all aspects of the growth and development of girls have been studied intensively in relation to the first menstrual period.

Boas (1932) called attention to the relations between the menarche and growth, but Shuttleworth (1937) published the first comprehensive analysis of the growth of girls on the basis of menarcheal age. Using the data collected by Dearborn and his associates in the Harvard Growth Study on a large number of girls whose age at first menstruation was known, Shuttleworth formed eight groups, the first including those who menstruated under ten and a half years and the eighth, those who did so at fourteen and a half years or over. Each intervening group included those who did so within half-year age intervals. He plotted the average curves of growth for each of these groups for different measurements against chronological age. All the curves show a striking similarity in form, but the curve for each advancing age group was displaced further to the right. The first group reached the peak of growth at the earliest age, and each succeeding group reached it a little later. Shuttleworth plotted these same curves on a base line of years before and after the menarche, with the menarcheal ages of all groups superimposed. Under this arrangement the curves for all are much more nearly alike in placement. The striking nature of this relation can best be appreciated by reference to Shuttleworth's graphs, two of which are reproduced in Figures 3 and 4.

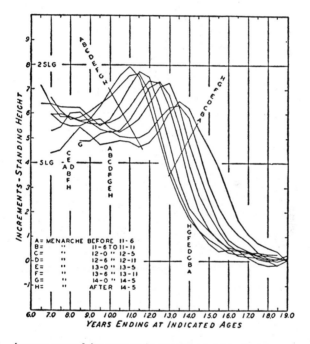

Fig. 3. Average annual increments in standing height of eight groups of patients menstruating at different ages (reproduced from Shuttleworth [1937] by permission of the author).

Figure 4 shows that there is still some difference between the extreme menarcheal groups in respect to the magnitude of the maximum growth and to its timing. The amount of maximum growth tends to be greater the earlier the menarche. The girls who menstruated earliest reached their peak of growth in height at or slightly after this event, whereas those who menstruated latest did so about a year in advance of it. The intervening groups reached the inflection point in growth between three and nine months before they menstruated. Shuttleworth (1938a) found the same timing of maximum growth in relation to the first menstrual period held for other body measurements, and even for the small bones of the hand as measured on x-ray films.

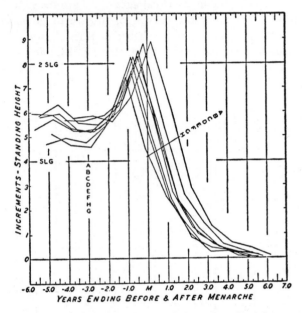

FIG. 4. Average annual increments in standing height of eight groups of patients menstruating at different ages (*reproduced from Shuttleworth [1937] by permission of the author*). The curves are arranged so that the points corresponding to the advent of the menarche are in the same vertical line.

*   *   *

[Pryor (1936), Simmons and Greulich (1943), and Stone and Barker (1937a) have reported other studies of the relationship between growth and sexual maturation in girls. Richey (1937) and Bayley (1943), using other criteria, have confirmed these general findings for boys also.]

ADOLESCENT CHANGES IN PHYSIOLOGIC FUNCTIONS

Basal Metabolism

There is general agreement that following the menarche in girls and maximum growth in boys the basal oxygen consumption falls sharply during the first year and to a lesser amount in the next two to five years. Talbot et al. (1937) state that between the menarche and the age of fifteen and a half years in girls the rate falls about 5 per cent below the average trend. Shock (1943) compared the curves of absolute oxygen consumption for early maturing girls and boys with those for late maturing groups. The boys had a higher average rate than the girls on an age basis, but the curves for both groups showed the same steady postpubescent decline. They became more uniform when plotted against the menarcheal age for girls and the maximum growth age for boys than when plotted against chronological age.

* * *

Other Physiologic Activities

Most of the physiologic processes that are unassociated with sexual development or with the basic endocrine activities related to sexuality have become well stabilized before adolescence, and relatively small changes take place in them during the latter years of growth.

Shock (1943) has obtained physiologic data based on studies of 50 girls every six months from the ages of twelve to eighteen years, with the age at the menarche known, and has plotted them on a menarcheal-age basis. These include pulse rates, systolic and diastolic blood pressures and pulse pressures, and basal respiratory volumes. His studies show that on the average among girls the systolic blood pressure rises steadily during the three years preceding the menarche—from 97 to 107 mm.—and remains at about the latter level during the ensuing five years. The diastolic pressure shows no constant change during either period. Hence, there is a net increase in pulse pressure during the premenstrual period, with little change thereafter. The average pulse rate shows a rise from 63 three years before the menarche to 73 one year before it and a slight drop to 70 at the menarche. The pulse falls further to 65 in the first three years and to 60 in the next two after the menarche. The basal respiratory volume expressed as liters per minute rises sharply in the two or three years before menarche—from 3.2 to 4.7 liters—and remains constant thereafter, but expressed as liters per square meter of body surface area per minute it presents an early rise followed by a gradual fall. Thus, in all these measurements except diastolic pressure there appears to be an increase during pubescence in girls.

In another publication, Shock (1944) presents norms for 50 adolescent boys and 50 adolescent girls on a chronological-age basis from eleven and a half years to seventeen and a half years. The principal sex difference appears to be that after fourteen years of age the average systolic pressure and pulse pressure are considerably higher for boys than for girls. Graham et al. (1945) also presents figures for blood pressures based on repeated determinations in 3580 children, from which he secured modal values as well as variability values with age. Variability tended to increase with age but was more pronounced among girls between ten and thirteen years old than among boys of the same age range. . . .

* * *

THE ENDOCRINE GLANDS

It has been recognized for many years that the processes of growth and maturation are influenced by, if not completely under the control of, hormones secreted by several of the endocrine glands. Extensive research during recent years, based largely on animal experimentation but supplemented by studies of grossly abnormal children and the clinical use of endocrine products, have done much to clarify understanding of the mechanisms involved. More recently the development of methods for determining the amounts of certain hormones excreted in the urine of normal as well as of abnormal children has especially helped to confirm certain hypotheses regarding the endocrine activities associated with growth and maturation during adolescence.

* * *

The glands that are of special interest . . . are the pituitary, the adrenals, the ovaries and the testes. The interactions of the hormones elaborated by these glands appear to be responsible, in large measure at least, for the progressive stages of adolescent development that have been described. The anterior lobe of the pituitary gland is known to elaborate several hormones, among which the growth hormone, the gonadotropic hormone—of which there are two or more fractions, follicle-stimulating and gonadotropic—and the adrenocorticotropic hormone have been most thoroughly studied. It appears that an increased secretion of the growth hormone is primarily responsible for the general acceleration of the rate of growth of the body as a whole and that a decrease in this secretion, probably brought about by action of the gonads, accounts in part for the sudden deceleration in growth. This conclusion is based primarily on studies showing that in its absence growth does not occur and that with excess secretion general uniform overgrowth takes place.

The initial stages of sexual differentiation, especially of the growth of the gonads, are believed to result from an increased production of the gonadotropic and adrenocorticotropic hormones, the former probably acting directly and the latter indirectly by stimulating the androgenic zones of the adrenal glands. Lack of these hormones during the prepubescent period results in some degree or type of hypogonadal state. An excess of these hormones prior to puberty produces manifestations of precocious sexual development, with or without early reproductive capacity. Some of these deviations from the normal may also occur as a result of abnormal levels of secretion of the specific part of the adrenals referred to, owing to disease in these glands.

The gonadotropic hormone is excreted in the urine, and repeated quantitative determinations have been made throughout adolescence on twenty-four-hour specimens of urine in several groups of normal boys and girls. The reports of Nathanson, Towne and Aub (1941) on studies at Harvard and of Dorfman, Greulich and Solomon (1937) on studies at Yale are of particular interest. These indicate that the gonadotropic hormones—measured by Nathanson as the follicle-stimulating hormone (F. S. H.) and by Dorfman as gonadotropin—do not appear in measurable quantities in girls until eleven years of age or in boys until thirteen years. Excretion of the hormones increases rapidly in amount after their first appearance, and this increase coincides with the dramatic increase in the hormones from the peripheral sex glands. Nathanson, Towne and Aub (1941) point out that the secretion of the follicle-stimulating hormones probably precedes that of the gonads, but that the methods available for their assay at the time of the study were not sufficiently precise for their presence to be recognized in their initial small concentrations.

Estrogens are the female sex hormones, which are probably produced both by the adrenal glands and by the ovaries, and androgens are the male sex hormones, measured as the 17-ketosteroids and produced both by the adrenal glands and by the testes. According to Nathanson, Towne and Aub (1941), estrogens and androgens are both present in both sexes in fairly constant but negligible amounts between three and seven years of age. The amounts of these excreted in the urine increase moderately and to a like degree in girls and boys between seven and nine years, the 17-ketosteroids on the average being slightly higher in boys and the estrogens in girls. Between nine and eleven years the 17-ketosteroid excretion increases more rapidly in boys and the estrogen excretion in girls, but individual differences are extremely wide. During the twelfth year on the average, but sometimes earlier, a cyclic variation in output of estrogens by girls becomes obvious [well before the first menstrual period but later in association with these periods]. The average values continue to rise in girls after eleven years, whereas the output of estrogens by boys remains relatively constant. During this same period boys excrete increasing quantities of the 17-ketosteroids, but the difference between the sexes in the excretion of androgens is not nearly so marked as that of estrogens becomes.

Nathanson and his co-workers conclude that there is a primary stimulation of the gonads and adrenal glands that causes a steady —noncyclic—increase in both androgens and estrogens in both sexes. The high values and cyclic excretions of estrogens occurring in girls result from a superimposed stimulation—presumably of the ovaries by the pituitary gland after the former have matured sufficiently to excrete quantitatively. Similarly, the high urinary values of the 17-ketosteroids occurring later in boys are thought to be the result of an added excretion from the maturing testes. Thus, the gonadotropic hormones of the pituitary apparently first stimulate the adrenal cortex to increased but steady excretion of 17-ketosteroids and estrogens. At the same time they stimulate the growth and maturation of the testes and ovaries and later stimulate these organs to hormonal activity. This causes a higher but relatively steady excretion of androgens by boys and a much higher and cyclic excretion of estrogens by girls, thereby leading to the ultimate marked differences between the sexes in the amounts of these hormones found in the urine.

Talbot et al. (1943) have also studied the excretion of 17-ketosteroids in relation to age and have emphasized that the amounts recoverable from the urine before ten years are negligible. They also found that little sex difference is discernible until fifteen years of age and that the output by boys increases up to eighteen years of age at least. It should be pointed out, however, that it has not been demonstrated that the gonads themselves secrete any hormones that affect the development of the sex organs or sex characteristics prior to the pubescent period. Moore (1944) has reviewed the evidence relating to the gonads during embryonic and prepubescent life, and concludes that they do not secrete hormones that affect sex-organ development during these periods. In considering the relations between the levels of these excretions and the physical changes associated with adolescence, the following observations have been made. First, the simple linear elevations in these excretions have progressed for several years, probably three or four, before the first clinical signs of sexual differentiation appear. This covers the period that I have referred to as prepubescence. Second, the sudden sharp rise of estrogens in girls, which precedes by a short interval the development of cyclic variations, is closely associated with the early physical changes of pubescence and rapid growth of the ovaries and may be said to mark the beginning of the pubescent period. Cyclic variations in excretion of estrogens are apparently taking place during much of the pubescent period in girls—that is, for a year or more prior to the menarche. It is therefore consistent with these occurrences to postulate that the ovarian follicular hormone is necessary before cyclic excretions can begin, and that under this stimulation uterine development must have progressed sufficiently before the menstrual cycle can be completed. The menarche thus follows a period of several years of gonadal endocrine development. Third, the first sharp increase in the excretion of 17-ketosteroids in boys is associated with rapid growth of the adrenal glands and precedes that of rapid growth of the testes. A further increase is associated with rapid growth of the testes and appearance of the secondary sex characteristics. This association of events lends support to the presumption that the former is primarily of adrenal origin and the second of testicular origin. Lastly, the shift from neuter configuration to greater differentiation in physical characteristics accompanies the changes in the levels of these hormonal excretions. Nathanson, Miller, Towne and Aub (1941) have reported a correlation of 0.8 between excretion of 17-ketosteroids and that of urinary creatinine in both boys and girls. Since the latter is a function of muscle mass, androgenic excretions are presumably closely correlated with amount of muscle. The greater development of muscles in boys over girls actually occurs during the years when the excretion of androgens is becoming markedly greater in boys than in girls. Both Nathanson and Dorfman have found that the individual variability in the excretion levels of these hormones is to some extent correlated with the physical development of the subjects.

With several hormones being produced and interacting on each other, the variations in the timing, character and magnitude of adolescent growth and sexual differentiation are readily understandable. Furthermore, with the production of both male and female sex hormones by both sexes, and in different amounts between individuals, various degrees of femininity in boys and masculinity in girls are to be expected. In considering many of the variables in

both sexes, as, for example, late development in girls with broad
shoulders, narrow hips and considerable body hair as contrasted
with early development in boys with broad hips, narrow shoulders
and sparse body hair, differences in the balance of the sex hormones
from the usual occurrence may be assumed. Nathanson, Miller,
Towne and Aub (1941) cite an example of striking change from obvious feminine identification in 2 boys toward masculinity associated
with a rise in the androgen-estrogen ratio from estrogen excess to
androgen preponderance. Further studies are required to demonstrate the relations between individual variability in hormonal
excretions and growth and maturation.

FACTORS CONTRIBUTING TO GROUP DIFFERENCES IN GROWTH AND DEVELOPMENT OF NORMAL ADOLESCENTS

A better understanding of the normal physical and physiologic
changes of adolescence, and particularly of the variability in their
manifestations, which is consistent with good health and satisfactory
ultimate development, would undoubtedly lead to more rational
management of many of the so-called "problems of adolescence." It
is not suggested that these problems do not require attention, but
rather that the recognition that they are in many cases essentially
physiologic would result in more conservative therapy and in
greater emphasis on hygienic living. Frank (1941) has called attention to some of the implications of what is known about growth and
development during the adolescent years in respect to the policy and
program of care for adolescents from a health standpoint. Shorr
(1941) approaches such endocrine problems from this point of
view and has discussed the management of the usual ones. He takes
the position that most of these can best be handled by a sane program of physical and mental hygiene, planned from the point of
view that they are in the main expressions of physiologic variations.

It is now fully established that hormones elaborated by the endocrine glands are primarily responsible for the events that have
been shown to occur in connection with the progress of a child toward maturity. Nevertheless, it is of interest to consider what conditions may lead to variations in hormonal activities and hence to
differences between individuals or groups during this period. Since
this report is concerned with normal occurrences, the effects of

congenital abnormalities, defects, accidents and disease will not be considered.

Racial and familial traits have long been recognized as important predeterminers of group as well as of individual characteristics. The extensive literature bearing on these hereditary factors cannot be reviewed here, but it is clear that any effects brought about by environmental factors can operate only within the limitations imposed by the genetically determined qualities and potentialities of the initial germ plasm. Boas (1928) devotes much attention to the parts played by heredity and environment in bringing about family and racial differences. He has found that certain traits, such as the form of the head and face, are much more strongly influenced by race or family pattern than are others like height and weight. From statistical analyses of extensive studies, however, he concludes that even facial characteristics are modified by changes in environment. Hence, it is unwise to assume that any physical attribute is entirely determined by heredity or cannot be modified by environment. In clinical practice it is important to recognize individual characteristics that are constitutional in character and that may impose physical limitations or lead to extreme deviations in physical status or growth progress. A carefully taken family history often makes it appear that these are intrinsic in nature, but this conclusion cannot be accepted until a careful investigation of environmental factors has been carried out and a serious effort has been made to correct unfavorable influences. It is also unsafe to compare two racial groups of children and to conclude that any differences found to exist between them are racial in origin. Several recent studies offer strongly suggestive evidence that dietary habits or factors associated with socioeconomic circumstances may have more to do with the differences found to exist between racial groups than has the factor of race itself.

Some writers have stressed the differences in size and build and rate of maturation between groups of children living under different climatic conditions, but here again one must be cautious in accepting climatic factors as responsible unless racial differences on the one hand and socioeconomic differences on the other have been taken into account. Mills (1937) has brought together considerable evidence in support of a climatic effect. This evidence deals not only with the average age of the menarche and with the rates of growth of children in different climates but also with these differences in animals reared in different atmospheric conditions. Mills states that in regions of depressing moist heat, both growth and the menarche are delayed and the final adult form is slender and small, whereas growth and pubescent development are most accelerated and the most robust body forms are seen in the stimulating, stormy temperate regions. He has obtained exactly similar differences in laboratory animals, where ease or difficulty in loss of body heat was the experimental variable.

Michelson (1944) has attempted to determine whether differences in the age at the menarche between Whites and Negroes are attributable to race or socioeconomic circumstances. He studied twelve separate population groups and showed that Negro girls born and living in the West Indies reached the menarche on the average at 13.99 years, those in the southern part of the United States did so at 13.68 years, those in New York State at 12.94 years, and a small well-to-do group in New York State at 12.85 years. White girls born and living in New York State reached the menarche on the average at 12.86 years. Although the average age at the menarche for all Negroes is considerably later than that for Whites, this breakdown into groups makes it seem extremely doubtful that race per se is primarily responsible.

Other students have reported differences in menarcheal ages for different socioeconomic groups, with very late occurrence among girls in the less favored groups. Larger samples and better selected groups must be studied, however, before the influence of socioeconomic factors can be considered to have been established. The same may be said of the recent reports from Europe to the effect that girls are now menstruating about one year later than was previously usual in countries subjected to severe dietary restrictions and other socioeconomic stresses during the recent war. The accumulating evidence suggests strongly, however, that prolonged undernutrition, especially in calories and protein, may retard maturation as well as physical growth. This is not surprising in view of the fact that chronic starvation leads to amenorrhea in women and to loss of the secondary sex characteristics in both men and women.

Meredith (1939a, 1941) and Meredith and Meredith (1944) have reviewed the evidence concerning the effects of race, region and socioeconomic factors on the height and weight of children. Using the Harvard Growth Study data, [they] compared children born and living in Massachusetts of North European ancestry with those of Italian ancestry in respect to stature. The former exceeded the latter at all ages from seven to seventeen years in both sexes. The increments of gain year by year were not significantly different dur-

ing this period, however, the racial difference having been established by seven years, the earliest age studied.

In [a] study based on more than 60 samples of boys between the
ages of nine and fourteen years representing differences in race,
class, time and region, Meredith (1941) found that boys in the
United States of various ethnic groups, otherwise roughly comparable, differ in average height between groups up to a maximum of
5 cm.; that white boys residing in different parts of the United
States vary little in average height and weight; and that white boys
of the professional and major managerial classes are taller and heavier than those of the unskilled and semiskilled classes, the differences
not exceeding 3 per cent for stature and 6 per cent for weight.

Meredith and Meredith's (1944) most interesting findings have to
do with a striking secular trend over the last fifty years. Their
analysis of the measurements obtained in Toronto school children
in 1892, 1923 and 1939 are of particular interest. The typical Toronto boy aged thirteen to fourteen years was taller in 1939 than was
the boy of 1892 by nearly 9 cm., and the typical boy of 1923 was
about midway between. The differences at all ages were in the same
direction, although of less marked degree. [They] also find that
boys in the United States today, both White and Negro, are 6 to 8
per cent taller and 12 to 15 per cent heavier than were boys half a
century ago. In general, secular differences in the United States
covering the last half-century are twice as large as any of the other
differences considered, whereas geographical differences are the
smallest of all. Several studies of the heights of college boys in recent years and of their fathers while in college, and similarly of col-
ege girls and their mothers a generation ago, have revealed a
considerable increase indicative of a secular trend. The causes for
these evidences of increasing size with time call for further study,
but they are doubtless related to differences in the incidence of illnesses in early life, to dietary habits, to habits of activity and to
other more obscure factors generally referred to as socioeconomic.

.... 10 ....

SOME PHYSIOLOGICAL ASPECTS OF
ADOLESCENCE

by Nathan W. Shock

How do adolescent boys and girls compare in their physical growth?
May temporary physical changes occur in the growth of normal adolescents? These are some of the questions that Nathan W. Shock of
the U. S. Public Health Service National Heart Institute discusses in
the following article, which presents the results of a series of repeated
measures he and his co-workers made of one hundred teen-age boys
and girls over a period of seven years. [From *Texas Reports on
Biology and Medicine*, 1946, *4*, 289-310. Reprinted by permission of
the author and the University of Texas. Abridged and edited by the
author and editor.]

The increase in growth rate followed by the attainment of sexual
maturity has long been regarded as the chief characteristic of adolescence. However, the physiological mechanisms upon which these
changes are based have received scant attention. Other than basal
metabolism and the inception of menarche in girls, few studies of
the physiological aspects of adolescence have been made in humans. In recent years, repeated measurements on the same children
during growth have demonstrated the individuality of the growth
process and the serious limitations of the average values usually regarded as "age-norms" (Shuttleworth, 1938a) obtained from averages of different children measured at successive ages. Recognition
of such individual differences in rates of growth and maturation is
essential to the proper interpretation of average curves which continue to serve as the background. The aim of the present report is
to present the results of a study made of some physiological changes
taking place in average children at adolescence.

*   *   *

AGE CHANGES IN CARDIOVASCULAR MEASUREMENTS UNDER BASAL CONDITIONS

Average curves, based on chronological age groups, were prepared for all measurements taken. In Figure 1 the average basal pulse rates for girls and boys are shown (Shock, 1944). In this figure, as in all other figures in this article, connected points were

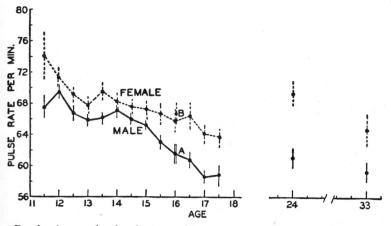

FIG. 1.   Average basal pulse rates of boys and girls *(from Shock, 1944)*.

obtained from measurements of the same children as they matured. Points shown at ages 24 and 33 years obtained from tests of other subjects. Points marked *A* and *B* are average values for 50 additional boys and 50 additional girls, aged 15.5-16.5 years, who were tested for the first time at this age. The length of the vertical line through each point indicates ±1 standard deviation of the mean. These curves show an average decrease of 8-9 beats per minute for boys and girls during adolescence. The average rate for girls is from two to six beats faster than for boys of the same age. This sex difference in pulse rate increases somewhat with age. The slight rise in pulse rate observed in girls between the ages of 13.0 and 13.5 years is not statistically significant when averages are calculated on the basis of chronological age, but when girls are grouped on the basis of physiological maturity (as estimated from the age at first menstruation) evidence of a rise in pulse rate just prior to menarche is obtained (See figure 11).

Figure 2 shows the average systolic blood pressure for adolescent boys and girls (Shock, 1944). Between the ages of 11½ and 13½ years the average blood pressure rises from 103 to 108 mm. Hg in both sexes. After the age of 13½ the systolic pressure of boys continues to rise, reaching a value of 114 mm. at the age of 17½, while

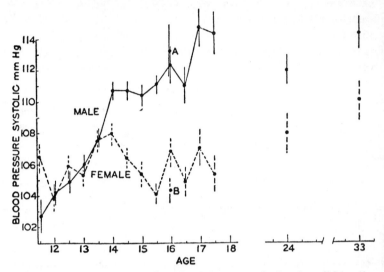

FIG. 2. Curves for average systolic blood pressure under basal conditions (*from Shock, 1944*).

that of girls drops slightly, reaching a minimum of 104 mm. at the age of 15½. Beyond this age there is a slight rise in pressure in girls reaching 106 mm. at 17½ years. Thus a sex difference in blood pressure develops during adolescence which persists throughout life.

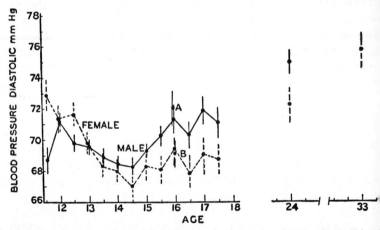

FIG. 3. Curves for average diastolic blood pressure under basal conditions (*from Shock, 1944*).

Changes in the diastolic blood pressure with age are shown in Figure 3. Between the ages of 12 and 14½ diastolic pressures of both boys and girls tend to diminish, reaching a minimum of 67-68 mm. at 14½ years. After this age, the average pressure rises again so that at 17½ years the values are practically the same as they were at 12 years. This gradual rise in diastolic pressure continues throughout life. The difference between girls and boys is not statistically significant at any age.

Figure 4 shows the development of a sex difference in pulse pres-

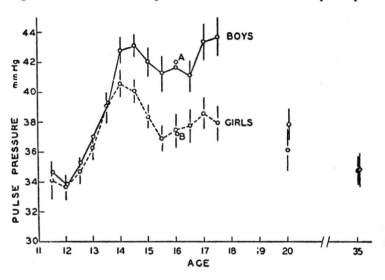

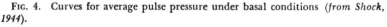

FIG. 4.   Curves for average pulse pressure under basal conditions (*from Shock, 1944*).

sure in adolescent children (Shock, 1944). The average pulse pressure rises from 34 mm. at age 11½ to 39 mm. at age 13½ in both sexes. Beyond this age the pulse pressure of boys continues to rise while that of girls falls, resulting in a significant sex difference between the ages of 15 and 17½ years. This sex difference disappears in adults.

*   *   *

AGE CHANGES IN RESPIRATORY
MEASUREMENTS UNDER BASAL CONDITIONS

During adolescence the average basal respiratory rate diminished from 16½ per minute at 11½ years to 14½ per minute at 17½ years

(Shock and Soley, 1939). No significant difference between girls and boys was observed. However, all measurements of respiratory volume show a definite sex difference. When no correction for differences in body size is made, differences in basal respiratory volume of boys and girls are quite marked, as shown in Figure 5. In boys the basal respiratory volume increases from 4.50 l./min. at age 11½ to 6.0 l./min. at age 17½, while in girls, little change with

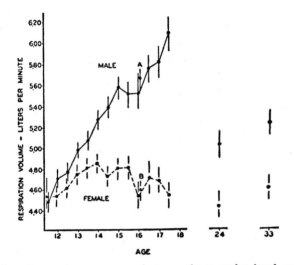

FIG. 5. Age changes in average respiratory volume under basal conditions. Liters per minute reduced to standard conditions.

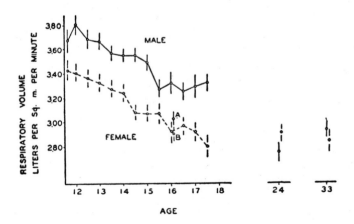

FIG. 6. Age changes in average basal respiratory volume corrected for body size. Liters per square meter of body surface per minute.

age is observed. When respiratory volumes are corrected for differences in body size by dividing by the surface area, the values for both boys and girls diminish with increasing age and the sex difference of about 400 cc. per sq. m. per minute remains uniform throughout adolescence (See Figure 6).

* * *

AGE CHANGES IN BASAL METABOLISM

From the correlations between the average of three determinations of basal metabolism on two successive days the probable error of estimate was computed. The error of estimate of basal metabolism determinations carried out under the conditions of our experiments varied between 1.26 and 1.99 calories per square meter of body surface per hour for both boys and girls between the ages of 11.5 and 17.5 years (Shock, 1942) (equivalent to 3-5 per cent deviation). Since no systematic change in reliability of measurement was found with increasing age in children subjected to repeated tests and since the probable errors of estimate for groups of children tested only once were no greater than for children of the same age who had been tested ten times previously, it may be concluded that the reliability of metabolism measurements is not significantly altered by repeated testing, provided a preliminary training test is given.

From the average of the six determinations of basal metabolism made on two successive days, average values were calculated for each half-year age interval. Figure 7 shows the average basal heat production for males and females. . . . Since the measurements made on the control groups of 16-year-old subjects (Groups *A* and *B* of Figure 7) do not differ significantly from measurements made on the children subjected to repeated testing, there is no reason to believe that the results obtained in the cumulative study have been significantly altered because of the extensive training or laboratory experience of these subjects.

These data show that the average basal metabolism decreases gradually throughout the adolescent period. In girls, the rate of fall of basal metabolism has become very small by the age of 16-17 years. In boys, however, the basal metabolism continues to decrease beyond the age of 18 years, thus offering additional evidence of earlier maturity in girls than boys.

* * *

While the curves shown in Figure 7 demonstrate that a gradual fall in basal metabolic rate is characteristic of the adolescent period, they provide no basis for predicting the pattern of age changes in individual boys and girls (Shock, 1944). In fact, only ten out of

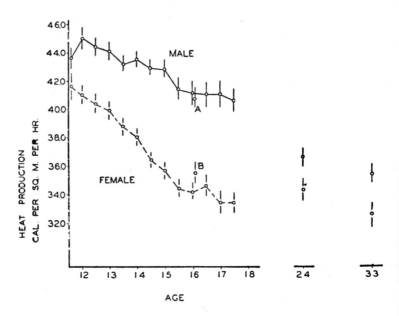

Fig. 7. Age changes in average basal heat production. Calories per square meter of body surface per hour (*from Shock, 1942*).

one hundred cases studied exhibited the uniform, even, decrease characteristic of the average curves. Over half of the subjects showed periods of very rapid change as illustrated in Figures 8 and 9. Because these periods of rapid change occur at different chronological ages in different subjects, distinctive individual patterns are lost in the averaging process. A few subjects revealed an age trend opposite to that of the average, that is an increase in basal metabolic rate with age. These subjects, five in number, tended to be small, slow-maturing and physiologically unstable as shown by poor agreement between measurements of metabolism made on successive days.

Similar discrepancies between individual and average growth curves have been found for other physiological variables as well. Hence it is important to bear in mind that wide individual differences in patterns and rate of physiological development occur among so-called "normal" children and that children of the same chronological age may be quite unlike in their degree of physiological maturity.

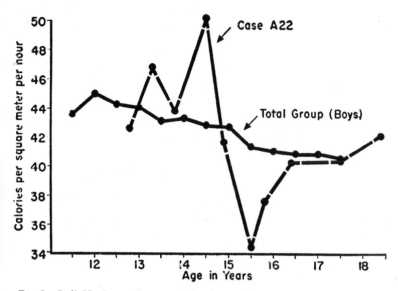

FIG. 8. Individual growth curve of basal metabolism of a boy compared with the average curve (*from Shock, 1944a*).

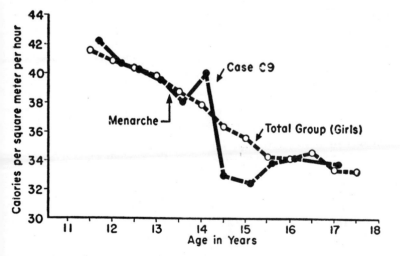

FIG. 9. Individual growth curve of basal metabolism of a girl compared with the average curve. The arrow indicates the age at which first menstruation occurred in this girl (*from Shock, 1944a*).

AGE CHANGES IN HORMONE EXCRETION

In view of the role of endocrine secretions in stimulating sexual development and maturity, information about the amount of such hormones present in the blood is of utmost importance. At the present time we do not have analytical methods of sufficient specificity and sensitivity to determine quantitative variations in the amounts of gonadotrophic, estrogenic or androgenic hormones present in the blood stream. Hence, attention has been directed to determining the amounts of these substances excreted in the urine. The methods used often depend on the biological response of immature test animals (rats, mice, chicks) to the injection of extracts prepared from urine samples. For such tests the total urine output must be collected over a period of several days in order to yield enough of the hormones to permit adequate bioassays. Furthermore, the meaning of increased urinary excretion of a hormone is difficult to assess. An increased excretion is usually taken as an indication of increased production of the hormone by the appropriate gland. There is no definite assurance, however, that the increased excretion is not the result of diminished utilization, since the hormone appearing in the urine represents the amount that is wasted or lost to the animal body. Since laboratory facilities were unavailable for hormone assays in the California study, no observations were obtained on the children under consideration. However, data from other studies will be briefly viewed.

There is no general agreement on the amount of gonadotrophic hormone excreted by different aged children. In perhaps the most adequate research reported, Greulich, Dorfman, et al. (1942) analyzed urine specimens of 64 boys aged 10-17 years. At ages less than $12\frac{1}{2}$ years all tests were negative for gonadotrophic hormones; at ages greater than $12\frac{1}{2}$ years some tests were positive, while at ages greater than 16 years all tests were positive. As would be expected, the boys were more homogeneous with respect to hormone excretion when classified into maturity groups than when classified on the basis of chronological age.

Both boys and girls excrete small amounts of estrogenic hormone. Before the age of 10 years the amount excreted is from 3 to 20 international units per 24 hours for each sex. After the age of 11 the daily excretion of estrogens increases rapidly in females, reaching values of 200-400 international units per 24 hours, while that of males increases only slightly. (See Figure 10).

Greulich, Dorfman, *et al.* (1942) . . . determined the daily excretion of male sex hormone in 82 boys between the ages of 8 and 17 years. The average daily excretion increased from 8.5 international

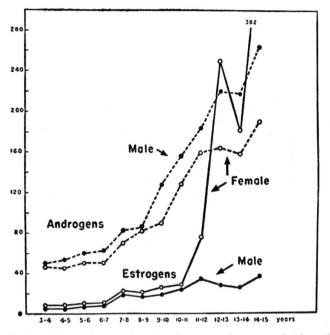

FIG. 10.   Age changes in excretion of androgens and estrogens in the urine of boys and girls (*from Nathanson, Towne, and Aub, 1941*).

units per 24 hours at age 8-14 to 10.8, 21.5 and 24.8 for 14, 15, and 16 year old boys respectively. The range of values, however, was very great: from 1-34 international units among 8-14 year old boys and from 2-57 international units per 24 hours among the older boys.

From these results we may tentatively conclude that before the age of 11 or 12 years both boys and girls excrete measurable amounts of both male and female sex hormones. Slightly greater amounts of male hormone are excreted by boys than girls and slightly greater amounts of female sex hormones are excreted by girls than boys, but the differences are not striking. After the age of 11 years, the excretion of female sex hormone markedly increases in girls and the excretion of male hormone increases correspondingly in boys so that a large difference between the excretory patterns of the two sexes becomes established.

EFFECTS OF SEXUAL MATURATION ON
OTHER PHYSIOLOGICAL FUNCTIONS

The effect of sexual maturation on other physiological functions was investigated in the following manner (Shock, 1943). For each girl the time (or age) at which the physiological tests were made was expressed as months before or after menarche instead of as chronological age. Mean values of blood pressure, pulse rate and basal heat production were computed for each six month interval before or after menarche. If at menarche there were a sudden change in physiological conditions within the body which produced changes in blood pressure, for instance, the average curve plotted in the manner outlined above would show a sudden change in slope or direction of trend at the time of menarche. The results of this analysis for 52 girls are shown in Figure 11. From this figure it may be

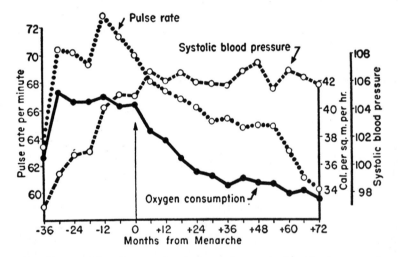

Fig. 11. Basal functions as related to sexual maturity in girls. Average values based on age deviation from menarche of the individual case. The vertical line at 0 indicates the beginning of menstruation (from Shock, 1944a).

seen that the progressive rise in systolic blood pressure characteristic of childhood ceases at menarche and thereafter maintains a uniform level. Pulse rate also rises during the premenarcheal years attaining a maximum value in the year preceding menarche. After menarche pulse rates decline. Perhaps the most striking non-sexual physiological change at menarche is the sudden fall in basal metabolism which commonly follows the beginning of menstruation. Thus the decrease in basal metabolism which characterizes the adolescent period actually takes place rather rapidly over the 2-3 years following menarche.

DISCUSSION AND SUMMARY

Some of the results obtained from repeated measurements of girls and boys taken during adolescence have been summarized in terms of average curves. This analysis has shown that some but not all differences between the sexes with respect to physiological measurements arise during adolescence. For instance the lower basal oxygen consumption of females is present before adolescence. On the other hand differences in blood pressure, respiratory volume, etc., first appear during the adolescent period. Examination of average curves gives the impression that the physiological changes taking place during adolescence are slow and gradual. However, when individual growth curves for certain physiological measurements are plotted, it is quite apparent that in many adolescents the physiological adjustments of this period are rapid and abrupt, and that wide variations above or below the average curves may be present in different individuals at different times. This information is of considerable value in interpreting the results of physiological measurements in individual cases. The increased variability in physiological measurements during adolescence may be taken as an indication that one of the important aspects of development is learning to maintain physiological equilibrium (Shock, 1944a). In adults, less variability in physiological measurements is encountered because the organism has learned to utilize all its available adaptive mechanisms in the maintenance of homeostasis. In the adolescent these processes are still being organized and synthesized. Thus it may be helpful to regard adolescence as a period of physiological learning. An example of such physiological learning is the regulation of menstrual periodicity. When menstruation first begins in adolescent girls it does not usually recur at uniform intervals. However, over a period of several years the physiological factors involved in menstruation become better coördinated and a greater regularity of interval is established (Bayer, 1940). The individual organism has learned to maintain the even homeostatic adjustment of the adult upon which certain physiological rhythms, such as that of menstruation, may be superimposed. As a result of such learning, physiological fluctuation is reduced and the uniformity of the adult state is attained.

NUTRITION AND GROWTH

by Marian E. Breckenridge and E. Lee Vincent

The quality and quantity of the food we consume affects our growth and general physical condition. If one's diet is improved, it may improve such factors of one's general physical make-up as height, weight, and bone development. In this brief excerpt from their book, Marian E. Breckenridge of the Merrill-Palmer School and E. Lee Vincent of Chatham College, Pittsburgh, explore the relationship between nutrition and growth, behavior, and mental performance. [From *Child Development*, Philadelphia: W. B. Saunders Company, 1955, pp. 116, 118-126. Reprinted by permission of the authors and W. B. Saunders Company.]

The potentialities for growth, as determined by heredity, cannot be realized without adequate food and conditions favorable to the physiologic processes which convert food into body tissues. Even the life processes of the first cell, or the beginning of life, depend upon specific chemical substances which are present in the cell itself. As the cell multiplies and differentiation takes place, different types of cells acquire different structures and, therefore, have specific needs. Bone, for example, must have calcium and phosphorus in relatively large quantities for its growth. Muscles demand proteins and certain inorganic salts while nerves require, among other things, a fairly large supply of fat-like substances, called lipids.

Going hand in hand with the structure of these tissues are their functions. These functions depend upon the constitution of the tissues plus the materials which are brought to them by the fluids in which they are bathed. Thus the normal beating of the heart depends upon the concentration of the calcium salts, and the quantitative relationship of calcium to sodium and potassium in the fluid which bathes the heart muscle. Nerve irritability, also, is dependent upon these minerals. The secretions of the digestive tract, and of the endocrine glands require supplies of specific substances, as will be shown later.

Food, the source of these necessary materials, becomes all important for the mother during the prenatal period and for the child after birth in providing the body with its needs for growth and activity.

FOOD AFFECTS HEALTH AND GROWTH

Studies of the dietary habits of groups and their growth, observations of deprivations in war-torn countries and under experimental conditions, and observations of the effect of supplements to the diet upon health and growth indicate the important effect food has upon the physical well-being and growth of individuals.

Dietary Habits and Physical Status

A study of the relationship between man's natural diet and his physical status has been presented by Orr and Gilks (1931). Two African tribes, the Masai and the Akikuyu, live side by side but have very different dietary customs. The Masai live largely on meat, milk and blood. Various roots and barks are used for "teas." The pregnant women are sent into the bush to eat berries. This diet is rich in growth-promoting substances. The Akikuyu diet consists chiefly of cereals, tubers, plants, legumes and green leaves. This diet is limited in growth-promoting substances, especially calcium. The men eat chiefly corn, sweet potatoes or other cereals and tubers. The young children, up to five years of age, are given edible earths from salt licks and ashes of certain swamp plants. One of these earths is especially high in calcium. The girls continue to use these sources of minerals and also have a monopoly on some kinds of green leaves rich in calcium. Even with the supplements for children the Akikuyu diet is not adequate for the best growth.

Comparing the adults, the mature Masai male is, on the average, five inches taller and twenty-three pounds heavier than the mature Akikuyu, and his muscular strength is 50 per cent greater. Deformities of the bones, decayed teeth, spongy gums, anemia, pulmonary diseases, tropical ulcer and other diseases fostered by poor nutrition, are more prevalent among the Akikuyu than among the Masai with a better diet. A study of the children up to eight years of age showed that more than 60 per cent of the Masai boys and girls were rated very good in general physical condition, while only 7 per cent of the Akikuyu boys and 29 per cent of the girls were so rated.

The value of a better diet is shown not only in the comparison of the two tribes but also in the difference between the boys and girls of the Akikuyu tribe. Further evidence of the inadequacy of the diet for promoting growth is shown in the comparison of the growth of the Akikuyu infants with that of English babies. It is found that during the first month the Akikuyu infants are about half a pound heavier than English babies. For ten months the rate of growth of both is similar. After ten months the rate of the Akikuyu infants is slower and at thirty months they are about 8 pounds lighter than the English. This is one of many examples cited in the literature on nutrition which indicate that differences in dietary habits among groups of people contribute to differences in physical status.

Such observations of the dietary habits and growth and health of a people suggest that differences in growth patterns in families and groups of families may have some dietary as well as hereditary basis. It seems probable that family food patterns carried over from one generation to another may be contributing to the differences in the growth of children. Generally speaking, children of today are taller and heavier than children of former generations (Meredith, 1949; Sebrell, 1953a) and are maturing earlier (Gould and Gould, 1932; Michelson, 1944). Nutrition is thought to be one of the factors associated with this increase.

In this period when children have been growing better, there have been shifts in the relative importance of various foods which have been consumed in the United States (Phipard and Stiebling, 1951). There has been increased consumption of dairy products other than butter, citrus fruits, green leafy and yellow vegetables, on the credit side, and refined sugar, on the debit side. These trends, except for the sugar, have enriched diets from the nutritional point of view, and indicate that people are eating more of foods which are important in promoting health. The enrichment of wheat flour (Wilder and Williams, 1944) and corn meal (Lease, 1953) with thiamine, riboflavin, niacin, and iron in both and additional calcium in the latter, of converted rice (Kik and Williams, 1945), the fortification of margarine with vitamin A and the fortification of some milk with vitamin D have also contributed to improving the quality of the American diet.[1]

There are vast differences in the food eaten in families. Income, availability of foods, family size, management and food habits are factors contributing to these differences (Phipard and Stiebling,

[1] Sebrell (1953) reports that the average American in 1945, compared with the period before enrichment was introduced, received in his food 27 per cent more thiamine, 19 per cent more niacin, 17 per cent more riboflavin, and 17 per cent more iron. The greatest increase occurred in the low income groups.

1951). Many families still have inadequate food[2] even though, according to Stiebling (1950) in 1949 the food available in the United States, if shared in accordance with need and used with discrimination, was sufficient to give everyone an adequate diet. Studies of differential growth in the different socio-economic levels point to nutrition as a contributing factor. More information regarding the long-term effects of diet upon human beings is needed.

Effect of Nutritional Deprivations during Wartime

Growth of children in weight and to a lesser degree in height has been shown to be affected during wartime by restrictions in food intake caused by scarcity of food.[3] The extent of the growth deficit is related to the severity of the undernutrition[4] or malnutrition. Older children tend to be affected more than the very young, perhaps because the younger children in the family may receive a relatively larger share of the available food than the older ones.

Evidence comes from observations during World War II in France (Trémolières, *et al.*, 1950), Belgium (Ellis, 1945), Greece (Valaoras, 1946), and Holland (Jonxis, 1946). In Holland in 1945, for example, most children over one year of age lost weight, and toward the end of the famine period they ceased growing in height. In Greece 55 per cent of the three- to eight-year-olds were underweight for height in 1942 and 1943 and 64 per cent in 1944. In a French study (Trémolières, *et al.*, 1950) of children from six to twenty years of age the thirteen-year-old girls were the most vulnerable. Following World War II observations of French children (Trémolières, *et al.*, 1950) and those of Dutch children liberated from Java and sent to

---

[2] An example of this condition is given in a survey of families living in rural areas in 1945 (a peak year of supply). In a county of Georgia the food of one third of the white families and two thirds of the Negro families provided less than two thirds of the dietary allowances for one or more nutrients as recommended by the National Research Council (Phipard and Stiebling, 1951).

[3] For a summary of evidence accumulated during World War I and World War II (Keys, *et al.*, 1950, Vol. II, Ch. 45).

[4] Undernutrition is a condition due to inadequate food in which the deficiency is quantitative rather than qualitative, i.e., a deficiency of calories with the nutrients fairly well balanced. Such was the condition in much of Europe during and directly following World War II, described in Studies of Undernutrition, Wuppertal, 1946–1949 (Cambridge University, Department of Experimental Medicine, 1951). In malnutrition, on the other hand, there is a deficiency of specific nutrients, e.g., the deficiency of vitamin B complex found in the Japanese prison camps (Smith and Woodruff, 1951).

Australia for rehabilitation (De Haas and Posthuma, 1946) indicate that children can recover from periods of deprivation, if they have not lasted too long, and will catch up in growth in height and weight. Keys, *et al.* (1950) states that from past experiences it can be safely assumed that the food crises of the 1940's in many parts of the world, *if they were not of too long duration,* will probably have no permanent harmful effect on the generation of growing children. However, children who continue to grow up with inadequate food will not have the opportunity for rehabilitation and thereby will be unable to achieve their potential for growth.

Minnesota Study of Human Starvation

The war studies cited above refer to the effect of underfeeding upon height and weight. Information of the effect of undernutrition upon the physiologic processes of such children is lacking except indirectly by the manifestations of such characteristics as chronic fatigue, lack of vigor, listlessness and inactivity as noted, for example, by Stuart (1944) during World War II in a group of French children between twelve and eighteen years of age. It seems pertinent, therefore, to cite briefly some of the results of the Minnesota Study of Human Starvation (Keys, *et al.,* 1950), which demonstrated the effect of severe underfeeding and later restoration of adequate food on a group of young men.[5]

It was found that all parts of the body underwent change during semi-starvation. Much of the fat disappeared, active tissues—especially muscles—decreased, more water was held in the tissues, while the bones changed relatively little. The men's physiques changed because of the loss of subcutaneous fat and muscle. Bodily processes slowed down, including circulation; basal metabolism was lowered; and blood sugar decreased. The skin was cold to touch and the men complained of feeling cold. Sexual functions were reduced; sperm were less mobile and lived a shorter time. Moderate anemia developed. Strength and endurance decreased markedly. The men complained of feeling weak. Slowing down of voluntary movements was observed. Coordination deteriorated whenever steadiness of the whole body was involved. On the other hand, no change was ob-

[5] Thirty-two mentally and physically healthy young men, living under carefully controlled conditions, were observed and tested during three successive periods: 12 weeks of adequate diet, 24 weeks of semi-starvation diet, 12 weeks of increased food intake.

served in accurate movements of small muscles nor were sensory mechanisms disturbed. Capacity for work, both in long, steady and in strenuous activity, decreased. This was shown both in the work done and the lowered efficiency of circulatory and respiratory mechanisms. These physical changes were accompanied by changes in behavior which will be discussed in the following section.

When the food was increased the men improved, although the response was not prompt nor synchronized for all structures and functions. After thirty-three weeks of rehabilitation the men were substantially back to normal. During that time water in the tissues decreased. Fat increased more rapidly than muscle. Muscle regained slowly. Likewise, muscular strength and endurance were slow to return. The extremely slow recovery of strength was reflected in a delayed return to the men's former capacity for work. After twenty weeks of rehabilitation the endurance of the men was still far below that at the beginning of the experiment. Functioning of heart and lungs and energy metabolism gradually improved. The anemia gradually disappeared. Sexual functions, as measured by mobility and longevity of sperm, also gradually improved and returned to normal generally about the time of renewal of sex interests and desires. This experiment has demonstrated that the body does not respond immediately to improving the food needs of men after a period of starvation, but rather that the process of recovery is gradual and tends to be slow. While the result of this experiment cannot be applied directly to children it seems reasonable to assume that functional changes occur in children as well as young adults under conditions of severe underfeeding.

Limited Calories Affect Growth of Healthy Children

That too few calories can be a limiting factor in growth has been demonstrated in healthy children living under satisfactory conditions. Macy and Hunscher (1951) in a study of children living in an excellent institutional environment found that too few calories may not only interfere with satisfactory weight gains but also may reduce the amount of nitrogen available for the building of body tissues. One boy who was losing weight and nitrogen gained weight and retained nitrogen when 10 calories for every kilogram (2.2 pounds) of his weight[6] were added to his diet daily.

---

[6] A total of little more than 200 calories, equivalent to about a glass of milk and a slice of bread with butter.

Supplementing the Diet

Studies have shown that improvement of inadequate diets can improve the health and growth of children. Spies and his co-workers (Spies and Dreisen, 1949; and Dreisen, *et al.*, 1950) have demonstrated that milk added as a supplement to poor diets of malnourished children will improve their growth. Children of four to fifteen years of age during a twenty-month period of supplementation[7] averaged an increased monthly gain of 3.6 per cent in height and 29 per cent in weight. When the milk was withdrawn for the following twelve months the improvement ceased. The children gained an average of 1.23 cm. (.48 in.) and 1.35 kg. (3 lb.) more than another group of ethnically and nutritionally comparable children. But even with the supplement very few of the children completely reduced their growth lag. This was thought to be due, separately or in various combinations, to too little additional food, too little time on the experimental diet, imbalances in the diet, and irreversible changes produced by long-term undernutrition.

A second study (Spies, *et al.*, 1953) was made of the skeletal maturation of 82 children, half of whom received a dietary supplement of dried milk equivalent in protein value to three quarts of milk per week for forty months after which the supplement was increased to twelve quarts of milk per week for six months. The other half of the children served as controls. During the forty months little difference in progress in bone maturation was found between the two groups. However, when 19 of the experimental group were given twelve quarts of milk a week they increased their rate of bone maturation by 80 per cent over that of the former period and far surpassed the other children who had no milk or only three quarts. Whole milk and skimmed milk were equally effective. Apparently the three quarts of milk per week did not supply sufficient bone-forming nutrients to produce a change. The quantity as well as the quality of a supplement is important.

Supplementation of a diet with a specific nutrient may correct a chronic deficiency. A survey in a community in Vermont (Browe and Pierce, 1950) revealed signs (conditions of the eye, the gums and the tongue of school children) indicating possible deficiencies in vitamin A, vitamin C and niacin. Half of the children showing

[7] Six quarts of milk per week were added to a diet deficient in calories and in several of the essential nutrients. The milk was given as reconstituted milk solids equivalent in protein value to that contained in six quarts of cow's milk. Some children received whole milk; some received skimmed or non-fat milk.

these signs were given vitamin A, vitamin C or niacin, depending upon the specific signs and the other half given placebos. The difference between the two groups in improvement was significantly in favor of those receiving the supplement. This study and the former ones cited indicate that improvement of an inadequate diet according to the nutritional needs for an individual child may very appreciably affect his health and growth.

NUTRITION AFFECTS BEHAVIOR AND MENTAL PERFORMANCE

Behavior

Nutrition can affect behavior and emotional adjustment.[8] However, to demonstrate a clear-cut relationship between nutrition on the one hand and behavior and emotional adjustment on the other is extremely difficult since nutrition is only one of a number of factors affecting the expression of interaction of the individual and his environment. Nevertheless the effects of undernutrition or malnutrition can be discernible in situations which are complicated by poor physical environment and emotional stresses and strains. Periods of severe underfeeding provide evidence. Spies, *et al.* (1952) describe a child whom they had observed from 5 to 12 years of age. He was a white boy, the fourth child in a family of ten that had lived on a diet consisting chiefly of cornbread, biscuits, fat pork, sugar, occasionally turnip greens, corn, tomatoes and berries in season. Rarely did this child have any milk, eggs, meat, fish or cheese. At 5 years of age he was retarded in growth and showed clinical evidence of deficiencies in thiamine, riboflavin and niacin. His mother reported that he had had "cracks"[9] at the corner of his mouth most of his life and frequently his tongue was red and sore.[10] During the following three years his mother complained that he was "fractious," and his teachers stated that he did not concentrate on his school work, had poor grades and was quarrelsome. At eight years and nine months he was given a skimmed milk supplement which increased his intake of protein, calcium, thiamine, riboflavin and niacin. No other changes were made in his life. During the first year there was little change in his lip and tongue condition, his disposition and his school grades. Following that year gradual im-

---

[8] See Keys, *et al.* (1950, Vol. II, Chas. 36–42).
[9] Symptom of riboflavin deficiency.
[10] Symptom of niacin deficiency.

provement in lip and tongue symptoms were noted. His mother reported great improvement in his disposition. His teachers said that he could concentrate better on his studies, his school grades had improved and his behavior was excellent. This relatively small improvement in his diet had contributed slowly to somewhat better living for this child even though it was insufficient to improve his growth rate in height and weight.

The behavior in school of children in Trier, Germany, during World War I is another example (Blanton, 1919). After three years of undernutrition the children showed a decrease in physical and nervous energy and an increase in nervous disorders. The teachers reported that the children grew tired more easily than in the pre-war days, were unable to concentrate, slower in comprehension, poorer in memory, inattentive and restless. Discipline was hard to maintain. One teacher reported that she could keep the attention of her class for only five minutes in contrast to thirty minutes formerly. The standard of school work was lowered. The number of children who failed to pass about doubled; the number of children doing superior work was not compatible with their mental capacity since the children apparently had not lost any of their mental capacity as measured by the usual mental tests. They lacked the staying qualities found in a well-nourished child.[11]

Observations during starvation in real life situations have been corroborated by the changes in behavior of the subjects of the Minnesota Study on starvation. The progressive anatomic and biochemical changes which produced sensations, drives and limitations to physical functions rendered the men increasingly ineffective in their daily life. During the period of semi-starvation men who had been energetic, even-tempered, humorous, patient, tolerant, enthusiastic, ambitious and emotionally stable became tired, apathetic, irritable, lacking in self-discipline and self-control. They lost much of their ambition and former self-initiated spontaneous physical and mental activity. They moved cautiously, climbed stairs one step at a time, and tended to be awkward, tripping over curbstones and bumping into objects. They lost interest in their appearance. They dressed carelessly and often neglected to shave, brush teeth and comb their hair. They became more concerned with themselves and less with others. It required too much effort to be social. Their interests narrowed. The educational program which was to prepare them for

[11] It should be noted that lack of food was also accompanied by unfavorable conditions at home and school due to the war.

foreign rehabilitation work collapsed. Humor and high spirits were replaced by soberness and seriousness. Any residual humor was of a sarcastic nature. They had periods of depression and became discouraged, in part because of their inability to sustain mental and physical effort. They were frustrated because of the difference between what they wished to do and what they could do. They found themselves buying things which were not useful at the time. They stopped having "dates." All sex feelings and expression virtually disappeared. All the time they were being distracted by hunger sensations and showing great concern about and interest in food.

When their food was increased during the rehabilitation period their psychologic recovery was somewhat faster than their physical improvement, although many months of unlimited diet passed before recovery was complete. Emotional stability and sociability were regained more rapidly than strength, endurance and sexual drive.

The sudden feeling of improvement, however, was temporary. Morale became low because many anticipated quick, complete recovery. As energy increased, they no longer were willing to accept conditions unquestioningly and showed annoyance at restrictions. Many grew argumentative and negativistic.[12] Humor, enthusiasm and sociability reappeared; irritability and nervousness diminished. The feeling of well-being increased the range of interest. The sense of group identity which had become strong during the semi-starvation period was dissipated as men began looking forward to making plans for their futures. An interest in activity and sex increased, their concern about food decreased after a period of insatiable appetite when they were first permitted to eat all they desired.

These were general trends in behavior changes, but considerable individual differences were noticed in the men's ability to withstand the stresses and strains of the experience, which appeared to bring out their innate strengths and weaknesses.[13]

Intelligence

It has been shown that undernutrition or malnutrition can affect

[12] In a study in Scotland of the effect of milk consumption on the growth of school children (Leighton and McKinlay, 1930) the teachers were asked to give their general impressions of the effect of the milk supplement upon the children. One teacher remarked, "In the playground buoyancy and pugnacity are developing to an alarming extent." No doubt these children had more available energy to expend.

[13] Some of these behavior changes were reflections of personality changes measurable by psychologic tests (Keys, et al., 1950).

mental activities or the way an individual uses his mental abilities. However, whether nutrition affects the mental capacity of children is a moot question. Mental capacity seems to withstand deprivations which will affect mental activity. The children in Trier, Germany, in spite of their poor school performance had still the same mental capacity as measured by tests. In the Minnesota Study, according to both clinical judgment and quantitative tests the men's mental capacity did not change appreciably during either semi-starvation or rehabilitation. The subjective estimates of loss of intellectual ability may be attributed to physical disability and emotional factors. Whether similar resistance exists at earlier ages when the nervous system is immature has yet to be demonstrated.[14]

The original promise that glutamic acid fed to mentally defective individuals might improve their level of intelligence has not been fulfilled. The conflicting results, due probably to differences in procedures and interpretation, and the mounting negative evidence seem to indicate that glutamic acid is not a "brain food."[15]

There have been some investigations of a relationship between some of the B-complex vitamins (i.e., riboflavin, thiamine and niacin) and intelligence. A well-controlled experiment (Guetzkow and Brozek, 1946) with men, planned to test deprivation of these vitamins and subsequent supplementation of thiamine, has been reported but no comparable experiments have yet been done with children. Young men were partially and then severely deprived of thiamine, riboflavin and niacin, after which thiamine was restored. A minimal drop in two out of six tests, in which speed appeared to be the essential factor, occurred during the period of deprivation. There was no evidence of an impaired rate of learning. However, there is little doubt that definite, prolonged vitamin deficiencies, especially of thiamine and niacin, will eventually result in mental retardation.[16]

Studies of the effect of thiamine supplements upon learning ability have given no assurance that adding thiamine to the diet of school-aged children will be followed by increased ability to learn.[17]

---

[14] An experiment (Bernhardt and Herbert, 1937) with rats deprived of vitamin B showed a varying response at different ages. During the 6th to 12th weeks such deprivation resulted in no difference in water-maze learning from that of a control group, but the rats deprived during their nursing period showed considerable retardation in learning.

[15] For specific references and summary of results see Nutrition Review (1951, 1953).

[16] See Spies, *et al.* (1943).

[17] For discussion of studies see Nutrition Review (1946, 1948, 1949).

Harrell's (1943, 1946) reported positive effects were not confirmed when Robertson *et al.* (1947), using identical twins and thus controlling the genetic factor, fed thiamine supplements to one of each of the twins, all of whom lived at home.

At the present time we have no means of ascertaining the effects of inadequate diets fed to children throughout their growing years. When the mental abilities of children thus deprived have been followed throughout their growth period there will be better evidence to ascertain to what degree nutrition affects the development of intelligence.

Evidence has been cited that underfeeding has a real effect upon the well-being of an individual and is reflected in his behavior. It would be wise, therefore, to keep in mind the nutritional needs of children and to meet them wherever possible. When lack of spontaneous activity, undue fatigue and irritability are apparent it would be profitable to investigate nutrition along with many other factors.

CHAPTER FIVE

Emotional Development

12

ADOLESCENT CONCERNS WITH PHYSIQUE

by Alexander Frazier and Lorenzo K. Lisonbee

Many people, young as well as old, are concerned about their physical appearance, for their acceptance by others depends in part upon the impressions derived from it. Alexander Frazier of Ohio State University and Lorenzo K. Lisonbee present here the results of their study of the concerns of ninth-grade adolescents with their physiques. [From *School Review*, 1950, *58*, 397-405. Reprinted by permission of the authors and The University of Chicago Press. One footnote has been omitted.]

A major task of adolescence is to adjust to the dramatic physical changes which mark the development of the child into the adult. In addition, the adolescent has, somewhere along the line, the problem of accepting his emerging shape and size as the physique with which he will have to proceed through life. Knowledge of the nature of adolescent physical changes is considerable; however, knowledge about the feelings of the adolescent seems less well documented. In searching for such evidence, the present writers were struck by the frequency with which the small, but intensively analyzed, sample represented in a California study is cited (Stolz and Stolz, 1944). In order to prepare materials for helping adolescents toward adjustment, it was felt desirable to collect local evidence that might be somewhat broader in its possible implications.

THE PRESENT STUDY

A Questionnaire

The present report covers the responses of all tenth-graders at North Phoenix High School for the year 1949-50. These 580 students, 309 girls and 271 boys, were enrolled in the required biology course. A questionnaire was drawn up to discover how these children saw themselves physically and how they felt about their conceptions of themselves. The major sections of the questionnaire dealt with weight, height and proportions, rate of development, facial appearance, and desire for self-improvement. All students answered anonymously.

For the first three sections, self-description was based on five choices. For example, in the section on height these choices were (1) short, (2) rather short, (3) about average, (4) rather tall, and (5) tall. In Section 4, facial appearance, the student was simply to check those of 59 items that he felt applied to him; items were grouped under "nose," "mouth," "skin," etc. Section 5, dealing with self-improvement, was designed to elicit a free written response. After each item of self-description in Sections 1 through 4, there followed a five-point scale for expression of worry or concern: (1) "Never think about it," (2) "Think about it now and then," (3) "Worry about it a little," (4) "Worry a good deal," and (5) "Worry a lot." To simplify reporting, the responses on this scale from 3 through 5 are combined and considered to represent what we will call *concern*.

Limitations of the Study

In reporting the findings of this survey, the writers acknowledge that whatever generalizations may be drawn must be regarded as highly tentative. The sample is not large. It represents only tenth-graders. The school population is largely middle-class. The attempt to measure concern is undoubtedly ambitious. Yet the need for studies of this kind is so great that the writers wish to offer their results to other persons who are working to collect evidence on the same problem.

Section 1: Weight

How do these tenth-grade boys and girls see themselves in terms of weight? If they think of themselves as heavy or thin, how do they feel about it? Students were asked to rate themselves both for their entire body and for various sections on a five-point scale: (1) too thin, (2) rather thin, (3) about right, (4) rather heavy, and (5) too heavy. They were also to indicate their degree of concern on the scale described above.

As shown in Table 1, almost one third of the girls see themselves

TABLE 1

PER CENT OF 580 TENTH-GRADE BOYS AND GIRLS GIVING CERTAIN DESCRIPTIONS
OF THEIR PHYSIQUES AND PER CENT EXPRESSING CONCERN ABOUT
THE CHARACTERISTICS DESCRIBED*

DESCRIPTION	PER CENT SO DESCRIBING THEMSELVES		PER CENT EXPRESSING CONCERN	
	Boys	Girls	Boys	Girls
Thin	21	16	22	48
Heavy	13	30	3	55
Short	26	27	39	22
Tall	28	22	4	49
Development early	19	24	6	15
Development slow	17	13	40	36

*The table is read as follows: 21 per cent of the boys and 16 per cent of the girls described themselves as thin; 22 per cent of the boys and 48 per cent of the girls so describing themselves expressed concern about this characteristic.

as heavy (combining "rather heavy" and "too heavy"), with more than half of them expressing some degree of concern. Only 13 per cent of the boys describe themselves in this manner, and little concern is expressed by them. Two-thirds of the boys describe themselves as "about right" compared to 54 per cent of the girls. Boys are more inclined than girls to rate themselves thin, although the girls express more concern over thinness. However, boys show more than seven times as much concern about being thin as about being heavy. Throughout this study, boys are found less expressive of concern than girls.

Boys and girls were also asked to describe themselves in terms of weight of body sections (face, neck, shoulders, chest, abdominal section, hips, upper arm, forearm, upper leg, lower leg, and ankles). When the two positions for heaviness and thinness at either end of the scale were combined, items checked as heavy or thin by as many as 25 per cent of the boys or girls served to reinforce the picture given above. Nearly half the girls (46 per cent) think they have heavy hips. Heavy abdominal sections (43 per cent) and upper legs (38 per cent) rank next. The forearm is the only section marked thin by any sizable number of girls (28 per cent). Supposed heaviness of these parts of the body greatly concerns the girls, just as it does in reference to the entire body. Of the girls who consider their hips heavy, 64 per cent express concern. Heavy upper legs bother half the girls so describing themselves; heavy midregions, a third.

Thinness of body sections is self-assigned by a considerable per cent of the boys, bearing out the inclination noted in the description of the entire body. One-third of the boys consider their upper arms thin; 30 per cent mark themselves as having thin forearms; 27 per cent, thin chests. One section, the mid-region, is marked heavy by a sizable number (28 per cent). Here again, concern is less pronounced for boys than for girls. Heaviness of abdominal sections concerns one-third of the boys so describing themselves; thinness of upper arm, 27 per cent; thinness of chest, 21 per cent; and thinness of forearm, 20 per cent.

The tenth-grade girls in this study tend to think of themselves as heavy, particularly in certain sections of the body. Girls express a high degree of concern about their weight. Boys tend to think they are "about right," with some inclination toward thinness, particularly in upper arms, forearms, and chests. Boys are less expressive of concern about weight than are girls.

Section 2: Height and Proportions

How do these students see themselves in terms of height and proportions, and how do they feel about their self-conceptions? The questionnaire asked tenth-graders to describe themselves in terms of a five-point scale for height, width of hips and shoulders, and length of arms, legs, trunk, and feet. The "worry" scale was the same for this section as for the others.

Most of the boys and girls saw themselves as "about average" in height. However, as shown in Table 1, girls were a little more inclined to think of themselves as short, boys as tall. As far as concern was expressed, it centered rather dramatically in tallness for girls (49 per cent of the girls who thought of themselves as tall expressed concern) and in shortness for boys (39 per cent concern). Tall boys felt little concern, not much more than did heavy boys.

The items which attempted to get at possible concerns over proportions revealed little, except that a rather large number of girls

(37 per cent) consider themselves to have wide hips and express a high degree of concern (60 per cent) about it. Such a self-conception and concern with width of hips is undoubtedly related to their consciousness of heaviness in that region, as revealed under weight. Large feet are accepted as their lot by 28 per cent of the girls, with an expressed concern of 37 per cent. Although 35 per cent of the boys think their feet are large, only 10 per cent of these express concern.

Half the tall girls among these tenth-graders are concerned about their height. Nearly 40 per cent of the short boys express concern. These findings are the most significant in this section of the questionnaire.

Section 3: Rate of Development

How many of these boys and girls think of themselves as slow or fast in development? How concerned are they? Both sexes were asked to describe themselves in terms of total growth. Boys were also asked to rate themselves as to growth of beard, muscular development, and voice change.

Most of these tenth-graders consider themselves average, as will be seen from the percentages for early and slow development given in Table 1. A larger percentage of girls than of boys think their rate early; more boys than girls see themselves as slow-developing. Concern over early development is not too large with either boys or girls, although more than twice as much for girls.

The most significant fact emerging from this section of the study is that 40 per cent of the boys who consider themselves slow-maturing express concern. This is the highest amount of concern expressed by boys, except that over blackheads and pimples. While the slow-developing girls express 36 per cent concern, the fact that boys of this group are even more expressive is highly indicative of the insecurity that faces slow-developing boys, even at the tenth-grade level. In actual per cents of total boys and girls, those who express concern over what they consider their slow rate of development is only 6 per cent. The number is not large, but the concern is great, particularly for boys.

Section 4: Facial Appearance

How do these boys and girls describe themselves in terms of facial appearance, and how much concerned are they? For each of the 59 items that might be checked, students were asked to mark also the usual five-point scale of concern.

As shown in Table 2, only 17 of the items were marked by as

TABLE 2

ITEMS OF SELF-DESCRIPTION CHECKED BY TEN PER CENT OR MORE OF 580 TENTH-GRADE BOYS AND GIRLS, WITH AMOUNT OF EXPRESSED CONCERN

	BOYS			GIRLS	
Item of description	Per cent checking	Per cent of concern	Item of description	Per cent checking	Per cent of concern
Blackheads or pimples	57	51	Blackheads or pimples	57	82
Lack of beard	34	2	Heavy eyebrows	24	11
Heavy eyebrows	27	1	Freckles	23	24
Scars, birthmarks, moles	20	13	Oily skin	22	52
Irregular teeth	17	39	Scars, birthmarks, moles	22	30
Heavy lips	14	5	Glasses	21	31
Protruding chin	13	6	High forehead	19	8
Ears stick out	13	6	Too round face	19	21
Oily skin	12	27	Too homely	18	42
Freckles	12	—	Dry skin	16	43
Heavy beard	11	13	Irregular teeth	16	42
Glasses	11	23	Thin lips	15	13
Dark skin	10	4	Low forehead	13	3
Receding chin	10	4	Too long nose	11	23
Gaps in teeth	10	26	Too big nose	11	44
Too long nose	10	8	Receding chin	10	13
Too thin face	10	15	Odd-shaped nose	10	23
Too large ears	10	8			

many as 10 per cent of the girls; 18 items by 10 per cent of the boys. In addition to the nine items common to both sexes (blackheads or pimples; heavy eyebrows; freckles; oily skin; scars, birthmarks, moles; glasses; irregular teeth; too long nose; and receding chin), the girls included high forehead, too round face, too homely, dry skin, thin lips, low forehead, too big nose, and odd-shaped nose. The boys listed lack of beard, heavy lips, protruding chin, ears stick out, heavy beard, dark skin, gaps in teeth, too thin face, and too large ears.

That 57 per cent of both sexes testify to having blackheads and pimples and that both boys and girls are more concerned about the problem than about any other item in the entire questionnaire is the outstanding fact revealed by this section. Both boys and girls express considerable concern also about oily skin, irregular teeth, and glasses. Concern is heavy for girls who think they have a nose that is too big, skin that is too dry, or that they are just too homely.

A few other facts are of interest. We note that nearly twice as many girls as boys wear glasses. Boys express no concern about freckles; girls, 24 per cent. Lack of beard, which a third of the boys acknowledge, causes little "worry," reinforcing what we had found on this item under rate of development.

Apparently, complexion problems form the chief physical worry of these tenth-grade boys and girls. Nothing else, in either this or other sections, looms as large in affecting so many and in "worrying" a majority of both boys and girls who are affected.

Section 5: Desire for Self-improvement

The fifth part of the questionnaire was designed to find out what tenth-grade boys and girls thought of the desirability of changing themselves. This question was asked: "Would you change your physical self in some way if you could?" As shown in Table 3, two-thirds of this group said they would.

TABLE 3

NUMBER AND PER CENT OF 580 TENTH-GRADE BOYS AND GIRLS DESIRING SOME CHANGE IN PHYSICAL SELVES

SEX	YES		NO		NO ANSWER		TOTAL	
	No.	Per Cent	No.	Per Cent	No.	Per Cent	No.	Per Cent
Boys	164	61	92	34	15	5	271	100
Girls	222	72	60	19	27	9	309	100
Both	386	67	152	26	42	7	580	100

What kinds of changes are desired? In a second question, students were asked, if they desired change, to specify in what ways. As shown in Table 4, the responses have been broken down and classified for both boys and girls by areas, number of items for each area, percentages, and rank order. However, before examining the total picture, it may be of interest to look at the desires of each sex separately.

THE CHANGES GIRLS WANT. Girls are highly specific about the ways in which they would like to change themselves, as the following samples indicate:

My hips and legs are too large and fat. If I could have smaller hips and legs, I'd have a much better figure. I'd also like to be a *little* more developed above the waist than I am, but I am not flat. I wish I didn't have so many pimples or had to wear glasses.

(1) I would make myself thinner. (2) I would make my ears lie back. (3) I would make my forehead lower. (4) I would take away my pimples and make my complexion clear and soft. (5) I would make my eyes just a little bigger. (6) I would make my feet smaller.

I would first of all change my nose, as it is huge. I think someday I will go to a plastic surgeon and get my nose changed. I would not be so tall. I would like a wider jaw. I thought when I got my teeth straightened my jaw would be wider, but it is still sharp and pointed. I would like a clear, unscarred complexion. I have blackheads and pimples. I may go to a dermatologist. My eyes are small with short lashes. I have many moles, which I saw a doctor about, but they cannot be removed without scars or pits.

I'd have cute legs, a cute figure, and a shorter forehead. I'd also be three inches shorter and smaller feet. I'd have blue eyes and blond hair fixed in page-boy. I would weigh 101 pounds.

I would rather not wear glasses. I would lose ten pounds. I would like a complexion that stays nice all the time.

TABLE 4

AREAS IN WHICH 222 GIRLS AND 164 BOYS IN GRADE X SPECIFY
DESIRE FOR SELF-IMPROVEMENT

| | GIRLS | | | BOYS | | |
CATEGORY	Number of items	Per cent of items	Rank order	Number of items	Per cent of items	Rank order
Proportions	122	20.6	1	81	24.4	1
Complexion	109	18.4	2	38	11.4	5
Weight	74	12.5	3	50	15.1	3
Hair	62	10.5	4	14	4.2	7
Height	59	10.0	5	55	16.6	2
Features	55	9.3	6	16	4.8	6
Eyes	52	8.8	7	10	3.0	9
Teeth	21	3.6	8	11	3.3	8
Daintiness	13	2.2	9	—	—	—
Strength	—	—	—	46	13.9	4
Personal qualities	9	1.5	10	3	0.9	11
Freedom from disease or deformity	1	0.2	11	5	1.5	10
Unclassified	15	2.5	—	3	0.9	—
Total	592	100.1	—	332	100.0	—

When these responses had been itemized and classified, it was plain that the desires of the girls to change were distributed through most of the categories. Since lack of space prohibits the listing of all the items grouped under each category, only the largest clusters can be mentioned.

Under the category Proportions in Table 4, with 122 items, these clusters were slimmer hips (31), smaller feet (24), smaller waist (17), and good shape (16). The major clusters under the category Complexion (109 items) were clear complexion (42), no pimples (21), no freckles (16). The category Weight (74 items) lent itself to simple subdivision, more slender (50) and fatter (24). Most of the items under the category Hair (62) were contributed by girls who wanted to have hair that was dark (15), blond (12), longer (12), or naturally curly (10). Under the category Height (59 items), the girls were chiefly desirous of being shorter (38), although some wished to be taller (17). The chief desire under the category Features (55 items) was to have a nice nose (16) or a pretty face (13). The desires under the category Eyes (52 items) centered in no glasses and better vision (21) and blue eyes (12).

THE CHANGES BOYS WANT. The questionnaire results consistently revealed that the boys were less expressive than the girls. The boys responded with answers that were analyzed into 332 items, as compared with 592 of the girls. A few of these statements in their entirety follow:

I would make my chest bigger than it is now and also my shoulders. I would like to weigh a little bit more, say about twenty to twenty-five pounds more than I do now.

Be bigger and have more muscular development. Be taller and get rid of skin blemishes.

I would make myself look handsomer and not fat. I would have wavy black hair. I would change my whole physical appearance so that I would be handsome, with a good build.

Well, I would start off by putting on some meat, next would be to get rid of my pimples, then to get some muscles, then to get rid of my glasses.

I would build up my upper arm, forearm, chest, shoulder, and abdomen muscles.

I would be taller, more muscular, slimmer, have better posture, lighter and more slowly-growing head of hair, big, broad shoulders, and heavier calves.

Categories of major importance for boys are shown in Table 4, as being Proportions, Height, Weight, Strength, and Complexion.

The clusters of items under each of these reveal the chief concerns. Under Proportions (81 items), the chief clusters are better build (17), broader shoulders (17), and larger chest (11). The category Height (55 items) is singularly centered in becoming taller (51). The items under the category Weight (50) are chiefly for heavier (36). The category Strength (46 items), perhaps poorly balanced by what we have termed "Daintiness" for girls, has two chief clusters, better muscular development (28) and stronger (10). For the boys, only one cluster emerges under the category Complexion (38 items), and that is no pimples (16).

These tenth-graders of both sexes are most conscious of a desire to conform to their conceptions of the ideal physical appearance in the areas of proportions, weight, height, and complexion, with a somewhat different rank order for each sex, chiefly notable for a switch in emphasis on complexion and height. Girls are more aware of complexion problems, boys of stature. In addition, a major category, which is plainly sex-determined, appears for both girls and boys among the top five categories. These categories are hair for girls; strength for boys.

Agreement in categories is not borne out, of course, in the clusters of items under weight and height. Girls desire to be thinner, boys heavier; girls want to be shorter, boys taller. In part, these differences may reflect the fact that girls of this age will be more mature than boys. Probably, the differences are largely differences in the ideal physique held in mind by each sex. An interesting check upon another section of the questionnaire is provided by the fact that proportions here rank first, whereas we had failed to elicit much response from the students for that aspect of Section 2. Our items there were apparently not the right ones.

SUMMARY

In order to collect more information about how adolescents think of themselves physically and how concerned they are over their self-conceptions, the writers questioned one tenth-grade group of 580 students in terms of weight, height, and proportions, rate of development, facial appearance, and desire for change. As reported here, the findings seem to justify the following generalizations:

1. The girls in this study are inclined to think of themselves as heavy and to express a high amount of concern about their supposed heaviness. Boys think of themselves as about right in weight

but incline toward describing themselves as thin, with considerable concern about thinness in the upper arms and chest.

2. Height concerns chiefly the girls who think of themselves as tall, the boys who consider themselves short. Short boys express what is, for their sex, a high degree of concern.

3. Fewer of these boys and girls consider themselves slow in maturing than think themselves early. Most of them see themselves as average in this respect. However, among both boys and girls, the slow-maturing children express high concern. This is particularly outstanding among the boys in comparison with other expressions of male concern.

4. Blackheads and pimples are self-ascribed by a majority of the group. The concern of both sexes is higher for this item than for any other item in the entire questionnaire.

5. Two-thirds of these tenth-graders express a desire for some change in themselves physically, with items relating to proportions leading the categories for both sexes. Weight, height, and complexion are the other top areas in which desired change is common to both boys and girls.

··· 13 ···

PHYSICAL MATURING AMONG BOYS AS
RELATED TO BEHAVIOR

by Mary Cover Jones and Nancy Bayley

Do adolescents who mature physically at an early age differ in their social adjustment from those who mature physically at a later age? Mary Cover Jones of the University of California (Berkeley) and Nancy Bayley of the National Institute of Mental Health seek an answer to this question by means of an investigation of two groups of boys, one early-maturing and one late-maturing. Their findings are presented in the following article. [From *Journal of Educational Psychology*, 1950, *41*, 129-148. Reprinted by permission of the authors and Warwick and York, Inc. Some of the footnotes have been omitted.]

The problems of adjustment which are usually attributed to the adolescent period center around the youth's need to develop heterosexual interests, to select a vocation, and, in general, to acquire the status of adulthood in the eyes of his peers and of his elders. The impetus for the attainment of independent and mature status is undoubtedly related to the adolescent's physical changes, but the process of growing up is so complex and so interwoven with cultural factors that we have not yet been able to demonstrate more than a rather general relationship between physical and psychological phases of development.

It is well known that children mature at different rates, and reach the period of pubescence at different chronological ages. Although the psychological accompaniments of these differences in maturing can be examined in terms of mass statistics (Stone and Barker, 1937, 1939), this approach to the problem is often disappointing because of its tendency to obscure the intricacies of the growth pattern and the dynamics involved in the process of integration. Case reports of individual children have been somewhat more successful in their attempts to disclose the processes involved in the attainment of maturity (Jones, 1943, 1949), but the accumulation of individual life histories is a slow way in which to arrive at useful generalities.

The present report deals with two groups of boys who fall at opposite ends of a normal sample distributed on the basis of one developmental characteristic (skeletal age). In an attempt to find differentiating behavior characteristics, statistical comparisons of the two groups have been made and illustrative case material has been assembled for individuals falling at each extreme. The method, while providing no touchstone, does enable us to consider group differences without losing sight of the individual behavior patterns of members of the group.

There are several ways in which children's physical maturity status may be expressed. One of the most commonly used for girls, is the age of menarche. As a possible comparable measure for boys, some investigators have used the age of appearance of pubic or of axilliary hair (Richey, 1937). Shuttleworth (1939) classified children in the Harvard Growth Study according to age at maximum growth in height. Height and weight have also been used as an index of physical maturity, although maturity differences may be obscured by genetic differences in measurements of gross body dimensions. This difficulty is avoided by the use of skeletal age norms, from x-rays of the long bones of the hand and knee (Todd,

1930, 1937). Skeletal age has the advantage of being a stable and reliably assessed indicator of physical maturity, closely related to other aspects of physical maturing (Flory, 1936), and applicable at all ages from birth to young adulthood.

Several studies have dealt with the relationship between skeletal maturity and intelligence (Abernethy, 1936; Simmons, 1944; and West, 1936). Comparisons with other psychological factors are relatively scarce. In one of the few investigations in this field, Stone and Barker (1939), using the age at menarche as a criterion, found greater maturity of interests among girls who were past the menarche, than among premenarcheal girls of the same age.

PHYSICAL CHARACTERISTICS OF THE EARLY- AND LATE-MATURING GROUPS

The selection of contrasting extreme groups for the present study was on the basis of physical maturity assessments by the Todd standards for hand and knee. The groups included sixteen boys who were most consistently accelerated and sixteen who were most consistently retarded during the four and a half years for which we had cumulative skeletal x-rays, beginning at an average age of fourteen years. The total distribution from which these extremes were truncated consisted of ninety cases, a normal classroom sample of boys in an urban public school system (Jones, 1949).

Figure 1 presents the comparative maturity assessments of the two groups at two age levels; each dot or circle indicates the skeletal age for an individual case. Some relevant physical data are given in Figure 2, which compares the distribution of the two groups in height at three age levels, and also with regard to adult height as predicted by the Bayley method (Bayley, 1946; Bayer and Bayley, 1947). The age levels used are grade placements (instead of more restricted age intervals) to facilitate comparison with the behavioral data which are of greater significance when kept in their original contexts.

On the average, the physically accelerated and the physically retarded boys are seen to be of the same age, but are separated by about two years in skeletal age (the criterion variable). Although some overlapping can be noted (Fig. 2) in the height of individual children at each age, the means of the groups (indicated by arrows) are widely different. Even as early as eleven years (grade H5 and L6) all of the late-maturing are shorter than the mean for the early-maturing. At the mean age of fourteen years (grade H8 and L9) the distributions show an extreme separation; in the later years of adolescence the differences tend to decrease, and the predicted mature heights of the early- and late-maturing are very similar.

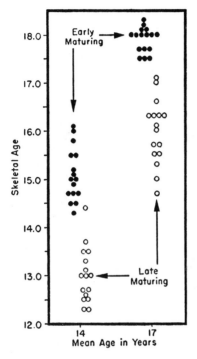

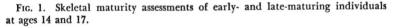

FIG. 1. Skeletal maturity assessments of early- and late-maturing individuals at ages 14 and 17.

There is also an obvious divergence (with no overlap) when the two groups are compared in terms of physical maturity ratings. This is seen when Greulich and Dorfman's (1942) five-point standards of maturity, based on ratings of pubic hair and external genitals, are applied to photographs taken at fourteen years of age. The characteristic rating at this age is 3. The mean of sixteen early-maturing boys was 4.5 (close to the maximum), with no rating below 4. The mean of the sixteen late-maturers was 2.0, with only two ratings of 3.

The boys who matured late were relatively very small from thirteen to fifteen years. In agreement with Bayley's (1943) study of body build in relation to skeletal maturing, they were characteristically slender built and long legged at all ages. Furthermore, their strength tests show them to have been relatively weak at the ages when they were lagging in size, and their scores in the Espenschade (1940) tests of athletic ability were in most instances below average. The early-maturing boys, on the other hand, were usually large, broad-built and strong, and tended to show good athletic

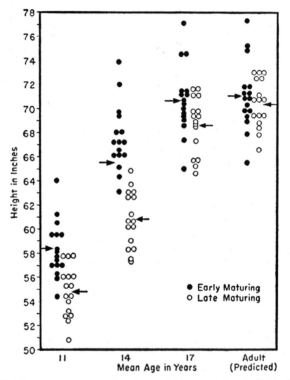

Fig. 2. Height measurements of early- and late-maturing individuals at four ages.

skill throughout the period of our records. Their superiority in strength and physical skills was greatest at ages thirteen to fifteen (Jones, 1946), when their early growth spurt accentuated their differences in size as compared with the slower-growing average and late-maturing boys. This is in agreement with a recent report by H. E. Jones (1949), who presents a variety of data for groups of boys in the Adolescent Growth Study, considered in relation to static dynamometric strength. Strong boys were found to be relatively mature in skeletal age, weak boys were immature.

SOCIAL BEHAVIOR IN BOYS' GROUPS

The psychological records examined in connection with the present study include both observational measures and reputation scores. We shall present first the ratings made independently by three staff members when the boys were in small groups (usually six) in a same-sex 'free play' situation. These will be referred to as ICW (Institute of Child Welfare) rating. The monograph by Newman (1946) contains a description of the rating scales and procedure. The observations and ratings were concerned, in general, with social behavior and personal attributes which are important in social relationships.

The ratings have been converted into standard scores in which 50 represents the mean of the total group, with a SD of ten points. The direction and the degree of a child's deviation from the mean of his group are thus expressed in such a way that comparisons can readily be made between accelerated and retarded subgroups.

Figure 3 and Figures 5 to 7 present cumulative standard score curves, from ages twelve to seventeen, for a series of traits involving personal appearance, expressiveness, attention-seeking, and emotional patterns. As shown in Figure 3, the early-maturing are con-

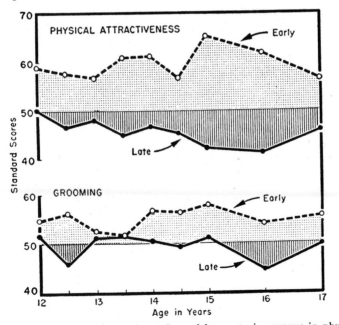

Fig. 3. Mean standard scores for early- and late-maturing groups in physical appearance.

sistently rated as superior in physical attractiveness, with average scores which reach their highest value at age fifteen. In general, the group is about one SD above the mean total sample of boys. The late-maturing fall somewhat below the group mean, increasingly so from age twelve to age fifteen or sixteen. These differences in attractiveness of physique are complexly influenced by factors of size and of body build. Early maturing is not only associated with a more rapid growth in height, but also with mesomorphy (Sheldon et al., 1940). The boys in this group tend to be 'well-built,' muscular, and athletic. By Sheldon's (1940) classification, the average body-build formula was 2.8–4.4–3.5 for the early-maturing; 2.4–3.9–4.0, for the late-maturing. By contrast the more slender, poorly-muscled build of the late-maturers was rated as relatively 'unattractive' by the adult observers.

When a comparison is made of the androgynic qualities of the builds of these two groups, the early-maturers are found to be on the average more 'masculine,' the late-maturers more 'childish' in their build. As shown in the lower half of Figure 3, early-maturing, as might be expected, is also associated with a somewhat greater attention to the amenities of personal grooming. This is expressed in cleanliness, attention to hair and nails, and neatness of clothing.

The difference between the two groups in physical attractiveness is most marked at ages fifteen and sixteen. Figure 4 presents com-

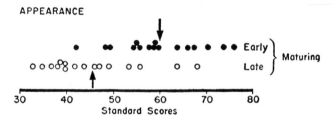

Fig. 4. Comparative distributions of early- and late-maturing in appearance (means indicated by arrows).

parative distributions at age sixteen for a composite based on physique, grooming, and attractiveness of facial appearance. Each circle represents an individual case; the means are indicated by arrows. So marked is the separation of the early- and late-maturing that all but one of the former fall above the average of the latter; only two cases among the late-maturing are rated above the central tendency of our total group of boys.

Another group of traits which may have developmental significance are those related to expressiveness. Ratings of 'animation'
and 'eagerness' are presented in Figure 5. In these characteristics

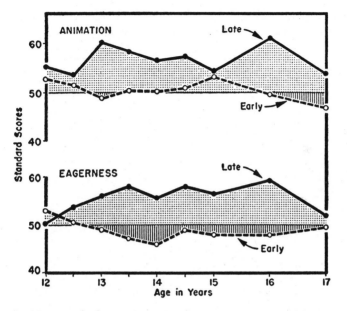

Fig. 5.   Mean standard scores for early- and late-maturing groups in expressive
traits.

the early-maturing are close to the group average, but the late-
maturing are consistently above the average. Similar differences
were found for other traits involving expressiveness; comparisons
were made for behavior defined, at contrasting extremes, as
talkative-silent; active-stationary; busy-idle; peppy-indifferent; and
laughing-sober. In each of these the early-maturing boys were distributed similarly to the total sample of boys, the late-maturing
were consistently on the 'expressive' side of the scale.

At least two factors are probably involved in determining this
deviate position of the late-maturing. The first is a persistence of
a childish activity pattern. A busy scurrying about and noisy interchange of shouts and comments is more characteristic of pre-
adolescence than of later years; the adolescent often looks down
upon such behavior as undignified, and adopts instead the role of a
lounger, observing with tolerant superiority the childish antics of
those younger than himself. A second factor is a reaction formation
to inferiority. The 'active small boy' may be expressing through his

activity not merely a survival of an immature culture pattern, but may also use this, as the only technique he knows, to hold the attention of others and to compensate for a physically less favored status.

In this connection, it is instructive to consider the evidence concerning attention-seeking behavior, as presented in Figure 6. In

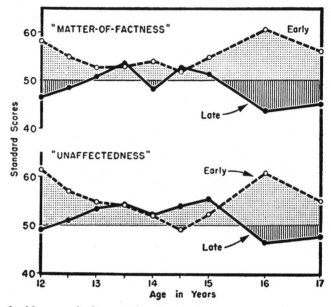

Fig. 6. Mean standard scores of early- and late-maturing groups in attention-seeking behavior.

the upper half of this figure, the late-maturing boys tend to vary around the average in the trait 'matter-of-factness.' Their lowest score is at age sixteen, when they fall on the 'show-off' side of the scale. In the lower half of the figure, their scores also vary around the average on the trait 'unaffectedness.' Again, they attain a low score at age sixteen; their expressiveness is judged to have a more affected quality at ages sixteen and seventeen than in the years immediately preceding. Although the differences are small, this would be consistent with an interpretation emphasizing a 'natural' or 'childish' expressiveness in the earlier years of adolescence, and a more compensatory attention-seeking expressiveness in the later years. In contrast, the early-maturing are at these ages judged to be relatively nonattention-seeking: unaffected and matter-of-fact.

Also pertinent are the ratings for inhibition and relaxation in

social situations (Figure 7). The late-maturing are relatively un-
inhibited, but they are also judged to be relatively tense. At age
sixteen, the early-maturing are on the average approximately one

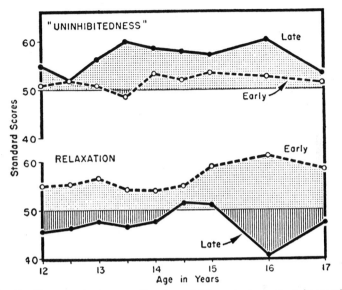

Fɪɢ. 7.   Mean standard scores of early- and late-maturing groups, in emotional
patterning.

SD above the group mean, in the direction of 'relaxation,' and the
late-maturing are a similar distance below the mean, in the direction of 'tenseness.' The early-maturing are consistently well-adjusted
in this trait, while the late maturing are in most semesters on the
less well-adjusted side of the scale.

Table 1 presents the significance of the differences between the
early- and late-maturing at age sixteen, based on *t* ratios. For all
but two traits on this list, differences are significant at the five per
cent level or better. In these two traits (animation and 'uninhibit-
edness') significant differences are obtained when results are considered for all nine semesters in which ratings have been recorded,
from ages twelve to seventeen, and analyzed in terms of the binomial test for consistency.[1] In attractiveness of physique, grooming,
and relaxation (higher for the late-maturing) differences are in

[1] Based on the probability that the difference in a series of paired measures
will occur in the same direction in a specified proportion of the instances (Fisher,
1946). Since the same subjects are involved, consistent differences are interpreted
as independent of errors in measurement, but they are not necessarily independent of initial sampling errors.

the same direction in each of nine semesters, with a significance level of .002. Differences of the same consistency were obtained for a number of other traits not included in Figures 3 to 7; these results show that the late-maturing are significantly more busy, more active, more 'peppy,' and more talkative. Differences at the two per cent level (in the same direction for eight of the nine semesters) were found for eagerness, social initiative, and

TABLE 1

MEAN STANDARD SCORES FOR EARLY- AND LATE-MATURING

	Early	Late	Significance of difference
Attractiveness of physique	60.6	45.0	.01
Grooming	54.6	49.8	.05
Animation	49.6	61.2	
Eagerness	47.9	59.3	.05
Uninhibitedness	52.5	60.2	
Matter-of-factness	60.5	43.6	.02
Unaffectedness	60.7	46.2	.05
Relaxation	61.1	40.6	.01

sociability, in favor of the late-maturing. Differences at the seven per cent level (in the same direction for seven of the nine semesters) occurred in several additional traits, indicating a possibly greater tendency for the early-maturing to be good-natured, and for the late-maturing to be attention-seeking and to enjoy games.

It may be noted that the two maturational groups show similar rather than different records in a number of traits of social importance. Thus, they present no marked nor consistent differences in observed popularity, leadership, prestige, poise, assurance, cheerfulness, or social effect on the group.

In view of the relation of maturing to physical abilities, and of the high valuation placed upon athletic performance in the adolescent culture (Tryon, 1939), it is perhaps surprising that differences in maturing are not reflected in such traits as popularity, leadership, or prestige. Case reports (Jones, 1943, 1949) have made it clear that late-maturing is sometimes a primary source of social and personal maladjustment. On the average, however, the late-maturing boy succeeds in maintaining a fairly adequate status among his age-mates; very likely he is helped in this by his activity and other compensations, and it is also probable that some of the early-maturing are handicapped at times by the fact that they have outgrown their age group.

DESCRIPTIVE DATA

In Figure 8, which presents unweighted composite values for various aspects of expressiveness (talkative-silent; active-stationary; peppy-indifferent; busy-idle; animated-stolid; eager-listless) at age sixteen, it can be observed that six of the late-maturing boys fall

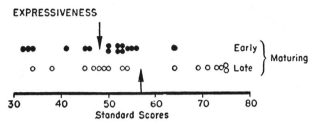

Fig. 8. Comparative distributions of early- and late-maturing in expressiveness (means indicated by arrows).

quite outside the distribution of the early-maturing. A brief description of each of these individuals will provide a more concrete indication of a behavior pattern characteristic of nearly half of the physiologically retarded boys. This pattern of 'boyishness' is fairly well illustrated by the case of Tom:

As a junior high school 'preadolescent' Tom was a chubby small boy, very rosy of cheek, sparkling-eyed, laughing and dimpled. His gaiety, good humor and dynamic activity were effective among his own equally boyish friends though most of his age-mates considered him to be quite immature in behavior.

Staff members made the following brief notations on the comment sheets recorded during free play situations (ages indicated in parentheses):

(13.4) In the nursery school yard: He seemed as delighted with the children of the nursery school as though someone had handed him a litter of puppies.

(13.4) At 'free' play with his own group: Tom played baseball with spirit if not with great skill. His activity was accompanied with continuous good-natured comments about the progress of the game and the 'boners' of his team-mates.

(13.9) Talking to another classmate: Tom Saylor chattered to Jim Cohn about his new job with as much enthusiasm as if he had found a gold mine. He is paid fifty cents a week to pass out handbills for a grocery store; this involves getting up at 5:30 every Friday morning. He was enthusiastic in urging Jim to "get in on it." The latter's indifference seemed to him like mild insanity.

(16.4) In senior high school: Still a small boy in comparison with most of his classmates, Tom's immaturity was obvious in many ways. His face was still cherubic, his lively and uninhibited activity more typical of younger boys. In the tenth grade an observer wrote: "He would seem to fit better in a junior high than a senior high school setting. Put him in a seventh or eighth grade classroom, and his appearance and behavior would be quite in keeping with that of the majority of his classmates."

Tom's clothes were misfits but he was as unconcerned about this as about his very dirty hands, although by this time most high school students were paying attention to clothes and cleanliness. His voice had not changed, as was very evident when he used it argumentatively in card games or jocularly in good humored razzing.

On the playground: Tom played pitching pennies with Ralph (an early-maturing boy) and seemed much more emotionally involved than the latter. He is often a conspicuous figure in childish scuffles; during a friendly tussle with several other boys he was disturbed at finding that he had lost his penny. He was ready to cry and fight about this, the only coin he had.

During most of this period (junior and senior high school) Tom seemed not to suffer from introspective misgivings about his adequacy. By some magical formula, he apparently had caught and prolonged that legendary will-of-the-wisp, 'happy childhood.' Tom seemed oblivious to the tide of events which swept most of his classmates into an earlier puberty. But his euphoric and carefree attitudes were not shown to an equal degree by all of the other six late-maturing who were also classified as exceptionally 'expressive.' Among these with relatively similar patterns of conspicuous and active behavior were several boys who seemed more obviously to be compensating for a sense of physical inadequacy or for loss of a social prestige which they had enjoyed in earlier years:

Lonnie was a boy previously described by H. E. Jones (1949) as one whose physical deficiencies in size and athletic prowess were a persistent source of tension and anxiety. His activity pattern was accompanied by excessive verbalizations and became more aggressive and compulsive as his status with the group declined and his home situation failed to support him during this difficult period.

Neal, another late-maturer, possessed a well-knit, athletic build, but was too small to play football or basketball on the team, as he had always been too small to compete with an older brother. His activity was chiefly limited to using athletic equipment; with other boys in a playground situation, he was inclined to be surly and on the defensive.

Bill and Teddy, two good friends from the same neighborhood, were active as nursery school children are active—they climbed, chased each other, hid and ran about. Often they were the ring leaders in mischievous hiding of the clothing or books belonging to other boys.

Milton was described as agile and quick, "climbed around like a monkey," ". . . his energy output seems to be twice that of an average healthy boy," he 'horsed around' in mixed group situations. In much of his group play he seemed to invite attack, to enjoy being teased and pummelled. At one time, however, he paid a mature classmate ten cents a week to protect him from some boys who were pestering him. An undisciplined child of somewhat elderly parents, he was disorganized, often rebellious, spent his energy in emotional outbursts as well as in random activity.

The six most 'expressive' late-maturing boys were conspicuous because of their activity in situations involving small groups of boys. They had chosen or were forced into what appeared, superficially at least, to be similar patterns of behavior. Yet the factors which determined the broad aspects of this behavior pattern were diverse and complex, altering in essential ways the details of the pattern from individual to individual.

Although expressiveness as exemplified by talkativeness, activity, eagerness and 'pep' is a form of behavior which many late-maturing boys easily assume or toward which they are predisposed, examples can be found of a quite opposite tendency. Two of the late-maturing boys are to be found near the extreme low end of the scale in expressiveness. These boys are brothers—Glenn and Charles. They were extremely self-contained and quiet, finding within themselves and their family satisfactions in behavior which did not require an audience or group participation.

Both boys were rated as non-attention getting and matter-of-fact; they were unsocial, and judged to have little effect upon their group of contemporaries. When most youngsters were seeking social satisfactions outside the family, Glenn and Charles were still enjoying congenial recreational interests with their parents. Their summer vacation was a family camping trip which involved packing into lonely country where the fishing and hunting was good. Glenn's response to the question, "Does your mother go camping with you?" was, "Yes, she likes to get away from people, too."

While in some respects Glenn and Charles resembled the early-maturing boys, their total complex of traits would never have led an observer to judge them to be among the more grown-up. In addition to having the lowest scores among the late-maturers on 'expressiveness, these brothers also had the lowest scores for 'sociability.' It is rather to be expected that girls would be outside their world. It was not until after they entered college that they began to take any initiative about dating girls. The mother, concerned with their 'backwardness' in this respect, tried to arrange for visits from families with girls of an appropriate age. After one such evening she was taken to task by her boys in this fashion: "Don't ever try that again. We didn't know what to talk about and it was a terrible bore."

Glenn and Charles are two boys who were late in reaching physiological and skeletal maturity and similarly slow to take on the social behavior of their peers. But in their slowness they remained aloof, bolstered by solid but solitary interests rather than by the energetic outgoing patterns of activity more common among the late-maturing boys of the study.

It is obvious that a statistical average which includes the social behavior scores of boys as different as Tom and the brothers—Glenn and Charles—will provide little understanding of the varieties of adjustment patterns adopted by late-maturing boys.

In analyzing the rating scores of the early-maturers, we find no clear-cut subgroup, such as our half dozen of conspicuously active little-boy late-maturers. This may be because the more grown-up boys are not required to over-react to an inadequate physical status and therefore have not tended to develop any one typical pattern in relation to this factor.

CLUBHOUSE RECORDS

Ratings and observations made in mixed group situations provide additional material for comparison of these two extreme groups of boys. These records were made in a variety of social situations, primarily in a clubhouse (Jones, 1940) maintained by the Adolescent Study near the school playground. In this situation it was possible to observe and rate a youngster's 'interest in the opposite sex,' based on approved behavior, participation in dancing and other mixed social situations, and talking about the other sex. As might be expected, marked differences were observed in this trait: in each of six series of records, beginning at age 13.5, the early-maturing obtained average scores above the group mean, and the late-maturing were consistently below the group mean. In this as well as in attention-seeking and other expressive behavior, a tendency could be noted for the late-maturers to show their widest deviation from the early-maturers during the period when they were most different in physical respects; in senior high school the apparent differences diminished, but as will be seen in the subsequent discussion of reputation records, the development of a more mature pattern in the late-maturers, does not necessarily imply a prompt change in their status in the peer culture.

The narrative records obtained in the clubhouse situation provide evidence of the numerous specific ways in which maturity differences are expressed. At a Saturday graduation party three of the early-maturers came to the party conspicuously late, a mark of sophistication not shown by any of the late-maturers. Three others had Saturday jobs, had been working all day and were eager to talk to adults about their work. Among the observer's comments about the early-maturers were such notations as 'he dances **well'**; 'seems to think of himself as an adult'; 'acts a bit condescending'; 'reserved, little energy output'; 'Ran sat in the corner and flirted with Myra'; 'cheek-to-cheek dancing'; 'gay and assured, tried to cut in.'

In contrast, these phrases described some of the boys who **were** of the same age but were late-maturing: 'the first time I've **ever** seen him with a girl'; 'he held his head tensely while dancing'; 'didn't dance at all'; 'acted extremely silly'; 'Ronnie admitted **he** had been to only three dances before'; 'Claude showed a beaming countenance at all times'; 'began to wiggle and giggle.'

REPUTATION WITH CLASSMATES

Another source of evidence concerning adolescent behavior **and** status is from the Reputation Test. For the same age range rep- resented in Figures 3 to 7, data are available from a series of **tests** in which classmates were asked to write down the name of anyone in the class conforming to certain descriptions (Tryon, 1939). **For** example, "Here is someone who finds it hard to sit still in class," or at the other extreme, "Here is someone who can work quietly without moving around in his seat." Scores were obtained by de- termining the percentage of times a person was mentioned on a given trait description, and these measures were then transformed into standard scores in which 50 represented the 'indifference point' (indicating no mentions at either extreme of the trait). Reputa- tion scores are less differentiating than ratings; they tend to iden- tify outstanding individuals, but may fail to distribute the middle range of cases who receive few or no mentions from their class- mates. As a result differences between early- and late-maturing in average reputation scores are less marked than in average ratings by adults. However, a number of traits show differences which occur in the same direction on six testings, and are significant by the binomial test.

The late-maturing are consistently more 'attention-getting,' **more** 'restless,' more 'assured in class,' more 'talkative,' less 'grown-up,' and less likely to have older friends. On five out of six tests **they** are more 'bossy,' and less 'good-looking.'

Less consistency is found for traits which have been established as especially important for adolescent prestiage. On judgments **of** 'popular,' 'leader,' 'friendly,' 'daring,' 'active in games,' and 'humor about self,' the late-maturing stand relatively well until the middle period of junior high school, and then tend to drop to lower status.

Table 2 presents a comparison of average standard scores for

TABLE 2

MEAN STANDARD SCORES FOR REPUTATION TRAITS

	Early-maturing	Late-maturing
Attention-getting	48.1	52.2
Restlessness	45.3	52.9
Talkativeness	47.9	53.0
Bossiness	47.1	52.6
Assurance in class	45.6	50.0
Popularity	54.0	50.7
Leadership	51.3	47.5
Humor (about self)	53.5	48.7
Having older friends	56.2	42.3
Good appearance	54.4	49.3

the two groups in the H 10 and L 11 grades. The differences are not statistically significant but they present a picture which is in general similar to that already found in the observations by adults: the late-maturing appear as assertive (in a small-boy extroverted way) but at this age are somewhat lower in prestige traits.

At the earlier ages the more active and energetic of those in the late-maturing group were not unsuccessful in winning social recognition. But the early-maturing were much more likely to get and maintain the kind of prestige accorded to athletes and officeholders. Two of the sixteen early-maturing boys became student body presidents, one was president of the boys' club (a position next in importance to that of student body president), several were elected to committee chairmanships, and four attained outstanding reputations as athletes. The sixteen late-maturing boys produced only one somewhat 'important' officeholder (a class vice-president), and one athlete.

CONCLUSIONS

A general picture emerges from the various ratings and characterizations of these two contrasting groups of boys. Those who are physically accelerated are usually accepted and treated by adults and other children as more mature. They appear to have relatively little need to strive for status. From their ranks come the outstanding student body leaders in senior high school. In contrast, the physically retarded boys exhibit many forms of relatively immature behavior: this may be in part because others tend to treat them as the little boys they appear to be. Furthermore, a fair proportion of these boys give evidence of needing to counteract their physical disadvantage in some way—usually by greater activity and striving for attention, although in some cases by withdrawal.

In interpreting the relationships reported above, it must be borne in mind that we have used somewhat imperfect tools, and that a more complete psychological study of each individual could be expected to reveal maturity differences in manifest traits and in behavior dynamics which are not clearly shown in the comparisons we have been able to make. The question may also be raised as to the adequacy of our criterion for selecting the early- and late-maturing.

It is doubtful if any single event in the maturing process for boys can be compared in psychological importance to the menarche in girls. Skeletal age, as a measure of maturing, is relatively satisfactory with regard to reliability and stability. It is applicable at all ages from birth to adulthood, and is therefore well adapted to longitudinal studies of the same individuals throughout their period of growth. But skeletal age is revealed only by x-ray. Individual differences in this variable are hidden, and hence have received no cultural value-assessments. Feelings of perplexity or inferiority may arise, in relation to early or late skeletal maturing, only in so far as skeletal age is related to other physical features (such as size, strength, primary or secondary sexual characteristics) or to psychological changes in adolescence. Although skeletal age is highly correlated with other (more external) aspects of physical maturing, we must expect some regression toward the mean in such factors as growth of pubic hair, or other sexual characteristics, among boys selected at the extremes in skeletal maturing.

It is not surprising that those who are retarded in skeletal development should often be directly aware of other aspects of physical retardation, and it is not surprising that this should lead to anxiety. We have seen, however, that there are many complicating factors, which make it difficult to predict the course which any individual adjustment will take. Some of our late-maturing boys enjoyed a degree of personal security, and status in other areas, which helped to balance their temporary physical inadequacies.

A boy like Lonny, whose support at home was withdrawn at the same time that his retardation in growth became important, had a more serious problem than Tom, whose general security was adequate. Some of the early-maturing boys with fine physiques, nevertheless had disturbing accompaniments of rapid growth (such as severe acne), which tended to offset other advantages.

Our findings give clear evidence of the effect of physical maturing upon behavior. Perhaps of greater importance, however, is the repeated demonstration of the multiplicity of factors, psychological and cultural as well as physical, which contribute to the formation of basic personality patterns.

·· 14 ··

SELF-CONCEPTIONS, MOTIVATIONS, AND INTERPERSONAL ATTITUDES OF LATE- AND EARLY-MATURING BOYS

by Paul Henry Mussen and Mary Cover Jones

The rate of physical maturing may affect personal-social development in crucially important ways. The present study by Paul Henry Mussen and Mary Cover Jones of the University of California (Berkeley) assesses the personality structure of early-maturing and late-maturing boys by means of the Thematic Apperception Test (TAT). The results indicate that the late-maturing boys are "more likely to have negative self-conceptions, feelings of inadequacy, strong feelings of being rejected and dominated, prolonged dependency needs, and rebellious attitudes toward parents." [From *Child Development*, 1957, *28*, 243-256. Reprinted by permission of the authors and Society for Research in Child Development.]

While many intensive case studies show that personal and social adjustment during adolescence may be profoundly influenced by rate of physical maturation, there is a scarcity of systematic data on the relationship between the adolescent's physical status and his underlying motivations, self-conceptions and interpersonal attitudes. There is, however, a small body of evidence which demonstrates that greater physical maturity is associated with greater maturity of interest among girls (Stone and Barker, 1939) and that early-maturing boys differ from their late-maturing peers in both overt behavior and reputational status. In one study (Jones and Bayley, 1950)[1] in which a staff of trained observers assessed a large group of adolescents on a number of personality variables, boys who were consistently retarded in physical development were rated lower than those who were consistently accelerated, in physical attractiveness, grooming, and matter-of-factness; and higher in sociability, social initiative (often of a childish, attention-getting sort), and eagerness. Reputation Test (Tryon, 1939) data indicated that classmates regarded the late-maturing boys as more attention-getting, more restless, more bossy, less grown-up and less good-looking than those who were physically accelerated.

On the basis of these findings, it may be inferred that adult and peer attitudes toward the adolescent, as well as their treatment and acceptance of him, are related to his physical status. This means that the sociopsychological environment to which late-maturers are subjected—and consequently the social learning situations they encounter—may be significantly different from that of their early-maturing peers. As a consequence, according to the ratings summarized above, they acquire different patterns of overt social behavior. It seems reasonable to hypothesize that groups differing in physical status will also differ in more covert aspects of behavior and personality.

Indirect evidence relevant to this hypothesis comes from an investigation of the long-term consequences of physical acceleration or retardation during adolescence. Jones (1957)[2] found that group differences in physique had practically disappeared by the time her early- and late-maturing subjects reached their early thirties. Nevertheless, young adults who had been physically retarded adolescents differed from those who had been accelerated in several important psychological characteristics. In general, it appeared that the adult subjects could be described much as they had been during adolescence. Thus, those who had been early-maturers scored higher on the good impression, socialization, dominance, self-control (low score on impulsivity), and responsibility scales of the California Psychological Inventory, while those who had been slow in maturing scored higher on the flexibility scale. On the Edwards Personal

[1] Selection 13 in this volume.
[2] Selection 71 in this volume.

Preference Schedule, early-maturers scored significantly higher on the dominance scale, while the late-maturing were high in suc-corance. Jones concludes that the early-maturing "present a con-sistently favorable personality picture with regard to . . . important social variables." Moreover, there was some evidence that these men had attained more stable vocational adjustments than those who had been late in maturing. These group differences in later adjust-ment suggest that the sociopsychological atmosphere in which the adolescent lives may have profound immediate and enduring effects on his personality structure as well as on his overt behavior.

The present study was designed to investigate the relationship between maturational status and certain important, covert aspects of personality during late adolescence. Personality structure was assessed by means of the Thematic Apperception Test (TAT) which seems to be the most appropriate and sensitive instrument for this purpose. More specifically, on the basis of the literature reviewed above and other general works on the psychology of adolescence (Farnham, 1951; Jones, 1943, 1949a), we formulated and tested a series of propositions relating to differences between the physically retarded and the accelerated in self-conceptions, underlying motiva-tions, and basic interpersonal attitudes. These variables were trans-lated into TAT categories—needs (*n*), press (*p*), and descriptions (defined briefly in Table 1)—and the scores of early- and late-maturers in each of these categories were compared. The propositions and the rationale underlying them, together with the TAT variables involved, follow.

1. In view of their obvious physical retardation, relatively un-favorable reputations and disadvantageous competitive position in many activities, the late-maturing boys are more likely to have feel-ings of inadequacy. Hence, more boys in this group than in the early-maturing group are likely to have negative self-conceptions (TAT category: *negative characteristics*).

2. The adolescent in our culture generally desires some inde-pendence and adult status. This may be the source of a major prob-lem for the late-maturer, however, since he is often regarded and treated as a small boy by adults and peers and is not likely to be granted independence as early as physically accelerated boys. There-fore, it may be anticipated that more late- than early-maturers regard adults, particularly their parents, as dominating, forcing them to do things they don't want to or preventing them from doing things they want to do (high scores in *p Dominance*). Moreover, the parental treatment these boys experience and parental refusal to grant them

independent status may be interpreted as personal rejection. Hence, we predicted that more late-maturing boys would score high in *p Rejection*.

3. These feelings of being dominated and rejected may result in attitudes of rebellion against the family and in feelings of hostility. We therefore expected that more of the late-maturing group would reveal strong aggressive needs (high scores in *n Aggression*) and desires to escape from (*n Autonomy—leaving parents*), or to defy, the family (*n Autonomy—defying parents*).

4. On the basis of the data indicating that slow-maturers showed a great deal of social interest (although often of an immature kind), we hypothesized that more members of this, than of the early-maturing group would reveal strong interests in friendly, intimate interpersonal relationships (high scores in *n Affiliation*).

5. Assuming that, as Jones and Bayley (1950) suggest, the social initiative and attention-getting devices of the late-maturers are of a compensatory nature, we would expect this group to be basically dependent and to have strong needs for support from others. These should be manifest by higher scores in TAT *n Succorance* and *p Nurturance*. The latter may be considered a more indirect measure of dependence, a kind of wish-fulfilling view of the world as helpful and friendly.

6. The early-maturer, being regarded and treated as more adult, is more likely to become self-confident, and to acquire high status goals. For these reasons, we predicted that more of the physically accelerated would give evidence of high achievement goals (high scores in *n Achievement*) and concern with personal recognition (high scores in *n Recognition*).

7. Late-maturing boys in our culture probably face more problems of personal adjustment than do their early-maturing peers. As a result of this, they may become more aware of their problems, and, as the high degree of flexibility of young adults who had been retarded in maturing suggests, more insightful. Hence we predicted that they would be more willing and able than early-maturers to face their own feelings and emotions (low scores in the TAT variable *denial of feeling*).

In summary, we attempted to test seven propositions related to differences in the personalities of early- and late-maturing boys. It was hypothesized that more late-maturers would score high in variables relating to negative self-conceptions, dependence, aggression, affiliation, rebelliousness, and feelings of being dominated and rejected. More early-maturers, on the other hand, were expected to reveal strong achievement and recognition needs, feelings of personal success, and tendencies toward denial of feelings.

PROCEDURE

The 33 seventeen-year-old male subjects of this investigation were members of the Adolescent Growth Study which included a normal sample of boys in an urban public school system (Jones, 1940). The subjects of the present investigation represented two contrasting groups, selected on the basis of their physical maturity status: 16 of them had been among the most consistently accelerated throughout the adolescent period; the other 17 had been among the most consistently retarded.[3] All of them took the Thematic Apperception Test, which provides the basic data of this study, at age 17.

The TAT consisted of 18 pictures: nine from the Murray set which is now standard (cards 1, 5, 6, 7BM, 10, 11, 14, 15, 17); five pictures from the set generally used in 1938 when these data were collected (a man and woman seated on a park bench; a bearded old man writing in an open book; a thin, sullen, young man standing behind a well-dressed older man; a tea table and two chairs; an abstract drawing of two bearded men); and four designed especially for this investigation (the nave of a large church; a madonna and child; a dramatic view of mountains; a boy gazing at a cross which is wreathed in clouds).

The tests were administered individually. Each card was projected on a screen while the subject told a story which was recorded verbatim. Standard instructions were given for the Murray cards, and subjects were asked to describe the feelings elicited by the other four pictures. Most of the stories were brief, consisting of only one or two sentences.

As we noted earlier, each of the personality variables involved in the seven propositions was translated into a TAT scoring category. The scoring scheme involved counting the relevant needs, press, and descriptions of the heroes of the stories, the assumption being that

[3] The present sample includes 27 of Jones and Bayley's (1950) 32 subjects (the 16 most consistently retarded and 16 most consistently accelerated boys in the study). The other five boys had not taken the TAT at age 17. The six subjects who were in the present study but not in Jones and Bayley's study are the three "runners-up" from each end of the physical maturity distribution, i.e., the three who were closest to the 16 most accelerated cases and the three cases next to the 16 most retarded.

the storyteller has identified with the hero: the hero's needs are the same as the boy's; the press that impinge upon the hero are the ones that affect the boy telling the story. A total of 20 needs, press, and descriptive categories, each defined as specifically as possible, was developed in the analysis of the protocols. A score for each subject for each TAT category was derived by counting the number of stories in which it appeared. A list of the categories used, together with brief descriptions of them, is found in Table 1.

To test the reliability of this analysis, one of the authors (PM) and another psychologist[4] independently scored 15 complete protocols (300 stories). The percentage of interrater agreement was 90, computed by the usual formula (number of agreements divided by number of agreements plus number of disagreements).

In order to eliminate bias, the scoring used in the present study was done "blind," that is, independently of knowledge of the subject's maturational status.

RESULTS

Frequency distributions of the scores of all subjects were made for all the TAT variables. Each distribution was then dichotomized at the point which most nearly enabled the placing of half of the 33 subjects above, and half of them below, the dividing point. Subjects having scores above this point were considered high in this particular variable; those with scores below this point were considered low in this variable. Chi square tests were used to test the seven propositions, i.e., to ascertain whether or not high scores in certain TAT variables were in fact more characteristic of one group (late- or early-maturers) than of the other.

Table 1 lists the TAT variables, the number of late- and early-maturers with high scores in the variable, the chi square value obtained and the level of significance. It should be noted that the hypotheses tested were one-sided hypotheses, while the chi square value is in terms of a two-sided hypothesis. When chi square has only one degree of freedom, the square root of chi square has a distribution which is the right hand half of a normal distribution. In order to test a one-sided hypothesis, the chi square test must be converted into the equivalent value in terms of a unit normal

---

[4] We are indebted to Dr. Virginia B. Ware for her participation in this aspect of the study.

TABLE 1

NUMBER OF EARLY- AND LATE-MATURERS SCORING HIGH IN TAT VARIABLES

TAT Variable	Definition of Variable	High Early-Maturers	High Late-Maturers	Chi Square Value	p
Proposition 1					
Negative Characteristics	H is described in negative terms (e.g., imbecile, weakling, fanatic)	5	13	6.80	<.01
Proposition 2					
p Dominance 1	H forced by parents to do something he doesn't want to	4	8	1.73	.09
p Dominance 2	H prevented by parents from doing something he wants to	6	8	.31	>.30
p Dominance 3	Total instances of H's being forced by parents to do something and/or prevented from doing something	7	11	1.46	.11
p Rejection	H rejected, scorned, or disapproved of by parents or authorities	5	11	3.69	.03
Proposition 3					
n Aggression 1	H is aggressive in physical, asocial way	8	3	3.88	.02
n Aggression 2	H is mad at someone, argues	7	4	1.52	.10
n Aggression 3	Total of all H's aggressive actions	11	8	1.26	.10
n Autonomy 1	H leaves home	7	10	.75	.20
n Autonomy 2	H disobeys or defies parents	7	11	1.46	.11
n Autonomy 3	Total of instances in which hero leaves and/or defies his parents	3	9	4.16	.02
Proposition 4					
n Affiliation 1	H establishes good relations with his parents	8	8	.00	>.50
n Affiliation 2	H falls in love, has a romance, marries	9	14	2.66	.05
n Affiliation 3	Total instances in which H establishes and/or maintains friendly relations	8	12	1.46	.11
Proposition 5					
n Succorance	H feels helpless, seeks aid or sympathy	7	12	2.43	.06
p Nurturance 1	H is helped, encouraged, or given something by parents	5	8	.93	.18
p Nurturance 2	H is helped, encouraged, or given something by someone else (not parents)	8	14	3.88	.02
Proposition 6					
n Achievement	H attempts to attain a high goal or to do something creditable	9	10	.02	>.50
n Recognition	H seeks fame and/or high prestige status	9	8	.28	>.30
Proposition 7					
Denial of Feeling	S states that picture elicits no thoughts or feelings	9	5	2.43	.06

deviate (Fisher, 1938). The levels of significance reported in Table 1 were evaluated in these terms.

Table 1 shows that, as had been predicted, more late-maturing than early-maturing boys revealed feelings of inadequacy and negative self-concepts, i.e., scored high in the TAT variable *negative characteristics*. Hence proposition 1 was confirmed. This finding is consistent with the frequently made clinical observation that retardation in physical maturation may be an important source of personal maladjustment and attitudes of inferiority.

Proposition 2 stated that more late-maturers regard their parents as highly dominating and rejecting. The evidence summarized in Table 1 substantially supported this proposition. While the difference was not statistically significant, more late- than early-maturers scored high in *p Dominance by parents* (total). There was a marked difference between the groups in the variable which involves parental domination by forcing the child to do something he does not want to do (*p Dominance by parents, forcing*). However, examination of the data with respect to the variable *p Dominance by parents (prevention)* makes it necessary to reject that part of the proposition which maintains that late-maturers are more likely to view their parents as highly restrictive of their activities.

That aspect of proposition 2 which deals with feelings of rejection was confirmed by our data. Compared with the early-maturing group, a significantly greater proportion of the late-maturers told stories in which the hero was rejected by parents or authority figures. These feelings of rejection may stem from different sources. In some cases, the parents' behavior may make it clear that they are disappointed in their physically retarded son whom they regard as immature. The boy, perceiving this attitude, may interpret it as rejection. In other cases, parental reluctance to allow the late-maturing boy to establish his independence may lead to considerable tension in the family and the boy's feelings of rejection may simply reflect the ongoing parent-child conflict.

It is possible that earlier in their teens, soon after the physical changes of adolescence became apparent, many of the early-maturing boys also experienced conflicts with their parents, arising from difficulties in establishing their independence or in handling emerging heterosexual interests. At that time they too may have felt dominated or rejected. However, by the age of 17, when these data were collected, these boys were ordinarily treated as adults and granted more freedom. Hence, they were more likely to have resolved many of their conflicts with their parents and to feel accepted and independent.

The hypothesis (part of proposition 3) that more late-maturers would be highly aggressive was rejected on the basis of the evidence given in Table 1. In fact, the differences between the two groups on all the TAT aggression variables were in the opposite direction from the prediction. High scores in the variables relating to aggression of the most overt and violent type were significantly more frequent among the early-maturers, and more members of this group also scored high in measures of milder (verbal) aggression and of total aggression. While late-maturers may experience more problems of adjustment and greater frustrations than their early-maturing peers, they apparently do not manifest greater aggressive motivation. It may be that their own feelings of inadequacy or fears of retaliation and punishment for aggression inhibit their expression of hostile feelings, even in fantasy. On the other hand, the early-maturers who feel more secure personally, and recognize their own relatively advantageous physical and social status, may feel freer to express their aggressive needs. Since agression is a culturally stereotyped masculine trait, it seems possible that the physically accelerated, being accepted as mature and identifying readily with adult males, are more likely to acquire this characteristic. In any case, the finding that early-maturers express higher aggressive motivation during late adolescence seems consistent with Jones' finding that, as young adults, they score high on the dominance scale of the Edwards Personal Preference test (Jones, 1957). Perhaps the relatively strong aggressive motivation of the early-maturer, or the mature sex-role identification it may imply, serves as a basis for the development of later qualities of leadership and persuasiveness (Jones, 1959).

As Table 1 indicates, the other aspect of proposition 3 was confirmed: a significantly greater proportion of late- than of early-maturers displayed strong motivations to escape from, or defy, their parents. These may be essentially aggressive reactions, stemming from feelings of parental domination and rejection, or they may reflect the late-maturers' awareness of their strife with their parents whom they perceive as blocking their drives for independence. These strong needs for escape and defiance may also be considered evidence of a generally immature way of handling parent-child conflicts. Perhaps, by the age of 17, the early-maturers have already resolved many of their conflicts with their families and/or have learned to handle these in less rebellious and in more direct and mature ways.

Proposition 4 stated that, compared with their early-maturing peers, more late-maturers would manifest strong needs for establishing close social contacts with others. While there was some confirmatory evidence, the results were not clear-cut. When all affiliative needs were considered together (score for *n Affiliation—total*), the group differences were in the predicted direction, but not statistically significant. Examination of the protocols revealed that almost all instances of affiliation concerned either parents or the opposite sex; there were very few stories involving close, friendly associations between like-sexed peers. The two major types of affiliation were scored separately. As Table 1 shows, late-maturers did not differ from early-maturers with respect to need for affiliation with parents, but a significantly greater proportion of the former group displayed strong motivation for heterosexual affiliation.

In view of the late-maturers' strong feelings of inadequacy and dependent needs (see below), it is surprising that a greater proportion of this group did not exhibit strong needs to establish and maintain close bonds with their parents. This may be due to the late-maturers' more intense conflicts with their parents at this age (17 years), their fears of being rejected and dominated by them, and their generally defiant attitudes which prevent them from admitting, even in fantasy, their strong underlying needs to form close contacts with them.

The significant difference between the groups in *n Affiliation* (*love, romance, marriage*) is subject to several possible interpretations. For one thing, this category may refer to general needs to establish close relations with others (with peers or adults other than parents) and not merely to desire for contact with the opposite sex. The set of stimulus cards may not have been adequate to elicit responses indicative of more general affiliative needs; hence, these were expressed through responses in the heterosexual affiliation category. If this is true, proposition 4 was confirmed, and the late-maturers' high scores in this variable indicate their greater general interest in establishing and maintaining friendly relationships.

It is also possible that the late-maturers' strong affiliative needs are actually directed only toward members of the opposite sex, i.e., that *n Affiliation* (*love, romance, marriage*) measures specifically heterosexual interests. Assuming that this is true, there is another plausible explanation for the discovered difference. As we saw earlier, the late-maturer may be afraid to admit that he desires close associations with his parents. He may also feel that his immaturity and poor reputational status prevent him from establishing successful social relationships with like-sexed peers. Hence, he may "displace" his affiliative needs to members of the opposite sex, who, in his fantasies, may seem more responsive.

A third possible explanation of the difference is based on Jones and Bayley's findings that the late-maturers show less overt interest in girls and are regarded as less good-looking (Jones and Bayley, 1950). From these data, it may be inferred that the physically retarded probably do not have successful and rewarding experiences with girls. Hence their heightened need for affiliation with the opposite sex, expressed in the TAT, may reflect their attempts to satisfy in fantasy needs which they cannot satisfy adequately in reality.

The data were generally supportive of proposition 5 which stated that late-maturers are likely to have strong underlying dependent needs. A higher proportion of this group than of their early-maturing peers scored high in *n Succorance,* the difference between the two groups approaching statistical significance ($p = .06$). Furthermore, high scores in the category involving receiving help and support from others (not including parents) (*p Nurturance—non-parents*)— an indirect measure of dependent needs—were significantly more characteristic of the physically retarded than of the physically accelerated. In view of the late-maturers' attitudes toward their parents, discussed above, it is not surprising to find that perceptions of parents as kindly and supportive (high scores in *p Nurturance-parents*) were not significantly more common in this group than in the early-maturing group.

On the basis of the data involving the TAT variables *n Achievement* and *n Recognition,* we rejected proposition 6 which stated that more early-maturers would be self-confident and have high needs for achievement and personal recognition. In our culture there is strong pressure to develop needs for achievement and personal recognition, and, according to our results, these needs and feelings may become intense regardless of—or perhaps in spite of—the child's maturational status, feelings of personal adequacy, dependency, and adjustment to parents.

Two interesting incidental findings from the TAT data seem to be consistent with the proposition that more early- than late-maturers are likely to be self-confident. Seven boys in this sample of 33 adolescents told stories in which the hero was helpful or kind to someone else (*n Nurturance*). Of this group, six were early-maturers, while only one as a late-maturer ($\chi^2 = 2.09$, $p = .07$). Insofar as *n Nurturance* may be a measure of the storyteller's own feelings that he can accept an active, mature role, more of the accelerated group feel self-assured with respect to having attained mature status.

The other incidental finding which seems to support propositon 6 is based on responses only to card 1 of the Murray series which depicts a young boy contemplating a violin which rests on a table in front of him. Eight of the subjects spoke of the boy (the hero) as a prodigy or a genius. Of these, seven were early-maturers; only one was physically retarded ($\chi^2 = 5.25$, $p = .01$). If the attribution of this prestige status and accomplishment to the hero reflects the subject's own feeling that he has been an achiever, it follows that more of the physically accelerated have positive self-concepts. In view of the small number of cases involved, both of these findings must be considered tentative, but they do offer some evidence in support of proposition 6.

Proposition 7, which stated that relatively few of the physically retarded boys are unwilling or unable to face their own feelings and emotions, received some support from the TAT data summarized in Table 1. A smaller proportion of the members of this group than of the physically accelerated group specifically denied that the pictures evoked any feelings or emotions (e.g., "It doesn't make me think of anything"). While this variable may not adequately measure *denial of feeling* as a major defense mechanism, this result seems to indicate that late-maturers are more sensitive to their own feelings and more ready to admit and face them openly. Since these qualities are basic to the development of psychological insight, it may be inferred that late-maturers, as a group, are more likely to become insightful individuals.

DISCUSSION

The results of the study support the general hypothesis that, in our culture, the boy whose physical development is retarded is exposed to a sociopsychological environment which may have adverse effects on his personality development. Apparently, being in a disadvantageous competitive position in athletic activities, as well as being regarded and treated as immature by others, may lead to negative self-conceptions, heightened feelings of rejection by others, prolonged dependent needs, and rebellious attitudes toward parents. Hence, the physically retarded boy is more likely than his early-maturing peer to be personally and socially maladjusted during

late adolescence. Moreover, some of his attitudes are likely to interfere with the process of identification with his parents, which is
generally based on perceptions of them as warm and accepting
(Payne and Mussen, 1956).[5] This, in turn, may inhibit or delay the
acquisition of mature characteristics and attitudes which are ordinarily established through identification with parents. Fortunately
for the late-maturers' subsequent adjustments, they seem more willing and able to face their feelings and emotions. This may be a result
of their awareness of others' attitudes toward their immaturity or
their feelings of personal inadequacy and dependency.

The physically accelerated boys, on the other hand, are likely to
experience environmental circumstances which are much more conducive to good psychological adjustment. Hence, their psychological
picture, as reflected in their TAT stories, is much more favorable.
By the time they were 17, relatively few early-maturers harbored
strong feelings of inadequacy, perceived themselves as rejected or
dominated by parents or authorities, or felt rebellious toward their
families. As a group, they appeared to have acquired more self-
confidence and had probably made stronger identifications with
mature adults. Hence, they perceived themselves as more mature
individuals, less dependent and in need of help, and more capable of
playing an adult male role in interpersonal relationships.

These findings assume additional, probably greater, importance
when they are considered in the light of Jones' findings on the early
adult (age 33) adjustments of boys who had been retarded or accelerated in physical maturing (Jones, 1957). It should be recalled that
by this age physical differences between the two groups had practically disappeared. Certain important psychological differences were
noted, however, and these were consistent with the differences at
age 17, reported in the present study. For example, the responses of
the early-maturing group to two paper-and-pencil tests revealed that,
as young adults, they were more dominant, more able to make a
good impression and more likely to be turned to for advice and
reassurance; more self-controlled; and more willing and able to carry
social responsibility. In short, they present a general picture of
psychological maturity. Moreover, more of the early-maturers seemed
to have made successful vocational adjustments. In contrast to this,
when the late-maturers became adults, they tended to be highly
dependent individuals who could be described, on the basis of their
test responses, as tending to be rebellious, touchy, impulsive, self-

[5] Selection 33 in this volume.

indulgent, and insightful. Most of these characteristics are indicative of poor adjustment and psychological immaturity. Fewer members of this group had made good vocational adjustments.

The striking correspondence between the two descriptions of the groups, derived from different kinds of tests and collected at widely separated periods of time, lends further support to Jones' conclusion that "the adolescent handicaps and advantages associated with late- or early-maturing appear to carry over into adulthood to some extent" (Jones, 1957). It seems clear that many attributes of adolescent personality (patterns of motivation, self-conceptions, and attitudes toward others) characteristic of late- and early-maturing boys are relatively stable and durable rather than situational and transitory. This may be attributable to the fact that in our culture adolescence is generally a critical and difficult period of adjustment. Within a relatively brief interval of time, the child must work out numerous complex and vitally important personal problems—e.g., adaptation to his changed biological and social status, establishment of independence, vocational adjustment. In dealing with these problems, he may acquire new behaviors and personality attributes which have broad ramifications, not only on his current adjustment, but also on his subsequent development. If the adolescent can cope with his problems without too much inner stress and turmoil, his self-esteem, feelings of adequacy, and consequently his subsequent adjustment, are likely to be enhanced. On the other hand, if his problems induce great tension and anxiety, he is likely to feel frustrated and inadequate, and, if these feelings are maintained, to adjust less satisfactorily as an adult.

Obviously, the adolescent's success or failure, as well as ease or tension, in handling his problems will be determined to a large degree by the sociopsychological forces to which he is subjected during this time, and these, as we have seen, may be significantly related to his rate of maturation. Thus, physical status during adolescence—mediated through the sociopsychological environment—may exert profound and lasting influences on personality. For this reason, many aspects of the adult's behavior and personality seem consistent with his adolescent adjustments, attitudes and motivations.

Insofar as our results permit generalization, they suggest that some important aspects of motivation, such as needs for achievement and personal recognition, are not significantly affected by maturational status. It may be that among subjects whose achievements are strongly encouraged and rewarded from very early childhood, the need to achieve becomes powerful and resistant to change even in the face of feelings of helplessness and inadequacy. The latter may inhibit the achievement-oriented overt behavior of some late-maturers, but the underlying motivation to achieve seems as strong in this group as it is among the physically accelerated.

In conclusion, it should be noted that, although rate of maturing and associated factors may affect personality development, the relationship between physical status and psychological characteristics is by no means simple. A vast number of complex, interacting factors, including rate of maturation, determine each adolescent's unique personality structure. Hence, in any specific instance, the *group* findings of the present study may not be directly applicable, for other physical, psychological, or social factors may attenuate the effects of late- or early-maturing. For example, an adolescent boy who is fundamentally secure and has warm, accepting parents and generally rewarding social relationships may not develop strong feelings of inadequacy even if he matures slowly. Analogously, the early-maturing boy who has deep feelings of insecurity, for whatever reasons, will probably not gain self-confidence simply because he matures early. In summary, in understanding any individual case, generalizations based on the data of the present study must be particularized in the light of the individual's past history and present circumstances.

SUMMARY

The present investigation was designed to test seven propositions concerning the relationship between rate of physical maturation and important aspects of personality structure, specifically, self-conceptions, underlying motivations, and basic interpersonal attitudes. The TAT protocols of 33 seventeen-year-old boys—16 who had been consistently physically accelerated throughout adolescence and 17 who had been consistently retarded—were analyzed according to a scoring schema involving 20 needs, press, and descriptive categories. The scores of early- and late-maturers in each of the categories were compared.

An earlier study (Jones and Bayley, 1950) demonstrated that late-maturing boys are more likely than their early-maturing peers to encounter a generally unfavorable sociopsychological environment. Analysis of the data of the present study indicates that this situation may have adverse effects on the personalities of the physically retarded. These boys are more likely to have negative self-conceptions, feelings of inadequacy, strong feelings of being rejected and dominated, prolonged dependency needs, and rebellious attitudes toward parents. In contrast, the early-maturing boys present a much more favorable psychological picture during adolescence. Relatively few of them felt inadequate, rejected, dominated, or rebellious toward their families. More of them appeared to be self-confident, independent, and capable of playing an adult role in interpersonal relationships. Early- and late-maturing groups did not differ significantly from each other in needs for achievement or personal recognition.

These findings make it clear that rate of physical maturing may affect personality development in crucially important ways. However, it is important to note that in any particular case the effects of early- or late-maturing may be significantly modified by the individual's psychological history and present circumstances.

CHAPTER SIX

Mental Growth and

Development

15

A NEW LOOK AT THE CURVE OF INTELLIGENCE

by Nancy Bayley

Recently, longitudinal studies have yielded results which do not follow the generally accepted form of the age-curve of intelligence. These deviations are summarized and discussed, and a new age-curve of intelligence is proposed by Nancy Bayley of the National Institute of Mental Health. Also described are the changing components of intellectual functioning and the environmental influences on intellectual growth. [From *Proceedings, 1956 Invitational Conference on Testing Problems,* Princeton, Educational Testing Service, 1957, pp. 11-23. Reprinted by permission of the author and Educational Testing Service, publishers of the *Proceedings* and sponsors of the annual Invitational Conference.]

In the past 30 years the accepted form of the age curve of intelligence has become pretty well stabilized, as the result of a number of studies in which many people of different ages were tested. Miles (1942) set the pattern which follows the course of increasing scores to the early 20's followed by a consistent but slower decline throughout the adult years. Subsequent studies have followed this pattern with minor variations. Notable among them are the studies of Jones and Conrad (1933), of Wechsler (1944), and of Foulds and Raven (1948).

In recent years repeated tests on the same persons as they grow older have yielded scores that do not follow this pattern, but indicate that at least some intellectual abilities may continue to increase slowly to 50 years of age or older. These, among other findings on early development, such as the instability of infant scores, are forcing us to reconsider the whole subject of age changes in intellectual abilities. As a part of this reconsideration we need to review the methods by which intelligence can best be tested and evaluated, at different ages and levels of complexity. We must investigate the limitations of current tests and develop more adequate and discriminating ones.

THE COMPLEX NATURE OF INTELLECTUAL ABILITIES

It is, of course, understood that the "curve of intelligence" is derived from performances on tests that measure samples of the whole range and variety of mental abilities. This means that all of the following discussion presupposes that the tests must be validated and re-validated, as occasion requires and permits, against useful outside criteria of intelligent behavior. That is, if we wish to know the nature of intellectual change over time, we must insure that we are using a valid measure of intelligence. It may be necessary, also, for us to re-evaluate our criteria of intelligence.

In formulating any adequate theory of the nature of intelligence it seems to me necessary to take into consideration the fact that the human organism, in all of its aspects, undergoes continual processes of change throughout its life span. These changes are more rapid at some periods of life than at others, and in some processes than in others. They involve increments and decrements in size and waxing and waning of functions. They also involve developmental increases in complexity, and processes of maturation of both structure and function, followed eventually by retrogressions, declines and other manifestations of senescence.

In the field of intelligence these processes are complex and difficult to work with, and hence have been only partially mapped out. For one thing, the concept of intelligence is very general, and covers a variety of intellectual functionings. It is necessary, then, for an adequate appraisal of the course of intelligence from birth to old age, that we consider not only the course of general intelligence, but also age changes in mental organization, and that we try to identify and independently to measure the various intellectual functions. When this has been done, it will become possible to trace the developmental changes in each function or factor, and to see how each fits in to any general, over-all curve.

Of course, many investigators have been working on the problem of analyzing intelligence into its component parts. Early in the history of intelligence testing efforts were made both to define intelligence and to construct tests that would sample and score separately its different aspects. At first the various intellectual faculties to be tested were selected on an *a priori* basis. But with experience, and the help of statistics, we have found ways of isolating and measuring relatively discrete intellectual functions.

Considerable work has been done on what seems to me the logical approach to building new test batteries, i.e., through the use of such methods as factor analysis, cluster analysis, or analysis of variance. But very few investigators have actually applied the results of such analyses to construct factorially independent scales. A notable exception, of course, is the series of Thurstone (1938) tests of Primary Mental Abilities. Following from such a start as this, by successive constructions, analyses, and additions of test items and test areas, we can hope to tease apart and thus to identify, measure, and label the different components of intelligence. Something very like this process has been reported recently by Guilford (1956) who presents an elaborate scheme for what he calls "The Structure of Intellect." [See the following selection in this book, page 198.] He reports systematic attempts to detect and to organize into a conceptual frame the various factors of intellect. With this schema as a basis, new types of function are hypothesized or identified, and appropriate tests are devised to measure them. It seems to me that Guilford reports the kind of research we badly need if we are to differentiate and understand the various intellectual processes that make up "intelligence." But in his elaborate analysis he does not take into consideration the further complications of age and maturational differences.

However, a number of investigators are interested in this developmental aspect of intelligence, and with the instruments available several studies have been made on age changes in intellectual ability and in mental organization (Garrett, 1946). Much of this work has been done on tests of cross-sectional samples: that is, on tests administered once to persons of different ages. But there are very pertinent data now available from a number of longitudinal studies in which the same persons have been tested repeatedly as they grew older. None of these longitudinal studies covers the entire age span, but some start as young as one month of age and others continue through 50 years and even older. By splicing together some of these data it should be possible to construct longitudinal age curves of several different intellectual factors.

A SUGGESTED AGE-CURVE OF INTELLIGENCE

Any curve of intelligence will be dependent upon the behavioral components included in the test scores on which it is constructed. The general curve which I presented last year in an article "On the Growth of Intelligence (Bayley, 1955), is based on total scores of fairly comprehensive tests. To the extent that these tests are broadly inclusive and representative of "general intelligence," this curve might be thought of as representing the usual course of age changes in general intellectual capacity.

Everyone agrees that intelligence grows throughout infancy and childhood, though with the accumulation of records we have had to move along (from a start at 13 years), the age at which growth was assumed to stop. As for the *form* of the childhood curve, minor differences from one investigator to another are probably related to differences in tests and sampling, but there is the further problem of constructing comparable units of growth. In the tentative curve I constructed, for the period one month to 25 years, I used the test scores of the Berkeley Growth Study. It was necessary to splice together the scores from a number of different tests by converting the scores into standard deviation units based on the mean and S.D. of the 16-year scale scores on the Wechsler-Bellevue Test.

This part of the curve shows rapid acceleration in the first year and again a moderate acceleration between 8 and 10 years. After about 10 years the rate slows down so that by 25 the increment is very gradual. Freeman and Flory's (1937) curve, although based on units derived in a different way, is similar to the Berkeley Growth Study curve for the ages it covers, 8 to 17 years. According to the V.A.C.O. curve, there is accelerated growth between about 10 and 12 years. This is later than the Berkeley Growth Study period of rapid growth. However, different tests were used, and when the subtests of the V.A.C.O. are considered, each has a different course of growth with different ages of greatest increment.[1]

[1] It is interesting to note that the childhood period of acceleration in both of these studies comes *before* the adolescent spurt of physical growth in boys. For the Berkeley study it occurs in both sexes at the same age and is over before physical acceleration starts.

By fitting on to the Berkeley Growth Study curve, the curves of either Owens' Iowa data, or of the scores made on the Concept Mastery test by the spouses of Terman's Gifted subjects, it was possible to construct a 50-year curve from just two longitudinal samples. Rather than choose between them, I put both adult studies onto the curve. Each one contributes something that the other lacks. The Alpha test probably samples a wider variety of abilities, but the Concept Mastery test offers more possibility of expansion into higher scores. Also, the Terman study subjects covered a sufficiently wide range of ages tested that it was possible to plot approximate scores by age at 5-year intervals from 20 to 50 years. Thus from the Terman material it appears that a relatively greater proportion of this adult growth occurs between 20 and 25 years, with the subsequent increments relatively smaller, and constant.

Of course, this curve can be viewed only as a tentative one based on limited tests and limited samples. In constructing more adequate curves we need to take into account many things. For example, different mental functions appear to have different rates of growth with different ages at maximal contribution to the total. In order to spell this out we need to have both more clearly defined and more adequately measured subtests or "factors."

CHANGING COMPONENTS OF THE CURVE

It seems to me probable that in the early part of the curve the independent factors tend to occur successively, with simultaneously developing and operating factors appearing only after some complexity of intellectual functioning has been achieved. For example, in the Berkeley Growth Study both the early age trends in standard deviations, and the patterns of correlations for consistency of scores, indicate age changes in the nature of abilities. These changes are also shown by Hofstaetter's (1954) factor analysis of my table of correlations for consistency of scores from birth through 18 years (Bayley, 1949). He obtained 3 distinct factors that operate successively. The first, which he named Sensory-Motor Alertness, is predominant for the first two years, with a very high loading at months 7 through 12. The second factor, "Persistence" is high from 2 to 4 years, while the third, "Manipulating Symbols" accounts for most of the variance after 4 years. The three factors are about equal in weight at two years.

This use of the total scores gives evidence for some age-specific factors and even indicates the beginnings of concurrent factors that operate over longer segments of growth. The total scores are made up from a variety of behaviors which could represent several different factors. Support for only general factors in infancy is lent by the study of Richards and Nelson (1939) who factored the Gesell Scale scores for 80 infants at 6, 12 and 18 months. In this scale they included gross motor coordinations that are left out of the California First-year Mental Scale. The fact that they obtained just two factors, "Alertness" and "Motor Ability" would make it appear that I had already separated the factorially independent functions in the first year by putting the gross motor coordinations into a Scale of Motor Ability. Therefore, the "Sensory Motor Alertness" factor of Hofstaetter and the "Alertness" factor of Richards and Nelson appear to be practically identical. This factor may very well represent the lion's share of "intelligence" for the first 9 months. After this Hofstaetter's factors II and III appear to be operating concurrently for a while.

I shall not attempt to cover the work on factor analysis of intelligence tests. There are others here far more able to do this. But it may be of interest to consider a few isolated bits from longitudinal studies that it seems to me contribute to our understanding of this general problem.

Freeman and Flory's (1937) longitudinal data show different slopes of increment for their four subtests and evidence for different ages at highest ability. Relative to the means and S.D.'s of the 17-year scores the Analogies score has shown most change during the 9-year interval, 8 to 17 years, with Opposites scores gaining second. The slopes of these curves indicate that they have approached close to their mature status. The slower-gaining Vocabulary and Completion tests appear to be still gaining at 17 years (Bayley, 1951).

Some data based on retest scores on the Wechsler-Bellevue for my small Berkeley Growth Study sample may be relevant in this same connection. This test was given at four ages (16, 18, 21 and 25 years), the number for the first three testings ranging from 35 to 45. So far, 24 have been given the test at 25 years. For the full scale and for the Verbal and Performance halves, there is no indication that these young adults have reached their intellectual ceiling. But for this group, the subtests of the Wechsler-Bellevue are unequal both in difficulty and in the slopes of their age curves (Bayley, 1957). Each appears to be following a different course of change with age. These differences show up most clearly when constant subsamples are selected, so that the same cases are included at all ages used in the growth curves.

Other subsamples, selected to be homogeneous in certain respects, show interesting differences in scores and growth rates. For example, in a division by sexes boys and girls do about equally well on the Full Scale but the boys are better on the Verbal, and the girls on the Performance Scale.

The group was divided into higher and lower intelligence halves on the basis of their average scores at 16, 17 and 18 years. The highly intelligent group was found to do equally well on the Verbal and Performance parts of the test. The lower-scoring less "intelligent" half, however, does much less well on the Verbal than on the Performance Scale. Both highs and lows exhibit increasing scores but with some indication that the high group is approaching a ceiling. This ceiling is at least in part due to a lack of top in the Wechsler-Bellevue scale.

If we consider the 11 subtests separately, for constant sub-samples, the greater differences between the higher and the lower intelligence groups occur in the 6 verbal tests. Among the 5 Performance tests the two groups differ most in Picture Arrangement and Block Design (tests that require organization of spatial relations) and least in Picture Completion and Digit Symbol substitution (tests that require recognition of patterns). Those subtests in which the highs do not show continued increase in scores are tests in which they have already reached the upper limits of the scale. The lows show continued growth in most subtests but appear to have reached their top capacities in the Vocabulary and Block Design subtests, and possibly Picture Arrangement. We may have here some indications of differential growth according to level of ability.

These comparisons are on a very small sample, and on a test that is not completely adequate for such purposes. The data therefore are only suggestive, but they do seem to indicate some probable differences in ability-tied growth rates for different intellectual functions. However, credence may be lent to these differences by the fact that they are in general congruent with those found by H. E. Jones for the Adolescent Growth Study for a similar age range on the subtests of the Terman Group test (Jones, 1955a).

To carry the picture beyond 25 years, we may turn to the consideration of age changes in both cross-sectional and longitudinal studies.

The cross-sectional studies tend to agree in the finding that some abilities, such as information and word knowledge, are maintained with little or no loss to an advanced age, while other abilities such as arithmetic, analogies, and organization of spatial relations, decline with age (after 20 or 30) at varying rates (Jones, 1955). Those functions that drop off most rapidly in the older subjects appear to differ with the tests used, and to some extent with the populations studied. The more recent the studies and the more complete the population sample included, the less do scores drop with advancing age. Other differences in age trends are often found to be related to general intellectual level of the subjects and to the amount of their education.

In the longitudinal studies, however, there is an invariable finding that the scores in at least some subtests are higher on the second testing. The earlier of these reports, such as the studies of Freeman and Flory (1937), and of R. L. Thorndike (1948), were usually on tests of young adults, mostly college students in their late teens and early twenties. But more recently repeat test scores have been secured on adults at later ages. These also show increased scores earned at the later testing after the subjects have grown older, with 12 to 30 years elapsed time between tests. I should like here to summarize some of these studies.

Owens (1953) repeated the Army Alpha test on fifty-year old men who had taken this same test thirty-one years before as college freshmen, and found an increase in tested ability at the later age, with greatest increase in the Information test, and least in Arithmetic. Bayley and Oden (1955) found increases on repeat tests after a 12-year interval, for gifted adults on Terman's (1956) difficult Concept Mastery test. When these scores are expressed in Standard Deviation units for each subtest at its initial administration, there was twice as much increase in the Synonym-Antonym (or word-knowledge) half as in the Analogies (or abstract relationships) half of the test. The increases occur in all age groups tested (20 to 50 years), though they are least in the Analogies test for the older ages. Nisbet (1956) reports repeat tests after a lapse of about 23 years, on 141 teachers in Aberdeen, Scotland, who were first tested as post-graduate students when about 22 years old. On a timed verbal group test (Simplex Group Intelligence Scale) improvement occurred on all 14 subtests; the increase was significant in all but one. Greatest increases, expressed in S.D. of the first testing, were in Substitution, .71 σ, Vocabulary, .67 σ, and Number Series, .65 σ; they were least in Digit Memory, .16 σ, Verbal Rearrangement, .21 σ, and Analogies, .26 σ. H. E. Jones (1955a) has reported increased Terman Group Test scores between the 16½ year tests and retests at 33 years for 83 cases of the Berkeley Adolescent Growth Study. He found smaller gains in the lowest-scoring quartile of his population and in those subtests involving problem-solving. The greatest gains were in Vocabulary. Thus, the studies cited, both the cross-sectional and the longitudinal, show similar age trends in changing organization. At the older ages the subjects do relatively better in tests of information and word knowledge and less well in tests of reasoning and seeing relationships.

EVALUATING INTELLECTUAL CHANGES IN ADULTS

The difference between the two methods of study is found in comparisons of the actual scores. In the longitudinal studies the subjects nearly always do better at the later testing, when they are older, on most of the subtests, as well as on total scores. Although the longitudinal studies were made on different populations and using different tests, they agree in finding that different intellectual functions show varying amounts of increase, ranging from no change to as much as a standard deviation between test and retest. In no instance do these studies show the precipitous decline in scores after the age 25 to 30 that occurs in most cross-sectional studies of age differences.

Let us consider some of the things that could account for this difference.

(a) When subjects of different ages are tested at one time, there is the problem of selecting comparable samples. Apparent changes in relative scores could be artefacts of differential sample selection for subjects of different ages. In the older age groups there may be selective elimination of certain segments of the population, through deaths or through lack of cooperation. It is true that when a complete population is tested, e.g., a whole Vermont community (Jones and Conrad, 1933), or an entire prison population (Corsini and Fassett, 1953), the curve of intelligence scores show less decline with age. We might conclude that when willingness to be tested is a selective factor the brighter older persons are less cooperative about taking tests or else more adept at finding excuses. In any event, when the same persons are retested at successive ages, whatever the selective factors in sampling, we do have a constant sample.

(b) But with a constant sample there is the ever-present problem in psychological testing, the inescapable fact that a test is never the same for a person the second time he takes it. When comparing retests it is necessary to take into account possible practice effects and generally increased familiarity with the testing procedures. However, in many studies practice effects are of little import. When the elapsed time between tests has been as much as 12 to 30 years (as in the Owens, the Nisbet, and the Bayley and Oden studies), it seems obvious that there can be very little, if any, direct memory of problems and their solutions from the first to the second test. Also, when alternate test forms are used there may be very little increase after short intervals. I have, for example, some data on practice effects of the Concept Mastery test. There was practically no carry-over from one form to the other after an interval of only 1 or 2 weeks for the sample of 148 on which the 2 forms of the scale were equated. The difference was less than two points or about 1/15 of the S.D. of scores.

(c) Another important difference between the longitudinal and cross-sectional data is the *temporal* one. Perhaps this has not been given enough weight. In cross-sectional studies all tests are given at the same time, while in longitudinal studies not only do the same subjects grow older before their retests, but with the lapse of time they have all experienced the same general changes in the environment, and have been responding to similar changes in such things as world events and means of communication.

It is relevant here to point out that the scores earned on the Concept Mastery test by Terman's Gifted Study subjects who were tested only once increased just as much in the 12-year interval, 1939-40 to 1950-52, as did the scores of the twice-tested subjects. One hundred-twenty-nine of the men who missed the first administration of the test but took it in 1950-52 earned scores averaging half an S.D. above the mean for the men tested in 1939. A similar increase over the 1939 means was found for 98 Gifted Study women who were first tested in 1950-52. For each testing date the means of the once-tested and twice-tested groups are very similar. Thus, there appears to have been no selective factor differentiating the groups: whether or not a subject was tested in 1939 and/or 1951 was pretty much a matter of his geographical availability. Furthermore, for these bright people the average scores earned at the later date and older age were evidently not dependent on the experience of having taken the Concept Mastery test at the earlier date. In general, then, it seems to me that we should consider very seriously the possibility that at least some kinds of intelligence may very well continue to improve slowly from 20 to 50 years or older.

ENVIRONMENTAL DETERMINERS IN INTELLECTUAL GROWTH

So far I have touched only briefly on the whole array of potential influences on intellectual growth that we may classify as environmental. This is a very general term, including both emotional climate and opportunities for intellectual stimulation and for practice in intellectual activities such as reasoning and problem solving. No organism develops in complete absence of stimulation, and up to a certain stage in infancy the minimal requirements for life furnish adequate stimuli to afford normal development. Ordinarily the human infant's environment is much richer than these minimal conditions. The infant responds to those parts of his environment that are relevant for his degree of maturity (neural, sensory-motor, perceptual and organizational). Also, as he grows the actively healthy child will interact with his surroundings, seeking stimulation to the extent of his capacities to utilize and cope with it. Those who are inherently gifted may well be the ones who continue to seek out and to find challenging intellectual problems and experiences in any normal life situation. However, there are probably here also inherent individual differences in this kind of active intellectual curiosity. Granting this, we may further explore the possibility that extreme environmental deprivation, or depressing emotional climate could restrict the growth of even the most intellectually alert, while optimal intellectual stimulation and emotional climate could enhance the development even of those with little inherent drive or capacity.

If we assume the relevance of these variables to the growth of intelligence, then we need to study the conditions of their effects on the course of mental development. We should inquire what kinds of emotional climate are optimal at what ages, what effects the attitudes of responsible adults such as parents and teachers have on intelligence, and whether certain attitudes are more important at some ages than at others. We should inquire further: What kinds of intellectual stimulation, or "environmental enrichment" are optimal for infants, pre-schoolers, children, adults? Is deprivation at certain stages crucial in determining whether development will be normal? That is, are there environmental "critical stages" for mental growth analogous to those embryological stages at which trauma can result in such deformities as cleft palate, ovarian agenesis, or possibly Mongolism and other conditions associated with feeblemindedness?

We have now some relevant information, offering tentative answers to some of these questions, but so far most of the information is based on casual observations or on studies that have not been sufficiently well designed and controlled to give us definitive answers.

A number of reports (Bowlby, 1951; Spitz, 1945) suggest the retarding effect on infants of life in institutions which offer little in either normal parental care or mental stimulation. But we do not yet know either the amount or generality of this effect, or on the other hand, what are the crucial aspects in regard to type of care, the nature of deprivation, or the ages at which the child experiences them. The fact that institutions do not invariably depress intelligence is brought out by Rheingold (1956) who studied the effects of a significant care-taking mother-figure on 6-month old institutional babies. The six babies she cared for 40 hours a week for 8 weeks, compared with 6 control babies, showed no significant differences in IQ at the end of care.

There are studies that show significantly low IQ's for children in backward rural communities (Sherman and Henry, 1933; Wheeler, 1942). The studies of racial differences in intelligence are plagued with the problems of environmental impoverishment in certain racial groups.

The many comparisons that show a correlation between socio-economic factors and IQ have made clear the fact of the relationship, but give little information about the specific ways in which such factors might effect mental growth.

Studies of the relation between intelligence scores and such personality factors as emotional tone, effort, and persistence, usually show a moderate positive correlation in young children. But so far we have little information on the effect of long-term emotional influences on the growth curve of intelligence. However, we do have reports of the differential effects of praise and blame on learning, and the depressive effect of anxiety on achievement in school (Palermo, Castenado, and McCandless, 1956). Ability to learn is often classed as one form of intelligence.

In the Berkeley Growth Study (Bayley, 1940) as well as in other studies, such things as the children's emotional tone and generally optimal conditions for testing yield r's with IQ that are in the neighborhood of about .30 (Honzik, Macfarlane, and Allen, 1948; Macfarlane, Allen, Honzik, 1954; Wittenborn, et al., 1956). However, when we considered individual children, and for each child correlated his "Optimal" and "Attitude" scores with his intelligence ratings for series of 10 to 15 ages we found a wide spread of r's from +.77 to −.46, with a mean of +.20. Evidently the children differed in the effect of current emotional state on performance, and for some children other factors (presumably maturational and hereditary) were of predominant importance for mental growth (Bayley, 1940).

As for the long-term effects of emotional climate, Schaefer, Bell and I (1956) are now in the process of getting some tentative information from the Berkeley Growth Study. Personality characteristics of the mothers, relevant to their behavior toward these children, have been rated. The ratings were made on a scale designed for use with descriptive protocols of the mothers, made at the times they came with their children for the tests when the children were between 1 month and 3 years of age. Some of these behavior traits were found to be relatively stable over a 10-year period that could be compared. The most stable of the maternal traits are: cooperativeness, use of fear to control the child, irritability, tendencies to ignore the child, to reject the homemaking role, to evaluate the child positively, to express affection toward the child, to treat him as an equal, and to be strict with him. The 32 traits could be clustered into two main variables, which we have labeled by the "good" end of the scale, (a) Positive Attitudes, and (b) Autonomy of the Child. The few correlations we have computed with intelligence indicate that there are relations with these maternal variables, but that the nature of the relationship changes with the age of the child. If these preliminary findings should hold up, it would appear that during the first year of life higher scores tend to be earned by babies whose mothers are intrusive, dominating and punitive, while by the time they reach school age the reverse is true and the high-scorers' mothers are characterized as cooperative, evaluating their children positively, expressing affection toward them, and allowing them autonomy as individuals.

This analysis is still so incomplete that I hesitate to mention it. But there are other studies that corroborate it in a general way, though they are not directly comparable in methods or in the variables used. For example, Macfarlane, Allen and Honzik (1954) report correlations between children's mental test scores and the number of their problems (as reported by the mothers). At 21 months and 3 years the r's with IQ tend to be positive, but from 4 through 14, the r's are negative (around $-.30$), indicating a tendency after 3 years for high IQ to go with fewer problems. There are no direct correlations reported here between the IQ's and parental attitudes. However, in another paper (Honzik, Macfarlane, and Allen, 1948) the same authors report individual cases whose IQ's appear to be related to parental behaviors. Wittenborn (1956), working on data from the Yale Clinic of Child Development, reports some r's between 5-year Binet IQ and certain characteristics of adoptive parents. These r's also vary around .30, with the adoptive parents' Ambition, Education-Occupation, and Age-Duration of marriage. These variables probably reflect some enduring attitudes and expectations of the parents.

If we were to develop an environmental criterion of conditions fostering high intelligence, it might be composed of scores on some of the following variables: 1. Characteristics of the parents (or responsible adults) in respect to: (a) Understanding of the child's capacities and readiness for tasks of given difficulties, (b) willingness to grant the child autonomy relative to his capacities, (c) ability to offer stimulating experiences without overly strong pressures to high achievement, (d) warm affectionate acceptance of child as an individual in his own right. 2. Environmental opportunities geared to the child's stage of development. These last will include good teaching and varieties of experience, perhaps through the media of such things as radio and television, as well as travel and discussions of ideas.

Wechsler (1956) has recently discussed the possible causes of the differences between the 1939 and 1955 age-curves of intelligence as measured by the two forms of his scale. The 1955 curve is at most ages higher than the earlier one, and scores do not start to drop until after 30 years. In addition to the usual reasons (sampling, educational level and testwiseness) for this generally increased performance, he offers a fourth of a very different kind. To quote from his abstract: "Finally, one may posit that the improved performance of the American adult on tests of intelligence could be due in part to the improving general health and virility of the population during the last two decades. Advances in medical and social hygiene have seemingly not only served to increase life expectancy but extended the period of intellectual as well as physical vigor into later maturity."

We find some support for this suggestion of Wechsler's from studies of children's nutritional status. Many studies report low positive r's with IQ of such variables as size, health and physical maturity (Ebert and Simmons, 1943; Knobloch and Pasamanick, 1953; Terman and Oden, 1947). It is, therefore, quite possible that generally improved health and living conditions in recent years are reflected, not only in generally greater physical size, but also in greater and more prolonged mental vigor.

I should like to suggest to Wechsler that he go a step further, and if his hypothesis is true, then possibly his curve falls off after 30 because, in his cross-section sample, his older subjects have not had the advantage of growing up in this generally more healthful world.

Another step beyond this is to suggest that not only is the physical environment improved in the last two decades but also the psychological environment. Perhaps in addition to more years of schooling for more people we have actually progressed in our educational effectiveness, grade for grade. Also, it seems rather obvious that the general environment in which children are now growing up is richer: there is more knowledge available and better communication of it; travel is easier, and more children can, with less trouble, have varied experiences. Possibly also our knowledge of child training and mental hygiene are influencing parental practices in a healthful way.

If these things are true in any significant degree, and if progress in mental and physical health continues, it may become necessary repeatedly to construct new norms for intelligence every decade or so. Furthermore, in considering age changes in older people, we may need to evaluate their scores according to norms standardized at appropriate calendar years, rather than for age only.

·································· **16** ··································

THREE FACES OF INTELLECT[1]

by J. P. Guilford

The following selection describes an attempt to identify and organize into a unified system the factors involved in intellectual performances. The structure of intellect is represented by a cubical model whose dimensions are: the kinds of materials or content dealt with by the individual, the kinds of processes or operations performed on the material, and the kinds of products achieved. The author, J. P. Guilford of the University of Southern California gives a number of examples of tests, each representing a factor. [From *American Psychologist*, 1959, *14*, 469-479. Reprinted by permission of the author and the American Psychological Association.]

My subject is in the area of human intelligence, in connection with which the names of Terman and Stanford have become known the world over. The Stanford Revision of the Binet intelligence scale has been the standard against which all other instruments for the measurement of intelligence have been compared. The term IQ or intelligence quotient has become a household word in this country. This is illustrated by two brief stories.

[1] The Walter V. Bingham Memorial Lecture given at Stanford University on April 13, 1959.

A few years ago, one of my neighbors came home from a PTA meeting remarking: "That Mrs. So-And-So, thinks she knows so much. She kept talking about the 'intelligence *quota*' of the children; intelligence *quota*'; imagine. Why, everybody knows that IQ stands for intelligence *quiz*.'"

The other story comes from a little comic strip in a Los Angeles morning newspaper, called "Junior Grade." In the first picture a little boy meets a little girl, both apparently about the first-grade level. The little girl remarks, "I have a high IQ." The little boy, puzzled, said, "You have a what?" The little girl repeated, "I have a high IQ," then went on her way. The little boy, looking thoughtful, said, "And she looks like such a nice little girl, too."

It is my purpose to speak about the analysis of this thing called human intelligence into its components. I do not believe that either Binet or Terman, if they were still with us, would object to the idea of a searching and detailed study of intelligence, aimed toward a better understanding of its nature. Preceding the development of his intelligence scale, Binet had done much research on different kinds of thinking activities and apparently recognized that intelligence has a number of aspects. It is to the lasting credit of both Binet and Terman that they introduced such a great variety of tasks into their intelligence scales.

Two related events of very recent history make it imperative that we learn all we can regarding the nature of intelligence. I am referring to the advent of the artificial satellites and planets and to the crisis in education that has arisen in part as a consequence. The preservation of our way of life and our future security depend upon our most important national resources: our intellectual abilities and, more particularly, our creative abilities. It is time, then, that we learn all we can about those resources.

Our knowledge of the components of human intelligence has come about mostly within the last 25 years. The major sources of this information in this country have been L. L. Thurstone and his associates, the wartime research of psychologists in the United States Air Forces, and more recently the Aptitudes Project[2] at the University of Southern California, now in its tenth year of research on cognitive and thinking abilities. The results from the Aptitudes Project that have gained perhaps the most attention have pertained to creative-thinking abilities. These are mostly novel findings. But to me, the most significant outcome has been the development of a unified theory of human intellect, which organizes the known, unique or primary intellectual abilities into a single system called the "structure of

[2] Under Contract N6onr-23810 with the Office of Naval Research (Personnel and Training Branch).

intellect." It is to this system that I shall devote the major part of my remarks, with very brief mentions of some of the implications for the psychology of thinking and problem solving, for vocational testing, and for education.

The discovery of the components of intelligence has been by means of the experimental application of the method of factor analysis. It is not necessary for you to know anything about the theory or method of factor analysis in order to follow the discussion of the components. I should like to say, however, that factor analysis has no connection with or resemblance to psychoanalysis. A positive statement would be more helpful, so I will say that each intellectual component or factor is a unique ability that is needed to do well in a certain class of tasks or tests. As a general principle we find that certain individuals do well in the tests of a certain class, but they may do poorly in the tests of another class. We conclude that a factor has certain properties from the features that the tests of a class have in common. I shall give you very soon a number of examples of tests, each representing a factor.

THE STRUCTURE OF INTELLECT

Although each factor is sufficiently distinct to be detected by factor analysis, in very recent years it has become apparent that the factors themselves can be classified because they resemble one another in certain ways. One basis of classification is according to the basic kind of process or operation performed. This kind of classification gives us five major groups of intellectual abilities: factors of cognition, memory, convergent thinking, divergent thinking, and evaluation.

Cognition means discovery or rediscovery or recognition. Memory means retention of what is cognized. Two kinds of productive-thinking operations generate new information from known information and remembered information. In divergent-thinking operations we think in different directions, sometimes searching, sometimes seeking variety. In convergent thinking the information leads to one right answer or to a recognized best or conventional answer. In evaluation we reach decisions as to goodness, correctness, suitability, or adequacy of what we know, what we remember, and what we produce in productive thinking.

A second way of classifying the intellectual factors is according to the kind of material or content involved. The factors known thus far involve three kinds of material or content: the content may be

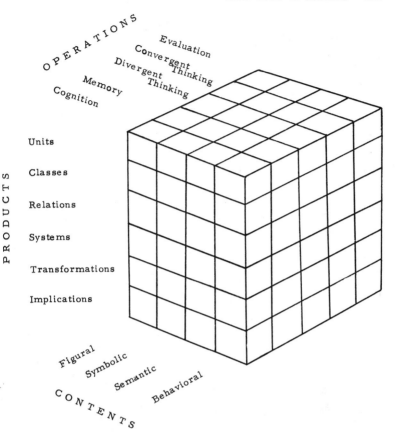

FIG. 1. Theoretical model for the complete "Structure of Intellect."

figural, symbolic, or semantic. Figural content is concrete material
such as is perceived through the senses. It does not represent anything except itself. Visual material has properties such as size, form,
color, location, or texture. Things we hear or feel provide other
examples of figural material. Symbolic content is composed of letters,
digits, and other conventional signs, usually organized in general
systems, such as the alphabet or the number system. Semantic content is in the form of verbal meanings or ideas, for which no
examples are necessary.

When a certain operation is applied to a certain kind of content,
as many as six general kinds of products may be involved. There is
enough evidence available to suggest that, regardless of the combi
nations of operations and content, the same six kinds of products
may be found associated. The six kinds of products are: units, classes,

relations, systems, transformation, and implications. So far as we have determined from factor analysis, these are the only fundamental kinds of products that we can know. As such, they may serve as basic classes into which one might fit all kinds of information psychologically.

The three kinds of classifications of the factors of intellect can be represented by means of a single solid model, shown in Figure 1. In this model, which we call the "structure of intellect," each dimension represents one of the modes of variation of the factors.[3] Along one dimension are found the various kinds of operations, along a second one are the various kinds of products, and along the third are various kinds of content. Along the dimension of content a fourth category has been added, its kind of content being designated as "behavioral." This category has been added on a purely theoretical basis to represent the general area sometimes called "social intelligence." More will be said about this section of the model later.

In order to provide a better basis for understanding the model and a better basis for accepting it as a picture of human intellect, I shall do some exploring of it with you systematically, giving some examples of tests. Each cell in the model calls for a certain kind of ability that can be described in terms of operation, content, and product, for each cell is at the intersection of a unique combination of kinds of operation, content, and product. A test for that ability would have the same three properties. In our exploration of the model, we shall take one vertical layer at a time, beginning with the front face. The first layer provides us with a matrix of 18 cells (if we ignore the behavioral column for which there are as yet no known factors) each of which should contain a cognitive ability.

The Cognitive Abilities

We know at present the unique abilities that fit logically into 15 of the 18 cells for cognitive abilities. Each row presents a triad of similar abilities, having a single kind of product in common. The factors of the first row are concerned with the knowing of units. A good test of the ability to cognize figural units is the Street Gestalt Completion Test. In this test, the recognition of familiar pictured objects in silhouette form is made difficult for testing purposes by blocking out parts of those objects. There is another factor that is known to involve the perception of auditory figures—in the form of

[3] For an earlier presentation of the concept, see Guilford (1956).

melodies, rhythms, and speech sounds—and still another factor involving kinesthetic forms. The presence of three factors in one cell (they are conceivably distinct abilities, although this has not been tested) suggests that more generally, in the figural column, at least, we should expect to find more than one ability. A fourth dimension pertaining to variations in sense modality may thus apply in connection with figural content. The model could be extended in this manner if the facts call for such an extension.

The ability to cognize symbolic units is measured by tests like the following:

Put vowels in the following blanks to make real words:

P _____ W _____ R
M _____ RV _____ L
C _____ RT _____ N

Rearrange the letters to make real words:

R A C I H
T V O E S
K L C C O

The first of these two tests is called Disemvoweled Words, and the second Scrambled Words.

The ability to cognize semantic units is the well-known factor of verbal comprehension, which is best measured by means of a vocabulary test, with items such as:

GRAVITY means _____
CIRCUS   means _____
VIRTUE means _____

From the comparison of these two factors it is obvious that recognizing familiar words as letter structures and knowing what words mean depend upon quite different abilities.

For testing the abilities to know classes of units, we may present the following kinds of items, one with symbolic content and one with semantic content:

Which letter group does not belong?
XECM   PVAA   QXIN   VTRO

Which object does not belong?
clam   tree   oven   rose

A figural test is constructed in a completely parallel form, presenting in each item four figures, three of which have a property in common and the fourth lacking that property.

The three abilities to see relationships are also readily measured by a common kind of test, differing only in terms of content. The well-known analogies test is applicable, two items in symbolic and semantic form being:

JIRE : KIRE : : FORA : KORE KORA LIRE GORA GIRE
poetry : prose : : dance : music walk sing talk jump

Such tests usually involve more than the ability to cognize relations, but we are not concerned with this problem at this point.

The three factors for cognizing systems do not at present appear in tests so closely resembling one another as in the case of the examples just given. There is nevertheless an underlying common core of logical similarity. Ordinary space tests, such as Thurstone's Flags, Figures, and Cards or Part V (Spatial Orientation) of the Guilford-Zimmerman Aptitude Survey (GZAS), serve in the figural column. The system involved is an order or arrangement of objects in space. A system that uses symbolic elements is illustrated by the Letter Triangle Test, a sample item of which is:

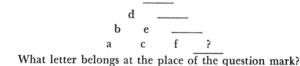

What letter belongs at the place of the question mark?

The ability to understand a semantic system has been known for some time as the factor called general reasoning. One of its most faithful indicators is a test composed of arithmetic-reasoning items. That the phase of understanding only is important for measuring this ability is shown by the fact that such a test works even if the examinee is not asked to give a complete solution; he need only show that he structures the problem properly. For example, an item from the test Necessary Arithmetical Operations simply asks what operations are needed to solve the problem:

A city lot 48 feet wide and 149 feet deep costs $79,432. What is the cost per square foot?

A. add and multiply
B. multiply and divide
C. subtract and divide
D. add and subtract
E. divide and add

Placing the factor of general reasoning in this cell of the structure of intellect gives us some new conceptions of its nature. It should be a broad ability to grasp all kinds of systems that are conceived in terms of verbal concepts, not restricted to the understanding of problems of an arithmetical type.

Transformations are changes of various kinds, including modifications in arrangement, organization, or meaning. In the figural column for the transformations row, we find the factor known as visualization. Common measuring instruments for this factor are the surface-development tests, and an example of a different kind is Part VI (Spatial Visualization) of the GZAS. A test of the ability to make transformations of meaning, for the factor in the semantic column, is called Similarities. The examinee is asked to state several ways in which two objects, such as an apple and an orange, are alike. Only by shifting the meanings of both is the examinee able to give many responses to such an item.

In the set of abilities having to do with the cognition of implications, we find that the individual goes beyond the information given, but not to the extent of what might be called drawing conclusions. We may say that he extrapolates. From the given information he expects or foresees certain consequences, for example. The two factors found in this row of the cognition matrix were first called "foresight" factors. Foresight in connection with figural material can be tested by means of paper-and-pencil mazes. Foresight in connection with ideas, those pertaining to events, for example, is indicated by a test such as Pertinent Questions:

> In planning to open a new hamburger stand
> in a certain community, what four questions
> should be considered in deciding upon its
> location?

The more questions the examinee asks in response to a list of such problems, the more he evidently foresees contingencies.

The Memory Abilities

The area of memory abilities has been explored less than some of the other areas of operation, and only seven of the potential cells of the memory matrix have known factors in them. These cells are restricted to three rows: for units, relations, and systems. The first cell in the memory matrix is now occupied by two factors, parallel to two in the corresponding cognition matrix: visual memory and auditory memory. Memory for series of letters or numbers, as in memory span tests, conforms to the conception of memory for symbolic units. Memory for the ideas in a paragraph conforms to the conception of memory for semantic units.

The formation of associations between units, such as visual forms, syllables, and meaningful words, as in the method of paired associates, would seem to represent three abilities to remember relationships involving three kinds of content. We know of two such abilities, for the symbolic and semantic columns. The memory for known systems is represented by two abilities very recently discovered (Christal, 1958). Remembering the arrangement of objects in space is the nature of an ability in the figural column, and remembering a sequence of events is the nature of a corresponding ability in the semantic column. The differentiation between these two abilities implies that a person may be able to say where he saw an object on a page, but he might not be able to say on which of several pages he saw it after leafing through several pages that included the right one. Considering the blank rows in the memory matrix, we should expect to find abilities also to remember classes, transformations, and implications, as well as units, relations, and systems.

The Divergent-Thinking Abilities

The unique feature of divergent production is that a *variety* of responses is produced. The product is not completely determined by the given information. This is not to say that divergent thinking does not come into play in the total process of reaching a unique conclusion, for it comes into play wherever there is trial-and-error thinking.

The well-known ability of word fluency is tested by asking the examinee to list words satisfying a specified letter requirement, such as words beginning with the letter "s" or words ending in "-tion." This ability is now regarded as a facility in divergent production of symbolic units. The parallel semantic ability has been known as ideational fluency. A typical test item calls for listing objects that are round and edible. Winston Churchill must have possessed this ability to a high degree. Clement Attlee is reported to have said about him recently that, no matter what problem came up, Churchill always seemed to have about ten ideas. The trouble was, Attlee continued, he did not know which was the good one. The last comment implies some weakness in one or more of the evaluative abilities.

The divergent production of class ideas is believed to be the unique feature of a factor called "spontaneous flexibility." A typical test instructs the examinee to list all the uses he can think of for a common brick, and he is given eight minutes. If his responses are: build a house, build a barn, build a garage, build a school, build a church, build a chimney, build a walk, and build a barbecue, he would earn a fairly high score for ideational fluency but a very low score for spontaneous flexibility, because all these uses fall into the same class. If another person said: make a door stop, make a paper weight, throw it at a dog, make a bookcase, drown a cat, drive a nail, make a red powder, and use for baseball bases, he would also receive a high score for flexibility. He has gone frequently from one class to another.

A current study of unknown but predicted divergent-production abilities includes testing whether there are also figural and symbolic abilities to produce multiple classes. An experimental figural test presents a number of figures that can be classified in groups of three in various ways, each figure being usable in more than one class. An experimental symbolic test presents a few numbers that are also to be classified in multiple ways.

A unique ability involving relations is called "associational fluency." It calls for the production of a variety of things related in a specified way to a given thing. For example, the examinee is asked to list words meaning about the same as "good" or to list words meaning about the opposite of "hard." In these instances the response produced is to complete a relationship, and semantic content is involved. Some of our present experimental tests call for the production of varieties of relations, as such, and involve figural and symbolic content also. For example, given four small digits, in how many ways can they be related in order to produce a sum of eight?

One factor pertaining to the production of systems is known as expressional fluency. The rapid formation of phrases or sentences is the essence of certain tests of this factor. For example, given the initial letters:

W_____ c_____ e_____ n_____

with different sentences to be produced, the examinee might write "We can eat nuts" or "Whence came Eve Newton?" In interpreting the factor, we regard the sentence as a symbolic system. By analogy, a figural system would be some kind of organization of lines and other elements, and a semantic system would be in the form of a verbally stated problem or perhaps something as complex as a theory.

In the row of the divergent-production matrix devoted to transformations, we find some very interesting factors. The one called "adaptive flexibility" is now recognized as belonging in the figural column. A faithful test of it has been Match Problems. This is based

Item from the test Match Problems.

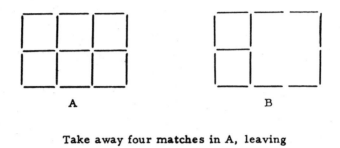

A   B

Take away four matches in A, leaving
three squares and nothing more. Answer: B.

Fig. 2. A sample item from the test Match Problems. The problem in this item
is to take away four matches and leave three squares. The solution is given.

upon the common game that uses squares, the sides of which are
formed by match sticks. The examinee is told to take away a given
number of matches to leave a stated number of squares with nothing
left over. Nothing is said about the sizes of the squares to be left. If
the examinee imposes upon himself the restriction that the squares
that he leaves must be of the same size, he will fail in his attempts to
do items like that in Figure 2. Other odd kinds of solutions are
introduced in other items, such as overlapping squares and squares
within squares, and so on. In another variation of Match Problems
the examinee is told to produce two or more solutions for each
problem.

A factor that has been called "originality" is now recognized as
adaptive flexibility with semantic material, where there must be a
shifting of meanings. The examinee must produce the shifts or
changes in meaning and so come up with novel, unusual, clever, or
farfetched ideas. The Plot Titles Test presents a short story, the
examinee being told to list as many appropriate titles as he can to
head the story. One story is about a missionary who has been captured by cannibals in Africa. He is in the pot and about to be boiled
when a princess of the tribe obtains a promise for his release if he will
become her mate. He refuses and is boiled to death.

In scoring the test, we separate the responses into two categories, clever and nonclever. Examples of nonclever responses are: African Death, Defeat of a Princess, Eaten by Savages, The Princess, The African Missionary, In Darkest Africa, and Boiled by Savages. These titles are appropriate but commonplace. The number of such responses serves as a score for ideational fluency. Examples of clever responses are: Pot's Plot, Potluck Dinner, Stewed Parson, Goil or Boil, A Mate Worse Than Death, He Left a Dish for a Pot, Chaste in Haste, and A Hot Price for Freedom. The number of clever responses given by an examinee is his score for originality, or the divergent production of semantic transformations.

Another test of originality presents a very novel task so that any acceptable response is unusual for the individual. In the Symbol Production Test the examinee is to produce a simple symbol to stand for a noun or a verb in each short sentence, in other words to invent something like pictographic symbols. Still another test of originality asks for writing the "punch lines" for cartoons, a task that almost automatically challenges the examinee to be clever. Thus, quite a variety of tests offer approaches to the measurement of originality, including one or two others that I have not mentioned.

Abilities to produce a variety of implications are assessed by tests calling for elaboration of given information. A figural test of this type provides the examinee with a line or two, to which he is to add other lines to produce an object. The more lines he adds, the greater his score. A semantic test gives the examinee the outlines of a plan to which he is to respond by stating all the details he can think of to make the plan work. A new test we are trying out in the symbolic area presents two simple equations such as $B - C = D$ and $z = A + D$. The examinee is to make as many other equations as he can from this information.

The Convergent-Production Abilities

Of the 18 convergent-production abilities expected in the three content columns, 12 are now recognized. In the first row, pertaining to units, we have an ability to name figural properties (forms or colors) and an ability to name abstractions (classes, relations, and so on). It may be that the ability in common to the speed of naming forms and the speed of naming colors is not appropriately placed in the convergent-thinking matrix. One might expect that the thing to be produced in a test of the convergent production of figural units would be in the form of figures rather than words. A better test of such an ability might somehow specify the need for one particular object, the examinee to furnish the object.

A test for the convergent production of classes (Word Grouping) presents a list of 12 words that are to be classified in four, and only four, meaningful groups, no word to appear in more than one group. A parallel test (Figure Concepts Test) presents 20 pictured real objects that are to be grouped in meaningful classes of two or more each.

Convergent production having to do with relationships is represented by three known factors, all involving the "eduction of correlates," as Spearman called it. The given information includes one unit and a stated relation, the examinee to supply the other unit. Analogies tests that call for completion rather than a choice between alternative answers emphasize this kind of ability. With symbolic content such an item might read:

pots   stop   bard   drab   rats   <u>?</u>

A semantic item that measures eduction of correlates is:

The absence of sound is _____.

Incidentally, the latter item is from a vocabulary-completion test, and its relation to the factor of ability to produce correlates indicates how, by change of form, a vocabulary test may indicate an ability other than that for which vocabulary tests are usually intended, namely, the factor of verbal comprehension.

Only one factor for convergent production of systems is known, and it is in the semantic column. It is measured by a class of tests that may be called ordering tests. The examinee may be presented with a number of events that ordinarily have a best or most logical order, the events being presented in scrambled order. The presentation may be pictorial, as in the Picture Arrangement Test, or verbal. The pictures may be taken from a cartoon strip. The verbally presented events may be in the form of the various steps needed to plant a new lawn. There are undoubtedly other kinds of systems than temporal order that could be utilized for testing abilities in this row of the convergent-production matrix.

In the way of producing transformations of a unique variety, we have three recognized factors, known as redefinition abilities. In each case, redefinition involves the changing of functions or uses of parts of one unit and giving them new functions or uses in some new unit. For testing the ability of figural redefinition, a task based upon the Gottschaldt figures is suitable. Figure 3 shows the kind of item for such a test. In recognizing the simpler figure within the structure of a more complex figure, certain lines must take on new roles.

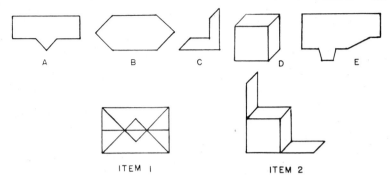

FIG. 3.   Sample items from a test Hidden Figures, based upon the Gottschaldt figures. Which of the simpler figures is concealed within each of the two more complex figures?

In terms of symbolic material, the following sample items will illustrate how groups of letters in given words must be readapted to use in other words. In the test Camouflaged Words, each sentence contains the name of a sport or game:

> I did not know that he was ailing.
> To beat the Hun, tin goes a long way.

For the factor of semantic redefinition, the Gestalt Transformation Test may be used. A sample item reads:

> From which object could you most likely make a needle?
> A. a cabbage
> B. a splice
> C. a steak
> D. a paper box
> E. a fish

The convergent production of implications means the drawing of fully determined conclusions from given information. The well-known factor of numerical facility belongs in the symbolic column. For the parallel ability in the figural column, we have a test known as Form Reasoning, in which rigorously defined operations with figures are used. For the parallel ability in the semantic column, the factor sometimes called "deduction" probably qualifies. Items of the following type are sometimes used.

> Charles is younger than Robert
> Charles is older than Frank
> Who is older: Robert or Frank?

Evaluative Abilities

The evaluative area has had the least investigation of all the operational categories. In fact, only one systematic analytical study has been devoted to this area. Only eight evaluative abilities are recognized as fitting into the evaluation matrix. But at least five rows have one or more factors each, and also three of the usual columns or content categories. In each case, evaluation involves reaching decisions as to the accuracy, goodness, suitability, or workability of information. In each row, for the particular kind of product of that row, some kind of criterion or standard of judgment is involved.

In the first row, for the evaluation of units, the important decision to be made pertains to the identity of a unit. Is this unit identical with that one? In the figural column we find the factor long known as "perceptual speed." Tests of this factor invariably call for decisions of identity, for example, Part IV (Perceptual Speed) of the GZAS or Thurstone's Identical Forms. I think it has been generally wrongly thought that the ability involved is that of cognition of visual forms. But we have seen that another factor is a more suitable candidate for this definition and for being in the very first cell of the cognitive matrix. It is parallel to this evaluative ability but does not require the judgment of identity as one of its properties.

In the symbolic column is an ability to judge identity of symbolic units, in the form of series of letters or numbers or of names of individuals.

Are members of the following pairs identical or not:
825170493_____825176493
dkeltvmpa_____dkeltvmpa
C. S. Meyerson_____C. E. Meyerson

Such items are common in tests of clerical aptitude.

There should be a parallel ability to decide whether two ideas are identical or different. Is the idea expressed in this sentence the same as the idea expressed in that one? Do these two proverbs express essentially the same idea? Such tests exist and will be used to test the hypothesis that such an ability can be demonstrated.

No evaluative abilities pertaining to classes have as yet been recognized. The abilities having to do with evaluation where relations are concerned must meet the criterion of logical consistency. Syllogistic-type tests involving letter symbols indicate a different ability than the same type of test involving verbal statements. In the figural column we might expect that tests incorporating geometric reasoning

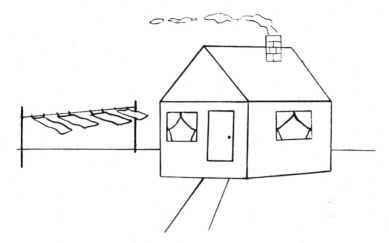

Fig. 4. A sample item from the test Unusual Details. What two things are wrong with this picture?

or proof would indicate a parallel ability to sense the soundness of conclusions regarding figural relationships.

The evaluation of systems seems to be concerned with the internal consistency of those systems, so far as we can tell from the knowledge of one such factor. The factor has been called "experiential evaluation," and its representative test presents items like that in Figure 4 asking "What is wrong with this picture?" The things wrong are often internal inconsistencies.

A semantic ability for evaluating transformations is thought to be that known for some time as "judgment." In typical judgment tests, the examinee is asked to tell which of five solutions to a practical problem is most adequate or wise. The solutions frequently involve improvisations, in other words, adaptations of familiar objects to unusual uses. In this way the items present redefinitions to be evaluated.

A factor known first as "sensitivity to problems" has become recognized as an evaluative ability having to do with implications. One test of the factor, the Apparatus Test, asks for two needed improvements with respect to each of several common devices, such as the telephone or the toaster. The Social Institutions Test, a measure of the same factor, asks what things are wrong with each of several institutions, such as tipping or national elections. We may say that defects or deficiencies are implications of an evaluative kind. Another interpretation would be that seeing defects and deficiencies are evaluations of implications to the effect that the various aspects of something are all right.[4]

SOME IMPLICATIONS OF THE STRUCTURE OF INTELLECT

For Psychological Theory

Although factor analysis as generally employed is best designed to investigate ways in which individuals differ from one another, in other words, to discover traits, the results also tell us much about how individuals are alike. Consequently, information regarding the factors and their interrelationships gives us understanding of functioning individuals. The five kinds of intellectual abilities in terms of operations may be said to represent five ways of functioning. The kinds of intellectual abilities distinguished according to varieties of test content and the kinds of abilities distinguished according to varieties of products suggest a classification of basic forms of information or knowledge. The kind of organism suggested by this way of looking at intellect is that of an agency for dealing with information of various kinds in various ways. The concepts provided by the distinctions among the intellectual abilities and by their classifications may be very useful in our future investigations of learning, memory, problem solving, invention, and decision making, by what ever method we choose to approach those problems.

For Vocational Testing

With about 50 intellectual factors already known, we may say that there are at least 50 ways of being intelligent. It has been facetiously suggested that there seem to be a great many more ways of being stupid, unfortunately. The structure of intellect is a theoretical model that predicts as many as 120 distinct abilities, if every cell of the model contains a factor. Already we know that two cells contain two or more factors each, and there probably are actually other cells of this type. Since the model was first conceived, 12 factors predicted by it have found places in it. There is consequently hope of filling many of the other vacancies, and we may eventually end up with more than 120 abilities.

The major implication for the assessment of intelligence is that

---

[4] For further details concerning the intellectual factors, illustrative tests, and the place of the factors in the structure of intellect; see Guilford (1959).

to know an individual's intellectual resources thoroughly we shall need a surprisingly large number of scores. It is expected that many of the factors are intercorrelated, so there is some possibility that by appropriate sampling we shall be able to cover the important abilities with a more limited number of tests. At any rate, a multiple-score approach to the assessment of intelligence is definitely indicated in connection with future vocational operations.

Considering the kinds of abilities classified as to content, we may speak roughly of four kinds of intelligence. The abilities involving the use of figural information may be regarded as "concrete" intelligence. The people who depend most upon these abilities deal with concrete things and their properties. Among these people are mechanics, operators of machines, engineers (in some aspects of their work), artists, and musicians.

In the abilities pertaining to symbolic and semantic content, we have two kinds of "abstract" intelligence. Symbolic abilities should be important in learning to recognize words, to spell, and to operate with numbers. Language and mathematics should depend very much upon them, except that in mathematics some aspects, such as geometry, have strong figural involvement. Semantic intelligence is important for understanding things in terms of verbal concepts and hence is important in all courses where the learning of facts and ideas is essential.

In the hypothesized behavioral column of the structure of intellect, which may be roughly described as "social" intelligence, we have some of the most interesting possibilities. Understanding the behavior of others and of ourselves is largely nonverbal in character. The theory suggests as many as 30 abilities in this area, some having to do with understanding, some with productive thinking about behavior, and some with the evaluation of behavior. The theory also suggests that information regarding behavior is also in the form of the six kinds of products that apply elsewhere in the structure of intellect, including units, relations, systems, and so on. The abilities in the area of social intelligence, whatever they prove to be, will possess considerable importance in connection with all those individuals who deal most with other people: teachers, law officials, social workers, therapists, politicians, statesmen, and leaders of other kinds.

For Education

The implications for education are numerous, and I have time just to mention a very few. The most fundamental implication is that we might well undergo transformations with respect to our conception of the learner and of the process of learning. Under the prevailing conception, the learner is a kind of stimulus-response device, much on the order of a vending machine. You put in a coin, and something comes out. The machine learns what reaction to put out when a certain coin is put in. If, instead, we think of the learner as an agent for dealing with information, where information is defined very broadly, we have something more analogous to an electronic computor. We feed a computor information; it stores that information; it uses that information for generating new information, either by way of divergent or convergent thinking; and it evaluates its own results. Advantages that a human learner has over a computor include the step of seeking and discovering new information from sources outside itself and the step of programing itself. Perhaps even these steps will be added to computors, if this has not already been done in some cases.

At any rate, this conception of the learner leads us to the idea that learning is discovery of information, not merely the formation of associations, particularly associations in the form of stimulus-response connections. I am aware of the fact that my proposal is rank heresy. But if we are to make significant progress in our understanding of human learning and particularly our understanding of the so-called higher mental processes of thinking, problem solving, and creative thinking, some drastic modifications are due in our theory.

The idea that education is a matter of training the mind or of training the intellect has been rather unpopular, wherever the prevailing psychological doctrines have been followed. In theory, at least, the emphasis has been upon the learning of rather specific habits or skills. If we take our cue from factor theory, however, we recognize that most learning probably has both specific and general aspects or components. The general aspects may be along the lines of the factors of intellect. This is not to say that the individual's status in each factor is entirely determined by learning. We do not know to what extent each factor is determined by heredity and to what extent by learning. The best position for educators to take is that possibly every intellectual factor can be developed in individuals at least to some extent by learning.

If education has the general objective of developing the intellects of students, it can be suggested that each intellectual factor provides a particular goal at which to aim. Defined by a certain combination of content, operation, and product, each goal ability then calls for certain kinds of practice in order to achieve improvement in it. This implies choice of curriculum and the choice or invention of teaching methods that will most likely accomplish the desired results.

Considering the very great variety of abilities revealed by the factorial exploration of intellect, we are in a better position to ask whether any general intellectual skills are now being neglected in education and whether appropriate balances are being observed. It is often observed these days that we have fallen down in the way of producing resourceful, creative graduates. How true this is, in comparison with other times, I do not know. Perhaps the deficit is noticed because the demands for inventiveness are so much greater at this time. At any rate, realization that the more conspicuously creative abilities appear to be concentrated in the divergent-thinking category, and also to some extent in the transformation category, we now ask whether we have been giving these skills appropriate exercise. It is probable that we need a better balance of training in the divergent-thinking area as compared with training in convergent thinking and in critical thinking or evaluation.

The structure of intellect as I have presented it to you may or may not stand the test of time. Even if the general form persists, there are likely to be some modifications. Possibly some different kind of model will be invented. Be that as it may, the fact of a multiplicity of intellectual abilities seems well established.

There are many individuals who long for the good old days of simplicity, when we got along with one unanalyzed intelligence. Simplicity certainly has its appeal. But human nature is exceedingly complex, and we may as well face that fact. The rapidly moving events in the world in which we live have forced upon us the need for knowing human intelligence thoroughly. Humanity's peaceful pursuit of happiness depends upon our control of nature and of our own behavior; and this, in turn, depends upon understanding ourselves, including our intellectual resources.

CHAPTER SEVEN

From Infancy to Adulthood

17

THE COURSE OF HEALTHY PERSONALITY

DEVELOPMENT

by Midcentury White House Conference on Children and Youth

A basic principle of human development is that growth, development, and behavior change are essentially gradual and continuous. The following article presents a theory of the course of personality development adopted by the Midcentury White House Conference on Children and Youth. Formulated by Erik H. Erikson of the Austen Riggs Center it is based on the hypothesis that in each of eight stages of human development there is a central problem that has to be solved, temporarily at least, if the person is to proceed with vigor and confidence to the next stage of development. [From *A Healthy Personality for Every Child—Fact Finding Report: A Digest*, pp. 8-25, prepared by the Midcentury White House Conference on Children and Youth; published by Health Publications Institute, Inc., 216 North Dawson St., Raleigh, N. C. Copyright, 1951, by Health Publications Institute, Inc.]

THE SENSE OF TRUST

The component of the healthy personality that is the first to develop is the sense of trust. The crucial time for its emergence is the first year of life. As with the other personality components to be described, the sense of trust is not something that develops independent of other manifestations of growth. It is not that the infant learns how to use his body for purposeful movement, learns to recognize people and objects around him, and also develops a sense of trust. Rather, the concept "sense of trust" is a short-cut expression intended to convey the characteristic flavor of all the child's satisfying experiences at this early age. Or, to say it another way, this psychological formulation serves to condense, summarize, and synthesize the most important underlying changes that give meaning to the infant's concrete and diversified experience.

Trust can exist only in relation to something. Consequently, a sense of trust cannot develop until the infant is old enough to be aware of objects and persons and to have some feeling that he is a separate individual. At about three months of age a baby is likely to smile if somebody comes close and talks to him. This shows that he is aware of the approach of the other person, that pleasurable sensations are aroused. If, however, the person moves too quickly or speaks too sharply the baby may look apprehensive or cry. He will not "trust" the unusual situation but will have a feeling of uneasiness, of mistrust, instead.

Experiences connected with feeding are a prime source for the development of trust. At around four months of age a hungry baby will grow quiet and show signs of pleasure at the sound of an approaching footstep, anticipating (trusting) that he will be held and fed. This repeated experience of being hungry, seeing food, receiving food, and feeling relieved and comforted assures the baby that the world is a dependable place.

Later experiences, starting at around five months of age, add another dimension to the sense of trust. Through endless repetitions of attempts to grasp for and hold objects, the baby is finally successful in controlling and adapting his movements in such a way as to reach his goal. Through these and other feats of muscular coordination the baby is gradually able to trust his own body to do his bidding.

The baby's trust-mistrust problem is symbolized in the game of peek-a-boo. In this game, which babies begin to like at about four months of age, an object disappears and then reappears. There is a slightly tense expression on the baby's face when the object goes away; its reappearance is greeted by wriggles and smiles. Only gradually does a baby learn that things continue to exist even though he does not see them, that there is order and stability in his universe. Peek-a-boo proves the point by playful repetition.

Studies of mentally ill individuals and observations of infants who have been grossly deprived of affection suggest that trust is an early-formed and important element in the healthy personality. Psychiatrists find again and again that the most serious illnesses occur in patients who have been sorely neglected or abused or otherwise deprived of love in infancy. Similarly, it is a common finding of psychological and social investigators that individuals diagnosed as a "psychopathic personality" were so unloved in infancy that they have no reason to trust the human race and, therefore, no sense of responsibility toward their fellow men.

Observations of infants brought up in emotionally unfavorable institutions or removed to hospitals with inadequate facilities for psychological care support these findings. A recent report says: "Infants under six months of age who have been in an institution for some time present a well-defined picture. The outstanding features are listlessness, emaciation and pallor, relative immobility, quietness, unresponsiveness to stimuli like a smile or a coo, indifferent appetite, failure to gain weight properly despite ingestion of diets which are entirely adequate, frequent stools, poor sleep, an appearance of unhappiness, proneness to febrile episodes, absence of sucking habits" (Bakwin, 1949).

Another investigation of children separated from their mothers at six to twelve months and not provided with an adequate substitute comes to much the same conclusion: "The emotional tone is one of apprehension and sadness, there is withdrawal from the environment amounting to rejection of it, there is no attempt to contact a stranger and no brightening if a stranger contacts him. Activities are retarded and the child often sits or lies inert in a dazed stupor. Insomnia is common and lack of appetite universal. Weight is lost, and the child becomes prone to current infections" (René Spitz, unpublished manuscript).

Most significant for our present point, these reactions are most likely to occur in children who up to the time of separation at six to nine months of age had a happy relation with their mothers, while those whose relations were unhappy are relatively unaffected. It is at about this age that the struggle between trusting and mistrusting the world comes to a climax, for it is then that the child first perceives clearly that he and his environment are things apart. That at this time formerly happy infants should react so badly to separation suggests, indeed, that they had had a faith which now was shattered. Happily, there is usually spectacular change for the better when the maternal presence and love are restored.

It is probably unnecessary to describe the numerous ways in which stimuli from without and from within may cause an infant distress. Birth is believed by some experts to be a painful experience for the baby. Until fairly recently doctors were likely to advise that babies be fed on schedule and that little attention be paid to their cries of hunger at other times. Many infants spent many of the waking hours of the first four months doubled up with colic. All of them had to be bathed and dressed at stated times, whether they liked it or not. Add to these usual discomforts the fact that some infants are handled rather roughly by their parents, that others hear angry words and loud voices, and that a few are really mistreated, and it will not be difficult to understand why some infants may feel the world is a place that cannot be trusted.

In most primitive societies and in some sections of our own society the attention accorded infants is more in line with natural processes. In such societies separation from the mother is less abrupt, in that for some time after birth the baby is kept close to the warmth and comfort of its mother's body and at its least cry the breast is produced. Throughout infancy the baby is surrounded by people who are ready to feed it, fondle it, otherwise comfort it at a moment's notice. Moreover, these ministrations are given spontaneously, wholeheartedly, and without that element of nervous concern that may characterize the efforts of young mothers made self-conscious and insecure by our scientific age.

We must not exaggerate, however. Most infants in our society, too, find smiles and the comfort of mother's soft, warm body accompanying their intake of food, whether from breast or bottle. Coldness, wetness, pain, and boredom—for each misfortune there is prompt and comforting relief. As their own bodies come to be more dependable, there is added to the pleasures of increasing sensory response and motor control the pleasure of the mother's encouragement.

Moreover, babies are rather hardy creatures and are not to be discouraged by inexperienced mothers' mistakes. Even a mother cat has to learn, and the kittens endure gracefully her first clumsy efforts to carry them away from danger. Then, too, psychologists tell us that mothers create a sense of trust in their children not by the particular techniques they employ but by the sensitiveness with which they respond to the children's needs and by their over-all attitude.

For most infants, then, a sense of trust is not difficult to come by. It is the most important element in the personality. It emerges at the most vulnerable period of a child's life. Yet it is the least likely to suffer harm, perhaps because both nature and culture work toward making mothers most maternal at that time.

THE SENSE OF AUTONOMY

The sense of trust once firmly established, the struggle for the next component of the healthy personality begins. The child is now twelve to fifteen months old. Much of his energy for the next two years will center around asserting that he is a human being with a mind and will of his own. A list of some of the items discussed by Spock under the heading "The One Year Old" will serve to remind us of the characteristics of that age and the problems they create for parents. "Feeling his oats." "The passion to explore." "He gets more dependent and more independent at the same time." "Arranging the house for the wandering baby." "Avoiding accidents." "How do you make him leave certain things alone?" "Dropping and throwing things." "Biting humans." "The small child who won't stay in bed at night."

What is at stake throughout the struggle of these years is the child's sense of autonomy, the sense that he is an independent human being and yet one who is able to use the help and guidance of others in important matters. This stage of development becomes decisive for the ratio between love and hate, between cooperation and wilfulness, for freedom of self-expression and its renunciation in the make-up of the individual. The favorable outcome is self-control without loss of self-esteem. The unfavorable outcome is doubt and shame.

Before the sense of autonomy can develop, the sense of trust must be reasonably well established and must continue to pervade the child's feeling about himself and his world. Only so dare he respond with confidence to his new-felt desire to assert himself boldly, to appropriate demandingly, and to hurl away without let or hindrance.

As with the previous stage, there is a physiological basis for this characteristic behavior. This is the period of muscle-system maturation and the consequent ability (and doubly felt inability) to coordinate a number of highly conflicting action patterns, such as those of holding on and letting go, walking, talking, and manipulating objects in ever more complicated ways. With these abilities come pressing needs to use them: to handle, to explore, to seize and to drop, to withhold and to expel. And, with all, there is the dominant will, the insistent "Me do" that defies help and yet is so easily frustrated by the inabilities of the hands and feet.

For a child to develop this sense of self-reliance and adequacy that Erickson calls autonomy, it is necessary that he experience over and over again that he is a person who is permitted to make choices. He has to have the right to choose, for example, whether to sit or whether to stand, whether to approach a visitor or to lean against his mother's knee, whether to accept offered food or whether reject it, whether to use the toilet or to wet his pants. At the same time he must learn some of the boundaries of self-determination. He inevitably finds that there are walls he cannot climb, that there are objects out of reach, that, above all, there are innumerable commands enforced by powerful adults. His experience is much too small to enable him to know what he can and cannot do with respect to the physical environment, and it will take him years to discover the boundaries that mark off what is approved, what is tolerated, and what is forbidden by his elders whom he finds so hard to understand.

As problems of this period, some psychologists have concentrated particularly on bladder and bowel control. Emphasis is put upon the need for care in both timing and mode of training children in the performance of these functions. If parental control is too rigid or if training is started too early, the child is robbed of his opportunity to develop, by his own free choice, gradual control of the contradictory impulses of retention and elimination.

To others who study child development, this matter of toilet training is but a prototype of all the problems of this age-range. The sphincters are only part of the whole muscle system, with its general ambiguity of rigidity and relaxation, of flexion and extension. To hold and to relinquish refer to much more than the bowels. As the child acquires the ability to stand on his two feet and move around, he delineates his world as me and you. He can be astonishingly pliable once he has decided that he wants to do what he is supposed to do, but there is no reliable formula for assuring that he will relinquish when he wants to hold on.

The matter of mutual regulation between parent and child (for fathers have now entered the picture to an extent that was rare in the earlier stage) now faces its severest test. The task is indeed one to challenge the most resourceful and the most calm adult. Firmness is necessary, for the child must be protected against the potential anarchy of his as yet untrained sense of discrimination. Yet the adult must back him up in his wish to "stand on his own feet," lest he be overcome by shame that he has exposed himself foolishly and by doubt in his self-worth. Perhaps the most constructive rule a parent can follow is to forbid only what "really matters" and, in such forbidding, to be clear and consistent.

Shame and doubt are emotions that many primitive peoples and some of the less sophisticated individuals in our own society utilize in training children. Shaming exploits the child's sense of being small. Used to excess it misses its objective and may result in open shamelessness, or, at least, in the child's secret determination to do as he pleases when not observed. Such defiance is a normal, even healthy response to demands that a child consider himself, his body, his needs, or his wishes evil and dirty and that he regard those who pass judgment as infallible. Young delinquents may be produced by this means, and others who are oblivious to the opinion of society.

Those who would guide the growing child wisely, then, will avoid shaming him and avoid causing him to doubt that he is a person of worth. They will be firm and tolerant with him so that he can rejoice in being a person of independence and can grant independence to others. As to detailed procedures, it is impossible to prescribe, not only because we do not know and because every situation is different but also because the kind and degree of autonomy that parents are able to grant their small children depends on feelings about themselves that they derive from society. Just as the child's sense of trust is a reflection of the mother's sturdy and realistic faith, so the child's sense of autonomy is a reflection of the parents' personal dignity. Such appears to be the teaching of the comparative study of cultures.

Personal autonomy, independence of the individual, is an especially outstanding feature of the American way of life. American parents, accordingly, are in a particularly favorable position to transmit the sense of autonomy to their children. They themselves resent being bossed, being pushed around; they maintain that everybody has the right to express his opinion and to be in control of his affairs. More easily than people who live according to an authoritarian pattern, they can appreciate a little child's vigorous desire to assert his independence and they can give him the leeway he needs in order to grow up into the upstanding, look-you-in-the-eye kind of individual that Americans admire.

It is not only in early childhood, however, that this attitude toward growing children must be maintained. As was said at the outset, these components of the healthy personality cannot be established once and for all. The period of life in which they first come into being is the most crucial, it is true. But threats to their maintenance occur throughout life. Not only parents, then, but everybody who has significant contact with children and young people must respect their desire for self-assertion, help them hold it within bounds, and avoid treating them in ways that arouse shame or doubt.

This attitude toward children, toward all people, must be maintained in institutional arrangements as well. Great differences in educational and economic opportunity and in access to the law, discrimination of all kinds are threats to this ingredient of mental health. So, too, may be the over-mechanization of our society, the depersonalization of human relations that is likely to accompany large-scale endeavor of all kinds.

Parents, as well as children, are affected by these matters. In fact, parents' ability to grant children the kind of autonomy Americans think desirable depends in part on the way they are treated as employees and citizens. Throughout, the relation must be such as affirms personal dignity. Much of the shame and doubt aroused in children result from the indignity and uncertainty that are an expression of parents' frustrations in love and work. Special attention must be paid to all these matters, then, if we are to avoid destroying the autonomy that Americans have always set store by.

THE SENSE OF INITIATIVE

Having become sure, for the time being, that he is a person in his own right and having enjoyed that feeling for a year or so, the child of four or five wants to find out what kind of person he can be. To be any particular kind of person, he sees clearly, involves being able to do particular kinds of things. So he observes with keen attention what all manner of interesting adults do (his parents, the milkman, the truck driver, and so on), tries to imitate their behavior, and yearns for a share in their activities.

This is the period of enterprise and imagination, an ebullient, creative period when phantasy substitutes for literal execution of desires and the meagerest equipment provides material for high imaginings. It is a period of intrusive, vigorous learning, learning that leads away from the child's own limitations into future possibilities. There is intrusion into other people's bodies by physical attack, into other people's ears and minds by loud and aggressive talking. There is intrusion into space by vigorous locomotion and intrusion into the unknown by consuming curiosity.

By this age, too, conscience has developed. The child is no longer guided only by outsiders; there is installed within him a voice that comments on his deeds, and warns and threatens. Close attention to the remarks of any child of this age will confirm this statement. Less obvious, however, are experts' observations that children now begin to feel guilty for mere thoughts, for deeds that have been imagined but never executed. This, they say, is the explanation for the characteristic nightmares of this age period and for the over reaction to slight punishment.

The problem to be worked out in this stage of development, accordingly, is how to will without too great a sense of guilt. The fortunate outcome of the struggle is a sense of initiative. Failure to win through to that outcome leaves the personality over-burdened, and possibly over-restricted, by guilt.

It is easy to see how the child's developing sense of initiative may be discouraged. So many of the projects dreamed up at this age are of a kind which cannot be permitted that the child may come to feel he is faced by a universal "No." In addition he finds that many of the projects are impossible of execution and others, even if not forbidden, fail to win the approval of the adults whom he has come to love. Moreover, since he does not always distinguish clearly between actuality and phantasy, his over-zealous conscience may disapprove of even imaginary deeds.

It is very important, therefore, for healthy personality development that much leeway and encouragement be given to the child's show of enterprise and imagination and that punishment be kept at a minimum. Boys and girls at this stage are extraordinarily appreciative of any convincing promise that someday they will be able to do things as well, or maybe better, than father and mother. They enjoy competition (especially if they can win) and insistence on goal; they get great pleasure from conquest. They need numerous examples of the kinds of roles adults assume, and they need a chance to try them out in play.

The ability that is in the making is that of selecting social goals and persevering in the attempt to reach them.

If enterprise and imagination are too greatly curbed, if severe rebukes accompany the frequently necessary denial of permission to carry out desires, a personality may result that is over-constricted. Such a personality cannot live up to its inner capacities for imagination, feeling, or performance, though it may overcompensate by immense activity and find relaxation impossible.

Constriction of personality is a self-imposed constriction, an act of the child's over-zealous conscience. "If I may not do this, I will not even think it," says conscience, "for even thinking it is dangerous." Resentment and bitterness and a vindictive attitude toward the world that forces the restriction may accompany this decision, however, and become unconscious but functioning parts of the personality. Such, at least, is the warning of psychiatrists who have learned to know the inmost feelings of emotionally handicapped children and adults.

This developmental stage has great assets as well as great dangers. At no time in life is the individual more ready to learn avidly and quickly, to become big in the sense of sharing obligation and performance. If during this preschool period the child can get some sense of the various roles and functions that he can perform as an adult, he will be ready to progress joyfully to the next stage, in which he will find pleasurable accomplishment in activities less fraught with phantasy and fear.

There is a lesson in this for later periods of personality development as well. As has been said before, these conflicts that come to a head at particular periods of a child's life are not settled once and for all. The sense of initiative, then, is one that must be continually fostered, and great care must be taken that youngsters and young people do not have to feel guilty for having dared to dream.

Just as we Americans prize autonomy, so too do we prize initiative; in fact, we regard it as the cornerstone of our economic system. There is much in the present industrial and political mode of life that may discourage initiative, that may make a young person think he had best pull in his horns. What these tendencies are and what they may do to youngsters and to their parents, who too must feel free if they are to cultivate the sense of initiative in their children, is a subject that warrants much serious discussion.

THE SENSE OF ACCOMPLISHMENT

The three stages so far described probably are the most important for personality development. With a sense of trust, a sense of autonomy, and a sense of initiative achieved, progress through the later stages is pretty well assured. Whether this is because children who have a good environment in their early years are likely to continue to be so favored, or whether it is because they have attained such strength of personality that they can successfully handle later difficulties, research has not yet made clear. We do know that nearly all children who get a good start continue to develop very well, and we know that some of those who start off poorly continue to be handicapped. Observations of this sort seem to support psychological theory in the conclusion that personality is pretty well set by about six years of age. Since, however, some children develop into psychologically healthy adults in spite of a bad start, and since some who start well run into difficulties later, it is clear that much research is needed before this conclusion can be accepted as wholly correct.

To return to the developmental analysis, the fourth stage, which begins somewhere around six years of age and extends over five or six years, has as its achievement what Erikson calls the sense of industry. Perhaps "sense of accomplishment" would make the meaning clearer. At any rate, this is the period in which preoccupation with phantasy subsides, and the child wants to be engaged in real tasks that he can carry through to completion. As with the other developmental stages, there are foreshadowings of this kind of interest long before six years of age. Moreover, in some societies and in some parts of our own society children are trained very early to perform socially useful tasks. The exact age is not the point at issue. What is to be pointed out is that children, after a period characterized by exuberant imagination, want to settle down to learning exactly how to do things and how to do them well.

In contrast to the preceding stages and to the succeeding ones, this stage does not consist of a swing from a violent inner upheaval to a new mastery. Under reasonably favorable circumstances this is a period of calm, steady growth, especially if the problems of the previous stages have been well worked through. Despite its unspectacular character, this is a very important period, for in it is laid a firm basis for responsible citizenship. It is during this period that children acquire not only knowledge and skills that make for good workmanship but also the ability to cooperate and play fair and otherwise follow the rules of the larger social game.

The chief danger of this period is the presence of conditions that may lead to the development of a sense of inadequacy and inferiority. This may be the outcome if the child has not yet achieved a sense of initiative, or if his experiences at home have not prepared him for entering school happily, or if he finds school a place where his previous accomplishments are disregarded or his latent abilities are not challenged. Even with a good start the child may later lapse into discouragement and lack of interest if at home or school his individual needs are overlooked—if too much is expected of him, or if he is made to feel that achievement is beyond his ability.

It is most important for health of personality, therefore, that schools be conducted well, that methods and courses of instruction be such as will give every child the feeling of successful accomplishment. Autobiographies of juvenile delinquents show time and again a boy who hated school—hated the fact that he was marked out as stupid or awkward, as one who was not as good as the rest. Some such boys find in jobs the sense of accomplishment they miss at school and consequently give up their delinquent ways. Others, however, are handicapped in job finding and keeping by the very fact that in school they did not develop the sense of industry; hence they have work failure added to their other insecurities. Nor is delinquency the only or the most likely outcome of lack of success in school. Many children respond in a quieter way, by passive acceptance of their inferiority. Psychologically they are perhaps even more harmed.

Our Puritan tradition maintains that children will not work except under the spur of competition, so we tend to fear the suggestion that all should succeed. To help children develop a sense of accomplishment does not mean, however, merely giving all of them good marks and passing them on to the next grade. Children need and want real achievement. How to help them secure it, despite differences in native capacity and differences in emotional development, is one of the school's most serious challenges.

School, of course, is not the only place in which children at this stage of development can secure the sense of industry. In work at home there are many opportunities for a child to get a feeling of mastery and worthwhile endeavor. Rural youth groups and their urban counterparts cater to this need, and many recreation programs put as much emphasis on work as on play. School, however, is the legally constituted arrangement for giving instruction to the young, so it is upon teachers that the professional responsibility for helping all children achieve a sense of industry and accomplishment rests.

In addition to aiding personality development in this way, teachers have many opportunities for reconfirming their pupils' sense of trust, autonomy, and initiative or for encouraging its growth in children who have been somewhat hampered by previous life experiences. Teachers cannot work alone, of course, either in aiding a child in the development of new capacities or in strengthening old ones. Jointly with parents and others they can do much, not only for children of already healthy personality but also for many whose development has been handicapped.

THE SENSE OF IDENTITY

With the onset of adolescence another period of personality development begins. As is well known, adolescence is a period of storm and stress for many young people, a period in which previous certainties are questioned and previous continuities no longer relied upon. Physiological changes and rapid physical growth provide the somatic base for the turmoil and indecision. It may be that cultural factors also play a part, for it has been observed that adolescence is less upsetting in some societies than in others.

The central problem of the period is the establishment of a sense of identity. The identity the adolescent seeks to clarify is who he is, what his role in society is to be. Is he a child or is he an adult? Does he have it in him to be some day a husband and father? What is he to be as a worker and an earner of money? Can he feel self-confident in spite of the fact that his race or religion or national background makes him a person some people look down upon? Over all, will he be a success or a failure? By reason of these questions adolescents are sometimes morbidly preoccupied with how they appear in the eyes of others as compared with their own conception of themselves, and with how they can make the roles and skills learned earlier jibe with what is currently in style.

In primitive societies adolescents are perhaps spared these doubts and indecisions. Through initiation rites, often seemingly cruel in character, young people are tested out (and test themselves out) and are then welcomed into a socially recognized age category in which rights and duties and mode of living are clearly defined. In our society there are few rituals or ceremonies that mark the change in status from childhood to youth. For those who have religious affiliations, confirmation, joining the church, may serve this purpose in part, since the young people are thereby admitted, in this one segment of their lives at least, to the company of adults. Such ceremonies serve, in addition, to reaffirm to youth that the universe is trustworthy and stable and that a way of life is clearly laid out.

Graduation ceremonies might play a part in marking a new status were it not that, in present-day America, status is so ill defined

What rules of law and custom exist are too diverse to be of much help. For example, legal regulations governing age of "consent," age at which marriage is permitted, age for leaving school, for driving a car, for joining (or being required to join) the Army or Navy mark no logical progressions in rights and duties. As to custom, there is so much variation in what even families who live next door to each other expect or permit that adolescents, eager to be on their way, are practically forced into standardizing themselves in their search for status. In this they are ably abetted by advertisers and entertainers who seek their patronage, as well as by well-meaning magazine writers who describe in great detail the means by which uniformity can be achieved.

In this urge to find comfort through similarity, adolescents are likely to become stereotyped in behavior and ideals. They tend to form cliques for self-protection and fasten on petty similarities of dress and gesture to assure themselves that they are really somebody. In these cliques they may be intolerant and even cruel toward those they label as different. Unfortunate as such behavior is and not to be condoned, intolerance serves the important purpose of giving the group members at least the negative assurance that there is something they are not.

The danger of this developmental period is self-diffusion. As Biff puts it in *The Death of a Salesman,* "I just can't take hold, mom. I can't take hold of some kind of a life." A boy or girl can scarcely help feeling somewhat diffuse when the body changes in size and shape so rapidly, when genital maturity floods body and imagination with forbidden desires, when adult life lies ahead with such a diversity of conflicting possibilities and choices.

Whether this feeling of self-diffusion is fairly easily mastered or whether, in extreme, it leads to delinquency, neurosis or outright psychosis, depends to a considerable extent on what has gone before. If the course of personality development has been a healthy one, a feeling of self-esteem has accrued from the numerous experiences of succeeding in a task and sensing its cultural meaning. Along with this, the child has come to the conviction that he is moving toward an understandable future in which he will have a definite role to play. Adolescence may upset this assurance for a time or to a degree but fairly soon a new integration is achieved, and the boy or girl sees again (and with clearer vision) that he belongs and that he is on his way.

The course is not so easy for adolescents who have not had so fortunate a past or for those whose earlier security is broken by a sudden awareness that as members of minority groups their way of life sets them apart. The former, already unsure of themselves, find their earlier doubt and mistrust reactivated by the physiological and social changes that adolescence brings. The latter, once secure, may feel that they must disavow their past and try to develop an "American" personality.

Much has been learned and written about the adolescent problems of the boys and girls whose early personality development has been impaired. How they can be helped, if their disorders are not too severe, is also fairly well known. The full implications of these findings for parents, teachers, and others who would guide youth are still to be worked out but, even so, there is considerable information.

Less well understood are the difficulties and the ways of helping adolescents who grew up in cultures that are not of the usual run. These boys and girls may have been privileged in having had a childhood in which there was little inhibition of sensual pleasures, and in which development proceeded by easy, unselfconscious stages. For them, difficulties arise if their parents lose trust in themselves or if their teachers apply sudden correctives, or if they themselves reject their past and try to act like the others. The new role of middle-class adolescent is often too hard to play. Delinquency or bizarre behavior mark the failure.

How to reach these boys and girls, how to help them attain their desire, is a matter not well understood. It is clear, however, that they should not be typed by pat diagnoses and social judgments, for they are ever ready to become the "bums" that they are called. Those who would guide them must understand both the psychology of adolescence and the cultural realities of the day. There is trust to be restored and doubt and guilt and feelings of inferiority to be overcome. The science of how to do this is still pretty much lacking, though here and there teachers, clergymen, probation officers, and the like are highly successful in the task.

Hard though it be to achieve, the sense of identity is the individual's only safeguard against the lawlessness of his biological drives and the authority of an over-weening conscience. Loss of identity, loss of the sense that there is some continuity, sameness, and meaning to life, exposes the individual to his childhood conflicts and leads to emotional upsets. This outcome was observed time and again among men hard pressed by the dangers of war. It is clear, then, that if health of personality is to be preserved much attention must be given to assuring that America makes good on its promises to youth.

THE SENSE OF INTIMACY

After the sense of identity, to a greater or less extent, is achieved, it becomes possible for the next component of the healthy personality to develop. This is the sense of intimacy, intimacy with persons of the same sex or of the opposite sex or with one's self. The youth who is not fairly sure of his identity shies away from interpersonal relations and is afraid of close communion with himself. The surer he becomes of himself, the more he seeks intimacy, in the form of friendship, love and inspiration.

In view of the early age at which boy and girl attachments are encouraged today, it may seem strange to put the critical period for the development of the sense of intimacy late in adolescence. The explanation is that, on the one hand, sexual intimacy is only one part of what is involved, and, on the other, boy-girl attachments of earlier age periods are likely to be of a somewhat different order. Regarding the latter point, it has been observed by those who know young people well that high-school age boys and girls often use each other's company for an endless verbal examination of what the other thinks, feels, and wants to do. In other words, these attachments are one means of defining one's identity.

In contrast to this use of friendship and companionship, boys and girls late in adolescence usually have need for a kind of fusion with the essence of other people and for a communion with their own inner resources. If, by reason of inadequacies in previous personality development, this sense of intimacy cannot be achieved, the youth may retire into psychological isolation and keep his relations with people on a formal, stereotyped level that is lacking in spontaneity and warmth or he may keep trying again and again to get close to others, only to meet with repeated failure. Under this compulsion he may even marry, but the role of mate is one he can rarely sustain, for the condition of true two-ness is that each individual must first become himself.

In this area of personality development as in the others, cultural factors play a part in sustaining or in discouraging the individual in his development. American culture is unusually successful in encouraging the development of the feelings of independence, initiative, industry, and identity. It is somewhat less successful in the area of intimacy, for the culture's ideal is the subordination of sexuality and sensuality to a life of work, duty, and worship.

Consequently, American adolescents are likely to be unsupported by their parents and to find little confirmation in story or song for their desire to sense intimately the full flavor of the personality of others. In many of them, then, the sense of intimacy does not develop highly and they have difficulty in finding in close personal relations the outlet for tension that they need.

There is some evidence that a change in conventions and customs in this respect is in the making, however. Too abrupt change in any such cultural matter is not to be urged, but it is to be hoped that gradual, frank discussion can bring about gradual alteration in attitude and overcome the dangers inherent in the traditional rigidity.

THE PARENTAL SENSE

"Parental sense" designates somewhat the same capacity as that implied in the words, creativity or productivity. The individual has normally come to adulthood before this sense can develop fully.

The parental sense is indicated most clearly by interest in producing and caring for children of one's own. It may also be exhibited in relation to other people's children or by a parental kind of responsibility toward the products of creative activity of other sorts. The mere desire for or possession of children does not indicate that this component of the healthy personality has developed. In fact, many parents who bring their children to child guidance clinics are found not to have reached this stage of personality development.

The essential element is the desire to nourish and nurture what has been produced. It is the ability to regard one's children as a trust of the community, rather than as extensions of one's own personality or merely as beings that one happens to live with.

Failure to develop this component of the healthy personality often results in a condition which has not been adequately categorized clinically. Although a true sense of intimacy has not developed, the individual may obsessively seek companionship. There is something of egotism in this as in his other activities, a kind of self-absorption. The individual is inclined to treat himself as a child and to be rivalrous with his children, if he has any. He indulges himself, expects to be indulged, and in general behaves in an infantile or immature manner.

There are both individual and social explanations of the failure to develop an adequate parental sense. Individually, the explanation may be found in the inadequate development of the personality components previously described. In some people this failure goes far back. Because of unfortunate experiences in childhood they did not arrive at a firm sense of trust, autonomy, and the rest. In others it is only inadequacies in later stages, especially in the development of the sense of intimacy, that are at fault.

Socially, as has been suggested throughout this analysis, healthy personality development depends upon the culture's ideals and upon the economic arrangements of the society. In order that most people may develop fully the sense of being a parent, the role of parent, both mother and father, must be a respected one in the society. Giving must rank higher than getting, and loving than being loved. The economy must be such that the future can be depended upon and each person can feel assured that he has a meaningful and respected part to play. Only so can most individuals afford to renounce selfish aims and derive much of their satisfaction from rearing children.

THE SENSE OF INTEGRITY

The final component of the healthy personality is the sense of integrity. In every culture the dominant ideals, honor, courage, faith, purity, grace, fairness, self-discipline, become at this stage the core of the healthy personality's integration. The individual, in Erikson's words, "becomes able to accept his individual life cycle and the people who have become significant to it as meaningful within the segment of history in which he lives."

To continue Erikson's description, "Integrity thus means a new and different love of one's parents, free of the wish that they should have been different, and an acceptance of the fact that one's life is one's own responsibility. It is a sense of comradeship with men and women of distant times and of different pursuits, who have created orders and objects and sayings conveying human dignity and love. Although aware of the relativity of all the various life styles that have given meaning to human striving, the possessor of integrity is ready to defend the dignity of his own life style against all physical and economic threats. For he knows that, for him, all human dignity stands or falls with the one style of integrity of which he partakes."

The adult who lacks integrity in this sense may wish that he could live life again. He feels that if at one time he had made a different decision he could have been a different person and his ventures would have been successful. He fears death and cannot accept his one and only life cycle as the ultimate of life. In the extreme, he experiences disgust and despair. Despair expresses the feeling that time is too short to try out new roads to integrity. Disgust is a means of hiding the despair, a chronic, contemptuous displeasure with the way life is run. As with the dangers and the solutions of previous periods, doubt and despair are not difficulties that are overcome once and for all, nor is integrity so achieved. Most people fluctuate between the two extremes. Most, also, at no point, either attain to the heights of unalloyed integrity or fall to the depths of complete disgust and despair.

Even in adulthood a reasonably healthy personality is sometimes secured in spite of previous misfortunes in the developmental sequence. New sources of trust may be found. Fortunate events and circumstances may aid the individual in his struggle to feel autonomous. Imagination and initiative may be spurred by new responsibilities, and feelings of inferiority be overcome by successful achievement. Even late in life an individual may arrive at a true sense of who he is and what he has to do and may be able to win through to a feeling of intimacy with others and to joy in producing and giving.

Evidence of such changes is found in the case records of psychiatrists and social workers. Common sense observation attests that similar changes in health of personality are sometimes accomplished without benefit of any form of psychotherapy. Much remains to be learned about this, however, especially about how life itself may serve as therapeusis.

For the healthy personality development of children and youth it is necessary that a large proportion of adults attain a sense of integrity to a considerable degree. Not only parents but all who deal with children have need of this quality if they are to help children maintain the feeling that the universe is dependable and trustworthy. Integrity is relatively easily attained and sustained when the culture itself gives support, when a meaning to life is clearly spelled out in tradition and ceremony, and roles are clearly defined. Our culture, with its rapidly changing technology and its diversity of value standards, leaves much for the individual to work out for himself. In the American dream, however, and Judaeo-Christian tradition on which it is based there are values and ideals aplenty. In the interest of the welfare of children and youth, in order that a generation of happy individuals and responsible citizens be reared, it is highly important that these values and ideals be brought into prominence and that the promise of American life be kept.

•••••••••••••••••••••••••••••• 18 ••••••••••••••••••••••••••••••

A VALIDATION OF DEVELOPMENT AND

ADJUSTMENT HYPOTHESES OF ADOLESCENCE

by Aileen Schoeppe and Robert J. Havighurst

This longitudinal study confirms two basic hypotheses about developmental tasks: performance on them is positively interrelated at any given age and performance in a given task area at one age is positively related to subsequent performance in that area. The authors are Aileen Schoeppe of New York University and Robert J. Havighurst of the University of Chicago. [From *Journal of Educational Psychology*, 1952, *43*, 339-353. Reprinted by permission of the authors and the American Psychological Association.]

THE PROBLEM

The concept of developmental tasks—those major common tasks which face all individuals in a given society or subgroup of society—is a useful tool for thinking about human development and about the education and guidance of children and youth. This concept seems to provide a framework within which knowledge about human behavior can be organized and this information can be used in learning optimum socialization processes. It has evolved from the recent efforts of students of the life sciences to understand social learning and the problems boys and girls face in becoming oriented to their cultural milieu. The developmental task concept originated in the Study of Adolescents of the Progressive Education Association, but was first elaborated in detail by Havighurst in 1948 in the monograph *Developmental Tasks and Education* (Havighurst, 1952). Since then it has been used rather widely. The most recently, thorough, and somewhat novel account is that by Tryon and Lilienthal (1950) in *Fostering Mental Health in Our Schools*. However, a complete survey of the literature shows it all to be theoretical.

The investigation herein reported was made in an attempt to learn more about the concept by studying intensively the achievement of thirty adolescents in Middle-western American society on five developmental tasks of adolescence; namely,

(1) Learning an appropriate sex rôle.
(2) Achieving emotional independence of parents and other adults.
(3) Developing conscience, morality, and a set of values.
(4) Getting along with age-mates.
(5) Developing intellectual skills.

THE HYPOTHESES

The study tested several hypotheses about the relationships of levels of achievement on developmental tasks at various ages, and among several tasks at the same age. The aim was to answer the following specific questions: Does a tendency to be high in achievement in one task relate systematically to the level of achievement in other tasks at the same age? What are the patterns of achievement? Is there a systematic relation among the levels of achievement on the tasks at various periods of adolescence? If so, what is the nature of this relationship?

A concern for finding answers to the above stated questions led to the formulation of definite hypotheses which, when tested, would yield the desired information:

(1) Good achievement on a developmental task at one age is followed by good achievement on similar tasks at subsequent ages.

(2) Good achievement on a developmental task tends to be associated with good achievement on other tasks at the same age.

(3) In a minority of cases good achievement on one developmental task may be used to compensate for poor achievement on other tasks.

As the study progressed, additional questions were raised. Chief among these were questions relative to the overlapping or discreteness of tasks. Specifically, are there basic underlying factors which may account for achievement in certain of the tasks and other basic factors which may account for achievement in other tasks? Does the "clustering" of tasks influence achievement on them?

THE DATA

As a part of the Midwest Community Study Research Project, a major interdisciplinary research carried on since 1942 by the staff of the Committee on Human Development of the University of Chicago for the purpose of investigating character and personality development during childhood and adolescence in a typical Midwestern community, rich and extensive data have been collected on a group of adolescents. These lent themselves to the purposes of the study and form the basic data for it.[1]

The subjects are fifteen boys and fifteen girls studied intensively in the Project. They are a selected sample, originally chosen on the basis of being "adjusted" or "unadjusted" as defined by arbitrarily determined composite criteria, from the original sample, which consisted of the one hundred fifteen children who had been born in 1932 and who in 1942 resided in the small city of "Midwest" or its surrounding rural territory. The data used in the present study were compiled at ages ten, thirteen, and sixteen.

The completed folder of case-study materials on each subject, representing the results of thirty-two instruments, included information in the following broad areas: interviews; psychometric data; subject's reports via check lists; subject's reports via free response; various ratings by acquaintances, teachers, and others; projective techniques; sociometric data; physical data; Clinical Conference and Moral Character Conference[2] summaries and reports; ratings by staff members on a "Trait Rating List" of forty-seven personality and social rôle items at age sixteen.

On the basis of these data eight or more Research staff members rated each subject on a ten-point scale on four developmental tasks; this scale represented a comparison by the rater of the subject against the Conference estimate of the norm for the American adolescent population with definitions set to place this norm at 5.5. At age sixteen separate ratings were made on the inner and outer aspects (i.e., covert and overt behavioral manifestations) of learning an appropriate sex rôle and assuming emotional independence of parents and other adults on the premise that these aspects were some-

---

[1] Without this previous work the present study could not have been possible; appreciation is expressed to all who worked on gathering and interpreting the primary data for the Midwest Community Study.

[2] The Clinical Case Conference studied the group from 1945 to 1947; it was followed by the Moral Character Conference. Both are part of the large Project and the latter integrated all the earlier data and their interpretation by the earlier Conference into its research.

what independent and might be discrepant, and that the data were sufficient to permit separate ratings of them at this age. Ratings were also estimated from the accumulated data on these recurrent tasks at the earlier ages of ten and thirteen.[3] All of his ratings on a task were averaged for each subject.

In addition, it was thought other available data on the subjects permitted rating on a fifth task, "Achieving intellectual skills." In actuality, in the light of the data, this task would probably be more correctly termed "Achieving academic skills," for the two measures determining the ratings are measures of academic achievement only and, at least in our present society, "intellectual skills" is a much more inclusive term and may have a connotation quite different from a narrow academic one. These ratings were not made by the Research staff, but were determined by decile rankings, made in terms of the entire original sample, on academic measures. For the school years ending in 1943 and 1946, this rating was made as follows: a numerical value was given to the average letter grade in each subject for the year, these numerical values were averaged, and the total scores of the entire sample ranked; this rank was then added to the individual's rank for the Metropolitan Achievement Test to give the total rank of the individual for the year; the total group for each year was then divided into deciles. For 1949 only school marks were available and these were in percentage form, rather than the letter grades of previous years; intellectual achievement for this year was rated by ranking these scores, then dividing the total group into deciles.[4] It is assumed these decile ratings thus determined are equivalent, for purposes of the present study, to the ratings on the other tasks on the ten-point rating scale.

The ratings on the five developmental tasks, thus obtained, furnish the sole data for the correlational analyses to test the adjustment and development hypotheses.

[3] It is recognized that ratings for earlier ages probably would have been somewhat more refined had they been made at those ages rather than attempting to arrive at ratings for those ages simultaneously with ratings for age sixteen, but practical considerations in the Project made such great precision impossible. It is also recognized that it would have been highly desirable to have had such ratings of inner and outer aspects for all ages as were made for age sixteen, but the Research staff thought the data from which to rate adequately on inner feelings were insufficient at earlier ages to warrant a separate rating.

[4] The correlations between ranks for the total group were made by Spearman's rank-difference correlation formula and the critical ratio for significance determined. For 1943 data C.R. = 6.8; for 1946 data C.R. = 9.1. Thus there is a significant relationship between rank in the achievement test scores and rank in the school grades.

METHODS OF ANALYZING DATA

To test the hypothesis of consistency of development, intercorrelations of ratings for all subjects on a task at each of the three age levels with each other age level were made to determine similarity of level of achievement of the task; this was repeated for all tasks.

To test the hypothesis of adjustment by considering simultaneous achievement on the several tasks, the ratings of subjects at each age level on all the tasks were intercorrelated to determine the degree of relationship between levels of achievement on the various tasks at given ages.

To check further on an adjustment hypothesis and the possibility of basic factors underlying certain tasks, intercorrelations were made of each task at all age levels with every other task at all age levels and these were organized by correlation profile analysis. In the same figure the profiles of congruent tasks at the same age were plotted. An attempt was then made by inference to determine an underlying factor which might be the causality for these task groupings.

To check on the hypothesis that good achievement on one task may be used to compensate for poor achievement on another or other tasks, rankings of levels of achievement were made for all individuals on all tasks at all ages. Those subjects who appeared simultaneously in the top quarter on one or more tasks and in the lowest quarter on one or more tasks were studied for a comparison of ratings, and an attempt was made to determine reasons for these discrepancies.

SUMMARY OF THE FINDINGS

Before considering relationships, it seems requisite to describe the central tendencies and dispersions of the group on the tasks at the various ages. Table 1 contains these data.[5]

From this table it can be observed that the group consistently averaged near the theoretical mean (5.5) for the American adolescent population, as designated by the Conference definitions. Thus, the group as a whole can be said to be, within the limits of the rationale of the study, quite average in their achievement on the developmental tasks rated, and the ranges indicate that the study includes cases from one extreme on the rating scale to the other extreme. Because of these wide ranges, opportunity is presented for studying all levels of achievement and for pointing up sharp contrasts.

[5] [Table omitted.]

TABLE 2. INTERCORRELATIONS OF RATINGS ON EACH TASK AT EACH AGE LEVEL WITH EACH OTHER TASK AT ALL AGE LEVELS*

	SRO 10	SRO 13	SRO 16	SRI 16	EIO 10	EIO 13	EIO 16	EII 16	CMV 10	CMV 13	CMV 16	A-M 10	A-M 13	A-M 16	IS 10	IS 13	IS 16
SRO 10	...	.61	.42*	(.34)	.68	.48	.50	.43*	.70	.44*	.42*	.83	.57	.49	.45*	.42*	.37*
SRO 13		...	.84	.59	.62	.83	.84	.86	.38*	.53	.52	.53	.82	.77	.54	.49	.46*
SRO 16			...	.70	.58	.71	.79	.75	.39*	.55	.53	.38*	.66	.73	.45*	.45*	.42*
SRI 16				...	.47	.76	.58	.68	.40*	.51	.49	(.28)	.44*	.48	(.34)	(.26)	(.18)
EIO 10					...	.83	.79	.69	.43*	(.23)	(.22)	.57	.47	.39*	.37*	(.29)	(.23)
EIO 13						...	.95	.84	(.26)	.38*	.37*	.45*	.64	.57	.51	.45*	.48
EIO 16							...	.93	(.35)	.50	.51	.51	.65	.63	(.30)	.55	.49
EII 16								...	.47	.63	.65	.43*	.63	.64	.66	.62	.55
CMV 10									...	.80	.78	.80	.55	.45*	.57	.64	.58
CMV 13										...	.98	.60	.68	.78	.71	.78	.76
CMV 16											...	.58	.70	.78	.75	.79	.78
A-M 10												...	.75	.71	.62	.58	.52
A-M 13													...	.94	.69	.62	.58
A-M 16														...	.74	.72	.69
IS 10															...	.92	.78
IS 13																...	.91
IS 16																	...

* An asterisk following a coefficient of correlation denotes it is significant only at .05 level; coefficients not so marked are significant at .01 level. A coefficient enclosed in parentheses indicates it is not significant at either .01 or .05 levels. With 28 degrees of freedom an r to be significant at .01 level must be .463 or greater; at .05 level .361 or greater.

The task abbreviations in the table are: SRO—Learning an appropriate outer sex rôle. SRI—Learning an appropriate inner sex rôle. EIO—Achieving outer emotional independence of parents and other adults. EII—Achieving inner emotional independence of parents and other adults. CMV—Developing conscience, morals, and a set of values. A-M—Getting along with age-mates. IS—Developing intellectual skills.

Table 2 presents the basic correlational data which permit testing of the first two hypotheses and of the possibility of basic factors underlying certain tasks.

DEVELOPMENTAL RELATIONSHIPS

The longitudinal study of relatedness of each task through the three age levels shows the hypothesis that good achievement on a developmental task at one age is followed by good achievement on similar tasks at later ages to be correct. In fact, all correlations except one are significant at the .01 level and that one—Sex Rôle (Outer) Task at ages ten, sixteen—is significant at the .05 level, that level of significance assumed as satisfactory for the study.

The one very clear-cut finding from the longitudinal study is the much greater variability among the tasks and the lower correlations for ages ten, thirteen than for ages thirteen, sixteen. The very high correlations at ages thirteen, sixteen show quite conclusively that the level of achievement on these particular tasks is practically fixed by age thirteen. Therefore, the period from ten to thirteen years seems the crucial period for adolescent changes and development in personality and socialization patterns in these subjects. A rather commonly accepted generality is that with puberty and physiological changes comes other adolescent development, but, if these correlations are valid, it appears that other adolescent changes may well forerun the physiological changes. There is need to extend the study to other earlier and also more advanced age ranges. But the findings suggest rather forcefully that the so-called "latency" period may be a latency period only in physiological development and that it is a critical, extremely important period in social and personality development. Recurrently throughout the literature on personality development are suggestions that the latency period needs to be studied much more intensively than it has been; certainly these correlations hint that it and the early adolescent years are the time when permanent patterns are being formed and socializing influences are most effective. Therefore it behooves those guiding children during this formative period to have as much information as is possible on how the child may be aided in the accomplishment of the developmental tasks at this age period. An encouraging step in this direction is the very recent appearance of a new summary and critical analysis of available literature bearing upon the development and psychology of preadolescents, drawn from the various disciplines, with a formulation of guiding principles (Blair and Burton, 1951).

Some other conclusions regarding development may also be made. The correlations between age levels for Sex Rôle (Outer) Task are lowest; plausibly, physiological factors over which the individual exercises little control enter importantly into this task.

The correlations between achievement of intellectual skills at the various ages are highest; the factor of basic intellective capacity, over which the individual also exercises little control, enters prominently, but makes for stability instead of fluctuation on the task.

An extremely high correlation (.98) shows great consistency in the Conscience, Morals, Values Task between ages thirteen and sixteen; the conscience and morality pattern one has established by age thirteen evidently remains virtually stable unless there are traumatic or other situational experiences.

ADJUSTMENT RELATIONSHIPS

Over-all Adjustment

The hypothesis that good achievement on one task tends to be associated with good achievement on other tasks at the same age appears to be correct. Table 3 presents a summary tabulation of the correlations between achievement on the tasks at each of the respective age levels.

The adjustment, and also the development, hypothesis is further substantiated by the fact that seventy per cent of the correlations at age ten, eighty per cent at age thirteen, and ninety per cent at age sixteen are significant at the .01 level. Allport has succinctly described this consistency of personality: "As if to offset the disunity that comes with differentiation in early childhood, there is a compensatory process of integration. . . . By virtue of the functional joining of psychical systems (through conditioning, generalization of habit, and all associational processes) integral units come into existence. For the most part these units represent coherent foci of development, found serviceable to adjustment and to mastery. . . . Functional units though to some extent independent tend, nevertheless, normally to converge into more embracing systems. Though perfect unity is never achieved, there may be said to be a constant progression in that direction." (Allport, 1937, pp. 344 f.)

A clear-cut conclusion is that satisfactory relations with peers is bound to accomplishment of the other tasks.

TABLE 3

SUMMARY TABLE OF CORRELATIONS OF TASKS AT VARIOUS AGES

	Age		
	10	13	16
Correlations Consistently High from Age to Age			
Sex Rôle (Outer) Task with Emotional Independence (Outer) Task	.68	.83	.79
Sex Rôle (Outer) Task with Age-Mates Task	.83	.82	.73
Emotional Independence (Outer) Task with Age-Mates Task	.57	.64	.63
Conscience, Morals, Values Task with Age-Mates Task	.80	.68	.78
Intellectual Skills Task with Age-Mates Task	.62	.63	.69
Correlations Consistently Low from Age to Age			
Sex Rôle (Outer) Task with Intellectual Skills Task	.45	.49	.42
Emotional Independence (Outer) Task with Conscience, Morals, Values Task	.43	.38	.51
Emotional Independence (Outer) Task with Intellectual Skills Task	.37	.45	.49
Correlations Inconsistent from Age to Age			
Sex Rôle (Outer) Task with Conscience, Morals, Values Task	.70	.53	.53
Conscience, Morals, Values Task with Intellectual Skills Task	.57	.78	.78

Basic Factors

From the correlation profile analyses, based on intercorrelations of each task at all age levels with each other task at all age levels,[6] the tentative conclusion is drawn that there may be three separate basic factors underlying the tasks studied, although much more definite scientific investigation must be carried on before this can be stated with certainty. These findings are merely suggestive of the possibility of merit in a factor analysis of the tasks; such an analysis might do much to define, delineate, and delimit the specific tasks.

A factor which may be basic to the Sex Rôle (Outer) Task, Achieving Emotional Independence (Inner and Outer) Tasks, and Getting Along with Age-Mates Task has an affective base. These seem to center around the "feeling" aspects of the individual—that part of his personality that, tragically, up to the present the schools have not generally deemed it their concern to develop. Physiological, emotional, and social maturity of the individual are all a consideration in this clustering, but the effect of each goes back to an emotional base and the individual's acceptance of his impulses.

[6] The method duplicated that described by Tryon (1939).

A second factor which may underlie the Conscience, Morals, Values Task and the Intellectual Skills Task plausibly may be intellectual in origin. It suggests rational acceptance of discipline, or possibly a degree of conformity. This embodies intellectualizing by the individual and his acceptance of the necessity to formulate a pattern, a system of discipline, for his living both in informal interpersonal relations and in formal societal institutions.

A third factor seems basic only to the Sex Rôle (Inner) Task. About all one can definitely say from the data and the measures considered in the study is that this task does not fit with the others and therefore one deduces that it must have a different underlying factor. It is very tentatively suggested that this may have largely a biologic origin in hormonal balance. This hypothesis comes rather from using other studies to explain this discrepancy than from any data in the study. The isolation of this task corresponds with what Kinsey (1948, 1953) seems to be concluding, and it is suggestive of Murphy's (1947, p. 106) approach to personality study and his specific suggestion, with David Levy's study as evidence, that sexual and maternal drives suggest a constitutional factor.

These are interesting data and may be valuable in suggesting approaches for further study to delineate in a more refined manner developmental tasks and to define them more precisely. But it must be reëmphasized that this is only an exploratory study suggested by the correlations resulting from the study of longitudinal development and cross-sectional adjustment on the tasks empirically defined by the Moral Character Conference and that more careful and extensive analyses must be made before accepting these as basic factors. However, this exploration does suggest that such research may prove fruitful.

Negative Relationships

Tentative but positive conclusions were reached substantiating the third hypothesis—that some individuals use good achievement on one task to compensate for poor achievement on another or others. The small number of such cases (according to criteria, described previously, that were used for selection) makes any truly definite conclusions impossible but the trend suggests even a greater homogeneity in adjustment than anticipated. Only five of the thirty cases might be considered compensators, and only one subject appeared in both top and bottom quarters of achievement on tasks at all three age levels; thus compensation would seem to be for the most part and for most adolescents a temporary mechanism of adjustment to alleviate differences in physical maturation. It may be that compensation is used with expediency and forethought more often than hypothesized and is helpful in making a subsequent adjustment. Perhaps by the compensatory behavior the individual makes himself acceptable to himself during this particular period of development and, when the crisis has passed, tension is reduced and there is no further need to compensate in the same manner for the same reasons. However, this prognostication is wholly theoretical, may be invalid, or may be relevant only to periods of major physiological change such as adolescence. It is based primarily on empirical observation that rapid or retarded maturers physiologically often experience grave temporary maladjustments which time generally mollifies. The amount of compensation at stages of more stable bodily functioning should be studied for purposes of comparison and validation. However, the results do tend to indicate that achievement on one task at one particular age may be being used by an individual as a compensation for lack of achievement on another in order to make himself an acceptable self.

Finally, a study of the patterns of the five compensating cases shows that the patterns of negative relationships may be similar, but for the same or totally different reasons. Two girls, while varying in actual ratings, have precisely the same patterns and the causes for their patterns seem to be similar; they rate high on Sex Rôle (Inner) Task but low on Relations with Age-Mates and Emotional Independence (Inner). Do they do this because they know that sex is an area in which they can achieve and they perceive that this will be socially acceptable behavior for females in our culture? Conversely, the achievements of a boy and a girl compensator form identical patterns but stem from very different reasons. The girl compensates neurotically, needing intellectual achievement to justify her proud isolation from good peer relations and acceptance of her sex rôle, while the boy seems to compensate because of immature development. These examples only serve to pose the question: what are patterns of compensation in our culture? They also serve to reiterate the need for studying individual cases and the dynamics of a particular situation.

SUMMARY

(1) The results of this empirical study tend to show the hypotheses about adjustment and achievement implicit in the concept of

developmental tasks to be correct. Some are so decisive as to leave little question; others suggest the need for further research to permit more definite conclusions.

(2)   The evidence seems clear-cut that the early period of adolescence is the crucial one in which changes in levels of accomplishment of these tasks are taking place, that levels of achievement are largely determined by age thirteen on these specific tasks.

(3)   Satisfactory relations with peers appear to be very closely linked to accomplishment of other tasks. Next in importance seems to be achievement of an appropriate sex rôle, and the findings indicate greater variability in achievement of this task at various adolescent age levels than variability in other tasks.

(4)   The analyses suggest the possibility of basic factors underlying the achievement of certain "clusters" of tasks which may group or belong together because of these basic factors. Three such factors are very tentatively isolated.

(5)   Finally, the paucity of negative relationships serves to substantiate further the hypothesis of over-all adjustment and to suggest that compensation may be to a greater extent than predicted a studied, oft times commendable means of temporary adjustment.

The study has raised questions and suggested further investigations. Similar comparable verification studies to test hypotheses for achievement and adjustment at other ages would be desirable. The possibility that there may be basic factors underlying the accomplishment of certain tasks which seem to cluster together needs further study, probably by factorial analysis. Finally, a much larger group of compensators must be studied through time before any very valid conclusions regarding negative relationships may be reached. Such studies should be fruitful in further defining the concept and giving it more specific meaning and perhaps wider application.

.... 19 ....

SENESCENCE AND THE EMOTIONS:
A GENETIC THEORY

by Katharine M. Banham

A theory of emotional development that embraces the total life span is outlined by Katharine M. Banham of Duke University. Starting with undifferentiated responses and random behavior in infancy, the account progresses through increasing differentiation and integration to maturity, then a period of consolidation followed by some disintegration, and a final stage of constricted response and perseverative behavior. [From *Journal of Genetic Psychology*, 1951, *78*, 175-183. Reprinted by permission of the author and The Journal Press.]

Recent studies of the psychological aspects of aging have revealed similarities between the emotional behavior of aged persons and that of neurotic individuals irrespective of age. In a monograph entitled *Social Adjustment in Old Age,* Otto Pollak (1948) says:

There is general agreement among both laymen and students of old age that a number of traits indicating maladjustments are more frequently found among old people than among younger groups in the general population. A partial list of these traits follows:

(1) Feelings of inadequacy.
(2) Feelings of rejection, of being unwanted.
(3) Feelings of depression, of self-pity.
(4) Hypochondria, including overvaluing genuine physical symptoms.
(5) Anxiety, worry.
(6) Emotional sensitivity (irritability, querulousness, tearfulness).
(7) Boredom, restlessness.
(8) Apathy, passivity.
(9) Negativism.
(10) Guilt feelings.
(11) Narrowing of interests.
(12) Social withdrawal.
(13) Rigidity, difficulty in adjusting to new conditions.
(14) Conservatism.
(15) Loss of social inhibitions (vulgarity, untidiness, uncleanliness, over-talkativeness).
(16) Regressive tendencies, especially sex (autoerotism voyeurism).

Pollak attributes these maladjustments partly to environmental frustrations and the limited opportunities of old people for the satisfaction of thwarted needs, and partly to changes in mental and physical capacities and functions.

Most observers have agreed that there seems to be a decline in mental functioning with old age (New York, Department of Educational Nursing, 1948). Thinking becomes slower; memory patchy and incomplete; ideas become confused; motivation, ambition, and range of interests are reduced; speech is repetitive; and attention tends to wander. This wandering of attention on the part of old folk, though apparently similar to that of the inattentive child, has certain qualitative differences. The young child is usually keenly aware of a number of things, and he does not concentrate or fixate his attention on any one of them for more than a few seconds. The old person, on the other hand, is blithely indifferent to many aspects of his environment or psychological situation. His attention fixes on one aspect and then upon another, in a fashion related in his past experience by contiguous occurrence, emotional bond, or conceptual thinking. His attention is narrowed and specific rather than diffuse or dispersed. But it may be no more concentrated and actively engaged in a process of mental organization than that of a restless and inattentive child.

The older person has been observed to fatigue more easily than the younger, physically as well as mentally. Speed of movement, strength, and endurance become reduced, and motor coördination becomes increasingly difficult (Cowdry, 1942). Possibly it is by way of adapting to this reduction in vitality that he tends to economize rather than squander his resources in excess activity. He sits quietly for hours at a stretch. He "cuts corners," does things the easiest way, sometimes carelessly and untidily. In handwriting his letters are often poorly formed and illegible, as much from carelessness as poor eye-hand coordination. Sometimes he appears to take the longest route in the pursuance of a task, as when clearing a desk of accumulated papers, he puts away one at a time instead of classifying and grouping them. Such organization would require more concentration and mental effort, it would involve new learning which he finds difficult to do.

Two characteristics of behavior frequently associated with old age are those of rigidity and difficulty in adjusting to new conditions. The former is expressed in perseverative and repetitive behavior, in prejudiced attitudes, and fixation of feeling tone. A variety of techniques have been devised, and reported in the literature, for the measurement of different forms of rigidity.[1] Scatter pattern analyses of results on intelligence scales, such as the Wechsler Bellevue, have revealed slowness and difficulty in new learning of a cognitive nature by old people, i.e., those over 65 years of age. Attitude inventories have provided evidence of poor emotional adjustment on the part of elderly people, possibly due in some measure to lack of affective adaptability (Cavan, et al., 1949).

In old age it would seem that there is a decreasing ability to form new associative bonds or new Gestalt patterns in acts of cognition, including perception and thought, in motor coördination and in feelingful attitudes. The older person misperceives objects and spoken words, translating them into what is familiar to him. His thinking and speech or repetitive, determined by past associations rather than present purpose or relevance. He has an inability to reject or eliminate the inessential in thought as well as in action. The elderly person forms new concepts and abstractions with great difficulty, but he makes use of old established ones quite freely in his conversation, thus giving the impression that he is more intellectually agile than he is. He uses vague general terms, abstract symbols and clichés quite glibly, although he may have forgotten the full significance of their meaning which he had known at one time. Old people, moreover, cling to their prejudices. Their emotional attitudes, like their habits of thought, persist with but slight bearing upon changed circumstances.

Schrier and Boyd, in their studies of rigidity, using the Bender Gestalt test and an arithmetical technique, obtained results which indicated some positive relationship (significant multiple correlation .556) between different rigidity measures (Rokeach, 1949). Rokeach suggests that there may be a "general rigidity factor." Thus, a person showing rigidity in one form of behavior may be expected to show it in another. There is a growing amount of evidence in the literature that a rigid "inability to shift" may apply to goal objectives and feelingful attitudes or prejudices as well as to cognitive and motor learning (Cohen, 1949).

Angyal, Shakow, and Rosenzweig have conducted investigations, the findings from which indicate that there is some relationship between rigidity of behavior and the functional neuroses and psychoses (Angyal, 1948). Since rigidity is also one of the traits associated with old age, it may be the common factor relating behavior of mentally

---

[1] Angyal, 1948; Cattell and Tiner, 1949; Cavan, et al., 1949; Fisher, 1949; Shakow and Rosenzweig, 1937.

disordered persons with that of the aged. It may be true that, as Pollak (1948) has suggested, there are more maladjusted persons among the aged than among younger folk. But it is also possible that rigidity is merely a characteristic of the normal process of aging. According to this view, persons suffering from some forms of psychoneurosis or psychosis, who behave in a rigid manner are showing signs of senility in this respect. Neurotics are by no means all rigid in their behavior. Some are exceedingly flexible and pliable. But all old people show a certain amount of rigidity, inflexibility, and narrowing of range of response. Individuals vary as to the specific nature and degree of their inflexibility, but, by and large, as they become older they become more set in their ways, their beliefs, attitudes, and emotional moods (Cavan, *et al.*, 1949).

In order to explain the apparent diminution of affective adaptability in old age, the theory is here postulated that emotional organization undergoes a certain amount of consolidation, constriction, and disintegration in later life. When an old person is stimulated by an exciting or a terrifying event, instead of becoming hyperactive or generally inhibited and tense in his responses like a young child, he acts in a specific, repetitive fashion. The excited child's behavior may be inappropriate because of its violent or random nature, but the disturbed older person behaves inappropriately because of the limited nature of his behavior and its unchangeability.

The young child, when recovering from the intense excitement or shock prompted by a startling event, such as a thunderstorm, has at his disposal a considerable amount of mobilized energy, which he may expend in diversified play or constructive pursuits. The old person, on the contrary, may be exhausted by the emotional shock, less able to turn to other things, and he may remain anxious or depressed for a long time. The emotions of old people are characterized by paucity rather than over-abundance of affective energy. The form of their behavior tends to narrow, like a stream in drought, into one channel rather than brim over into general hyperactivity or tension.

A commonly accepted theory of explanation of neurotic behavior, among psychiatrists and psychologists, is that it is regressive in nature. It represents either a fixation at, or return to more childish and primitive ways of behaving in a difficult and emotionally disturbing situation. Neurotic adults are considered to be manifesting emotional immaturity. The writer considers that this explanation may be adequate for some cases, particularly overexcitable and anxious types. But certain obsessive and compulsive neurotics exhibit behavior more characteristic of elderly persons than of young children. They are rigid and inflexible in their behavior. They might be described as prematurely sensile in their reactions to distressing situations, rather than emotionally immature.

It is a tenable hypothesis, then, in the absence of adequate proof, that older persons are no more apt to be neurotic than younger ones. The data so far accumulated, which indicates that more old people show signs of maladjustment than younger groups, may be accounted for largely by the fact that they have more frustrations to face both in social restrictions and their own personal limitations. The evidences of rigidity in the behavior of older people may be normal characteristics of advancing age, and not necessarily signs of neurotic personality.

Indeed, the great majority of elderly people are happily adjusted to their social environment and personal limitations. Partly on account of the wisdom of experience, habits based on successful solution of difficulties in the past, and partly on account of reduced emotional excitability, the older person is much less disturbed by discomfort, frustrations, and inconveniences than young children. He knows more, is better prepared to meet an emergency, and so is less easily frightened. His tendency to "single track" thinking and action makes him less likely to experience the anxiety that accompanies conflicting impulses. In some ways his reduced affective sensitivity and changeability may actually be helpful factors in adjustment, rather than drawbacks. Unkind treatment by others, economic privations, and diminished physical and mental capacities are often accepted with resignation, and without the emotional turmoil that such conditions would provoke in younger people.

Accepting the hypothesis that repetitiveness in behavior and lack of affective adaptability, two of the manifestations of rigidity, are normal attributes of aging, it follows that younger people who exhibit these traits are showing signs of senility rather than immaturity. This holds for "normal" individuals restricted in their outlook on life as well as for mentally disordered persons. Feebleminded persons, also, regardless of age, are apt to be rigid in their performance and inflexible in their emotional attachments (Kounin, 1941). In these respects they may be considered to be more senile than child-like in behavior.

Just as there appears to be a process of maturation of behavior in early infancy (Gesell and Thompson, 1934), with a neurological counterpart in myelination of axon sheaths, so also there seems to be

TABLE 1

SCHEMATIC PRESENTATION OF A GENETIC THEORY OF LIFE-SPAN EMOTIONAL CHANGES

Infancy		Maturity		Old Age
Undifferentiated response. Random behavior.	Processes of differentiation and integration.	Mature emotional sensitivity and control. Maximum differentiation of response and aesthetic feeling.	Processes of consolidation and some disintegration.	Constricted response. Perseverative behavior.

Excitement

Distress-Disgust
- Anxiety
- Fear
- Shame
- Anger
- Jealousy
- Disappointment
- Restless uneasiness

Delight
- Joy
- Elation
- Hopeful anticipation
- Affection
- Sex love

Old Age:
- Grief
- Worry
- Self-pity
- Guilt feelings
- Querulousness-Depression
- Irritability
- Boredom

- Mystical ecstasy
- Possessive satisfaction-Content
- Benevolence
- Gustatory sensuousness

Apathy and Passivity

a process of psychobiological senescence in the later years of life (Hall, 1922). This maturation and senescence shows in affective behavior as well as in motor coördination and processes of thought. The behavior of an infant in an emotionally disturbing situation is general and random in nature. It is undifferentiated and undiscriminating (Bridges, 1930, 1931, 1932). In terms of Gestalt psychology, the part is confused with the whole. The child reacts vaguely to the total situation. Gradually during the first few months of life emotional reactions become more differentiated and specific in nature, and related to certain definite events, such as threatening dangers, interfering restrictions, or refreshing movement. Thus the emotions of fear, anger, and joy evolve. Actual experiences in life determine largely the pattern of emotions and the form of their expression which each individual develops (Table 1).

During the years of maturity emotional behavior is at its most adaptive level. Certain situations, for example, such as the loss of a pocket book or an invitation to a banquet, are dealt with appropriately and in a variety of different ways by the same individual on different occasions. Some emotion may be expressed in visceral and behavioral response, but not too much, and none is wasted in useless movement or tension as in the case of young children and emotionally immature persons. There is maximum sensitivity to environmental conditions and refinement of aesthetic appreciation in emotional maturity. Behavior responses are most varied, but purposefully and adaptively related to the stimulating event, to individual and social needs.

The aged person, when emotionally stimulated, is generally less responsive than a younger one. He shows less enthusiastic zest and less emotional concern in his later years. His responses to a disturbing situation are specific, like those of any mature adult, but they are less varied and sometimes less appropriate than those of a younger person. The older person tends to react to the part rather than the whole situation. When emotional maladjustment occurs in old age, the writer suggests, it may be an outcome of too great specificity and constriction, a paucity of affective energy and lack of flexibility in behavior. Emotional responses of old people are inadequate because they are not comprehensive and varied enough to deal with a new situation. There is insufficient drive or desire to experiment. The maladjusted child's behavior, on the other hand, is inappropriate because of its all-or-none nature, its lack of discrimination, over-exuberance or active general resistance.

As many observers have already pointed out, there are regressive tendencies in older people, and on occasion their behavior may show signs of emotional immaturity. But all neurotic maladjustments whether in old or young people cannot be accounted for in this way. Some so-called emotionally immature adolescents manifest in their behavior an inflexible specificity, characteristic of senescence. Elderly people, on the other hand, at times regress to child-like negativistic or excited behavior. They show explosive temper, become immobile with fear, or hyper-active and talkative with excitement. For the most part, however, their emotions are attenuated, and are stimulated only through a few ideational associative patterns.

The foregoing theory may be applied in consideration of the problem presented by the psychoses. It may, for example, offer a psychological explanation of what occurs in the mental functioning of a patient who improves in adjustment after shock treatment or after a pre-frontal lobotomy operation. It is suggested that the effect of a shock, whether electric, insulin, heat or other form, is to reactivate many old pattern reactions that have fallen into disuse during the psychotic periods. In this way, a greater variety of responses becomes available for use by the patient in dealing with current situations. Among these reactivated patterns may be the grosser and less differentiated emotional responses of early childhood that serve to further mobilize mental energy. Shock may also broaden the perceptions, thus making the individual more keenly aware of the total external and internal situation, and this in turn helps him to act appropriately and to deal more adequately with life's daily problems.

Psychotic patients who show improvement in their social relations and emotional expression after pre-frontal lobotomy may do so for a different reason from that explaining general improvement after shock. It is suggested that during the psychosis the person's emotional responses have become narrowly specific and stereotyped, associatively tied to one ideational system. When certain nerve connections are cut between the cerebrum and thalamus which controls bodily response in emotion, the stereotyped emotional patterns are broken up and the individual is freer to act in a more general way. While affective responses were being channeled into the patient's psychotic symptoms, other emotional responses were inhibited or dormant. The release of inhibited responses, and reactivation of dormant ones, after operation frees the patient's attention to perceive more of his environment and allows him to vary his behavior. He has still, however, to build up new sentiments and affective patterns to deal with emergencies as they arise.

If there is any truth in the foregoing theory that premature senile rigidity and inflexibility are dynamic factors in certain psycho-neuroses and psychoses, checks could be made by means of treatment calculated to increase flexibility of behavior, motivation and versatility of response, applied to patients in different age groups. Physical treatments which would improve blood circulation in the brain and other organs, physiotherapy, and endocrine therapy to regulate metabolism, might all have some effect in reducing rigidity. Psychological treatment should also be even more effective, in the form of perceptual and motor stimulation, through color, sound, rhythmic movement, manual and creative activities. If these were accompanied by play or analytic therapy to release the tied and channeled emotion, old stereotypes might be broken down, and more integrated and appropriate behavior developed. Improvement, however, would not be anticipated in the case of very deteriorated psychotics, feeble-minded, and aged and demented patients.

SUMMARY

The relationship of certain characteristics of the behavior of elderly persons and of maladjusted persons has been briefly discussed. The theory has been presented that a tendency to rigidity, i.e., to perseveration and inflexibility, is part of the normal process of aging. The rigidity is manifest in affective behavior as well as motor performance and thought. It may appear in extreme form or prematurely early in cases of mental disorder and maladjustment. A genetic theory of emotional changes that take place during the life span of an individual has been outline. These changes include increasing differentiation and integration of affective response from infancy to maturity, and reduction in intensity, variety and flexibility of response towards old age. Suggestions for a psychological explanation of improvement in emotional adjustment following shock and lobotomy treatment of psychotic patients, has been given, using as a basis the genetic theory and its implications. A schematic diagram, representing the genetic theory of life-span emotional changes, is given in Table 1.

Part Three

....

THE ADOLESCENT
AND HIS PEERS

CHAPTER EIGHT

Social Role

20

A NOTE ON SEX DIFFERENCES IN THE DEVELOPMENT OF MASCULINE AND FEMININE IDENTIFICATION

by David B. Lynn

How do American boys and girls develop their masculine and feminine identification? In this selection David B. Lynn of the University of Colorado differentiates the concept of identification by introducing the concepts of sex-role preference, sex-role adoption, and sex-role identification. Also proposed are several hypotheses generally supported by research findings which may help clarify "previously confusing and seemingly contradictory data." [From *Psychological Review*, 1959, *66*, 126-135. Reprinted by permission of the author and the American Psychological Association.]

The purpose of this note is to contribute to the theoretical formulation of sex differences in the development of masculine and feminine identification, and to review research findings relevant to this formulation. The concept of identification has held a prominent position not only in psychoanalysis, but also in other psychological theories (Cava and Raush, 1952; Fenichel, 1945; Lazowick, 1955; Martin, 1954; Mowrer, 1953; Sanford, 1955; Stoke, 1950; Tiller, 1958; Tolman, 1943). Sanford said of the term "identification":

A term that can be employed in so many different ways and that, as Tolman says, has been accepted by most psychologists and sociologists, could hardly mean anything very precise. It might be proposed, quite seriously, that we give up the term "identification" altogether. . . . We must in any case specify "what kind" [of identification] . . . (Sanford, 1955, p. 107).

In this paper an attempt is made to comply with Sanford's latter suggestion rather than throw out the term "identification" altogether. Such widespread use of the term suggests, if nothing more, its potential utility with adequate clarification.

The present formulation differs from the classical Freudian position which postulates that girls experience greater difficulty than boys in developing appropriate sexual identification because of their envy of the genital organ possessed by little boys. It also differs from the Freudian position that, because the girl has the same-sex parent (the mother) as her first love-object, she must therefore overcome a homosexual hurdle in developing same-sex identification (Fenichel, 1945). The position taken in this paper is in agreement with those who hold that, on the contrary, the early closeness of the girl to the same-sex parent (the mother) gives her an initial advantage in progressing toward appropriate identification (Brown, 1956; Mowrer, 1953). This initial advantage is thought to be counterbalanced, to a large extent, by later learning experiences in this masculine-oriented culture.

Before developing this formulation further, let us differentiate the concept of identification from other similar concepts. Brown (1956) clarified the concept of sex-role identification considerably by contrasting it to *sex-role preference*. Sex-role preference refers to the desire to adopt the behavior associated with one sex or the other, or the perception of such behavior as preferable or more desirable. This concept has been measured by simply asking Ss whether they have ever wished to be of the opposite sex (Fortune survey, 1946; Gallup, 1955; Terman, 1938). It has also been measured by having children state their preference for objects, or pictures of objects, characteristic of one sex or the other (Brown, 1956, 1957; Rabban, 1950). Let us add the concept of *sex-role adoption*. This concept refers to the actual adoption of behavior characteristic of one sex or the other, not simply the desire to adopt such behavior. Women, for example, sometimes wear clothes usually associated with males, e.g., trousers. Men sometimes become beauty operators, a vocation usually associated with women. This concept refers to one's overt behavior, not to one's sex-role preference. An individual may, for example, *adopt* behavior characteristic of his own sex because it is expedient to do so, not because he *prefers* doing so. Sex-role preference is, to this extent, irrelevant to this particular concept. The sex role one actually incorporates, i.e., the role one identifies with, may, in some cases, also be irrelevant to sex-role adoption.

Sex-role identification is reserved to refer to the actual incorporation of the role of a given sex, and to the unconscious reactions characteristic of that role. Thus, a person may be identified with the opposite sex, but for expediency adopt much of the behavior characteristic of his own sex. He may even prefer the role of his own sex, although identified with the opposite-sex role. One would expect such a person, being identified with the opposite sex, to have many unconscious reactions characteristic of the opposite-sex role despite his adopting much of the behavior characteristic of the same-sex role. On the other hand, the woman who, on appropriate occasions, adopts aspects characteristic of the opposite-sex role, such as wearing trousers or wearing short hair, is certainly not necessarily identified with the male role. Thus, *sex-role adoption* refers to overt behavior characteristic of a given sex, and *sex-role identification* refers to a more basic process characteristic of a given sex. Sex-role identification is much more difficult to measure that sex-role preference or adoption. Attempts have been made to measure what is here referred to as sex-role identification through projective techniques, such as human figure drawings (Brown and Tolor, 1957; Jolles, 1952; Morris, 1955; Tiller, 1958; Tolor, 1955; Weider and Noller: 1950, 1953), and through measuring the similarity between responses of parents and their children (Gray and Klaus, 1956; Lazowick, 1955).

It is probably true that most individuals may be said to prefer, adopt, and identify with their own sex role. Most psychologists associate psychological disturbances with a lack of harmony among aspects of an individual's sex role. With the present conceptual scheme a variety of combinations are theoretically possible, e.g., a person might identify with and adopt the pattern of his own sex, but still prefer the opposite-sex role. On the other hand, a person might identify with the opposite-sex role, adopt the behavior of his own sex, and also consciously prefer the same-sex role, etc. These sex-role definitions should become better clarified in the body of the paper.

THEORETICAL FORMULATION

Before stating specific hypotheses let us briefly formulate the position taken in this paper concerning the development of masculine and feminine identification. The developmental processes, as presented here, are not considered inevitable nor universal. If these processes are appropriately described for the U. S. culture of today, they may not fit a significantly altered U. S. culture of the future. Moreover, if these processes are appropriately described for the U. S. culture, they may, nevertheless, be inappropriate to many other cultures. Cross-cultural studies should help verify and amplify the hypotheses presented in this paper.

First, it is assumed that the process of identification follows the laws of learning. Next, it is postulated that, for both male and female infants, learning to identify with the mother (or the person playing the mother-role) is among the earliest learning experiences. In this formulation, it is considered one of the major sex differences in the development of identification that the boy must shift from his initial identification with the mother to identification with the masculine role, whereas the girl need make no such shift.

The shift from mother to masculine identification is begun when the boy discovers that he somehow does not belong in the same sex-category as the mother, but rather as the father; that he is no longer almost completely in a woman's world characterized by the maternal care received during infancy, but is now increasingly in a man's world. It is true that in early childhood, as well as in infancy, the child's life is mainly peopled with women rather than men, but the ideology of our culture in general, and the demands made on the little boy in particular, are masculine in nature. Despite the shortage of male models, a somewhat stereotyped and conventional masculine role is nonetheless rather clearly spelled out for him. A study by Sheriffs and Jarrett (1953) indicated that men and women share the same stereotypes about the two sexes. They found that ". . . virtually no behavior or quality escapes inclusion in either a male or female 'stereotype,' and that these stereotypes are substantially the same whether held by men or women" (Sheriffs and Jarrett, 1953, p. 161).

If the boy behaves like a "little man," say by not crying when hurt, this "brave" behavior is reinforced. Perhaps he is rewarded by being called "Mommy's nice little man." If, on the other hand, he does not behave in a masculine-stereotyped fashion, say he cries when hurt, this behavior may be negatively reinforced, e.g., by being called a sissy. If he behaves in a feminine-stereotyped fashion, say by playing with dolls beyond a certain age, he may be similarly ridiculed. Moreover, he is rewarded simply for having been born masculine through countless privileges accorded males but not females. The boy learns to prefer the masculine role to the feminine one, to adopt the masculine role, and, in time, to identify with it. Sex-role identification, being a more deeply rooted process than either sex-role preference or sex-role adoption, is consequently more slowly changed. However, through the reinforcement of the culture's highly developed system of rewards and punishment, the boy's early learned identification with the mother eventually weakens and becomes more or less replaced by the later learned identification with a culturally defined, somewhat stereotyped masculine role.

The development of the appropriate sex-role identification for the girl is considered, in many ways, the converse of that for the boy. When the girl leaves infancy she goes from a woman's world of mother care to a man's world. Being feminine, she thus moves from a same-sex- to an opposite-sex-oriented world, whereas the boy, conversely, moves from an opposite-sex- to a same-sex-oriented world. Unlike the situation for the boy, whose sex role is well spelled out for him, the girl, upon leaving infancy, does not receive adequate reinforcement through distinct rewards for adopting the feminine role, and definite punishment for adopting the masculine one. On the contrary, she is, in a sense, punished simply for being born female, whereas the boy is rewarded simply for being born male. Findings in *Patterns of Child Rearing,* by Sears *et al.* (1957), support the suggestion that the girl is, in a way, punished for being female. The girls were found to be treated less permissively than boys and more conformity was demanded of them. Hubert and Britton (1957) also found mothers of boys to be less strict with them, expect less understanding of rules, and to allow more activity. The girl quickly learns to prefer the masculine role since our culture, despite definite changes, is still masculine-centered and masculine-oriented, and offers the male many privileges and much prestige not accorded the female. As Brown pointed out,

The superior position and privileged status of the male permeates nearly every aspect, minor and major, of our social life. The gadgets and prizes in boxes of breakfast cereal, for example, commonly have a strong masculine rather than feminine appeal. And the most basic social institutions perpetuate this pattern of masculine aggrandizement. Thus, the Judeo-Christian faiths involve worshiping God, a "Father," rather than a "Mother," and Christ, a "Son," rather than a "Daughter" (Brown, 1958, p. 235).

Smith (1939) found results to suggest that children, as they grow older, increasingly learn to give males prestige. Smith asked children from eight to 15 to vote on whether boys or girls had desirable and undesirable traits. He found: (a) with increase in age, boys have a progressively poorer relative opinion of girls, and girls have a progressively better relative opinion of boys; (*b*) with increase in age, boys have a progressively better opinion of themselves, and girls have a progressively poorer opinion of themselves. Kitay (1940) found that women share with men the prejudices prevailing in our culture against their own sex.

Not only does the girl learn to prefer the masculine role because of its many advantages, but she, unlike the boy, is not given the degree of negative reinforcement for adopting certain aspects of the opposite-sex role. Although restricted in many ways more than boys, girls are nevertheless allowed more freedom than boys in opposite-sex role adoption. For a girl to be a tomboy does not involve the censure that results when a boy is a sissy. Girls may wear masculine clothing (shirts, trousers), but boys may not wear feminine clothing (skirts, dresses). Girls may play with toys typically associated with boys (cars, trucks, erector sets, guns), but boys are discouraged from playing with feminine toys (dolls, tea sets).

Data from two national sample interview studies of adolescents, reported by Douvan (1957a, 1957b), suggest that the role for the adolescent girl is very poorly defined by the culture. Since she is typically not yet married, the adolescent girl cannot play her primary role of wife and mother. Furthermore, the culture discourages her from taking action to realize this primary role. The female is not supposed to take the major initiative in choosing a mate. She must, to a large extent, be chosen as a mate rather than actively choosing. Moreover, because her primary goal is marriage and family, the girl's vocational plans do not imply the same career commitment that the boy's vocational plans imply for him. Douvan concludes that "girls . . . can do little about the central aspect of feminine identity before marriage" (1957b, p. 190).

The girl, however, has the same-sex parental model for identification (the mother) with her more than the boy has the same-sex parental model (the father) with him. Both boys and girls usually spend more time with their mothers than with their fathers. They see the mother engaging in many activities, and under many circumstances in which they do not see the father. There is much incidental learning which takes place from such contact with the mother. Although both boys and girls doubtless learn a great deal in this incidental fashion, it is only the girls, not the boys, who can, later on at the appropriate time, apply such latent learning in a direct fashion in their lives. The boys, being separated more from their fathers than girls from their mothers, tend to identify with the stereotype of the masculine role which the culture in general, not simply the father in particular, spells out for them. The girl, on the other hand, tends to identify with aspects of her own mother's role specifically.

However, the girl is still affected by many cultural pressures despite the fact that she need not shift identification, and despite the physical presence of the mother during her development. In this formulation it is predicted that the prestige and privileges afforded males but not females, and the lack of punishment for adopting aspects of the masculine role, have a slow, corrosive, weakening effect on the girl's feminine identification. Conversely, the prestige and privileges accorded the male, the rewards offered for adopting the masculine role, and the punishment for not doing so, are predicted to have a strengthening effect on the boy's masculine identification.

HYPOTHESES

The following hypotheses emerge from this formulation:

1. The young boy's same-sex identification is at first not very firm because of the shift from mother to masculine identification. On the other hand, the young girl, because she need make no such shift in identification, is relatively firm in her initial feminine identification. However, the culture reinforces the boy in developing masculine identification much more adequately than it does the girl in developing feminine identification. *Consequently, with increasing age, males become relatively more firmly identified with the masculine role and females relatively less firmly identified with the feminine role.*

2. The culture offers higher prestige and more advantages to the male than to the female. *Consequently, a larger proportion of females than males will show preference for the role of the opposite sex.*

3. Not only is the male role accorded more prestige than the female role, but boys are more likely to be punished than girls for adopting aspects of the opposite-sex role. *Therefore, a higher proportion of females than males adopt aspects of the role of the opposite sex.*

4. The girl has the same-sex parent (the mother) with her more than the boy has the same-sex parent (the father) with him as a model for identification. However, a stereotyped sort of masculine role is spelled out rather clearly for the boys by the culture. *Consequently, males tend to identify with a cultural stereotype of the masculine role, whereas females tend to identify with aspects of their own mothers' role specifically.*

TEST OF HYPOTHESES

Let us now see how consistently these hypotheses fit previous findings and whether this formulation helps clarify seeming contradictions.

If Hypothesis 1 is valid, that with increasing age, boys become relatively more firmly identified with the masculine role and girls relatively less firmly identified with the feminine role, and assuming that figure drawings constitute an adequate measure of identification, then this hypothesized trend should be reflected in the sex of the figure drawn first. The data do seem, in fact, to support this hypothesis. Brown and Tolor (1957) reviewed a number of studies on human figure drawings. The studies on figure drawings with children (Jolles, 1952; Morris, 1955; Tolor and Tolor, 1955; Weider and Noller: 1950, 1953) show that, with younger children, a higher proportion of girls than boys drew the same-sex figure first, and with older children this trend is reversed, and a larger proportion of boys than girls drew the same-sex figure first. A study by Jolles (1952), using a wide age range, might be specifically cited in this regard. Jolles found that with children between five and 12, a significantly higher proportion of younger boys drew the opposite-sex figure first than did older boys. A significantly higher proportion of 11- and 12-year-old girls drew the opposite-sex figure first than did boys of the same age.

Lynn, D. B., and Sawrey, W. L., in an unpublished study in which eight- and nine-year-old Norwegian children were asked to draw a family (in contrast to drawing a person), found that a higher proportion of girls than boys drew the same-sex parent figure first, largest, and in most detail.

Despite the fact that with younger children a higher proportion of girls than boys drew the same-sex figure first, studies with adults consistently show a higher proportion of men than women drawing the same-sex figure first. Brown and Tolor (1957) combined findings from several studies of figure drawings with College Ss and found that 91% of the men drew the male figure first while only 67% of the women drew the female figure first.

Thus, the findings on figure drawings support the hypothesis that with increasing age males become more firmly same-sex identified and females relatively less firmly same-sex identified. However, Brown and Tolor (1957) found evidence leading them to suggest that human figure drawings may be an inadequate test of identification. Confidence in the validity of this hypothesis must await substantiation through further research findings.

In this formulation it is considered one thing to show a sex-role preference, and quite another to form a sex-role identification. Hypothesis 2 predicts that, because of higher prestige and greater privileges accorded the masculine role, a higher proportion of females than males will show opposite-sex-role preference. In this connection Rabban (1950) asked 300 children between 30 months and eight years of age to choose the toys they liked best from a number of toys. Some of the toys were judged to be typically associated with boys and others with girls. All of the Ss were also asked to pick a doll which resembled them most and to indicate the sex of the doll. In addition, they were asked whether they would like to be a "mama" or "daddy" when they grow up. The results showed no significant differences between three-year-old children, but otherwise boys showed significantly more masculine preferences than girls feminine preferences.

Brown (1957) administered the It Scale for Children to 303 boys and 310 girls between the ages of approximately $5\frac{1}{2}$ and $11\frac{1}{2}$. The It Scale is composed of pictures of various objects and figures typical of and associated with the role of one sex in contrast to the other. A card with a child-figure drawing on it, referred to as "It," is used by having each S make choices for It. Brown found that boys showed a much stronger preference for the masculine role than girls for the feminine role, particularly in all grades below the fifth. He found that girls at the kindergarten level showed a preference pattern characterized by relatively equal preference for masculine and feminine elements, and girls from the first grade through the fourth grade showed a stronger preference for the masculine role than for the feminine role. In contrast to girls in all earlier grade levels, girls in the fifth grade showed a predominant preference for the feminine role.

The Lynn Structured Doll Play Test (Lynn, 1955, 1957a, 1957b; Lynn and Lynn, in press; Lynn and Sawrey, in press; Tiller, 1958) was used in the study of 80 eight- and nine-year-old Norwegian children mentioned above in connection with an unpublished study by Lynn and Sawrey. The Structured Doll Play Test (SDP) is a projective test in which the S is presented with dolls representing family and peer group figures in a series of typical family and peer group situations. The S resolves these situations through doll play. One of the SDP situations required the S to choose either the boy or girl doll as the one for the ego-doll to play with. The results showed a significantly higher proportion of girls choosing the boy doll (the opposite-sex child doll) than the girl doll (the same-sex child doll). Thus, despite the fact that these same Norwegian girls had drawn the same-sex parent figure first, largest, and in most detail, they nevertheless showed a preference for the opposite-sex child doll.

These results are consistent with studies of sex-role preference in adults in which men and women were asked whether they had ever wished to belong to the opposite sex. These studies show that below 5% of adult males as contrasted to as high as 31% of adult females recall consciously having been aware of the desire to be of the opposite sex (Fortune survey, 1946; Gallup, 1955; Terman, 1938).

Thus, the research findings in general support the hypothesis that more females prefer the masculine sex role than males the feminine role.

Hypothesis 3 predicts that more females not only prefer, but also adopt the masculine role than males do the feminine role. Emmerich (in press) used a structured doll play interview with 31 Ss between $3\frac{1}{2}$ and 5 years of age. Emmerich measured the degree of similarity between the S's conception of his parent's nurturance-control attitude and the S's own nurturance-control attitude. The S's parent's nurturance-control attitude was indicated by the doll play fantasy of the parent doll's actions toward a child doll. The S's own nurturance-control attitude was indicated by the fantasy of the child doll's actions toward a baby doll. The degree of similarity between the parent's and S's attitude was the difference between the parent doll's and the child doll's nurturance-control scores. In the present conceptual framework this is considered a measure of fantasied sex-role adoption. Emmerich found that only the boys but not the girls showed a significant tendency to select the same-sex parent as a model more than the opposite-sex parent. Thus, the boys adopted (in fantasy) the father role more closely than they did the mother role. In this way the hypothesis tended to be supported, at least for young children.

As was pointed out above, the mother is typically with the children more than the father is, thus making herself available as a model for identification more frequently than the father. Largely for this reason, Hypothesis 4 predicts that males tend to identify with a cultural stereotype of the masculine role whereas females tend to identify with aspects of their own mothers' role specifically. Gray and Klaus (1956) did a study relevant to this hypothesis, using responses to a sentence completion test and to the Allport-Vernon-Lindzey Study of Values filled out by 34 female and 28 male college students, their parents, and by the students as they believed their mothers and fathers would respond. They found much more similarity between the women and their mothers than between the men and their fathers, both as tested and as perceived.

Hypothesis 4 was also supported in a study by Lazowick (1955). The Ss in this study were 30 college students. These Ss and their mothers and fathers were required to rate concepts, e.g., "myself," "father," "mother," etc. The degree of similarity between "meanings" of each concept as rated by Ss and their parents was then determined. It was found that the similarity between fathers and their own children was not significantly greater than between fathers and children randomly matched. On the other hand, the similarity between mothers and their own children was greater than between mothers and children randomly matched.

Thus, despite the fact that data on figure drawings suggest that more men are same-sex identified than women, these results suggest that women are more closely identified with aspects of the role of their own same-sex parent (mother) specifically than men are with their own same-sex parent (father).

What are some of the ways this theoretical formulation may clarify seemingly contradictory or confusing findings? This paper reviewed studies showing that a higher proportion of girls than boys chose objects and pictures of objects characteristically considered masculine (Brown, 1956, 1957; Rabban, 1950); and yet, in the study by Lynn and Sawrey, a higher proportion of eight-year-old girls than boys drew the same-sex parent figure first, largest, and in most detail. These findings are very confusing if the term "identification" is used in connection with both the operations "sex-role object choice" and "parent drawings." The differentiation suggested by Brown (1956), and also used in this formulation, between sex-role preference and sex-role identification may eliminate the contradiction in these results. The studies of choice of masculine and feminine objects are considered, in this formulation, studies of *sex-role preference;* whereas the studies of figure drawings are considered studies of *sex-role identification.*

The results in which a higher proportion of adult males than females drew the same-sex figure first are in seeming contradiction with data reviewed showing a closer similarity between responses of women and their mothers' responses, than of men and their fathers' responses (Gray and Klaus, 1956). The contradiction is removed by the hypothesis that the male identifies with a stereotype of the masculine role, and the female with her mother's role specifically.

The data showing that females responded with more similarity to their own mothers' responses than males to their fathers' responses (Gray and Klaus, 1956) may also seem to contradict the data in the study by Emmerich (in press) in which young boys, but not girls, showed a significant tendency to select the same-sex parent as a model more than the opposite-sex parent. There is, however, a great deal of difference between the operations involved in these two studies, viz. in the S's *fantasy* of the father doll's actions (Emmerich, in press), and the *actual* responses of real fathers to the materials used in the study by Gray and Klaus (1956). In the framework of the present formulation the boys in the doll play study *adopted,* in fantasy, the father role significantly more closely than they did the mother role; whereas in the study by Gray and Klaus the adult males did not *identify* as closely with their own fathers' role as the women with their own mothers' role.

SUMMARY

The purpose of this note is to contribute to the theoretical formulation of sex differences in the development of masculine and feminine identification, and review research findings relevant to this formulation.

There was a differentiation made among the concepts of *sex-role preference, sex-role adoption,* and *sex-role identification.*

The process of identification was assumed to follow the laws of learning. Both male and female infants were hypothesized to learn to identify with the mother. Boys, but not girls, must shift from this initial identification with the mother to masculine identification. Despite the fact that the girl need not shift her identification, and despite the physical presence of the mother during her development, the girl is still affected by many cultural pressures. The prestige and privileges offered males but not females, and the lack of punishment for adopting aspects of the masculine role, are predicted to have a slow, corrosive, weakening effect on the girl's feminine identification. Conversely, the prestige and privileges accorded the male, the culture's systematic rewards for adopting the masculine role, and punishment for not doing so, strengthen the boy's masculine identification.

The following hypotheses emerged:

1. With increasing age, males become relatively more firmly identified with the masculine role, and females relatively less firmly identified with the feminine role.

2. A larger proportion of females than males will show preference for the role of the opposite sex.

3. A higher proportion of females than males adopt aspects of the role of the opposite sex.

4. Males tend to identify with a cultural stereotype of the masculine role, whereas females tend to identify with aspects of their own mothers' role specifically.

These hypotheses were generally supported by the research findings which were reviewed. This formulation may help clarify previously confusing and seemingly contradictory data.

·· **21** ··································

CULTURAL CONTRADICTIONS AND SEX ROLES:

A REPEAT STUDY

by Paul Wallin

Some college women are expected to fill mutually exclusive roles—for example, the feminine role of homemaker and the modern role of career girl. In some cases the conflicting expectations come from the family and friends, causing uncertainty, insecurity, and conflict. In the following article Paul Wallin of Stanford University repeats an earlier study assessing the incompatible sex roles of women college students. [From *American Sociological Review*, 1950, *15*, 288-293. Reprinted by permission of the author and the American Sociological Society.]

This article reports an approximate replication of a study by Komarovsky (1946) in 1942-43 on incompatible sex roles in the social environment of the college girl. The article describes Komarovsky's investigation and the repeat study and then compares them in terms of (*a*) their quantitative findings and (*b*) their interpretations of the findings.

KOMAROVSKY'S STUDY

Komarovsky concluded from her data that college women are exposed to two contradictory roles. These are characterized by her as the "feminine" and the "modern" roles. In describing the former, she states that, "While there are a number of permissive variants of the feminine role for women of college age ('the good sport,' 'the glamour girl,' 'the young lady,' 'the domestic home girl,' etc.), they have a common core of attributes defining the proper attitudes to men, family, work, love, etc., and a set of personality traits often described with reference to the male sex role as 'not as dominant, or aggressive as men,' or 'more emotional, sympathetic'" (pp. 184-185). The modern role, on the other hand, "partly obliterates the differentiation in sex. It demands of the woman much the same virtues, patterns of behavior, and attitudes that it does of the men of a corresponding age" (p. 185). During the college years the conflict between the feminine and modern roles "apparently centers about academic work, social life, vocational plans, excellence in specific fields of endeavor, and a number of personality traits" (p. 185).

Komarovsky studied the nature and incidence of some components of these roles in 153 women seniors. (The socio-economic characteristics of the group are not reported.) Half the women were members of an undergraduate family course who wrote autobiographical papers on the topic. The other were all the students of a class in social psychology at the same eastern institution. Each of these women was interviewed for approximately an hour. The autobiographical and interview documents ranged from five to thirty typewritten pages. The general conclusion derived from the materials has already been presented; the more specific findings are discussed below following the description of the repeat study.

THE REPEAT STUDY

A replication of Komarovsky's investigation seemed worthwhile for two reasons: (1) because the original sample consisted of seniors in a single institution who were taking a course in the family or social psychology, there was some question as to whether the findings were more generally applicable, and (2) since the subjects of Komarovsky's research did not participate anonymously, what they wrote or said conceivably might have been influenced by their conception of what would present them in the most favorable light to the investigator or the interviewer.

The repeat study was carried out in 1949 in a western coeducational university where the ratio of men to women is about 3 to 1.

A ten per cent random sample of unmarried, undergraduate female students was drawn from the campus directory. The 163 women so selected were asked to fill out a brief anonymous questionnaire and were given a short interview. The questionnaires were distributed—and the interviews conducted—by 54 members (33 men, 21 women) of a family class as part of the course work. Each person was assigned three subjects in such a way as to preclude his obtaining subjects known to him. The large majority of the subjects lived on or close to the campus and there was little difficulty in contacting them. Most of them were seen at their place of residence.

The questionnaire was two sides of a page in length. It was kept to a minimum size to encourage cooperation. It contained a number of questions about background characteristics as well as those concerned with the subjects' roles. The anonymity of the questionnaire was emphasized by the fact that subjects were told that on completing it, they were to seal it in an envelope to be returned to the writer.

The interviews were not meant to be used as a source of data because the interviewers were untrained. However, since reports of the interviews provided some suggestive ideas for interpreting the questionnaire data a few words about the interview are in order.

The student interviewers were given a few general questions to put to the subjects and were requested to try to obtain a verbatim record of the answers. The questions were: (1) What do you consider appropriate behavior in your social relations with men? (2) What is your conception of the relative importance of academic and social activities? (3) What is your attitude toward marriage and a career? Each question was followed by an inquiry as to what was regarded as the source of the subject's ideas, conceptions or attitudes.

No precise check could be made of the representativeness of the sample of 163 women. Only one refused to cooperate and substitutions had to be made for a few who for various reasons could not be reached. There was a 4 per cent overrepresentation of lower-division students and a corresponding underrepresentation of upper-division women, but since school year was found to have no relation to the dependent factors of the study, this aspect of the sampling did not affect the findings.

About a third of the subjects were majoring—or intending to

major—in one of the social sciences, the remainder being distributed in the humanities (29 per cent), education (20 per cent), physical sciences (12 per cent), and in other fields (6 per cent). All but a negligible percentage were between 18 and 21 years of age, the majority being 19 or 20. Their parents were predominantly native born (93 per cent), Protestant (70 per cent), and of college level (both parents with one or more years of college, 70 per cent). Their fathers were largely in the professions, in managerial and executive positions, or had their own business.

FINDINGS OF THE TWO STUDIES

Komarovsky does not report either the specific directions given the subjects who wrote accounts of their conflicts in roles or the questions asked those who were interviewed. In trying to duplicate her study with questionnaire data the writer attempted to deduce from the article the particular topics to which the subjects addressed themselves and to formulate some questions bearing on these topics.

The first set of items used for this purpose in the repeat study focused on the frequency with which women pretended inferiority to men. Such pretense involves a clash of the modern and feminine roles described by Komarovsky. In the modern role the college woman is defined as the equal of the male and is expected to strive for scholastic honors and for leadership in many student activities. But insofar as in dating and other paired relationships with men the college woman is required to adopt the inferiority and subordinacy of the more traditional feminine role, she is exposed to contradictory expectations. The responses to the questions, reproduced in Table 1, show that many college women, although conceiving of themselves as the equals of their male companions, feel called upon to pretend inferiority to them.

The percentages in Table 1 can be compared with one of the quantitative findings of Komarovsky's research. Forty per cent of her subjects indicated that they "have occasionally 'played dumb' on dates, that is, concealed some academic honor, pretended ignorance of some subject, or allowed the man the last word in an intellectual discussion" (p. 187).

The question in the repeat study touching this area most directly is that on frequency of pretended intellectual inferiority (Item 2, Table 1). Combining the percentages of women who checked "Several Times" or "Once or Twice" we get 43.2 per cent, a figure which is strikingly close to the 40 per cent of Komarovsky's sample. The latter percentage also corresponds closely to the equivalent percentages for the other three items in Table 1. It is interesting that about half the women in the repeat study pretended inferiority, even in the realm of artistic knowledge or taste in which presumably men adopt a permissive attitude to women's equality if not superiority.

TABLE 1

PERCENTAGE OF 163 WOMEN GIVING INDICATED RESPONSES TO
QUESTIONS ON PRETENDED INFERIORITY TO MEN

Question	Frequency					
	Very often or often	Several times	Once or twice	Never	No answer	Total
1. When on dates, how often have you pretended to be inferior in artistic knowledge or taste (in music, art, literature, etc.)?	8.1	15.6	23.2	51.9	1.2	100.0
2. How often have you pretended to be intellectually inferior to the man?	14.3	16.9	26.3	41.9	0.6	100.0
3. How often have you "played dumb" on dates because you thought the man preferred you that way?	7.5	11.2	22.6	58.7	—	100.0
4. How often have you pretended to be athletically inferior when participating in some sport with a man?	6.9	8.1	29.4	55.6	—	100.0

Additional evidence in the repeat study of the pressure experienced by women students to assume a subordinate role to the male, although regarding themselves as equal or superior to him, is provided by the replies of the 163 subjects to the following two questions:

(a) In general, do you have any hesitation about revealing your equality or superiority to men in intellectual, artistic or athletic competence?

Have considerable hesitation, 5 per cent; have some, 30.0 per cent; very little, 39.4 per cent; none at all, 25.6 per cent.

(b) In your opinion, to what extent is it damaging to a girl's chances for dates if she is known to be outstanding in academic work?

Very much so, 2.5 per cent; somewhat, 24.5 per cent; a little, 37.6 per cent; not at all, 35.4 per cent.

The answers to these questions as well as those in Table 1 indicate that a substantial proportion of the women believe they are penalized in their relations with men if they manifest equality or superiority with respect to the latter in knowledge or ability in various areas.

Another question in the repeat study which intended to get at the role conflict of the college woman was: How often have you been advised to act more "feminine"? This advice implies that its recipients were regarded by their "advisers" as over-playing the modern role, which, as Komarovsky points out, tends to be more masculine than feminine in character. Less than half the women (45.1 per cent) had "never" been told this. Of the remainder, about 31 per cent had been so advised "once or twice," 21 per cent "several times," and 4 per cent "often" or "very often." The sources of the advice were: mother 66.7 per cent, father 24.2 per cent, brother or brothers 10.3 per cent, sister or sisters 9.2 per cent, boy friend or friends 19.5 per cent, and others 6.9 per cent. The percentages total to more than 100 because some of the women reported getting the advice from two or more sources.

The second quantitative finding in Komarovsky's study was that 26 per cent of her respondents had "some grievance against their families for failure to confront them with clearcut and consistent goals. The majority, 74 per cent, denied having had such experiences" (p. 185). The questions in the repeat study touching on this area and the responses to them are given in Table 2.

It should be noted that there is a divergence between Komarovsky's study and the present one in this phase of the inquiry. The former concerned itself with the conflict or contradiction in the conceptions held by the college woman's parents (or other family members) as to what her primary goals (her role) should be while in college. The present study investigated the contradiction between the conceptions of the college woman and those of her parents and others close to her. Inconsistency of parental expectations can be a source of difficulty, but so can parental expectations that are in complete accord when they are at variance with the college woman's own conception of what she should be doing. The critical question, therefore, is whether there is any incompatibility between the young woman's conception of what she should be doing in col-

TABLE 2

PERCENTAGES OF 163 WOMEN REPORTING CONFLICT WITH FAMILY MEMBERS
ON COLLEGE ACTIVITIES AND POST-COLLEGE PLANS

| | | Extent of Contradiction | | |
Question	None	A little	Considerable	Total
1. How much contradiction is there between what you think and what the following think about how you should be spending your time in college?				
Father	66.3	27.4	6.3	100.0
Mother	70.1	25.5	4.4	100.0
Other family member whose opinion you respect	85.6	13.2	1.2	100.0
Boy friend or fiancé	83.2	15.6	1.2	100.0
2. How much contradiction is there between what you would like to do and what the following would like you to do when you finish college?				
Father	83.8	13.1	3.1	100.0
Mother	77.5	20.0	2.5	100.0
Other family member whose opinion you respect	89.3	8.8	1.9	100.0
Boy friend or fiancé	87.5	8.8	3.7	100.0

lege (and what she wishes to do after college) and the conceptions with which she is confronted by mother, father, other family members, boy friends or the man she expects to marry.

Actually, of course, the college woman will find herself in disagreement with at least one of her parents when her father and mother differ in their expectations. Consequently, the 26 per cent of the girls in Komarovsky's sample reporting inconsistent parental expectations can be assumed to have been at odds on what they were doing in college with one or both of their parents. This figure can be compared with the percentages (Table 2, question 1) of women in the repeat study reporting some contradiction between their conceptions of their college activities and those of their parents. About 34 per cent indicate some incompatibility with the views of their fathers, and 30 per cent some incompatibility with the views of their mothers.

But discrepancies between the conceptions of the college woman and those of *either or both parents* are present in 43 per cent of the cases, a significantly larger percentage than was found in Komarovsky's group. This difference, however, can be accounted for in part, at least, by the fact that the 26 per cent incidence of disagreement assumed for Komarovsky's sample does not include the women whose parents were in agreement with one another but whose expectations differed from those of their daughters. Twenty-three per cent of the women in the repeat study fell in this category.

Komarovsky's study did not distinguish between goals set by parents in the present and those urged for the future. The data of the present study indicate greater consensus between the college woman and her parents on her orientation to the future than on her present course of activities. Only 30 per cent of the subjects report some conflict with one or both parents in regard to what the latter would like them to do after finishing college.[1]

The data also revealed that conceptions of the college woman as to her present role in college are more likely to be in conflict with those of her father than with the conceptions of other family members whose opinion is respected and those of boy friends or fiancés.[2]

In order to ascertain the nature of the contradictions, subjects were allowed space in the questionnaire to state them briefly. Their statements show quite clearly that the incompatibility of views about goals while in college revolve about the question of the relative emphasis to . . . be given academic and social activities. In the majority of cases where there is some contradiction with the views of father or mother (or both), the parents are reported as favoring more attention to studies (the modern role) and less to dating and other social activities (the feminine role). This emphasis is also reported for other family members. Relatively few women indicated incompatibility with the views of their boy friends or fiancés.

The contradictions between the post-college goals of the subjects and those espoused by their parents, other family members, and

---

[1] The C.R. of the difference between 43 per cent and 30 per cent is 2.5.
[2] The C.R. of the difference between percentages of fathers and "other family members" with whom no contradiction is reported is 4.2. The corresponding differences between fathers and "boy friends or fiancés" has a C.R. of 3.2.

boy friends or fiancés varied considerably in content. There is little or no evidence that the incompatibility of views in this sphere tends to involve the conflict of the modern and feminine roles.

INTERPRETATION OF THE FINDINGS OF THE TWO STUDIES

The findings of the questionnaire data of the repeat study are in essential agreement with those of the original study based on case materials. They agree (a) that a substantial proportion of college women feel called upon on occasion to pretend inferiority to men while conceiving of themselves as equal (or superior) to them, and (b) that many college women are exposed to inconsistent parental expectations or (in terms of the repeat study) have views contradictory to those of either or both their parents as to how they should be spending their time in college. This congruence of findings from studies employing different methods and using samples from two institutions in opposite regions of the country argues for the presumption that the condition to which the findings refer is rather widespread. However, the interview data of the repeat study dispose the writer to the tentative conclusion that the problem is less momentous for the college woman than is suggested by Komarovsky's report.

The impression derived from Komarovsky's analysis and some of the excerpts quoted from her personal documents is that the college woman faced with incompatible expectations tends to be considerably disturbed by the experience. The writer's viewpoint is that in the large majority of cases the incompatibility either is not taken seriously or is rather readily resolved.

This judgment is based on the fact that in all but a few cases the subjects of the repeat study when interviewed expressed no grievance or resentment against parents or other persons for confusing or creating a conflict in them about the course they were to pursue in college or afterwards. The relatively unemotional statements made by subjects in regard to differences between them and their parents suggest that as a rule the differences are not pressed by the latter and at most are regarded as an annoyance by the former.

There is likewise little indication in the interview data that most college women who sometimes simulate inferiority to the male are at all agitated by the contradiction between their behavior and their conception of themselves as equals of the male. The interview data point to some considerations which may account for this. There appears to be a selective process at work which leads women to whom this contradiction would be upsetting to favor the company of male companions with whom they feel simulation is not necessary. The women who simulate may not be unduly troubled because they tend to regard their occasional pretense of inferiority as part of a "line" which is appropriate to the dating situation in which it characteristically occurs. Because she is not deeply involved in the casual dating relationship, the college woman seems to be able to use the "line" without being perturbed by the thought that in doing so she is not "being herself," namely the equal of the male. But when her association with a particular male develops into a more meaningful companionship or love relationship, the dating role and its "line" are no longer called for and she *can* be herself. It is only in the probably infrequent instances when a woman temperamentally or otherwise strongly disposed to the modern role becomes emotionally involved with a male who requires the feminine role of her that great psychological stress might be anticipated.

There are a number of possible explanations of the difference between Komarovsky's evaluation and that proposed here of the psychological consequences for the college woman when she is exposed to conflicting role conceptions. The writer's interpretation may not be valid because of the inadequacies of the interview data on which it is based. Or Komarovsky's case history excerpts—from which her evaluation has, in part, been inferred by the writer—inadvertently may not be typical of her entire sample in regard to the particular issue at question. Finally the possibility must be considered that there are some critical differences between the women of the original and repeat studies. The women investigated in the latter research are almost unanimously oriented to marriage, a home and children, and unlike college women oriented to a career one would not expect them to be militantly attached to the modern role. If Komarovsky's group included an appreciable number of career women, their vested interest in the modern role would have weighted the sample with persons for whom a conflict between the modern and feminine roles would be a matter of greater consequence.

·································· **22** ··································

MEN'S AND WOMEN'S BELIEFS, IDEALS,
AND SELF-CONCEPTS

by John P. McKee and Alex C. Sherriffs

A finding of this selection that may have important sociological and psychological implications is: Women are exerting pressure on men to modify their role by incorporating more of the traditionally "feminine" qualities such as orientation toward interpersonal relations and expression of human feelings. John P. McKee and Alex C. Sherriffs of the University of California (Berkeley) describe the changing roles of men and women and the disequilibrium in the relationship between the sexes. [From *American Journal of Sociology,* 1959, *44,* 356-363. Reprinted by permission of the authors and The University of Chicago Press.]

This paper is the report on the third of a series of studies of sex roles in American society. These are investigations of the status, content, developmental aspects, and implications of the stereotypes of males and females.

We have previously determined by each of three quite different methods, and for procedural variations within each, that college men and women regard the male more highly than the female sex group (McKee and Sherriffs, 1957). These results are consistent with findings reported by Komarovsky (1946, 1950, 1953) based on yet another approach and on a different college population. We consider the higher evaluation of males by college students of both sexes as established beyond reasonable doubt.

We have also examined the characteristics that college men and women ascribe to themselves and to each other (Sherriffs and McKee, 1957). When such subjects were asked to indicate on an adjective check list those characteristics that are true of men in general and of women in general, the resulting male "stereotype" contained many more individual favorable characteristics than did the female "stereotype." Male subjects particularly emphasized males' favorable characteristics, but female subjects emphasized females' *un*favorable characteristics. Furthermore, women's self-descriptions also emphasized their unfavorable characteristics much more than did men's. In general, these stereotypes were confirmed by means of a different method when each of one hundred subjects was asked to list ten characteristics for each sex. It was possible to sort the many individual responses into a limited number of rational categories which differentiated the sex groups.

While undertaking our investigations, we accept without hesitation two basic assumptions made by nearly every writer in this field: that the roles of the two sex groups are changing today and that the relationship between the groups is in disequilibrium. Our data themselves give confirming evidence for these assumptions.

Our aim in this, the third investigation, is to study certain aspects of the attitudinal and belief systems of our subjects which might be expected to reflect the changes in roles of, and the disequilibrium between, the sex groups. Recognizing the differential status still accorded the groups and possessing empirical evidence regarding the definitions currently given the sex roles, we believe that we can find meaning in the resulting information.

We ask these questions about beliefs: What do men and women believe the other sex wants them to be? To what degree does each sex group believe that the other *wants* it to conform to the sex-role stereotype? Our subjects certainly subscribe to stereotypes when describing men and women. This we had found earlier. And the stereotypes closely resembled those outlined by Komarovsky and Mead. In a period of cultural change for sex roles, however, we would expect to find differences between what are thought to be the characteristics of the sex groups and what is thought by members of one sex group to be desired of them by members of the other sex group. More specifically, we ask: Do women really believe that men are jealous of the characteristics that are allegedly masculine? Komarovsky and Mead (1949) argue that women hold such beliefs; Wallin (1950) does not go so far. And what about men? What characteristics do men believe women would like them to have? Komarovsky (1953, p. 299) writes: "We place an intolerable burden upon men by re-emphasizing a model of 'masculinity' which is increasingly difficult to attain in modern society." But do men believe that women want them to demonstrate superiority and to personify virile and adequate masculinity to the extent that this writer suggests? We suspect that the situation will by now have been modified by the realities of the new social goals which have emerged for both men and women and by the very cultural contradictions which Komarovsky describes so well.

In the literature on sex differences there are statements that one sex must conform more rigidly to society's traditional mold than the other. However, in the literature there are nearly as many arguments for this sex's being male as for its being female. Belief about what the other sex wants should indicate some significant pressures for conformity—and conformity to what. How do the sex groups compare?

Questions about sex-typing in the subjects' beliefs immediately raise questions about the correspondence between such sex-typing and the sex-typing that the two sexes actually do want in each other. Examination of this correspondence will throw light on the relative awareness by the sex groups of each other's desires. Further, examination of what each sex actually wants in the other will reveal whether the two sexes are equally insistent that the traditional roles be maintained.

Finally, it is of interest to see how these matters relate to the sex-typing in what men and women say they would *like* to be. Are men and women equally able to express and exhibit the characteristics that they desire? "Equally able" in terms of what they believe the other sex wants and "equally able" in terms of what the other sex really does want?

SUBJECTS AND PROCEDURE

One hundred unmarried men and one hundred unmarried women enrolled in introductory courses in psychology at the University of California were given four cards on which Sarbin's (no date) Adjective-Check List was printed. The responses to the ACL's are the basic data for this investigation. The subjects were asked to check on the first card "those adjectives which describe what you would *ideally* like to be." On the second card subjects checked "those adjectives which describe yourself as you really are." On the third card they checked "those adjectives which describe your ideal woman" ("man" for female subjects). On the fourth card men checked "those adjectives which *you think* describe the ideal man for women of your age," and women checked their beliefs about the desires of *men* of their own age.

We explained to the subjects that they were to try to predict, or guess, what members of the other sex had checked on the preceding card. For the sake of brevity we refer to card 1 as indicating the

"Ideal Self," card 2 as "Real Self," card 3 as "Ideal Member of Other Sex," and card 4 as "Belief." Ideal Self was given before Real Self largely because this seemed the least threatening task. Cards 3 and 4 were placed in order to help clarify the instructions for card 4. In presenting the results, we shall follow the order of our logic rather than the order of procedure. Thus, we shall go from Belief to Ideal Member of Other Sex (or what other sex "really" wants) to Ideal Self and finally to Real Self.

RESULTS

We have analyzed the data as follows. Each adjective received a score based on the proportion of subjects who chose it. These proportions were then transformed (arc sine transformation) and the resulting distributions subjected to a "Subjects $\times$ Words" analysis of variance. The subject categories are "men" and "women"; the word categories are "male" and "female." A "male" or "female" word is one that is agreed by *both* men and women to characterize the stereotypes of men or of women (Sherriffs and McKee, 1957). With *masculine* and *feminine* eliminated, there are twenty-nine favorable "male" words and twenty favorable "female" words in the stereotypes. There are eight unfavorable "male" words and seventeen unfavorable "female" words.[1] The requirement that *both* men and women agree on the stereotypic character of a word was made to facilitate the computation and interpretation of the analyses of variance. Since this requirement eliminates those adjectives that only one sex or the other includes in a stereotype, we shall present subsidiary findings to augment the analysis.

With four sets of instructions and with the favorable and unfavorable words analyzed separately, there result eight different analyses of variance. Table 1 presents the four means (given in percentages corresponding to the means of the transformed scores) for each of the eight analyses. We shall consider the favorable words first.

The table shows that for favorable words there is a significant subjects effect under each set of instructions: men select a larger number of favorable adjectives than women when indicating their Belief about what the other sex wants; for all other instructions women

[1] Favorableness or unfavorableness was determined by the judgments of members of a different sample from the same student population. For details see McKee and Sherriffs (1957).

TABLE 1

SUBGROUP MEANS FOR FAVORABLE WORDS

Subjects	I Belief Words		II Ideal Member of Other Sex Words		III Ideal Self Words		IV Real Self Words	
	Male	Female	Male	Female	Male	Female	Male	Female
Men	78**	76	63	78	76	65	53	51
Women	58	86	82***	80	75**	82	46**	68
Interaction	***		**		***		***	

SUBGROUP MEANS FOR UNFAVORABLE WORDS

Subjects	I Belief Words		II Ideal Member of Other Sex Words		III Ideal Self Words		IV Real Self Words	
	Male	Female	Male	Female	Male	Female	Male	Female
Men	5	4	2	5	5	2	25	17
Women	3	9	8	4	4	5	23**	27
Interaction	*		***				*	

* p < .05.
** p < .01.
*** p < .001.

select a larger number of favorable adjectives than men.[2] Table 1 also shows significant words ✕ subjects' interactions for the favorable words for each set of instructions. For the unfavorable words there is one significant main effect: to describe the Real Self, women choose a larger number of unfavorable words than men do. There are also significant interactions for the unfavorable words for all instructions except Ideal Self.

Belief

What sort of sex-typing do members of one sex believe that members of the other sex want in them? Column I of Table 1 suggests that men believe that women want them to have the favorable qualities of both sexes and about equally. But women believe that men want them to possess favorable feminine characteristics to a much greater degree[3] than favorable masculine characteristics. In fact, women's choices of sex-*in*appropriate adjectives is so reduced that the over-all subjects effect is significant in favor of men, while in columns II, III, and IV, it favors women. In short, Komarovsky's view of women's beliefs about the amount of sex-typing demanded of them appears to be confirmed: women *do* think men wish to restrict them from characteristics that are thought to be masculine.

But what about men's Beliefs? For men the picture is different. Where women believe they are restricted by men, one might almost say that men believe that in the eyes of women the ideal male is one who exemplifies not only much that society alleges to be masculine *but also much that society alleges to be feminine.*

Ideal Member of Other Sex

And the men are correct. At least they are correct if we take women's description of their Ideal Man as the criterion. In column II

[2] That the significant judges effect for Belief is different from the judges effect under other instructions gives us a good deal of confidence that the ACL reflects motives and attitudes and not simply verbality or *n* check adjectives. We do not assume the ultimate validity of a self-description (or any other description) given on an ACL, but to some extent the proof of the pudding is in the eating, and the qualitative aspects of previous findings seem to us to make good sense. So do the qualitative findings presented in later sections of this paper.

[3] Technically, the term "degree" is perhaps misleading. The scores are based on the percentage of the subjects who selected each adjective in the two stereotypes. Theoretically, all subjects could select an item, but none of them feels very strongly about it. Marbe's Law suggests that this possibility is not in fact likely. Consequently, we have used this simplest terminology.

of Table 1 we find that, when women describe the ideal male, he is almost exactly what men believe women would have him be. He has the favorable characteristics of both sexes equally, and he has most of them. Significantly more is asked of him than he himself asks of women. And most of this over-all subject difference is due to women's greater choice of the sex-*in*appropriate characteristics. In fact, the median (but not the mean) discrepancy between women's choices of favorable female characteristics for the Ideal Self and for the Ideal Male is *negative*.

To some extent the women's Beliefs are also correct: men do restrict women. But women's Beliefs exaggerate the degree of this restriction. On the average, the favorable female characteristics are selected by 78 per cent of the men for the ideal woman, while the favorable male characteristics are selected by only 63 per cent. But this 15 per cent differential is not nearly so large as the 28 per cent differential that women *believe* to be the case.

There are qualitative aspects of men's "restrictions" which help to clarify the picture. In describing the ideal woman, men selected ten of the twenty-nine adjectives in the male stereotype significantly less often than other male words. These ten words are *aggressive, courageous, daring, deliberate, dominant, dynamic, forceful, independent, rugged,* and *sharp-witted*. On the average, these words were selected by only 31 per cent of the men to describe their Ideal Woman. Eight of these words, all save *deliberate* and *sharp-witted*, are members of our (Sherriffs and McKee, 1957) twelve adjective, third masculine "cluster" which appears to represent action, vigor, and a kind of almost "muscular" effectiveness. *Deliberate* and *sharp-witted* are from the twelve-item "cluster" of rational competence and effectiveness, and there are no items from the small "cluster" involving uninhibited social style. In short, if men are somehow jealous of their masculinity or feel that some characteristics are simply inappropriate in women, that feeling seems to apply primarily to those characteristics related to strength and personal force.

Ideal Self

The data for the Ideal Self cast more light on just which characteristics seem to be peculiarly masculine and peculiarly feminine. Women's Ideal Self is a trifle less differentiated than men's. That is, for favorable words men show an 11 per cent differential between their average choice of sex-appropriate and sex-inappropriate characteristics, while for women the differential is 7 per cent. We had expected the sex difference to be somewhat larger; that is, we had expected women to show a much greater interest in male characteristics than men showed in female characteristics. This was apparently just somewhat naïve: to some extent women simply accept men's pre-emption of the cluster involving strength and personal force. Well under 50 per cent of the women choose *aggressive, daring, dominant, forceful,* and *rugged* for the Ideal Self. And each of these is in the upper half of the distribution of discrepancies between women's choices for the Ideal Self and their choices for the Ideal Man. Furthermore, three additional adjectives from the same cluster are also in the upper half of this distribution of discrepancies, even though they are chosen by over half of the women for the Ideal Self. These three are *adventurous, ambitious,* and *individualistic.* In other words, for eight of the twelve items in the strength and personal force cluster, there is evidence that women, even as men, feel them to be more appropriate in men than in themselves. But this is as far as the women go. They choose the remaining four words in the cluster (*courageous, dynamic, independent,* and *self-confident*) at least as often for the Ideal Self as for the Ideal Man, and the vast majority of women choose them. And much the same is true of the remaining favorable items in the male stereotype—most women choose them for the Ideal Self, and they choose them as frequently for the Ideal Self as for the Ideal Man.

But, while this is true for women's choices of adjectives in the male stereotype, the converse is not true for men's choices of adjectives in the female stereotype. In every case but one, men select favorable female characteristics less often for the Ideal Self than for the Ideal Woman. Since fifteen of these twenty female characteristics are chosen for the Ideal Self by over half of the men, one can hardly say that they *reject* female traits. But we do suspect that simple positive affect in themselves, or at least the thought of it, is a little unsettling to men—*affectionate, lovable, sentimental, sensitive,* and *soft-hearted* are the five words for which men's choices for Ideal Self and Ideal Woman are most discrepant, and the discrepancies are very large (mean = 31 per cent). Compelling as this is, it is not quote conclusive, for, while *gentle* and *kind* are also in the top half of the distribution of such discrepancies (speaking now only of female words), the magnitude of the discrepancy for these two words is only 12 per cent. And for *warm* and *sympathetic* the discrepancies are less than for the average female word.

In any event, and for whatever reasons, it is true that, apart from the strength and forcefulness cluster, women do desire allegedly male characteristics more than men desire allegedly female characteristics. If one's *ideals* be taken as the criterion of one's conformance to a social norm, then, rather surprisingly, it is men who conform to the norm more than women, rather than the other way around.

Real Self

But if one's self-description be the criterion, then women are the conformers. The data for the Real Self (col. IV of Table 1) show that for the favorable characteristics there is a significant interaction and a significant subjects effect favoring women. The key to both effects is women's choice of female words. On the average, female words are chosen by 68 per cent of the women, while male words are chosen by only 53 per cent of the men. It is this difference between men's and women's choices of the sex-appropriate items which must be responsible for the main effect, for the sex difference in choice of sex-*in*appropriate items would give a subjects difference in the other direction—one favoring men rather than women. Another way of putting it is to say that women, so far as the favorable elements of their self-descriptions are concerned, are more exclusively feminine than men are exclusively masculine. This, of course, corresponds to the subjects' Beliefs about what the other sex wants and also to what the other sex "in fact" does want. When *all* the favorable adjectives are examined (as opposed to only those which both men and women agree to be stereotypic), we find that, on the average, the sex-appropriate adjectives are selected by 55 per cent of the men and 67 per cent of the women; neutral words, by 55 per cent of the men and 61 per cent of the women; and sex-inappropriate words, by 52 per cent of the men and 49 per cent of the women.[4] Thus, men show an average difference of only 3 per cent between their choices of sex-appropriate and sex-inappropriate items, while for women this differential is 18 per cent. For all favorable words combined the values are 55 per cent for men and 59 per cent for women, and the difference is not significant.

One other feature of the self-descriptions calls for comment. This is the fact that women choose a significantly larger number of *un*favorable characteristics than men do. The effect is present for both male and female words and somewhat more marked for the sex-inappropriate ones (6 per cent) than for the sex-appropriate (2 per

[4] For this analysis "sex-appropriate" and "sex-inappropriate" refer to those adjectives which members of the *subjects' own sex* ascribe significantly more often to own sex or the other sex.

cent). However, the somewhat greater effect for the sex-inappropriate adjectives turns out to be due to the fact that the analysis is based on only those characteristics which *both* men and women agree to be stereotypic. Examination of *all* the unfavorable characteristics reveals that the sex-appropriate ones are selected by 22 per cent of the men and by 29 per cent of the women, while the sex-inappropriate ones are selected by 21 per cent of the men and 23 per cent of the women. Thus the differential is greater (7 per cent) for the sex-appropriate ones than for the sex-inappropriate (2 per cent), which is in keeping with the results for favorable characteristics.

SUMMARY AND DISCUSSION

1. For all instructions except Belief, women check more favorable stereotyped adjectives than men. For Belief instructions, men check more. This finding does not relate to questions raised earlier except, perhaps, to reflect a greater person-orientedness on the part of women —an expression of the role for which they are trained in our society (and these words *do* describe people).

2. Women believe that, from men's point of view, the Ideal Woman is markedly sex-typed. This corroborates the thinking and findings of other investigators. Here, as in the case of our other variables, we have quantitative results for the present day which we will be able to compare with responses to the same method in future years.

3. Men believe that, from women's point of view, favorable male characteristics and favorable female characteristics are equally desirable.

4. And when women describe their Ideal Man, they do select favorable female characteristics as often as they select favorable male characteristics.

Two findings above are new to us. They suggest not only that the "model of masculinity [is] increasingly difficult to attain in modern society" (Komarovsky) but that there are now in fact strong pressures to bring about a change. We do not have evidence for a decrease in pressure on men to maintain their masculine qualities, but we find a pressure by women to have men more oriented to interpersonal relations and more expressive of human (feminine in the stereotype) feelings. If college women now exert such pressure and if they have communicated it to men, then both men and women should, as they become parents during the next few years, teach these values in rearing the new generation of sons (and daughters).

Our findings do not support that part of Komarovsky's (1953, p. 76) statement which refers to boys: "If the more rigid masculine model penalizes the boys who have feminine tendencies, it also has its advantages. Once a boy can adjust himself to the masculine model, he will be spared the contradictory pressures which tend to impinge upon the growing girl no matter which model she accepts in childhood." The masculine model no longer seems so rigid.

5. Men, when they describe their Ideal Woman, include favorable male characteristics considerably less often than they include favorable female characteristics. However, when we examine the data which led to this conclusion along with our information concerning women's beliefs in this regard, we see that men are—or at least claim to be—somewhat less restrictive than women believe them to be; they allow women to have some "masculine" characteristics. The fact that there is least "give" by men on what are probably the most basically masculine variables (action, vigor, and achievement effectiveness) suggests the hypothesis that a change in the traditional female sex role stereotype may be under way, with the most crucial variables to be affected last, if at all.

6. Women's Ideal Self is a trifle, and by statistical test insignificantly, *less* sex-typed than men's. Close examination of individual items of the ACL suggests that women, though often including male attributes in their Ideal Self, do not yet, by and large, desire a life of robust and vigorous masculinity. Similarly, men, though valuing for themselves such traits as "warm" and "sympathetic," and accepting the virtue of being "gentle" and "kind," balk at attributes which would require open demonstration of personalized feelings or which might suggest sentimentality. When those adjectives most related to such "essence of sex-role" traits are set aside, then, for the large remainder women's Ideal Self is, indeed, less sex-linked in its content than men's.

7. Women's Real Self is more sex-typed than men's. We subscribe to the interpretation made by Komarovsky that in their everyday life women still feel that they must behave according to the traditional stereotype; and men, we would guess, though behaving less like this hypothetical norm, are probably uneasy in their failure to do so.

8. Women's Real Self is also more unfavorable than men's; this we have found before.

In summary, the findings are completely consistent with the assumptions that the roles of men and women are changing and that there is disequilibrium in the relationship between the groups. During a time of such change it is to be expected that attitudes will shift more rapidly than overt behaviors, that beliefs about the demands of others will reflect both the present facts and the traditional expectations (and therefore not perfectly predict either), that the sex with higher status in the society will be able to express overt change sooner than the sex with less security, and, finally, that those attributes which are at the core of the sex-role stereotypes will change least and last. We would interpret the discrepancy which we have found between college women's ideals for themselves and the attributes they say they actually express as reflecting in addition the dual training of American daughters: preparation to meet economic exigencies and the responsibilities of modern life (emphasized in the Ideal Self) and training to be feminine in the tradition of the female stereotype (emphasized in the Real Self).

Thus far our findings are either supportive of or consistent with the ideas of Komarovsky, who has published widely on such questions as they relate to the American scene.

However, we also present data which indicate that there is no inconsiderable pressure on men to modify their role by incorporating more of the traditionally "feminine" qualities. This pressure we assume to be present because of the wishes of our women subjects—wishes of which the men are well aware. This important fact has hitherto been understressed, but it seems to us eminently reasonable under present circumstances of social change. Also, we observe that men subjects are more perceptive of what women desire in them as attributes than are women subjects insightful about the current desires of men for characteristics in them. The often-made generalization about the greater social perceptiveness of women may require modification under particular psychosociological circumstances.

························· **23** ·························

THE ROLE OF MEMBER IN CLUBS OF LOWER-
CLASS AND MIDDLE-CLASS ADOLESCENTS

by Henry S. Maas[1]

Lower-class adolescent members of neighborhood clubs relate to their adult leaders in a manner similar to middle-class adolescent relationships with their peers who are club presidents. Other social class differences in relationships to peers, leader, and club president are discussed in this experimental study by Henry S. Maas of the University of California (Berkeley). [From *Child Development*, 1954, *25*, 241-251. Reprinted by permission of the author and the Society for Research in Child Development.]

Is the type of role-adaptation adolescents make as members of formally organized groups related to their social class affiliation? Specifically, is the role of member fulfilled in different ways in neighborhood center teenage clubs in the slums and in middle-class areas? In the sizeable body of empirical studies on children's group behavior and on social class influences upon adolescent life, one finds few generalizations that bear directly upon this problem.

In their informal associations with peers, adolescents value certain behaviors and attributes that vary with social class membership (Hollingshead, 1949; Neugarten, 1946; Pope, 1953). In addition to peer culture mores, however, role-adaptation in teen-age clubs is theoretically dependent upon the formal structure of such groups, including a president or chairman, members who are clearly so designated, and an adult leader whom the neighborhood center assigns to foster youth's practice in democratic decision-making and for other purposes. Slum area street gangs, which may be in their own

[1] The writer is indebted to the following persons who were members of the year's graduate seminar in which this study was executed: Robert T. Blazejack, Evelio Grillo, Robert J. Hagest, Margie B. Herman, Genevieve C. Hoffman, Donald Z. Miller, Charles O'Shea, Irving M. Piliavin, Joseph H. Solis, Memya Thoren, and William B. Ward. The study was done as a Group Research Master's Project at the School of Social Welfare, University of California, Berkeley, under the writer's faculty supervision. The graduate students served as group observers and in many other roles in the course of the investigation.

way as clearly structured as the neighborhood center clubs, have been vividly described by Thrasher (1927), Whyte (1943), and others, but comparable accounts on middle-class neighborhood youth groups are lacking, and none of these groups, of course, has a responsible adult regularly in attendance. Membership in formally organized groups and other components in the social participation patterns of middle- and lower-class youth have been studied (MacDonald, McGuire, and Havighurst, 1949; McEntire, 1952), but research on role-adaptation *within* such groups has failed to utilize social class as an independent variable. Instead, when the social class concept has been used, it has been for purposes of experimental control, as for example in Lippitt's first laboratory study on children's groups.[2] Lacking systematic empirical inquiry, the relationship of social class status to role-adaptation in formally organized groups is open to such speculative generalization as: "The worker [working class] group tends to remain relatively unstructured—roles are ill-defined and quite fluid, preventing fruitful specialization and growth (Bellin and Reissman, 1949, p. 29)."

Drawing upon Davis' (1944; Davis and Dollard, 1940) research on social class theory and adolescent development, one might postulate that lower-class teenage club members express more aggression, engage more frequently in digressions from the central activity of a meeting, and are generally less collaborative as a total group during club meetings than are comparable middle-class club members. Prior research, in Chicago (Bancker, 1951; Maas, 1951a, b; Olson, 1951), of which the current study is a continuation, reveals that this simple formulation does not stand up under testing. Rather, the prior research suggests that the roles of member, club president, and adult leader are quite differently perceived by slum area and middle-class neighborhood center adolescents. A proposition on role inferred from narrative records of club meetings and interviews with a cross-section of members, early in the Chicago research, seemed to be confirmed when all the data on twelve clubs were in. Since the current

---

[2] Lippitt (1940, p. 65) describes the children in both groups as though none came from lower-class families. "With one or two exceptions, equally true for both clubs, we may roughly generalize . . . [for all subjects]: (1) a home of good socio-economic status, few siblings, and consistently moderate discipline; (2) an unorganized neighborhood play life with no hint of gang membership; (3) rather inactive membership in a Club pack; and (4) membership in a progressively inclined university school system." With subjects of this type of background, one may question Lippitt's (1940, pp. 190-191) generalizing, albeit with caution, about behavior of "the authoritarian group members" and "the democratic group." What might have happened had some lower-class children been included in each of these groups?

study aims to re-test, with more refined research techniques, certain parts of this formulation, its quotation here is appropriate:

> In the middle-class groups, pre- and early adolescents seem primarily directed toward working out relationships with peers. At home their proximate relationships with parents in joint activities—going places and doing things together—and the freedom to express verbally their negative reactions, to gainsay parental requests, and to manipulate parents in ways that suggest their equal status and power with parents make relations with the adult adviser in youth group settings developmentally less significant. In the lower-class groups, however, the adult adviser becomes a more significant and conflictful person, someone in a sense who is supra-human—to be tried, or challenged more or less openly. Relations among peers in the lower-class groups are characterized by repeated obvious attempts at status seeking. . . . This pattern in the lower-class groups may be traced to the increasing distance lower-class boys and girls in growing up have attained from adults; earlier on their own (as Davis and others have shown), they seem to have gotten out of communication with adults. Physical aggression in their homes, when parents are at home together with their pre- and early adolescent children, continues to assure them the adult is boss. Personal relationships are seen in a hierarchical framework, definitely non-equalitarian and non-collaborative, and the power struggle between adults and early adolescents carries over into the youth groups, with much hostility, overt, covert, and smothered (Maas, 1951b, p. 12).

For the current study, the concept of role has been operationalized as having structural and functional properties. Structurally, the role of member is fulfilled in reciprocal relationships with the roles of adult leader, president, and other member. Functionally, each role may include behaviors that are primarily collaborative, in the process of democratic decision-making; hostilely aggressive, in the authoritarian tradition of might-is-right; or digressive, an asocial or anarchic mode of interaction. The psychological counterparts of these three modes of social process appear in Horney's (1945, p. 42) statement that "a child can move *toward* people, *against* them or *away from* them." In a teenage club, these three modes of interaction can be directed by a member in any one of three structural directions: to the adult leader, president, or other member(s). The functional and structural properties of role seem adequately operationalized if every interaction is seen as having conjointly a mode and a direction.

If the role of member and its reciprocal roles are differentially perceived by lower-class and middle-class adolescents, the modes and directions of interaction that members initiate and receive should reflect this differential pattern. Members may sanction or taboo more or less interaction with the adult leader or the president. The mode of such interaction theoretically depends upon the perception of each role. "Toward" behavior or collaboration is assumed to imply respect or trust; as a group-integrative or centripetal mode of interaction that leaders to the resolution of an issue, it includes the behaviors of suggesting, asking, yielding, approving, deciding, and the incorporating of oppositional or excluded persons. (See Figure 1.)

Observer _____   Club Name _____

Time Started _____   Date _____

Time Ended _____   No. Members _____

Observation No. 1 2 3 (circle)   Co-observer _____

	Leader		President		Member(s)			
TOWARD (collaboration)	P	M	L	M	L	P	M	
1. suggest								
2. ask for								
3. yield								
4. approve								
5. decide								
6. incorporate								
AGAINST (aggression)	P	M	L	M	L	P	M	
1. compel, force								
2. resist								
3. attack ...... verbal								
non-verbal								
AWAY FROM (digression)	P	M	L	M	L	P	M	
1. non-group relevant interaction verbal								
non-verbal								
2. silence								

FIG. 1. Observational tally-sheet used by observers for each six-minute observation period.

"Against" behavior or hostile aggression implies distrust or threat and is manifest by compelling or forcing, resisting, and either verbal or non-verbal attack; interaction which aims to superordinate the initiator and subordinate the object of the interaction, such as compelling, is thus considered hostilely aggressive. "Away from" behavior or digression is group-disintegrative or centrifugal interaction in the process of movement away from threatening or disapproved others and/or central activity of the group at a given time; it may appear as subgrouping or fragmentation of members who engage in tangential "horse-play" or other non-group relevant interaction during discussion on the planning of future events. Collaboration, aggression, and digression are three modes of behavior that may be incorporated with greater or lesser frequency into the role of member in different groups and directed with greater or lesser frequency to the correlative roles of adult leader, club president, or other member.

Specifically, then, drawing upon what is known and postulated about lower-class and middle-class adolescent group life, the following hypotheses are proposed on the lower-class, as compared with the middle-class, club member:

Hypothesis 1: In lower-class groups, the member directs to the adult leader (a) more collaboration, (b) more aggression, and (c) more digression. The adult is developmentally "a more significant and conflictful person" for him (Maas, 1951b, p. 12).

Hypothesis 2: In lower-class groups, the member directs to the president (a) less collaboration, (b) less aggression, and (c) less digression. More obvious in his status-seeking among peers (ibid., p. 12), the lower-class club member is likely either quickly to conform with or to ignore a president, depending on his true status in the peer society; whether high or low, he is not likely to be the focus of more frequent interactions than his counterpart in middle-class groups who may be either approved or disapproved, but in either case is seen as the occupant of a position that must be dealt with, may be widely aspired to, and seems essential to the achievement of club and neighborhood center goals. Such postulates are at least in line with Davis' concept of "social anxiety" among middle-class youth (Davis, 1944).

Hypothesis 3: In lower-class groups, the member directs to other members (a) less collaboration, (b) more aggression, and (c) more digression. This follows from the characteristically more overt expression of aggression and lesser degree of impulse control found among lower-class youth today (Davis, 1944).

Each of these hypotheses is the converse of a hypothesis on the role of member in middle-class adolescent clubs.

METHODS

To test the hypotheses, ten clubs averaging a total attendance of 126 adolescent members were selected and paired in the San Francisco Bay Area. An observational instrument (Figure 1) was developed and used in three successive mid-year meetings in each club.

For the selection of clubs, criteria which provide control of factors theoretically related to members' role-adaptation were set up, members' social class status being the independent variable. The criteria that could be met in the field are as follows: (a) all clubs have scheduled weekly meetings in a neighborhood center attracting primarily either slum area or middle-class adolescents; (b) all clubs have an agency-designated adult leader regularly in attendance; (c) all club meetings are presided over by an adolescent in the role of president; (d) all club meetings include a forum-type discussion for the members' planning of their own programs, thus excluding from this study all groups with highly ritualized procedures and agency-imposed programs as in some Scout troops; (e) all clubs are organized and meeting for a minimum of four months by the time that research observations begin, thus excluding from this study all very newly organized clubs still in the process of initial group formation and role-definition; and (f_1) all clubs are composed of either boys or girls, ages 12 to 16, with a median attendance of not fewer than 6 and not more than about 20 members, but (f_2) all clubs paired for co-observation are to be of the same sex, not more than about a year apart in median age of members, not too disparate in numbers attending, and each composed predominantly of lower-class or middle-class adolescents. These criteria are in certain ways a broadening of the initial theoretically-set controls, but limits had to be expanded in view of the clubs available for pairing in the 21 canvassed urban neighborhood centers. Matching of the adult leaders in paired clubs was considered a theoretically questionable and operationally infeasible procedure in this field investigation, if only because of evidence that the role of adult leader is more a function of the structure and process of the group than a direct correlate of any as yet isolated personal or ego-structure factor in the leader as an individual (Maas, 1950). Data on the leaders of the ten clubs, obtained after their selection, reveal

TABLE 1

AGE, SEX, ATTENDANCE, PARENTAL OCCUPATION, AND SOCIAL CLASS OF ADOLESCENT MEMBERS IN TEN PAIRED CLUBS

Club	Age Range (years)	Median Age	Sex	Median Attendance (N = 126)	Median Parental Occupation*	Social Class
A	12–13	12.8	M	10	2	lower
B	11–13	12.5	M	6	6	middle
C	14–16	14.7	M	15	3	lower
D	12–14	13.5	M	18	6	middle
E	13–16	14.0	M	8	3	lower
F	13–14	13.5	M	21	7	middle
G	16–17	16.5	M	8	4	lower
H	14–17	15.7	M	12	7	middle
I	13–15	13.8	F	17	4	lower
J	12–13	12.6	F	11	7	middle
Lower class (mean)		14.4	—	11.6	3.2	—
Middle class (mean)		13.6	—	13.6	6.6	—

* See footnote 3 for rating scale.

that the adults working with the lower-class and the middle-class adolescents were roughly comparable as to prior experience as adult leader, educational level, and prior personal experience as member of a youth group.

Lower-class and middle-class clubs were paired, as shown in Table 1. Each pair of clubs was observed by the same team of two observers, thus reducing the possibility of ascribing observed differences to differences among observers. Both observers in each team were of the same sex as the members of the paired clubs they observed.

TABLE 2

RELIABILITY OF TALLY-SHEET OBSERVERS INDICATED BY RANK ORDER CORRELATIONS OF TYPE OF MODE AND DIRECTION OF INTERACTIONS

Observers	Pre-test 1		Pre-test 2		Pre-test 3		Mean
	Type of mode	Direction	Type of mode	Direction	Type of mode	Direction	
I–II	—*	.69	.84	.71	.68	.71	.73
I–IV	—*	.90	.64	.76	.74	.84	.78
II–IV	.74	.61	.37	.38	.82	.50	.57
III–V	.97	.88	.78	.88	.63	.90	.84
VI–VII	.94	.45	.92	.83	.70	.74	.76
VIII–IX	.97	.79	.73	.77	.86	.73	.81

* Coefficient not obtained because of error by Observer I in recording.

Social class estimates of club members were made first by comparative evaluation of neighborhood (dwelling area) and then by occupational rating[3] of club members' parents, the latter rating for all clubs confirming the former estimates. While all the middle-class clubs were predominantly Caucasian and non-ethnic, clubs A, C, and I (see Table 1) were composed of Negroes, and clubs E and G met in a neighborhood center that served a large percentage of Italian ethnics.[4]

In each team of co-observers, one wrote a narrative record and one used the observational tally-sheet (Figure 1) to obtain three spaced six-minute observations in each of three successive meetings. (Data from the narrative records are not discussed in this report.) To obtain samples of early, middle, and later interactions in each meeting of each club, the first six-minute observation on a tally-sheet began five minutes after each meeting had begun; the second, twenty minutes after the beginning of each meeting; and the third, as close to the termination of each meeting as possible. In the development of the tally-sheet, its validity was judged non-quantitatively in pre-tests on club meetings role-played by members of the research group; pre-planned interaction patterns and narrative reports of these "clubs" in action were compared with the tally-sheet records. The reliability of an instrument like the tally-sheet is determined primarily by the reliability of its users. Rank order correlation of the thirteen types of interaction (horizontal items, Figure 1) and the seven direction totals (vertical items, Figure 1) revealed that all but two of the pre-test observers (II and IV) could use the tally-sheets with some degree of objectivity (Table 2). Observers I, III, V, VII, and IX were chosen to do the tally-sheet recording in the field; the others, and observer X, became the narrative report co-observers.

FINDINGS AND CONCLUSIONS

The role of member is differently fulfilled and apparently differ-

[3] Ratings are based on a scale developed for the U.S. Bureau of the Census (1950). Higher ratings are for proprietors, managers, and professionals, 8 or 7; sales and clerical workers, 6; and skilled craftsmen and foremen, 5. Lower ratings are for semi-skilled and unskilled workers: operatives, 4; household and service workers, 3; laborers, 2; and relief recipients, 1.

[4] Minority group ethnicity is a factor in urban lower-class culture that Warner has built into his social class theory (Warner, 1952, pp. 118-140) and that Davis and Havighurst (1946) have found for Negroes and Caucasians in no way obfuscates social class differences in child-rearing.

TABLE 3

FREQUENCY BY MODE AND DIRECTION OF INTERACTIONS INITIATED BY
MEMBERS IN LOWER-CLASS AND MIDDLE-CLASS CLUBS

Direction Mode	Lower class	Middle class	Total	Chi-square value
To Adult Leader:				
Collaboration	94	64	158	5.70*
Aggression	44	31	75	2.25
Digression	10	10	20	. . .
To Club President:				
Collaboration	50	85	135	9.07†
Aggression	18	42	60	9.60†
Digression	5	5	10	. . .
To Other Member(s):				
Collaboration	208	240	448	2.29
Aggression	84	55	139	6.05*
Digression	270	243	513	1.42
TOTAL	783	775	1558	36.38‡

Significant at: * .02 level   † .01 level   ‡ .001 level

ently perceived by the lower- and the middle-class adolescents, as may
be seen in Tables 3 and 4.

Hypothesis 1: The lower-class adolescent club member directs more
collaborative interactions to the adult leader than does the middle-
class member (Table 3). The data do not support parts (b) and (c) of
this hypothesis in regard to more aggression and digression directed
to the adult leader in slum area groups. It should be noted that the
adult leader reciprocally directs more collaborative interactions to
lower-class than to middle-class members (Table 4).

Hypothesis 2: The middle-class adolescent club member directs
more collaborative and more aggressive interactions to the president
(Table 3). The data do not support part (c) of this hypothesis on
digressive interactions. The president, in turn, is more collaborative
and aggressive with members in middle-class than in lower-class
groups (Table 4).

Hypothesis 3: The lower-class adolescent club member is more
aggressive with other members (Table 3). The data do not support
part (a) of this hypothesis on less collaboration among lower-class
adolescents. There is some slight evidence (Table 4, at the .10 level
of confidence) that there is more member-member digression in the
lower-class clubs.

The data validate only parts of the initial proposition. The over-all pattern of quantitative findings is largely, however, in the expected directions. The initial formulation may thus be refined in the following ways:

1. The role of member among lower-class adolescents in neighborhood center clubs is fulfilled in a relationship to the adult leader that is comparable to the relationship the middle-class adolescent member has with his peer in the role of club president. In slum area clubs, the adult leader would seem to be a more significant figure to members than in middle-class neighborhood centers where adolescent members ostensibly have less need for interaction with the adult.

2. The role of member among middle-class adolescents apparently sanctions less aggression and digression in member-to-member interactions than does the comparable role among lower-class adolescents. This much squares with existing social class theory. It should be noted, however, that the total amount of aggression expressed by members in the two types of group is not significantly different, since the club president in the middle-class groups is the target (and initiator) of significantly more aggressive interactions than is his counterpart in the lower-class groups. One must conclude, therefore, that the role of member among both lower- and middle-class adolescents offers equal opportunity but different directional outlets for the expression of aggression in teenage clubs.

TABLE 4

FREQUENCY BY MODE AND DIRECTION OF INTERACTIONS RECEIVED BY
MEMBERS IN LOWER-CLASS AND MIDDLE-CLASS CLUBS

Direction	Mode	Lower class	Middle class	Total	Chi-square value
From Adult Leader:					
	Collaboration	249	164	413	21.40‡
	Aggression	49	51	100	...
	Digression	7	12	19	1.12
From Club President:					
	Collaboration	135	221	356	17.10‡
	Aggression	48	112	160	23.10‡
	Digression	10	20	30	2.94**
From Other Member(s):					
	Collaboration	208	240	448	0.57
	Aggression	84	55	139	7.30†
	Digression	270	243	513	2.70**
TOTAL		1060	1118	2178	76.23‡

Significant at: ** .10 level   † .01 level   ‡ .001 level

3. Differences found between lower-class and middle-class adolescents in the role of member and its relationships with the reciprocal roles of adult leader and club president may be explained in terms of differential cultural training and experience relevant to role-adaptation in formally organized groups. The initial proposition on differences in adolescent-adult and peer relationships in lower-class and middle-class child life is not invalidated by the findings of this study.

CHAPTER NINE

Status

24

CONTINUITIES AND DISCONTINUITIES IN CULTURAL CONDITIONING

by Ruth Benedict

Some positions in a group are valued more highly than others. In American society, one's occupation, income and wealth, education and skill, family, place of residence, home ownership, and clique membership are some of the major determinants of status. Ruth Benedict (1887-1948), late of Columbia University, shows the relationship between child-rearing practices in America and values placed upon status, from infancy to adulthood. After pointing out that there is no single, "natural" path to maturity, she describes how the discontinuities in the cultural conditioning of children as well as physiological factors may contribute to maladjustment and personality upheavals. [By permission from *A Study of Interpersonal Relations,* edited by Patrick Mullahy. Copyright 1949, by the publisher, Hermitage Press, Inc.]

All cultures must deal in one way or another with the cycle of growth from infancy to adulthood. Nature has posed the situation dramatically: on the one hand, the new-born baby, physiologically vulnerable, unable to fend for itself, or to participate of its own initiative in the life of the group, and, on the other, the adult man or woman. Every man who rounds out his human potentialities must have been a son first and a father later, and the two roles are physiologically in great contrast; he must first have been dependent upon others for his very existence, and later he must provide such security for others. This discontinuity in the life cycle is a fact of nature and is inescapable. Facts of nature, however, in any discussion of human problems, are ordinarily read off not at their bare minimal but surrounded by all the local accretions of behavior to which the student of human affairs has become accustomed in his own culture. For that reason, it is illuminating to examine comparative material from other societies in order to get a wider perspective on our own special accretions. The anthropologist's role is not to question the facts of nature, but to insist upon the interposition of a middle term between "nature" and "human behavior"; his role is to analyze that term, to document local man-made doctorings of nature, and to insist that these doctorings should not be read off in any one culture as nature itself. Although it is a fact of nature that the child becomes a man, the way in which this transition is effected varies from one society to another, and no one of these particular cultural bridges should be regarded as the "natural" path to maturity.

From a comparative point of view, our culture goes to great extremes in emphasizing contrasts between the child and the adult. The child is sexless, the adult estimates his virility by his sexual activities; the child must be protected from the ugly facts of life, the adult must meet them without psychic catastrophe; the child must obey, the adult must command this obedience. These are all dogmas of our culture, dogmas which, in spite of the facts of nature, other cultures commonly do not share. In spite of the physiological contrasts between child and adult, these are cultural accretions.

It will make the point clearer if we consider one habit in our own culture in regard to which there is not this discontinuity of conditioning. With the greatest clarity of purpose and economy of training, we achieve our goal of conditioning everyone to eat three meals a day. The baby's training in regular food periods begins at birth, and no crying of the child and no inconvenience to the mother is allowed to interfere. We gauge the child's physiological make-up and at first allow it food oftener than adults, but, because our goal is firmly set and our training consistent, before the child is two years old it has achieved the adult schedule. From the point of view of other cultures, this is as startling as the fact of three-year-old babies perfectly at home in deep water is to us. Modesty is another sphere in which our child training is consistent and economical; we waste no time in clothing the baby, and, in contrast to many societies where the child runs naked till it is ceremonially given its skirt or its pubic sheath at adolescence, the child's training fits it precisely for adult conventions.

In neither of these aspects of behavior is there need for an individual in our culture to embark before puberty, at puberty, or at some later date upon a course of action which all his previous training has tabooed. He is spared the unsureness inevitable in such a transition.

The illustration I have chosen may appear trivial, but, in larger and more important aspects of behavior, our methods are obviously different. Because of the great variety of child training in different families in our society, I might illustrate continuity of conditioning from individual life histories in our culture, but even these, from a comparative point of view, stop far short of consistency; and I shall, therefore, confine myself to describing arrangements in other cultures in which training which with us is idiosyncratic is accepted and traditional and does not, therefore, involve the same possibility of conflict. I shall choose childhood rather than infant and nursing situations, not because the latter do not vary strikingly in different cultures, but because they are nevertheless more circumscribed by the baby's physiological needs than is its later training. Childhood situations provide an excellent field in which to illustrate the range of cultural adjustments which are possible within a universally given, but not so drastic, set of physiological facts.

The major discontinuity in the life cycle is of course that the child who is at one point a son must later be a father. These roles in our society are strongly differentiated; a good son is tractable, and does not assume adult responsibilities; a good father provides for his children and should not allow his authority to be flouted. In addition, the child must be sexless so far as his family is concerned, whereas the father's sexual role is primary in the family. The individual in one role must revise his behavior from almost all points of view when he assumes the second role.

I shall select for discussion three such contrasts that occur in our culture between the individual's role as child and as father: (1) responsible-non-responsible status role; (2) dominance-submission; (3) contrasted sexual role. It is largely upon our cultural commitments to these three contrasts that the discontinuity in the life cycle of an individual in our culture depends.

RESPONSIBLE—NON-RESPONSIBLE STATUS ROLE

The techniques adopted by societies which achieve continuity during the life cycle in this sphere in no way differ from those we employ in our uniform conditioning to three meals a day. They are merely applied to other areas of life. We think of the child as wanting to play and the adult as having to work, but in many societies the mother takes the baby daily in her shawl or carrying net to the garden or to gather roots, and adult labor is seen even in infancy from the pleasant security of its position in close contact with its mother. When the child can run about, it accompanies its parents still, doing tasks which are essential and yet suited to its powers, and its dichotomy between work and play is not different from that its parents recognize, namely the distinction between the busy day and the free evening period. The tasks it is asked to perform are graded to its powers, and its elders wait quietly by, not offering to do the task in the child's place. Everyone who is familiar with such societies has been struck by the contrast with our child training. Dr. Ruth Underhill tells me of sitting with a group of Papago elders in Arizona when the man of the house turned to his little three-year-old-grand-daughter and asked her to close the door. The door was heavy and hard to shut. The child tried, but it did not move. Several times the grandfather repeated: "Yes, close the door." No one jumped to the child's assistance. No one took the responsibility away from her. On the other hand there was no impatience, for after all the child was small. They sat gravely waiting till the child succeeded and her grandfather gravely thanked her. It was assumed that the task would not be asked of her unless she could perform it, and, having been asked, the responsibility was hers alone just as if she were a grown woman.

The essential point of such child training is that the child is from infancy continuously conditioned to responsible social participation, while at the same time the tasks that are expected of it are adapted to its capacity. The contrast with our society is very great. A child does not make any labor contribution to our industrial society except as it competes with an adult; its work is not measured against its own strength and skill but against high-geared industrial requirements. Even when we praise a child's achievement in the home, we are outraged if such praise is interpreted as being of the same order as praise of adults. The child is praised because the parent feels well disposed, regardless of whether the task is well done by adult standards, and the child acquires no sensible standard by which to measure its achievement. The gravity of a Cheyenne Indian family ceremoniously making a feast out of the little boy's first snowbird is at the furthest remove from our behavior. At birth the little boy was presented with a toy bow, and from the time he could run about serviceable bows suited to his stature were specially made for him by the man of the family. Animals and birds were taught him in a graded series beginning with those most easily taken, and as he brought in his first of each species his family duly made a feast of it, accepting his contribution as gravely as the buffalo his father brought. When he finally killed a buffalo, it was only the final step of his childhood conditioning, not a new adult role with which his childhood experience had been at variance.

The Canadian Ojibwa show clearly what results can be achieved. This tribe gains its livelihood by winter trapping, and the small family of father, mother, and children live during the long winter alone on their great frozen hunting grounds. The boy accompanies his father and brings in his catch to his sister as his father does to his mother; the girl prepares the meat and skins for him just as his mother does for her husband. By the time the boy is twelve, he may have set his own line of traps on a hunting territory of his own and return to his parent's house only once in several months—still bringing the meat and skins to his sister. The young child is taught consistently that it has only itself to rely upon in life, and this is as true in the dealings it will have with the supernatural as in the business of getting a livelihood. This attitude he will accept as a successful adult just as he accepted it as a child.

DOMINANCE—SUBMISSION

Dominance-submission is the most striking of those categories of behavior where like does not respond to like, but where one type of behavior stimulates the opposite response. It is one of the most prominent ways in which behavior is patterned in our culture. When it obtains between classes, it may be nourished by continuous experience; the difficulty in its use between children and adults lies in the fact that an individual conditioned to one set of behavior in childhood must adopt the opposite as an adult. Its opposite is a pattern of approximately identical reciprocal behavior; the societies which rely upon continuous conditioning characteristically invoke this pattern. In some primitive cultures, the very terminology of address between father and son, and, more commonly, between grandchild and grandson or uncle and nephew, reflects this attitude. In such kinship terminologies, one reciprocal expresses each of these relationships so that son and father, for instance, exchange the same term with one another, just as we exchange the same term with a cousin. The child later will exchange it with his son. "Father-son," therefore, is a continuous relationship he enjoys throughout life. The same continuity, backed up by verbal reciprocity, occurs far oftener in the grandchild—grandson relationship or that of mother's brother—sister's son. When these are "joking" relationships, as they often are, travellers report wonderingly upon the liberties and pretensions of tiny toddlers in their dealing with these family elders. In place of our dogma of respect to elders, such societies employ in these cases a reciprocity as nearly identical as may be. The teasing and practical joking the grandfather visits upon his grandchild, the grandchild returns in like coin; he would be led to believe that he failed in propriety if he did not give like for like. If the sister's son has right of access without leave to his mother's brother's possessions, the mother's brother has such rights also to the child's possessions. They share reciprocal privileges and obligations which in our society can develop only between age mates.

From the point of view of our present discussion, such kinship conventions allow the child to put in practice from infancy the same forms of behavior which it will rely upon as an adult; behavior is not polarized into a general requirement of submission for the child and dominance for the adult.

It is clear from the techniques described above, by which the child is conditioned to a responsible status role, that these depend chiefly upon arousing in the child the desire to share responsibility in adult life. To achieve this, little stress is laid upon obedience but much stress upon approval and praise. Punishment is very commonly regarded as quite outside the realm of possibility, and natives in many parts of the world have drawn the conclusion from our usual disciplinary methods that white parents do not love their children. If the child is not required to be submissive, however, many occasions for punishment melt away; a variety of situations which call for it do not occur. Many American Indian tribes are especially explicit in rejecting the ideal of a child's submissive or obedient behavior. Prince Maximilian von Wied, who visited the Crow Indians over a hundred years ago, describes a father's boasting about his young son's intractibility even when it was the father himself who was flouted; "He will be a man," his father said. He would have been baffled at the idea that his child should show behavior which would obviously make him appear a poor creature in the eyes of his fellows if he used it as an adult. Dr. George Devereux tells me of a special case of such an attitude among the Mohave at the present time. The child's mother was white and protested to its father that he must take action when the child disobeyed and struck him. "But why?" the father said, "He is little. He cannot possibly injure me." He did not know of any dichotomy according to which an adult expects obedience and a child must accord it. If his child had been docile, he would simply have judged that it would become a docile adult—an eventuality of which he would not have approved.

Child training which brings about the same result is common also in other areas of life than that of reciprocal kinship obligations between child and adult. There is a tendency in our culture to regard every situation as having in it the seeds of a dominance-submission relationship. Even where dominance-submission is patently irrelevant we read in the dichotomy, assuming that in every situation there must be one person dominating another. On the other hand some cultures, even when the situation calls for leadership, do not see it in terms of dominance-submission. To do justice to this attitude, it would be necessary to describe their political and especially their economic arrangements, for such an attitude to persist must certainly be supported by economic mechanisms that are congruent with it. But it must also be supported by—or what comes to the same thing, express itself in—child training and familial situations.

CONTRASTED SEXUAL ROLE

Continuity of conditioning in training the child to assume responsibility and to behave no more submissively than adults is quite possible in terms of the child's physiological endowment if his participation is suited to his strength. Because of the late development of the child's reproductive organs, continuity of conditioning in sex experience presents a difficult problem. So far as their belief that the child is anything but a sexless being is concerned, they are probably more nearly right than we are with an opposite dogma. But the great break is presented by the universally sterile unions before puberty and the presumably fertile ones after maturation. This physiological fact no amount of cultural manipulation can minimize or alter, and societies, therefore, which stress continuous conditioning most strongly sometimes do not expect children to be interested in sex experience until they have matured physically. This is striking among American Indian tribes like the Dakota; adults observe great privacy in sex acts and in no way stimulate children's sexual activity. There need be no discontinuity, in the sense in which I have used the term, in such a program if the child is taught nothing it does not have to unlearn later. In such cultures, adults view children's experimentation as in no way wicked or dangerous, but merely as innocuous play which can have no serious consequences. In some societies such play is minimal and the children manifest little interest in it. But the same attitude may be taken by adults in societies where such play is encouraged and forms a major activity among small children. This is true among most of the Melanesian cultures of Southeast New Guinea; adults go as far as to laugh off sexual affairs within the prohibited class, if the children are not mature, saying that since they cannot marry there can be no harm done.

It is this physiological fact of the difference between children's sterile unions and adults' presumably fertile sex relations which must be kept in mind in order to understand the different mores which almost always govern sex expression in children and in adults in the same culture. A great many cultures with pre-adolescent sexual license require marital fidelity, and a great many which value pre-marital virginity in either male or female arrange their marital life with great license. Continuity in sex experience is complicated by factors which it was unnecessary to consider in the problems previously discussed. The essential problem is not whether or not the child's sexuality is consistently exploited—for even where such exploitation is favored, in the majority of cases the child must seriously modify his behavior at puberty or at marriage. Continuity in sex expression means rather that the child is taught nothing it must unlearn later. If the cultural emphasis is upon sexual pleasure, the child who is continuously conditioned will be encouraged to experiment freely and pleasurably, as among the Marquesans; if emphasis is upon reproduction, as among the Zuñi of New Mexico, childish sex proclivities will not be exploited, for the only important use which sex is thought to serve in his culture is not yet possible to him. The important contrast with our child training is that, although a Zuñi child is impressed with the wickedness of premature sex experimentation, he does not run the risk as in our culture of associating this wickedness with sex itself rather than with sex at his age. The adult in our culture has often failed to unlearn the wickedness or the dangerousness of sex, a lesson which was impressed upon him strongly in his most formative years.

DISCONTINUITY IN CONDITIONING

Even from this very summary statement of continuous conditioning, the economy of such mores is evident. In spite of the obvious advantages, however, there are difficulties in its way. Many primitive societies expect as different behavior from an individual as child and as adult as we do, and such discontinuity involves a presumption of strain.

Many societies of this type, however, minimize strain by the techniques they employ; and some techniques are more successful than others in ensuring the individual's functioning without conflict. It is from this point of view that age-grade societies reveal their fundamental significance. Age-graded cultures characteristically demand different behavior of the individual at different times of his life, and persons of a like age-grade are grouped into a society whose activities are all oriented toward the behavior desired at that age. Individuals "graduate" publicly and with honor from one of these groups to another. Where age society members are enjoined to loyalty and mutual support, and are drawn not only from the local group but from the whole tribe, as among the Arapaho, or even from other tribes as among the Wagawaga of Southeast New Guinea, such an institution has many advantages in eliminating conflicts among local groups and fostering intratribal peace. This seems to be also a factor in the tribal military solidarity of the similarly organized Masai of East Africa. The point that is of chief interest for our present discussion, however, is that by this means an individual who at any time takes on a new set of duties and virtues is supported not only by a solid phalanx of age mates but by the traditional prestige of the organized "secret" society into which he has now graduated. Fortified in this way, individuals in such cultures often swing between remarkable extremes of opposite behavior without apparent psychic threat. For example, the great majority exhibit prideful and non-conflicted behavior at each stage in the life cycle, even when a prime of life devoted to passionate and aggressive head hunting must be followed by a later life dedicated to ritual and to mild and peaceable civic virtues.

Our chief interest here, however, is in discontinuity which primarily affects the child. In many primitive societies, such discontinuity has been fostered not because of economic or political necessity or because such discontinuity provides for a socially valuable division of labor, but because of some conceptual dogma. The most striking of these are the Australian and Papuan cultures where the ceremony of the "Making of Man" flourishes. In such societies it is believed that men and women have opposite and conflicting powers, and male children, who are of undefined status, must be initiated into the male role. In Central Australia the boy child is of the woman's side, and women are taboo in the final adult stages of tribal ritual. The elaborate and protracted initiation ceremonies of the Arunta, therefore, snatch the boy from the mother, dramatize his gradual repudiation of her. In a final ceremony he is reborn as a man out of the men's ceremonial "baby pouch." The men's ceremonies are ritual statements of a masculine solidarity, carried out by fondling one another's *churingas*, the material symbol of each man's life, and by letting out over one another blood drawn from their veins. After this warm bond among men has been established through the ceremonies, the boy joins the men in the men's house and participates in tribal rites. The enjoined discontinuity has been tribally bridged.

West of the Fly River in southern New Guinea, there is a striking development of this Making of Men cult which involves a childhood period of passive homosexuality. Among the Keraki it is thought that no boy can grow to full stature without playing the role for some years. Men slightly older take the active role, and the older man is a jealous partner. The life cycle of the Keraki Indians includes, therefore, in succession, passive homosexuality, active homosexuality, and heterosexuality. The Keraki believe that pregnancy will result from post-pubertal passive homosexuality and see evidences of such practices in any fat man, whom, even as an old man, they may kill or drive out of the tribe because of their fear. The ceremony that is of interest in connection with the present discussion takes place at the end of the period of passive homosexuality. This ceremony consists in burning out the possibility of pregnancy from the boy by pouring lye down his throat, after which he has no further protection if he gives way to the practice. There is no technique for ending active homosexuality, but this is not explicitly taboo for older men; heterosexuality and children, however, are highly valued. Unlike the neighboring Marindanim, who share their homosexual practices, Keraki husband and wife share the same house and work together in the gardens.

I have chosen illustrations of discontinuous conditioning where it is not too much to say that the cultural institutions furnish adequate support to the individual as he progresses from role to role or interdicts the previous behavior in a summary fashion. The contrast with arrangements in our culture is very striking, and against this background of social arrangements in other cultures the adolescent period of *Sturm und Drang* with which we are so familiar becomes intelligible in terms of our discontinuous cultural institutions and dogmas rather than in terms of physiological necessity. It is even more pertinent to consider these comparative facts in relation to maladjusted persons in our culture who are said to be fixated at one or another pre-adult level. It is clear that if we were to look at our social arrangements as an outsider, we should infer directly from our family institutions and habits of child training that many individuals would not "put off childish things"; we should have to say that our adult activity demands traits that are interdicted in children, and that, far from redoubling efforts to help children bridge this gap, adults in our culture put all the blame on the child when he fails to manifest spontaneously the new behavior or, overstepping the mark, manifests it with untoward belligerence. It is not surprising that in such a society many individuals fear to use behavior which has up to that time been under a ban and trust instead, though at great psychic cost, to attitudes that have been exercised with approval during their formative years. Insofar as we invoke a physiological scheme to account for these neurotic adjustments, we are led to overlook the possibility of developing social institutions which would lessen the social cost we now pay; instead, we elaborate a set of dogmas which prove inapplicable under other social conditions.

.... 25 ....

FAMILY BACKGROUND AND BEHAVIOR

by August B. Hollingshead

From his study of adolescents and their families in a midwestern American community, August B. Hollingshead of Yale University, concludes that the social behavior of adolescents is related to the positions of their families in the social structure of the community. For purposes of the study, the positions the families occupy are determined by members of the community who rate them into one of five social classes, designated by Roman numerals, the upper class being I and the lower class V. In this excerpt from his book Hollingshead compares the behavior of the adolescents from the three upper classes with that of Class V adolescents. [From *Elmtown's Youth: The Impact of Social Classes on Adolescents,* New York: John Wiley and Sons, Inc., 1949, pp. 441-447. Reprinted by permission of the author and John Wiley and Sons, Inc.]

*   *   *

We can conclude with confidence that adolescents who have been reared in families that possess different class cultures may be expected to follow different behavior patterns in their responses to situations they encounter in their participation in the community's social life. Furthermore, this study, if it has done nothing else, has demonstrated clearly that, for a complete cross section of a relatively homogeneous age and sex group in one community in contemporary America, the home an adolescent comes from conditions in a very definite manner the way he behaves in his relations with the school, the church, the job, recreation, his peers, and his family.

We believe that one of the important things this study highlights is the diversity of behavior exhibited by adolescents in the different classes in their day-to-day activities. We might have assumed that in a community the size of Elmtown with a stable, white, native-born population, there would be more uniformity in the behavior of this age group than we found. Common-sense judgments might have inclined us to think that in such a narrowly restricted age group social behavior would fall into a more or less common pattern in each sex group. That it did not was a surprise. In view of this fact, we shall attempt to explain tentatively how we think the functional relationship between class position and behavior develops.

To begin with, we must recognize that the child receives the vast majority of his experiences during the pre-school years in his parental home and in the immediate neighborhood around his home. During these years essential aspects of the class culture which characterize the family are transferred through the subtle processes of informal learning from the parents to the child. What the child learns in the home is carried out of it to the neighborhood, and the child is not aware of the connection between home influence and what he does. In this way, family background goes along with the child wherever he goes, and what he has learned in the home acts as a powerful influence on his behavior in non-family social situations.

The class aspect of this learning process is intensified in Elmtown by the fact that families in a given neighborhood belong, with few exceptions, either to the same or an adjacent class; inevitably, they possess the same or similar class cultures. Consequently, the neighborhood children, with whom a child is prone to play, tend to have the same or similar traits and attitudes. As a result, children in the same class, living in the same neighborhood, learn similar definitions of acceptable and unacceptable behavior relative to the family, the job, property, money, the school, the government, men, women, sex, recreation. It is thus perfectly normal for families in the same or an adjacent class, concentrated in a particular residential area (the 400 area for classes I and II, and "down by the canal" or "below the canal" for class V) to provide their children with significantly different learning situations from those of families in other classes who live in other residential areas. Moreover, children in a given neighborhood who belong to the same or adjacent classes, and who are associated intimately in their play groups, also tend to develop similar conceptions of themselves, of other children, of adults, and of society.

The behavior patterns and conceptions of right and wrong, of self, of others, and of society learned by the child in the home and the neighborhood are carried into the school, the church, and other areas of community life. In these situations the child encounters children from other neighborhoods who have other behavior patterns and other definitions of behavior. In these non-family, non-neighborhood situations, the attitudes and behavior patterns associated with certain classes are more acceptable than others. In the school situation, for example, the behavior patterns of classes I, II, and III are generally acceptable, whereas those of class V are tabooed. This means that children from the three higher classes are not only socially acceptable to the school and to one another, but also that the things they have learned at home and in the neighborhood are not abhorred. On the contrary, the little class V boy or girl is not acceptable socially, nor are the things he has learned "across the tracks" approved in the classroom or on the playground. Thus, from his earliest years in school the class II youngster knows what is "right"; he also knows he is "right." On the other hand, the class V youngster is "wrong" socially, and he is soon taught that he is "wrong." Furthermore, he is never allowed to forget that he is "wrong."

Children reared in class I, II, and III homes are taught to be "polite," to have "good manners," to be "refined," and to use "judicious" speech. They are taught also that personal aggression is extremely dangerous from the viewpoint of social acceptance. By precept and example, they learn that one's aims are to be achieved by stratagem and subterfuge rather than by combativeness. They are taught not to play with hoodlums, to watch their manners, to select carefully their friends, hobbies, and recreational pursuits. There is continual pressure from parents to study, to avoid the lower classes, to go to Sunday School regularly. The parents generally know the parents of the children with whom their children associate. If these friendships do not meet with their approval they ordinarily bring pressures to bear on the child to drop the friends and activities which do not conform with parental expectation. They are not always successful, but the pressure is active. On the whole, though, children in these three classes are guided by their parents along lines approved by the class cultures with remarkable success.

By way of contrast, the class V child reared "below" or "near" the canal learns very soon that his family is stigmatized in many ways—area of residence, kind of residence, occupation, reputation, number of children—and that he is held in contempt by boys and girls in the higher classes. He learns to resent his family, but he must rely upon it for food, clothes, and shelter. However, he has almost unlimited freedom to do as he desires, for his father is generally away from home, at work, or in search of pleasure, many times in jail, and his mother is busy trying to eke out a bare existence for her many children by means of a job outside the home. Since there is little or no room in the severely overcrowded small house where he may play, he plays along the river and the canal, in and near the coal chutes, and along the railroad tracks. His parents admonish him to be a "good" boy (a "little lady" in the case of a girl), but there is little effective control over his play. From the age of 5 or 6 he is faced with the responsibility of looking out for himself in the neighborhood, in school, and around the community. By the time adolescence is reached he has assumed full control of himself and his activities. He earns his own money, makes his own choices, and believes that he is acting as a "free agent." Actually he does what he and his fellows have learned they must do if they are to play the roles appropriate for their age and class statuses. In his thoughts and actions, he is bolstered by his clique mates (and it is not coincidence that almost all are class V's, and the rest are class IV's) as well as by older youths and adults in the social circles in which he moves. He insists upon absolute freedom in the spending of his money. If one tells him he is foolish to spend his money for old cars, flashy clothes, liquor, gambling, and sex, one will be told forcibly—we experimented on this point with a few class V's we knew well—"No one can tell me how I am going to spend my money. Did you earn it?" This insistence upon freedom to do what he desires brings him into conflict with the law with significantly greater frequency than the other classes. This situation, however, is accepted by the class V youngster as something he must expect for he has seen it happen with parents, relatives, and friends.

Our points are: first, children's behavior patterns are established primarily by their early experiences in the family and secondarily in the neighborhood; and, second, similar experiences in family and neighborhood mold children into similar social types because their learning in both areas tends to be strongly associated with class. The great majority of these adolescents have had most of their childhood experiences in the intimate, limited area of family and neighborhood. In this world of close, interpersonal relationships they have learned how their families are regarded in the larger non-family area of society. In the neighborhood they also come in contact with persons, both children and adults, from other classes and neighborhoods. It is here that they first become aware that there are people socially different from themselves.

Thus, we infer that the family and neighborhood sub-cultures not only set the stage upon which the child acts, but they also provide him with ways of acting and definitions of action. In addition, they make him realize that he will be rewarded for some kinds of behavior and punished for others. They provide him with roles, teach him how to play them, and accord him different status positions as he plays such roles as child in the family, pupil in the school, and little boy on the street. As he participates in successive social situations, he learns to act in certain ways, to regard himself as a valued member of the group or as an unwanted person. Unconsciously, he is being molded into a personality that is simultaneously a creature of his experiences and a creator of new situations in which he will act as a molder of conduct.

The child, as actor in the social process, *manipulates* what he has learned from his associates in previous situations as he strives to adjust to new situations which make demands upon him moment by moment, hour by hour, day by day, week by week, and so on through the years. By the time he reaches adolescence his personality is formed. Also he has developed conceptions of (1) himself; (2) the social structure; (3) his place in it along with appropriate roles and statuses; (4) forms of behavior, approved and disapproved; and (5) means of doing what he desires even though it involves the violation of law and the mores.

Conceived of in this way adolescent behavior is a complex response to a series of definitions the child has learned in the family, the play group, and the school which have varying degrees of relevancy in recurrent and new social situations to which he has to adjust. Situations which children face daily are defined in a general way by the communal, the class, and the family cultures, but they are defined explicitly by the clique in which a child plays. Within the clique, definitions are placed on a situation which influence the child's behavior in that situation. The adjustments he makes to these definitions appear to be determined by the meaning each has for him, in relation to the others, as it applies in the situation of the moment. The effective definition that he follows appears to be more closely related to the definitions other children place upon the situation, at least what he thinks the others think, than it is to definitions his parents, teachers, ministers, police, and other adults place upon it. Therefore, the specific behavior traits exhibited by adolescents tend to be along lines approved by their clique mates, who also tend to be members of the same class.

The definition the child thinks his associates place upon the behavior demanded of him cannot be ignored, nor should it be separated from the complex, for the social situation the child participates in is a shared experience, and the definition placed upon it is shared generally by the participants. Moreover, the form it takes is often a response to what the group has learned previously in similar situations. Thus, past learning is redefined, when necessary, to fit the present. This process results in the constant projection of past learning into the present, the adolescent's present behavior being an adjustment to past learning interpreted in terms of the demands of the moment.

If this theoretical position is sound, the effects of differential learning in the home and the neighborhood during the childhood years are the basic conditioning factors which give rise to the highly significant differences in social behavior observed among the adolescents in the different classes. We shall conclude with the general proposition that, if an adolescent has been trained in the home and the neighborhood to act, let us say, like a class I person, and his clique associations are with class I boys or girls, that adolescent will reveal a class I behavior pattern in his non-family social activities. We believe that this generalization will apply to each class and to each area of social behavior. In view of it, we may expect adolescents reared in a given class to exhibit the behavior characteristics peculiar to that class. However, if these persons are presented with a different set of conditions in later years which come to have value for them in their efforts to adjust to new conditions, we may expect that there will be significant changes in their behavior. This implies that social mobility may be expected when a new set of definitions is learned in response to a new set of social conditions. This is a problem we have not touched in this study, but it is of great importance theoretically to sociologists and psychologists. It is also of interest from a practical viewpoint, because of its supposed prevalence in American society.

·········· **26** ··········

THE STATUS OF ADOLESCENTS IN AMERICAN

SOCIETY: A PROBLEM IN SOCIAL IDENTITY[1]

by Robert D. Hess and Irene Goldblatt

How are adolescents viewed by parents and by adolescents themselves? How accurate is each in predicting the response of the other group? These are among the questions explored in the following

[1] Support from the Social Science Committee of the University of Chicago is gratefully acknowledged.

experimental study by Robert D. Hess of the University of Chicago and Irene Goldblatt of the Institute for Juvenile Research. [From *Child Development,* 1957, *28,* 459-468. Reprinted by permission of the authors and the Society for Research in Child Development.]

Adolescents occupy an ambiguous position in American society. As a phase in personal and social development adolescence is a recognized period experienced by every American youth. As a status in the social structure, however, it is loosely defined at both entry and exit transition points and offers a set of vague and often conflicting roles. The age behaviors expected of adolescents by adults are viewed by society with ambivalence and anxiety. With the possible exception of old age, no other phase of individual development is so clearly marked by negative connotations and lack of positive sanctions.

It is obviously one of the central objectives of socialization to bring pre-adult members to equal status in the adult society. However, the

Table 1

MEAN ITEM RESPONSE BY ADOLESCENTS

	Ratings of		Predictions of Adults' Ratings of	
Traits	Teen-Agers	Adults	Teen-Agers	Adults
1. Neat–untidy	4.81	5.88	3.17	5.68
2. Patient–impatient	2.94	4.72	2.23	5.06
3. Cooperative–uncooperative	4.59	5.38	3.37	5.86
4. Serious–frivolous	4.50	5.56	2.70	5.41
5. Responsible–irresponsible	4.62	6.22	2.76	6.07
6. Courteous–rude	4.81	5.81	3.17	5.83
7. Mature–immature	4.62	6.06	2.87	6.00
8. Cautious–impulsive	2.69	5.44	2.10	5.28
9. Consistent–inconsistent	3.56	5.44	2.37	5.76
10. Grateful–ungrateful	4.81	5.72	3.00	5.83
11. Reliable–unreliable	5.19	5.97	3.40	5.93
12. Stable–unstable	4.35	5.47	2.90	5.93
13. Moral–immoral	5.16	5.53	3.80	5.79
14. Self-directed–easily influenced	3.72	5.28	3.17	5.68
15. Respectful–disrespectful	4.78	5.75	3.37	5.79
16. Unspoiled–spoiled	3.97	5.03	2.67	5.72
17. Considerate–inconsiderate	4.44	5.62	3.07	5.83
18. Self-controlled–wild	4.59	5.88	2.80	6.11
19. Thoughtful–thoughtless	4.66	5.66	3.13	5.86
20. Loving–angry	4.81	5.69	3.60	5.72
Means	4.38	5.60	2.80	5.71

difficulty of achieving this transition is affected by the subordinate individual's perception of the relative position of his status group in the structure of the society and by the attitudes of adults and their willingness to permit expressions of autonomy on the part of subordinate members.

Although there has been little systematic research on the status of adolescents in American society, as viewed by adults or by adolescents themselves, it is generally assumed that the attitudes of the society toward its teen-age members are characteristically depreciatory and often hostile. Our preliminary interviews with adolescents revealed their awareness of a presumed inferior reputation among adults. Adolescents frequently expressed the belief that they are, as a group, subject to condemnation, criticism and general devaluation by adults and that there exists among adults a stereotype of adolescents as sloppy, irresponsible, unreliable, inclined toward destructive and

TABLE 2

MEAN ITEM RESPONSE BY PARENTS

Traits	Ratings of		Predictions of Teen-Agers' Ratings of	
	Teen-Agers	Adults	Teen-Agers	Adults
1. Neat–untidy	3.98	5.00	4.93	5.00
2. Patient–impatient	2.48	3.69	5.14	2.58
3. Cooperative–uncooperative	4.45	4.84	5.96	3.84
4. Serious–frivolous	4.80	5.20	5.62	5.82
5. Responsible–irresponsible	4.87	5.24	6.02	6.09
6. Courteous–rude	4.44	4.86	5.48	4.30
7. Mature–immature	3.98	5.02	5.60	5.36
8. Cautious–impulsive	2.72	4.78	4.11	5.18
9. Consistent–inconsistent	3.57	4.18	5.53	3.18
10. Grateful–ungrateful	4.59	4.82	5.60	3.66
11. Reliable–unreliable	4.98	5.10	5.91	4.93
12. Stable–unstable	4.45	4.76	5.64	4.98
13. Moral–immoral	5.98	5.46	5.87	5.51
14. Self-directed–easily influenced	4.18	4.32	5.85	5.18
15. Respectful–disrespectful	4.50	5.22	5.56	4.70
16. Unspoiled–spoiled	3.70	4.31	5.54	4.22
17. Considerate–inconsiderate	4.22	4.78	5.66	3.77
18. Self-controlled–wild	4.62	5.34	5.32	5.16
19. Thoughtful–thoughtless	4.09	5.24	5.54	4.49
20. Loving–angry	4.83	5.14	5.32	4.57
Means	4.27	4.86	5.51	4.63

anti-social behavior. It was the objective of our research to explore the evaluation of adolescents by both teen-agers and parents and the relationship between opinions of parents and teen-agers within the same family.

RESEARCH PROCEDURE

The Instrument

To obtain evaluations of adolescent and adult reputations, a set of rating scales of 20 pairs of adjectives was constructed. These pairs were selected from comments offered by teen-agers and adults in interviews about the problems of parent–teen-ager interaction. The adjectives represent socially desirable aspects of character and personality, and define in part the standards toward which the middle-class child is directed by his elders and, to a lesser extent, the terms in which the adolescent evaluates himself. The members of each pair can be viewed as positive and negative ends of a specific behavior continuum. Each pair of adjectives was set up on a seven-point scale, 7 representing the highest, or most desirable, rating, and 1 the lowest (*see* Table 1).

Testing Procedure

Each subject was asked to use the scales in making ratings on (a) the "average teen-ager," (b) the "average adult," (c) "teen-agers" from the viewpoint of an adult, and (d) "adults" from the viewpoint of an adult. This resulted for each adolescent in a set of ratings on teen-agers and adults and his prediction of the manner in which teen-agers would be rated by adults.[2] Similarly, each parent was instructed to rate (a) the average "teen-ager," (b) the "average adult," (c) "teen-agers" from the viewpoint of a teen-ager and (d) "adults" from the viewpoint of a teen-ager.

The testing procedure gave rise to the following sets of data:
A. Actual evaluation of own status group, or "self-rating"
   (1) adolescents' rating of teen-agers
   (2) parents' rating of adults
B. Evaluation of the other status group, or "actual reputation"
   (1) adolescents' ratings of adults
   (2) parents' rating of teen-agers

[2] The rating scales were administered twice over a three-week interval to a group of six adolescents. Ninety-two per cent of the scores shifted only one scale step or less from the first to the second administration of the scales.

C. Predictions of how the other status group would rate own status group, or "expected reputation"

    (1) adolescents' predictions on how adults would rate teen-agers

    (2) parents' predictions on how teen-agers would rate adults

D. Predictions of how members of the other status group would rate themselves, or "predicted self-rating"

    (1) adolescents' predictions of how adults would rate adults

    (2) parents' predictions of how teen-agers would rate teen-agers

Sample

Ratings were collected in conjunction with an interview study of 32 families, a study concerned with exploring beliefs and attitudes about teen-agers as these affect parent-child relationships during the adolescent period. The sample was composed of 32 adolescents, 16 boys and 16 girls, and 54 parents, 30 mothers and 24 fathers. In each family, interviews and rating scales were administered to the mother and her teen-age child. The father was interviewed in slightly more than one-half of the families. However, whenever possible, rating scales were obtained from fathers, even if they were not accessible for interviewing. All interviews were taken in the home and the rating instrument was administered in the course of the interview.

The families in the sample were upper-middle and middle class in a metropolitan area. Twenty-three of the families were Protestant, one was Catholic, and seven were Jewish. There was one mixed marriage, Protestant and Jewish.

Average age of the boys was 15.9 years; the average of the girls, 15.5 years. The average high school grade of both boys and girls was 2.8. Two of the adolescent subjects attended private, non-denominational schools, one attended a parochial school, and the remaining 29 were enrolled in a public high school.

FINDINGS

PERCEPTION OF THE STATUS DIFFERENCE BETWEEN THE TWO GROUPS

Ratings of the Two Groups on "The Average Teen-Ager"

Both adolescents and parents rated teen-agers in a mildly favorable manner. Fifteen of the ratings by adolescents fell above the scale mean (4.0) and five below (Table 1). The mean rating that adolescents gave to teen-agers, on all items, was 4.38. Parents rated teen-agers above the scale mean on 14 of the items and below on six (Table 2). Expected differences between the ratings of parents and those of adolescents did not emerge. Only three of the differences between adolescent and parent ratings were statistically significant at the .05 level of confidence (items 1, 7, 13). On one of these, the moral-immoral continuum, the parents gave teen-agers a significantly higher (more positive) rating than did the adolescents themselves.

Ratings by the Two Groups on "The Average Adult"

Both adolescents and parents believe that adults are superior to the teen-ager on all but one (item 13) of the 20 characteristics. Not only did both groups rate the adult more favorably than they rated the teen-ager, but the adolescent subjects gave much higher mean ratings to adults than did the parents. The mean rating on all items by adolescent subjects was 5.60; that of the parents was 4.86. Adolescents rated adults higher than did the parents on each of the 20 items. Sixteen of these item differences were statistically significant. Only items 4, 8, 13, and 19 showed insignificant differences.

The Extent of Perceived Differences between Teen-Agers and Adults

The difference between each group's rating of teen-agers and its rating of adults (Tables 1 and 2, col. 2 minus col. 1) can be considered an expression of the distance in status as it is differently perceived by the two groups. It has already been noted that teen-agers are rated in a mildly favorable manner by both groups, and that adults are be-

TABLE 3

COEFFICIENTS OF ASSOCIATION (TAU) BETWEEN THE RATINGS

OF PARENTS AND OWN CHILDREN

	Children			
	Expectation of Underevaluation (Table 1, col. 1—col. 3)			
	Girls	N	Boys	N
Parents: Perception of Status Difference (Table 2, col. 4—col. 1)				
Mother	.55*	(13)	.59*	(13)
Father	.13	(11)	.00	(10)

* $p < .01$.

lieved to be superior to teen-agers. However, adolescents accentuate in their ratings the relative superiority of adults over teen-agers. In scale terms, the distance between adults and teen-agers is perceived by the adolescents to be almost twice as large as that seen by parents. These differences apparently represent the different concerns of the two groups. Both groups share the opinion that teen-agers have a relatively long way to go before they reach the adult level of self control. However, the adolescent subjects seem to feel that they are much less "responsible" and less "self-directing" than adults, while the parents seem relatively unconcerned about these characteristics.

EXPECTED REPUTATION

The Attempt to Predict the Ratings of the Other Group

The adolescent's view of his status in the social system is a function of the reputation he anticipates from adults as well as his own view of his age group. It is significant, then, that the adolescents of our sample predict that teen-agers will be evaluated in a generally unfavorable manner by the adult group.

All of the ratings which the adolescent subjects anticipate will be given to teen-agers by adults fall below the scale mean (Table 1, col. 3). Adolescents expect that the lowest ratings will describe them as impulsive, impatient, inconsistent, spoiled, frivolous, irresponsible, and wild. In contrast to the unfavorable reputation adolescents believe the teen-ager has, the parents in the sample believe that their own status group has a mildly favorable reputation among teen-agers.

Disparity between Expected Reputation and Self-Ratings

The difference between the adolescents' own rating of teen-agers and their predictions of the average adults' rating of teen-agers can be regarded as a measure of the extent to which teen-agers will feel underrated or depreciated. The data indicate that adolescents expect to be underrated on each of the items. On 18 of the items (all except 8 and 14) the difference between self-ratings and expected ratings is statistically significant (Table 1). By contrast, parents predict that teen-agers will significantly underrate adults on only six items (2, 3, 9, 10, 17, 19; Table 2, col. 2 minus col. 4).

The items on which the parents feel that adults will be underrated can be seen as relating to tension in interpersonal relationships. However, parents believe that qualities of maturity which are relatively independent of interpersonal relationships will either be accurately perceived by the teen-ager or even overrated. These ratings suggest that parents feel they will be seen as mature but unsympathetic or ill-intentioned in interpersonal affairs. They feel that they will be seen as more "uncooperative," "ungrateful," "impatient," and "thought-less" than they really are.

RATINGS INDICATING EXPECTED PERCEPTION OF STATUS DIFFERENCES

Predictions of the Self-Ratings of the Other Group

The disparities already mentioned are emphasized by the belief each group has about the ratings which they think members of the other group will give themselves. Two sets of predictions are in-volved: the adolescents' predictions of how adults will rate them-selves, and the parents' predictions of the ratings teen-agers will give themselves (Table 1, col. 4; Table 2, col. 3). Both groups believe that members of the other status group will have very favorable opinions of themselves. Parents predict that teen-agers will rate them-selves above the scale mean on all items. Adolescents believe that adults will rate themselves above the mean on all items. The differ-ence between the two sets of predicted self-ratings is very small.

Disparity between Predicted Self-Ratings and Own Ratings

The parents' predictions of the teen-ager's favorable opinion of himself represents a belief that teen-agers will overestimate them-selves on the traits in question, since the parents themselves give a generally lower rating to teen-agers. In contrast the adolescent expects that parents will see themselves in the same favorable light as he sees them. In effect, teen-agers are expressing confidence in the parents' judgment, even when the parents are evaluating themselves. By the same rationale, parents expect that teen-agers will be conceited, or, at best, unrealistic when judging themselves. This expectation is expressed by significant differences on 17 of the 20 items (exceptions are 13, 18, and 20; Table 2, col. 1 minus col. 3). There is only one reversal: parents say that teen-agers will underrate themselves on "moral" behavior.

Comparison of the rank ordering of items revealed that parents believe teen-agers will emphasize items having to do with readiness for emancipation from parental control. Such items as "responsible," "mature," "consistent," "stable," and "self-directed" rank higher in the predicted self-estimate than in the parents' ratings of adolescents. In complementary fashion, parents expect that adolescents will rate themselves *relatively* low on "self-controlled," "cautious," "neat," and "patient." This indicates that these parents believe that teen-agers think of themselves as ready to lead their own lives—but along rather hedonistic lines.

The Expected Perception of Status Difference

A measure of predicted status differential between the two groups may be obtained by a comparison between the view the adolescent has of his reputation with adults and the view he thinks adults will have of themselves. This is the teen-ager's prediction of his relative status in the eyes of the adults.

Considered in these terms, the data show that *adolescents think adults will see themselves as vastly superior to the average teen-ager* (Table 1, cols. 3 and 4). Further, adolescents predict that adults' opinion of the status difference will be much greater than adolescents believe it is (Table 1, cols. 1 and 2 compared with cols. 3 and 4).[3]

PARENTAL ATTITUDES AND THE RATINGS BY OWN TEEN-AGERS

It was assumed that the ratings given by adolescents to the "average adult" and to the "average teen-ager" were not unaffected by the attitudes encountered in their own family experience. The ratings of parent-child pairs were examined, therefore, to determine the degree of association between mother-child pairs and between father-child pairs.

The resulting coefficients offer evidence that the mother's attitudes are more influential than the father's in determining the attitudes of the teen-agers. The mother's perception of status difference (Table 2, col. 2 minus col. 1) correlates significantly with the extent to which her teen-agers feel underrated (Table 1, col. 1 minus col. 3). That is, the larger the status difference that the mother perceives between adults and teen-agers, the lower the reputation that her adolescent

---

[3] An indication of the characteristic adolescent attitude toward their status in adult minds is seen in the relatively small range that appeared in the predicted ratings. In rating their own group and the adult group, the range between highest and lowest mean rating is three scale steps; in the predicted ratings this range is two scale steps. The adolescents, then, are predicting that the average adult will show little discrimination in evaluating teen-agers and will underrate them even on traits on which the teen-agers feel most competent and acceptable. The parents do not make a comparable assumption in the ratings they expect from teen-agers.

predicts teen-agers have. This relationship is highly significant and holds for both mother-daughter and mother-son pairs (Table 3). However, the father's perception of the adult–teen-ager status difference appears to have virtually no effect upon the attitudes of his children as indicated by insignificant coefficients with both sons and daughters.[4]

Although adolescents appear to be sensitive to their mothers' evaluations, their own ratings of teen-agers are relatively independent of parental opinion. The comparison between the ratings of parents and their children on the "average teen-ager" reveals no significant association between adolescents and either father or mother (Pearson r's of .062 and .067 respectively). The teen-ager's feeling about his group's reputation among adults thus appears to be determined in part by the attitudes of his own mother toward teen-agers as a group but he resists her influence in making his evaluation of his own group.

Summary of Findings

1. Adolescents and parents agree in expressing mildly favorable opinions of teen-agers.

2. The adolescents tend to idealize adults, i.e., they have much higher opinions of adults than do the parents.

3. Adolescents see a relatively greater status difference between teen-agers and adults than do the parents.

4. Adolescents believe that the average adult has a generalized tendency to depreciate teen-agers. They feel that teen-agers have a uniformly low reputation among adults.

5. Parents anticipate that teen-agers will have a selective tendency to undervalue adults. They predict that adults will get lower ratings than they merit on items which refer to interpersonal relationships, but that they will be accurately evaluated on non-interpersonal maturity items.

6. Adolescents believe that the adults will evaluate themselves relatively accurately.

7. Parents believe that teen-agers have unrealistically high opinions of themselves.

8. Both adolescents and parents believe that the status difference

[4] The attitudes of fathers about teen-agers are significantly related to those of the mothers in the sample (Pearson $r = .44$) but their perception of the status difference between the two groups is not (Pearson $r = .18$).

between teen-agers and adults will be distorted to approximately the same extent by the other group.

9. The attitude of the adolescent about the relative status of teen-agers is significantly associated with the opinions of his mother about the adult–teen-age status difference. However, the opinion of his parents is not related statistically to his evaluation of the "average teen-ager."

10. The attitude of the father as expressed in the rating scales is not significantly associated with ratings of his own teen-age children.

Three trends in the data stand out as particularly relevant to parent-adolescent relationships and to theories of adolescent socialization: (a) the agreement between the two groups in their evaluation of teen-agers; (b) the perceptual distortions of both groups in predicting the response of the other group; and (c) the immense status difference between the groups that teen-agers believe exists in the minds of adults. The prominence of these trends emphasizes the difficulties faced by the adolescent in his effort to effect a transition from adolescence to adult roles and behavior.

From their own point of view, the adolescents credit themselves with an acceptable degree of achievement which, nevertheless, places their group in a subordinate position with respect to adults. This willingness to admit a differentiation between their own status and that of adults is in agreement with the views of adults, though it tends to exaggerate the status distance.

The assumption by parents that teen-agers have unrealistically high opinions of themselves is not corroborated by the data obtained from adolescents themselves. This parental belief may, to some extent, simply represent a response to, and acceptance at face value of, a protective bravado and air of competency which the adolescent assumes to protect himself, both from arousing parental anxieties and from his own feelings of inadequacy.

Our data suggest that one of the central problems in parent–teen-ager relations lies not so much in disparity between their respective evaluations of adolescents as in the fact that each group mistrusts or misunderstands the opinions of the other. Parents and adolescents thus interpret teen-age behavior and problems in different, and often contradictory, terms. For the adolescent, teen-age problems are expressed in terms of *ego functions*—autonomy, self-control and judgment based upon exploratory experience with adult roles. For the parent, the problems of teen-agers are primarily concerned with control of *id impulses* for which, they believe, parental supervision and control are essential. Both views, of course, are to a degree realistic and the families of our study which displayed a minimum of parent-child conflict were those in which parents and teen-agers were willing to recognize the importance of both viewpoints.

The status difference between the groups probably serves a positive socializing function for the teen-ager. A moderate overestimation of the attributes of adults offers a lever for the parent in the socializing process and provides motivation for the adolescent towards increased autonomy and maturity. However, the extreme idealization of the adult by the adolescent, when it is joined with a belief that personal achievements he has made are not recognized by adults, may retard ego development and encourage behaviors which defeat the objectives of both parents and adolescents themselves.

CHAPTER TEN

Sex Information, Attitudes, and Behavior

27

THE SEX INFORMATION OF YOUNGER BOYS

by Glenn V. Ramsey

What do teen-age boys know about sex? What are their sources of information and at what ages do they acquire the information? These are some of the questions that Glenn V. Ramsey of Austin, Texas, attempts to answer in the article that follows. [From *American Journal of Orthopsychiatry*, 1943, *13*, 347-352. Reprinted by permission of the author and the American Orthopsychiatric Association.]

Data are presented in this report concerning: (1) the nature of the sex information of 291 pre-adolescent and early adolescent boys; (2) ages at which the information was acquired; (3) sources of information; (4) the sex vocabularies of these boys. The data are drawn from the complete sex histories of these boys. All of the histories were obtained by personal interview. Ages ranged from 10 to 20 years, although 85 per cent of the population ranged from 12 to 16 years of age. Five of the boys were Negro and 286 were white. Approximately 75 per cent of the group was Protestant, 7 per cent Catholic, 3 per cent Jewish, and 15 per cent of no religious affiliation. The population was composed primarily of boys from the middle and upper-middle socio-economic levels of a Middle

Western city of over 100,000 people. One-half of the boys, 146 to be exact, comprised the whole of the seventh and eighth grade male populations in one of the junior high schools of the city. This hundred per cent sample afforded an unusually valuable measure of the adequacy of the whole series used in the study. The remainder of the population (145) was a random sample drawn from organized neighborhood groups which meet in various sections of the city. The present data and generalizations are offered as interpretations of the boys we studied, and it should be recognized that further information is needed before generalizations are made for boys in general.

AGE AND SEX INFORMATION

There are relatively few published data concerning the extent of sex information of younger boys. Hattendorf's report (1932) concerning questions asked during an 18 month period by 563 boys revealed that sex questions appeared as early as the second year and that such questions were most frequent during the years six, seven, and nine. Hamilton (1929) made several inquiries concerning the sex education of the 100 men in his study. The responses to the question concerning age at which first information about sex matters was received produced the following percentages:

Under age 6	14%
6 to 11 inclusive	68
12 to 15 inclusive	13
16 and older	3
Unknown	2

Bromley and Britten (1938) state that two-thirds of the 1,364 college students included in their study had obtained information concerning abortions and birth control methods before leaving high school. Terman, et al. (1938) reports as follows on the time that information concerning the origin of babies was secured by 678 men.

Before age 6	8%
Ages 6 to 11	60
Ages 12 to 16	30
Over age 16	2

In the present study each boy reported the age at which he first secured information concerning nine specific items of sex, as shown below.

TABLE 1

SEX INFORMATION OF 291 BOYS BY AGE GROUPS

Age	Total population passing through each age	Ejaculation	Mother origin of babies	Nocturnal emissions	Contraceptives	Menstruation	Masturbation	Intercourse	Prostitution	Venereal disease
5	291	0 %	4.8%	0 %	0 %	0 %	4.2%	.3%	0 %	0 %
6	291	0	12.4	.3	0	0	8.9	8.3	.7	0
7	291	1.0	20.6	1.0	.4	.4	14.2	16.6	1.4	0
8	291	3.0	33.1	2.4	2.2	.9	23.6	27.7	2.7	0
9	291	6.5	47.1	5.9	5.2	2.6	33.2	41.9	8.9	1.3
10	291	14.4	69.1	10.7	10.0	4.8	43.2	57.5	23.4	3.1
11	290	33.7	84.8	24.0	34.6	14.1	62.7	79.5	43.1	10.1
12	283	56.7	94.7	40.0	56.3	22.6	80.4	90.8	66.5	21.3
13	237	78.8	97.9	57.6	76.6	32.2	90.9	96.2	89.0	39.1
14	165	92.7	100.0	72.8	86.5	37.8	95.7	98.8	96.9	57.2
15	104	99.0		84.6	88.4	48.8	99.0	99.5	100.0	62.2
16	64	100.0		95.3	88.4	87.5	100.0	100.0		76.5
17	42			97.6	93.8	100.0				90.0
18	24			96.1	100.0					

It is evident from Table 1 that most of the boys were introduced to the various topics of sex information before they reached senior high school age. A considerable amount of information was had before they reached age 10. By age 14, nearly all had a fair idea of the processes of human reproduction, and considerable information concerning other items of human sexual behavior. Over 95 per cent at the age of 14 knew about the origin of babies, masturbation, intercourse, and prostitution. Over 86 per cent at age 14 knew about contraceptives. Approximately half of the boys at age 14 had secured at least some information concerning venereal diseases. At all ages the boys had more knowledge of male than of female sexual physiology.

It should be pointed out, however, that a mere introduction to some fact or an experience with some form of sexual phenomenon does not in itself indicate that the individual is equipped with the necessary information and interpretation that will enable him to meet his individual and social needs. The above data indicate that any program of sex instruction which is designed to provide the initial information for a boy, must reach him well before the onset of adolescence. Otherwise companions and other miscellaneous sources will have contributed to his early education. The histories of these boys show considerable variation in their ages at the onset of adolescence, and the ages at which they need information **and** guidance will, in consequence, vary considerably.

SOURCES OF SEX INFORMATION

The sources contributing to the sex information of boys have received more study than the ages at which that information is acquired. The studies of Hughes (1926), Exner (1915), Achilles (1923), and Peck and Wells (1923), indicate that companions are the chief source of such information for most males. Companions were reported as the primary source of information in 78 per cent of the 1,029 boys in the Hughes study (1926), and by 85.4 per cent of the 948 college men in the Exner investigation (1915). Two-thirds of the 596 males in the Achilles (1923) study reported contemporaries or self experience as their primary source of information concerning masturbation and nocturnal emissions. The sources of information as given by 168 college men in the Peck and Wells study (1923) were: companions, 28 per cent; home, 27 per cent; school, 12 per cent; books, 12 per cent; and the remaining percentages were scattered. These data were all acquired by the questionnaire method. First sources of information for nine specific items about sex are given in the following table.

TABLE 2

FIRST SOURCES, SEX INFORMATION OF 291 BOYS

First source of information	Origin of babies %	Ejacu-lation %	Noc-turnal emis-sions %	Con-tracep-tives %	Men-strua-tion %	Mas-turba-tion %	Inter-course %	Prosti-tution %	Vene-real dis-eases %
Conversation, male companions	52.5	67.4	68.0	92.1	57.6	44.2	90.9	93.0	65.5
Conversation, female companions	.7	—	—	.5	4.3	—	1.7	—	—
Mother	27.5	1.3	2.8	2.7	20.2	1.0	.5	1.5	4.8
Father	3.5	2.6	2.8	1.6	4.3	—	1.0	1.9	4.8
Printed matter	4.4	2.2	1.6	1.0	5.1	2.1	2.1	1.3	14.3
Adults	3.0	1.3	2.4	.5	4.3	.4	.5	1.3	6.8
Observation	4.1	11.3	—	—	2.1	21.2	.7	—	—
Actual experience	—	10.9	22.4	—	—	30.7	—	—	—
Others (school, movies, radio, etc.)	2.2	—	—	—	—	—	—	—	3.8
Indefinite or unknown	2.1	3.0	—	1.6	2.1	‡	2.6	1.0	—

The data from the present study are in accord with those previously reported in finding male companions as the primary source of the sex information of boys. Approximately 90 per cent of the first information that boys receive is acquired from male companions or their own experience. On less personal matters of sex (origin of babies, venereal diseases, menstruation) other sources of information become slightly more important, but even with these items companions rank first as the initial source of information. Parents are rarely reported as the first source of information for the particular items explored in this study. When instruction is given by parents, it is given by the mother more often than by the father. Schools, church, radio, printed material, and adults other than parents appear only rarely as the first source of the boys' information, except for one item, namely, venereal diseases. In general, the data indicate that those sources which might be considered most reliable are not the ones that contribute to the early information which boys have in this area of knowledge.

PARENTS AND SEX INSTRUCTION

The published data concerning the later contributions of parents and guardians to the sex education of their children show (from reports given by children) that approximately 50 per cent of the families make *no* attempt to give instruction in this field. Percentages reported for parents that offered *no* sex instruction to their children follow.

Hamilton (1929)	100 males	40%
Butterfield (1939)	98 males and females	48
Bromley and Britten (1938)	1,364 college students	over 50
Hughes (1926)	1,029 boys	50
Terman et al. (1938)	768 men	62

In the present study 55 per cent of the boys stated that neither parent had contributed anything to their sex education (see Table 3).

TABLE 3

BOYS' RATINGS OF PARENTS' CONTRIBUTION TO SEX EDUCATION *

Source	None	Little	Fair	Adequate
Mother	60%	29%	10%	1%
Father	82	13	4	1
Either parent	55	32	12	1

* Percentages based on 287 boys.

In order to evaluate the adequacy of parental sex instruction, each subject was asked to rate the amount of sex information he had received from each parent as "adequate," "fair," "little," or "none." The results are presented in the above table. Only 13 per cent of the boys rated their parents' efforts in sex education as fair or adequate. This figure is in close agreement with previous reports on this point. The similar figures as reported by Hamilton (1929), Bromley and Britten (1938), Achilles (1923), and Terman, et al. (1938), would range from 7 per cent to 15 per cent. The fact is evident that the majority of parents make little or no effort to give sex instruction to their children and that only one of every ten parents is rated by the children as doing a fair or adequate job.

A SEX VOCABULARY SURVEY

A sex vocabulary check list was used in an attempt to determine the extent to which a selected vocabulary was known to 128 boys of the one hundred per cent group (see Table 4).

The results of this survey show that the boys in this study had a very limited vocabulary of standard terms about sex. Many, however, revealed during individual interviews that they were acquainted with many of the phenomena which appear in the lower percentages of words known. Vernacular terms or awkward euphemisms are employed by them to discuss reproductive system and sexual behavior. These boys would find it difficult to read the simplest printed matter concerning sex and reproduction. In any sex instruction, by printed or oral methods, effort would have to be directed toward the development of an adequate sex vocabulary.

SUMMARY

In this report on 291 boys, data are presented showing that most of the boys had acquired considerable sex information during their pre-adolescent years. Male companions were reported by the boys as the primary source of sex information. Approximately 55 per cent state that neither parent had contributed to their sex instruction, and only 13 per cent rated their parents' efforts at sex instruction as fair or adequate. The sex vocabulary survey shows that the boys as a group had a very limited knowledge of recognized words and phrases which pertain to sexual biology and sexual behavior.

TABLE 4

SEX VOCABULARIES OF SEVENTH- AND EIGHTH-GRADE BOYS*

Word	Known	Not clear	Unknown
1. Female	96%	2%	2%
2. Male	95	2	3
3. Animal	87	5	8
4. Fertilize	53	21	26
5. Sex	46	31	23
6. Urine	44	18	38
7. Circumcision	28	19	53
8. Reproduction	26	27	47
9. Urinate	23	16	61
10. Wet dreams	22	19	59
11. Labor pains	21	23	46
12. Penis	19	25	56
13. Erection	14	20	66
14. Operation	13	11	76
15. Sperm	13	34	53
16. Intercourse	11	17	72
17. Premature	10	15	75
18. Ovum	9	16	75
19. Testes	8	31	61
20. Ovaries	8	17	75
21. Vagina	6	3	91
22. Scrotum	6	8	86
23. Emissions	4	8	88
24. Abortion	3	6	91
25. Conception	3	7	90
26. Oviduct	3	3	94
27. Semen	2	19	79
28. Menstruation	2	16	82
29. Masturbation	2	2	96
30. Pregnancy	2	14	84
31. Embryo	2	17	81
32. Ejaculation	2	7	91
33. Uterus	0	12	87

* Each percentage based on 127 or 128 responses.

·············· **28** ··············

DATING BEHAVIOR OF COLLEGE STUDENTS

by Winston W. Ehrmann

What is the dating behavior of college students? To what extent do they engage in physical intimacies and to what degrees? In the following selection, Winston W. Ehrmann of Colorado State University reports the results of his study of more than eight hundred unmarried college students of both sexes on their physical love-making during dating. He describes the most intimate physical stage to which the student goes or has ever gone (according to this research) in his dating, who initiates the activity leading into a given stage, and who or what stops the activity from going into a more intimate stage. Details of the findings and interpretations of these premarital sexual activities have been published by Ehrmann (1959). [From *Marriage and Family Living*, 1952, *14*, 322-326. Reprinted by permission of the author and of the National Council on Family Relations.]

. . . The fact that this behavior falls into highly compartmental stages of increasing "degrees of intensity" both with respect to physical intimacy and to moral judgment, from no physical contact at the lower limit to sexual intercourse at the upper limit, readily lends itself to analysis in terms of control.

The control of this highly compartmentalized behavior can be measured both (1) in terms of the most advanced stage to which a person goes in his current behavior or has ever gone in his life, and (2) in terms of who initiates the activity leading into a given stage and who or what stops the activity from going into a more advanced stage. Attitudes can be studied in terms of why a person does or does not engage in these activities. The writer used as subjects samples of single students not previously married who were enrolled in his classes in Marriage and the Family. In all we had an exploratory group, a schedule group, and an interview group.

The exploratory group consisted of thirty males in 1946 when the university was not coeducational. Exploratory interviews were held with these subjects solely for the purpose of testing the practicability of collecting information about dating behavior in accordance with the technique described in this paper. It was found that the method for recording dating behavior and its control was feasible. Many of the students in this group made invaluable suggestions about the proposed oral and written instructions and about the format and content of the tentative schedule. It was decided to administer the schedule to a sufficient number of students, the schedule group, so that at least two hundred usable ones would be obtained from each of these three groups: male veterans, male non-veterans, and females. The problem of obtaining over two hundred female subjects was solved when the state legislature made the university coeducational beginning in the fall semester 1947.

Over a period of three years subjects were selected by random sample from the classes in Marriage and the Family. The schedule was administered to them on a purely voluntary basis either individually or in sex segregated groups. Of about one thousand students to whom the schedule was given only two students, both girls who were among the first subjects, returned the blanks unanswered. The number of students that subsequently completed schedules was 985. Therefore, including the exploratory group, a total of 1015 took part in the study. The 841, or 85.4 per cent, of the schedules that were sufficiently complete to be used in the final tabulation consisted of data from 302 male veterans, 274 male non-veterans, and 265 females.

In order to test the degree of reliability of the data and, even more importantly, to investigate certain interrelated aspects of the individuals' attitudes, it was decided to select a smaller sample, the interview group, from the schedule group and to have with each a personal interview. The interview was to cover precisely the same material that was covered on the written schedule, and in addition the interviewer was to obtain from each subject his attitudes on many aspects of dating behavior which centered around the individual's moral evaluation of this behavior and its control, and which, because of its complex nature, could not be readily obtained from a written schedule until some simplified standardization of technique can be devised. Eventually interviews were had with 100 students: 50 males (25 veterans and 25 non-veterans) and 50 females.

The most important matter in the organization of the data was to determine the classification of the physical love-making activities in dating into various categories which are here called "stages." The ideal classification would be to have each distinct behavior pattern as a separate stage. From the practical consideration of the ease with which the average subject could codify his own behavior this arrangement was found to be impractical. It was discovered, as a result of the exploratory interviews and as might be expected, that the subject could give the best response with the use of the fewest number of categories. Adjustment between theoretical considerations and practical matters had to be made. The most satisfactory solution seemed to be to have the following eight categories which were used in Schedule *A*:

Stage   *Description*

A   No dates within specified period.

Dates involving:

B   No physical contact or only holding of hands.
C   Kissing and hugging, or boy fondling the girl's breast with his hands outside her clothes, or both.
D   Boy fondling girl's naked breast, as well as any activity in *C*.
E   Boy fondling girl's genitals or naked area around genitals, as well any activity in *C* or *D*.
F   Sexual intercourse, as well as any activity in *C*, *D*, or *E*.
(Stages *B*, *C*, *D*, *E*, and *F* are mutually exclusive)

G   Female fondling male's genitals through his clothes.
H   Female fondling male's naked genitals.
(Stages *G* and *H* are not mutually exclusive either to the other or to *B*, *C*, *D*, *E*, and *F*)

Although the classification into stages is an essential and integral part of the study, it is in addition the means whereby a more specific pattern of control can be determined. In order to obtain this information each subject indicated for the dates in each stage (1) who initiated the behavior, male or female, and (2) who or what situation prevented it from going beyond that stage; in other words, who starts and who or what stops the behavior in each compartmentalized pattern. The *positive control* of the behavior is represented by who initiates the behavior, male or female, and the *negative control* by who or what prevents the behavior from going beyond a particular stage. The negative control is divided into four categories: the behavior went no farther because (1) there was no opportunity (inappropriateness of the situation), (2) the girl would not, (3) the boy would not, and (4) neither tried to go farther. A summary of controls of all dates of all individuals is given in Table 1.

PATTERN OF CONTROL FOR ALL DATES

	As reported by males	As reported by females
P. Percentage of dates on which behavior initiated by		
P1 boy	75.3	78.9
P2 girl	24.7	21.1
	100.0	100.0
N. Percentage of dates on which behavior went no farther because		
N1 no opportunity	22.9	13.0
N2 girl would not	29.6	30.1
N3 boy would not	4.9	2.2
N4 neither tried	42.6	54.7
	100.0	100.0

(NOTE: The above figures are based upon the sum of all dates of all individuals.)

As a result of student reactions and suggestions, during the first part of the data-collecting phase, certain aspects of the instructions and the schedule were modified at two different times. The first modification came after about two hundred schedules, mainly from men, had been received. Requesting the subjects to report their behavior for a typical or representative month during the preceding year was not a satisfactory procedure for many. For those who had had a fairly regular pattern of behavior over this period it was satisfactory, but not for the rest. As a result of discussions with many of these students, it was determined that the "current behavior pattern," as reported on a monthly basis, was a more definite entity to the subjects than "a typical or representative month." All subsequent subjects were instructed to complete this part of the schedule on this basis and also to report the length of time covered by their current behavior pattern.

The second modification was made after approximately thirty per cent of the eventual total of schedules had been completed. At this point it was decided to make certain minor though important additions to Schedule *A* to construct Schedule *B* primarily because of certain criticisms raised by many of the female subjects, particularly the interview group. Their major criticisms were (1) that whether a person is going steady or not should be included on the schedule (this information had already been obtained in all of the interviews), and (2) that Stage C should be divided into two stages.

In view of the final empirical findings of the study, reclassification of Stage C in Schedule A into Stages C1 and C2 in Schedule B proved to be highly significant. The really critical point in dating behavior was found to exist between Stage C1 (kissing and hugging) and Stage C2 (boy fondling the girl's breast) according to Schedule B rather than between Stage C (kissing, hugging, or boy fondling girl's breasts) and Stage D (boy fondling girl's naked breasts) as had been originally inferred in the construction of Schedule A. The reason that this condition had not been established initially arose in part because the exploratory group were males and because the writer in an attempt to keep the number of different stages small erred in consolidating two behavior patterns that have quite different moral values placed upon them by students, particularly the females. Placing more than one behavior pattern in one stage is a satisfactory procedure as long as approximately the same moral evaluation is attached to each pattern. To the males in the exploratory group the consolidation of kissing, hugging (general bodily embrace), and the male feeling the female breast into a single stage seemed to be a reasonable procedure although they gave the unanimous opinion that kissing and hugging were somewhat more acceptable patterns of behavior than the male feeling the female breast. On the other hand when Schedule A was administered to the first group of females, the majority either suggested or protested that these activities ought to be placed into different stages.

Although this reclassification of stages is significant in determining the most advanced stage to which a person goes or has ever gone in his behavior, it is not so discriminating in influencing control in terms of who starts and who or what stops the behavior because these determiners tend to be similar in adjacent behavior patterns along the continuum. The classification of subjects according to the most advanced stage to which the individual goes in his current behavior is given both for the entire group of subjects (Schedules A and B) and for the second group only (Schedule B) in Table 2. These tables show quite vividly that although an apparent critical transition point occurs between Stages C and D, the more significant turning point is between C1 and C2, and the degree of difference is much more pronounced for the females than the males. This fact was, of course, foretold by the pronounced peronal reactions of the females. It must, of course, be emphasized that Table 2 gives the most advanced stage to which the individual goes. The greatest number of dates fall into Stage C; approximately ifty percent of the dates of the males and sixty percent of the females occur in this stage.

TABLE 2

THE MOST ADVANCED STAGE TO WHICH INDIVIDUAL GOES IN HIS
CURRENT BEHAVIOR

IIa. The Entire Group (Schedule A and B groups)

		A	B	C	D	E	F	Total
Males	%	3.9	4.7	30.6	5.4	16.6	38.8	100.0
Females	%	0.7	4.5	59.7	8.3	17.7	9.1	100.0
Males	f	23	27	176	31	96	223	576
Females	f	2	12	158	22	47	24	265

(d.f. = 5 $P < .001$ $X^2 = 102.02$)

IIb. The Second Group (Schedule B group only)

		A	B	C1	C2	D	E	F	Total
Males	%	4.4	4.2	22.8	11.0	5.0	16.2	36.4	100.0
Females	%	1.0	3.0	45.5	17.0	5.0	18.0	10.5	100.0
Males	f	17	16	87	42	19	62	139	382
Females	f	2	6	91	34	10	36	21	200

(d.f. = 6 $P < .001$ $X^2 = 62.92$)

One of the most frequently asked questions about these figures is, "Why are the figures for male and female students so different? Are the males boasting and the females lying; or is it because the girls who 'go all the way' are promiscuous with a great many different boys?" The assumption in these questions is that the male and female students have dates only with one another. If this situation were true, then the suppositions in the above questions would also be true, but the basic assumption is not correct. Furthermore, the writer was impressed by the fact that the overwhelming majority probably told the truth. The primary reason for the difference arises from the fact that the majority of the men students do not date coeds and that for many of the men who do, a majority of their dates are with girls who are not coeds. This result is to be expected in a situation where the men outnumbered the women students sixteen to one at the beginning and six to one at the end of the study. Most of the males have dates only or principally with girls in their home towns or in the towns in the adjacent region and then only on week ends. The male students are highly mobile and think nothing of traveling several hundred miles on a week end to go home for a date or to go to some other town—also for a date. In fact, the mass exodus on week ends is quite marked.

Prior to the construction of the original schedule two methods of analyzing dating behavior in terms of social class were considered, and both were subsequently utilized. Since it was not feasible to ascertain the social status of the family of each subject, the occupational class of the father was employed as a rough classification of social status. On the basis of prior knowledge of student dating habits gained largely through premarital and marital counseling experience, it appeared to the writer that a more significant determiner of dating behavior and its control depended upon the comparative social class position of the couple involved. In this framework of reference a person may have a date with a person of the same, lower, or higher social status. The recording of this information was made relatively easy by the simple device of having three appropriately marked columns for recording dating behavior in each stage. It was subsequently discovered that individuals, except in rare instances, definitely evaluate the relative class status of their dates in accordance with their own individual framework of reference.

The social class of the individual and the comparative social class of the companion, particularly in the dates of the males, plays a significant part in the pattern of the dating behavior and its control. The social class position of the individual as measured by the occupational group of the father showed little correlation with dating behavior. One reason for this lack of variation may be that although the sample had representatives from most economic groups, the middle and upper class groups predominated, and another and perhaps more important reason may be that all college students regardless of class origin are strongly influenced by middle-class standards. On the other hand, whether dates are with companions of the same, lower, or higher class seems to be an important determiner of behavior among these individuals. It is interesting to note that this finding was also foreshadowed by the net impressions gained from association with students and from the data supplied by the exploratory group. Furthermore, the crossing of class lines is in this study a much more important factor in the dating behavior of males than females. Almost forty percent of the males and only twenty percent of the females crossed class lines in their current dating behavior. The female crossers showed a slight or moderate tendency to have dates more frequently with boys of a higher social status, whereas the male crossers showed a more pronounced preference for girls of a lower social status. These males also tended to have more experiences in the more advanced stages of dating behavior than the others.

The type of control also varied. Only one illustration of this is given here. The male crossers cited that "the girl would not go farther" as a more frequent reason, comparatively speaking, for control, both for dates with girls of the same and of different social class; whereas the males who had dates only with girls in their own class gave more often that "neither tried to go farther." The fact that girl refusal is a relatively more important item of control among those males who cross class lines and who also actually have more sexual activity seems to be a contradiction. A closer inspection reveals, however, that these facts are consistent. It appears that more of these boys look upon dating primarily as a source of overt sexual gratification. Although they seek girls who are more likely to and who do satisfy their desires, they are so extremely persistent in their demands that they are more frequently refused. This fact was epitomized by one of the boys in the interview group. In the discussion of controls, he had stated that girls refusing to go farther had been the reason he had not been able to go farther. When asked if there were any other reasons, he blurted in response, "Jeepers, creepers, I didn't know there was any other reason!" Among boys who have dates only with girls in their social class, although the second most important reason of control is girl refusal, the primary reason is that neither tried to go farther. As repeatedly brought out in the interviews, this reason was also primarily a female determined phenomenon, but the attitudes about it were different. This type of control represented usually an equilibrium point that was acceptable to both parties. The male did not try to go beyond it because he knew that the girl would not go farther or because he felt that he ought not to try to go farther in consideration for her moral attitudes.

Before this study was started the writer had some misgivings about the willingness of students, especially girls, to participate in it. During the entire course of the investigation, he was constantly amazed at the cooperative attitude taken by both males and females. This spirit was also characteristic of those students who were

in the classes from which subjects were not taken. Although the
general nature of the study was outlined to them, many expressed
the view that they, too, "ought to be" subjects. Any misgivings
about the girls' reactions were completely dispelled by their whole-
hearted cooperation during the schedule-administering sessions and
during the interviews. At the end of the interview each girl was
asked what she thought of the interview. Every one of them emphatically stated that they were glad to have had the opportunity to
talk about their dating affairs. All expressed the opinion that it
had done them a great deal of good.

A very large number of the students have wanted to know why
more studies had not been made of dating behavior. Lowrie (1948)
expressed the need for factual studies in this field. The writer in
speaking for his students and for himself concurs completely with
Lowrie's view.

······························ **29** ······························

A SLUM SEX CODE

by William Foote Whyte

Men living in slum areas tend to have an elaborate and binding sex
code. Women are classified into categories, and for each category there
is an appropriate form of sex behavior that is supported by social sanctions. These are some of the findings reported in the article that follows, by William Foote Whyte, a professor in industrial and labor
relations at the New York State School of Industrial and Labor Relations, Cornell University. [From *American Journal of Sociology*, 1943,
49, 24-31. Reprinted by permission of the author and of the University of Chicago Press.]

Respectable middle-class people have very definite standards of
sex behavior. They are inclined to assume that behavior which does
not conform to these standards is unorganized and subject to no
set of ethics. It is my purpose to point out that, in one particular
area commonly thought to be characterized by laxness of sex behavior, there is an elaborate and highly developed sex code. A study

of the social and sex life of the slum will also yield certain clues as to the nature of the process of assimilation of an alien people into American society.

My information is based upon a three-and-a-half-year study of the Italian slum district of "Cornerville" in "Eastern City." By discussions with a number of men in corner gangs, in which I was a participant observer, I was able to learn the sex code of the slum, as it appears to the corner boys.

The story must be told against a background of local social life. In peasant Italy, as in other peasant societies, the family group undertook to regulate the social and sexual relations of the children. Marriages were arranged by the parents of the couple, and no young man was allowed to visit a girl's home unless he had been accepted as her suitor. The influence of this system is still to be observed in Cornerville. Parents try to keep a strict watch upon their daughters. In most cases they are unable to arrange the marriages for their children, but they retain control over the home. The corner boy knows that if he once visits a girl in her home it will be assumed by her parents (and by everyone else) that he intends to marry her. Consequently, until he is completely sure of his own intentions, the corner boy remains outside of the house. He even hesitates to make a date with a girl, for if he does take her out alone it is assumed that he is her "steady."

Dances given by local clubs mark the high point of the social activities. Except for those who are "going steady," groups of men and groups of girls go separately to the dances. The man chooses his girl for each dance and, at the conclusion of the number, leaves her with her friends. There is no cutting in. When the dance is over, the men and women go home separately. Parties in a girl's home, picnics, evenings at the bowling alleys, and other social activities all tend to take this group form.

When a man centers his attention upon one girl, he arranges to meet her on the street corner. Good girls are not expected to "hang" on the corner, but the men consider it perfectly respectable for them to keep appointments on the corner. Most parents object to this practice more or less strongly and try to insist that the man shall come to the home. The insistence of the parents and the reluctance of the corner boy place the girl in a difficult position. Of course, she herself may not wish to give the relationship the permanent form which a visit to the home would involve. If they work outside of the home, most girls are able to insist upon some right to govern their own social relations; but this always involves friction with the parents, its seriousness depending upon the strength of parental control and the strenuousness of the daughter's efforts to gain independence.

The sex life of the corner boy begins when he is very young. One of them writes:

> In Cornerville children ten years of age know most all the swear words and they have a good idea of what the word "lay" means. Swearing and describing of sex relations by older people and by the boys that hang on the corner are overheard by little children and their actions are noticed and remembered. Many of the children when they are playing in the streets, doorways and cellars actually go through the motions which pertain to the word "lay." I have seen them going through these motions, even children under ten years of age.
>
> Most all the boys that I know and all my friends carry safes [condoms]. Most boys start carrying safes when they are of high school age.
>
> Safes are purchased from necktie salesmen as cheap as a dozen for fifty cents. Some boys buy them and then make a profit by selling them to the boys at school. You can get them in some of the stores around here.

The sex play of young boys is relatively unregulated. The code of sex behavior crystallizes only as the corner boys reach maturity.

Relations between corner boys and women cannot be described in uniform terms, since there are tremendous variations in behavior, depending upon the category in which the woman is placed and the man's qualifications for access to women of various categories. The local classification of women which is explicit or implicit in corner-boy attitudes and behavior may be represented in the three categories shown in the accompanying tabulation. The most highly valued type of woman is placed at the top of each category.

Sex experience	Physical attractiveness	Social- and ethnic-group position
1. "Good girls"	Beautiful	1. Superior groups
2. "Lays"		2. Italian nonslum
a) One-man girls	to	3. Italian slum
b) Promiscuous		
c) Prostitutes	ugly	

One evening the corner boys were discussing a beautiful girl in the neighborhood. Danny said that he would take three months in any jail in the country, even Alcatraz, for the privilege of being in bed with her for eight hours. Doc said that Danny felt this way because the girl was a virgin. Danny agreed but added: "I would take one week in any jail even if she was a lay; that's how good I think she is." The difference between three months and one week strikingly illustrates the different valuations placed upon "good girls" and "lays." Doc explained the desirability of a virgin in this way: "No one has been there before. You are showing her the way. It's a new discovery. . . . We all say we would like to lay a virgin, but we really wouldn't."

The corner-boy code strongly prohibits intercourse with a virgin. Thus the most desirable of women is also the most inaccessible. A good girl may submit to a limited amount of kisses and caresses without compromising her reputation. She must not be a "teaser" (one who attempts to excite the man as much as possible without granting him sexual access). The virginity of a "teaser" is thought to be only a technicality, and if she is raped it serves her right. Otherwise a girl's virginity must be protected.

"Good girls" are the kind that one marries. A man who takes her virginity from a "good girl," seriously affecting her marriageability, will marry her because he is responsible. The man who seeks to evade his responsibility, especially if he has made the girl pregnant, may be forced into marriage by the priest and the girl's parents. The alternative is going to jail and being held liable for the support of the child to the age of twenty-one.

While strong legal and institutional sanctions uphold virginity, corner boys do not abide by the code simply from fear of the consequences of violation. They have strong sentiments supporting the sanctity of virginity. It is felt that only the lowest type of man would have intercourse with a virgin.

If the ban on intercourse with virgins were never violated, the only nonvirgins would be girls who had had sex relations with men outside of the district. This is obviously not the case. Several stories indicate that some early-adolescent boys and girls introduce each other to sex activity. The young boy who has never had intercourse himself does not feel so strongly the protective attitude toward virgins that he will assume later. There are a few local men who break the rule, but the danger of entanglements within the district is so great that most such activity must be confined to outsiders. In any case a corner boy cannot admit having "laid" a virgin without incurring the scorn of his fellows.

The corner boys believe that a man's health requires sexual intercourse at certain intervals. "Good girls" are not available for this purpose, and even casual social relations with them are likely to lead to commitments and responsibilities that the man is not prepared to assume. The corner boy has much more freedom, and much less responsibility in dealing with "lays"; freedom increases and responsibility decreases as he establishes relations lower down in this class.

From the standpoint of prestige and social advantage, the ideal girl in the "lay" class is the one who will have sexual relations with only one man in one period, but there are great risks involved in such relationships. As one corner boy said:

> If you go with a girl too long, even if she lays, you're bound to get to like her. That's human nature. I was going out with a girl, and I was banging her every date. After about four months, I saw I was really getting fond of the girl, so I dropped her just like that.

While a man should marry only a good girl, he may become attached to the one-man girl and allow his emotions to override his judgment. Furthermore, if it is not widely known that the girl is a "lay" and she consequently enjoys a good reputation, her family will be able to exert a good deal of pressure to force a marriage. If he makes her pregnant, marriage is hardly to be avoided.

The promiscuous girl is less desirable socially, but there is also less risk in having relations with her. Only pregnancy can impose a responsibility; and, since the identity of the father is difficult to prove, such entanglements may frequently be avoided.

In practice it is hard to distinguish between these two types of "lays," because the promiscuous girl usually tries to pass herself off as a one-man "lay" and one-man girls are constantly slipping into the lower category. Nevertheless, there is a real distinction in the mind of the corner boy, and he acts differently according to his conception of the girl's sexual status. He talks freely about the promiscuous girl and is glad to share her with his friends. He keeps the higher type of "lay" to himself, says little about his relations with her, and treats her with more respect. The reputation of the one-man "lay" is not, however, permanently protected. If she breaks off with the corner boy and takes up with another man, the corner boy is likely to boast openly that he had her first.

The professional prostitute or "hustler" is the least desirable of women. I have heard some men advocate having relations with prostitutes on the ground that no social risk is involved; but generally the corner boys feel that to go to a house of prostitution would be to admit that they could not "pick up" any girls. One corner boy expressed his opinion in this way:

I never go to a whorehouse. What do you get out of that? It's too easy.
ɔu just pay and go in and get it. Do you think the girl gets any fun out
that? . . . I like to take a girl out and bull her into it [persuade her].
hen when you lay her, you know she's enjoying it too. . . . And after
ɔu're through, you feel that you have accomplished something.

Another had this to say:

You might pay a hustler a dollar and that's all there is to it, it's a business
ɔoposition. If you pick up a girl, you may spend three to five dollars on
ɔod and drinks, but I'd rather do that any time. . . . You figure, the other
ay, it's just a business proposition. When you go out with a girl that ain't
hustler, you figure, she must like you a little anyway or she wouldn't
ɔ out with you. A hustler will take any man she can get, but this girl is
ɪst for you tonight anyway. You take her out, have something to eat and
ɪink, you go for a ride, you begin muggin' her up, then you get in there.
. . That's the way I like to do it. You're staking out new territory. You
ɪt the feeling you really done something when you get in there.

The corner boys make a distinction between a house of prostitu-
ɔn and a "line-up." In a line-up one of the men brings a prosti-
ɪte to some room in the district and allows his friends to have in-
ɪrcourse with her, each man paying the girl for the privilege.
Vhile this is a commercial arrangement, nevertheless, it is handled
y the boys themselves, and some who would not think of going to
house of prostitution are willing to participate with their friends
ɪ a line-up.
The code not only differentiates different types of women in cor-
ɪr-boy attitudes; it also involves strikingly different behavior with
ɪomen of the different categories, as the following stories indicate.
Danny had picked up a "hustler" and taken her to his gambling
ɔint on the understanding that she would receive a dollar a man.
Vhen she was finished, he handed her an envelope containing the
ɪills. She had counted the bills when he pretended to be alarmed
ɪd snatched the envelope away from her, replacing it in his pocket.
ɪe protested. Danny handed her another envelope of the same size
ɪhich contained only slips of paper. She was satisfied and went
ɪway without looking into the envelope. Danny felt that he had
ɪlayed a clever trick upon the girl.
Doc told me another story about Danny:

There are some noble things down here, Bill. . . . You take Danny's
ɪife, as we call her. She goes to church all the time—what a good kid she
ɪ, and she's nice looking too. She goes for Danny. She wants to marry him.
ɪow she goes for him so much that he could probably belt her if he wanted

to. But he doesn't want to marry her. He hasn't a job to support a wife. So he stays away from her. . . . Then take Al Mantia. He was a hound. He was after women all the time. One time he and Danny went out with a girl—she said she was a virgin. She had one drink, and she was a little high. They were up in a room, and they had her stripped—stripped! She still said she was a virgin, but she wanted them to give her a belt. But they wouldn't do it. . . . Can you imagine that, Bill? There she was stripped, and they wouldn't do anything to her. . . . The next day she came around and thanked both of them. They can't be such bad fellows if they do that.

The Danny who spared the virgin is the same Danny who cheated the "hustler." In one case the code imposed a strong responsibility; in the other case no responsibility was involved.

The physical-attractiveness criterion needs little comment, for here the corner boys are simply evaluating women in much the same terms as those used by men everywhere in their society. The only significant local variation is found in the strong preference for blondes in sexual relationships. Most of the local Italian girls tend to have black hair and olive complexions. While a good example of this type may appear strikingly attractive to the outsider, the corner boys are more impressed by blonde hair and a fair skin.

In the social- and ethnic-group category, the most desirable woman for non-marital sex relations is the girl of old American-stock background, preferably blonde, who has a higher status than the corner boy. Once I was walking through the aristocratic section of Eastern City with a corner boy when we passed a tall and stately blonde, fashionably dressed, and very attractive. My companion breathed deeply as he said: "The old Puritan stock! . . . The real McCoy! Wouldn't I like to give her a belt."

The attraction of the native stock is not confined to the lower-class Italian. Mario Martini was born in Cornerville, but as he became successful in business he moved out to a fashionable suburb. He married an Italian girl and raised a family, sending his children to private school. He had many business relations and some social relations with upper-class Yankees. He made a practice of hiring only girls of native background for his secretarial work, and on some of his business trips he would take one of these girls along—for sexual as well as secretarial purposes. One of Martini's former secretaries, who told me this story, was a girl of rather plain features, which emphasizes the prestige of the native background even for a man who was as successful as Mario Martini.

If an old-stock American girl is not accessible, then a socially superior member of an ethnic group living outside of Cornerville is the next best thing. There is little prestige involved in having relations with a Cornerville "lay," unless she is especially attractive on a physical basis.

The three categories so far discussed give us a rating scale in terms of feminine desirability. There is one important factor which limits access to certain women, however desirable they may be in terms of these categories. We must consider the social ties between the man and the woman. The incest taboo operates in Cornerville, as elsewhere, to prohibit access to females of certain specified familial ties. While marriages may be contracted beyond these incest limits, the corner-boy code also prohibits nonmarital access to relatives who are not blood relations (for example, the brother-in-law's cousin) and to relatives of friends. A corner boy described such a case to me. He was careful to explain that his friend, the girl's cousin, knew that she was a "lay" and would have been glad to have him enjoy himself. Furthermore, the girl was chasing after him so that she was practically forcing the sex relationship upon him. When he was about to have intercourse, he thought of his friend, and, as he says, "I couldn't do a thing." It is only with an outsider, with someone who is not related to him or to a friend, that the corner boy feels free to have sexual relations.

The three categories of "Sex Experience," "Physical Attractiveness," and "Social- or Ethnic-Group Position" are not, of course, the product of any individual's evaluation. They represent, implicitly, the standards of the group—the corner gang. The standards are being continually defined in action and in group discussion. The corner boys are continually talking over the girls that they know and others that they have observed in terms of all these categories. Consequently, a high degree of consensus tends to arise in placing the individual girl in her position in each category. The men then know how they are supposed to act in each case; and the observer, equipped with this conceptual scheme, is able to predict how, as a general rule, the men will attempt to act.

One feature of this classificatory scheme should be noted. The standards for marriage and for nonmarital sex relations are quite different. For nonmarital sex relations the ideal girl is a one-man "lay," blonde and fair skinned, belonging to a socially superior old-stock group, and having no familial connection with the corner boy or any of his friends. For marriage, preference is for the virgin of Italian extraction and having some family connection with friends or relatives of ego. (The girl fitting this description would usually, but not always, be a dark brunette.)

Different sorts of evaluation are involved in the two cases. The corner boy thinks of casual sex relations in terms of personal prestige as well as physical satisfaction. If he were able to persuade an attractive blonde to drive down to his corner and pick him up in an expensive-looking car, he could make a great impression upon his fellows. Wives are thought of in terms of long-run compatibility and utility. Corner boys express their preference for a wife of Italian extraction because "she would understand my ways," "she would know how to cook for me," and "I could trust her more than the others"; "the Italian women make faithful wives; it's their upbringing."

The corner boy's relations with the opposite sex are not determined simply by his evaluation of feminine desirability. He must possess certain qualifications in order to gain access to the most desirable women. Talk is important. The man who can talk entertainingly and "bull the girl to her ears" gains in prestige with his fellows, as well as in his social opportunities. However, talk is not enough. Social position, money, and possession of a car weigh heavily in the balance. It is a common complaint of the corner boys that the most desirable women are most difficult of access because they demand more in position, money, and a car than most corner boys can provide. I once asked a corner boy if it was necessary to have a car in order to pick up a girl for sexual purposes. He answered:

No, you can take her up to a room. . . . But no nice girl will go up to a man's room. If you take her out in the car, that's all right. If she goes up to your room with you, she's really a bum.

Under the influence of a car, a ride in the country, drinks, and heavy petting, a girl can allow a man to have sexual intercourse with her without any premeditation on her part. But if he suggests to her that they go to a room she can no longer pretend that she does not know what he is about. By consenting, she stamps herself as the kind of girl who goes to rooms with men. Even the most promiscuous like to maintain the pretense that they do it seldom and never in such a premeditated fashion. Thus the man with a car is generally able to have intercourse with a more desirable class of women than are available to the man who must rely upon rented rooms.

If the observer can classify the corner boy in terms of these criteria and classify the women within his social orbit in terms of the categories described above, then the individual's social and sexual behavior becomes still more subject to close prediction. No invariable rules can be set up, for the corner boy's code, like all other codes, is sometimes violated; but the discussion so far should clearly indicate that the relations between the sexes in the slums are subject to definite rules of behavior. The corner boys, while deviating from respectable middle-class standards, lead an organized sex life.

Our discussion has been confined to pre-marital sex and social relations. Little change is required in order to apply our conclusions to the post-marital behavior of the corner boy. The wife is expected to be completely faithful, and even the slightest flirtations are seriously regarded. The husband is expected to be a good provider and to have an affection for his wife and children. Nevertheless, the field of sexual adventure is not barred to him, and he endeavors to keep this quite separate from his married life. While the wives object, the men see nothing wrong in extra-marital sex relations, as long as they are not carried to the extremes of an open scandal or serious neglect of the family. Within these limits, the married man looks upon the feminine world just as he did before marriage.

While the slum sex code has now been described in outline form, it remains for us to consider the effect of this code and of the behavior it involves upon some of the broader social processes.

It is not easy for the Cornerville girl to maintain a good reputation if she has social relations with Cornerville men. Once I went to a dance outside of the district with two corner boys and three girls. It was late when we drove back to Cornerville. The driver stopped the car just outside of the district, and all the girls and one of the men got out to walk home. Later I asked why the girls had not been driven home. The driver answered:

Well, you know, Bill, the people of Cornerville are very suspicious people. They can make up a story about nothing at all. . . . If the girls came home alone, people would talk. If we all drove up in a car at one o'clock in the morning, they would wonder what we had been doing. . . . If the three of them walk home with Nutsy, then people will say, "Well, they have been in good company."

It is not only the older generation which gossips about the girls. The corner gang is continually defining and redefining reputations. Not even the "good girl" is safe from suspicion, and her local field of action is sharply circumscribed if she does not want to commit herself to marriage at an early age. As we have seen, the one-man "lay" cannot afford to have her "boy friend" in Cornerville because, if the relationship broke down, her reputation could be destroyed.

While social life outside of Cornerville has a great appeal to most girls, those who center their activities beyond the local boundaries seem to fit largely into two categories that represent the top and the bottom of Cornerville feminine society. There are a number of "good girls" who work outside of the district and use contacts made in this way in order to move into superior social circles. Then there are the "lays," who find greater freedom elsewhere. Most of the "good girls," being limited by their backgrounds, are unable to build up a social life outside of Cornerville. They have a romantic picture of a non-Cornerville, non-Italian of superior educational and economic status who will some day come along and marry them. While the social restrictions of Cornerville weigh particularly heavily upon the girls and influence many of them to wish for an escape through marriage outside the district, most marriages are contracted within Cornerville or between Cornerville and adjoining districts of similar social background. Nevertheless, the character of Cornerville social life operates to withdraw a significant number of local women from the orbit of the corner boys.

This situation is recognized by the corner boys. One of them commented:

> There are lots of lays in Cornerville. You take Market Street from Norton Street down; nine out of ten of those girls will lay. But they won't lay for a Cornerville fellow. You know why? Because they figure if they lay for me, I'll tell my friends the girls lay, and they'll want to lay her, and it'll get around. . . . Can you beat it, Bill, they're all around us yet we can't get them.

My informant was disgruntled over his failure to "get" Cornerville girls, and his 90 per cent figure is not to be taken seriously. If these girls actually did go outside of the district, he was in no position to know their sexual status, and any estimate can be no more than a guess. Probably the percentage of "lays" among local girls is very small. In any case, the fact remains that Cornerville men find most local girls barred to them except for marriage. In this situation they also must look outside of Cornerville for social and sexual satisfactions. The men, with their highly organized and localized corner gangs, tend to be even more restricted than the women in their social movements, and only a minority are able to operate at all effectively outside of Cornerville. However, even that minority contributes toward changing the social structure of Cornerville and Eastern City.

The restrictions of the peasant Italian family mores, plus the close watch kept upon their behavior, tend to push some of the young Italian girls out of Cornerville. Finding local fields restricted, some of the young men follow the girls in reaching for outside social contacts. This operates to stimulate intermarriage, illegitimate births out of interethnic sex relations, and social mobility. The study of the assimilation of the Italian population would be incomplete if we did not analyze the social and sex life of the slums in these terms.

Part Four

....

MULTIPLE GROUP
MEMBERSHIP

CHAPTER ELEVEN

The Adolescent and His Family

30

THE CONTEMPORARY AMERICAN FAMILY

AS AN ANTHROPOLOGIST SEES IT

by Margaret Mead

The family is the primary agent of socialization which may be defined as the process by which the person learns the ways of his society and thus becomes able to take his place as a member in good standing. In this selection, Margaret Mead of the American Museum of Natural History acquaints us with the family in the United States, describing a number of its distinguishing features, how it has changed, and the more important consequences of these changes. [From *American Journal of Sociology*, 1948, *53*, 453-459. Reprinted by permission of the author and The University of Chicago Press. The footnote has been omitted.]

An anthropologist looks at the American family as one of the many forms which the family has taken throughout human history since human beings first invented ways in which adult males could become more or less permanently responsible for the care of females and their children. With a few exceptions, which are so curious and contrived that they only emphasize the ubiquitousness of the institution of the family, all human societies have patterned the relationship between sexually paired adults and dependent young.

The tie between the father and child may not be recognized as biological. It may be conceived as fostering only or as a spiritual contribution only in which the father gives spirit, the mother body. The children of other men may be accepted readily; children of several brothers may be regarded as having equivalent claims on the care of one of the brothers; brothers may be treated interchangeably in their access to each other's wives; or sisters may be regarded as potential wives of the same man. The primary fostering tie between parent and child may be extended to include a three-generation family with many collateral lines or shrunk to the tiny biological family of the modern three-room apartment dwellers who have no kin within a thousand miles. The authority of the father may last until death, or all social relations between father and son, even speech, may end at puberty. Women may become completely absorbed into the kin group of their husbands, taking their names and their burial places, or they may even retain control over their own dowries. The life of the next generation may be minutely described in terms of family relationships or family choices made by the parents, or each generation may construct its family life for itself. Marriages may be for life between one man and one woman, or serially monogamous, or between one man and several women, or, less usually, between one woman and two or more men.

But nowhere are these crucial relationships, within which women are protected and cared for during childbearing and little children nurtured and reared, left unpatterned and unregulated. During periods of very rapid social change, of migration, of war and epidemic, the carefully devised and delicate patterns, which rely far more for their preservation on the habituated bodies and vivid expectations of those who were reared within them than upon any external sanctions, may break down. Then, for a period, the primary unit tends to become what it is among the primates, females and young, with the males exercising a nonspecific dominative and protective function in regard to the whole group. During such periods or in certain sections of a population almost the whole support of the children may fall on the mother, as in certain lower economic groups in large cities, or among ethnic groups at the moment of cultural breakdown. Old forms of legal marriage may become so expensive and cumbersome that a large part of a population may be said, at some period, to be living out of wedlock, but the new, altered, or simplified form will in time again become the recognized form of the family for that group.

Traditionally, societies have depended upon reproducing their orderly forms of family life by rearing children within families, who will regard that form of family life within which they were reared as normal, natural, and desirable. Children absorb during infancy and early childhood the whole pattern of family interrelationships which they then will be able to repeat, subject to the distortions introduced by hiatuses in their own experience, or idiosyncrasies of their own constitution and personality. Even in a society which changes as rapidly as our own, a large proportion of our patterns of family life are attempts—often faulty attempts because circumstances are so changed or the other partner has learned such different patterns—to reproduce the family behavior learned in childhood. A large part of the disorganization of family life today, the frequency of divorce, the incidence of neurosis and disease, may be laid to the discrepancies and contradictions between the expectations learned in childhood and the actualities of the present time.

The American family pattern is an urban middle-class pattern, although upper-class patterns occur, and lower-class practice deviates sharply from middle-class standards, and rural family life still retails the stamp of an earlier historical period. Films, comic strips, radio, and magazines presuppose a middle-class family. This family is typically formed at marriage, when young people finally cease to speak of "my family" as referring to the parental family and begin to look toward a family of their own. It is expected to consist exclusively of husband, wife, and minor children, with the presence of in-laws to be prevented if possible and almost universally to be deplored, particularly by the unrelated spouse. Support from parents to married children is not expected, and, where married children have to give support to their parents, this is regarded as a handicap, a burden on the young marriage. Nor are married children expected to plan their lives on the expectation of ultimately inheriting from either set of parents-in-law; such inheritances when they come along are windfalls, good luck rather than something which may be properly looked forward to. While married children will acknowledge some responsibility for the support of aging parents, especially when widowed, almost no responsibility is taken for brothers and sisters and their children, except in cases of extreme emergency or disaster. Unmarried adult women are expected to support themselves and are often also expected to assume a larger share of the support of a parent than that which is shouldered by married sons and daughters.

The orientation of the new family is forward, and the young couple are normally expected to provide their own establishment. The parents may provide for a wedding or give them a house or a car, but these are works of supererogation, not expected parental behavior, such as is expected in countries in which the parents have to set the young couple up with full household equipment. The assumption is that the parents have given their children of both sexes a "good education" which equips them to choose a mate, earn a living, and manage their lives for themselves with a minimum of help, advice, or interference.

The new family is expected to be formed entirely on the choice of the young people, with the young man taking the formal initiative in making the actual proposal. In selecting a mate, the primary considerations are personal attractiveness in the girl and attractiveness and ability as a breadwinner in the boy; all other considerations, even health, are regarded as subsidiary to them. Common background is very often subsumed under personal attractiveness and congeniality, and the skills which may be necessary to homemaking and mating are regarded as appropriately learned after marriage by practicing them on and with the chosen partner. Here a convention of premarital chastity for the girl, and a preference for minimal premarital experience for the boy, combine with an equal expectation that the girl will know nothing about running a house or a man about budgeting his income and that during the early years of marriage romantic ardor must balance ignorance and lack of skill. Young people may, without criticism, marry without any accumulation of property of any sort, without any certainty of where they are going to live, and, provided they have a little cash in hand and the man has proved earning power, without his having a job at the moment. Very few human societies have encouraged young people to start a new family with such very small backing from parents and the wider kin group. Actually a great deal of help, both formal and informal, is given to new marriages, but it is not only not something which may be legitimately expected but is actually something about which young people may feel considerable hesitation if not a real sense of inadequacy in accepting.

The American wife is expected to be educated, as well educated although not as highly trained as the husband, for there is more expectation that he will have a special money-bringing skill than that she will. Differences in education between men and women vary from couple to couple, and the only consistencies are a generally accepted delegation of earning to the husband and management of consumption to the wife. Which spouse prefers driving the car, listening to the radio, keeping up with the news, or participating in the community is a matter of individual adjustment subject to the rules of local groups or cliques but not a matter which is patterned by role for husband and wife. Until marriage the girl has been almost as free as her brother; if she has had a job, she has spent her money as she wished, giving her family something for her board where circumstances dictate such a course, and in recent years often leaving home to work and live in another city, with steadily decreasing protests from parents. For an unmarried son to leave home is still regarded as more usual than for an unmarried daughter. Until her decision to marry she is expected to be guided by the same considerations in the choice of a job which influence her brother—chance for advancement or security, interest, or money, or any combination of these. Once engaged, however, her life-orientation is expected to undergo a sharp change—ambition to shift from job to home.

The new home, so unsupported by parents or kin, is designed and planned by the young couple, very often an ill-assorted compromise between home memories and the new standards of contemporaries, of the department stores, and of women's magazines. Even the simplest middle-class home in the United States is a sort of stage set, constructed with thought, on which the family are going to enact their parts, against which the wife sees herself and the rest of the family. If the furniture is not new, it is at least newly bought second hand, and refurnished and rearranged with care. Within this home, the wife is expected to occupy herself, using it also as a platform from which she goes out into community life, of which, however, she has very little during the early years of her marriage. Where marriages have not taken place inside an existing youthful clique, it is expected that former friends of either spouse will prove trying and uncongenial and that new social groups will be formed based on neighborhood and community ties cultivated by the wife and on business ties cultivated by the husband. The claims of the wife for the local ties grow stronger when there are children and when their neighborhood companionships have to be considered. Husband and wife are expected to rely exclusively on each other as far as cross sex relationships are concerned and never to go out in mixed company without the other partner. On the whole, where men continue social relations with men after marriage, they are either labeled rather dubiously as "business" or frankly regarded as periods of relaxation—fishing, card-playing, yarning—antithetical to the more regulated home life. Women's relations with women outside the home are patterned either as parts of a local prestige game or as earnest endeavors to "do something worth while," and the grounds upon which men and women resent their spouses' outside interests tend to be very different.

A small family, with at least one child of each sex, for whom the parents can make adequate educational allowance, is regarded as more commendable than a larger family of children in which the children have to forgo an education. A large family, however, all of whom receive good educations through a combination of parental help and their own energies is a great credit to everyone. It is regarded as unfortunate when children are born within the first two years after marriage, as this ties the young couple down too soon. Parenthood is a responsible anxious matter, in which the mother must keep herself continually up to date with changing standards of child care. Having children, for a woman, is pretty close in feeling to having a job, for a man—a necessary proof of adequacy and wholeness as a human being, something which one does not so much enjoy but something which one would be unwilling not to have done. Unemployed married women without children are under some compulsion to explain their lack of occupation to themselves or to their neighbors; until recently women who had successfully reared even one child felt that they had made an appropriate and dignified social contribution for which they deserved recognition and support for the rest of their lives. When the children marry and leave the home, the American woman is faced with the same type of readjustment as that facing her husband perhaps two decades later when he retires. The discrepancy in the timing of the husband's and wife's retirement periods presents one of the problems of American marriage, as it is motherhood rather than housewifeliness which is the source of pride and self-sacrifice in the urban married woman. The period between the children's leaving home and old age is the main source of voluntary civic and social activity in the United States, as the married woman, trained to years of responsible social behavior in the care of family, finds her task cut in half while her strength is still unimpaired.

Marriage is for life, and all breaks in marriage are treated as failures, and failures which involve some degree of moral turpitude—either sexual or economic irresponsibility. At the same time, the extremely wide prevalence of divorce means that the possibility of divorce, defined as failure and as a disaster, is included in the picture of marriage. Women learn that they must keep their husbands, not merely from casual adventures or time spent wastefully elsewhere, but as husbands; and men learn that it is their wives' duty to keep them and that the world is filled with other women, married or unmarried, who, having failed or decided not to keep their own husbands, will try to attract them away from their present wives. This question of a wife's maintaining her attractiveness, in the face of the domestic routines, the sick bay, the broken drain, the unwashed coffee cups after last night's party, is felt to be a test of her adequacy and her sense of responsibility. A wife is not expected to try to keep her husband's love simply because love is a warm and pleasant thing or simply because she loves him and wants him to love her. Rather she must be continually on the alert to be a successful wife who is making a good job of her marriage. The moral alternatives are whether a woman is regarded as selfish because she "is just interested in keeping her husband" or is "unselfishly working to make a success of her marriage," which includes a sense of responsibility to her husband and children. With this burden of making the marriage relationship a continuous articulately happy experience in which each partner would choose the other over again each day—which puts a premium on never being unshaven or in curlers—there goes an explicit recognition that it is wrong to insist on the trappings of success where one has failed. The husband or wife who holds an unwilling partner—whatever the reason for the unwillingness—to a marriage from which he or she is trying to escape is regarded as behaving in an unsportsman-like manner. It is the wife's duty to make her husband want to stay and to shy away from taking too great risks with other women's efforts to impress him with their superior attractiveness. Similarly it is the husband's duty to provide for his wife and children so that she will want to stay with him. But, except within orthodox religious groups who still regard marriage as a sacrament, it is neither husband nor wife's duty to stay, once they are sure they want to leave, and, indeed, they may be regarded as doing harm to the other spouse and the children by bringing them up in a "home without love." The average American male's job insecurity, the fear that his maturity, which is based on his ability to earn his own living and provide completely for his family, may be taken from him by personal failure or by a depression, is matched by the average American wife's fear that she may fail at her job of homemaking and end up without a husband and perhaps with children to support.

Within this family, children are given an extraordinary amount of attention when judged by the standards of most other societies. Their needs, their wishes, and their performances are regarded as central and worthy of adult attention. The mother is the principal disciplining and character-molding parent and must both give love, comfort, and care and stimulate and goad the child to achievement and outside contacts. Her inevitable oscillation between demanding achievement as a proof of the child's love and threatening to withhold her love if the child does not achieve produces some of the typical conflicts in American character which were especially apparent in young draftees in World War II. The mother also has to train the male child in assertiveness, bidding him at the same time to be peaceful and co-operative and to stand up for himself, which training is responsible for some of the characteristic American uncertainties about their own strength. The father's role is to provide at one time a more horizontal fraternal relationship, supporting the growing child, especially the son, in conflicts with his mother when her demands are excessive or she is too unwilling to let the child grow up, and occasionally introducing a sharp unpredictable bit of violent disapproval in reinforcement of the mother's discipline. While the relationship to the mother introduces into the American child's character the principal strains and conflicts in regard to ethical behavior and giving and receiving of love, the relationship to the father provides a fairly steady, although not very aggressive, support of the child's individuality and pressure toward maturity. Both parents offer the child an appreciative audience for his growing independence, achievement, and autonomy and thus establish firmly his habit of acting, while young, weak, and inexperienced, with the overemphasis which is not regarded as inappropriate because the child is so small that it is all right to show off.

In the training of the young child there is a strong emphasis upon habit training, his learning to eat and eliminate and to sleep at the right times, and an enormous interweaving of beliefs about health and hygiene with morality. Next in importance is the attainment of some degree of motor autonomy. Training of the emotions is a matter more of teaching a child that it should not feel disapproved emotions, like jealousy, hate, or envy, than of any great attending to manners or minutiae of interpersonal relationships, and an ethical insisting that the other person's feelings, rights, etc., must be taken into account. Children are expected to develop consciences modeled upon the admonitions and supported by the rewards and punishments administered by parents. Each child is given its own property; a room to itself is the ideal, and toys and books and tools are personal possessions, respect for which is enforced among brothers and sisters. The custom of paying children for small jobs in the home, and encouraging them to undertake small money-earning jobs outside the home as good for their characters, is widespread. Children are permitted to exert considerable pressure upon the family's choice of food, magazines, and radio programs, and American advertisers regularly exploit this willingness to take consumption cues from children. Weaning is a gradual matter, punctuated by new privileges granted on birthdays and culminating in the period when either son or daughter becomes self-supporting. Self-support is defined not as actual ability to support one's self outside the home but as having a full-time paid job, all of which may actually go into clothes and pleasure, while the parents continue to provide most or all of the board. The tendency to overestimate and overstate an earning child's own money —so sharply contrasted with urban working-class practice in many European countries—has a later reflection in the tendency to treat a married woman's earnings as in some peculiar sense her own and not simply the resource of the whole family—which is the view held of the husband's earnings. The expectation is that children will press toward maturity and that parents will provide an admiring audience, practical help, and a certain check on their impetuosity, which, however, should actually serve as a further stimulus to make them take on more responsibilities.

The relationship between the character formation of the child and the life-history of its own immediate family, its financial ups and downs, accidents, illnesses, etc., is extraordinarily close, because of the isolation of each small family. Events which would be blurred or reinterpreted by the behavior of neighbors and relatives here become crucial in forming the personalities of the children. This extreme importance of the small, intimate family is to some degree compensated for by the great importance of the age group and by the extent to which group standards supersede family standards at adolescence.

The theme of American parenthood was well summarized by the head of a great high school, who turned to the group of assembled parents, many of them foreign born, many of them showing the marks of sacrifice which had made it possible for their children to attend high school, and said: "Let us rise to greet the children," and then added: "They offer you, their parents, the only thing they have to offer you—their success."

Two major readjustments are taking place in the American family pattern today. The first is the new ways of life which are becoming necessary as the isolated biological family becomes more and more usual, at a period when the demands made on the housewife as a result of new knowledge of nutrition, pediatrics, psychology, and home management in general have also greatly increased. Society is expecting more of the wife and mother at the very period when she, through isolation and lack of help and resources, is less able to meet these demands. Community services of all sorts—all-year-round school facilities, housekeeping services, twenty-four-hour boarding for children during illness in the home, prepared foods, expert advisory services to supplement the homemaker's traditional behavior, which is no longer adequate—are the results.

These innovations find cultural support in our American focus on the welfare of children and in the major contribution to future success which is given by careful education in childhood. Resistance to these changes and a continued insistence that, because families managed in the past to meet every emergency of illness, unemployment, insanity, accident, death, without formalized outside help, they should continue to do so now are rooted in the American cultural belief in the importance of autonomy, independence, and responsibility. Only by a widespread recognition that the family of today is being asked to do a much more difficult task of child-rearing, with much fewer resources than were available to the farm and small-town family, nested among relatives and neighbors and informed by a trusted tradition, can this resistance be shifted.

The second great readjustment which is occurring in the family pattern is the terminability of American marriage. As the old religious sanctions which enjoined fidelity until death, regardless of such ephemeral considerations as congeniality or "happiness," have faded for large sections of the population and have been powerless to save many more marriages from dissolution, new ways of holding marriages together are developing. The life of a family is coming to be seen as a ship which may be wrecked by any turn of the tide unless every member of the family, but especially the two parents, are actively and co-operatively engaged in sailing the boat, vigilantly tacking, trimming their sails, resetting their course, bailing in storms—all to save something which is worth their continuous care. This new ideal, in which all the members of a family work together to keep alive an ever changing relationship, may in time provide us with the necessary new ethical sanction within which to give our changing family dignity and safety.

.... 31 ....

THE SOCIOLOGY OF PARENT-YOUTH
CONFLICT

by Kingsley Davis

What are the causes of conflict between adolescents and their parents? In the following selection, Kingsley Davis of the University of California (Berkeley), expounds his views on this question. After pointing out the constants, or universal conditions, that are basic to all parent-child conflict and the variable conditions that depend upon the specific society, he shows how conditions in American society tend to produce friction between parents and their children. [Abridged from *American Sociological Review*, 1940, 5, 523-535. Reprinted by permission of the author and of the American Sociological Society.]

. . . Why does contemporary western civilization manifest an extraordinary amount of parent-adolescent conflict? In other cultures, the outstanding fact is generally not the rebelliousness of youth, but its docility. . . . What, then, are the peculiar features of our society which give us one of the extremest examples of endemic filial friction in human history?

Our answer to this question makes use of constants and variables, the constants being the universal factors in the parent-youth relation, the variables being the factors which differ from one society to another. Though one's attention, in explaining the parent-youth relations of a given milieu, is focused on the variables, one cannot comprehend the action of the variables without also understanding the constants, for the latter constitute the structural and functional basis of the family as a part of society.

THE RATE OF SOCIAL CHANGE

The first important variable is the rate of social change. Extremely rapid change in modern civilization, in contrast to most societies, tends to increase parent-youth conflict, for within a fast-changing social order the time-interval between generations, ordinarily but a mere moment in the life of a social system, become historically significant, thereby creating a hiatus between one generation and the next. Inevitably, under such a condition, youth is reared in a milieu different from that of the parents; hence the parents become old-fashioned, youth rebellious, and clashes occur which, in the closely confined circle of the immediate family, generate sharp emotion.

*   *   *

THE BIRTH-CYCLE AND DECELERATING SOCIALIZATION

Note, however, that rapid social change would have no power to produce conflict were it not for two universal factors: first, the family's duration; and second, the decelerating rate of socialization in the development of personality. "A family" is not a static entity but a process in time, a process ordinarily so brief compared with historical time that it is unimportant, but which, when history "full" (i.e., marked by rapid social change), strongly influences the mutual adjustment of the generations. This "span" is basically the birth-cycle—the length of time between the birth of one person and his procreation of another. It is biological and inescapable. It could, however, have no effect in producing parent-youth conflict, even with social change, if it were not for the additional fact, intimately related and equally universal, that the sequential development of personality involves a constantly decelerating rate of socialization. This deceleration is due both to organic factors (age—which ties it to the birth-cycle) and to social factors (the cumulative character of social experience). Its effect is to make the birth-cycle interval, which is the period of youth, the time of major socialization, subsequent periods of socialization being subsidiary.

Given these constant features, rapid social change creates conflict because *to* the intrinsic (universal, inescapable) differences between parents and children it adds an *extrinsic* (variable) difference derived from the acquisition, at the same stage of life, of differential cultural content by each successive generation. Not only are parent and child, at any given moment, in different stages of development, but the content which the parent acquired at the stage where the child now is, was a different content from that which the child is now acquiring. Since the parent is supposed to socialize the child, he tends to apply the erstwhile but now inappropriate content. He makes this mistake, and cannot remedy it, because, due to the logic of personality growth, his basic orientation was formed by the experiences of his own childhood. He cannot "modernize" his point of view, because *he* is the product of those experiences. He can change in superficial ways, such as learning a new tune, but he cannot change (or *want* to change) the initial modes of thinking upon which his subsequent social experience has been built. To change the basic conceptions by which he has learned to judge the rightness and reality of all specific situations would be to render subsequent experience meaningless, to make an empty caricature of what had been his life.

*   *   *

PHYSIOLOGICAL DIFFERENCES

Though the disparity in chronological age remains constant through life, the precise physiological differences between parent and offspring vary radically from one period to another. The organic contrasts between parent and *infant,* for example, are far different from those between parent and adolescent. Yet whatever the period, the organic differences produce contrasts (as between young and old) in those desires which, at least in part, are organically determined. Thus, at the time of adolescence the contrast is between an organism which is just reaching its full powers and one which is just losing them. The physiological need of the latter is for security and conservation, because as the superabundance of energy diminishes, the organism seems to hoard what remains.

Such differences, often alleged (under the heading of "disturbing physiological changes accompanying adolescence") as the primary cause of parent-adolescent strife, are undoubtedly a factor in such conflict, but, like other universal differences to be discussed, they form a constant factor present in every community, and therefore cannot in themselves explain the peculiar heightening of parent-youth conflict in our culture.

The fact is that most societies avoid the potential clash of old and young by using sociological position as a neutralizing agent. They assign definite and separate positions to persons of different ages, thereby eliminating competition between them for the same position and avoiding the competitive emotions of jealousy and envy. Also, since the expected behavior of old and young is thus made complementary rather than identical, the performance of cooperative functions as accomplished by different but mutually related activities suited to the disparate organic needs of each, with no coercion to behave in a manner unsuited to one's organic age. In our culture, where most positions are *theoretically* based on accomplishment rather than age, interage competition arises, superior organic propensities lead to a high evaluation of youth (the so-called "accent on youth"), a disproportionate lack of opportunity for youth manifests itself, and consequently, arrogance and frustration appear in the young, fear and envy, in the old.

PSYCHOSOCIAL DIFFERENCES: ADULT REALISM VS. YOUTHFUL IDEALISM

The decelerating rate of socialization . . . , when taken with rapid social change and other conditions of our society, tends to produce certain differences of orientation between parent and youth. . . .

Though both youth and age claim to see the truth, the old are more conservatively realistic than the young, because on the one hand they take Utopian ideals less seriously and on the other hand take what may be called operating ideals, if not more seriously, at least more for granted. Thus, middle-aged people notoriously forget the poetic ideals of a new social order which they cherished when young. In their place, they put simply the working ideals current in the society. There is, in short, a persistent tendency for the ideology of a person as he grows older to gravitate more and more toward the status quo ideology, unless other facts (such as a social crisis or hypnotic suggestion) intervene. With advancing age, he becomes less and less bothered by inconsistencies in ideals. He tends to judge ideals according to whether they are widespread and hence effective in thinking about practical life, not according to whether they are logically consistent. Furthermore, he gradually ceases to bother about the *untruth* of his ideals, in the sense of their failure to correspond to reality. He assumes through long habit that, though they do not correspond perfectly, the discrepancy is not significant. The reality of an ideal is defined for him in terms of how many people accept it rather than how completely it is mirrored in actual behavior. Thus, we call him, as he approaches middle age, a realist.

The young, however, are idealists, partly because they take working ideals literally and partly because they acquire ideals not fully operative in the social organization. Those in authority over children are obligated as a requirement of their status to inculcate ideals as a part of the official culture given the new generation. The children are receptive because they have little social experience— experience being systematically kept from them (by such means as censorship, for example, a large part of which is to "protect" children). Consequently, young people possess little ballast for their acquired ideals, which therefore soar to the sky, whereas the middle-aged, by contrast, have plenty of ballast.

This relatively unchecked idealism in youth is eventually complicated by the fact that young people possess keen reasoning ability. The mind, simply as a logical machine, works as well at sixteen as at thirty-six. (Shuttleworth, 1938, Figs. 16, 230, 232, 276, 285, 308.) Such logical capacity, combined with high ideals and an initial lack of experience, means that youth soon discovers with increasing age that the ideals it has been taught are true and consistent are not so in fact. Mental conflict thereupon ensues, for the young person has not learned that ideals may be useful without being true and consistent. As a solution, youth is likely to take action designed to remove inconsistencies or force actual conduct into line with ideals, such action assuming one of several typical adolescent forms—from religious withdrawal to the militant support of some Utopian scheme—but in any case consisting essentially in serious allegiance to one or more of the ideal moral systems present in the culture. An illustration of youthful reformism was afforded by the Laval University students who decided to "do something about" prostitution in the city of Quebec. They broke into eight houses in succession one night, "whacked naked inmates upon the buttocks, upset beds and otherwise proved their collegiate virtue. . . ." They ended by "shoving the few remaining girls out of doors into the cold autumn night" (*Time*, October 19, 1936).

A different, usually later reaction to disillusionment is the cynical or sophomoric attitude; for, if the ideals one has imbibed cannot be reconciled and do not fit reality, then why not dismiss them as worthless? Cynicism has the advantage of giving justification for behavior that young organisms crave anyway. It might be mistaken for genuine realism if it were not for two things. The first is the emotional strain behind the "don't care" attitude. The cynic, in his judgment that the world is bad because of inconsistency and untruth of ideals, clearly implies that he still values the ideals. The true realist sees the inconsistency and untruth, but without emotion; he uses either ideals or reality whenever it suits his purpose. The second is the early disappearance of the cynical attitude. Increased experience usually teaches the adolescent that overt cynicism is unpopular and unworkable, that to deny and deride all beliefs which fail to cohere or to correspond to facts, and to act in opposition to them, is to alienate oneself from any group, because these beliefs, however unreal, are precisely what makes group unity possible. Soon, therefore, the youthful cynic finds himself bound up with some group having a system of working ideals, and becomes merely another conformist, cynical only about the beliefs of other groups.

While the germ of this contrast between youthful idealism and adult realism may spring from the universal logic of personality development, it receives in our culture a peculiar exaggeration. Social change, complexity, and specialization (by compartmentalizing different aspect of life) segregate ideals from fact and throw together incompatible ideologies while at the same time providing the intellectual tools for discerning logical inconsistencies and empirical errors. Our highly elaborated burden of culture, correlated with a variegated system of achieved vertical mobility, necessitates long years of formal education which separate youth from adulthood, theory from practice, school from life. Insofar, then, as youth's reformist zeal or cynical negativism produces conflict with parents, the peculiar conditions of our culture are responsible.

SOCIOLOGICAL DIFFERENCES: PARENTAL AUTHORITY

Since social status and office are everywhere partly distributed on the basis of age, personality development is intimately linked with the network of social positions successively occupied during life. Western society, in spite of an unusual amount of interage competition, maintains differences of social position between parent and child, the developmental gap between them being too clearcut, the symbiotic needs too fundamental, to escape being made a basis of social organization. Hence, parent and child, in a variety of ways, find themselves enmeshed in different social contexts and possessed of different outlooks. The much publicized critical attitude of youth toward established ways, for example, is partly a matter of being on the outside looking in. The "established ways" under criticism are usually institutions (such as property, marriage, profession) which the adolescent has not yet entered. He looks at them from the point of view of the outsider (especially since they affect him in a restrictive manner), either failing to imagine himself finding satisfaction in such patterns or else feeling resentful that the old have in them a vested interest from which he is excluded.

Not only is there differential position, but also *mutually* differential position, status being in many ways specific for and reciprocal between parent and child. Some of these differences, relating to the birth-cycle and constituting part of the family structure, are universal. This is particularly true of the super- and subordination summed up in the term *parental authority*.

Since sociological differences between parent and child are inherent in family organization, they constitute a universal factor potentially capable of producing conflict. Like the biological differences, however, they do not in themselves produce such conflict. In fact, they may help to avoid it. To understand how our society brings to expression the potentiality for conflict, indeed to deal realistically with the relation between the generations, we must do so not in generalized terms but in terms of the specific "power situation." Therefore, the remainder of our discussion will center upon the nature of parental authority and its vicissitudes in our society.

Because of his strategic position with reference to the new-born child (at least in the familial type of reproductive institution), the parent is given considerable authority. Charged by his social group with the responsibility of controlling and training the child in conformity with the mores and thereby insuring the maintenance of the cultural structure, the parent, to fulfill his duties, must have the privileges as well as the obligations of authority, and the surrounding community ordinarily guarantees both.

The first thing to note about parental authority, in addition to its function in socialization, is that it is a case of authority within a primary group. Simmel has pointed out that authority is bearable for the subordinate because it touches only one aspect of life. Impersonal and objective, it permits all other aspects to be free from its particularistic dominance. This escape, however, is lacking in parental authority, for since the family includes most aspects of life, its authority is not limited, specific, or impersonal. What, then, can make this authority bearable? Three factors associated with the familial primary group help to give the answer: (1) the child is socialized within the family, and therefore knowing nothing else and being utterly dependent, the authority of the parent is internalized, accepted; (2) the family, like other primary groups, implies identification, in such sense that one person understands and responds emphatically to the sentiments of the other, so that the harshness of authority is ameliorated; (3) in the intimate interaction of the primary group control can never be purely one-sided; there are too many ways in which the subordinated can exert the pressure of his will. When, therefore, the family system is a going concern, parental authority, however, inclusive, is not felt as despotic.

A second thing to note about parental authority is that while its duration is variable (lasting in some societies a few years and in others a lifetime), it inevitably involves a change, a progressive readjustment, in the respective positions of parent and child—in some cases an almost complete reversal of roles, in others at least a cumulative allowance for the fact of maturity in the subordinated offspring. Age is a unique basis for social stratification. Unlike birth, sex, wealth, or occupation, it implies that the stratification is temporary, that the person, if he lives a full life, will eventually traverse all of the strata having it as a basis. Therefore, there is a peculiar ambivalence attached to this kind of differentiation, as well as a constant directional movement. On the one hand, the young person, in the stage of maximum socialization, is, so to speak, *moving into* the social organization. His social personality is expanding, i.e., acquiring an increased amount of the cultural heritage, filling more powerful and numerous positions. His future is before him, in what the older person is leaving behind. The latter, on the other hand, has a future before him only in the sense that the offspring represents it. Therefore, there is a disparity of interest, the young person placing his thoughts upon a future which, once the first stages of dependence are passed, does not include the parent, the old person placing his hopes vicariously upon the young. This situation, representing a *tendency* in every society, is avoided in many places by a system of respect for the aged and an imaginary projection of life beyond the grave. In the absence of such a religio-ancestral system, the role of the aged is a tragic one.

Let us now take up, point by point, the manner in which western civilization has affected this *gemeinschaftliche* and processual form of authority.

Conflicting Norms

To begin with, rapid change has, as we saw, given old and young a different social content, so that they possess conflicting norms. There is a loss of mutual identification, and the parent will not "catch up" with the child's point of view, because he is supposed to dominate rather than follow. More than this, social complexity has confused the standards *within* the generations. Faced with conflicting goals, parents become inconsistent and confused in their own minds in rearing their children. The children, for example, acquire an argument against discipline by being able to point to some family wherein discipline is less severe, while the parent can retaliate by pointing to still other families wherein it is firmer. The acceptance of parental attitudes is less complete than formerly.

Competing Authorities

We took it for granted, when discussing rapid social change, that youth acquires new ideas, but we did not ask how. The truth is that, in a specialized and complex culture, they learn from competing authorities. Today, for example, education is largely in the hands of professional specialists, some of whom, as college professors, resemble the sophists of ancient Athens by virtue of their work of accumulating and purveying knowledge, and who consequently have ideas in advance of the populace at large (i.e., the parents). By giving the younger generation these advanced ideas, they (and many other extrafamilial agencies, including youth's contemporaries) widen the intellectual gap between parent and child.

Steps in Parental Authority

Our society provides little explicit institutionalization of the progressive readjustments of authority as between parent and child. We are intermediate between the extreme of virtually permanent parental authority and the extreme of very early emancipation, because we encourage release in late adolescence. Unfortunately, this is a time of enhanced sexual desire, so that the problem of sex and the problem of emancipation occur simultaneously and complicate each other. Yet even this would doubtless be satisfactory if it were not for the fact that among us the exact time when authority is relinquished, the exact amount, and the proper ceremonial behavior are not clearly defined. Not only do different groups and families have conflicting patterns, and new situations arise to which old definitions will not apply, but the different spheres of life (legal, economic, religious, intellectual) do not synchronize, maturity in one sphere and immaturity in another often coexisting. The read-justment of authority between individuals is always a ticklish proc-ess, and when it is a matter of such close authority as that between parent and child it is apt to be still more ticklish. The failure of our culture to institutionalize this readjustment by a series of well-defined, well-publicized steps is undoubtedly a cause of much parent-youth dissension. The adolescent's sociological exit from his family, via education, work, marriage, and change of residence, is fraught with potential conflicts of interest which only a definite system of institutional controls can neutralize. The parents have a vital stake in what the offspring will do. Because his acquisition of independence will free the parents of many obligations, they are willing to relinquish their authority; yet, precisely because their own status is socially identified with that of their offspring, they wish to insure satisfactory conduct on the latter's part and are tempted to prolong their authority by making the decisions them-selves. In the absence of institutional prescriptions, the conflict of interest may lead to a struggle for power, the parents fighting to keep control in matters of importance to themselves, the son or daughter clinging to personally indispensable family services while seeking to evade the concomitant control.

Concentration within the Small Family

Our family system is peculiar in that it manifests a paradoxical combination of concentration and dispersion. On the one hand, the unusual smallness of the family unit makes for a strange in-tensity of family feeling, while on the other, the fact that most pursuits take place outside the home makes for a dispersion of ac-tivities. Though apparently contradictory, the two phenomena are really interrelated and traceable ultimately to the same factors in our social structure. Since the first refers to that type of affection and antagonism found between relatives, and the second to activi-ties, it can be seen that the second (dispersion) isolates and in-creases the intensity of the affectional element by sheering away common activities and the extended kin. Whereas ordinarily the sentiments of kinship are organically related to a number of com-mon activities and spread over a wide circle of relatives, in our mobile society they are associated with only a few common activi-ties and concentrated within only the immediate family. This makes them at once more instable (because ungrounded) and more intense. With the diminishing birth rate, our family is the world's smallest kinship unit, a tiny closed circle. Consequently, a great deal of family sentiment is directed toward a few individuals, who are so important to the emotional life that complexes easily develop. This emotional intensity and situational instability increase both the probability and severity of conflict.

In a familistic society, where there are several adult male and female relatives within the effective kinship group to whom the child turns for affection and aid, and many members of the younger generation in whom the parents have a paternal interest, there appears to be less intensity of emotion for any particular kinsman and consequently less chance for severe conflict (Mead, 1930; Spencer, 1939). Also, if conflict between any two relatives does arise, it may be handled by shifting mutual rights and obligations to another relative.

Open Competition for Socioeconomic Position

Our emphasis upon individual initiative and vertical mobility, in contrast to rural-stable regimes, means that one's future occupation and destiny are determined more at adolescence than at birth, the adolescent himself (as well as the parents) having some part in the decision. Before him spreads a panorama of possible occupations and avenues of advancement, all of them fraught with the uncertainties of competitive vicissitude. The youth is ignorant of most of the facts. So is the parent, but less so. Both attempt to collaborate on the future, but because of previously mentioned sources of friction, the collaboration is frequently stormy. They evaluate future possibilities differently, and since the decision is uncertain yet important, a clash of wills results. The necessity of choice at adolescence extends beyond the occupational field to practically every phase of life, the parents having an interest in each decision. A culture in which more of the choices of life were settled beforehand by ascription, where the possibilities were fewer and the responsibilities of choice less urgent, would have much less parent-youth conflict (Mead, 1928, pp. 200 ff.).

Sex Tension

If until now we have ignored sex taboos, the omission has represented a deliberate attempt to place them in their proper context with other factors, rather than in the unduly prominent place usually given them (Frank, 1928; Mead, 1928, pp. 216-217, 222-223). Undoubtedly, because of a constellation of cultural conditions, sex looms as an important bone of parent-youth contention. Our morality, for instance, demands both premarital chastity and postponement of marriage, thus creating a long period of desperate eagerness when young persons practically at the peak of their sexual capacity are forbidden to enjoy it. Naturally, tensions arise—tensions which adolescents try to relieve, and adults hope they will relieve, in some socially acceptable form. Such tensions not only make the adolescent intractable and capricious, but create a genuine conflict of interest between the two generations. The parent, with respect to the child's behavior, represents morality, while the offspring reflects morality *plus* his organic cravings. The stage is thereby set for conflict, evasion, and deceit. For the mass of parents, toleration is never possible. For the mass of adolescents, sublimation is never sufficient. Given our system of morality, conflict seems well-nigh inevitable.

Yet it is not sex itself but the way it is handled that causes conflict. If sex patterns were carefully, definitely, and uniformly geared with nonsexual patterns in the social structure, there would be no parent-youth conflict over sex. As it is, rapid change has opposed the sex standards of different groups and generations, leaving impulse only chaotically controlled.

The extraordinary preoccupation of modern parents with the sex life of their adolescent offspring is easily understandable. First, our morality is sex-centered. The strength of the impulse which it seeks to control, the consequent stringency of its rules, and the importance of reproductive institutions for society, make sex so morally important that being moral and being sexually discreet are synonymous. Small wonder, then, that parents charged with responsibility for their children and fearful of their own status in the eyes of the moral community, are preoccupied with what their offspring will do in this matter. Moreover, sex is intrinsically involved in the family structure and is therefore of unusual significance to family members *qua* family members. Offspring and parent are not simply two persons who happen to live together; they are two persons who happen to live together because of past sex relations between the parents. Also, between parent and child there stand strong incest taboos, and doubtless the unvoiced possibility of violating these unconsciously intensifies the interest of each in the other's sexual conduct. In addition, since sexual behavior is connected with the offspring's formation of a new family of his own, it is naturally of concern to the parent. Finally, these factors taken in combination with the delicacy of the authoritarian relation, the emotional intensity within the small family, and the confusion of sex standards, make it easy to explain the parental interest in adolescent sexuality. Yet because sex is a tabooed topic between parent and child, parental control must be indirect and devious, which creates additional possibilities of conflict.

SUMMARY AND CONCLUSION

Our parent-youth conflict thus results from the interaction of certain universals of the parent-child relation and certain variables the values of which are peculiar to modern culture. The universals are (1) the basic age or birth-cycle differential between parent and child, (2) the decelerating rate of socialization with advancing age, and (3) the resulting intrinsic differences between old and young on the physiological, psychosocial, and sociological planes.

Though these universal factors *tend* to produce conflict between parent and child, whether or not they do so depends upon the variables. We have seen that the distinctive general features of our society are responsible for our excessive parent-adolescent friction. Indeed, they are the same features which are affecting *all* family relations. The delineation of these variables has not been systematic, because the scientific classification of whole societies has not yet been accomplished; and it has been difficult, in view of the interrelated character of societal traits, to seize upon certain features and ignore others. Yet certainly the following four complex variables are important: (1) the rate of social change; (2) the extent of complexity in the social structure; (3) the degree of integration in the culture; and (4) the velocity of movement (e.g., vertical mobility) within the structure and its relation to the cultural values.

Our rapid social change, for example, has crowded historical meaning into the family time-span, has thereby given the offspring a different social content from that which the parent acquired, and consequently has added to the already existent intrinsic differences between parent and youth, a set of extrinsic ones which double the chance of alienation. Moreover, our great societal complexity, our evident cultural conflict, and our emphasis upon open competition for socioeconomic status have all added to this initial effect. We have seen, for instance, that they have disorganized the important

relation of parental authority by confusing the goals of child control, setting up competing authorities, creating a small family system, making necessary certain significant choices at the time of
adolescence, and leading to an absence of definite institutional
mechanisms to symbolize and enforce the progressively changing
stages of parental power.

If ours were a simple rural-stable society, mainly familistic, the
emancipation from parental authority being gradual and marked
by definite institutionalized steps, with no great postponement of
marriage, sex taboo, or open competition for status, parents and
youth would not be in conflict. Hence, the presence of parent-
youth conflict in our civilization is one more specific manifestation of the incompatibility between an urban-industrial-moble
social system and the familial type of reproductive institutions.

.... **32** ....

THE ADOLESCENT AND HIS HAPPY FAMILY

by John Levy, M.D., and Ruth Munroe

We hear and read so much about clashes between adolescents and
their parents that some of us may lose our perspective and believe that
little if anything can be done to understand and improve adolescent-
parent relations. In the following article, an excerpt from their book
pleasantly entitled *The Happy Family,* John Levy (1897-1938) and
Ruth Munroe, of the College of the City of New York, reassure parents that the adolescent "revolt" is but a healthy preparation for
marriage and suggest what parents can do to assist their children in
successfully hurdling this period of their development. [From *The
Happy Family,* New York: Alfred A. Knopf, Inc., 1938, pp. 4-17. Reprinted by permission of Ruth Munroe and Alfred A. Knopf, Inc.]

First impressions are strong impressions. Adults cannot help re-
living in some fashion the kind of life they knew in childhood. The
warmth and intimacy of the family group become synonymous with
life itself. Even if the warmth seems suffocating at times and the intimacy contentious, we are so bred up to them that we cannot exist
in any other atmosphere any more than the proverbial fish out of

water. My daughter does not reject the Follies out of a reasoned conviction that the joys of maternity are superior to the joys of the footlights. She simply doesn't know any better, since her experience to date has been confined to family life. Nor does she have an incestuous passion for daddy which leads her to choose him as the father of her children. I must admit reluctantly that her choice is due largely to the fact that I am first in the field and have to date very little competition. She thinks of life in terms of the family, and the family in terms of her own parents. Her affections, her expectations of happiness and pain, are being molded constantly by the little group into which she happened to be born. By the time her worldly knowledge has progressed far enough to make her critical about the family, it will be too late for her to change her basic feelings. Whether she likes it or not, her emotional bias toward family living will be so strong that she cannot overcome it.

Idealists, troubled by the obvious deficiencies of the marriages they see around them, are forever devising new systems guaranteed to run with an oiled precision. Free love, companionate marriage, easy divorce, state care of children—these projects and many others like them are designed to solve the problems of people seeking to live happily together. Logically almost any one of these schemes is superior to the curious institution we call holy matrimony. Institutions which have grown haphazard out of the necessities of succeeding generations never make sense if you look at them rationally. Unfortunately logic is not very effective in ordering people's lives. Psychologically these Utopian systems of marriage make a fundamental blunder. They ignore the point we have just been making: that marriage begins in infancy. People who have learned about family loves and hates and rivalry and devotion in their parents' home carry the lessons into their own homes. The most perfect system fails if it does not meet the expectations formed in childhood. We make ourselves wretched very frequently by adhering to foolish outworn ideas about marriage, but I fear we should be even more miserable without them. My little daughter in her twenties will still want a family, and her family will somehow or other continue the emotional atmosphere of her present home.

Nevertheless there comes a time when the orderly sequence of development from one generation to the next is sharply interrupted. The little girl who planned cheerfully for a family of five becomes a slightly gangling young lady who turns up her nose at all boys. She's not going to tie herself down with children. If she can't manage to be a nurse or an author or an explorer, she'll get a job in Woolworth's. So many parents come to me in alarm about the behavior of their teen-age children, boys and girls alike, that I would like to chat at some length about the meaning of this adolescent revolt.

Their children, parents complain, have suddenly become impossible. Affectionate, dutiful daughters treat their homes "like a hotel." They sleep there and occasionally "grab a meal," but their real life is lived elsewhere. They fly into a fury when mother mildly suggests helping with the dishes. Johnny's conversation is almost exclusively of the "gimme" variety. His resentment knows no bounds if he cannot have the family car or a dress suit. Parents I see are about equally divided between those who worry because their daughters won't look at a boy and those who are distracted because their girls stay out till all hours with the crowd doing heaven knows what. Listening to these lurid tales about the young, one gets the impression that the whole institution of the family is going on the rocks for want of a new generation to carry on.

It is usually possible to give full reassurance to these anxious parents. While the adolescent revolt is so common as to be almost universal, the family has maintained itself for a very long time. As a matter of fact, the revolt is an essential preliminary to the business of getting married. I should be more concerned about those children who remain wholly docile and affectionate during this period. Growing up means growing away from the old family in preparation for founding a new one. The child who remains safely cradled in the parental home becomes the man who never establishes a home of his own. Or who, if he happens to marry, is forever trying to force his new life into the mold of the old—to make his wife exactly like his mother, and his children exactly like himself. Since his wife is after all not his mother, he is perpetually dissatisfied, while she, poor woman, is frustrated at every turn.

A new marriage must not be hampered by old loyalties and attitudes. The adolescent has to shift gears from the low speed of childhood to the high speed of parenthood. All his life he has been dependent and protected. As a father he must do the protecting. His childish devotion to his parents must change to a mature affection, very much less intense in quality. His absorbing emotional relationships must be focused on his contemporaries. Gears very often grind badly during a shift, but they are rarely stripped. The unpleasant noise we hear from our teen-age children is just the grinding of the gear shift—cacophonous, but useful.

The adolescent revolt is healthy preparation for the serious task of finding a mate. None the less, parents and children alike find it difficult to bear. Let us consider the parents' side first. They cannot be expected to preserve an Olympian calm while their youngsters engage in sprightly adventures which can easily lead to serious trouble. Parents are used to taking care of their children, and the habit of protection persists after the same type of care is no longer possible. The mother who held little Tommy's hand crossing Fifth Avenue to the park just a short time ago, cannot help being at least a back-seat driver when Tommy whizzes past the red lights in his new sport roadster. Habits are made of durable stuff. It takes more than Tommy's first pair of long pants to change his parents' attitude toward him. Tom may appear to himself and his schoolfellows practically gray-haired, but his parents still see him in rompers. They have looked after him for years and they continue to look after him even when their care has become an insult to his manhood. They have obtained a fair measure of obedience and respect in the past. The impertinence and ingratitude of the adolescent come therefore as a painful shock. Young people are apt to ascribe most of their difficulties with their parents to this cause: "They can't realize that we're grown up."

Parents have more to overcome during this period, however, than habits of protection. Parents, especially mothers, *need* dependent children. They have built their life around them and cannot help feeling like an empty shell when the children have grown away from their home ties. Almost always rearing a young brood means curtailing other interests. Mothers with little children are too busy to keep up with outside affairs, hobbies, or even close friendships. Moreover, they are so intent upon their children, so emotionally absorbed in them, that these extraneous matters seem unimportant. I used to commute with a group of women who illustrated this point very nicely. They were highly trained and highly intellectual college teachers, but many of them had young children of their own. During the relaxed moments on the train the forthcoming election, the tense European situation, or the latest college gossip did indeed receive some attention. But if you listened in on the most animated and bright-eyed discussions you found that these so-called bluestockings talked about Jimmy's feeding problem, or the cute thing little Betty did last night. The really important conversation was in no way different from that of the little knot of suburban mothers down the aisle, going to town for a day's shopping.

Small children need a great deal of attention and a great deal of emotion. They get it, too, one way or another, from every mother I know. Older children have no use for this emotion. Indeed, they suffer from it, since they are trying desperately to get on their own feet. But you cannot turn a parent's love for children on and off like a faucet. When it is dammed up, the backwaters choke the parents, and the children still get wet from the overflow. My friends the college teachers are going to find their discussions of the European situation pretty thin gruel after the rich diet to which they have accustomed themselves during the childhood of their youngsters. Perhaps their professional interests and hobbies will help if they are firmly connected with the main stream of their emotional life. At best, though, they are in for a bad time, like all parents. No mother ever delivered a child at adolescence with less pain than at the hour of birth. It is impossible to give up without pain a creature which has matured as part of ourselves.

Perhaps the hardest thing parents have to face during this period of adolescent revolt is the way their children refuse help and discipline which they obviously need. If Tommy drives so recklessly his mother is sure he'll get killed. If Mary carries on with the boys at her present pace she'll get into trouble and ruin her whole life. You can't let Johnny tie himself up for life with a fast girl like Charlotte. He'll be wretched later on.

Very often—not always, but very often—parents are quite right. Tommy may get killed, and Mary is spoiling for trouble. But almost always there seems to be very little parents can do about it. Their old techniques for handling their children have become distressingly ineffective. Discipline during the period of the revolt is anathema to the young girl or boy—discipline from parents. Mary's sorority sisters may tell her to behave herself or else—and get her to behave. But if mother tries the same methods she meets a storm of protest and frequently finds herself outwitted into the bargain. The mother of one Mary I know sent her to her first football game with a chaperon. The chaperon, it was learned later, went quietly to bed at ten and didn't even wake up when Mary came in at five slightly the worse for a few highballs. Reasoning is rarely successful because neither party can stay reasonable long. Calm analysis of Mary's behavior soon degenerates into a series of high-pitched recriminations and self-justifications on both sides. Mary complains that you "just can't talk to mother," and mother confidentially tells you the same thing about Mary. Appeals to Mary's affection and sense of fair play in an effort to elicit obedience are perhaps the most ill-advised of all, since Mary is quite properly trying to outgrow her affection and naturally resents the fact that she is still in many ways dependent on her parents.

No, parents during the adolescent revolt just have to "take it." I do not mean that they should relax all attempts to control their children. On the contrary we shall soon see that their guardianship is still of major importance psychologically. Continued effort to guide these obstreperous youngsters in the way the individual parent feels to be best is, I think, essential to their best development. But the apparent results, for the time being, are sure to be disappointing. Disputes, accusations, rebellious and sulky withdrawals follow upon any course of action in the majority of homes.

I wish I could offer a pain-dispelling drug to mothers during this second birth, this delivery of children into the adult world. Or that I could at least, like a good obstetrician, tell the mother exactly what to do every step of the way. More than one woman has said to me grimly: "I'm at my wits' end. What*ever* I do for Mary, it seems to be wrong." Exactly! Mary is rebelling against mother, not against anything special mother is doing. (We'll soon talk about Mary's side of it.) It does follow, then, that whatever mother does is wrong—or right, since no other plan of guidance works any better. That is why a set of psychological rules of conduct would not help. The real problem of the adolescent revolt is this: a particular kind of love relationship—namely, that of mother and dependent child —is in process of dissolution. Mother and child are frankly suffering, the mother even more than the child because it is harder for her to find substitutes for her loss.

The help I can offer, as a psychiatrist, to these mothers is an understanding of the problem and assurance that all parents of adolescent children suffer alike. Mothers are bound to be worried about the escapades of their rebellious offspring. But they do not have to feel the added torment of a sense of guilt, and they do not have to feel that the children turn against them because of their own shortcomings. "I've tried so hard to be a good mother," they wail, "and just look at the result." The result is as natural as the dropping of leaves in autumn. Indeed, as we shall see, the more Johnny has loved his mother, the more necessary it is for him to fight against her for a time until he has freed himself for a new love. His childhood love was good, his new love will be successful, and the fight is the necessary bridge between them. Johnny *wants* a fight. He *needs* a fight. So let him have it. Heartache and worry and vexation come to all parents during the adolescent revolt. It is not their fault, and there is nothing much they can do about it except continue to be the kind of parent they have always been. They just have to "take it."

Johnny has a difficult time during this period too. He gets into plenty of scrapes, and he does have a good deal to put up with from parents who cannot help giving him more care than he wants. But his main problem is that half of him *likes* to be protected and loved, while the other half is trying to be independent. He is not really rebelling so much against mother as against his own love for his mother. Growing up is a fearsome task. It is safer and pleasanter to remain a little boy, coddled by parents who love him and tell him what to do. The adventurous part of him that wants to grow up and do things is in constant war against this timorous self that wants familiar affection and security. Civil warfare is bitter warfare. The adolescent revolt is a fight against oneself. The conflict would not be half so violent if it were a simple struggle between children and parents. Its virulence comes from the revolt of the maturing self against the baby self. Parents are dragged into the strife because they are all mixed up in young folks' minds with the baby self.

Young people cannot admit, even to themselves, that they do not wholly want freedom, that they are—to be blunt—scared of it. They cannot admit that in part they do not want to grow up. So they pretend that their parents are over-anxious and won't give them freedom. This guile is unconscious. They do not know that they are putting off their own feelings on their parents. They genuinely believe that they are whole-hearted in their desire for independence and are only held down by dominating adults. I have often observed that parents are frequently less dominating than their children think. Florrie's mother brought her to me because she would have nothing to do with men. At her first visit Florrie told me with tears in her eyes that she could never marry—her parents wouldn't allow it. She was an only child and so dear to them that they couldn't give her up. At first sight Florrie's story was quite plausible. Parents often do reproach their children for behavior which they themselves unconsciously encourage. Careful study of this family revealed, however, that Florrie's parents were no more selfish and absorbing in their love than the rest of us. They had, perhaps, cherished their only daughter a little more protectively than was good for her. But the protection was not holding Florrie back as much as her own fear of leaving them. Florrie was afraid to grow up and assume the responsibilities of wifehood. Unwilling to face her own timidity frankly, she had managed to fool herself into believing that she was not allowed to go out into the world. Florrie herself *wanted* dominating parents.

Parents and educators, impressed by the voluble reproaches of their charges and also by modern theories of freedom in child-training, frequently grant a high degree of independence during adolescence. The results show that Florrie is not alone in her rejection of freedom. Many students in our "progressive" colleges clamor for marks, examinations, and all the paraphernalia of discipline which in conservative colleges cause rebellion. Looking back on a wasted semester, they say: "Why didn't you *make* me work?" Forgetting that they selected the college because it sponsored student initiative, and also that they had vigorously resisted any efforts of the college to enforce its academic regulations. Parents suffer the same censure. A college freshman writing a paper on "How I was Brought Up" concluded with this remarkable sentence: "My parents have given me everything except punishment." She was quite innocent of any attempt at humor or irony. She regretted that she had not been forced to behave properly. When young girls discuss with me the scrapes their friends get into, their most frequent comment is this: "Their parents shouldn't have *allowed* them to get into such a mess."

When we understand the adolescent revolt as a revolt against the baby self as well as against parents, we can sympathize with these reactionary youngsters. Too great leniency in adolescence increases anxiety. If a boy has the independence he wants without fighting for it, he comes perilously close to realizing that he doesn't really want it. Love and protection that you struggle against are nevertheless love and protection—and very comforting at times. Going away to college, starting out in the business world, deciding on a career, learning about sex and choosing a wife—these are the tasks of adolescence. At no other time of life do people have to make so many decisions of far-reaching importance. It is natural that young people should want to work out these choices independently and establish themselves as adults. But it is also natural that they should frequently feel frightened and dismayed. When things go wrong they are glad enough to "pass the buck" to parents—to be forced to make certain choices without the painful necessity of making up their minds, and to be relieved of responsibility for mistakes. If they can obtain real help without sacrificing their feeling of independence they can handle their dilemma with a minimum of discomfort.

The adolescent revolt accomplishes just this sleight-of-hand. Since the young person is apparently fighting tooth and nail for freedom, he can preserve his own feeling of independence and growing maturity. At the same time he receives from his parents the support he needs—and wants in an undercover way. As his real independence grows, he becomes less noisy but more decisive in his demands for freedom. Meantime parents have become accustomed to the loss of their babies and usually are ready to grant full adult status. In this wise the painful struggle of the parent to renounce his protective attitude is really very helpful to the child. The boy gains security while he fights free of his own need for parental love. It is much easier for the child to liberate himself than to be forcibly emancipated by an over-progressive parent.

Falling out of love with parents is, then, the first step toward falling in love with a mate and beginning a new family. Of course we never fall out of love with our parents entirely, never quite reach that man-to-man affection which is our goal. The adolescent revolt is not completely over by the time serious courtship begins. Frankly, it is never entirely put down, nor does it start with a sudden *coup d'état* at the age of fourteen, as I have perhaps suggested. The toddler has sporadic moments of rebellion, and the baby self still carries on its underground campaign when old age returns us to the toddler stage. None of us gets entirely free from his childhood way of loving. We still crave the all-encompassing warmth and protection of our earliest years. We still cover our own fear of a cold world with a blustering independence. But the most dramatic years of revolt are those of adolescence. We say that the American Revolution lasted from 1775 to 1783, though everyone knows that serious tension existed between England and America for many years before and many years after. The war period brought hostile feelings into the open. Just so the adolescent revolt permits parents and children to recognize their antagonisms. Everyone knows too that America remained dependent on England, culturally and economically, long after she declared herself a free state. The two countries are still interdependent and at times show both the exaggerated affection and the bitterness of a dissolved mother-child relationship. But America after 1783 was outwardly free to conduct her affairs with other nations as she would. So the adolescent, while still subtly influenced by his relationship with his parents, proceeds to fall in love on his own, to pick a mate and guide his new family as best he may.

····························· 33 ····························

PARENT-CHILD RELATIONS AND FATHER
IDENTIFICATION AMONG ADOLESCENT BOYS

by Donald E. Payne and Paul Henry Mussen

In this study, Donald E. Payne of Dunlap and Associates and Paul Henry Mussen of the University of California (Berkeley) find that adolescent boys who identify closely with their fathers perceive their fathers and mothers as highly rewarding and warm. Those who identify most closely are more calm and friendly and have more characteristically masculine attitudes than their less highly identified peers. Also, masculine mothers tend to inhibit strong father identification in their sons. [From *Journal of Abnormal and Social Psychology*, 1956, 52, 358-362. Reprinted by permission of the authors and the American Psychological Association.]

Workers in the field of child development, personality theory, and clinical psychology agree that identification is a fundamental concept. While there are some differences in the way the term is used, it generally implies that "a child gives its emotional allegiance to one of its parents and attempts to duplicate in its own life the ideals, attitudes, and behavior of the parent with whom it is identifying" (Stoke, 1950, p. 163).

According to several theorists, children of both sexes initially identify with their mothers since they are most likely to develop emotional attachments to her and to find participation in, and imitation of, her activities rewarding (Mowrer, 1950; Sears, 1953). Later on, the father is likely to become the chief source of rewards for the male child. He associates more with his son and allows the boy to participate in more activities with him. At the same time, society demands that the boy adopt the proper sex role. For these reasons, the boy shifts from identification with his mother to identification with his father (Mowrer, 1950; Sears, 1953).

Sears, Pintler, and Sears (1946) have shown that if the father is absent from the home his preschool-age son is likely to be delayed in acquiring sex-appropriate behavior patterns. But, according to the theory, mere presence of the like-sexed parent in the home is not

enough to promote identification with him. It has also been hypothesized that the process is influenced by "the degree of affection accorded to the child by the person with whom identification is attempted" and "the extent to which the child's needs are gratified by
the person with whom identification is attempted" (Stoke, 1950,
p. 166).

Although there are many case histories which seem to lend support
to these hypotheses, there are no published data, based on normal
subjects, which test them directly. Sears (1953) has presented some
indirect evidence, however, which is highly relevant. She found that
the five-year-old sons of warm, affectionate fathers tend to play the
father role in doll-play activities more frequently than boys whose
fathers are relatively cold. Insofar as extent of playing this role may
be an index of the degree of identification with the father, it may be
inferred that warm fathers are likely to foster strong father identification in their sons.

Clinical observation indicates that boys who prefer their mother
(i.e., see her as more rewarding and more affectionate) throughout
childhood are not likely to shift their identifications to their father.
In such cases they are apt to adopt sex-inappropriate behavior patterns or to become conflicted about their sex roles (Seward, 1946).

Direct rewards for imitation of the father's behavior also play an
important role in the adoption of masculine behavior patterns. If
the child is frequently and consistently rewarded for "acting like
daddy" he develops a generalized tendency to imitate his father. As
Mowrer (1950) has pointed out, the extent to which the child is
rewarded for sex-appropriate behavior depends not only on the
actions of the like-sexed parent but also on generally harmonious
interparental relationships.

Most clinicians and theorists agree that the child who achieves sex-
appropriate identification is more likely to become well adjusted
subsequently than the child who fails to achieve such identification.
Several systematic studies also present evidence relevant to this
notion. In one study of adolescent boys, low perceived father identification (measured in terms of the similarity between the subject's
own MMPI responses and those he thought his father would give)
was found to be related to more abnormal MMPI profiles (Sopchak,
1952). In another study, boys who perceived themselves as being
similar to their fathers with respect to Strong Vocational Interest
Inventory patterns manifested fewer conflicts in their Blacky Test
stories (Cava and Raush, 1952). However, as Child (1954) has pointed
out, both of these studies may be criticized on the grounds that the

techniques used may be measuring only projection, i.e., the child's projected, rather than actual, resemblance between himself and his father.

The present study which made use of actual father-son similarities as a measure of identification was designed to test four specific hypotheses derived from the theoretical considerations discussed above: I. The degree to which boys identify with their fathers is related to the degree to which they perceive him as rewarding, i.e., the extent of his kindness, helpfulness, warmth. II. The degree of father identification is related to the differential reward values of the two parents, or, more specifically, to the extent to which the father is seen as relatively *more* rewarding than the mother. III. The degree of father identification in boys is related to the extent to which they perceive their families (parents as a unit) as rewarding. IV. Among boys, a high degree of father identification is conducive to adequate social and emotional adjustment.

METHOD

Measures of Identification

Initially, 182 boys, juniors and seniors in a public high school in a medium-sized city, completed questionnaires consisting of 50 items, each of which was to be checked as true or false. The items were selected from three scales of the California Psychological Inventory (Gough, 1951): 18 from the Tolerance Scale (e.g., "Disobedience to any government is never justified"); 17 from the Social Participation Scale (e.g., "I am a good mixer"); and 15 from the Masculinity-Femininity Scale (e.g., "I prefer a shower to a bath tub").

Copies of the same questionnaire were sent to the boys' mothers and fathers who were requested to complete them independently and return them by mail. In 72 cases, both parents complied with the request.

Thus, a sample of 72 boys was available whose attitudes, orientations, and preferences could be compared with those of their mothers and fathers. The number of father-son and of mother-son agreements (identical answers) was counted. Each boy's father-identification score consisted of the number of father-son agreements *minus* the number of mother-son agreements. This difference score seemed more appropriate as a measure of identification than the number of father-son agreements alone because it reflected the differential adoption of paternal rather than maternal or general familial attitudes. However, this score was highly correlated with the number of father-son identical responses ($r = +.74$). As would be anticipated, most boys (58) had positive scores; that is, they had adopted more of their fathers' than of their mothers' attitudes.

The 20 boys most highly identified with their fathers (father-identification scores ranging from $+6$ to $+14$ with a mean of $+7.7$) and the 20 who were least highly identified (scores of $+1$ to -6 with a mean of -1.9) were selected for further study. The two groups were matched in age (mean age for both groups, 17.0 years), grade placement (eight seniors and twelve juniors in each group), and approximate socioeconomic status.

Measures of Parent-Child Relations

Each of the 40 boys completed five projective incomplete stories dealing with parent-son relationships. For example, in one story, "A boy wants to use the family car for a date on Friday evening. He knows that neither of his parents plans to use the car. . . . Which of his parents would he ask for the car, and what would happen then?" It was assumed that the boy's responses revealed his perceptions of his own experiences with his parents.

In order to test the hypotheses, the nature of the boy's attachments to his father, mother, and parents (as a unit) were assessed objectively by scoring the incomplete stories in two ways. First the stories were examined for the presence of concrete rewards (gifts, praise, demonstrations of affection, permission to use the car) from the mother, father, or parents (undifferentiated). The total number of stories in which the father was seen as the source of a reward constituted the boy's father-reward (FR) score; the number in which the mother was seen as the source was the mother-reward (MR). A family-reward score (FamR) was derived from the sum of the stories involving rewards by parents (mentioned without designating mother or father specifically) plus the MR and FR scores.

It is, of course, quite possible that a child may become attached to, and dependent upon, a parent who does not give him many concrete rewards, but who maintains a generally satisfying relationship with him. For this reason, the stories were also scored in another way. Two judges rated each story independently with respect to presence or absence of positive relationships with mother, father, or parents (undifferentiated, taken as a unit). Presumably the judges used clinical criteria such as parental understanding, mutual respect, and affection in making their judgments.

TABLE 1

CORRELATIONS BETWEEN FAMILY VARIABLES
AND FATHER-IDENTIFICATION SCORES

Variable	tet-r
FR	.30*
PRF	.37**
FR minus MR	.31*
PRF minus PRM	.15
FamR	.37**
PRFam	.39**

* $p = .05$.
** $p = .02$.

Three scores, closely paralleling the three scores based on the first method of scoring, were derived from these ratings of the psychological soundness of relationships. These were: PRF, the number of stories in which there was evidence of a positive father-son relationship; PRM, the number of stories reflecting positive mother-son relationships; and PRFam, the sum of PRF, PRM and the number of stories involving positive relationships with parents (father and mother not referred to separately).

Measures of Adjustment

Each subject's home-room teacher rated him on nine traits presumably related to social and emotional adjustment. These were: calmness, friendliness, sensitivity, popularity, masculinity, persistence, tolerance, assertiveness, and emotional adjustment.

The traits were rated on five-point linear scales having descriptive comments at each of the points. Scores on these traits, derived from the ratings, ranged from one to five, a score of one indicating the lowest degree of the trait, five the highest. Since only one teacher rated each boy, it was impossible to check the reliability of these ratings.

RESULTS AND DISCUSSION

The first three hypotheses dealt with the influence of the boy's perceptions of the reward values of members of his family on the strength of his identification with his father. Translated into the operations of the present study, Hypothesis I stated that the degree of father identification is positively related to the number of perceptions of the father as a gratifying, rewarding individual. To test this, father-identification score (high or low) was correlated with high and low scores (above or below the median for the total group of 40 subjects) on FR and PRF.[1] Hypothesis II was tested by correlating father-identification status with high and low (above or below the median for the entire group) scores on the measures of the extent to which the father was seen as the predominant source of reward (*more* rewarding or gratifying than the mother; FR—MR; PRF—PRM). In order to test the third hypothesis, father-identification status was correlated with high or low status (above or below median for the entire group) with respect to the two measures of the perceived reward value of the family as a whole (FamR, PRFam).

The findings, which generally support the hypotheses, are summarized in Table 1.

The significant positive correlations between father-identification scores and the two measures of the reward value of the father are clearly consistent with Hypothesis I. As had been predicted, boys are more likely to identify with fathers whom they perceive as rewarding, gratifying, understanding, and warm than with fathers who are not perceived in these ways. If the son's perceptions are in fact determined by the father's behavior toward him, it may be inferred that fathers who are the source of many rewards and who have established sound psychological relationships with their sons facilitate the boys' identifications with them.

The results only partially support the second hypothesis. Most of the boys (87 per cent) saw their fathers as more rewarding than their mothers, i.e., had positive FR minus MR and PRF minus PRM scores. According to the second hypothesis, the perceived differential between the father's and mother's reward values would be greater for highly father-identified than for less highly father-identified boys. Only one of the two correlations relevant to the hypothesis was significant. Boys who are strongly identified with their fathers see the mother-father differential with respect to concrete rewards as a relatively great one. Less highly identified boys tend to regard the difference as smaller. The hypothesized relationship does not hold with regard to the differential in general psychological soundness of relationships, however.

The significant correlations between father-identification scores

---

[1] All relationships between familial variables and degree of father identification were measured by means of tetrachoric correlations for extreme groups, according to the method described by Peters and Van Voorhis (1940, p. 375).

and the two total family variables lend support to the third hypothesis. Compared with boys who have relatively weak father identifications, those who are highly identified with their fathers obtain greater concrete reward scores, that is, regard their families as generally more rewarding in concrete ways. Moreover, according to their stories, they have stronger feelings than their less highly father-identified peers that they have established close, warm relationships with their parents.[2]

It seems quite likely that boys who perceive their parents as important sources of reward and express a great deal of satisfaction about their relationships with them are from generally harmonious families. This is the type of family in which, as Mowrer (1950) suggests, both the mother and father reward the boy's imitation of his father. Our data clearly support the hypothesis that boys who feel comfortable in their relationships with their parents adopt more of their father's behavior and attitudes than boys who experience less favorable parent-child relationships.

While these relationships between familial variables and strength of identification clearly support the first three hypotheses, the data do not enable us to specify antecedents and consequents. That is, the findings may be interpreted to mean that favorable perceptions of the father and the family unit are the antecedents of strong father identification. On the other hand, it is possible that such identification itself is antecedent, leading to favorable, but perhaps distorted, perceptions of other members of the family. The former interpretation seems the more plausible to us, since it is consistent with much of the theory regarding the determinants of identification, with clinical observation, and with findings such as those reported by Sears (1953). Independent, nonprojective measures of the reward values of various family members, correlated with indices of identification, would help to clarify the problem.

The fourth hypothesis, dealing with the relationship between degree of father identification and social and emotional adjustment, was tested by correlating identification status with the teachers' ratings on each of the nine personality characteristics. Tetrachoric correlations were again used since the psychological trait ratings had been dichotomized into high and low categories (above and below median for all 40 subjects).

[2] It should be noted that this relationship cannot be attributed only to the correlation between identification and father rewards scores (FR), since FR and FamR were not highly correlated ($r_{tet} = +.23$, which is not significant). Thus, although rewards from the father contribute to the total family rewards, another factor (such as general reward value of the family) must be introduced to account for the significant correlation between FamR and identification.

Only two of the nine personality characteristics, calmness and friendliness, were significantly correlated with identification status ($r_{\text{tet}} = +.44$ and $+.39$, respectively). The other seven correlations did not differ significantly from zero. While strength of identification may be more highly correlated with other more valid and more reliable measures of adjustment, the present findings are at least partially supportive of the hypothesis. If higher ratings on these characteristics are indicative of better social and emotional adjustment, it may be inferred that substantial father identification is conducive to more adequate personal adjustment.

Some other findings, not directly related to the hypotheses, are also of interest. It will be recalled that the questionnaires to which the boys, their mothers, and their fathers responded contained 15 masculinity-femininity items from which masculinity scores could be derived. The boys' masculinity scores were highly correlated with father-identification scores ($r_{\text{tet}} = +.60$), indicating that boys who are closely identified with their fathers tend to have more characteristically masculine attitudes than their peers who are less highly identified with their fathers. In spite of this they apparently do not appear to be more masculine in their everyday behavior, for ratings of masculinity were not significantly correlated with father-identification scores.

Surprisingly, the fathers of the highly identified boys did not have significantly higher masculinity scores than the fathers of the less strongly father-identified boys. The correlation between boys' identification scores and fathers' masculinity scores ($r_{\text{tet}} = .00$) shows that boys may identify with their fathers and adopt many of their attitudes if these fathers are seen as warm, understanding, and rewarding, regardless of whether or not they have highly masculine attitudes. Since the highly identified boys are generally more masculine in attitudes it may be inferred that good identification with the father is basic to learning these attitudes. Perhaps the boy who has been rewarded for imitating his father's behavior begins, through generalization, to emulate behavior of other men also. The attitudes he holds when he is an adolescent are adopted partially from the father but also from other, often more masculine, models.

On the other hand, mothers' masculinity scores were significantly negatively correlated with their sons' identification scores ($r_{\text{tet}} = -.38$). The more masculine the mother, the less strongly the boy tends to identify with his father. This finding is entirely consistent with what would be predicted on the basis of learning-theory hypotheses concerning identification. The more masculine woman tends to be more dominant in the home and may be perceived as the principal source of reward and gratification for her son as well as her daughter. When this is the case, the male child remains attached to her and dependent upon her and is consequently less able to establish a close relationship with his father. Hence, he is not as likely to identify with his father and to adopt his behavior and attitudes.

SUMMARY

Fifty items from the California Psychological Inventory were administered to junior and senior high school boys and their parents. Extent of identification with the father was measured by subtracting the number of items to which mother and son had responded identically from the number of items to which father and son had responded identically. The 20 boys with highest father-identification scores and the 20 boys with lowest father-identification scores were then given an incomplete-stories test. Judges rated each story for the presence of concrete rewards and psychologically sound relationships with the parents (considered individually and as a unit).

Three hypotheses dealing with antecedents of high and low father identification were tested. Analysis of the data revealed a significant relationship between high father identification and perception of the father as a highly rewarding, affectionate person (Hypothesis I). There was some evidence that the differential between perceived reward value of the father and mother (in favor of the father) would be greater for highly father-identified boys than for those less strongly father identified (Hypothesis II). Strong identification with the father was associated with perceptions of relationships with parents (considered together) as highly rewarding and warm (Hypothesis III).

For these subjects, degree of father identification was highly correlated with masculinity of attitudes. Relatively masculine mothers tended to inhibit strong father identification in their sons. According to teachers' ratings of the subjects on nine personality characteristics, boys who were strongly father-identified were significantly more calm and friendly than their less highly identified peers.

STUDENT QUESTIONNAIRE

Directions:
 1. Please read each of the following statements carefully, decide how you feel about it, and then mark your answer.

2. If you *agree* with the statement, or feel that it is *true* about you, put a circle around the letter *T* before the statement.

3. If you *disagree* with the statement, or feel that it is *not true* about you, put a circle around the *F* before the statement.

Remember: Be sure to circle either the T (true) or the F (false) for every statement, even if you have to guess at some.

T F 1. People who are supposed to be experts are often no better than other people.

T F 2. It is certainly all right for anyone to grab all he can get in this world.

T F 3. I enjoy social gatherings just to be with people.

T F 4. Most people are honest chiefly through fear of being caught.

T F 5. I am very slow in making up my mind.

T F 6. People are often jealous of good ideas just because they did not think of them first.

T F 7. I like mechanics magazines.

T F 8. Most of the time I would rather stay at home evenings than go out with friends.

T F 9. I think I would like the work of a clerk in a large department store.

T F 10. There is only one true religion.

T F 11. I usually take an active part in the entertainment at parties.

T F 12. I would like to be a soldier.

T F 13. I think I would like the work of a dress designer.

T F 14. I prefer a shower to a bathtub.

T F 15. Parents are much too easy on their children nowadays.

T F 16. I am a good mixer.

T F 17. The man who provides temptation by leaving valuable property unprotected is about as much to blame for its theft as the one who takes it.

T F 18. I am not likely to speak to people until they speak to me.

T F 19. I think I would like the work of a librarian.

T F 20. I like to boast about my achievements now and then.

T F 21. Women should not be allowed to drink in cocktail bars.

T F 22. I like adventure stories better than romantic stories.

T F 23. I find it easy to drop a friend.

T F 24. I seem to be about as capable and smart as most others around me.

T F 25. Disobedience to any government is never justified.

T F 26. Most people would lie to get ahead.

T F 27. People can sometimes change me even though I thought my mind was made up on a subject.

T F 28. A person needs to show off a little now and then.

T F 29. I like to go to dances.

T F 30. I have no patience with people who argue with me on things that I know more about than they do.

T F 31. It makes me uncomfortable to do a stunt at a party even when others are doing the same sort of thing.

T F 32. I must admit I enjoy playing practical jokes on people.

T F 33. I don't really care whether people like me or dislike me.

T F 34. I should like to belong to several clubs or lodges.

T F 35. It is hard for me to act natural when I am with new people.

T F 36. Minority groups will misuse their privileges if they are given too much freedom.

T F 37. In school I was sometimes sent to the principal for cutting up.

T F 38. I like to be the center of attention.

T F 39. People should be more definite about things.

T F 40. I think I would like the work of a garage mechanic.

T F 41. I would like to be a nurse.

T F 42. When I am in a group I usually do what the others want to do.

T F 43. It is very hard for me to tell anyone about myself.

T F 44. [omitted]

T F 45. I have no sympathy for someone who is always doubting and unsure about things.

T F 46. Only a fool would want to change our American way of life.

T F 47. I like to go to parties and other affairs where there is lots of loud fun.

T F 48. I want to be an important person in the community.

T F 49. People pretend to care more about one another than they really do.

T F 50. When in a group of people I have trouble thinking of the right things to talk about.

PARENTS QUESTIONNAIRE

Instructions for Parents:

1. *Each* parent is to fill out one of the surveys.
2. Fill them out independently—*do not discuss them with each other.*
3. After finishing the survey, place the survey questionnaire in the enclosed stamped envelope, and return it *immediately.*

SURVEY QUESTIONNAIRE

How to fill out this survey:

1. Read each of the statements below. Decide whether the statement is *true* or *false*.
2. If you think the statement is *true*, put a circle around the *T* (true) in front of the statement.

3. If you think the statement is *false*, put a circle around the *F* (false) in front of the statement.

Sample:

T F 1. I like to get up early in the morning.

If you *do* like to get up early in the morning, you would put a circle around the *T*, like this:

(T) F 1. I like to get up early in the morning.

If you *do not* like to get up early in the morning, you would put a circle around the *F*, like this:

T (F) 1. I like to get up early in the morning.

Remember: Put a circle around the T if you agree with the statement, and a circle around the F if you disagree. *Be sure to answer all the items, even if you have to guess at some.*

(The items used in the Parents Questionnaire were identical with those in the Student Questionnaire.)

INCOMPLETE STORIES

Incomplete Story Number 1:

A boy wants to use the family car for a date on Friday evening. He knows that neither of his parents plan to use the car. Which of his parents would he ask for the car, and what would happen then?

Incomplete Story Number 2:

It is report-card time, and a boy has brought home a report-card with all "A's." What might his parents say when he shows it to them? What might his mother say or do? What might his father say or do?

Incomplete Story Number 3:

A boy came home from a date at three o'clock one morning. His parents had told him to be home by midnight. His father and mother are waiting up for him when he gets home. What might the boy say or do when he meets them? Then what would his mother and father say or do? How would the story end?

Incomplete Story Number 4:

One boy's parents went out for an evening. While they were gone, some of the boy's friends dropped in. By accident, a valuable lamp was broken, and before there is time to clean up the pieces the parents return home. What might his mother and father say or do?

Incomplete Story Number 5:

Most boys have problems which they cannot figure out at some time or another. If a boy had such a problem, what might it be? Which of his parents might he go to for advice or help? What advice would this parent give him?

TEACHERS' RATING SCALE

Name of boy being rated_____His grade_____

Your name_____

Instructions:

1. Please do not consult anyone else when making your ratings.
2. Place a check mark on the scale at the point which you feel best describes the boy you are rating. It is important that you make your judgments independently for each quality rated; try not to allow your general impression of the boy influence you in the specific ratings
3. One suggestion which may be of help to you when making judgment is to rate *all* of the boys on the first scale; then start over and rate all of the boys on the second scale; etc. It has been found that this method gives more precise results than rating each boy on all the scales at one time.

1. Friendliness:

1	2	3	4	5
genial, outgoing, tries very hard to make friends	sociable, likes people	average degree of friendliness	less friendly than average, seldom makes new friends	markedly unfriendly, avoids others, solitary

2. Persistence:

1	2	3	4	5
won't try, or doesn't care, gives up easily	lackadaisical, doesn't put forth much effort	about average amount of effort	tries harder than most, willing to work hard	tries very hard sticks it out in spite of difficulties

3. Sensitivity:

1	2	3	4	5
supersensitive, feelings hurt extremely easily	more sensitive than average	average sort of response to approval & disapproval	matter-of-fact, feelings not easily hurt	callous, insensitive, thick-skinned

4. Tolerance:

1	2	3	4	5
extremely sympathetic to new ideas & persons	open-minded, liberal outlook	about normal degree of tolerance	tends to be narrow-minded	bigoted, very intolerant

5. Intelligence:

1	2	3	4	5
extremely dull, very slow to grasp ideas	duller than average	average intelligence	better than average, bright	extremely bright, very quick to grasp ideas

6. Masculinity:

1	2	3	4	5
very masculine in appearance & behavior	more masculine than average	average amount of masculinity	somewhat effeminate	marked effeminacy, a sissy

7. Nervousness:

1	2	3	4	5
extremely calm & relaxed, never seems upset	tends to take things in his stride	occasionally upset, tension appropriate to the situation	tense & nervous, gets upset easily	very nervous, fidgety, many nervous mannerisms

8. Popularity:

1	2	3	4	5
very unpopular, a social isolate	somewhat unpopular, seldom sought out by others	about as popular as average	more popular than average, well-liked by others	very popular, a social leader

9. Assertiveness:

1	2	3	4	5
extremely dominating, always directs & controls others	more assertive than average	normal amount of assertiveness	rarely in control, tends to submit to others	very submissive, invariably directed by others

10. Emotional adjustment:

1	2	3	4	5
well-adjusted	better than average	average adjustment	not so well-adjusted	has many personality problems

CHAPTER TWELVE

The Adolescent in School

34

RELIEVING ANXIETY IN CLASSROOM

EXAMINATIONS

by W. J. McKeachie, Donald Pollie, and Joseph Speisman[1]

The anxiety of the student as he faces his teacher who has the power
to thwart him in his goal, that of completing the work satisfactorily,
is well known to both students and teachers. The sequence of experiments in this selection shows that the teacher may reduce or dissipate
anxiety in his students by encouraging them to write comments about
their objective examination questions. The authors are W. J. Mc-
Keachie of the University of Michigan, Donald Pollie of Washington
University, and Joseph Speisman of the University of California
(Berkeley). [From *Journal of Abnormal and Social Psychology*, 1955,
50, 93-98. Reprinted by permission of the authors and the American
Psychological Association.]

The concept of anxiety has been one of the most widely used concepts in recent psychological theory. In this paper we will use anxiety
to mean the state of an individual in a threatening situation from
which he cannot immediately escape. In an earlier paper (McKeachie,
1951) the senior author suggested some of the ways in which student
anxiety may be mobilized by the classroom situation and its possible
effects upon his performance. This paper reports a series of investi-

[1] Louis Berman, Ann Neel, and Richard Teevan also carried out experiments
in this group.

gations concerned with student performance on objective-type class-room achievement examinations. Our basic assumption in these investigations was that such a high degree of anxiety is mobilized by classroom tests that the students' performance is adversely affected.

Theory

Basically our theory was this: Most students begin a test with some anxiety as a result of their uncertainty about the outcome of the test and their high degree of motivation for achieving a "good" grade in the course. As they progress through the test they inevitably encounter some questions that are too difficult or ambiguous for them to answer. Each such item adds to the student's anxiety. As he attacks the succeeding items either the anxiety, or the Zeigarnik effect aroused by the items which he has failed to pass, interferes with his performance, or in Maier's (1949) terms, his behavior becomes frustration-instigated, rather than motivated problem-solving behavior.

If the effects of failing items could be diminished in some way, test performance should be improved.

EXPERIMENT I

Purpose

Our first experiment was based on the theory that if students could "blow off steam" about items that cause them difficulty, performance on succeeding items would be improved. Permitting students to write comments about difficult or ambiguous items might act to discharge feelings or to give the student more closure on the item.

Thus, our hypothesis was: Students who are encouraged to write comments about test items on their answer sheets will make higher test scores than students who have no opportunity to make comments.

Procedure

The tests upon which the experiments were performed were the regular classroom examinations in our general psychology course. They consisted of multiple-choice questions to which students responded by checking the appropriate letter on a separate answer sheet. They were given during the regular class period, and with few exceptions students completed the test in less than the class hour. Those who wished it were given additional time. In this experiment, half of the answer sheets were of the usual form, while the other half contained a blank line beside each place for responding. The instructions for the latter, or experimental group, contained these words "Feel free to make any comments about the items in the space provided."

Results

The results of the experiment confirmed our hypothesis. Students who used the answer sheets with spaces to comment (even though many made no comments) made significantly higher scores on the test than those who used conventional answer sheets (see Table 1). Note that this experiment did not directly test our theory about discharge of anxiety, but merely indicated that an opportunity to comment was beneficial.

Discussion

The results of Experiment I were gratifying; yet in view of the many experiments in which different teaching methods failed to produce differences in objective test scores, our results seemed too good to be true. Consequently we asked ourselves a number of questions:

1. Would we get the same results if we repeated the experiment? The obvious way to find out was to repeat the experiment. We did this three times, obtaining results comparable to those of Experiment I.

2. Did the mere appearance of the answer sheet somehow influence scores on the test? To answer this question, Experiment I was repeated with the control group using answer sheets which were identical to those used by the experimental group except that instead of the instructions, "Feel free to comment . . ." their answer sheet con-

TABLE 1

EFFECTS OF DIFFERING TYPES OF ANSWER SHEETS UPON TEXT SCORES

Answer Sheet	N	Mean	SD
Usual type	83	29.65	3.9
With space for comments	83	31.09	3.6

Note.—Difference significant at .01 level.

tained the instructions, "Do not mark in this space." Again the group with instructions, "Feel free . . ." made significantly higher scores.

TABLE 2

EFFECT OF DIFFERING SETS TOWARD TEST

Set	Answer Sheet	N	Mean	SD
Counts for grade	Space for comments	94	20.1	3.7
	Usual type	131	18.4	4.1
Just for practice	Space for comments	69	19.3	3.4
	Usual type	34	17.5	2.8

EXPERIMENT II

Purpose

If anxiety interferes with test performance, increasing student anxiety should decrease test scores. This was the hypothesis which governed Experiment II.

Procedure

The procedure used in Experiment II was the same as that in Experiment I except that some of the students were told that the test to be given would count as part of the course grade and some were told that this would be a practice test which would not count on their grades. Both groups had been warned several days in advance of the test that a test would be given, but the information that this was to be only a practice test was given to one group in the examination period. Both types of answer sheets used in Experiment I were used in both groups.

Results

While the effect of the differences between the two types of answer sheets was again significant, our hypothesis (for which we had planned to use a one-tailed test of significance) was not confirmed. The group which thought the test counted toward the course grade did not make lower scores (see Table 2).

Discussion

To attempt to explain negative results is a fascinating but dangerous pastime. One explanation was that the students' experiences with tests had generally been so anxiety ridden that our different sets were not enough to neutralize the effects of the many cues for anxiety present when the student actually took the test. Another was that the announcement that the test was "just for practice" may have so reduced motivation that performance was less. This explanation is congruent with findings that people with high need for achievement do not perform up to capacity in nonachievement situations (McClelland, *et al.*, 1953).

EXPERIMENT III

Purpose

In our early experiments we had been so amazed that the experiment worked that we had not attempted further conceptualization of the way it worked. We thought that allowing students to comment reduced their anxiety, but we had never measured anxiety, and our one attempt to manipulate anxiety had failed to produce differences in behavior. Thus we were eager to learn more of the way in which permitting students to write comments about questions improved their test scores. We had four ideas:

1. When students write a comment about a test item, they must think further about that item. In thus reorganizing their thoughts about the item, they are more likely to be able to select the correct alternative.

2. In commenting about the item the student can explain the reasons for choosing the alternative, and even though this may not make the instructor mark the item right, he will see that the student has some knowledge. Thus the student does not have as great a feeling of failure and may develop a greater sense of closure about the item. This will reduce interference with later items.

3. In commenting on an item, the student can vent his emotions. Since emotions may interfere with problem solving, this release of emotional tension will permit a more rational approach to subsequent items.

4. The fact that the student is allowed to comment changes his perception of the test. He is less likely to feel that the test is intended to be punitive. He is more apt to perceive the instructor as trying to facilitate his success. Thus his anxiety about the test is reduced, and whether or not he writes comments, he will be able to perform more rationally.

Our next experiment was designed to test these ideas. Specifically our hypotheses were:

1. Students' performances on a test will be improved if they are permitted to write their feelings about test items, but are not permitted to write explanations, as compared with students who have no opportunity to write comments.

2. Students' performances on a test will be improved if they are permitted to write explanations of their answers, but are not permitted to write their feelings, as compared with students who have no opportunity to write comments.

3. Giving students the opportunity to write comments affects their scores on items succeeding the item which is commented on rather than on the item upon which comments were made.

Procedures

Our procedures were much the same as in previous experiments except that we now had two experimental groups. The instructions on their answer sheets read as follows:

Group 1: "In the space provided please state your feelings, only, concerning the question. Do not explain your answer. Your comments may consist of anything whatever you feel about the question—its fairness, clarity, importance, triviality, etc. Your comments will be of aid to us in evaluating your test. Remember you may say whatever you feel."

Group 2: "In the space provided please state your explanations, only, of how you arrived at your particular answer. Do this only in those cases where a solution of the answer entails the application of a principle, fact, or method you have learned about. In other words, explain your answer wherever explanations seem necessary. These will be of aid to us in evaluating the complexity of the questions we have asked you. Use the space for explanations only."

To test Hypothesis 3, the obvious procedure would be to compare scores of the experimental groups with the control group on the items about which most comments were written as well as on the items immediately following. To insure that some items would attract comments and that they would not be too closely bunched together, we inserted six items which had proved very difficult to previous classes in general psychology and spaced these well apart. Unfortunately, even with these insertions no more than 20 per cent of the students wrote comments about any one item, and differences in scores on that or the succeeding item were insignificant. This led us to a different procedure for testing Hypothesis 3. If failing an item creates tension, this tension should increase throughout the test. If having an opportunity to write comments aids in reducing or releasing this tension, the improvement in performance should be more marked on the last half of the test than on the first half. Hence separate scores for each half of the test were computed.

Results

Our attempt to restrict students' comments to feelings (Hypothesis 1) or to explanations (Hypothesis 2) appeared from our results to have dissipated much of the effect of permitting comments. As indicated in Table 3, differences between the groups were not significant. However, Hypothesis 3 was verified. The groups that had been given opportunities to write comments were significantly superior to the control group on the last half of the test even though they were not superior on the first half (see Table 4).

In a retest of this hypothesis with other groups, comparable results were obtained with the difference in scores on the last half of the test between "feelings" and "no comments" groups having a probability of .16 and that between "explanations" and "no comments" groups having a probability of .005.

Discussion

This experiment was partly encouraging and partly discouraging. Our prediction was verified. The effects of the opportunity to comment were most pronounced on the last half of the test. Since there were no more comments on the last half of the test than on the first half, this seemed to demonstrate that comments did not affect the scores on the items about which comments were written, but rather succeeding items. This fitted in with our theory that tension is built up throughout the test and that giving opportunity to comment reduces the increasing tension. But we were surprised to find that in general neither the instructions to write explanations nor to write feelings about items seemed to have been as effective as our usual instruction to "Feel free to comment. . . ." We repeated this part of

TABLE 3

TEST SCORES FOR GROUPS GIVEN DIFFERENT INSTRUCTIONS

Group	N	Mean	SD
Feelings	66	20.78	2.75
Explanations	75	20.86	2.25
No comments	70	20.07	2.72

TABLE 4

SCORES ON FIRST AND LAST HALVES OF TEST FOR
GROUPS GIVEN DIFFERENT INSTRUCTIONS

Group	N	First-Half Mean	Last-Half Mean	Mean of Differences	SD of Differences
Feelings	66	10.79	9.99	.80	1.7
Explanations	73	10.63	10.23	.40	1.8
No comments	70	10.72	9.40	1.32	1.9

Note.—Difference of differences: Feelings vs. no comments, $p = .11$; explanations vs. no comments, $p < .01$.

the experiment (Teevan and McKeachie, 1954) with the added variation of giving one group answer sheets with the instructions: "In the space provided please state your feelings about a question *and* an explanation of how you arrived at the answer you used. Whenever you come to a question that bothers you, give any feelings you have about its clarity, fairness, triviality, etc., and also an explanation of how you arrived at the answer you used. This will help us to evaluate your test and also help in making out future tests." Surprisingly enough, none of the experimental groups was significantly superior to the group with conventional answer sheets.

The results of this follow-up were disconcerting. It now appeared that the important variable was not whether or not students released emotional feelings or gained closure by explaining their answers. Rather, it now appeared that the over-all set given by the instructions to comment was more important. Obviously, another experiment needed to be done.

EXPERIMENT IV

Purpose

Based on our previous results we now developed the hypothesis that specific instructions to comment actually increase a student's anxiety since they ask him to perform an additional task upon which he may be evaluated. Additional restraint is felt, especially when these instructions specify the kind of comment to be made. Our original instructions to "Feel free to comment" must have worked because they made the situation a permissive one. Our hypothesis for

Experiment IV, then, was: Students given answer sheets with the instructions, "If you wish to make any comments about the questions on this exam, do so in the space provided," will make higher test scores than students with instructions to give their feelings and explanations of their answers on difficult items or students who are instructed not to comment.

Procedures

Our procedures were the same as in the preceding experiments. One-third of the students were given answer sheets with the instructions, "If you wish to make any comments about the questions on this exam, do so in the space provided"; one-third of the students

TABLE 5

EFFECT ON PERFORMANCE OF DIFFERING INSTRUCTIONS

Group	Mean	F	df	p
Explanations and feelings		(1 vs. 2)		
	32.73	2.5	1 and 281	NS
Do not comment		(2 vs. 3)		
	33.56	2.4	1 and 286	NS
Free comment		(1 vs. 3)		
	34.45	10.5	1 and 267	< .01

Note.—The F ratio when all three means were taken together was 4.89, which is just beyond the .01 level of confidence.

received answer sheets with instructions, "In the space provided, please state your feelings about a question *and* an explanation of how you arrived at the answer you used. Whenever you come to a question that bothers you, give any feelings you have about its clarity, fairness, triviality, etc., and also an explanation of how you arrived at the answer you used. This will help us to evaluate your test and also help in making out future tests"; and the remaining third of the students received answer sheets with instructions, "Do not mark in the space to the right of your answers." Except for the instructions all answer sheets were identical.

Results

As indicated in Table 5, our hypothesis was confirmed by our results. The students with permissive instructions made significantly higher scores than students receiving the other two types of answer sheets. Since all students in this and the other experiments finished the examination in the allotted time, the results were not due to differences in the time required to write comments.

EXPERIMENT V

Purpose

The results of the four experiments conducted up to this point convinced us that test performance is influenced by the stress of the testing situation, and that this stress could be reduced by giving students the opportunity to make comments about the test. At the same time we were interested in personality variables that might make for individual differences in the amount of stress which a student feels in taking a test. To us one of the most interesting possible personality variables was the student's need for achievement. The findings of McClelland *et al.* (1953) indicated that their measure of the achievement motive could differentiate students who felt motivated to excel from students who feared failure in achievement situations. We hypothesized that this latter group (low need achievement) would find the test situation more stressful, and that the

TABLE 6

ERRORS ON FIRST AND LAST HALVES OF EXAM

Group	N	First Half		Second Half	
		Mean	SD	Mean	SD
Fear-failure	12	6.5	3.6	5.6	2.8
High need achievement	12	2.8	1.9	4.6	1.8

Note.—Difference of differences, $p = .11$.

opportunity to write comments would be of more aid in improving their scores than it would be for students with less anxiety about achievement.

Procedure

Students who took part in the replication of Experiment III were given the measure of achievement motivation. Students were divided at the median on this measure into two groups: (*a*) a high n Achievement group, and (*b*) a low n Achievement (fear of failure) group (*ibid.,*). All of these students had been given answer sheets which requested that they write comments about difficult or ambiguous items. The scores of the two groups were compared for the items on the first half of the test and for the items on the last half of the test.

Results

The results were not conclusive but tended to support our hypothesis. On the first half of the test, the high-achievement students scored significantly higher than the fear-of-failure group. On the last half of the examination, there was no significant difference between the scores of the two groups. The probability of the difference in gains was .11 (see Table 6). Moreover, the correlation between scores on the last half of the examination and number of comments was .73 for the fear-of-failure group and only .05 for the high–need-achievement group.

DISCUSSION AND GENERAL CONCLUSIONS

What do our experiments add up to? In the sequence of experiments our theory had been building up step by step. We now had ideas about (a) the sources of anxiety in the testing situation, (b) the effect of anxiety upon performance, and (c) methods of reducing the deleterious effects of anxiety upon problem solving.

Sources of Anxiety

As we see it, the student's anxiety in the testing situation derives from his helplessness in relation to the instructor's power. The power of the instructor to assign a grade means that the instructor can, by assigning a low grade, bar the student from attaining some of his most important goals, such as admission to graduate professional training, the prestige of college graduation or of Phi Beta Kappa, and the material advantages of good grades in securing a job. While all student-instructor relationships possess some possible threat, the focus of the student's anxiety is course examinations, which are usually the primary basis for grade assignment. The degree of the student's anxiety will be a function of his perception of the instructor's arbitrariness and punitiveness in the use of his power. Our finding that freedom to make comments results in higher test scores could be at least partially explained, we believe, if our instructions

o "Feel free to comment . . ." influenced students to perceive the
nstructor as being a person who was not punitive, not attempting
o maintain his superior status, but one who wanted to give students
every opportunity to communicate to him.

In addition, the student's anxiety is a function of uncertainty (as
Sinha [1950] and Cohen [1953] have demonstrated). When we asked
or a specific type of comment, e.g., "only feelings" or "only explanations," we did not get the improved performance which we consistently obtained when our instructions were "Feel free to comment. . . ." In retrospect, we suspect that these specific instructions
were actually more ambiguous than the free-comment instructions.
The student was uncertain as to how much he was expected to comment and how much his comments would influence his instructor's
evaluation of him.

Finally, anxiety is a function of individual differences in motivation and security in the situation. Our results indicate that our
experimental variation of instructions had little effect upon the person with high need achievement, who in need-achievement theory, is
presumed to be stimulated but secure in achievement testing situations. However, students fearing failure were aided by the opportunity to make comments. These results are in harmony with those
of Hutt (1947), who found that maladjusted children achieved higher
IQ's when he followed each failed test item with an easy item. However, such a procedure did not significantly influence scores of normal children.

The effect of anxiety upon performance. While we had no direct
measure of anxiety, our findings do appear to support those of Deese
and Lazarus (1952), Lazarus, Deese, and Osler (1952), Sarason (1952),
and Maier (1949), who have reported decrements in various tasks as a
result of anxiety.

How can the decrement in performance due to anxiety be reduced?
Obviously, reducing anxiety should reduce the detrimental effects
of anxiety, and as we pointed out earlier, this is, we believe, one of
the functions of giving students opportunity to comment on test
questions. But the fact that scores of students who were allowed to
comment improve relatively in the second half of the test suggests
that commenting in itself may also be of some value in improving
performance. We suspect that when a person is frustrated or anxious,
the discharge of the tension through almost any available response
will help decrease the effect of the anxiety on later problems. However, we cannot help speculating about the fact that each time we

compared instructions to write feelings against instructions to write explanations, the explanations group made slightly, but not significantly, better scores. Can it be that merely "blowing off steam" is not effective, and that catharsis, whether of these superficial feelings or of deeply repressed emotions, should involve verbalizing cognitive as well as affective elements? Or, does the expression of negative feelings arouse fear of incurring the instructor's displeasure? Or is the important thing that the student feels that he is communicating to the person having power over him? Perhaps expression of feelings seems to communicate less than an explanation? Such speculations need to be tested by further research.

SUMMARY

The present experiments attempted to influence student scores on classroom tests by setting up conditions which would permit reduction or dissipation of anxiety.

The results showed that students who were encouraged to write comments about their questions made higher scores than students who had conventional answer sheets. Since students who could write comments did not differ significantly from the control group in their scores on the first half of the test but performed significantly better on the second half of the test, it was concluded that the effect of the comments was not to improve scores on the items about which the comments were written. When students were given specific instructions as to the type of comments to write, their test scores were lower than those of students who were told "Feel free to write comments."

On the basis of the McClelland, Atkinson, et al. test for achievement motivation, students who feared failure were distinguished from those with positive achievement motivation. When given opportunity to comment, students with fear of failure made lower scores on the first half of the test than students with high need achievement, but did not differ significantly on the last half of the test.

It is suggested that classroom examinations help determine the students' perception of the manner in which the instructor's power to assign grades will be used. Individual anxiety in the situation is partially a function of achievement motivation. Anxiety inhibits performance. Giving students an opportunity to write comments aids not only in reducing the threat but also in channeling the release of anxiety.

.... 35 ....

A FURTHER INVESTIGATION OF THE
RELATIONSHIP BETWEEN ANXIETY
AND CLASSROOM EXAMINATION
PERFORMANCE

by Allen D. Calvin, F. J. McGuigan, and Maurice W. Sullivan

In this repetition of an earlier experiment on the relationship between student anxiety and performance on classroom examinations,[1]
Allen D. Calvin, F. J. McGuigan, and Maurice W. Sullivan of Hollins
College confirm the earlier findings and introduce an improvement
in experimental design: a direct measure of anxiety. [From *Journal
of Educational Psychology*, 1957, *48*, 240-244. Reprinted by permission
of the authors and the American Psychological Association.]

In a recent paper McKeachie, Pollie, and Speisman (1955) found
that students who were given the opportunity to write comments
about their objective examination questions performed better on the
last half of their examination than students who were not given
an opportunity to comment. They pointed out that this finding
". . . fitted in with our theory that tension is built up throughout the
test and that giving opportunity to comment reduces the increasing
tension" (p. 95). They also reported a relationship between examination scores and McClelland's (1953) "need for achievement" personality variable. On the basis of their results they concluded:
"Anxiety inhibits performance. Giving students an opportunity to
write comments aids not only in reducing the threat but also in
channeling the release of anxiety" (p. 98).

Since McKeachie et al., themselves, noted after their first experiment that "our results seemed too good to be true," an attempt to
replicate their findings seems called for. In addition, the fact that

[1] See selection 34 in this volume.

they had no direct measure of anxiety indicates the need for an experiment where such a measure is provided. The following study is therefore an attempt to replicate McKeachie et al.'s results, and to test their "anxiety reduction" hypothesis.

METHOD

Subjects

The Ss, one hundred and fifty-two undergraduate female students from Hollins College, were taken from five classes as follows: sixty-one and thirty-five from two introductory psychology classes, seventeen and twenty-one from two introductory Spanish classes, and eighteen from a Spanish literature class. In each case the entire class participated.

Procedure

In an attempt to distinguish between high anxious and low anxious Ss, the A-Scale with the biographical inventory as described by Taylor (1953) was given. The Otis (1950) Higher Examination of Mental Abilities was also given. Both tests were administered at the beginning of each course. The rest of the procedure was similar to that used by McKeachie et al., who modified their methodology slightly from group to group. The specific procedure used in our experiment was as follows: The examination consisted of randomly presented, multiple choice items and was the first examination given in the course for each group. Each class was divided at random into an experimental and a control group. The experimental group in each class received answer sheets with the instructions: "Put an X through the best answer for each item. Feel free to make any comments about the items in the space provided," and the control group received answer sheets with the instructions: "Put an X through the best answer for each item. Do not mark in the space to the right of your answers."

RESULTS[2]

[2] Data gathered in connection with another study made it possible to test McKeachie et al.'s "anxiety reduction" hypothesis on a limited number of Ss using another measure of "anxiety" [the Palmer perspiration index described by Mowrer (1953)]. This analysis yielded non-significant results.

In all five classes, the experimental group made fewer errors on the last half of the examination than did the control group. Tests between experimental and control groups in each class, however, failed to reach the 5% point of significance. An F test between classes was made and no significant difference obtained, so the findings for all the classes were combined and the one-tailed binomial expansion indicated that the present results could be expected by chance approximately three times out of one hundred. Accordingly, the null hypothesis that there was no difference in performance between experimental and control groups on the last half of the examination was rejected.

The largest introductory psychology class permitted us to make an analysis in terms of the A-Scale. The sixty-one Ss were divided at the median and classified as low and high anxiety groups. The high anxiety Ss in the experimental group were significantly worse ($p < 0.04$, one-tailed t test) on the first half of the examination, but did not differ significantly from the low anxiety Ss on the second half (See Table 1). An evaluation, in terms of gain from the first half of the examination to the second, showed that the high anxious experimental Ss were significantly superior to the low anxious experimental Ss ($p < 0.005$). When a covariance to remove the effect of initial scores on gain scores was run the resulting F was still significant ($p < 0.02$). This difference in gain scores is indicated in Table 1 by the sharp reduction in errors for the high anxiety experimental group on the second half of the test, and by the slight increase in errors for the low anxiety experimental group. For the control group, the high anxiety Ss made more errors than the low anxiety Ss (although not significantly more) on *both* the first and second half of the test; while the high anxiety Ss did improve somewhat on the second half of the test the low anxiety Ss improved even more.[3]

The correlation between total number of comments and number of errors on the second half of the examination was −0.19 for the high anxiety experimental group, and −0.40 for the low anxious experimental group, neither of which was significant.

The correlation between Otis scores and anxiety scores was −0.05.

[3] In a personal communication from W. F. Smith, we have learned that he and F. C. Rockett, did a related study using the Sarason anxiety scale. They did not analyze their results to see if high anxiety Ss showed a greater gain than low anxiety Ss on the second half of the examination, but they varied type of instruction and although the effect of type of instruction was not significant, they found a significant interaction between type of instruction and anxiety level. High anxiety Ss benefited more from anxiety reducing instruction.

TABLE 1

ERRORS ON FIRST AND LAST HALVES OF EXAMINATION

Group	First Half	Second Half
Experimental		
High anxiety	9.58	7.25
Low anxiety	7.24	7.35
Control		
High anxiety	9.00	8.82
Low anxiety	8.43	6.78

DISCUSSION

The finding that all five experimental groups were superior to their corresponding controls corroborates the findings of McKeachie et al. The failure of the individual intra-class comparisons to reach acceptable levels of statistical significance may well be due to the smaller Ns in our classes than in McKeachie et al.

The sharp drop in errors for our high anxiety experimental group on the second half of the examination is similar to the behavior of McKeachie et al.'s low need for achievement group and supports their anxiety reduction hypothesis.

McKeachie et al. report a correlation for their low need for achievement group of 0.73 between scores on the last half of the examination and number of comments, and for their high need for achievement group of 0.05. Our correlations, between number of errors on the last half of the examination and number of comments, of course, reverses the sign so that in both McKeachie et al.'s Ss, and ours, those Ss who made the most comments performed the best. Neither of our correlations, however, approached the magnitude of McKeachie et al.'s low need achievement group, and our low A-Scale group actually had a higher correlation than our high A-Scale group, although neither of our correlations was significant. Rather than speculate on these results at this time, it seems wiser simply to note that there is a trend for those Ss who make more comments to make fewer errors on the last half of their examinations.

The practically zero correlation between Otis scores and anxiety scores certainly does not point toward any relationship between anxiety and intelligence in our sample, although we cannot of course definitely rule out the possibility that there may exist differences in intellectual makeup between our high and low anxiety Ss which are not shown by the Otis (Calvin et al., 1955; Taylor, 1955).

The present results, taken together with those of McKeachie et al., indicate the applicability of "drive reduction learning theory" to the classroom situation.

SUMMARY

In an effort to confirm findings by McKeachie et al., five undergraduate classes were divided into experimental and control groups. The experimental groups were allowed to comment on items in an objective examination while the control groups were not. When the results of the five classes are combined, the experimental Ss performed significantly better than the controls on the second half of the examination. The largest class with an N of sixty-one was divided into high and low anxious Ss on the basis of their A-Scale scores. Anxiety was found to be a significant variable in terms of improvement from the first half of the test to the second in the experimental group. It was also found that those Ss who made the most comments showed the greatest improvement, but this relationship was not significant. Implications of these findings are discussed.

································ **36** ································

VALIDITY OF TEACHERS' RATINGS OF

ADOLESCENTS' ADJUSTMENT AND ASPIRATIONS[1]

by David P. Ausubel, Herbert M. Schiff, and Marjorie P. Zeleny

What is the relationship between teachers' ratings and various objective and projective measures of adolescents' adjustment? How valid are teachers' ratings of pupils' academic and vocational aspirations? These are the two major problems explored in the following selection by David P. Ausubel of the University of Illinois, Herbert M. Schiff

[1] This research was supported by grants from the Bureau of Educational Research and from the University Research Board of the University of Illinois.

of the Idaho State Hospital South, and Marjorie P. Zeleny of Tucson, Arizona. [From *Journal of Educational Psychology*, 1954, *45*, 394-406. Reprinted by permission of the authors and Warwick & York, Inc.]

This study was concerned with the relationship between teachers' ratings of adjustment and aspirational traits in adolescents and various other self-report, objective, and projective measures of the same characteristics.

Teachers' ratings are frequently used for diagnostic, prognostic, guidance, and research purposes because of their ready accessibility and quantifiability. Moreover, when employed as averages of several raters and in relation to traits (a) which are overtly manifest and objectively observable in everyday behavior and (b) which can be specifically and unambiguously defined (Cronbach, 1949; Symonds, 1931; Terman and Oden, 1949), such ratings enjoy considerable reliability. A further advantage of teachers' ratings is the fact that they can be based on frequent and prolonged observation of behavior under a variety of conditions.

With respect to teachers' ratings of adjustment, the main problem was to ascertain the kinds of relationships that prevail between these observational appraisals of personality traits involved in adaptation to the school environment and such other criteria of adjustment as absence of overt behavioral symptomatology or relatively low degree of deviancy with respect to the more general personality trends measured by projective instruments. To what extent do these different instruments measure similar, overlapping, or even entirely discrete aspects of the global concept of adjustment? A secondary problem had to do with the bases on which teachers' ratings of adjustment are made. To what extent are they related to ratings of aspirational traits and to pupils' scholastic competence and sociometric status?

The second major problem dealt with in this study was the relationship between teachers' ratings of aspirational traits and "real life" measures of level of aspiration. In a sense this question raises the problem of the validity of such ratings.

METHOD

Population

The subjects in this study consisted of fifty students comprising, with the exception of a few absentees, the entire junior class of University High School[2] in Urbana, Illinois. The mean age of these students was 15.8 years, and the distribution by sex was twenty-four boys and twenty-six girls. A majority of students in this school come from professional homes, the parents generally holding academic appointments at the University of Illinois. Admission to the school, however, is unrestricted except for the payment of a small nominal tuition fee.

Teachers' Ratings

Five current teachers of each student were asked to make ratings at the end of the school year. In all, the ratings of fifteen teachers (eight male and seven female) were involved. Students were rated on a five-point scale on general adjustment (defined in terms of personality integration and emotional stability) and on three aspirational traits (persistence, scholastic competitiveness and academic aspiration). To minimize "halo effect," the teachers were requested to rate all students on a single trait before proceeding to consideration of the next trait. The ratings of five teachers were averaged to provide a mean rating for each student on four traits.

"Real Life" Measures of Aspiration

"Real life" indices of aspirational level included both academic and vocational measures. The former consisted of (a) academic goal discrepancy—the algebraic difference between the student's expressed academic aspiration for the current school year and his composite grade point average for the preceding four semesters; and (b) academic performance estimate—the algebraic difference between the student's estimate of his cumulative high-school standing and his actual four-semester grade point average. Prediction of academic standing was made on a six-point scale (well below average to upper few), and academic aspiration was expressed in terms of a five-point scale (get by to upper few). Grade point average was computed from actual grades which in this school are officially recorded on a five-point scale but are not divulged to students.

Three measures of level of vocational aspiration were utilized: (a) vocational prestige needs—the student's total weighted score on the level of interests part of the Lee-Thorpe (1946) Occupational

[2] The authors acknowledge the coöperation and administrative assistance of Professor Charles M. Allen, Principal, and of the staff of University High School in collecting these data.

Interest Inventory,[3] (b) vocational tenacity—a composite standard score on a hypothetical level of aspiration test consisting of three hypothetical situations in which the subject is successively requested to suppose that he is preparing for a career in medicine, engineering, and a skilled trade, respectively, and that in the course of his vocational preparation he meets serious obstacles of a specified nature. In each of these situations, four alternatives are presented ranging from maintenance of the original goal at all costs (high vocational tenacity) to complete abandonment of the original vocational goal (low vocational tenacity). The subject's choice in each situation, appropriately weighted, is converted into a standard score, and all three standard scores are added to yield a composite score, (c) vocational unreality—the total discrepancy between each of the subject's nine percentile scores on the Kuder (1946) Preference Record and the corresponding mean percentile scores of persons in his occupation of choice as given in the manual for this test.

Measures of Adjustment

In addition to teachers' rating of adjustment, the following indices of adjustment were employed: (a) M.M.P.I. adjustment score—total adjustment score on the Minnesota Multiphase Personality Inventory (Hathaway and McKinley, 1943). In deriving total adjustment scores, raw scores on each of the subscales were first converted into standard scores. Since a positive standard score on a given subscale indicated a degree of deviancy with respect to the trait measured that was greater than the mean score characterizing our population, a measure of total personality deviancy could be computed for each subject by merely summing all of his positive standard scores on the various subscales.[4] Finally, by reversing the sign of the total standard score, a measure of adjustment was obtained in which a high score was indicative of relatively good adjustment. (b) Rorschach adjustment score—an adjustment score derived from the Rorschach group test

[3] This is a measure of general level of job prestige desired by an individual. The subject is presented with thirty triads of occupational activities in each of which area of work involved is held relatively constant while level of job prestige is varied. Total score is computed from the subject's preferences in each triad appropriately weighted in terms of job prestige.

[4] Since a negative standard score is indicative of deviancy on the masculinity-femininity subscale, negative standard scores on this scale were added to the other standard scores to obtain total M.M.P.I. adjustment score (prior to final reversal of sign).

administered in accordance with the procedure developed by Harrower and Steiner (1945), and scored in accordance with the system developed by Klopfer and Kelley(1946). The adjustment score represents the total number of entries made in Munroe's (1945) check list[5] expressed as a standard score with the sign reversed so that a high score is indicative of good adjustment. (c) Rorschach anxiety score—the total number of occasions specified signs of anxiety appeared in the subject's protocol. Criteria of anxiety included fifteen commonly accepted signs such as diffuse shading responses, signs of shading shock, high number of card rejections, threatening or evasive responses, high percentage of oligophrenic responses, etc. (Eichler, 1951; Klopfer and Kelley, 1946; Rapaport, 1945). Each time one of these fifteen anxiety signs occurred, the subject was credited with one point. Thus, high Rorschach anxiety scores are indicative of relatively high levels of anxiety and vice versa. (d) Composite adjustment score—the algebraic sum of the subject's standard M.M.P.I, Rorschach adjustment and teachers' adjustment rating scores. (e) I.P.I. anxiety score—total score on a paper-and-pencil inventory designed to measure anxiety level (Illinois Personality Inventory). (f) Sociometric status—the mean sociometric rating earned by each student when rated sociometrically by all of his classmates on a five-point scale ("definitely not wanted as a friend" to "wanted as a best friend"). (g) Grade point average—the student's cumulative grade point average over four semesters computed on a five-point scale. As in the case of sociometric status, a numerically high score is at the desirable end of the scale.

RESULTS AND INTERPRETATION

Reliability and Generality of Measures

The reliability (generality over-raters) of teachers' ratings is shown in Table 1. For each trait the mean intercorrelation (computed by the squared r method) between the ratings of five teachers on the same pupils was obtained. This was corrected by the Spearman-Brown formula to indicate the predicted reliability of the average rating of five teachers. Application of the correction formula was considered justifiable since an average of five ratings is more reliable

[5] This check list proposes criteria for a "normal" range of responses for each type of scoring determinant. Entries in the check list, therefore, represent deviancy from the proposed limits of normalcy.

than a single rating in the same sense and to the same predictable degree that a ten-item test is more reliable than a two-item test. The resulting reliability coefficients approximate the range of magnitude generally obtained with combined teachers' ratings.

TABLE 1

INTERCORRELATIONS AMONG PERSONALITY TRAITS AS RATED BY TEACHERS

	Adjustment	Persistence	Scholastic Competitiveness	Academic Aspiration
Adjustment	.90*	.71	.60	.42
Persistence	—	.87*	.81	.73
Scholastic Competitiveness	—	—	.83*	.79
Academic Aspiration	—	—	—	.90*

NOTE: All coefficients of correlation in this table are significant beyond the one per cent level of confidence.

* Mean intercorrelation between five teachers' ratings of subjects on same trait computed by "square r" method, and corrected by Spearman-Brown formula to indicate the predicted reliability of the combined judgments of five raters.

Table 1 also shows that teachers' ratings exhibit considerable generality over traits. This is not necessarily indicative of "halo effect" since the three aspirational traits both closely resemble each other and are not logically unrelated to adjustment. Furthermore, the intercorrelations among aspirational traits are higher than the correlations between these latter traits and adjustment.

The reliability[6] of academic goal discrepancy and of academic performance estimate scores could not be ascertained, but there was a high degree of relationship between these two different indices of level of academic aspiration. Vocational tenacity scores on the three different kinds of situations (i.e., medicine, engineering, and skilled trade) exhibited a degree of generality which was proportionate to the degree of similarity between the vocations. The test-retest reliability of the level of interests scores on the Occupational Interest Inventory (identical with our measure of vocational prestige needs) is given as .88 in the test manual (Lee and Thorpe, 1946). The reliability of vocational unreality scores could not be determined. Vocational prestige needs were significantly related to both vocational

[6] A more definitive presentation and discussion of the reliability, generality, and psychological significance of "real life" measures of level of aspiration are given in a previous paper (Ausubel, Schiff, and Zeleny, 1953). The more relevant findings are summarized here to provide some objective basis for appraisal of these measures.

unreality and vocational tenacity in boys, but correlations between academic and vocational measures of level of aspiration were not significant.

It was not feasible for either technical or administrative reasons to obtain reliability coefficients for the Rorschach measures, the M.M.P.I. adjustment score, or the composite adjustment score. Intercorrelations among Rorschach adjustment score, M.M.P.I. adjustment score and teachers' rating of adjustment (see Table 2) were

TABLE 2

INTERCORRELATIONS AMONG ADJUSTMENT SCORES

	Rorschach Anxiety		M.M.P.I. Adjustment		Teachers Adjustment		Anxiety Level (I.P.I.)		Sociometric Status		Composite Adjustment	
	Boys	Girls	Boys	Girls	Boys	Girls	Boys	Girls	Boys	Girls	Boys	Girls
Rorschach Adjustment	—.24	—.19	.31	—.21	—.26	—.09	*—.40	—.32	—.17	.30	**.59	.40
Rorschach Anxiety	—	—	—.11	.01	—.21	—.16	.36	.06	—.17	—.22	—.21	—.20
M.M.P.I. Adjustment	—	—	—	—	.05	**.57	—.06	**—.56	.04	.13	**.79	**.61
Teacher Adjustment	—	—	—	—	—	—	.03	**—.52	**.75	**.64	*.40	**.79
Anxiety Level (I.P.I.)	—	—	—	—	—	—	—	—	.03	.01	.17	*—.45
Sociometric Status	—	—	—	—	—	—	—	—	—	—	*.44	**.59

* Significant at the one per cent level.
** Significant at the five per cent level.

generally non-significant except for the correlation between the latter two measures in our female subjects. The correlations between each of these three measures and composite adjustment score were spuriously high because each measure was a component part of the composite score. M.M.P.I. adjustment score was the most representative component of the composite measure in boys, and teachers' rating of adjustment enjoyed comparable status among girls.

Thus, it appears that the aspects of adjustment measured, respectively, by teachers' observational ratings of classroom behavior, a self-report index of behavioral deviancy with respect to various syndromes in psychopathology, and a projective measure of general personality integration are relatively unrelated to each other in our sample of adolescents. If all three measures are equally valid, they must all be measuring quite different aspects of adjustment which (except for M.M.P.I. and teachers' ratings in girls) show no significant overlap whatsoever. The same type of relationship holds true for self-report (I.P.I.) and Rorschach measures of anxiety which were

TABLE 3

CORRELATIONS BETWEEN TEACHERS' RATINGS AND VARIOUS
MEASURES OF ADJUSTMENT

Measures of Adjustment	Adjustment		Persistence		Teachers' Ratings Scholastic Competi- tiveness		Academic Aspiration	
	Boys	Girls	Boys	Girls	Boys	Girls	Boys	Girls
M.M.P.I. Adjustment	.05	**.57	—.06	—.02	—.01	—.05	—.16	—.24
Rorschach Adjustment	—.26	—.09	—.03	—.14	—.28	.22	—.12	.30
Rorschach Anxiety	—.21	—.16	—.19	.02	—.14	—.10	—.12	—.17
Anxiety Level (I.P.I.)	.03	**—.52	—.30	**—.52	—.38	—.20	—.30	—.34
Composite Adjustment	*.40	**.79	*.44	**.57	.23	**.53	—.04	**.70
Sociometric Status	**.75	**.64	**.54	*.48	*.46	*.42	*.40	*.39
Grade Point Average	**.59	**.61	**.78	**.72	**.92	**.84	**.61	**.71

* Significant at the one per cent level.
** Significant at the five per cent level.

not significantly correlated. This latter datum is not in accord with the previously reported finding of a significantly positive relationship between these two measures of anxiety in a population of college students (Ausubel, Schiff, and Goldman, 1953).

More in accordance with expectations, I.P.I. anxiety scores correlated negatively with composite and M.M.P.I. adjustment scores, and with teachers' ratings of adjustment in girls, and with Rorschach adjustment scores in boys. The relationships between Rorschach anxiety scores and other measures of adjustment were not significant. At least among our adolescent girls, therefore high levels of anxiety as measured by the I.P.I. tended to be associated with poor adjustment and vice versa. A possible explanation for this sex difference might lie in the prevailing cultural attitude that high levels of striving (and of the anxiety that accompanies such striving) are more acceptable and compatible with good adjustment in boys than in girls. In support of this interpretation was the fact that teachers' adjustment ratings were more consistently negatively related to boys' than to girls' academic goal discrepancy scores and academic performance estimates (see Table 4).

Relationship Between Teachers' Ratings and Other Measures of Adjustment

As already noted, teachers' rating of adjustment was not significantly related to Rorschach adjustment score in either sex, but was positively related to M.M.P.I. adjustment score in girls (p. < .01). Teachers' rating of adjustment was also significantly more highly related to composite adjustment score in girls than in boys, although in each case the coefficient of correlation was spuriously high. Rorschach anxiety score was not significantly correlated with teachers' rating of adjustment, but I.P.I. anxiety score was negatively related to the latter score in girls (p. < .01).

It would appear, therefore, that for our population of adolescents, teachers' ratings of adjustment are a more valid and psychologically meaningful measure in relation to girls than in relation to boys. Appraisal of boys' adjustment status is very possibly complicated in the minds of teachers by the fact that certain traits related to extremely high levels of striving (and the associated anxiety) are regarded as unfavorable for adjustment by mental hygienists, but are nevertheless accepted as desirable in connection with our cultural ideal of masculine success. In the case of girls, on the other hand, teachers are apparently less confused by contradictory criteria of adjustment. Supporting this interpretation are (a) the significantly negative correlation between girls' I.P.I. anxiety scores and teachers' adjustment ratings, in contrast to the approximately zero coefficient of correlation between the corresponding scores of boys, and (b) the more consistent tendency for teachers' ratings of adjustment to be correlated negatively with objective indices of academic level of aspiration in the case of girls (see Table 4).

A clue regarding the bases on which teachers' ratings of adjustment are made appears in the moderately high degree of positive relationship found between these ratings and (a) ratings on aspirational traits (see Table 1), and (b) pupils' sociometric status and grade point aver-

TABLE 4

CORRELATIONS BETWEEN TEACHERS' RATINGS AND "REAL LIFE" MEASURES OF LEVEL OF ASPIRATION

"Real Life" Measures of Level of Aspiration	Adjustment		Persistence		Scholastic Competitiveness		Academic Aspiration	
	Boys	Girls	Boys	Girls	Boys	Girls	Boys	Girls
Academic Goal Discrepancy	*—.43	*—.49	**—.57	**—.59	**—.52	**—.57	—.30	*—.44
Academic Performance Estimate	—.20	*—.46	—.20	*—.43	—.38	*—.48	—.15	—.31
Vocational Prestige Needs	—.25	—.10	.16	.11	.31	.23	.35	.25
Vocational Tenacity	—.11	—.19	—.04	—.15	.22	*.45	.34	.37
Vocational Unreality	—.31	—.22	—.13	.37	—.08	.27	—.03	.33

* Significant at the one per cent level.
** Significant at the five per cent level.

age (see Table 3). The composite portrait of a pupil who receives a high teachers' rating on adjustment is an individual who is perceived by teachers as persistent and scholastically competitive, who is highly accepted by his classmates and who has a superior scholastic record. Table 4 also shows that his academic aspirations tend to be more commensurate with his past academic performance as evidenced by the negative correlation between academic goal discrepancy and teachers' adjustment rating. In addition, if the pupil is a girl, she will tend to have high M.M.P.I. and composite adjustment scores and a low I.P.I. anxiety score.

Table 3 also shows the relationships between teachers' ratings of aspirational traits and other non-rating scale indices of adjustment. Aspirational ratings were not significantly related to M.M.P.I. and Rorschach adjustment scores or to Rorschach anxiety ratings. A puzzling negative relationship (p. $< .01$) prevailed between girls' I.P.I. anxiety scores and teachers' ratings on persistence. Teachers' ratings of aspirational traits were significantly correlated with composite adjustment in girls; in the case of boys this was only true with respect to persistence.

In general, as one might expect, grade point average was more highly correlated with aspirational ratings than with ratings of adjustment, but the reverse held true for sociometric status (see Table 3).

Relationship Between Teachers' Ratings and "Real Life"
Measures of Aspiration

Table 4 shows that there is a pronounced tendency for academic goal discrepancy scores to be negatively correlated with such highly related teachers' ratings as scholastic competitiveness, persistence, and academic aspiration. Thus, students who expressed relatively high academic aspirations for the future in the light of previous scholastic performance tended to receive ratings from teachers which were indicative of relatively low aspirational level. This same tendency prevailed with respect to academic performance estimate, but was significant only for girls, and in only two out of three instances. Generally speaking, relationships between teachers' ratings of aspirational traits and measures of vocational aspiration were not statistically significant and exhibited no consistent trend with respect to direction.

This negative relationship between "real life" measures of academic aspiration and teachers' ratings of aspirational traits (ostensibly based on motivational behavior in an academic setting) cast doubt upon the validity of the latter measures. It confirms findings in a previous study with intellectually gifted sixth-graders (Ausubel, 1951) in which the writer failed to obtain significant relationships between teachers' ratings of aspirational traits and a measure of prestige motivation (i.e., relative tendency to respond to an incentive of personal prestige by increasing work output over the level achieved under conditions of anonymity). Another supportive finding in this latter study was a zero correlation between these same ratings and pupils' self-ratings on aspirational traits (Ausubel, 1951). Lewis (1941), on the other hand, obtained very significant differences between "educationally retarded" and "educationally accelerated" gifted children aged nine to fourteen with respect to teachers' ratings on perseverance and ambitiousness.

Although educational performance (holding other factors constant) is perhaps a more definitive criterion of the validity of ratings of aspirational traits than either self-ratings or objective test measures, it should be realized that such evidence of validity is largely circular when the ratings are made by teachers. Since teachers' ratings of motivation are substantially based on academic performance, the latter criterion can hardly be considered independent. In the present study, correlations of .61 to .92 were obtained between teachers' ratings of aspirational traits and grade point average (see Table 3).

Taking all of the evidence into consideration, there is certainly good reason for questioning the validity of teachers' ratings of pupils' aspirational characteristics. This lack of validity is apt to be even more serious in the case of adolescent pupils, judging from the findings of the present study and from the relatively poor insight of teachers into high-school pupils' interests (Baker, 1938) and sociometric status (Bonney, 1947). Also, at least with respect to the latter function, teachers' perceptual ability has been shown to decrease markedly with increasing age of pupils (Ausubel, Schiff, and Gasser, 1952; Moreno, 1934).

SUMMARY AND CONCLUSIONS

Teachers' ratings of adjustment and aspirational traits were obtained for a class of fifty juniors in a University high school and related to various other self-report, objective, and projective measures of the same characteristics. The following conclusions can be reached with respect to our particular sample of adolescent boys and girls, and deserve to be tested on a more representative population:

(1) Averages of five teachers' ratings of adjustment and aspiration traits enjoyed high split-half reliability.

(2) Rorschach adjustment score, teachers' adjustment rating, and M.M.P.I. adjustment score were not significantly intercorrelated except for the latter two measures in the case of girls. Thus, all three instruments appear to be measuring quite different aspects of adjustment showing little or no overlap.

(3) High level of anxiety, as measured by the Illinois Personality Inventory (I.P.I.) was consistently associated with poor adjustment in girls. This was not true of boys. The suggestion was offered that anxiety, especially the variety associated with high striving, is more compatible with and culturally acceptable as evidence of good adjustment in boys than in girls.

(4) Teachers' ratings of adjustment appear to be more meaningful and psychologically valid for girls than for boys in as much as they were correlated in the appropriate direction with M.M.P.I. and composite adjustment scores and with I.P.I. anxiety score. This sex difference is attributed to the prevailing cultural ambivalence regarding the adjustive value of anxiety for boys in the light of their social sex rôle. In the case of girls, teachers' ratings of adjustment also tended to be more consistently correlated in the negative direction with "real life" measures of level of academic aspiration.

(5) Teachers tended to give high adjustment ratings to pupils whom they perceived as persistent and scholastically competitive, who were highly accepted by their classmates, who had superior scholastic records, and whose academic aspirations were commensurate with past academic achievement.

(6) Teachers' ratings of pupils' aspirational traits were very highly related to the latter's scholastic standing. Hence, academic performance can not be used as an independent criterion of the validity of these ratings.

(7) In view of the reliably negative correlations obtained between "real life" measures of level of academic aspiration and teachers' ratings of aspirational traits, the validity of the latter measure seems highly questionable.

37

THE CLASS AS A GROUP: CONCLUSIONS FROM
RESEARCH IN GROUP DYNAMICS

by William Clark Trow, Alvin F. Zander, William C.
Morse, and David H. Jenkins

How can teachers develop in their classrooms the best possible environment for learning? What are some of the implications of viewing
the class as a group? To what extent do student attitudes and behavior find their anchorage in the school or peer group? In the
following article, William C. Trow, Alvin F. Zander, and William C.
Morse, all of the University of Michigan, and David H. Jenkins, of
Temple University, attempt to answer these questions by reviewing
some of the findings in group dynamics that are practical and applicable to classroom situations. [From *Journal of Educational Psychology*, 1950, *41*, 322-338. Reprinted by permission of the authors
and Warwick and York, Inc.]

*   *   *

Although teachers work with groups and are daily troubled or
aided by group phenomena in their classrooms, there has been
strikingly little research on the dynamics of classroom groups. It
is often difficult to identify and study the many forces at work in
a classroom situation, but recent research in group dynamics indicates that it is possible to develop the necessary theoretical formu-
lations, hypotheses, and measuring methods for testing these hypotheses. The task remains to identify those areas in which we feel
the presence of group phenomena is most relevant to the classroom setting. We have much to learn about the forces involved in
the relationships among students, and between students and teacher.
Since the relationship between teacher and class-groups, for example, is by its very nature changing and flexible, it is important
that the concepts employed be adequate to deal with the dynamics

of relationships, involving changing relationships among persons, and changing perceptions of the teacher and the class, as the members acquire new insights and learnings.

A number of assertions from recent research in group dynamics have both theoretical and practical value for the field of educational psychology and teaching methods. This list is not exhaustive and there will be no attempt to describe the nature of the studies from which these data are derived. Many of these findings are from laboratory investigations with groups, but a sufficient number of them were obtained in field-experiment settings to indicate that work of this nature can readily be done in the actual classroom setting, as well as in the laboratory. Some of these assertions are well-tested and validated Others are less well proven. All of them have relevance and promise for educational psychology.

(1) The attitudes of an individual have their anchorage in the groups to which he belongs. Present evidence makes it apparent that many attitudes can be changed more easily by making changes in certain properties of the group than by directly teaching the individuals, as individuals, even in a classroom audience situation (Lewin, 1947, 1948, Chap. 4).

(2) The conduct and beliefs of pupils is regulated in large measure by the small groups within a classroom, such as friendship cliques, and the cohesive groups of students within a school. These groups demand conformity from their members to certain group standards, and the more cohesive the group, the greater is its power over the member (Coch and French, 1948; Festinger, Back, and Schachter, 1950).

(3) In some instances failure to learn may be advantageously conceptualized as resistance to change, using resistance here in the same sense as the therapist uses it in his relationships with a patient. For example, the group standards developed by persons who were learning a motor task quite similar to a previously perfected one, and who were simply told what they were to do, were entirely different from the group standards developed in a group in which the learners participated in a discussion and made group decisions about the necessity for, and the nature of, the new task to be learned. Those who participated in the discussion learned much more, more rapidly, and with much less aggression and resentment toward the persons inducing them to make this change (Coch and French, 1948; Zander, 1950).

(4) When frustrations are met, highly cohesive groups maintain their effort in movement toward the group goal much more vigor-

ously and effectively than do groups of low cohesiveness (French, 1944).

(5) Groups, especially those similar to classroom groups, can be disrupted into separate cliques; or this threat of disruption can be eliminated, by the alteration of forces which determine the attractiveness of the group for the members. (For example, helping them to become aware of the strength of attraction they have for each other, or the degree to which membership in the group provides a way to achieve things they value highly.) This condition can be brought about most easily when the members become aware of the forces influencing them, but it can also be effected by an outsider, such as a teacher, who adroitly helps the group to change the impact and strength of these forces surrounding and within their group (Thibaut, 1949).

(6) The training of persons for effective social action such as performance in school or civic service, can lead to greater effectiveness of effort by the trainees if they are members of a group which is being trained to work as a group, than will result if they are merely individuals in an audience situation (Lippitt, 1949).

(7) The amount of interaction among students in a class is determined in part by group factors. For example, in highly cohesive groups arriving at a decision that has general approval, the person whose viewpoint is too different from that of the rest will be rejected—that is, ignored. In a less well knit group, in which the discussion is not directed to a group decision, the deviate member is likely to get more comments directed to him than the person whose ideas are quite similar to those of the rest of the group (Schachter, 1950).

(8) When the members see themselves competing for their own individual goals which make coöperative effort impossible, there is disruption of the ready communication of ideas, the coördination of efforts and the friendliness and pride in one's group which are basic to class harmony and effectiveness. The competitive grading system commonly used today is an illustration in that it creates mutually exclusive goals among the members of a class group (Deutsch, 1949, 1949a).

(9) The group climate or style of group life can have an important influence on the member's personalities. One such style of group life can develop hostile, obedient, uncreative, "goldbrickers"; another can produce confused, purposeless, competitive, drifters; and still another can mould coöperative, flexible, purposeful, turn-taking, we-spirited persons. The group climate that produces such

effects is created by the resultant of a number of group properties which can be combined in various ways, among which are the leadership style of the teacher or that of those who function most as group leaders, the degree of cohesiveness, which has already been mentioned, the group-member-skills, the suitability of the group process for the task in hand, the techniques employed by the teacher to satisfy his ego and other needs, and the tension-release patterns used by the group (Lippitt and White, 1947; Zander, 1947).

(10) The reasons for the occasional failure of project methods, and other teaching procedures which depend upon effectively functioning groups often lie in the ineffective use of group problem-solving methods, or in the unskillful handling of group procedures. Groups can help themselves to mature and improve their ability as a learning or producing team by diagnosing their own failures and planning ways of repairing their own deficiencies. Students of group development have devoted much attention to methods of group diagnosis, ways of presenting the findings to a group, and methods for alleviating a group's procedural difficulties (Jenkins, 1948).

(11) Certain forms of classroom behavior may be recognized as mechanisms developed for relieving tensions somewhat similar to those employed by an individual in relieving his tensions. For example, they employ patterns of group behavior which help avoid difficult tasks or unpleasant situations. These mechanisms are often difficult to identify since they may either be wrongly perceived by the teacher as signs that the group is keeping busy, or they may be accepted as the usual troubles one gets into by the use of committee methods (Main and Nyswander, 1949).

(12) Difficulties in the transfer of verbal learning to social behavior, can often be overcome by the use of that form of rôle playing referred to as reality practice, in which the participant tryout the behavior they are expected to use in a situation from which all threat has been removed. Inhibition blindnesses, or fears of "learning" certain content, or behaving in unaccustomed ways can be removed by the use of a "cultural-island," a situation where new group standards are generated while away from the source of the inhibitions. This procedure is effectively used in excursions, conferences, summer camps, and other group activities in which the person is under the pressure of group standards that are different from those at home, and so he dares to adopt forms of behavior which might be quite desirable for him, but which he

might hesitate to try out in his accustomed environment for fear of adverse criticism (Hendry, Lippitt, and Zander, 1944).

Thus we can safely accept the view that group phenomena definitely affect the progress of learning, as well as the kind of learning that takes place. The educational significance of this view derives from the fact that the pupil's attitudes as well as his behavior patterns are modifiable. Increased motivation in participating in the classroom activities, and consequently in learning, derives from several different potential sources in a group atmosphere where good mental hygiene prevails.

Three such potential sources of increased motivation will be considered. The first of these sources lies in method of *goal determination*—the extent to which the goals of the class are determined by the entire group including both pupils and teachers, in a truly co-participant sense. When this procedure is followed, the child will feel that he has some control over his own destiny and, therefore, is able to accept the group goals which he helped select as being his own personal goals. They are things which he himself wants to do and, therefore, he is more likely to follow through on them. The absence of such codetermined objectives does not mean the absence of group standards, but some of these standards are not likely to be the ones which the teacher would choose, or the ones which best promote learning. Such group standards as the "gentlemen's mark" of "C," and the group rejection of the student who is too "eager," are familiar to all. Thus group standards in a classroom may inhibit good learning as well as accelerate it.

The second source of increased motivation lies in the extent to which the teachers and the pupils build a *supportive atmosphere* in the classroom, one which helps each child to realize that he is an accepted group member. When this condition maintains, each child has his own "area of freedom," within which he is free to make his own decisions. This area can often be much wider than is ordinarily supposed by teachers who are constantly making pupils' decisions for them. Although the group may not approve of everything a pupil does, it still accepts him as a person. In this kind of an atmosphere the child is able to develop a greater feeling of security with his fellows. In addition—and this is the important contribution to learning—he is likely to feel freed from personal threat and criticism and, therefore, more willing to go ahead and try new things without fear, realizing that if he fails he will not be rejected either by the class or by the teacher. Thus failure can be a very positive learning experience because, once the emotional threat is removed, the child can look at his abilities and limitations far more objectively and with greater awareness of what next steps are required for his learning. It would seem that little learning can occur if the child is denied positive opportunities to make errors.

A third potential source of increased motivation lies in the extent to which the various members of the class are accepted as *participating members*. When they are so accepted, each can benefit from the knowledge, skills, and abilities of all the other members. They are no longer dependent primarily or solely on the teacher for all information and guidance. Besides offering the possibility of the development of broader understandings, this gives to each pupil the opportunity to be a contributor to the group, and the classroom becomes, then, a situation for mutual exchange, for mutual sharing. Research is beginning to show the increased productivity of groups which have this coöperative pattern of relationship (Deutsch, 1949). Goal determination by the group, a supportive atmosphere, and a participating membership, then constitute three conditions of group organization of great effectiveness in developing motivation which contribute to the promotion of effective learning.

●   ●   ●

CHAPTER THIRTEEN

The Adolescent and the World of Work

38

THE PROCESS OF VOCATIONAL DEVELOPMENT

by Donald Super, John Crites, Raymond Hummel, Helen Moser, Phoebe Overstreet, and Charles Warnath

Using a developmental frame of reference Donald Super of Teachers College, Columbia University and his co-workers construct a theory of vocational development and behavior and suggest three types of factors which tend to influence it: role factors, personal factors, and situational factors. [From *Vocational Development: A Framework for Research*, New York: Bureau of Publications, Teachers College, Columbia University, 1957, pp. 39-53. Reprinted by permission of the authors and the Bureau of Publications, Teachers College, Columbia University.]

THE PROCESS OF VOCATIONAL DEVELOPMENT

An Ongoing, Continuous, Generally Irreversible Process

The outline of vocational development as a series of life stages, presented in Table 1, is not meant to imply that the process is discontinuous. The behavior depicted in each stage is based on the potential developed in the preceding stages. As Beilin (1955) has pointed out, vocational development is like development in general

TABLE 1[1]

VOCATIONAL LIFE STAGES

1. *Growth Stage* (Birth–14)
Self-concept develops through identification with key figures in family and in school; needs and fantasy are dominant early in this stage; interest and capacity become more important in this stage with increasing social participation and reality-testing. Substages of the growth stage are:
FANTASY (4–10). Needs are dominant; role-playing in fantasy is important.
INTEREST (11–12). Likes are the major determinant of aspirations and activities.
CAPACITY (13–14). Abilities are given more weight, and job requirements (including training) are considered.

2. *Exploration Stage* (Age 15–24)
Self-examination, role tryouts, and occupational exploration take place in school, leisure activities, and part-time work. Substages of the exploration stage are:
TENTATIVE (15–17). Needs, interests, capacities, values, and opportunities are all considered. Tentative choices are made and tried out in fantasy, discussion, courses, work, etc.
TRANSITION (18–21). Reality considerations are given more weight as the youth enters labor market or professional training and attempts to implement a self-concept.
TRIAL (22–24). A seemingly appropriate field having been located, a beginning job in it is found and is tried out as a life work.

3. *Establishment Stage* (Age 25–44)
Having found an appropriate field, effort is put forth to make a permanent place in it. There may be some trial early in this stage, with consequent shifting, but establishment may begin without trial, especially in the professions. Substages of the establishment stage are:
TRIAL (25–30). The field of work presumed to be suitable may prove unsatisfactory, resulting in one or two changes before the life work is found or before it becomes clear that the life work will be a succession of unrelated jobs.
STABILIZATION (31–44). As the career pattern becomes clear, effort is put forth to stabilize, to make a secure place, in the world of work. For most persons these are the creative years.

[1] Table 1 presents, in outline form, a synthesis of the ideas of Buehler (1933), Miller and Form (1951), and Ginzberg and associates (1951). It gives a brief description of the nature of the vocational behavior which seems characteristic of each life stage and it indicates the approximate age limits of the stages. As additional data on each life stage and substage are gathered, Table 1 may be filled in more fully with the details of vocational behavior that may be expected at each life stage, showing the sequences through which vocational development passes.

4. *Maintenance Stage* (Age 45–64)

Having made a place in the world of work, the concern is now to hold it. Little new ground is broken, but there is continuation along established lines.

5. *Decline Stage* (Age 65 on)

As physical and mental powers decline, work activity changes and in due course ceases. New roles must be developed; first that of selective participant and then that of observer rather than participant. Substages of this stage are:

DECELERATION (65–70). Sometimes at the time of official retirement, sometimes late in the maintenance stage, the pace of work slackens, duties are shifted, or the nature of the work is changed to suit declining capacities. Many men find part-time jobs to replace their full-time occupations.

RETIREMENT (71 on). As with all the specified age limits, there are great variations from person to person. But, complete cessation of occupation comes for all in due course, to some easily and pleasantly, to others with difficulty and disappointment, and to some only with death.

in that it is continuous. It is a process which continues through time, and it is manifested in a sequence of vocational behaviors, occurring throughout the life span of the individual. One type of behavior may give way to another; not all the behaviors appropriate at one life stage are appropriate at another. The direction of development generally cannot be reversed.

An Orderly, Patterned Process

While in some ways development is strictly an individual process, its essentials can be observed in the patterning of the behavior of all members of a society. In this sense the process of vocational development is an orderly one, as the material in Table 1 suggests. The patterning of behavior can be explained through the concept of *developmental tasks*. A developmental task, as defined by Havighurst (1953, p. 2) is: ". . . *a task which arises at or about a certain period in the life of the individual, successful achievement of which leads to his happiness and to success with later tasks, while failure leads to unhappiness in the individual, disapproval by the society, and difficulty with later tasks.*"

It has been stated before that growth and learning are the major determinants of development. Most individuals experience a normal physical growth process, and they meet and succeed with the physical developmental tasks, such as learning to walk and eat. A failure with a developmental task of this sort is readily observed, and attempts to remedy or eliminate the difficulty may be made.

While behavior resulting from physical growth is basic to development, it represents only a part of the behavioral repertoire. Much of behavior is learned through responding to external stimuli, and there is therefore some societal control over what is learned. This control of learning is accomplished through social example and pressure and is referred to as socialization. Society expects its members to master certain developmental tasks. Developmental tasks of this type are most often thought to be externally imposed. But as the individual

TABLE 2

OUTLINE OF VOCATIONAL DEVELOPMENT TASKS IN CHRONOLOGICAL ORDER*

Preschool Child
 1. Increasing ability for self-help
 2. Identification with like-sexed parent
 3. Increasing ability for self-direction

Elementary School Child
 1. Ability to undertake cooperative enterprises
 2. Choice of activities suited to one's abilities
 3. Assumption of responsibility for one's acts
 4. Performance of chores around the house

High School Adolescent
 1. Further development of abilities and talents
 2. Choice of high school or work
 3. Choice of high school curriculum
 4. Development of independence

Young Adult
 1. Choice of college or work
 2. Choice of college curriculum
 3. Choice of suitable job
 4. Development of skills on the job

Mature Adult
 1. Stabilization in an occupation
 2. Providing for future security
 3. Finding appropriate avenues of advancement

Older Person
 1. Gradual retirement
 2. Finding suitable activities for skills to occupy time
 3. Maintaining self-sufficiency insofar as possible

* The idea for this table was adapted from Stratemeyer, Forkner, and McKim (1947).

matures, he comes to internalize some of society's expectations and to set goals for himself. He becomes more self-directed. As this happens, developmental tasks resulting from social pressure may be considered internally imposed. Differentiation, integration, and the development of independence are involved in meeting developmental tasks.

Developmental tasks are much the same for all the individuals of a society. The degree to which the development of any one individual follows an orderly sequence depends upon how adequately the individual handles the developmental tasks with which he is faced. Differences between individuals in the success obtained with specific developmental tasks should account for many of the differences that occur in the over-all development of these same individuals.

Vocational developmental tasks are those developmental tasks which relate directly or indirectly to the world of work. A list of vocational developmental tasks may be compiled in several different ways: by considering only those tasks which are directly related to work, such as the making of an occupational choice, or by including also the more inferentially related tasks, such as the development of a sense of responsibility; by concentrating on all the vocational developmental tasks facing an individual at one period of time, or by constructing a chronological picture of all those tasks which face an individual during his lifetime. A brief chronological listing of vocational development tasks appears in Table 2.

An examination of this list makes clear that until adolescence almost all the vocational development tasks are only indirectly related to future work. Beginning in adolescence, with entry into high school as a convenient starting point, the tasks become more and more directly related to vocations. In adulthood, during the periods of establishment, maintenance, and retirement, they are directly related to vocations.

A Dynamic Process

The process of development is marked by a progressive increase and modification of the individual behavioral repertoire. To an extent, Table 2 obscures this fact. The statement that the child must walk before he can run has been made too often to need repetition. New behavior is based on old behavior. Furthermore, learning new behavior does not necessarily mean forgetting the old. Development is not the occurrence of a series of changing but unrelated behaviors, but rather the occurrence of additions to and modifications of the existing behavioral potential. In the process, some old behaviors are eliminated: crawling is abandoned when walking is mastered.

The behavioral repertoire is increased and modified through mastery of the successive developmental tasks faced by the individual. The changes that occur in the behavioral repertoire are descriptive of the process of development: it is a process of interaction and compromise or synthesis. The dynamics of the process may be viewed as follows: (1) The individual, faced with a new task of vocational development, (2) brings to bear upon that task his potential for and his repertoire of behavior, (3) has some degree of success or failure in handling the task, (4) incorporates whatever has been learned in this experience, and (5) uses this learning to add to or modify his existing repertoire. In this way, the behavioral repertoire is modified and/or expanded. Many repetitions of this sequence throughout the life span represent the process of vocational development.

To summarize, vocational development may be described as an orderly and patterned process, ongoing, continuous, generally irreversible, and dynamic, involving interaction of the behavioral repertoire, vocational developmental tasks, and other factors.

FACTORS AFFECTING VOCATIONAL BEHAVIOR AND DEVELOPMENT

In order to understand, to evaluate, and to predict ongoing vocational behavior or development, it is necessary to examine a number of their possible determinants. Some of these will be discussed below.

The Concepts of Roles and Self

Occupations may be viewed as organizations of social roles. They are, as Sarbin (1954, p. 225) defines them, positions, ". . . systems of rights and duties," sets of expectations, as these are sometimes specified in the job descriptions of civil service or of business and industrial concerns. These job specifications, Sarbin points out, describe the actions expected of the worker and the actions which he may expect from others with whom he is working. Another way of stating it is that positions and occupations are organizations of role expectations. The role, as Sarbin goes on to say, is what the person does, "a patterned sequence of learned *actions* or deeds performed by a person in an interaction situation." Vocational development may therefore be partly understood in terms of the ways in which a person meets the expectations of his occupational role.

Development is partially determined by the occupying of positions, since role expectations are organized around positions. Thus, the child occupies the position of boy (at school age he has short hair and wears trousers) or girl (she has long hair and wears a dress) and is called upon to play certain roles (e.g., to be brave and strong or to be kind and gentle). Role-taking is both conscious and unconscious: children and adults emulate role models sometimes by design, sometimes without awareness of the identification. Parents are typically the first role models: the father for a boy, the mother for a girl. As Tyler (1951) has demonstrated, the girl's role model is primarily a sex model, while the boy's begins as a sex model and develops into a differentiated occupational model. Vocationally related roles are thus practiced in childhood play and fantasy as well as in later school and free-time work and activities. Positions as team members, school officers, participants in clubs and similar activities, and as part-time employees carry with them role expectations with which the boy or girl must deal. All positions provide new opportunities for identification and the finding of role models.

The self may be viewed as what the person is, just as the role is what the person does. But the self is always conceived by someone. Thus Sarbin (1954), following James, Symonds, Brewster Smith, and others, defines the self as a phenomenal experience of identity. The self-concept is what the person under consideration conceives himself to be, the self-as-inferred-by-self. It is communicated to others by "I . . ." sentences. The self-concept is differentiated from the self-as-inferred-by-others. The self is the result of interaction between growth processes and personal-social development, the interaction of the person with others around him. As the individual takes roles in daily living and plays other roles in fantasy or play, as he identifies with role models and strives to emulate idealized persons, some of these roles and some of the associated traits are internalized as self-percepts, and his concept of self develops (Mowrer, 1950). For instance, a boy's father may consider playing baseball appropriate for boys (role expectation associated with a sex position), plays ball with him and other boys to get them started (provides a role model), and thus helps the boy develop a concept of himself as an athlete. In similar fashion, girls help with preparing meals, boys with household repairs, etc., and so they develop concepts of themselves as homemakers, craftsmen, and the like.

Tyler's study of the development of interests, referred to earlier, has been interpreted by Darley and Hagenah (1955, pp. 178-179) as indicating that most boys, even in first grade, begin to see themselves and their roles according to the different kinds of positions which they might occupy in adult life; most girls see themselves as home-makers like their mothers, regardless of special abilities. In this way, the role expectations of children help to form their self-concepts.

Even in adulthood, it seems likely that the concept of self may be modified by role-taking (actually occupying a position) or even by role-playing (playing the role in fantasy or play). Merton (1940) has made a logical analysis of the manner in which occupying a position in a bureaucracy depersonalizes and makes rigid the incumbents, and Sarbin (1954) has reviewed a number of studies of the experimental effects of role-playing in hypnosis on self-percepts, but adequate studies of the effects of occupational membership on self-concepts have not been carried out.

The self-concept is not only in part a product of social roles, but also seems to be a major determinant of occupational role-taking, that is, of occupational choice (Super, 1951). Just as one third-grade boy balked at sewing his torn trousers on the grounds that "boys don't sew" (i.e., "I am a boy, sewing is a girl's role"), so vocations are viewed favorably or unfavorably because they are considered appropriate or inappropriate to the self. Bordin (1943) has developed a theory of vocational interests based on self-concept theory: he hypothesizes that an individual responds to items in an interest inventory in terms of his concept of himself and in terms of his concept of his preferred occupation. Strong (1943) and Super (1949), on the other hand, view responses to the items in an interest inventory as self-percepts which, when scored, yield a description of the individual's self-concept in occupational terms: the occupational stereotype does not ordinarily contribute to the individual's mental set. Super (1951) has thus defined vocational choice as the "implementation of a self-concept."

Three types of factors appear to play a major part in vocational behavior and development: *role factors, personal factors,* and *situational factors* or factors external to the individual and not necessarily involving role expectations. Economic conditions and accidents are illustrations of situational factors. Role factors have just been considered; the rest of this discussion will therefore deal with personal and situational factors.

Personal Factors

Intelligence is one factor which has great influence on individual vocational behavior. Intelligence is related to educational success and, therefore, indirectly to job opportunities and job level (Pintner, 1931, Chapters 10-12; Strang, 1934, pp. 72-92). To some degree it is related to success on the job (Super, 1949). Intelligence is related to the appropriateness of individual vocational objectives, for the studies of Grace (1932), Sparling (1933), and others indicate that the more intelligent individuals tend to select occupational goals more wisely. Many studies have indicated the relationship between intelligence and occupational attainment (Proctor, 1937; Stewart, 1947). Intelligence also seems related to job satisfaction. Not only will dissatisfaction be felt when an individual attempts to handle a job beyond his capabilities and thus puts himself under constant stress, but there is evidence that ability in excess of that demanded by the job can also lead to frustration and loss of interest (Anderson, 1929; Pruette and Fryer, 1923). Thus, in several ways, direct and indirect, intelligence affects the vocational life of the individual.

Special Aptitudes, the ability to draw, for example, may greatly affect an individual's career, because they may influence not only his occupational choice but also his occupational attainment. Less dramatic but probably of significance to a larger number of individuals are those aptitudes which are important in a variety of occupations. Among these aptitudes are spatial visualization, perceptual speed and accuracy, and manual dexterity of various types. Possession or lack of these aptitudes affects the variety of occupations which the individual will be able to handle successfully, and also determines to some extent the degree of success he may attain in them.

Interests have been shown to be of importance in vocational choice. One might assume that an individual would enter the occupation which held the most interest for him. But because other factors also act as determinants of vocational choice, the role of interests in vocational development is one of synthesis or compromise. As illustration: A boy's interests may be like those of engineers, while his intelligence is not high enough for success in a college course or his funds are not sufficient for the extra years of schooling. He may, therefore, set his sights lower; he may become a mechanic or perhaps a crane operator. In this way, occupational choice is made in the *field* of greatest interest, while ability and opportunity (among other factors) determine the occupational *level* of the job choice within the field. In some instances the values of a subculture outweigh individual interests even in the selection of the vocational field (Jordaan, 1949; McArthur, 1954).

Interests also function, however, in determining occupational level. Factor analysis of the Strong Vocational Interest Blank (Strong, 1943) shows that the interests of engineers, physicists, and mathematicians are more like each other than like those of mathematics–science teachers and industrial arts teachers. The factor analysis of the Strong Blank would seem to indicate that interests are grouped to some degree by level. Thus, there are professional–scientific, professional–technical, and subprofessional–technical groups, as well as others. Interests seem related to both the field and the level of occupational choice.

Values closely resemble interests, and tests designed to measure them can be used almost interchangeably. Values, however, seem to represent something more basic than interests. They permeate all aspects of life, they concern life's goals, and in some instances they seem to be closely related to needs and drives. Ginzberg (1951) has classified work values into three types: (1) related to the work activity itself; (2) related to the returns of work, as exemplified by pay and the way of life a job permits; or (3) related to the concomitants of work, what is associated with the job, such as co-workers or supervisors. In adolescence, values begin to stabilize and, according to Ginzberg (1951), by sixteen seem to be an important factor in vocational choice. The goals the individual sets for himself, the things in life that are important to him, begin to influence him and to affect the choices indicated by his abilities and interests.

Attitudes are affected by the environment, for they are to a large extent a reflection of it. They are learned from the words and actions of others who are significant to the individual and from various events. One such event or one key figure can affect an attitude already held. In the relationship between the worker and his work, some of the conditions which seem to determine attitudes are the appropriateness of the job to the worker's intelligence (Fraser, et al., 1947), the degree of skill or responsibility demanded by the job (Hull and Kolstad, 1942), and the quality of supervision (Roethlisberger and Dickson, 1939). The attitudes a worker has toward his job are of importance not only to the worker himself but also to his employer. The Hawthorne study (Roethlisberger and Dickson, 1939) provided evidence that attitudes toward work affect both productivity and conduct on the job. According to this study, there seems to be a circular relationship between productivity and work attitudes. Good productivity gives men a feeling of accomplishment, which in turn results in increased effort (Katz and Hyman, 1947).

Personality includes not only intelligence, special aptitudes, interests, values, and attitudes, as discussed above, but also such factors as personality traits (reaction tendencies), needs, and self-concept. These last are believed by many to have considerable effect on vocational behavior. Familiar social stereotypes might lead one to expect a close relationship between personality types and vocational choice and adjustment. The meek, introverted bookkeeper and the extroverted, dominant salesman are examples that readily come to mind. A recent summary of relevant research by Darley and Hagenah (1955) shows that the stereotypes have some validity, and along the same line is the finding that salesmen tend to be somewhat more dominant than clerks (Dodge, 1937; Paterson and Darley, 1936). However, few other such differences have been found, and specific patterns of traits or needs have not yet been shown clearly to differentiate members of one occupation from those of another. The interrelationship between personality and vocation appears more complex and less obvious than might be expected (Super, 1949, p. 484).

According to certain surveys of employment records (Brewer, 1927), emotional problems are the most common cause of discharge from employment. This indicates that personality characteristics are indeed related to occupational success. However, general adjustment would be expected to affect success in almost any occupation, as Friend and Haggard's (1948) study seems to suggest, rather than operating as a particular influence in certain occupations. It may be that the individual is satisfied and successful in his work to the extent that he is able to adapt his personality, at least in his overt behavior, to the job, or is able to adapt the job to his personality. Although placement in a job means being cast in a role, each actor portrays the part in his own way. Moreover, the personality demands which are made upon an individual by his work are frequently as much a function of his work environment, including the people with whom he has to interact, as of the kind of work. For example, a secretary with a strong personality trait of dominance may be dissatisfied in a job in which a very dominant employer allows her to exercise little initiative or authority, but may be quite happy as a secretary to an employer who allows her more responsibility.

Another reason for the lack of evidence of a marked relationship between personality patterns and occupational choice and adjustment (except for the general role of adequacy of personal adjustment) may be the inability of present methods of personality assessment to differentiate pertinent factors with sufficient accuracy to demonstrate a relationship. With improved instruments, it is quite possible that the findings will be more positive than they are at present. However, clear-cut, rigidly defined vocational personality types will probably not be discovered even with better testing methods. Fortunately, the personality demands made by different occupations are varied and flexible, so that there is room for many kinds of personalities within the same occupation.

Some of the personal factors which may be determinants of vocational development have been mentioned here. They represent that part of the behavioral potential which has received the most attention from psychologists in studies of vocational choice and adjustment.

Situational Factors

A discussion of factors determining vocational behavior and development would not be complete without some mention of factors external to the individual.

Reference has already been made to studies by Miller and Form (1951) and by Davidson and Anderson (1937) of parental socioeconomic status and its effect on vocational development. Similar findings are reported by Bell (1938). In addition, Centers (1950) found that the higher the socioeconomic status of the parents, the more the attitudes of the adolescent tended to favor individualism as opposed to collectivism. These are just a few of the findings concerning socioeconomic status.

Factors which have so far been given little systematic study but which appear to affect vocational behavior and development are: religious background, atmosphere of home (warm, hostile, broken), parental attitudes toward the individual (acceptance or rejection), and parental attitudes toward schooling. There are many more situational factors. Changing factors in the environment may enable an individual to develop the strength needed in future problem situations, or the individual may have to do the best he can in spite of his immediate circumstances.

Other situational factors which may affect the individual include the general economic situation, such as depression or prosperity, and the international situation, such as war or peace. Although the individual may be able to do little to alter these conditions, he can be profoundly affected by them. The influence which these factors can have is seen in the following examples: veterans' legislation, making needed training available, can open up professional opportunities for men from lower socioeconomic levels; war needs can create new employment opportunities in heavy industries; and union control of the number of apprentices to be trained can restrict some trades to a favored few.

SUMMARY

In this chapter, an attempt has been made to clarify the concepts of vocational behavior and vocational development. Behavior has been defined, in general terms, as the responses the individual makes to the stimuli that impinge upon him. Throughout his life, the individual builds up a behavioral repertoire, and development is the process of progressive increase and modification of the behavioral repertoire. Vocational behavior and vocational development are aspects of behavior and development in general, the behavior involved pertaining directly or indirectly to the world of work.

Borrowing from Buehler's concept of life stages, vocational development through a series of vocational life stages has been described. With this concept in mind, the nature of vocational development has been discussed. It is an ongoing, continuous, generally irreversible, orderly, patterned, and dynamic process, which involves interaction between the individual's behavioral repertoire and the demands made by society, that is, by the developmental tasks. Vocational development is essentially a process of compromise or synthesis.

Finally, factors which influence vocational behavior and development have been considered. Three types of factors have been described: role factors, those imposed by society and involving role expectations; personal factors, those originating within or internalized by the individual, including the self-concept; and situational factors, economic and social factors which are external to the individual and over which he has no direct control. Some of the studies which relate these factors to vocational behavior and development have been briefly mentioned.

····························· 39 ·····························

LOOKING AT OCCUPATIONS[1]

by Willa Freeman Grunes

How do American high school students see the world of occupations? To answer this question Willa Freeman Grunes formerly of the University of California (Berkeley) uses two group-administered devices— the Grouping Test and the Pick-A-Job Test—and a theoretical framework which may be adaptable to other problems in social perception. The subjects reveal a perceptual structure consisting mainly of seven overlapping job clusters. Social class, sex, and regional differences in the structure are analyzed [From *Journal of Abnormal and Social Psychology*, 1957, *54*, 86-92. Reprinted by permission of the author and the American Psychological Association.]

How does the young American look at jobs? What groups of jobs appear in his psychological field? What do these groups look like to the perceiving individual? Do different social classes see these things differently? These are phenomenological questions, of the sort MacLeod (1947) meant when he suggested that the phenomenological method, found so fruitful in approaching classical problems in perception, be applied also in the field of social psychology. They concern the social world which is psychologically "there" for the subject, quite apart from what the experts might say is, or ought to be, there.

There have been few studies that attempt to answer such questions about aspects of the social world by attempting to discover perceived units and their characteristics. Methods for such investigation are woefully lacking and difficult to invent. The present study is pre-

[1] The material discussed is adapted from a doctoral dissertation (Grunes, 1954) done under the guidance of Professor Mason Haire. Especially extensive assistance was given by H. D. Mugass, R. R. Lange, W. C. Rasmussen, Dorothy W. Gottlieb, Katherine M. Cavanagh, Leon Festinger, and Camille J. Miller, as well as by the administrators and their staffs of the schools involved.

sented as suggestive of new ways for mapping perceived social worlds.

If we can determine what people see, we can better understand what they think and do. Specifically, in the realm of occupations, we can better see why they make their particular vocational choices, and why too many choose certain types of overcrowded fields while too few choose others.

Occupational perceptions were selected for this study partly because they seem important for revealing the psychological meaning of social class memberships. Such meaning has long been neglected in research on class in America. These perceptions also offer a meeting place between psychology and economics and hence offer a promising area for mutual enrichment of both fields.

METHOD

Sample

About 150 students in each of eight high schools were tested in 1952-53. Four Northern California schools were included: Oakland, McClymonds, San Lorenzo, and Hayward. There were also two Southeastern schools: Talladega in Alabama and Orangeburg in South Carolina; one Northwest Central school: Bismarck in North Dakota; and one Northeastern: Clifton Heights in Pennsylvania. The communities of the school vary widely in size, social class, race, and in degree and type of industrialization. The diversity seemed desirable in order to assess the generality of the findings.

Procedure

Two group-administered devices, the Grouping Test and the Pick-A-Job Test, were developed and pretested for purposes of revealing the way perceived occupations tend to be grouped by high school students; i.e., the perceived structure of the world of jobs. Both were indirectly inspired by various studies by Krechevsky (1932) [and recent unpublished work] on the way rats and also men structure the world around them. In order to make it easy and threatless for subjects to reveal their perceptions, both devices are disguised on purpose. The subject is provided with an incomplete situation, out of which he must make some sense of his own in order to deal with it. Such a disguised and unstructured approach seems appropriate to an area of content in which subjects may be unable or unwilling to verbalize what they perceive. Through these two devices, a perceptual structure was sought which could be regarded as common to most high school students. The assumption was nevertheless avoided that all social classes—or all individuals—possess a similar structure, or that any perceived structure necessarily reflects objective social reality. In this respect the method differs from that used by Lloyd Warner (1949) and his associates to study class structure.

Grouping Test. On the Grouping Test, the subject was presented with a list of 51 varied occupations, selected to represent each of the major categories in the Dictionary of Occupational Titles (U. S. Bureau of Employment Security, 1949). He was given the following written instructions (somewhat abridged here) along with some oral clarification:

> Let us see how fast you can think about various occupations. Group the following occupations as many ways as you can. For example, make groups according to what kinds of people work at the jobs, what kinds of work they do, etc. Give each group a title that tells what kinds of jobs belong under it. . . . At least two jobs must be in each group you make. You may use the same jobs under as many titles as you wish. For example: People who would probably know how to give first aid: airline stewardesses, doctors, nurses, physical education teachers. . . .
>
> The more groups you make within the time limit (15 minutes) the higher your score. You can use any types of groups you can think of. . . . Be sure to include all of the occupations on the list that belong under each of your titles, because you also get a higher score for every job you list that belongs there. Here is the list of occupations. . . .

The resulting data were tabulated and coded to indicate the jobs which tend to be placed together in the same groups, the grouping categories reflected in the titles, and the jobs most frequently placed under each type of title. A set of job clusters common to most students' view of the world of occupations was discovered. Content analysis of the titles was done by two coders working independently, using only categories which yielded at least 80 per cent agreement.

Since completing the present study, the author has learned of a similar effort by Campbell (1952) to develop a method for establishing subjective occupational groupings. His study failed, however, to reveal any common job clusters. The present method differs from his in permitting the subject to use each occupation in as many groups as he wished and to make as many (overlapping) groups as he could, as well as in the procedures used to analyze the data. These provisions appear more appropriate than Campbell's to the presumably complex nature of the perceived structure of the occupational world.

Pick-A-Job Test.[2] The Pick-A-Job Test offered the subject brief descriptions of six different people and asked him to assume the role of vocational counsellor and to suggest five appropriate jobs for each one. For example, the first description appeared thus:

A. Man   1._____
good-looking   2._____
clean   3._____
well-educated   4._____
self-confident 5._____

Results were analyzed to indicate the typical sorts of jobs suggested for each description.

The personality descriptions used on the Pick-A-Job Test were derived from earlier use of what may be called the Haire Describe-A-Person method, a modification of a procedure originally developed by Haire and described by Haire and Grunes (1950). High school students were given a few rather neutral facts about a fictitious person, and also his occupation, and were asked to guess the sort of person he was. Their guesses were coded for content and compared with descriptions obtained from similar subjects when the occupation was omitted from the given facts. Differences between the two sets of descriptions revealed stereotypes associated with the occupations selected for study. The Pick-A-Job Test was based on the typical descriptions thus obtained of businessman (Description 1 above), ditch-digger, actress, and farmer. Additional descriptions based on the typical businessman and ditch-digger were included, with the characteristics ascribed in each case to a woman.

Besides these procedures, the Gough (1949) Home Index, a measure of relative social status of high school students, was administered. It yields a continuous distribution of scores, but was here employed to classify subjects into three status groups (low, middle, and high) by cutting the distribution for each school at the two points where the large central frequencies began to call off.

[2] Instructions for *Pick-A-Job Test* are: This is a test of how good you are at picking the right job or occupation for other people when you know just a few facts about them. Each of the little lists below describes one person. Try to get an idea of what the person is like; then pretend that you are a vocational counsellor trying to help that person choose the right kind of occupation. Let us say that, if you think they should, they can take the time to get any training they may need. Under the description, next to the No. 1, write down your first choice for his occupation, then your second choice next to No. 2, and so on, till you have 5 choices for each person. [This footnote inserted by editor.]

TABLE 1

SOCIAL CLASS DIFFERENCES IN FREQUENCY OF GROUPING OTHER
OCCUPATIONS WITH DOCTOR

(Entries represent percentage of groups involving "doctor"
made by each social class)

Co-Member	Home-Index Social Class		
	Lower	Middle	Upper
Nurse	31	66	53
College Professor	38	59	80
Teacher	44	56	73
Social Worker	13	24	47
Air Line Stewardess	56	38	33

RESULTS

Deriving the Job Clusters

Data were compiled on each job listed on the Grouping Test, showing, for each social class, the other jobs with which a given job was grouped and the types of titles under which it was listed.[3] As a sample, the following information was gathered about the "doctor":

In at least 50 per cent of the instances in which doctor was listed, the following jobs appeared in the same group: nurse, college professor, and teacher. In at least 40 per cent, the engineer and minister were in the same group.

The dish-washer, ditch-digger, farmer's wife, hired man on farm, rancher, and janitor were in the same group with doctor less than 5 per cent of the times it appeared.

Doctor appeared in at least 50 per cent of the groups in which each of the following jobs appeared: nurse, college professor, teacher, engineer, social worker, reporter, businessman, and business-woman.

Table 1 shows the percentage of groups made by each social class that included both the doctor and each of the five occupations listed. Note that the higher status subjects tended to group doctor with other professionals more consistently than did the lower status subjects.

The categories of Grouping Test titles under which doctor was listed at least 50 per cent of the times they occurred include: educa-

---

[3] All the data are available in tabular form in the author's dissertation (Grunes, 1954).

tional barriers, much education, good looking, lot of money, personality barriers, social skills, ability barriers, brains, verbal skills, "skilled," "trained," training barriers.

Doctor was listed under less than 50 per cent of the titles categorized as follows: charm, strong, physical barriers, little or no education, "common labor," dumb, not own boss, little money.

From the above data, it was predicted that the first Pick-A-Job description, as given above, would elicit the suggestion of doctor,

TABLE 2

A SAMPLE JOB CLUSTER MATRIX: CLUSTER A

	Job Title									
	Doc.	Nur.	Coll.	Teach.	Eng.	Min.	Social	News.	Busm.	Busw.
Co-Members										
Doctor	X	++	++	++	++	++	++	++	++	++
Nurse	++	X		++	+	++	++	+		+
College Professor	++	++	X	++	++	++	+	++	++	++
Teacher	++	++	++	X	++	++	++	++	+	++
Engineer	+				X	+				
Minister	+	++	++	+	+	X	++	+		+
Social Worker					+	+	X			
News Reporter						+	+	X		+
Businessman			+	+		+	+	+	X	++
Business Woman			+			+	+	+	++	X
Air Line Stewardess		+				+	++	+		
Phys. Ed. Teacher				+	+			etc.*	etc.*	etc.*
Nonmembers										
Dish Washer	—		—	—	—	—		—	—	—
Ditch Digger	—	—	—	—	—			—	—	—
Farmer's Wife	—		—	—	—			—	—	—
Hired Man, Farm	—		—	—	—			—	—	—
Rancher	—		—	—	—			—	—	—
Married Woman	—	—	—					—	—	—
Welder	—				—			—	—	—
Truck Driver	—	—						—	—	—
Maid	—			—				—	—	
Housewife	—			—				—	—	
Janitor	—	—						—		
Garbage Collector	—							—		
Factory Worker	—				—					
Farmer	—									
Cleaning Woman	—									

Note—.++ means that 50 per cent or more of the times that the occupation at the top of the column was listed, it appeared in the same group as the occupation at the left of the row.

+ means that such co-grouping occurred in at least 40 per cent, but not as many as 50 per cent of the total listings of the occupation at the top.

— means that the occupation at the left appeared in fewer than 5 per cent of the groups in which the occupation at the top occurred.

* In the case of news reporter, businessman, and business-woman, associations were found with additional co-members not listed here. Data for the other occupations are complete.

among others. Actually, although the students had the whole world
of occupations from which to choose, and five different choices to
make, doctor accounted for fully 10 per cent of all jobs chosen for
that description.

Similar data for each job were combined to define and characterize
the commonly perceived job clusters. Table 2 gives, for example, the
matrix of relationships which led to the definition of the cluster
(Cluster A) to which the doctor belongs. The data presented also
provide some evidence that Cluster A overlaps with another cluster.

A complete matrix, similar to Table 2 but including all 51 jobs
on the Grouping Test, was used in determining the commonly perceived clusters.[4] Unless an occupation was grouped with at least one
member of a cluster at least 40 per cent of the time, it was not considered to be even a borderline member of that cluster. To be considered a clear member, it had to be grouped at least 50 per cent of
the time with most of the other clear members of the cluster.

A number of jobs were found to be borderline or clear members
of two clusters, and these jobs were taken as evidence that the clusters
overlap. No jobs were found to be even borderline members of more
than two clusters.

Confirmation of the clusters thus derived was found in the "non-
members," which always came from "distant" (nonoverlapping)
clusters, and in the data from the Pick-A-Job Test. Students tended
to choose jobs from a highly restricted set of clusters for each description on the Pick-A-Job Test. These clusters were found to be predictable from a knowledge of the cluster membership of the job the
stereotype of which had been drawn upon in formulating the description. For example, Description 1 (given above) elicited almost exclusively members of the cluster (A-B) to which "businessman" belongs
and members of the two clusters (A and B) with which A-B overlaps.

Implicit criteria in grouping. Characteristics of the clusters were
determined by an analysis of the type of titles under which the cluster
members were most frequently grouped—or not grouped—on the
Grouping Test. As shown by the types of titles they choose for their
groups, students typically show consciousness of certain dimensions
in thinking about jobs, most notably: barriers to attaining the jobs
(especially educational barriers), status, skill and knowledge, and the
nature of the work.

The empirical job clusters. The overlapping job clusters and the
outstanding characteristics ascribed to them, as revealed by the

---

[4] The matrix composes Part IV of the Appendix of the dissertation, pp. 307-
316 (Grunes, 1954).

Grouping Test and confirmed by the Pick-A-Job procedure, are as follows:

Cluster A. These jobs are characterized as requiring much education, ability, brains, social and verbal skill, and as yielding much money; they are almost never seen as requiring physical strength. Included from the list provided are college professor, minister, doctor, nurse, teacher, and less clearly engineer, social worker, reporter, and businessman.

Cluster A-B. These jobs have characteristics similar to those of Cluster A, but with much less stress on educational barriers. They include businessman (also a member of A), and business-woman (also a member of B).

Cluster B. These jobs are seen as "business" and as requiring verbal skills. They include business-woman, office-worker, secretary, stenographer, bank clerk, and, less clearly, salesman, saleswoman, and store clerk.

Cluster C. These jobs are seen as divided into two subclusters: C-1, characterized by skill and strength, and C-2, seen as hard work and "common labor" done by a worker who is strong and not his own boss. C-1 includes carpenter, mechanic, and welder; C-2 the farmer, rancher, hired man on a farm, truck-driver, and less clearly, ditch-digger.

Cluster C-D. These jobs are seen as involving hard work, "common labor," and as requiring little education or anything else except strength. The workers are seen as stupid and as not their own bosses. They include ditch-digger (also a member of C), garbage-collector, and janitor.

Cluster B-D. These jobs are seen as "business" and as requiring social skill. They include salespeople and store clerks (also in Cluster B) and also waiters and waitresses.

Cluster D. These jobs are seen as requiring little (not even strength), as "common labor," and hard work, and their holders as stupid people of little education who are not their own bosses. They include dish-washer, cook, maid, housewife; married woman who stays home and keeps house, cleaning woman and, less clearly, elevator operator, waitress (also a member of B-D), and janitor (also a member of C-D).

Certain occupations on the list could not be placed in the above system of interrelated clusters, including one rather weak group including actresses, airline stewardesses, and models, and a strong one including only policemen and firemen. Jobs which seemed to stand completely alone were factory worker (distantly related to

C-D and D), aviator, musician, physical education teacher, farmer's wife, tailor, barber, foreman, railroad conductor, and baseball player. A still more exhaustive list of occupations might well reveal further relationships.

Prestige Hierarchy

In the characteristics ascribed to the clusters, the prestige hierarchy inherent in the common cognitive structure is revealed, with positive and barrier-type characteristics both tending to be concentrated in the A and A-B Clusters, and least in Cluster D and the clusters overlapping it. Physical strength is an interesting exception to this rule. This prestige hierarchy agrees well with the conclusions of other investigators (Counts, 1925; Deeg and Patterson, 1947) who have asked various samples of Americans to rank lists of jobs according to their "social standing."

There is a large gap between the perception of professionals, business, and office people (Clusters A, A-B, and B, but not B-D) on the one hand, and manual and mechanical workers on the other, with only relatively rare cases occurring in which they are seen as members of the same group. Some of the evidence for this deep gap may be seen by studying the "non-members" in Table 2. All of these cases of

TABLE 3

OCCUPATIONS MOST COMMONLY GROUPED WITH COLLEGE PROFESSOR
ON THE GROUPING TEST BY SOCIAL CLASS

		Percentage of groups which contain both the occupation listed and college professor		
Co-Member	Cluster	Lower Class	Middle Class	Upper Class
Doctor	A	53%	70%	75%
Minister	A	33	53	63
Teacher	A	73	68	81
Engineer	A	30	44	58
Businessman	A-B	50	47	44
Business-woman	A-B	60	43	42
Office worker	B	33	26	17

Note.—Few of the differences in percentage shown are statistically significant, but they seem important because of their consistency. Those for college professor are typical of those for all other Cluster A occupations. There were *no* relevant cases showing an opposite trend.

extremely rare grouping with Cluster A occupations are from Clusters C, D, and C-D. The gaps between skilled and unskilled workers and between clerical and professional workers are not nearly so wide.

Stereotyped Job Choices

Students agree remarkably well on the occupations and clusters of occupations seen as appropriate for the people described on the Pick-A-Job Test. For each description, their choices are sharply limited to a few salient possibilities out of the thousands of occupations from which they were free to choose. In answer to Description 1, for example, the following job categories accounted for about 70 per cent of all the suggestions: salesman, manager, businessman, teacher, doctor, lawyer, and "office worker."

For Description 2—a man who is hard-working, strong, not very bright, and likes to follow orders—students mainly choose jobs from Clusters C and C-D, which contain mostly masculine occupations. The woman with the same traits is steered mainly toward Clusters B-D and D. For the other descriptions,[5] however, the sex of the person described changes the particular jobs selected, but not the clusters from which they come.

Group Differences in Perception of Occupations

Class differences. Although there is considerable agreement among students about the common pattern of clusters, there are some social class differences in cognition of the occupational world. Most notably, students from the upper classes tend to make a sharper distinction between business and professional people than do the lower classes. The latter tend to lump Clusters A and A-B and B into one high-prestige cluster. They also tend to exclude from that cluster certain occupations often placed there by upper classes—such as the social worker, minister, engineer, reporter, and musician. Table 3 presents a sample of the evidence for these conclusions, using the occupations grouped with college professor on the Grouping Test as examples. Each value in the table represents the percentage of the total number of groups, made by the subjects in a particular social class, which contain both the occupation at the left and "college professor." Note that the college professor is grouped with other professionals more

---

[5] Woman (charming, ambitious, good-looking, likes excitement); woman (clean, self-confident, attractive, well-educated); man (dependable, serious, hard-working, eager to learn new things).

consistently, and with business people less frequently, as status rises. (See also the data on doctor listed above.) In general, the upper classes seem to be more finely differentiated about the upper occupational strata. There is also some less clear evidence that the lower classes are more differentiated about the lower prestige jobs.

The class differences in characteristics attributed to particular jobs follow lines predictable from the class differences in the job clusters themselves. Subjects from the lower classes tend more often to include jobs from Clusters A-B and B—as well as A, which all classes stress—when listing jobs that share certain positive and barrier-type characteristics, especially those concerning education and ability.

Certain particular occupations on the Grouping Test list were placed in different clusters by different classes. The clearest example is the "engineer," interpreted as a professional by upper classes and as a skilled mechanical worker by lower.

These class differences are evident in coherent patterns in the data, but could not feasibly be subjected to statistical test. The group differences described below, except where otherwise noted, were found to be significant at the .05 level of confidence.

Subjects higher in social status appear to be relatively lacking in both status and barrier consciousness, but relatively strongly conscious of skill and knowledge, pace of work, and money. It may be that students are less aware of the job aspects about which they feel less insecure. The fact that students whose breadwinners are in manual or mechanical work are relatively less conscious of strength seems to support this inference.

The Pick-A-Job Test results reflect the greater tendency of the lower classes not to differentiate the top three job clusters. While higher status subjects restrict themselves closely to professionals and business people for both the male and female version of Description 1, clerical occupations are often selected by lower classes. For example, clerical work is suggested for the male version by 31.3 per cent of the lower-class subjects, by 15 per cent of the middle class, and by only 2.6 per cent of the upper class (difference significant at the .01 level). For Description 2, upper classes tend to name more stereotypically low-prestige jobs like the garbage-collector and ditch-digger —perhaps again indicating their coarser distinctions among lower-strata occupations.

Sex differences. The study revealed some outstanding differences in the way boys and girls see the world of jobs. Through the titles they used on the Grouping Test, girls showed more awareness—or at least more articulateness—concerning all the common types of job aspects, with the exceptions of security, money, and hours of work.

If the female is more status conscious, as has been claimed, she is also more conscious of a large number of other perceptual dimensions of jobs.

Sex differences were also found in the answers to Description 1 and its feminine counterpart on the Pick-A-Job Test, with the girls showing a stronger tendency than boys to name teaching jobs for both versions. Boys tend to select clerical rather than professional jobs for the female version, while girls choose mostly professional jobs, as do both sexes for the male version—perhaps a sex difference in willingness to limit capable females to lower social position.

Regional differences. In broad outlines, students in all eight schools see the same world of occupations. But consistent trends in the data indicate that those in the large industrialized communities tend, like higher status subjects, to see a relatively sharp professional business distinction. Students in the Southeastern schools appear, through their Grouping Test titles, to be more conscious of status and education than the others tested; but otherwise there is considerable regional similarity in the types and relative potencies of dimensions used for categorizing occupations. The social worker is the outstanding example of a job that is grouped differently in different regions: it is much more clearly professional in the large Northern cities.

Despite the class, sex, and regional differences mentioned, in general the students seem to agree rather closely in their basic perceptual structure concerning occupations.

DISCUSSION

The Grouping Test technique, in which a collection of items is set before the subject for him to record the groups or units that he perceives spontaneously, is easily adaptable to many problems of social perception. Instead of occupations, one could list, for instance, names of political figures, nationalities, religions, brands of food, business corporations, or periodicals. The general method of the Pick-A-Job Test is likewise adaptable. Since it involves giving the subject hypothetical group characteristics and asking him to name members of the group, it could be called the Pick-The-Members technique. In other adaptations, subjects could be asked to name, instead of jobs, clubs to which the described individual might belong, public policies he might be likely to favor, movies he might enjoy, etc.

The Haire method (Describe-The-Person or Describe-The-Member), used here in conjunction with the Pick-A-Job Test, seems generally adaptable for yielding hypotheses about the characteristics of

perceived groups. Together the two methods can be used to confirm
Grouping Test data about the composition and characteristics of
the perceived units. If the conclusions from the Grouping Test are
valid, use of the Pick-The-Members technique on the same subjects
should yield the members of the appropriate Grouping Test cluster,
when that cluster's characteristics are used to form the description on
the Pick-The-Members Test. And the Describe-The-Person method
should tend to yield the characteristics found through the Grouping
Test for the group of which the Person is seen as a member. The various methods were used in this manner in the present study to com-
plement and validate each other.

Some of the implications of the study for vocational guidance are
discussed elsewhere (Grunes, 1956).

SUMMARY

A phenomenological study of the way American high school students perceive occupations is presented. A perceptual structure consisting mainly of seven overlapping job clusters is found to be characteristic of most subjects. Class and regional differences in the structure are analyzed and the different attributes ascribed to each cluster
are examined. Two original types of methods are used which are
adaptable to many other problems in social perception.

•••••••••••••••••••••••••••••• 40 ••••••••••••••••••••••••••••••

SATISFACTIONS IN WORK

by Jerome M. Seidman and Goodwin Watson

Perhaps one of the most important series of problems confronting
youth is that of choosing a vocation, preparing for it, finding a job,
liking it, and keeping it. A study of one part of this sequence—the
reasons why certain jobs are liked—was made by Jerome M. Seidman
of Montclair State College, and Goodwin Watson of Teachers College, Columbia University. The results of their study of single men
sixteen to twenty-four years of age are presented in the following
selection. [From *Journal of Consulting Psychology*, 1940, *4*, 117-120.
Reprinted by permission of the authors and the American Psychological Association.]

Orientation to everyday life situations is vitally affected by the degree of satisfaction derived from one's job and the general attitude toward the work experience. A popular literature documenting the complex interrelations of the job and day-to-day living has been rapidly accumulating, apexed recently by the autobiographical *Christ in Concrete* (DiDonato, 1939) and the sociological novel, *The Grapes of Wrath* (Steinbeck, 1939). In a more objective vein the social scientist has also approached the problem, delving more specifically into the importance of the job as it affects what one does, whom one knows, and often, how one thinks. The findings reveal how significantly the job impinges upon and frequently alters one's opinions, attitudes, and even one's system of values. In this category may be mentioned Hersey's (1932) study of workers' emotions in shop and home, Bakke's (1934) analysis of employment in England, and the American Youth Commission survey of Maryland youth (Bell, 1938). All tend to stress the focal importance of the job, so aptly termed by the Lynds (1937) "the watershed down which the rest of one's life tends to flow."

Research in job satisfaction has been concerned chiefly with simple questionnaires and rating scales which have dichotomized the subjects into those who are satisfied and those who are dissatisfied with their present jobs. Relations between these categories and such indices as age, sex, marital status, intelligence, education and various personality variables have been extensively investigated. Hoppock (1935) and Hoppock and Spiegler (1938) have summarized the literature in this field.

The present study seeks to ascertain the casual factors of job satisfaction as ascertained from the total work experience. The subjects were 190 young men, American-born and unmarried, between the ages of 16 and 24. All were unemployed high school graduates who had held two or more full-time jobs during a total work experience of at least one year. They were clients of the Adjustment Service, an organization which provided a program of aptitude testing and vocational counseling for more than 10,000 men and women in New York City in 1933-1934.

The study was facilitated by the interest and rapport of the subjects as indicated by:

1. The reasons they gave for coming to the Adjustment Service: 68 per cent for vocational guidance, 17 per cent for confirmation of their own plans, 5 per cent for job placement advice, 10 per cent for miscellaneous purposes.

2. The manner in which they learned of the Service: 30 per cent through other clients and friends; 10 per cent through the radio, newspapers, magazine articles, public libraries and museums; 60 per cent through the cooperation of various recreational, religious and educational agencies.

3. The number of different occasions upon which the subjects appeared for interviews: 76 per cent, three times; 10 per cent, four or more times.

The data for this report were obtained from the occupation record sheets which were part of the clients' Adjustment Service records. After filling out a comprehensive occupation blank each subject indicated the job he favored in reply to the written question, "Which of the jobs you have held appealed to you most, or proved most interesting?" Reasons for job satisfaction were designated in answer to the subsequent query, "Why?"

FINDINGS

The percentage distribution of the various reasons given for satisfactions in work is shown in Table 1. One hundred and fifty-

TABLE 1

SATISFACTIONS IN WORK

Reasons	Per cent
Vocational aspiration	29
Congenial work conditions and social contacts	24
Initiative, responsibility and prestige	19
Variety of tasks	12
Opportunity for promotion	8
Short working hours	4
Salary	4
$N=157$	

Seventy-two per cent gave one reason; 23 per cent, two reasons; 4 per cent, three; 1 per cent, four. Each subject received a score of one. It was not intended in this study to analyze qualitative differences in intensity and in range of statement.

seven subjects (83 per cent) gave specific replies; 33 (17 per cent) did not. Twenty-eight of those who failed to give specific replies, or 15 per cent of the total group, stated that no job proved interesting; five, or 2 per cent of the total group, stated that all jobs proved interesting.

The following quotations show vividly the varied and, at times, unique individuality of the responses:

Vocational aspiration
I am naturally artistically inclined and I hoped to become a comic artist and newspaper writer and thought it would be good training.

Because I am mechanically inclined and the actual work is interesting to me.

Congenial work conditions and social contacts
The place of business was pleasant and the people working with me were pleasant and cooperated with me.

The work was interesting in that I came in contact with many types of people during the day.

Initiative, responsibility, and prestige
It permitted me to use my own judgment freely.

The responsibility and the knowledge that upon the successful completion of my duties rested, in a small measure, the well being of the bank.

It took me out among people and gave me an importance that many men never achieve.

Variety of tasks
Work was not stereotyped. There were always new situations in which one had to adjust himself.

It was not monotonous work. There were new things always coming in which made the routine a little different every day.

Opportunity for promotion
While the details were somewhat monotonous banking as a whole would interest anybody who might advance himself above a routine position.

It held the most promise for advancement at the time.

Short working hours
Hours were such as permitted time for study in the evening.

Plenty of spare time.

Salary
Because of the greater earning possibilities.

Larger salary.

Three types of evidence support the finding that salary plays a relatively minor role in reasons for satisfactions in work. First, a comparison of the salaries of 131 favored jobs and 325 less-favored jobs (all other jobs) yielded a critical ratio of .61, revealing no significant relationship (Table 2). Second, a collateral study on *Dissatisfactions in Work* (Watson and Seidman 1941), [see the reading that follows] in which 132 of the same subjects were used, indicated that salary was least important of eight factors, accounting for one per cent of the replies. Third, 170 of the subjects who selected the three least important factors affecting work (from a prepared list of ten from the Strong Vocational Interest Blank, Part VI, Section 2), again designated salary as least important.

TABLE 2

COMPARISON OF SALARY OF FAVORED AND LESS-FAVORED JOB

	N	Range	Mean	σ	Diff. σ Diff.
Favored job	131	5–45	17.01	6.76	
Less-favored job	325	3–40	16.59	6.53	.61

The finding that salary is relatively unimportant in reasons for job satisfaction is not in accord with the results obtained by Brissenden and Frankel (1922). Their compilation of reasons for voluntary separation from service, advanced by over 8,000 employees, ranked dissatisfaction with wages first, accounting for 25 per cent of the replies. However, salary may be converted into a symbol of resentment against conditions which are emotionally charged, conditions often so complex that they do not readily manifest themselves during the interpersonal relations of the interview; nor do they fit adequately into the rigidly defined categories of the usual questionnaires and rating scales. Consequently, these conditions tend to become channelized, consciously or unconsciously, into the more convenient and concrete category, salary. Since salary in our culture constitutes such an obvious criterion of achievement and of social status, it is too likely to be overemphasized as a dominant satisfaction in work.

SUMMARY

One hundred and ninety unemployed male youths indicated reasons for selecting one of their work experiences as the most appealing or interesting. The findings are as follows:

1. Seventeen per cent gave "all-or-none" replies: 15 per cent found no job interesting; 2 per cent found all jobs interesting.

2. Reasons for satisfactions in work in the order of importance were: vocational aspirations; congenial work conditions and social contacts; initiative, responsibility and prestige; variety of tasks; opportunity for promotion; short working hours; salary.

3. The status of salary as the least important factor accounting for satisfactions in work was corroborated by three supplemental indices: A comparison of the salaries of the favored job and the less-favored job; a collateral study on dissatisfactions in work; the selection of the three least important factors affecting work from a prepared list of ten.

·································· 41 ··································

DISSATISFACTIONS IN WORK

by Goodwin Watson and Jerome M. Seidman

Some young people are well satisfied and happy with their jobs and work experience; others, however, are dissatisfied and unhappy. Why do adolescents dislike some of their jobs? Goodwin Watson of Teachers College, Columbia University and Jerome M. Seidman of Montclair State College, sought answers to this question in their study of sixteen- to twenty-four-year-old boys who came voluntarily to a free vocational service to get information about their abilities. The results are presented in the article that follows. [From *Journal of Social Psychology*, 1941, *13*, 183-186. Reprinted by permission of the authors and The Journal Press.]

The work experience, a necessary concomitant to the feeling of happiness, plays a significant role in the development of personality and character. Current research in social psychology and trends in vocational guidance demonstrate vividly the complex interrelations of the individual's reactions to the job and changes in temperament, opinion, attitude, and even system of values.

This report explores the factors believed responsible for having been "not entirely successful" on some of the jobs held. It is based on the opinions of 132 young men, clients of the Adjustment Service, sponsored by the American Association for Adult Education and conducted in New York City during 1933 and 1934, who, after filling out a comprehensive occupation blank, replied to "If you feel that you were not entirely successful on some of the jobs held, to what do you attribute that fact?" The subjects were between the ages of 16 and 24, American-born, single, unemployed high school graduates who had had two or more full-time jobs during a total work experience of at least one year. They showed no gross physical disorders and gave no evidence of psychiatric symptoms.

The distribution of opinions is shown in Table 1. Nine (7%) replied they had always been successful on their jobs; 1 (1%) that he had never been successful. Of the remaining 122 subjects[1] [see per cent column (1)], 54 (44%) stated that the nature of the job proved

TABLE 1

DISSATISFACTIONS IN WORK

Reasons	Number	Per cent	(1) Per cent
Nature of the job	54	41	44
Personality and attitude of the subject	29	22	24
Lack of education, guidance, experience, skill	11	8	9
Uncongenial work conditions	11	8	9
No opportunity for promotion	11	8	9
Tasks monotonous	4	3	3
Insufficient salary	1	1	1
Long hours	1	1	1
Always successful	9	7	
Never successful	1	1	
Total	132	100	100

unsatisfactory; 29 (24%) mentioned their personalities and attitudes as hindering success; three groups of 11 (9%) each cited lack of education, uncongenial work conditions, no opportunity for promotion; four (3%) designated monotony of tasks; one (1%) chose insufficient salary; and one (1%) long hours.

The frankly critical expressions of opinion that follow show marked differences in range and intensity. Noteworthy is the rapport revealed, especially the evaluations of the self under *personality and attitude of the subject.*

[1] Ninety-three gave one reason; 28 two; 1 three. A score of one was allotted to each subject.

Nature of the Job
I could not help but feel that any capabilities I have were being wasted.
Lack of interest in my work. It was not the work I wanted to do.
Not particularly suited to the job which made me indifferent to it.
I did not prefer a white collar job, such as office work . . . because I aspire to something better than working in a store or a factory.
Lack of interest and happiness in work.
Dislike for or disinterest in work often causes bad performance.
. . . I didn't care for that type of work.

Personality and Attitude of the Subject
Due to my early start in business, I didn't take it seriously.
I believe that lack of personality and aggressiveness were some of the reasons.
Lack of serious thought regarding future. Youth.
Habitual tardiness; undue slowness in completing tasks; fussiness over minor details.
Failure to realize importance of opportunities. Conceit.
I did not realize that excellent work alone is insufficient to hold a position.
. . . an unstable temperament.
My nervousness when it came to speaking.
. . . no tact. Tendency to disagree orally with boss.
Lack of spirit; no real driving force.

Lack of Education—Guidance—Experience—Skill
Lack of proper training in interior decorating.
Lack of skill.
Not enough experience. No guidance.
Inability to take shorthand and typewriting.
Lack of proper educational background.
Insufficient education.
Lack of business training and experience.

Uncongenial Work Conditions
Too many restrictions.
Lack of cooperation from some of the other employees.
. . . the curbing of ability by my immediate supervisor.
Lack of help in situations that were beyond my experience.
Racial prejudice; . . . working for relatives.
Because I knew my work and did not want to be lectured to at all occasions.
. . . the environment about the place.
. . . lack of cooperation on the part of superiors.

No opportunity for promotion
Most of the jobs I held were stop-gaps until I could do the work I really cared for.
No future in view.
I feel that I was not successful because I knew there was no advancement.

Lack of opportunity. It is difficult to find a job with chances for advance
ment.

Tasks Monotonous
. . . no brain work was required.
Doing the same thing mechanically without any change.
. . . distaste for routine.
. . . monotonous occupation.

Insufficient Salary
I believe it was due to the fact that I did not receive sufficient income
at the time.

Long hours
Long hours, lack of recreation.

Always successful
I have never felt that way.
Always successful.
I have always attained success on my jobs.
I have always seen myself progressing.
I was very satisfactory to all of my employers.
I feel that I did my duty wherever employed.

Never successful
I did not feel successful or contented to any degree in either position.

One hundred thirty-two male youth expressed reasons why they
had been "not entirely successful" on some of their jobs. It was
found that:

1. Nine (7%) were always successful.
2. One (1%) was never successful.

Of the remaining 122 subjects:

3. Forty-four per cent disliked the nature of the work.
4. Twenty-four per cent attributed dissatisfaction to deficiencies in their personality and social attitudes.
5. Nine per cent each mentioned lack of education, uncongenial
work conditions, no opportunity for promotion.
6. Monotony of tasks, long hours, insufficient salary, ranked
lowest, aggregating five per cent of the replies.

CHAPTER FOURTEEN

The Adolescent in the Community

42

TIME ORIENTATION IN DELINQUENTS

by Robert J. Barndt and Donald M. Johnson

In this experimental study a group of delinquent boys produces stories with significantly shorter time spans than matched nondelinquent boys. The authors, Robert J. Barndt of Lake Forest College and Donald M. Johnson of Michigan State University suggest further research on short time perspective as part of the pattern of delinquency. [From *Journal of Abnormal and Social Psychology*, 1955, *51*, 343-345. Reprinted by permission of the authors and the American Psychological Association.]

If we admit that an active imaginative human being constructs his own environment, selecting from the possibilities offered by reality, the temporal organization of this personal environment takes on considerable importance. Lewin (1948), for example, maintained that a person is likely to be future oriented if he feels that a highly valued goal is accessible to him, while a belief that the goal is beyond his reach restricts him to a present orientation.

This orientation toward the future is acquired, of course, by incidental learning during childhood and adolescence. Hence the different family atmospheres typical of different social classes would be
expected to produce different time orientations. Schneider and
Lysgaard (1953) recently reported some evidence from opinion polls
on a "deferred gratification pattern" in middle-class families, characterized by educational aspirations, saving habits, and the like, not
common in working-class families. Some time ago Davis and Dollard
(1940), speaking of the lower-class adolescent boy, said that "the
long-range goals do not seem to be 'there' in his world; he does not
see other people in his class attaining them, or practicing the behavior required of him, and he feels his parents and teachers are
'crazy' when they demand it of him."

Following up leads of this sort LeShan (1952) reported in this
Journal a comparison of lower-class and middle-class children in
respect to time orientation, using a story-telling technique. He found
that the time spans covered by the action of the stories of the middle
class children were significantly longer than those of the lower class
children. Fink (1953) found the story-telling technique applicable
also to research with the aged. His institutionalized subjects made
fewer references to the future in their stories than his noninstitution-
alized control group.

LeShan speculated that delinquents in general and psychopaths in
particular would have short time perspectives. They seem to live in
the here and now, unconcerned about rewards and punishments in
the future. The present study was designed to test the hypothesis that
delinquent boys would have shorter time orientations than ordinary
boys. Do delinquent boys have a short time orientation that is more
than a consequence of their social class background?

METHOD

Subjects

The experimental subjects (Ss) in this study consisted of 26 delinquent boys, ranging in age from 15 years, 7 months, to 17 years, 11
months, who had been committed to a state rehabilitational school
by court action.[1] All had appeared before the courts at least four

[1] We appreciate the cooperation of Mr. E. L. V. Shelley, Chief Psychologist,
Boys Vocational School, Lansing, Michigan, and Mr. Harold Barr, Superintendent
of Schools, Bath, Michigan, in securing subjects for this study.

times and 21 had been committed previously, either to the state
school or to semiprivate correctional schools, and were assigned to
the living unit reserved for recidivists. The group was selected in

TABLE 1

MEANS AND STANDARD DEVIATIONS OF DELINQUENTS
AND CONTROL GROUPS ON MATCHING VARIABLES

Variable	Delinquents		Controls	
	M	SD	M	SD
Age	16–8	6.8 mo.	16.9	10.3 mo.
IQ	91.9	3.3	92.1	3.3
School Achievement	6.1	2.4	6.4	2.2
Status Index	62.2	3.2	61.6	4.0

this way so as to eliminate nondelinquents and boys committed for
minor infractions.

At this rehabilitational school the sentences are of indefinite
length, but it is common knowledge among the boys that they will
go home in about six months. Since there is a continuous psychological program, the boys are familiar with psychologists and their
tests. Thus, except for their legal status as delinquents, these boys
live in an atmosphere more like an ordinary high school than a
prison.

The control group of 26 boys with no court history was made up
from the population of a small high school by selecting boys within
the IQ and age ranges of the experimental group. To check on academic achievement the scores of the experimental group on the
Stanford Achievement Test (Intermediate Form D) were obtained
from the school records and the same test was administered to the
control group. Means and standard deviations are shown in Table 1.
To check on social status the Index of Status Characteristics, as developed by Warner, Meeker, and Eells (1949), was used. This technique
assigns weighted scores to occupation, source of income, type of
dwelling, and dwelling area. The weighted scores are added and the
total is considered an index of socioeconomic status. According to
this scale the means of both groups fall approximately at the dividing
line between the lower-lower and upper-lower classes. As Table 1
shows the two groups are quite similar except for the larger age
variation of the control group. All differences between means were
far below statistical significance.

A check on place of residence showed that in the delinquent group

16 boys came from urban homes and 10 from rural homes. In the control group there were 14 from urban homes and 12 from rural homes. This difference also is a minor one.

Procedure

To investigate the span of future time orientation, a projective method was utilized, similar to that used by LeShan. Preliminary work showed, however, that the delinquent boys were unable or unwilling to respond to the instructions given by LeShan: "Tell me a story." After considerable trial and error, instructions were adopted to which the subjects could respond readily but which remained ambiguous enough to permit personal projection. As finally standardized the instructions were as follows.

"I want to see what kind of a story you can tell. I'll start a story and then let you finish it any way you want to. You can make it any kind of story you wish. Let's see how good a story you can tell. I'll start it now. 'About 3:00 o'clock one bright, sunny afternoon in May two boys were walking along a street near the edge of town.' Now you start there and finish the story any way you want to."

In response to these verbal instructions, stories were produced by all Ss of both groups. The stories were recorded stenographically or on a sound-disk recorder, from which they were later transcribed in full.

In the many instances in which a specific time interval was mentioned by S in telling the story, no inquiry was made. If no time or time interval was included, an inquiry was made following the end of the story. The standard question asked was: "How long was this from the start of the story?" In this way it was possible to score the stories in terms of specific time intervals dating from three o'clock.

After all were collected, the stories were assigned score values depending on the length of time covered by the action of the story. To avoid the overlapping intervals reported by LeShan, slightly different intervals were used. The scoring categories were as follows:
1. Under one hour
2. One hour or more but less than five hours
3. Five hours or more but less than twelve hours
4. Twelve hours or more but less than one week
5. One week or more but less than three months
6. Three months or more

Thus each story was given a score from one to six. As a check on

TABLE 2

TIME ORIENTATION SCORES FOR STORIES OF
DELINQUENT AND CONTROL BOYS

Score	Delinquents	Controls
1	6	0
2	6	6
3	4	9
4	8	3
5	1	6
6	1	2
Mean	2.8	3.6
SD	1.4	1.3

the reliability of the scoring, the stories were scored independently
by three graduate students in psychology.[2] There was complete agreement among the three judges, presumably because of the simplicity
and explicitness of the scoring categories and because an inquiry had
been made in doubtful cases.

RESULTS

Frequency distributions of the scores for the delinquent and control groups are shown in Table 2. It is clear that the sample of stories
from the delinquent boys took place in shorter times than the sample
of control stories. The t ratio of the difference between the means
was 2.08, which is significant by a two-tailed test ($p < .05$). Since the
distributions may not be normal, a chi-square test was also applied.
This yielded a chi square of 14.10, which is also significant ($p < .02$).

To check on the matching, the three variables, age, IQ, and school
achievement, were correlated with the scores for time orientation in
each group. The six correlations ranged from —.06 to .05. Hence the
difference between the groups in time orientation could not be due
to bias of the samples in respect to these variables.

Content differences in the stories of the two groups were marked.
Of the 26 subjects of the delinquent group 15 produced stories with
crime themes or unhappy endings. In the control group of 26 stories
there was only one with a crime theme and three others with unhappy outcomes.

[2] We are indebted to Leo Gladin and Lawrence Walker for their help in the
scoring.

So little is known about the development of time orientation that speculation is hardly profitable. We can conclude that short time perspective is part of the pattern of delinquency, but we cannot say which is cause and which is effect. We have demonstrated that useful results on time orientation can be obtained by this story-completion method with a simple scoring system. Perhaps research with younger children will be possible. A study of time orientation in nondelinquent siblings of delinquents would be instructive.

SUMMARY

A group of 26 delinquent boys was equated with 26 nondelinquents in terms of age, IQ, academic achievement, and socioeconomic status. Stories were obtained from all subjects in response to verbal instructions which included the beginning of the story. The stories were recorded and then scored in six categories in terms of the length of time covered by the action of the stories. Reliability of scoring was high. Analysis of the results showed that the delinquent boys did produce stories with significantly shorter time spans than the control boys.

······························· **43** ······························

THE IDENTIFICATION AND MEASUREMENT
OF PREDISPOSITIONAL FACTORS IN CRIME
AND DELINQUENCY

by Harrison G. Gough and Donald R. Peterson

Can predisposition to delinquency and crime be identified and measured? Several attempts have been made to construct instruments for this purpose. One of these is described in the following article, by Harrison G. Gough, of the University of California (Berkeley), and Donald R. Peterson, of the University of Illinois. They show how a questionnaire was constructed capable of differentiating significantly between delinquents and control groups. [From *Journal of Consulting Psychology*, 1952, *16*, 207-212. Reprinted by permission of the authors and the American Psychological Association. Some of the footnotes have been omitted.]

The value of a theory or concept resides in the range and scope of the facts it is capable of subsuming, and in the extent, number, and accuracy of the hypotheses it implies. The particular analogies employed, the vocabulary utilized, and the palatability of the constructs themselves are all of secondary importance when set against this first criterion.

The role-taking theory of psychopathy which the senior author outlined in an earlier paper (Gough, 1948) represents an attempt to meet these first requirements in a direct and straightforward manner. Without restating the details of this theory, it may be said that the role-taking theory did appear to synthesize and accommodate all the known clinical and psychopathological phenomena observed in psychopathy. Furthermore, it provided a basis for an inferential diagnosis, one freed from a barren dependence on any particular symptom or pattern of symptoms.

The key element in the role-taking theory was an incapacity to look upon the self as a "social object"—where the terms "self" and "social object" are used as defined by G. H. Mead—and the resulting failure to elaborate an adequate and realistic set of social expectancies and critiques. It is not contended that the psychopath (as specified by role-taking theory) is deficient in role-*playing* ability, in the sense of being unable to dissimulate, to feign, and to deceive others. Unfortunately, the language of the social psychological analysis here employed occasionally gives rise to that misperception. On the contrary, what the theory asserts is that the capacity to build up, to sustain, to integrate, and to organize the *residuals* which ordinarily accrue as a consequence of interactional experience is lacking.[1]

Perhaps a word of caution should be interjected that we are not attempting to define the essential nature of psychopathy, or to explain just what psychopathy "really is." The futility of such an enterprise is obvious. The present goal, rather, is to develop a

---

[1] The theory, it should be mentioned, is neutral with respect to the origin of this incapacity. It may be constitutional, developmental, idiosyncratic, reactive, etc., in origin. The present argument is merely that the role-taking position is a heuristic way of conceptualizing the behavior specified. (For a discussion of the origins of role-taking skills, see (Sarbin, 1952).

workable, useful, and reliable theory which can, in fact, unify the generally accepted findings in the conventional use of the concept of psychopathy, and which can, moreover, be used in an efficient and practical way in understanding and predicting the behavior of persons thus diagnosed.

We should not, of course, neglect the possibility that the new perspectives opened up by the theory may suggest a change or modification in the diagnostic conventions previously employed. Such a revision has, indeed, occurred in the present instance. One of the major implications of the role-taking theory is that the essential diagnostic factor is *not* social maladjustment, friction, or delinquency, as so often assumed, but rather a deficiency in role-taking capacity which is peculiarly liable to manifestation in social interaction.

In the present study, the task is to apply role-taking theory to the problem of delinquent and criminal behavior. It is not assumed that delinquency and psychopathy are synonymous—actually each can, and should be, defined independently of one another—or that all delinquents are psychopaths. The only assumption made is that the total delinquent and criminal population includes a large enough proportion of psychopathic types to make feasible the application of role-taking theory.

The particular goal was to determine whether a personality assessment device based on role-taking theory could be developed which would yield reliable and dependable predictions of delinquent and criminal behavior. Success, or partial success, in such an effort would represent a rather important step forward. According to a systematic review by Schuessler and Cressey (1950) of 113 studies in the last 25 years attempting to differentiate criminals from noncriminals on the basis of personality tests, the results of such endeavors have been consistently negative. Their over-all conclusion was that, "The doubtful validity of many of the obtained differences, as well as the lack of consistency in the combined results, makes it impossible to conclude from these data that criminality and personality elements are associated." Concurrence with this opinion was voiced in the last published paper of the noted criminologist, E. H. Sutherland (1951).

PROCEDURES

The first step in the present study was the creation of a pool of personality test items which would incorporate the salient features of the role-taking theory, as well as items believed on intuitive grounds to hold promise for the differentiation of delinquents from nondelinquents. The item "I often think about how I look and what impression I am making upon others" is an example of the former type, and the item "I used to steal sometimes when I was a youngster" is an example of the latter. This scale was then administered to a series of criminal, delinquent, behavior problem, and control samples, as follows:

Males
1. 43 high school boys from a small Minnesota community.
2. 125 high school boys from two Minneapolis schools.
3. 19 behavior problem boys from these three schools.
4. 243 young delinquents committed to the Minnesota Youth Commission.
5. 698 reformatory inmates.

Females
1. 44 high school girls from a small Minnesota community.
2. 134 high school girls from two Minneapolis schools.
3. 19 behavior problem girls from these three schools.
4. 105 reformatory inmates.

An item analysis of all control versus all delinquent samples (one at a time, separately by sex) was carried out. Sixty-four of the items showed good differentiating power, and were retained for a delinquency "scale." These items, and the direction of response indicative of delinquency, are listed below:

1. I get nervous when I have to ask someone for a job (F). 2. I sometimes feel that I made the wrong choice in my occupation (T). 3. I would never play cards (poker) with a stranger (F). 4. I would have been more successful if people had given me a fair chance (T). 5. I think Lincoln was greater than Washington (F). 6. Life usually hands me a pretty raw deal (T). 7. A person is better off if he doesn't trust anyone (T). 8. My family has objected to the kind of work I do, or plan to do (T).

9. Sometimes I used to feel that I would like to leave home (T). 10. If the pay was right, I would like to travel with a circus or carnival (T). 11. I would do almost anything on a dare (T). 12. As a youngster in school I used to give the teachers lots of trouble (T). 13. My parents were too strict with me when I was a child (T). 14. Even when I have gotten into trouble I was usually trying to do the right thing (F). 15. My parents never really understood me (T). 16. My home life as a child was less peaceful than those of most other people (T).

17. I think I am stricter about right and wrong than most people (F). 18. I often feel that I am not getting anywhere in life (T). 19. Even the

idea of giving a talk in public makes me afraid (F). 20. It is very important to me to have enough friends and social life (F). 21. I never worry about my looks (T). 22. I hardly ever get excited or thrilled (T). 23. I have very strong likes and dislikes (T). 24. My parents have often disapproved of my friends (T).

25. My home life was always happy (F). 26. I often act on the spur of the moment without stopping to think (T). 27. I seem to do things that I regret more often than other people do (T). 28. I would rather go without something than ask for a favor (T). 29. I have more than my share of things to worry about (T). 30. I go out of my way to meet trouble rather than try to escape it (T). 31. When I meet a stranger I often think that he is better than I am (F). 32. It is pretty easy for people to win arguments with me (T).

33. Before I do something I try to consider how my friends will react to it (F). 34. I have never been in trouble with the law (F). 35. In school I was sometimes sent to the principal for cutting up (T). 36. I keep out of trouble at all costs (F). 37. I often think about how I look and what impression I am making upon others (F). 38. I find it easy to "drop" or "break with" a friend (T). 39. I spend a good deal of time planning and thinking about my career (T). 40. I enjoy work as much as play (T).

41. It is hard for me to act natural when I am with new people (F). 42. When something goes wrong I usually blame myself rather than the other fellow (T). 43. I have often gone against my parents' wishes (T). 44. I have never done any heavy drinking (F). 45. I have been in trouble one or more times because of my sex behavior (T). 46. When I work at something I like to read and study about it (T). 47. Most of the time I feel happy (F). 48. My table manners are not quite as good at home as when I am out in company (F).

49. I know who is responsible for most of my troubles (T). 50. I get pretty discouraged with the law when a smart lawyer gets a criminal free (F). 51. I have used alcohol excessively (T). 52. When I was going to school I played hooky quite often (T). 53. People often talk about me behind my back (T). 54. I often feel as though I have done something wrong or wicked (T). 55. I don't think I'm quite as happy as others seem to be (T). 56. I used to steal sometimes when I was a youngster (T).

57. I am somewhat afraid of the dark (F). 58. I never cared much for school (T). 59. The members of my family were always very close to each other (F). 60. I sometimes wanted to run away from home (T). 61. With things going as they are, it's pretty hard to keep up hope of amounting to something (T). 62. My parents have generally let me make my own decisions (F). 63. I was often punished unfairly as a child (T). 64. My home life was always very pleasant (F).

The 64 items appear to group themselves into several rather distinctive clusters, such as the following:

1. Role-taking deficiencies, insensitivity to interactional cues and the effects of one's own behavior on others.

2. Resentment against family, feelings of having been victimized and exploited in childhood.

3. Feelings of despondency and alienation, lack of confidence in self and others.

4. Poor scholastic adjustment, rebelliousness.

Not all of the items are necessarily included in these particular four clusters. A more systematic statistical analysis of item intercorrelations might reveal additional, or perhaps different, clusters. The four clusters listed, however, do appear to be clearly suggested by a subjective appraisal and can probably be accepted as having clinical validity.

The test answer sheets of all subjects were next scored for this 64-item key, with the results indicated in Table 1. The progression of mean scores in Table 1 evidences a clear trend from lower scores for the control samples through intermediate scores for the behavior-problem samples to highest scores for the overtly delinquent samples. Analyses of variances yielded F ratios of 62.5 for the male samples and 91.3 for the female samples. Both of these values are significant well beyond the .01 level of confidence.

TABLE 1

MEAN SCORES ON THE De SCALE FOR THE CRITERION SAMPLES

Samples	N	M	SD
I. Males			
A. Comparison			
1. School A	43	18.70	5.11
2. Schools B and C	125	22.67	6.13
B. Delinquent			
1. School behavior problems	19	28.95	6.87
2. Young delinquents	243	30.40	6.20
3. Reformatory inmates	698	29.83	6.65
II. Females			
A. Comparison			
1. School A	44	16.20	4.80
2. Schools B and C	134	18.85	6.23
B. Delinquent			
1. School behavior problems	19	22.00	7.83
2. Reformatory inmates	105	30.26	5.63

Combining all the delinquent and all the control cases, for each sex separately, permits the evaluation of the screening efficiency of the Delinquency Scale. Table 2 presents these data. For these samples it would be possible to identify as many as 75 per cent of the delinquent and behavior problem subjects at the cost of only 23 per cent "false positives" for males and 12 per cent false positives for females. A cutting score of 26 would correctly classify 78 per cent of the total sample of 1,430 cases. The screening efficiency of the scale is thus quite good for these samples.

TABLE 2

SCREENING EFFICIENCY OF THE *De* SCALE

PROPORTION OF CASES WHICH WOULD BE CALLED "DELINQUENT" WITH VARIOUS CUTTING SCORES

Scores	Males		Females	
	Delinquents N=960	Controls N=168	Delinquents N=124	Controls N=178
28 and over	63	17	60	7
27 " "	68	19	65	10
26 " "	74	23	73	12
25 " "	79	31	79	17
24 " "	83	39	83	20
23 " "	87	45	85	21
22 " "	90	51	89	25

The next step in the project was the obtaining of cross-validational evidence. Forty-two randomly chosen items, out of the total of 64, were administered to a sample of 1,092 incoming recruits at Fort Ord, California. The same item subset was also given to 99 stockade prisoners who were tested in a group on a single day. The distributions of scores for these two samples are given in Table 3. The difference between the two means is 7.26, and the critical ratio 11.52, again significant well beyond the 1 per cent level.

The cross-validational screening efficiency of the *De* scale is indicated in Table 4. The cutting score proposed for the original samples was 26, out of a possible 64. In the abbreviated version used in this cross-validation, a cutting score of 17 would be proportional. A division at 17 would properly identify 66 per cent of the prisoners and would misclassify 22 per cent of the controls. The corresponding figures for the male subjects in the original samples were 74 and 23, so it can readily be seen that the amount of "shrinkage" in cross validation has been remarkably small. An inspection of the other proportions in Table 4 will suggest various ways of using the *De* scale. For example, if one wished to minimize

TABLE 3

COMPARISON OF ARMY RECRUITS AND STOCKADE PRISONERS ON AN ABBREVIATED FORM OF THE *De* SCALE

Scores	Recruits	Prisoners
33-35		2
30-32		5
27-29	5	9
24-26	20	13
21-23	48	18
18-20	102	15
15-17	163	17
12-14	284	14
9-11	276	4
6- 8	156	2
3- 5	37	
0- 2	1	
	———	———
N:	1,092	99
M:	12.75	20.01
SD:	4.66	6.11

TABLE 4

CROSS-VALIDATIONAL SCREENING EFFICIENCY OF THE *De* SCALE

Scores	PROPORTION OF CASES FALLING ABOVE VARIOUS CUTTING SCORES	
	Army Recruits *N=1,092*	*Army Prisoners* *N=99*
20 and over	9	52
19 " "	12	57
18 " "	16	63
17 " "	22	66
16 " "	26	71
15 " "	31	80
14 " "	38	84

false positives, but desired to identify at least 60 per cent of known prisoners, then a cutting score of 18 would be employed.[2]

A second cross-validational sample was obtained when a 58-item version of the scale was administered to 353 stockade prisoners at the Lackland Air Force Base, Texas. In this 58-item version a cutting score of 24 would be proportional to the score of 26 used for the total test. Sixty-four per cent of the Lackland prisoners scored at or above 24, and 36 per cent below. A control sample was not available at Lackland, but it was possible to determine from the stockade records whether or not a prisoner had any previous military offenses. The "first offense" group included 209 prisoners, and the repeaters numbered 144. The means and standard deviations were 25.74 and 6.55 for the first offenders, and 28.19 and 7.03 for the recidivists. The difference between the two means was 2.45, critical ratio 3.31, a value significant well beyond the .01 level of probability. This difference, with the recidivists having higher scores, again confirms the theoretical expectations.

The validity of the scale in both the original and the cross-validational samples thus appears to be adequate.[3] The scale does differentiate delinquent from control samples, in terms of both mean differences and per cent overlap. The evidence from the Army samples, in fact, suggests that the scale possesses practical screening efficiency. Furthermore, military recidivists score significantly higher, on the average, than first offenders.

These findings with respect to validity may now be reviewed briefly in reference to the role-taking theory upon which the largest portion of the items was based. The theory dictated the exploration of new areas of item content, with special emphasis on social interaction and expectancies. Many of the items derived from these considerations were phenotypically unrelated to criminal and delinquent behavior; that is, they made no reference to legal or illegal acts, rules, acceptance of authority, and the like. Yet, in spite of this phenotypical irrelevance, items such as these did, in fact, turn out under empirical analysis to relate to delinquency in the manner specified by the theory. Evidence such as this, perhaps particularly the practical screening efficiency of the scale, consti-

---

[2] The particular cutting scores discussed here would refer only to the abbreviated 42-item version used in the Army investigation. The expectation would be, however, that cutting scores for the total scale would be proportional to these.

[3] The only evidence for reliability so far obtained is an uncorrected split-half r of .72 for a random sample of 200 of the male reformatory inmates.

tutes a strong argument for the utility and pragmatic value of the role-taking theory of psychopathy.[4]

Any number of interesting follow-up studies are suggested by the results of the present investigation. For example, one would predict that low-scoring prison inmates on the *De* scale would be better parole risks than higher-scoring inmates. Or, a systematic comparison of nondelinquent but high-scoring subjects versus equally high-scoring and overtly delinquent subjects could be made. One would expect to find some interesting Rosanoff-type control factors in the former group. Then there is always the possibility of a configural analysis of the dimension isolated by the *De* scale with other variables. Consider, for example, the differences one would expect to find between subjects high on the *De* scale and on a femininity index, and subjects high on *De* but low on the femininity index.

ADJECTIVES

In using a scale such as the one for delinquency described here, or any other instrument for that matter, one of the needs of the user is to know what significance to attach to high and low scores, over and above the general implications which derive from the test's validity and reliability.

In an attempt to provide information of this type for the *De* scale, an exploration of the "social stimulus values" of high and low scores was undertaken. That is, the question was raised, "What sort of impression can a person who scores either high or low on the *De* scale be expected to make on his friends and associates?"

In order to accomplish this phase of the study, the scale was administered to 40 subjects who were participating in an intensive project being conducted by the Institute of Personality Assessment and Research, at the University of California, Berkeley. From this group of 40, the 10 highest and 10 lowest scoring subjects on the *De* scale were selected for special consideration. Then a systematic

---

[4] A conclusion such as this is not intended to rule out the possibility of accounting for the observations by other theories and points of view. The unique contribution of the role-taking theory in this instance was that it indicated a specific new area of item content, one which turned out, under analysis, to possess considerable validity. Once these relationships have been demonstrated, their meaning and significance can undoubtedly be fitted into and explicated by other viewpoints. The value of the role-taking theory is not that it is the only one which can "explain" these relationships, but rather that it led directly to their discovery and identification.

comparison was made of what observers had said *about* each subject, in order to discover consistent and reliable differences between the high and low scorers.

During the assessment periods, each of six Personality Institute staff members had completed an adjective check list for each assessee, giving as complete and accurate a picture as possible of his reactions to and conceptions of the assessee's personality structure and characteristics. The six "observer check lists" for each assessee were then consolidated into a single "composite observer check list" by considering each adjective with checks by two or more of the staff as being "present," and those with one or no checks as being "absent." The composite observer check lists for each of the 20 designated assessees were then split into the two criterion subsamples and an item analysis of the adjectives was completed.

All adjectives showing a statistically significant difference between the two subsamples were selected, and are listed below:

A. Adjectives checked more frequently about high scoring subjects.

affected	emotional	sensitive
anxious	headstrong	tense
defensive	persevering	wary
dissatisfied	rebellious	

B. Adjectives checked more frequently about low scoring subjects.

calm	good-natured	obliging
considerate	helpful	patient
conventional	moderate	peaceable
dependable	modest	tactful
frank	natural	unassuming

The social stimulus value of higher scores on the *De* scale appears to include an emphasis on characteristics such as dissatisfaction, rebelliousness, defensiveness, etc. On the other hand, lower scores "come through" socially as considerateness, dependability, moderateness, patience, and tactfulness. High and low scores on the *De* scale can, accordingly, be taken as predictive of the two patterns of social stimulus values indicated.

SUMMARY

A role-taking theory of psychopathy was applied to the practical problem of the identification and measurement of predispositional factors in crime and delinquency. An assessment device was constructed which was capable of differentiating significantly between delinquents and controls in both original and cross-validational samples.

Some possibilities for additional studies were suggested, and an analysis of the "social stimulus values" of the test instrument was conducted.

·································· 44 ··································

THE ROLE-TAKING HYPOTHESIS

IN DELINQUENCY[1]

by Charles F. Reed and Carlos A. Cuadra

The hypothesis upon which a scale for the detection of potentially delinquent behavior[2] is based, that role taking deficiency and social insensitivity are characteristic of psychopaths, is tested in this study by Charles F. Reed of the Upstate Medical Center, State University of New York, and Carlos A. Cuadra of Rand Corporation. Using a "normal sample" it is found that the scale discriminates between subjects on their ability to "see themselves as others see them." [From *Journal of Consulting Psychology*, 1957, *21*, 386-390. Reprinted by permission of the authors and the American Psychological Association.]

On the basis of an hypothesis concerning psychopathy, Gough has devised a scale for the identification of predisposition for delinquent behavior (Gough, 1948; Gough, 1957; Gough and Peterson, 1952). The present study is an experimental examination of the operation of the hypothesized variable in the production of scores on the scale.

Gough finds the psychopath unable to "look upon the self as a 'social object'" or to "elaborate an adequate and realistic set of social expectancies and critiques" (Gough and Peterson, 1952, p. 207).

---

[1] This study was inaugurated while both investigators were members of the staff of the Clinical Psychology Service of the VA Hospital, Downey, Illinois. The authors wish to acknowledge the support and assistance of the hospital administration and the Nursing Education Service throughout the course of the project.

[2] See selection 43 in this book.

For some clinical observers, however, one of the chief characteristics of psychopaths is their singular facility for slipping from one role to another, assuming the demeanor most opportune for the moment. Gough emphasizes that it is not a deficiency of role-playing ability to which he refers, but an absence of the "residuals which ordinarily accrue as a consequence of interactional experience . . ." (Gough and Peterson, 1952, p. 207). However, these residuals are not identified specifically, and Gough's concern seems to remain with the supposed inability to see one's self as seen by others.

Gough's Delinquency Scale (De)[3] incorporates this hypothesis and appears to have practical screening efficiency in differentiating between delinquent and nondelinquent samples (Gough, 1954; Gough, 1957; Gough and Peterson, 1952). The item "I often think about how I look and what impression I am making upon others" (answered False) is given as an example of a cluster of items reflecting "role-taking deficiencies, insensitivity to interactional cues and the effects of one's own behavior on others" (Gough and Peterson, 1952, p. 209). Items such as this seem rather to be reports of indifference to the opinion of others, not direct manifestations of incapacity in role-taking. Whatever the basis for the efficacy of De for screening, the data presented by Gough do not warrant the conclusion that incapacity in role-taking has been demonstrated. It could be argued with equal justification that part of the scale's power lay in items admitting past delinquencies, e.g., "I have never been in trouble with the law" answered False, since seven items in the scale are of this nature.

Data pertaining to the relative social sensitivity of subjects who receive high scores on De will be presented in this report. Social sensitivity was defined experimentally as the ability of a subject to predict descriptions made of him by peers. A normal sample was chosen instead of a sample of delinquent subjects for methodological reasons concerned with equivalence of task and with acquaintance-ship variables. The study deals with the examination of a delinquency scale rather than with delinquents themselves. References to "High De scorers" are not intended to convey the impression that these subjects were delinquent.

PROCEDURE

Successive classes of student nurses undergoing training at a VA neuropsychiatric hospital were used as Ss. Each class was tested near

[3] Now renamed the Socialization (So) Scale and scored in reverse in the California Psychological Inventory (Gough, 1957).

the close of three months' residence at the hospital, where the students had worked on wards, attended classes, and lived together. There was ample opportunity for observation of each other in a variety of working conditions, some of them stressful.

For the purposes of this study, each S was assigned to a group of four Ss. Each S was asked to describe herself on an adjective checklist (I), marking every adjective in the list with a plus when it was true or generally true, with a minus when it was false or generally false. As a second task (II), the S described each of the other members of her group of four. Finally, she attempted to predict how she would be described by the members of the small group as a group (III). Precautions of anonymity and seating were taken to foster candid appraisals.

The forced-choice technique was used because, in a pilot study with Navy hospital corps students in which the adjectives were checked only when they applied to a subject, there seemed to be a spurious accuracy in predicting group description. The fewer adjectives chosen, the higher the accuracy score. By employing forced choices, the correlation between accuracy and the number of adjectives marked plus was reduced to zero.

The California Psychological Inventory, of which the scale is a part, was administered as a final procedure. Complete data were available for 204 Ss; partial data existed for 25 more Ss.

Quantitative Data

The correspondence between an S's predicted description (III) and the descriptions which are made of the S by her peers (composite II's) is the variable of chief interest. A score was given whenever, on a given adjective, two of the three peers recorded the same sign as that recorded by the S. Total score, Predictive Accuracy, is the sum of the adjectives on which such agreement occurred.

The correspondence between S's self-description (I) and the peer-description (composite II's) was scored in a similar manner and the total score called Self-peer Correspondence.

Additional scores were evolved in the course of analysis of the data. They will be described after the report of initial results.

Peer-nomination Data

A second major source of data was provided by material gathered some months after the initial part of the study was completed. All Ss were contacted by mail and asked to select from a list of their classmates five whom they considered the most insightful of the class and five whom they considered least insightful. Insight was defined as

TABLE 1

COMPARISON OF SCORES OF HIGH-DE GROUP AND LOW-DE GROUP

| Variable | High-De group | | Low-De group | | |
	Mean	SD	Mean	SD	CR
Predictive Accuracy (III vs. II)	161.08	20.45	178.38	13.81	4.90**
Self-peer Correspondence (I vs. composite II's)	161.56	17.70	173.21	15.66	3.44**
Conventional-word Count (on III)	356.73	199.62	519.46	133.91	3.41**
Conventional-word Count (on I)	382.95	148.36	509.50	119.50	3.25**
Stereotyping	126.12	32.46	148.39	25.08	3.79**
Favorable Self-description	20.58	7.83	26.45	6.71	3.99**
Favorable Peer-description	29.52	5.41	30.15	5.19	.58
Favorable Expected Peer-description	19.24	9.20	26.09	6.00	4.36**
Anticipated Disagreement	47.40	16.95	37.32	14.07	3.20**

** $P < .01$.

follows: "An insightful person has the ability to recognize and understand the motives underlying her behavior and is aware of the effects of her behavior on other persons. She is alert to what other people think of her as a person. (In making judgments, do not be influenced by intelligence, likeability, etc., which are not necessarily related to insight. An unpleasant person, for example, still could be an insightful person.)" Approximately 60 per cent of the rating forms were returned.

RESULTS AND DISCUSSION

Comparison of the scores of Ss at the extreme quartiles of the De distribution yielded the results summarized in Table 1.

Accuracy Scores

The finding of chief interest is the relative inaccuracy of the high De scorers in predicting how they will be described by their peers.

The difference is significant beyond the .001 level. Even if the highest quartile is compared with the remainder of the sample in a one-tailed test the difference between means on Predictive Accuracy yields a critical ratio of 2.72, significant at .003. The correlation between Predictive Accuracy and *De* for the entire sample is —.41.

Several factors which might attenuate the inference to be made from this finding were examined.

The task of describing another person may be restricted by certain unverbalized conventions. Some characteristics may be assumed by most members of a group to be properties of most other members of the group and of themselves. In the present sample, for example, the adjective "intelligent" was generously used. A spuriously high accuracy score may be obtained by the S who is not responding to the particular members of her group of four, but who is accurately gauging the probability of an adjective being checked plus or minus when any S was describing any other S.

In this regard, it is interesting that the Self-peer Correspondence score also shows the high *De* scorers differing significantly from the low scorers. Correlation between the two scores for the entire sample is —.29. Apparently, the difference between the extreme groups is not solely a matter of anticipating the verbal responses of peers. The high *De*'s do not just mis-guess the descriptions that will be made of them. Their "private" self-descriptions differ more from the descriptions made by their peers than do the self-descriptions of the low *De*'s from their peer-descriptions.

To investigate further the possible effects of the popularity or unpopularity of adjectives, a Conventional-word Count was made. Each adjective was ranked according to frequency of use in the peer-descriptions (Checklists of Task II) and assigned a corresponding scoring weight. Self-descriptions (I) and predicted-descriptions (III) were scored for the sum of the weighted scores of adjectives marked with a plus. A high score indicates that S marked adjectives in the direction which conformed to the group's conventional usage.

High *De*'s marked adjectives less conventionally, both in the prediction task and in describing themselves. Conventional-word Count on Task III correlates .35 with Predictive Accuracy for the total sample. When Conventional-word Count is held constant, the correlation between *De* and Predictive Accuracy drops from —.41 to —.31, a coefficient still significantly different from zero at the .01 level. Conventionality of description—if it is to be construed as an attenuating factor—still fails to delete the differences in accuracy between the *De* extremes.

Stereotypy is a score based on the number of adjectives which an S checked in the same direction in describing all three peers in her group. A high score would seem to indicate either a failure to discriminate or a highly homogeneous group. High De scorers earn significantly lower scores. This score may simply be another reflection of venturing from popular responses.

The adjective checklists were scored for use of favorable and unfavorable items on the basis of the ratings procured from a group of judges by Gough (1955). Favorable Self-description refers to the relative emphasis on favorable adjectives in describing self. Favorable Expected Peer-description refers to the relative emphasis on favorable adjectives in Task III; Favorable Peer-description indicates the relative representation of favorable adjectives ascribed to S by her peers.

The results summarized in Table 1 indicate that while high De scorers described themselves in less favorable terms and expected to be described in less favorable terms than did the low scorers, the descriptions which were made of them were not less favorable.

A final score, Anticipated Disagreement, is the sum of adjectives given opposite signs by an S and I and III. A high score may be interpreted as indicative of an expectation that the group will differ from the S's self-description. High De scorers expect to be misdescribed or perhaps misunderstood. This is not the same phenomenon of describing self in unfavorable terms and expecting to be described in unfavorable terms, since this score is based on adjectives which differ in sign between self- and expected-description. This apparent psychological isolation may be related to characteristics Gough found in high scorers: "feelings of despondency and alienation, lack of confidence in self and others" (Gough and Peterson, 1952, p. 209).

Peer-nomination Findings

Nominations for insightfulness were tallied for each S and converted into T scores. The ratings for insight for the Ss in extreme quartiles on the De distribution showed a difference significant beyond the .02 level, Ss with high De scores being rated less insightful.

Content of Adjectives

The following adjectives are associated with scores in the extreme quartiles of the De distribution of the sample. Adjectives discriminating at the .01 level are listed before the ellipsis, those at the .05 level after the ellipsis.

STUDENT NURSES

High De

Described self as: Absent-minded, complicated, forgetful, head-strong, indifferent, temperamental, withdrawn . . . flirtatious, pleasure-seeking, quarrelsome.

Described by peers as: No adjectives significantly discriminating.

Expected to be described as: Absent-minded, changeable, confused, forgetful, indifferent, irritable, moody, restless, temperamental . . .

Low De

Described self as: Confident . . .

Described by peers as: No adjectives significantly discriminating.

Expected to be described as: Ambitious, confident . . .

NAVY STUDENTS

High De

Described self as: No adjectives significantly discriminating.

Described by peers as: Confused, impatient, lazy . . . dreamy, immature, interests narrow, irresponsible, self-centered, tactless, careless, foolish, impulsive.

Expected to be described as: Indifferent . . . confused, high-strung, immature, impatient, reckless.

Low De

Described self as: Conscientious, contented, cooperative, gentle, mild, practical, praising, peaceable, pleasant, relaxed, reliable, responsible, steady, tactful, thoughtful . . . clear-thinking, conservative, conventional, capable, cautious, efficient, dependable, moderate, jolly, kind, mannerly, mature, opportunistic, organized, reasonable, resourceful, self-confident, self-controlled, simple, stable, sympathetic, thorough, wholesome.

Described by peers as: Conservative, cooperative, capable, forgiving, generous, helpful, thoughtful, wise . . . alert, clear-thinking, clever, calm, cautious, easy-going, foresighted, frank, initiative, moderate, modest, obliging, kind, mannerly, mature, practical, patient, peaceable, poised, progressive, realistic, reasonable, relaxed, responsible, serious, steady, trusting.

Expected to be described as: Clear-thinking, capable, dependable, patient, peaceable, reliable . . . conservative, cooperative, cautious, honest, planful, reasonable, stable, steady, understanding.

The Navy sample was used in a pilot study and some differences between Ss and procedures prevent direct comparison of the adjectival content. The Navy sample consisted of 100 Ss, male and female. They represented approximately the same age range as the student nurses (17-21).

Nevertheless, qualities of indifference and impulsivity appeared in the peer-descriptions of both samples. In the Navy group, some of the adjectives which distinguish the expectations of the high scorers find verification in the peer-descriptions, e.g., "confused," "immature," and "impatient." A correct appraisal of group opinion was made in regard to these characteristics at least. Although the adjective checklist employed in this study has a broad range of description, there may be other self-appraisals on which the high *De* scorers do well.

SUMMARY

The purpose of the study was to test the hypothesis upon which a scale for the detection of potentially delinquent behavior had been based: that role-taking deficiency and social insensitivity were characteristic of psychopaths. More properly, the investigation concerned the association of social insensitivity with high scores on the scale. The scale had been demonstrated to possess satisfactory screening efficiency, but the operation of the assumed variable, it was suggested, had not been demonstrated.

A total of 204 normal female Ss used adjective checklists to describe themselves, described three other acquaintances specified by the investigators, and predicted how they themselves would be described in the composite checklists of the group. A second source of data was obtained by using the peer-nomination technique for designating low and high "insight" Ss.

Subjects from the extreme quartiles of the Delinquency (*De*) Scale distribution were compared for predictive accuracy and other variables with the following results and conclusions:

1. Subjects who score high on *De* are significantly less accurate in predicting how they will be described by others than are Ss who score low.

2. When peer-nomination ratings of insight were compared with

De scores, high *De* scorers were rated significantly less insightful than low scorers.

3. High *De* scorers expect to be described by peers in unfavorable terms, and so describe themselves. This expectation is not supported in the descriptions which are actually made by the peers.

4. High *De* scorers tend to use relatively fewer adjectives as they are used by the sample as a whole. Even with conventionality of description held constant, however, they are poorer in predictive accuracy than are other members of the sample.

5. High *De* scorers seem to expect to be misunderstood by their peers.

6. High *De* scorers in a pilot study characteristically expected to be described as confused, immature, and impatient, and were described in these terms by their peers.

If incapacity in role-taking implies a relative inability to understand and predict one's own social stimulus value in a particular setting, the findings of this study support indirectly the theoretical assumption upon which the *De* scale is based. The scale itself apparently discriminates between *S*s on their ability to "see themselves as others see them."

Part Five

....

INTERESTS, ATTITUDES, AND IDEALS

Chapter Fifteen
INTERESTS

Chapter Sixteen
RELIGIOUS BELIEFS

Chapter Seventeen
IDEALS AND VALUES

Chapter Eighteen
SOCIAL ATTITUDES AND OPINIONS

Chapter Nineteen
PERSISTENCE AND CHANGE OF ATTITUDES

CHAPTER FIFTEEN

Interests

45

READING INTERESTS: GRADES SEVEN THROUGH NINE

by Alice R. Wickens

This survey aims to assist adults in understanding and helping children with a major objective of the educative process: to develop a permanent interest in reading. Alice R. Wickens of the Tenafly, New Jersey, public schools reviews the recent changes in the reading preferences of adolescents and the influences of sex, age and intelligence, and environmental and personality factors as they relate to the quality and quantity of reading. [From Developing Permanent Interest in Reading, Helen M. Robinson, Editor, *Supplementary Education Monographs*, 1956, No. *84*, Chicago: University of Chicago Press, pp. 60-64. Reprinted by permission of the author and The University of Chicago Press.]

Teachers of reading hope to develop in children the variety of skills needed for reading many different kinds of material, as well as abiding interest and continuing pleasure in extensive reading as a useful and as a leisure-time activity. It is not encouraging that research has disclosed that the majority of adults do little reading of any significance. Teachers therefore should look carefully at the reading interests of adolescents, to find clues to the development and maintenance of a desirable quality of reading as an adult activity.

RELATION OF AGE TO READING INTERESTS

Research reports over a period of years show amazing agreement on the nature and effect of certain factors on reading interests. The first of these factors is chronological age. The junior high school years bring the peak in amount of reading done. Only a very few children do no reading at all during this three-year period.

Although this is the period of maximum reading, it is also the period in which reading definitely declines. The amount of individual reading increases rapidly toward the middle and upper grades then begins to drop off in Grade IX. Pupils in junior high school read an average of 19 per cent more than do pupils in senior high school. This pattern has been repeatedly verified.

A current survey of individual reading over the past year for these three grades at the Laboratory School of the University of Chicago shows a seventh-grade range of 5 to 79 books read, an eighth-grade range from 1 to 108, and a ninth-grade range from 1 to 155.

In an interview with this writer, Mrs. Yolanda Federici, young people's supervisor for the South Side Division of the Chicago Public Library system, notes that a similar decline occurs at the ninth-grade level in the general population, except in isolated instances. With this conclusion, Miss Catherine Adamson, general supervisor at the central library, concurs.

Both the literature and the opinion of experts advance reasons for this decrease in reading. Academic expectations increase considerably at this age, requiring additional homework and reducing time available for free reading. There are more extra-curriculum activities in school and a marked increase in the demands of social life outside of school.

In our culture, reading once tended to be looked upon as a waste of time as youth began to assume adult responsibilities. But since current living puts a rather high premium upon the ability to read, it is quite likely that these young people literally do not have time to read. This conclusion would imply that, since the decrease in quantity cannot be prevented, steps should be taken to insure a high quality of the reading done.

What is the quality of reading during early adolescence? In 1928 Jennings noted the wide range of interests and the general preference for wholesome reading on the part of junior high school boys and girls. Holy (1936, pp. 139-142) found a much wider range of interests in the junior high school than in the senior high school. For

example, more magazines are read at age thirteen. Newspaper-read
ing shows the beginning of a genuine interest in world events. Rather
specialized interests begin to appear at fourteen. Esther Anderson
(1948) called this the age of exploring. All the research studies agree
that the major interest is in fiction, mostly juvenile, with a dawning
interest in adult fiction. Among the top favorites in all reported
lists, however, are the classics, both juvenile and adult.

Data indicate that young people select books because of interesting
titles or pictures or because they know and like the author. Literary
elements with appeal for them include action, human interest,
imagination, humor, direct discourse, colorful descriptions and
names. Particularly they dislike preaching or moralizing. Other
interest factors are suspense, happy endings, and situations in which
students can imagine themselves. Elements of style which appeal
are a free and easy manner of writing, brevity, sincerity, and
straightforwardness of language, joined with rapidity of movement.

Norvell (1950, p. 38) determined the order of preference for types
of literature as follows: novels, plays, short stories, biographies,
essays, poetry, letters, and speeches. He summarized the changes in
interests when he stated: "The results of five studies . . . indicate
that the year-to-year changes in children's reading interests between
Grades VIII and XI are usually gradual and small."

At the junior high school level, Lyness (1951) found that certain
interest patterns tended to cluster in certain subject-matter areas
and to carry over from one area of mass communication to another.
Included were violence and adventure, educational content, love,
private life, and glamour.

Josette Frank (1954, pp. 138–168) summarizes the general areas
of interest in a descriptive and comprehensive manner. Young teen
agers enjoy the series books, stories of families, of life in other lands,
and of adventure on land and sea. They like stories with historical
backgrounds, stories about animals, and the teenage and career
books. They are interested in informative and how-to-do-it books, in
biographies, science, and discovery. Stories about school and about
sports have appeal. Students read the classics, both juvenile and
adult. They read mysteries, science fiction, poetry, and comic books.
Since they do read comics, it is well to note Arbuthnot's (1947)
opinion: "There is probably little cause to worry about children and
their comic strips as long as they are also enjoying good books."

Recently public librarians have observed some trends suggestive of
interest changes. Career books have dropped from eighth-grade to
sixth-grade level in popularity, while teen-age girls are increasingly
demanding books about the ballet and about ways in which to de

velop personality and popularity. Science fiction has also moved from junior high school level to the elementary school, where both boys and girls read it. The demand for biography has increased, with emphasis upon the lives of living persons. There is considerable increase in requests for informative books. It has been suggested that television is largely responsible for these changes. Librarians have noted that television stimulates areas of interest among young people on the one hand, while on the other hand the vast publishing industry turns out more and more books to meet this interest demand. These new books, in turn, provide television with additional subject matter. A dynamic interrelationship exists between the various media of mass communication, each stimulating the other.

SEX DIFFERENCES AND READING INTERESTS

At adolescence, differences in reading interests of boys and of girls sharpen. Norvell (1950, p. 46) has pointed out that the influence of sex differences upon selection of reading material is a dominant and highly significant factor. Girls read more than boys, but their interests are more homogeneous; boys cover a wider range of subjects and read more nonfiction than do girls.

Girls read boys' books, but boys do not like girls' books. Boys like biography and history, inventions and mechanics, adventure stories, and tales of athletic prowess. Girls read stories of home and school life, with *Little Women* reaching its height of popularity. Girls read adventure stories, too, but prefer them to be of the mild variety rather than the grim and desperate type which engross boys. Both sexes read biography, girls preferring the life-stories of women, although they read about men. Boys will not read biographies about women if they can avoid it.

About 90 per cent of the reading of both sexes is fiction. Of this, boys prefer outdoor adventures, mystery and detective stories, stories about sports and about animals, especially wild animals. They enjoy comic books, the boys' series, tales of war and patriotism, and those of humorous incident. They turn to adult fiction about a year later than girls, usually to the adult adventure story. In nonfiction, boys read over a wide range: biography, history, science, travel, and sports.

Girls also read mystery and detective stories, comic books, adventure and animal stories. The adventures, however, are mild, and the animals are pets or domestic animals. They read the girls' series, stories or home and family life, and romance. They read adult fiction

earlier than boys, generally turning to adult romance. Much of it
is likely to be sentimental trash. So heavily do girls read in this area
that, unless they have some guidance, they are in danger of developing a persistent habit of inconsequential reading. Girls read and like
drama and poetry much more frequently than do boys. Their
narrower range of nonfiction tends to be confined to biography, some
history, and subjects related to feminine interests.

INFLUENCE OF INTELLIGENCE ON
READING INTERESTS

A third factor having some influence upon reading interests is
intelligence. Exceptionally bright children read an average of three
or four times as many books as do children of average intelligence,
and the bright children generally read books of better quality. The
socioeconomic status of bright children is usually high and may
influence the amount of reading done. Lazar (1937, p. 101) found
that bright children from homes of lower socioeconomic status read
a great deal but that the quality tends to be less satisfactory.

Girls read more than boys, bright children more than average
children, average children more than dull children, while dull girls
read more than dull boys. Dull children tend to choose simpler and
less realistic materials, while bright children seem to be more interested in the realities of life. Bright and average boys usually read
adventure, history, and science. Slow boys tend to read history,
mysteries, fairy tales, and stories of home and school life. There is
little difference between the reading done by bright, average, and
slow girls, except that the slower girls read more fairy tales and
seem especially interested in useful feminine activities.

In surveying the reading of the bright population in Grades
VII-IX in the Laboratory School, the most interesting observation
about their reading was the catholicity of interest of both boys and
girls. It was as though they were dipping into, and savoring, all
kinds of literature, almost all of it good quality and much of it
classic.

READING AND ENVIRONMENTAL FACTORS

There are also certain environmental factors which determine
reading interests, such as the influence of parents and the recom-

mendations of friends, librarians, or teachers. More reading and a better quality of reading are associated with higher socioeconomic level. They are also correlated with the education of parents and their occupational and leisure-time pursuits, as well as with the amount of value which families accord educational attainments. Availability of books is a factor which librarians stress. Possession of library cards varies with the proximity of libraries. The kind of books available is of utmost importance. It has been found that amount and quality of reading are related to the number and kinds of books, magazines, and newspapers found in the home. A less measurable environmental factor is the early experiences of children with reading. Woellner (1949, p. 117) reported that 91 per cent of the children in her study had enjoyed having books and stories read to them.

We must not fail to take into account, as an environmental factor, the influence of television, mentioned earlier. Josette Frank (1954, p. 19) has this to say about it:

> More young people are growing up with an appreciation of the arts because, through the mass media, more children are exposed to them. . . . Books, newspapers, magazines, television, and radio bring the world into their homes.

INDIVIDUAL PERSONALITY DIFFERENCES

Personality is the last factor considered here, and one of extreme importance. Certain aspects of personality are characteristic of children of junior high school age. Other aspects are highly individual, but all of them operate to determine activities and interests. Children at this age read to satisfy personal curiosity and to satisfy deep needs and wishes. Reading can be a refuge from unpleasant circumstances, a source of companionship, a "ladder to the stars."

Woellner (1949, pp. 73-75) found that the reading attitudes of young people can be classified into three major groups. One is a tendency toward excessive reading, which results from emotional difficulties, with indiscriminate choice or an inadequate balance between purely recreational and purposeful reading. The opposite attitude is avoidance of reading, also rooted in personality problems, with poor reading habits, careless selections, and little progress in critical or creative thinking. Normal interest, the third, is associated with emotional poise, lack of rigidity in intellectual and emotional satisfactions, and versatility in general interests.

It cannot be stressed too heavily that these personality differences must be understood and accepted by the teacher. Each adolescent is still himself, no matter what the generalizations about reading patterns and interests for his age group may be. What, then, are the implications for teachers?

CONCLUDING STATEMENT

It is quite clear that the definite taste for reading characteristic of early adolescence is a guidepost. But if each child is to select the reading materials that will make the most of his personal capacities and interests, the teacher must provide careful guidance. Lack of time will inevitably diminish the quantity of the adolescent's reading. Careful guidance may help him to maintain worthy quality.

Paul Hazard's (1947) *Books, Children and Men* is a must for teachers in whose hands lies this intricate problem of motivating children to read and to like reading. The spirit of such leadership and the theme of Hazard's (1947, p. 4) book are both expressed in these sentences from it:

"Give us books," says the children; "give us wings. You who are powerful and strong, help us to escape into the faraway. . . . We are willing to learn everything that we are taught at school, but, please, let us keep our dreams."

·········· **46** ··········

CHILDREN'S MUSICAL PREFERENCES

by Vincent R. Rogers

The following selection investigates the musical preferences of children in relation to grade level, socioeconomic status, sex, and suburban or rural residence. Two findings are that popular music is preferred at all ages and preference for classical music decreases with age. The report raises an interesting question: To what extent can musical preferences be changed? The author is Vincent R. Rogers of the University of Massachusetts. [From *Elementary School Journal*, 1957,

57, 433–435. Reprinted by permission of the author and The University of Chicago Press.]

In spite of the large body of available knowledge concerning children's developmental interests and abilities in such important areas as reading, children's literature, spelling, arithmetic, and the social studies, there appears to be a need for significant research in the field of music. To help meet this need, the writer conducted an investigation which attempted to answer the following questions: (1) What are the musical preferences of children at succeeding grade levels? (2) What factors are related to these preferences, and what is the extent of these relationships?

Music educators, as a group, are not satisfied with today's programs in school music. They realize that there are many inadequacies both physical and otherwise, and many unsolved problems. It is hoped that this study will enable music educators to consider more scientifically the following problems:

1. Should all children be exposed to fundamentally the same music program, or should the music program be individualized, perhaps as reading is in the modern public school? For example, we know the effects of socioeconomic status on children's reading ability and interests, and we consider this factor in our teaching. The present study will better enable music educators to evaluate the effects of this particular factor on children's musical interests.

2. At what ages are children most open-minded or receptive to *all* kinds of music?

3. Are there certain developmental periods during which children display preferences for one type of music rather than another?

4. Are there differences between the musical preferences of boys and girls at various age levels? If so, are these differences large enough so that they, too, should be considered in our teaching?

METHOD OF THE STUDY

In order to carry out this study, it was necessary to create a test which would measure children's musical preferences. This test would, of course, have to be of reasonably short length (both in terms of total number of items and in terms of number of individual items) and simple enough so that a young child would be able to answer it without having his ability to read or write affect his responses. To meet these qualifications, a paired-comparisons technique was decided upon; that is, each item on the test was paired with every other item, round-robin fashion.

For the purposes of this study, music was divided into four basic categories: (1) seriously classical, (2) popular classical, (3) dinner music, and (4) popular music. Three items were chosen for each category, by members of the faculty of the School of Music at Syracuse University, as being representative of that particular type of music. With twelve individual excerpts (of approximately forty-five seconds each) and with three practice items, the use of the paired-comparisons technique resulted in a fifty-seven-item test requiring about one and one-half hours to administer. These items, along with all the necessary directions, were recorded on tape.

The test was initially given to fifty-one children in Grades I, IV, and VII. Two weeks later, a short form of the test was administered to the same children. The high degree of consistency of response that was found in this test-retest situation indicates that the test is a reasonably reliable instrument.

The final experiment was conducted using a group of 635 pupils in Grades IV, VII, IX, and XII from six different school systems. Approximately 25–30 children were randomly selected at each grade level in each of the six schools. Information was obtained concerning each child's grade, school, sex, and father's occupational status.

The data obtained upon administering the test to the population described above were analyzed in terms of the proportions of items chosen in each category when two categories were compared. For example, when popular music was compared with seriously classical music, the proportion of items chosen for each category was computed, and the significance of the difference between the two proportions was determined.

RESULTS

The musical preferences of children in Grades IV, VII, IX, and XII are reported for the following groups: (1) children at the various grade levels, (2) children from rural schools versus children from suburban schools, (3) children of upper versus lower socioeconomic status, and (4) boys versus girls.

In the first classification it was found that children increased

heir preferences for popular music and dinner music as they grew
)lder. Conversely, their preferences for seriously classical and popu-
ar classical music decreased as they advanced from Grade IV to
XII. By the twelfth-grade level, their preferences for popular music
vere so strong that critical ratios well beyond the .001 level of
ignificance were found.

In the second comparison (rural versus suburban) statistically
ignificant differences indicated that rural children in Grade IV
)referred popular music to a greater degree than did the suburban
:hildren in Grade IV. However, these differences gradually de-
:reased with age, and by Grade XII they had disappeared.

In the third area (upper socioeconomic status versus lower) it was
'ound that both groups preferred the popular music to a greater
legree than they did the classical. However, there was a persistent
lifference between the amount of preference for classical music
lisplayed by both groups. The upper-class group in Grades IV, VII,
and XII preferred classical music to a statistically greater degree
than did the lower-class group.

In the fourth area (boys versus girls) there were no significant
differences between the two groups in Grade IV. However, in Grade
VII the girls preferred popular music to a much greater degree than
did the boys, with critical ratios exceeding the .001 level of significance. This difference was also in evidence at the ninth-grade level.
At the twelfth-grade level, however, there were no statistically significant differences between the preferences of boys and girls.

CONCLUSIONS

1. There is an overwhelming preference for popular music at all
grade levels and by all groups regardless of type of school, sex, or
socioeconomic status.

2. There is a corresponding and sharp decrease in children's
preferences for classical music as they grow older regardless of sex,
type of school, or socioéconomic status.

3. With increased age, children exhibit a tendency to conform
more and more to a single pattern of musical preferences; that is,
there are much greater differences at the fourth-grade level than
there are at the twelfth-grade level, even though the pattern is
similar.

4. Physical maturity is a factor, though indirectly, in determining

musical preferences. It is common knowledge that girls generally mature sexually before boys. This earlier concern for the opposite sex apparently influences the girls' musical preferences, not because they show any innate musical ability (or lack of it), but because the popular music heard by the seventh-grade girls takes on an entirely new social meaning to them.

5. Socioeconomic status is an important factor in children's musical taste. While this factor is not strong enough to break the basic pattern of preferences, it is apparently strong enough to cause a considerable difference in the musical preferences of the children studied in this experiment, as evidenced by the consistently larger number of choices for classical music made by the upper-class group. This is a strong and steady influence which does not lessen even at the twelfth-grade level.

6. Our modern society, with its advanced means of communication, has apparently done away with any differences which might have existed between the musical preferences of rural and suburban school children, at least as far as the population studied here is concerned.

CONCLUDING REMARKS

Music educators are faced with a tremendous task if we accept the idea that "open-mindedness" toward music is good; that is, that children ought to enjoy listening to many kinds of music and ought to value serious music to the same degree as they do popular music. It would seem that music programs in the schools ought to be revamped so that children may be exposed to all kinds of music at the earliest possible time, thus counteracting the rather one-sided influence of our mass media of communication.

Educators have done a great deal of influential work in showing parents the importance of home environment as related to success in reading. They have helped parents to locate the best in children's literature, for example, and have attempted to convey the idea that, in a home barren of books, it is sometimes wishful thinking to expect one's children to become avid readers. The same technique might well be employed by music educators if we hope to develop in children real and lasting appreciation for all kinds of music.

.... *47* ....

CHILDREN AND TV—A NINTH REPORT

by Paul Witty and Paul Kinsella

What is the relationship of televiewing to school grades and reading habits? To what extent do teachers associate behavior and adjustment problems with TV? These are some of the questions that Paul Witty of Northwestern University and Paul Kinsella of the Skokie, Illinois, public schools attempt to answer in the following article. [From *Elementary English*, 1958, *35*, 450-456. Reprinted by permission of the authors and the National Council of Teachers of English.]

The almost universal interest in TV in America is one of the most phenomenal developments of modern times. A number of surveys made throughout the past decade have revealed the persistent popularity of TV. As early as 1949, Thomas E. Coffin (1949) reported that the average amount of time children devoted each week to TV was more than 24 hours. Among junior and senior high school pupils, surveys showed large amounts of televiewing, too. In 1950, a study by Gertrude Young (1950) disclosed a range of 1½ hours to 5½ hours given daily to TV by junior high school pupils. One writer compared the time spent televiewing with that required by the entire school curriculum. The school schedule occupied 27 hours and 55 minutes each week; the average time spent weekly in televiewing by pupils in homes having TV sets was 27 hours! (Gould, 1950.)

REACTION OF PARENTS AND TEACHERS TO TV

Parents and teachers were quick to react to TV. To some TV seemed to be a great menace. "TV is converting our children into a race of spectators," said one parent. "Life should be lived not watched," remarked another. And a discouraged teacher wrote: "Competing with TV for the attention of children is impossible." However, some parents and teachers found TV to be desirable and

stressed its value in extending children's experience and in culti
vating their interests. Nevertheless, the adverse effects of excessive
televiewing were repeatedly set forth in magazine and newspaper
accounts which appeared about mid-century.

One of the most widely quoted surveys utilized a team of research
workers who "monitored" all the TV programs presented by New
York City's seven stations during one week in January, 1951. It
was found that children's programs represented only about 12 per
cent (70) of the 564 hours of presentations. However, almost half
of the children's programs were westerns, thrillers, or animated
cartoons. During the entire week, only 3 hours could be identified
that were informative or instructive. One station alone included
programs for pre-school children.

The results of such studies were viewed by many people as an
indictment of TV. Yet even the most severe critics acknowledged
the strong appeal of TV to children. And others saw great potentialities for worthwhile recreation and education in this popular
new medium of mass communication.

It is almost ten years since TV made its advent and captivated
the children in the Chicago area. It is possible now to see some of
the effects of TV through comparison of the results of studies made
throughout the past decade.

In this paper, the writers will present the ninth in a series of
studies which began in 1950. They will also compare some results
of the latest study with those of earlier investigations.

RESULTS OF STUDIES MADE IN THE
CHICAGO AREA

This series of studies aimed to disclose the amount of time devoted
to TV and the programs preferred by elementary and secondary
school pupils, their parents, and their teachers. Questionnaires and
interviews were used to obtain data about televiewing. Additional
information was sought which related to children's grades in school,
the nature and amount of their reading, their educational attainment, and their conduct and behavior. The first and second studies
were made during 1950 and 1951, and were summarized in *Elementary English*, May, 1952. The third study, conducted during April
and May, 1952 was published in *Elementary English*, December,
1952. Subsequent studies appeared in *Elementary English* during
each of the following years.

In 1958 our studies were made in the Evanston Public Schools and in the Skokie, Illinois Schools. In this latest study, there were about 2800 pupils distributed throughout grades 1 to 12. Inquiries were directed to children and to their parents and teachers.

AMOUNT OF TELEVIEWING

TV came to the Chicago area in 1949. By the spring of 1950, 43 per cent of the pupils had TV sets. In 1951, 68 per cent reported sets at home; in 1952, 88 per cent; in 1955, 97 per cent. In 1958, the average was also 97 per cent.

In 1950, the children said that they devoted on the average 21 hours per week to TV. This figure dropped to 19 in 1951, but it went up again after new channels made more diverse programs available. In 1955, the average was 24 hours, and in 1957, 22 hours. For 1958 the average was 20 hours per week.

High school students in Evanston, as in earlier studies, were found to devote less time than elementary school pupils to TV. The average in 1957, as shown in Table 1, was 12 hours per week and in 1958, it was 13. Less time is given to TV in the summer than during the other seasons. According to our studies, the drop in televiewing during the summer months is about 20 to 25 per cent in total time per week. This drop has occurred rather consistently from year to year.

TABLE 1

AVERAGE HOURS SPENT WEEKLY WITH TELEVISION

	1951	1953	1955	1957	1958
Elementary School Pupils	19	23	24	22	20
High School Pupils	14	17	14	12	13
Parents	20	19	21	20	19
Teachers	9	12	12	12	12

THE FAVORITE PROGRAMS

Of course, favorite programs change, and year by year new offerings become popular. In 1950, the children's favorites were (in order): *Hopalong Cassidy, Howdy Doody, Lone Ranger, Milton Berle, Arthur Godfrey,* and *Small Fry.* In 1952, *I Love Lucy* became

TABLE 2

TEN FAVORITE TV PROGRAMS - 1958
EVANSTON AND SKOKIE TOTALS
(ELEMENTARY SCHOOLS)

1. Zorro
2. Disneyland
3. Bugs Bunny
4. Shock Theatre
5. Mickey Mouse Club
6. Blue Fairy
7. Father Knows Best
8. Lassie
9. Maverick
10. Susie

the best-liked program of both boys and girls and *My Friend Irma* and *Roy Rogers* were also very popular.

I Love Lucy continued in first place until 1955, when acclaim went to *Disneyland. Rin-Tin-Tin* and *Lassie* were also extremely well-liked. In 1956, *Disneyland* again held first rank, with *I Love Lucy*, third. In 1957, the children expressed these preferences: *Disneyland, Mickey Mouse Club, I Love Lucy*, and *Lassie*.

The ten most popular programs of the children in 1958 are given in Table 2. The exciting presentation *Zorro* has attained first place and has replaced *Disneyland*, which had been given top ranking during the preceding three years. *Disneyland* is in second place, with third and fourth ranks given to *Bugs Bunny* and *Shock Theatre*. Fifth and sixth rankings went in 1958 to *Mickey Mouse Club* and *Blue Fairy*.

The foregoing list includes children's responses for grades 1-6:

TABLE 3

TEN FAVORITE TV PROGRAMS - 1958

Grades 1-3	Grades 4-6
1. Zorro	1. Zorro
2. Bugs Bunny	2. Shock Theatre
3. Mickey Mouse	3. Father Knows Best
4. Blue Fairy	4. Disneyland
5. Disneyland	5. Maverick
6. Lassie	6. Dick Clark
7. Susie	7. Colt 45
8. Shirley Temple	8. American Bandstand
9. Superman	9. Cheyenne
10. Mighty Mouse	10. Leave it to Beaver

TABLE 4

TEN FAVORITE TV PROGRAMS · 1958
JUNIOR HIGH SCHOOL · SKOKIE

1. American Bandstand
2. Shock Theatre
3. Dick Clark Show
4. Maverick
5. Gunsmoke
6. Father Knows Best
7. Playhouse 90
8. Steve Allen
9. Ozzie and Harriet
10. Have Gun · Will Travel

When the group is divided into primary and intermediate levels, some noticeable differences appear. Comparison of the two lists in Table 3 reveals that *Zorro* is the number one choice in both groups and that *Shock Theatre* has great appeal in the middle grades. *Bugs Bunny* and *Mickey Mouse Club* are of course favorites with the younger group.

The following programs listed in Table 4 proved the favorites of pupils in grades 7 and 8: *American Bandstand, Shock Theatre, Dick Clark Show, Maverick,* and *Gunsmoke.* It will be observed that *Maverick, Shock Theatre,* and *Father Knows Best,* popular in the elementary grades, continue to be well liked at this level. Differences between the choices of the boys and the girls may be noted in Table 5.

Table 6 presents the ten favorites of high school students in 1958. *Steve Allen,* given first place in 1957 has been assigned to

TABLE 5

TEN FAVORITE TV PROGRAMS · 1958
JUNIOR HIGH SCHOOL · SKOKIE

Girls	Boys
1. American Bandstand	1. Shock Theatre
2. Dick Clark Show	2. Maverick
3. Father Knows Best	3. Gunsmoke
4. Shock Theatre	4. Zorro
5. Playhouse 90	5. American Bandstand
6. Maverick	6. Dick Clark Show
7. Ozzie and Harriet	7. Have Gun · Will Travel
8. Dinah Shore Show	8. Sports
9. Movies	9. West Point Story
10. Steve Allen	10. Sgt. Bilko

TABLE 6

TEN FAVORITE TV PROGRAMS - 1958
EVANSTON TOWNSHIP HIGH SCHOOL (9-12 GRADES)

1. Maverick
2. Gunsmoke
3. Steve Allen
4. Shock Theatre
5. Father Knows Best
6. Playhouse 90
7. Perry Como
8. American Bandstand
9. Dick Clark Show
10. Meet McGraw

third place. In first and second place are *Maverick* and *Gunsmoke*, while *Shock Theatre* is fourth. *Shock Theatre, Father Knows Best,* and *Maverick* were among the ten favorites of the elementary as well as the secondary school pupils.

The parents studied from year to year have averaged approximately 20 hours per week televiewing. When TV was new, their average was one hour more than now. The group studied in 1958 reported 19 hours each week as the average. The favorite programs of 1958 differ somewhat from those of previous years. High in popularity are the following: *Playhouse 90, Father Knows Best, Perry Como,* and *Dinah Shore.* These programs are cited among the ten favorites given in Table 7. The most notable change from 1957 is the omission of *I Love Lucy* in this year's list of favorites.

Only 25 per cent of the teachers had TV sets in 1950. An increase in TV ownership gradually raised the percentage until in 1958 it was

TABLE 7

TEN FAVORITE TV PROGRAMS - 1958
PARENTS (COMBINED LIST)

1. Playhouse 90
2. Father Knows Best
3. Perry Como
4. Dinah Shore
5. Lawrence Welk
6. Sports
7. Movies
8. Omnibus
9. What's My Line?
10. Person to Person

TABLE 8

TEN FAVORITE TV PROGRAMS - 1958
TEACHERS - COMBINED

1. Playhouse 90
2. Bold Journey
3. Perry Como
4. News
5. Wide Wide World
6. Person to Person
7. Lawrence Welk
8. What's My Line?
9. Omnibus
10. Climax

96. *What's My Line?* appeared as the first choice in 1951 and continued as a favorite in 1952, 1953, and 1954. The teachers showed less enthusiasm for *I Love Lucy* than did their pupils and the parents during the years 1952-1957. In 1956, the *$64,000 Question* shared first place with *What's My Line?* while Lawrence Welk was the most popular program in 1957. The ten programs favored by the teachers in 1958 are found in Table 8. These include: *Playhouse 90, Bold Journey, Perry Como, News,* and *Wide Wide World.*

PROBLEMS IN ADJUSTMENT AND BEHAVIOR

In the earlier studies, large numbers of parents and teachers reported behavior problems associated with TV. Cited were such items as: increased nervousness in children, impoverishment of play, disinterest in school, and eye strain. As the years have gone by, the frequencies of such reports have decreased.

Some parents and teachers too have pointed out that the TV offerings this year have included an unfortunate high frequency of westerns and other over-exciting presentations featuring violence and crime. However, both groups mention certain types of programs that they believe have distinct merit for children. In Table 9 the desirable children's programs suggested by the parents are set forth.

Despite the unfortunate characteristics of some programs, the teachers are reluctant to regard TV as the primary source of children's misdemeanors and undesirable conduct. Some of them have studied carefully, with special reference to TV, those children in their classes who display serious problem behavior. In every case of serious maladjustment, they have found that other factors, such as an unfavorable environment, seem to contribute to the child's undesirable conduct or behavior. But these teachers and many parents too, stressed their feeling that too many crime and western programs are being presented; and they deplored the type of movies that children now see so frequently on TV.

Among the kinds of programs teachers would like to see more often, a preference was displayed for more opera, travelogues, great plays, good music, news and science programs. The parents' desires were very similar in that they also wanted more travelogues, plays, science, and good music. The parents stated a desire too for more family situation programs. The children seemed to echo their fav-

TABLE 9

DESIRABLE PROGRAMS FOR CHILDREN
SUGGESTED BY PARENTS IN 1958

Program	Type
Mickey Mouse Club	Combination
Disneyland	Variety - Animated
Lassie	Animal
Captain Kangaroo	Variety - children
Mr. Wizard	Science
Ding Dong School	Pre-school
Blue Fairy	Fantasy
Shirley Temple	Fairy Tales
Father Knows Best	Family situation
Leave it to Beaver	Family situation

orite programs in asking specifically for more *Disneyland, Zorro,* and *Lassie.*

In various reports of favorite children's programs made over the past nine years, one may note high frequency of westerns and other offerings which feature crime and violence. Despite protests from parents and teachers, producers have continued to make very large numbers of such pictures for use on TV. In 1954, *The National Association for Better Radio and Television* stated that programs featuring crime and violence had increased 400 per cent during the preceding three years. In a sixty hour study, 26 hours of programming were found to be "objectionable." And five shows were classified as "most objectionable."

In 1955, the Association reported some improvement traceable to (1) "the steadily declining audiences for crime shows and (2) the availability of programs with positive values." The association has continued to emphasize the undesirability of many westerns, crime presentations, and other presentations. In 1957, the Association noted "the rapidly increasing number of crime-westerns being broadcast when children are listening."

Because of the great variation in TV offerings as well as the questionable nature of some presentations, it is clear that parent and school guidance are needed if children are to learn to make the most of TV and to choose programs with discrimination. Moreover, children should be encouraged to develop balanced and individually suitable patterns of leisure activity. These patterns should include not only TV but also outdoor play, desirable group pursuits, and reading and study activities.

TELEVIEWING, GRADES IN SCHOOL, AND READING

There are some conflicting reports published from time to time concerning the relationship of televiewing to grades in school. Our studies have rather consistently shown little relationship between the amount of televiewing and the school grades received by boys and girls.

Similarly, there has been much speculation about the relationship of televiewing to reading. From a number of sources, it seems evident that children today are reading a little more than they did a decade ago. This is shown by reports of librarians and teachers as well as by the pupils' own statements. Of course many children can not remember a time when they did not have access to TV. But of those who now can recall pre-TV days, 45 per cent stated that they read more, 26 per cent about the same, and 29 per cent less.

From these and other investigations, it appears that children are reading somewhat more at the present time than before TV came to their homes. There are of course some who read less now; these children are considered a real problem by their parents and teachers, who often look on TV as a threat to reading.

The threat of TV to reading can be met in part by constructive efforts of teachers. Seventy-nine per cent of the children in the Evanston study report that teachers are offering them guidance and valuable suggestions for televiewing. These teachers are encouraging their pupils to note new words heard on TV and to select presentations related to school work. They are guiding them also to books associated with TV programs, and are encouraging boys and girls to seek out excellent programs in science, current events, and world affairs. As a result, many children are deriving benefits from TV. The acquisitions of such pupils offer a glimpse of what TV at its best can mean to children and youth especially when individual guidance and encouragement are given. TV presents some problems, it is true, but it also offers unparalleled opportunities to promote the educational and avocational interests of boys and girls.

There seems to be among some parents a curious mistrust of their own ability to deal with the problems created by television. They observe with apprehension the appeal TV has for children, but sometimes question the effectiveness of their efforts to provide guidance. The inescapable conclusion seems to be that television is a real problem or liability largely in homes where it is permitted to become one. And, it is proving an asset in many homes in which parents are planning varied ways in which TV can be used to yield greater benefits and satisfactions. Employing methods similar to those utilized by teachers, parents are increasingly guiding the televiewing of children and are suggesting programs for them to see and relate to constructive endeavor. Some parents are using to advantage interests engendered by televiewing to promote reading. As a result, more and more children are deriving benefits from televiewing. But it should be pointed out too that many programs are inferior and that relatively few are available which can be used to stimulate worthwhile educational effort. Accordingly, parents, teachers, and commercial agencies should work together to develop more desirable and provocative offerings for children. The widespread appeal of TV provides an unparalleled opportunity for influencing children in positive ways. To do this, programs must be planned and developed through cooperative efforts of capable and interested adults.

48

CLOTHING AND APPEARANCE

by Sylvia S. Silverman

The attention adolescent girls give to their appearance—their choice of clothes and use of cosmetics—are subjects much discussed by adolescents and adults. What are the clothing and grooming practices of adolescent girls? What motivates them in their choice of clothing and in their attention to their appearance? How do these practices relate to the age of the girl, her economic level, her personality? Sylvia S. Silverman, a psychologist, sought answers to these questions in her study of teen-age girls, the results of which are presented in the following selection. [From *Clothing and Appearance: Their Psychological Implications for Teen-Age Girls*, New York: Bureau of Publications, Teachers College, Columbia University, 1945, pp. 114-119. Reprinted by permission of the Bureau of Publications, Teachers College, Columbia University.]

The purpose of this study was to gain insight into the clothing and grooming behavior of adolescent girls, an area which a review of related literature revealed to be one of major importance to girls during this life period but of relatively minor interest to researchers in the field of psychology.

THE PROBLEMS AND FINDINGS

Four problems seeking factual information as well as relationships were studied. These problems are stated below together with the major finding for each.

1. The first problem was concerned with girls' actual clothing and grooming behavior: their use of cosmetics, choices of clothing, preferences in jewelry. A distinction was made between the choices and practices for daily use or wear and those for week-end use to determine whether differences were apparent for the two situations. Three hundred seventy-three girls, ranging in age from 12 through 18 in grades 7 through 12 of a suburban six-year high school, responded to the questionnaire drawn up to study these choices. The data were treated with respect to age differences and significant trends with age were sought. The findings revealed the following:

a. Close conformity in the style of dress for daily wear was prevalent not only within the age groups but among the groups, girls at 12 and at all ages through 18 tending to dress in like fashion. Differences in dress among the age groups were evident in their week-end apparel, when the older girls were wearing higher heeled shoes, stockings instead of socks, and dresses rather than sweaters and skirts. Older girls also tended to wear fewer items of underwear, eliminating bulky underclothes and wearing foundation garments instead.

b. The girls did not tend to go in for heavy use of make-up although certain items were used almost universally. Age difference rather than conformity to a pattern was the dominating factor in the use of cosmetics. The use of lipstick, powder, and rouge tended to increase with age, the first two items being used even at age 12. There was also an increase in the use of most cosmetics for week-end occasions over daily wear, 38 per cent of the 12-year-olds using powder and lipstick, and the use of these items increasing to 94 per cent or more for girls aged 16 and over. Hand care appeared to play an important part in grooming practice, a considerable proportion of the group using hand lotion and nail polish. Eyes seemed to receive least attention, the use of eye cosmetics being negligible for daily use and relatively low for week ends. Items designed to heighten natural color were used to a greater extent than those meant for skin care.

c. Regular beauty parlor attendance was not considered part of the group's grooming needs at any age. Only 7 per cent of the total group went to a beauty parlor regularly, although 74 per cent went in preparation for some special event.

d. No item of jewelry reached the same degree of popularity for self-decoration as that achieved by several types of cosmetics. For the group as a whole, no single item of jewelry was worn by more than two-thirds of its members. Purely decorative items, such as rings, bracelets, and necklaces, tended to be more popular than tokens of membership or allegiance, such as club pins, school keys, and patriotic emblems.

2. Motivating factors influencing girls' choices of clothing and their attention to appearance constituted the second problem. Girls' interest in, their preference for, and their attitudes toward clothing, the psychological satisfactions they seek through their clothing and appearance, and the values they associate with them, their judgments concerning clothing, and their relationships to their mothers in this respect, were studied with reference to the changes apparent as the girls grew older. A supplementary question was attached to the questionnaire inquiring into the problems girls encounter in relation to their clothing and appearance, and asking them to cite questions on which they would like help. The findings are based on the responses of the same group referred to in Problem 1.

a. The desire for approval, the internal satisfactions of feelings of poise, self-confidence, and happiness, and the belief in advantages in vocational and social areas to be achieved from good clothing and an attractive appearance were found to be factors operating in the motivation of clothing choices and attention to appearance for the major portion of members of the 12- and 13-year-old groups, and throughout the total group with relatively slight differences for age.

b. The desire for sexual attractiveness was found to be a motivating factor in attention to dress and appearance at all ages, including ages 12 and 13.

c. The desire for modesty was not an underlying motive in girls' clothing choices, but was specifically related to the current fashion values of the particular article of clothing. Immodesty was condoned where the article had high fashion value and disapproved in out-of-date styles.

d. The liking for bright colors and effects in dress was rather high among girls in their early teens but tended to decrease as the girls grew older.

e. The group tended to be inconsistent rather than slavish in its attempt to keep in step with incoming or waning fads.

f. Older girls tended to be more affected in their social relationships by their clothing and to attach more importance to appearance as a factor in social selection than younger girls.

g. Other changes in response with age tended to come largely in the desire for greater independence in the choice of clothing, less dependence on the mothers, and the desire for an allowance and for more clothes.

h. Of the total group 92 per cent were opposed to the wearing of a school uniform, indicating a desire for individuality in dress.

i. For the most part, younger girls tended to exhibit as much interest in clothing and appearance as did older girls.

j. As a group, the girls tended to agree with their mothers concerning the suitability and choice of their clothing, but many felt their mothers were overcritical of the girls' attention to their appearance.

k. The problems with which girls wished help were oriented largely from the point of view of individual self-expression and self-improvement. The chief problems cited related to suitability to age and adaptation of style. Budgeting, clothing construction, and clothing care, problems which comprise the curriculum of most clothing courses, were given little attention by the girls.

3. The third problem considered the influence of the economic factor in relation to clothing and grooming behavior, to determine whether there were different modes of dress or grooming in cases where the economic differences were broad. A questionnaire designed to measure economic status was devised, and the extreme groups on the resulting economic scale were compared for differences in their choices and practices.

The economic factor was found to be of relatively slight importance in the choice of most clothing items and in grooming practices. Aside from a few luxury items, such as wrist watches, silk dresses, and fur-trimmed coats (the last two for week-end wear), which were more prevalent in the upper economic group, the two groups tended to wear most types of clothing and use most cosmetics to the same extent. The girls, therefore, seemed to be more affected by their desire to conform to group modes of behavior than by the availability or lack of funds.

4. The major problem was concerned with the study of the relationship between care of appearance and aspects of personality, to determine whether care of appearance was a form of behavior reflecting internal emotional states or feelings. A group ranking highest on appearance and a group ranking lowest on appearance were established on the basis of teachers' ratings of the 170 girls in the 11th and 12th grades in the same school situation on six components of appearance, chosen to indicate care and attention to clothing and grooming rather than physical beauty. The two groups were then compared for differences in personality characteristics as demonstrated by their responses to the Sheviakov and Friedberg

(1939) "Interests and Activities" scales. Differences for the two groups were also sought in relation to intelligence, age, economic status, participation in school activities, and prominence as leaders. Six case studies were made to investigate the meaning and significance of clothing and appearance for three girls in each of the two appearance groups.

a. As compared with the good-appearing group, the poor-appearing group tended to show a greater dislike for companionship with other girls, for boy-girl relationships, and for social contacts in group activities both at school and in the community. They also tended to dislike being in situations which gave them prominence in the group. On the whole they tended to be negativistic in their responses, to dislike giving free play to their imaginative powers, and to show a relatively smaller capacity for establishing friendships. They also gave indications of lack of self-love and of feelings of self-effacement.

b. The group rated high in appearance tended to place a higher value on activities involving their own sex, to like activities including the companionship of boys, and to enjoy the clubs and committee work that make up the social aspect of school life.

c. Good-appearing girls tended to be brighter than poor-appearing girls. The two groups were almost identical with respect to age.

d. Good-appearing girls tended to have a slightly higher economic background, but the correlation between appearance and economic standing was so slight (.103) as to be almost negligible.

e. Good-appearing girls tended to participate to a greater degree in school activities, such as clubs, sports, and dramatic presentations, and to be sought as leaders more frequently than poor-appearing girls.

f. Study of the individual case histories bore out some of the findings of the group study and gave indication that behavior with regard to care of appearance was purposive and rooted in the girl's life story. Appearance behavior seemed to serve as a means of expressing psychological mechanisms, such as compensation, identification, and attention-getting. There was also evidence to suggest that appearance was used as a means of impressing others, of winning favor with them, or as a weapon against them. In the cases studied the girls rated as giving much attention to appearance seemed to have a higher estimate of themselves than the girls who were rated low in appearance. In each instance appearance behavior gave indications of having significance as a means of meeting the girls' needs or as a way of working out some conflict.

CHAPTER SIXTEEN

Religious Beliefs

49

AGE DIFFERENCES IN RELIGIOUS BELIEFS
AND PROBLEMS DURING ADOLESCENCE

by Raymond G. Kuhlen and Martha Arnold

It is believed by some that adolescence is a period of generally increased religious doubts and problems. This is not substantiated in the following article by Raymond G. Kuhlen of Syracuse University, and his collaborator, who made a study of sixth-, ninth-, and twelfth-grade pupils to discover the relationship between age and religious beliefs and problems. [From *Journal of Genetic Psychology*, 1944, 65, 291-300. Reprinted by permission of the authors and of The Journal Press.]

Problems in the realm of values, philosophy of life, and religion have long been considered a major area of adjustment confronting adolescents. Marked changes in religious views are assumed to occur and many crucial problems to arise. At the college level it has been fairly well demonstrated that, on the average, profound change does not occur. That seniors are only slightly more liberal in outlook than freshman has been demonstrated in studies by Katz and Allport (1931), Dudycha (1933), and others. However, adequate evidence indicating age differences in beliefs held and problems faced during the adolescent period is not available for ages below college. Dimock (1936; 1937, p. 168) who has reported one study of younger adolescents, concludes that his data reveal "the relatively static nature of religious ideas of the adolescent during the four-year period (12–16) encompassed by this study," thus apparently contradicting popular opinion. It is probable, however, that the type of analysis followed by Dimock in his research has obscured a number of trends, and his data can hardly be accepted as evidence demonstrating religious ideas not to change during adolescence. Franzblau (1934) has shown that beliefs of Jewish adolescents become more liberal with increased age, and MacLean (1930) has presented data indicating the percentage of children of adolescent years who hold certain specific beliefs.

The research summarized in the present paper was an attempt to explore the nature of religious beliefs held during the adolescent period, and to test by at least one type of evidence the hypothesis that adolescence is a period of increasing religious problems. It differs from other investigations in that the results have been analyzed both with respect to specific problems faced and beliefs held, and with respect to relative age periods during adolescence, thus providing an age perspective in which to view such specific changes as might occur.

PROCEDURE

A questionnaire was prepared which listed 52 statements representing various religious beliefs (sample statements are contained in Table 2) which were to be marked according to whether the subject "believed" the statement, did "not believe" the statement, or did not know whether he believed it or not but had "wondered about" it. A second part of the questionnaire listed 18 problems of a religious sort taken from the Problem Check List (Junior and Senior High School Forms) prepared by Dr. Ross Mooney of the Ohio State University, with directions asking the subject to circle an "N," an "S," or an "O" depending upon whether he felt that a particular problem troubled or bothered him "never," "sometimes," or "often."

Responses from 547 sixth, ninth, and twelfth graders were obtained. The exact number of subjects and the mean age of each grade group are contained in Table 1. The significance of the use of these three grade groups in the study of adolescence lies in the fact that the sixth-grade group is largely prepubescent, the ninth-grade group pubescent (at least for boys; girls mature somewhat earlier), and twelfth-grade group post-pubescent. The sampling of these three phases of development during the age range in which adolescence normally occurs should be sufficient to provide evidence of any marked trend occurring during this period. During the discussion to follow, these groups will be referred to as 12-, 15-, and 18-year-olds. As might be expected, the groups were quite heterogeneous with respect to church membership. Among the 12-, 15-, and 18-year-old groups respectively there were 19, 33, and 10 Catholic boys and 26, 19, and 18 Catholic girls. The rest were scattered among Protestant denominations, with an occasional child of Jewish faith, or who indicated no church attendance.

TABLE 1

NUMBER OF CASES, MEAN AGE, AND STANDARD DEVIATION IN YEARS OF
GROUPS STUDIED

		Boys			Girls		Total
Grade	N	Mn. Age	SD	N	Mn. Age	SD	No.
6	80	12.4	1.2	94	12.0	0.9	174
9	128	15.2	1.0	115	14.9	1.0	243
12	49	18.1	0.8	81	17.8	1.0	130

CHANGES IN RELIGIOUS BELIEFS

The findings were analyzed first by ascertaining what proportion of each age group checked each statement indicating belief, disbelief, or uncertainty regarding that statement. Certain results of this analysis are summarized in Table 2. An examination of these findings indicates clearly that a number of rather significant changes have occurred. First to be noted is the fairly marked discarding of such beliefs as "Every word in the Bible is true," "It is sinful to doubt the Bible," "God is someone who watches you to see that you behave yourself, and who punishes you if you are not good." Roughly two-thirds (close to 70 per cent) of the 12-year-olds believed these statements to be true; only a third or less of the 18-year-olds would agree. Other statements which were notably less frequently believed by 18- than 12-year-olds are "Only good people go to heaven," "Hell is a place where you are punished for your sins on earth," and "Prayers are to make up for something wrong you have done." Thus many rather specific beliefs taught to, or picked up by, young children are no longer held by most of those in the late teens.

Second, a greater tolerance with respect to religious beliefs and practices is apparent with development into adolescence. Thus

more 18- than 12-year-olds agree that "Catholics, Jews, and Protestants are equally good," that "It is not necessary to attend church
to be a Christian." Fewer 18- than 12-year-olds believe that "People
who go to church are better than people who do not go to church,"
that "Young people should belong to the same church as their
parents," and that "Good people say prayers regularly."

TABLE 2

CHANGES IN SPECIFIC RELIGIOUS BELIEFS DURING ADOLESCENCE AS SHOWN BY
THE PERCENTAGE OF 12-, 15-, AND 18-YEAR-OLD CHILDREN WHO CHECKED
VARIOUS STATEMENTS INDICATING (a) BELIEF, (b) DISBELIEF,
OR (c) UNCERTAINTY (WONDER)*

Statement	"Believe" 12	15	18	"Not Believe" 12	15	18	"Wonder About" 12	15	18
God is a strange power working for good, rather than a person.	46	49	57	31	33	21	20	14	15
God is someone who watches you to see that you behave yourself, and who punishes you if you are not good.	70	49	33	18	37	48	11	13	18
I know there is a God.	94	80	79	3	5	2	2	14	16
Catholics, Jews and Protestants are equally good.	67	79	86	9	9	7	24	11	7
There is a heaven.	82	78	74	4	5	5	13	16	20
Only good people go to heaven.	72	45	33	15	27	32	13	27	34
Hell is a place where you are punished for yours sins on earth.	70	49	35	16	21	30	13	27	34
Heaven is here on earth.	12	13	14	69	57	52	18	28	32
People who go to church are better than people who do not go to church.	46	26	15	37	53	74	17	21	11
Young people should belong to the same church as their parents.	77	56	43	13	33	46	10	11	11
The main reason for going to church is to worship God.	88	80	79	6	12	15	4	7	6

* Discrepancies between the totals of "Believe," "Not Believe," and "Wonder
About," and 100 per cent represent the percentages who did not respond to the
statements. Differences of 8 or 9 will ordinarily yield a *CR* of 2.0, depending upon
the magnitude of the percentages involved.

CHANGES IN SPECIFIC RELIGIOUS BELIEFS DURING ADOLESCENCE AS SHOWN BY
THE PERCENTAGE OF 12-, 15-, AND 18-YEAR-OLD CHILDREN WHO CHECKED
VARIOUS STATEMENTS INDICATING (a) BELIEF, (b) DISBELIEF,
OR (c) UNCERTAINTY (WONDER)—Continued

Statement	"Believe"			"Not Believe"			"Wonder About"		
	12	15	18	12	15	18	12	15	18
It is not necessary to attend church to be a Christian.	42	62	67	38	23	24	18	15	8
Only our soul lives after death.	72	63	61	9	11	6	18	25	31
Good people say prayers regularly.	78	57	47	9	29	26	13	13	27
Prayers are answered.	76	69	65	3	5	8	21	25	27
Prayers are a source of help in times of trouble.	74	80	83	11	8	7	15	10	9
Prayers are to make up for something that you have done that is wrong.	47	24	21	35	58	69	18	17	9
Every word in the Bible is true.	79	51	34	6	16	23	15	31	43
It is sinful to doubt the Bible.	62	42	27	18	31	44	20	26	28

Third, it will be noted that drops in the proportion "believing"
a statement are not necessarily compensated for by increases in
the proportion "not believing" that statement. With respect to certain beliefs, at least, the issues are far from settled even by 18
years of age. More of the 18-year-old group, for example, "wonder about' the statement "Every word in the Bible is true," than
who agree with the statement or who disbelieve it. In the case of 12
of the 19 statements contained in Table 2, there is a trend toward
increased "wondering." Such is true of beliefs involving the hereafter (death, heaven, and hell), certain concepts of God, certain
beliefs with respect to prayer and belief in the Bible.

It is evident from these data that the religious views of adolescents in the late teens differ from those of 12-year-old children in a
number of very significant ways. In fact, of the 52 statements included in this study, changes were great enough in 36 statements to
be two or more times their standard errors. It would have been desirable to study age changes for particular groups, especially Catholic and non-Catholic, but there were too few cases in any particular
category to make such analysis significant. That even the 18-year-old
group have not yet reached a satisfactory religious philosophy is
suggested by the amount of uncertainty that exists with respect to

various beliefs and concepts. However, it must be admitted that many a person with a "satisfactory" set of religious beliefs would check "wonder about" when asked to react in one of three stated ways to statements such as those of this study.

RELIGIOUS DOUBTS AND PROBLEMS

It might be expected in view of the data thus far presented that there would be a general increase during development in adolescence in the proportion of statements "wondered about" and probably also in the number of problems faced. Both expectations are in line with the beliefs apparently held by many writers in the field of adolescent psychology. Two lines of evidences are presented regarding this question. First a "wonder score" was obtained for each subject by counting the number of items he checked as "wondering about." Second, a "problem score" was obtained by an analysis of the responses of each subject to the second portion of the questionnaire. Responses to the problems there listed were summarized by giving weights of zero, one, and two respectively to responses of "never," "sometimes," and "often," and summing the 18 responses. The results of such analyses are summarized in Table 3.

TABLE 3

TRENDS DURING ADOLESCENCE IN THE GENERAL EXTENT OF DOUBT AND CONCERN REGARDING RELIGIOUS ISSUES AS SHOWN BY MEAN "WONDER" AND "PROBLEM" SCORES OF THE THREE AGE GROUPS

	Age			CR Diff.
	12	15	18	12–18
Wonder scores	7.9	8.1	8.7	1.1
Problem scores	9.7	9.9	9.9	0.3
No. of cases	174	243	130	

A slight trend is noticeable in the case of the average number of statements wondered about, but the difference between the 12-year-old and the 18-year-old groups is so small compared to the amount of sampling error probably present that it cannot safely be considered more than a chance difference. In the case of the "problem scores" no difference appeared in the means for the three age groups. Thus insofar as these findings are concerned the hypothesis that adolescence is a period of *generally* increased religious doubts and problems is clearly not substantiated. Since age trends here (and also sex differences) are slight, it was decided to compare Catholics with non-Catholics by grouping sixth, ninth, and twelfth grades and both sexes together. When this was done, it became apparent that Catholics had lower scores in both "wonders" and "problems" than did the non-Catholics. In the case of "wonder scores" the mean difference was 3.0 (CR 4.9); in the case of "problem scores" the mean difference was 1.2 (CR 2.2).

That age trends exist with respect to the particular problem faced is to be expected, and appropriate data revealing such trends are presented in Table 4. Over half of the 18-year-old group of sub-

TABLE 4

FREQUENCY WITH WHICH PARTICULAR RELIGIOUS PROBLEMS EXIST AT VARIOUS AGES THROUGH ADOLESCENCE AS SHOWN BY PERCENTAGE OF DIFFERENT AGE GROUPS WHO CHECK EACH PROBLEM AS SOMETIMES OR OFTEN PRESENT

		Age		$CR_{Diff.}$
Problem	*12*	*15*	*18*	*12–18*
Having a different religion from other people	34	25	27	1.3
Disliking church service	33	47	60	4.9
Being forced to go to church	30	31	27	0.6
Disliking parents' religion	11	8	12	0.7
Failing to go to church	67	67	67	0.0
Changing my idea of God	29	25	31	0.4
Losing faith in religion	27	32	31	0.8
Doubting prayer will bring good	37	44	35	0.4
Getting help on religious problems	53	54	56	0.6
Choosing a religion	21	20	15	1.5
Parents' objection to church membership	23	14	11	2.6
Wanting to know the meaning of religion	53	48	60	1.2
Wanting communion with God	59	47	57	0.3
Heaven and hell	53	53	66	2.3
Sin	71	62	72	0.2
Conflicts of science and religion	42	50	57	2.6
Being teased about my religious feelings	26	22	18	1.5
Wondering what becomes of people when they die	67	56	80	2.3
Number of cases	174	243	130	

jects indicate that the following problems trouble them sometimes or often: disliking church service; failing to go to church; getting help on religious problems; wanting communion with God; wanting to know the meaning of religion; heaven and hell; sin; conflicts of science and religion; wondering what becomes of people when they die. It would seem as though adolescents do have certain religious problems regarding which they would like help, but apparently find conventional religious programs unsatisfying. Three of the problems listed—disliking church services; heaven and hell; and wondering what becomes of people when they die—become more prevalent with increased age, the critical ratios of the 12- to 18-year-old differences in these cases being over 2.0. One problem—parents' objection to church membership—decreases sufficiently to show fair statistical reliability. Just what is meant by this response is not clear. It may be that parents of twelve-year-olds consider them too young to join a church.

DISCUSSION

It is not implied by the selection of age groups of varying statuses with respect to pubescence, that the differences shown are a function of pubescence. Rather, it would seem more reasonable to assume that they are the result of accumulated experience in combination with increasing intellectual maturity which makes the adolescent more capable of interpreting the environment of ideas and facts in which he is becoming increasingly immersed. Greater intellectual maturity might be expected to increase sensitivity to inconsistencies either among the beliefs and views an individual contacts, or between his already established beliefs and new learnings. Also with greater maturity the adolescent is more capable of abstract generalizations which might result in discarding some specific beliefs in favor of more general ones.

Do such findings have any practical value? To the psychologist and others interested in human development such data are of interest as descriptions of how development proceeds. But are there any implications for those interested in religious education? Two obvious implications may be mentioned. First, those issues represented by statements which are increasingly "wondered about" as age increases may give clues as to appropriate topics for consideration in the teen years in both Sunday School classes and young people's groups. Second, beliefs discarded by children as they grow older may well be studied for their implications for teaching at earlier ages. Children's concepts regarding religion are more concrete and specific than are those of adults, the latter tending to be abstract and general. This change represents the normal growth of concepts. It would seem desirable that the specific and concrete beliefs taught to children be beliefs compatible with the more abstract adult views, and not beliefs later to be discarded because of incompatibility.

A few comments now regarding methods of studying adolescence. In studies of adolescent development it is necessary to include a sufficient age range in the sample to give perspective to the findings. Because a group of high school students have certain characteristics is no indication that those characteristics are peculiar to adolescence. It may well be that young children and adults as well show the same characteristics. The need for such an age perspective is interestingly demonstrated in data collected by Symonds and published by Shuttleworth (1938, Fig. 317). "Philosophy of life" which is ordinarily assumed to be a problem and interest typical of adolescents, was demonstrated to be of more interest *at 50* than at 15. The present study has not involved such a wide age range as did Symonds', but some perspective is given. The situation in adult years needs also to be studied.

However, certain difficulties are encountered in attempting to study wide age ranges by comparable procedures. It is desirable to get reactions of different age groups to essentially the *same situation*. But 10-, 11-, or 12-year-old youngsters may be unable to comprehend many statements entirely clear to adolescents in the middle or late teens. The question may well be raised regarding the present study as to whether the youngest group could adequately comprehend the questionnaire used. The writers believe that their comprehension was adequate. No more of the youngest group than the middle or oldest group failed to respond to the statements, and the responses of the 12-year-olds were, on the average, either comparable to the older age groups or continued trends apparent in the 15- and 18-year-old comparisons.

It is worth-while also to point out that in research of this sort, average scores may very well obscure more facts than they reveal. This is the writer's criticism of Dimock's study. In contrast to his conclusion of the relatively static nature of religious ideas in adolescence, the present findings reveal rather significant shifts during the ages considered. The need for detailed analysis is revealed even within the present study. Average "wonder scores" and "problem scores" showed little change. Yet analysis of responses to specific beliefs and problems indicated changes of high statistical reliability. The meaning of any "score" rests to a considerable extent upon the particular questions or items which that score summarizes.

When items showing increasing frequency of checking are added in with other items of a decreasing trend, the differences cancel and a fairly stable over-all score may conceal the actual change. It is probable that the use of a questionnaire dealing exclusively with religious issues has momentarily focused the subjects' attention upon a rather narrow range of human experience, and by taking these experiences out of the context of everyday living may give a biased picture of the importance of such issues and problems in the lives of adolescents. Three of the problem items used in the present study were included in a modified form of the Mooney *Problem Check List* (Junior High Level) used by the senior writer in another study. Although 22, 48, and 25 per cent of ninth graders in the present study checked these items as bothering them sometimes or often, only 9, 18, and 20 per cent of a group of 100 ninth graders so checked the same items when they were included among a great variety of other kinds of problems. This is simply another illustration of the part the instrument used plays in determining the "facts" discovered, and warns against too literal an interpretation of the absolute figures presented in this paper. The differences noted and trends revealed, however, may more safely be depended upon. One report by Mooney (1942) suggests that religious and moral problems are relatively minor in importance in adolescence when compared with other types of problems.

SUMMARY

Five hundred forty-seven children and adolescents, in three groups which averaged 12, 15, and 18 years of age, responded to a questionnaire which listed 52 statements representing various religious beliefs and 18 problems dealing with religious issues. Many significant differences appeared in religious beliefs when 12-year-olds and 18-year-olds were compared. A greater tolerance with respect to religious beliefs and practice, a discarding of a number of specific beliefs and increased "wondering about" statements regarding the hereafter (death, heaven, hell) constituted the major trends. An analysis of responses of "wondering about" particular beliefs and "problems" did not substantiate the commonly accepted hypothesis that adolescence is a period of generally increased religious doubts and problems. Catholics "wondered about" fewer beliefs and checked fewer problems than did non-Catholics. However, the specific problems checked by the subjects indicated that many do have problems of a religious sort, want help (in fact, one of the greatest problems seemed to be getting such help), but are dissatisfied with conventional church services.

.... 50 ....

THE RELIGION OF THE POST-WAR

COLLEGE STUDENT

by Gordon W. Allport, James M. Gillespie, and Jacqueline Young

To what extent do college students express their need for religious belief? What are their attitudes toward the Church? What is the relationship between their religious beliefs and their religious practices? To what extent do they believe in God? How do their beliefs in God compare with their attitudes toward the supernatural? These are some of the questions Gordon W. Allport, of Harvard University, James M. Gillespie, of Colby College, and their collaborator seek to answer in this investigation of Harvard University and Radcliffe College students. [Adapted from *Journal of Psychology*, 1948, *25*, 3-33. Reprinted by permission of the authors and The Journal Press.]

DO STUDENTS FEEL THAT THEY NEED RELIGION?

The pivotal question in our scale is Number 3 [the questionnaire follows the article]. Table 1 states the question and reports the results obtained.

The basic finding with which we start is that roughly seven out of every ten students (82 per cent of the women, 68 per cent of the men) feel that they need religion in their own lives. This statement does not imply that this proportion of students in theistic, orthodox, or in any sense conventional in their views; but only, given a chance to define religion in any way they choose, approximately seven in ten regard themselves as actually or potentially religious. Thus it is clear that the majority of young intellectuals—ordinarily regarded as the most "emancipated" and "religiously radical" element in the population—definitely consider the religious sentiment as appropriate to their own developing personalities.

TABLE 1

"DO YOU FEEL THAT YOU REQUIRE SOME FORM OF RELIGIOUS ORIENTATION OR BELIEF IN ORDER TO ACHIEVE A FULLY MATURE PHILOSOPHY OF LIFE?"

Percentages

	Harvard (N = 412)	Radcliffe (N = 85)	Male veterans (N = 289)	Male nonveterans (N = 123)
Yes	68	82	64	76
No	19	12	22	14
Doubtful	13	6	14	10

Table 1 shows also that *women are more religious than men.* . . . Although 14 per cent more women than men feel the need for religion, this difference is accounted for partly by the fact that men express themselves as "doubtful" twice as often as do women. As a matter of fact, only about one in ten among women, and two in ten among men, give definitely negative replies, i.e., regard religion as having no part to play in their lives. . . .

Veterans seem less religiously inclined than non-veterans. (The difference is not due to the age factor, for we find no appreciable difference in response between veterans 20 or under and 21 or over. In other words the difference between veterans and non-veterans is clearly due to war experience.) It will be noted throughout our series of tables that veterans seem consistently to be 10 to 15 per cent "less religious" than non-veterans.

*   *   *

ARE RELIGION AND SCIENCE FELT TO BE IN CONFLICT?

In Question 12 the subjects were asked to evaluate the conflict between science and religion. Although the modal response was that the *conflict is negligible,* all possibilities received a fair number of choices. Table 2 states the question and the percentages of men selecting each of the alternative answers. The responses from women were very similar.

The subjects were also asked to explain their answers briefly. Their comments seem to indicate five different frames of mind.

(a) *Perplexed.* In these cases, the conflict is keenly felt, and personal in nature. "Either science or religion must be wrong." There is evidence of confusion and doubt, and the student feels unable to 'take sides."

TABLE 2

'HOW DO YOU FEEL ABOUT THE FREQUENTLY MENTIONED CONFLICT BETWEEN THE FINDINGS OF SCIENCE AND THE PRINCIPAL (BASIC) CONTENTIONS OF RELIGION?"

Alternative	Percentage (N = 386)
Religion and science clearly support one another	21
Conflict is negligible (more apparent than real)	32
Conflict is considerable but probably not irreconcilable	17
Conflict is very considerable, perhaps irreconcilable	14
Conflict is definitely irreconcilable	16

(b) *Pro-religion.* Some subjects, requiring a strong religious orientation for effective living, cannot embrace the "cold finality" of science. Here we find mention of the past errors of science, and of its "destructive weapons," likewise of its inadequate explanations of the universe, or of the "life principle." "Science is on the wrong track."

(c) *Pro-science.* This group takes a strong stand, offering as a basis for their position such arguments as "lack of empirical verification" for religion, "uselessness of prayer," "science either can now, or soon will be able to explain everything," "revelation is inconceivable," "immortality and virgin birth impossible," "*orgone* takes care of the 'life principle,'" etc. Here are also mentioned the "bigotry, intolerance, ignorance" fostered by the church.

(d) *Dualistic.* Here the conflict is solved by compartmentalization. Science and religion are held completely apart. "Religion is feeling; science is knowing." "Science tells how; religion tells why." "Science leads us to a certain point; religion takes over from there."

(e) *Conciliatory.* In this group, as in the preceding, there is no onesided favoring of either science or religion. "There is a lack of knowledge in *both* spheres," "both satisfy those who want to believe," "they each answer the same questions, but in a different way, so that both are justifiable." These subjects often indicate how in their own minds specific conflicts have been resolved: artificial insemination as a justification for belief in virgin birth; allegory as an aid in interpretation of the Bible.

Although we have no certain evidence on the point, it seems very likely that the century-old quarrel between religion and science has abated. Fully 70 per cent of the students do not feel that the two provinces of human belief and action are irreconcilable. In part, the situation may be due to the fact that students no longer feel bound to such orthodox doctrines as did their student predecessors in previous college generations. In part, it may be due to the fact that present-day religion, including orthodoxy, has grown more flexible in accommodating the discoveries of science.

If we may report a further impression, we would say that the clash between religion and science is of less concern to present-day students than the clash between religion and the social order. . . . Judging from our open-ended questions (especially Item 18) "religion has failed" is a more common accusation than "religion is scientifically false."

STUDENTS' SELF-KNOWLEDGE

An interesting bit of evidence concerning the excellence of students' insight into the strength of their own beliefs is seen in Table 3.

TABLE 3

"HOW WOULD YOU SAY THAT YOUR OWN RELIGIOUS SENTIMENTS AND NEEDS COMPARE WITH THOSE OF OTHER YOUNG PEOPLE OF YOUR OWN AGE?"

	Percentages	
	Radcliffe	Harvard
Stronger than average	34	26
About average	34	40
Less strong than average	32	34

Just about the expected percentages report themselves as stronger than average, or less strong than average in religiosity. If anything, the insight of Harvard students is somewhat superior, since in comparison with all young people (male and female) we should expect somewhat more men to have sentiments somewhat "less strong than average."

Question 10 asked whether students feel that their views mark them off from their contemporaries, so that they are sometimes isolated or embarrassed by them. Table 4 shows that only about two-thirds of the students are clearly free from self-consciousness in this respect.

Membership in minority religious groups is a matter with which many developing personalities have to come to terms. According to our results the problem seems to cause concern to women more frequently than to men.

TABLE 4

"DO YOU FEEL THAT YOUR VIEWS REGARDING RELIGION, NO MATTER WHAT THEY ARE, IN ANY WAY MARK YOU OFF FROM YOUR CONTEMPORARIES, SO THAT YOU SOMETIMES FEEL EMBARRASSED OR ISOLATED BECAUSE OF THESE VIEWS?"

	Percentages	
	Radcliffe	Harvard
Yes	28	17
No	59	73
Doubtful	13	10

WHAT DO STUDENTS BELIEVE?

Roughly only about one-quarter of the students subscribe to the orthodox theological positions of the Catholic or Protestant churches. (In interpreting this finding it is well to bear in mind that approximately one-sixth of our subjects were reared in the Roman Catholic faith, and one-sixth in some branch of the Jewish faith.) Our evidence is derived from various doctrinal questions, Nos. 13 to 16. The percentages of students subscribing to each of the positions described are presented in Tables 5 to 9. The items employed in Question 13 were taken bodily from a questionnaire employed at the University of Wisconsin with both male and female students in 1930 (Sheldon and Stevens, 1942).

Table 5 shows that Harvard and Radcliffe students in 1946 seemed on the whole more favorably disposed toward the Church than did Wisconsin students 16 years earlier. . . .

Question 14 is derived in a slightly modified manner from the scale employed by Katz and Allport (1931) at the University of Syracuse in 1926. Although the modification in our scale does not permit direct comparison, it is evident that actually more of our students endorse the orthodox theistic position than did the Syracuse students 20 years ago, although at the same time more likewise subscribe to the positions of agnosticism and atheism. It is important to bear in mind that not only is there a difference in time involved between the two studies, but also a difference in the constituent college populations.

Although only about one-fifth of the men and two-fifths of the women in our study subscribe to the extreme theistic position, the great majority believe in a Deity of some kind. Only about 12 per

TABLE 5

STUDENTS WITH VARIOUS VIEWS CONCERNING THE NATURE OF THE CHURCH (QUESTION 13)

	Percentages		
	Harvard (N = 170)	Radcliffe (N = 63)	Wisconsin 1930 (N = 3010)
The Church is the one sure and infallible foundation of civilized life	6	6	4
On the whole the Church stands for the best in human life	36	40	24
There is certain doubt. Possible that the Church may do a good deal of harm	18	13	38
The total influence may be on the whole harmful	6	2	14
Stronghold of much that is unwholesome and dangerous to human welfare	10	6	14
Insufficient familiarity	4	8	6*
A different attitude	20	25	

*Wisconsin students were urged to avoid the last two options on this scale. Harvard and Radcliffe students were freely allowed to elect them.

TABLE 6

STUDENTS ENDORSING VARIOUS VIEWS OF THE DEITY (QUESTION 14)

	Percentages		
	Harvard veterans (N = 290)	Harvard nonveterans (N = 123)	Radcliffe (N = 86)
There is an infinitely wise omnipotent creator	17	25	40
There is an infinitely intelligent and friendly Being	25	27	19
There is a vast, impersonal spiritual Source	11	10	7
I neither believe nor disbelieve in God	23	17	12
The only power is natural law	8	7	9
The universe is merely a machine	5	2	2
None of these alternatives	11	12	11

cent consider themselves atheists and an additional 20 per cent agnostics, saying that "because of our necessary ignorance in this matter, I neither believe nor disbelieve in God."

In this connection we report (on the basis of Question 17c) that there is little support for the Marxist position that religion is the opiate of the people, and that active resistance to organized religious forces is therefore in order. Twelve per cent agree with this extreme position and an additional 12 per cent express no opinion. Seventy-six per cent disagree sharply with it.

Even though the majority have a belief in God of some kind, the majority likewise, with seeming inconsistency, subscribe to the humanistic proposition, as expressed by John Dewey (Question 17a), "If religion is to play a useful rôle in life, it should be regarded entirely as a natural human function; it should have nothing whatever to do with supernatural notions." Perhaps Dewey's unfortunate word "notion" in this statement helps explain why the proposition wins 55 per cent agreement among men, and 47 per cent agreement among women; for who wishes his religion to deal with mere "notions"— supernatural or otherwise? And yet an element of clear confusion remains. The majority have some type of belief in God, and at the same time, wish to rule out the supernatural.

To interpret this inconsistency we should probably regard the rejection of supernaturalism as an additional expression of dissatisfaction with the specific brand of supernaturalism taught in the traditional churches (as the students understand it). Discontent with historic theological positions has been evident in most of our results. Added evidence comes from the fact that the majority agree with the proposition that "denominational distinctions, at least within Protestant Christianity, are out of date, and may as well be eliminated as rapidly as possible" (Question 17b). Fifty-seven per cent of all students agree with the ecumenicists in this matter; only 19 per cent disagree, and the remainder have no opinion.

Turning next to the Christological problem, we find that only about one-quarter of the Harvard students and two-fifths of the Radcliffe students endorse the historic doctrinal position. Well over half the students prefer the view that "Christ should be regarded merely as a great prophet or teacher, much as the Mohammedans accept Mahomet, or as the Chinese accept Confucius."

A final doctrinal issue concerns belief in immortality. Here again roughly only about one-quarter of the students are orthodox in their positions.

TABLE 7

STUDENTS SUBSCRIBING TO VARIOUS VIEWS OF THE NATURE OF CHRIST
(QUESTION 15)

	Percentages		
	Harvard veterans (N=289)	Harvard nonveterans (N=122)	Radcliffe (N=86)
The human incarnation of God	23	30	42
A great prophet or teacher	58	51	50
Probably a mythical figure	2	4	0
None of these alternatives	17	15	8

TABLE 8

STUDENTS SUBSCRIBING TO VARIOUS VIEWS OF IMMORTALITY
(QUESTION 16)

	Percentages		
	Harvard veterans (N=288)	Harvard nonveterans (N=123)	Radcliffe (N=85)
Personal immortality	21	28	34
Reincarnation	1	2	1
Continued existence as part of a spiritual principle	10	11	8
Influence upon children and social institutions	40	34	35
Disbelieve in any of these senses	11	5	3
None of these alternatives	17	20	19

STUDENTS' RELIGIOUS PRACTICES

That students are more conventional in their religious practices than in their beliefs is indicated from the results in Table 9, based on the replies from Question 11.

It is evident that the great majority of students engage in some religious activities. Especially interesting is the fact that four-fifths of the women and three-fifths of the men report at least occasional experience of reverence, devotion, or dependence on a Supreme Being. It is apparent that religious inclination, as well as traditional religious practice, is considerably more prominent than is orthodoxy of belief. Only 15 per cent of the students deny altogether engaging in any religious practices or experiencing any religious states of mind during the preceding six months' period.

TABLE 9

STUDENTS REPORTING VARIOUS DEVOTIONAL PRACTICES DURING
PAST SIX MONTHS   *Percentages*

	Harvard veterans (N=290)	Harvard nonveterans (N=123)	Radcliffe (N=86)
Attended Church			
About once a week	14	25	39
About every other week	7	7	9
Average once a month	11	20	10
Once or twice only	34	28	26
Not at all	34	20	16
Prayed			
Daily	13	22	35
Fairly frequently	10	14	18
Occasionally	15	14	8
Rarely	22	26	12
Never	40	24	27
Experienced feeling of reverence			
Daily	8	13	17
Frequently	13	14	23
Occasionally	19	26	29
Rarely	20	17	9
Never	40	30	22

We conclude that fully half the students who, in some sense, lead religious lives do so without firm doctrinal convictions. This situation might be interpreted in one of two opposite ways. It may be that in many cases we are discovering the persistence of childhood religious feelings and practices after the rational groundwork is outgrown. In such cases we are dealing with individuals who are still in the process of losing their faith—vestigial feelings and activity outliving conviction. On the other hand, in some cases, we are undoubtedly dealing with individuals who have not yet found a mature structure of faith to support the religious experiences they have and the practices to which they hold. Since theological reasoning deals with the most difficult and least tangible of life's riddles, satisfactory results in this domain of thought are often achieved relatively late in the development of personality.

The fact that the students' theological views, such as they are, have shifted markedly toward the "liberal" position may also be interpreted in either of two ways. The result may be declared evidence of the distaste the modern generation has for what they consider to be "superstition." It may also be taken as evidence that the students of today are ignorant of what theology in reality teaches. . . . But, we have no way of telling what proportion of our subjects are dissenting "advisedly," and what proportion are rejecting historic doctrine out of ignorance concerning its nature as interpreted by the master theologians of the ages.

Table 10 will interest readers who wish to know how belief and practice vary among students who now subscribe to different systems of faith. In this table we have grouped beliefs and participation into categories that represent "more" and "less" religiosity.

TABLE 10

RELIGIOUS BELIEF AND CONDUCT OF HARVARD STUDENTS WHO EXPRESS NEED FOR RELIGION—ACCORDING TO CHOICE OF RELIGIOUS SYSTEM

| | Percentages | | | |
	Roman Catholic (N = 43)	Protestant Christianity (N = 71)	Judaism (N = 21)	New type needed (N = 48)
Belief in Deity				
Theistic or Deistic	98	85	68	25
All other positions	2	15	32	75
Belief in immortality				
Personal, or reincarnation	86	44	19	15
All other positions	14	56	81	85
Church attendance				
Monthly, or more often	100	61	33	25
Once or twice, or never	0	39	67	75
Prayer				
Daily, frequently, occasionally	95	71	33	30
Rarely, or never	5	29	67	70
Reverence				
Daily, frequently, occasionally	93	78	40	35
Rarely, or never	7	22	60	65

Without a single exception we find a steady progression: Roman Catholics are most religious by all these measures; Protestants less so; Jews still less; and those who declare themselves as favoring a new type of religion are least religious of all.

THE RELIGION OF VETERANS

In order to find out the effects of active war service Question 18 was asked of the veterans in our sample. Did the war make you more or less religious, it asked; also did it make you more or less interested in the problems religion seeks to solve? The results are presented in Tables 11 and 12.

TABLE 11

EFFECT OF WAR EXPERIENCES ON THE RELIGIOSITY OF VETERANS

	Percentages	
	Harvard	Princeton
	(N = 266)	(N = 199)
Made *more* religious	26.3	25.1
Made *less* religious	19.2	18.6
No effect in this regard	54.5	53.3
		(3.0 no opinion)

TABLE 12

EFFECT OF WAR EXPERIENCES ON INTEREST IN PROBLEMS OF RELIGION

	Percentages Harvard (N = 267)
More interested	58.4
Less interested	4.9
No effect	36.7

It is fortunate that comparable data at Princeton became available through the investigation of Crespi and Shapleigh (1946). The almost identical results indicate that our Harvard sample may in fact be typical of large numbers of collegiate veterans.

These tables contain surprising results. More students report that the war caused them to become increasingly religious than reported the opposite; and a sizable majority say that their interest in the problems dealt with by religion is increased. Yet, in Table 1 it was reported that veterans felt a need for religion in their lives less often than did non-veterans or women. Furthermore (though we have not always given a separate breakdown of the veterans' replies), on every single one of our questions they show themselves *less* formally religious and less orthodox than either non-veterans or women. The differences are ordinarily 10 to 15 per cent.

The apparent contradiction is not difficult to explain. (*a*). While war experience did have a mildly adverse effect on the religious beliefs and practices of veterans as a group, yet this finding is not incompatible with the discovery (Table 11) that in the case of *certain* veterans there was an intensification of religious feeling. (*b*). Although there was a loss in orthodoxy and formal religious participation, yet an interest grew in the social aims of religion, in the problems of evil, of immortality, of the existence of God and like ethical and philosophical riddles.

*   *   *

More light on the veteran's state of mind comes from the open-ended portion of Question 18 which asks "the principal type of effect war experience had (if any at all) upon your religious views." Three contrasting statements follow. The first is representative of the common negative reaction toward deficiency of religion in practice.

War is final proof: (*a*) that there is no God; (*b*) that religion is a failure. How can you believe in a beneficent deity when millions of innocent people are dying needlessly? If religion were effective, there could be no war, hatred, persecution, bigotry, starvation, selfishness, imperialism, and colonial exploitation.

Religion has tried for centuries to establish a brotherhood of man. It has had its day. The people should wake up and realize how futile it is and what hypocrites they are.

The problems religion tries to solve need solving, but religion has failed. I am interested in seeing them solved, but must look to other institutions.

The second takes a subjective and favorable view of religion.

If I had not had a personal religious philosophy when I entered combat, I do not believe I would have lasted at all. For me it was most definitely a source of strength. I require no one else to hold my beliefs but I experience intense personal comfort from them myself. I can think of no other single thing that sustains me day by day so much as my personal belief in God. I can't hold it out to other people because I really can't explain it.

The third reflects the frequent turning away from theological, but not from an ethical, Christianity.

I find myself highly confused. Don't believe in any organized religion, but do believe in the innate goodness of man. I believe in the Christian virtues, but not in the Christian religion.

During the war I was struck by how untouched the majority appeared to be by the basic and simplest principles of charity to one's neighbor, etc. I was convinced therefore that the only possible way to change or to improve this situation is to substitute some system of reasonable ethics for present denominational beliefs.

Among the veterans who had decided that their personalities required no religious faith, and among those who were doubtful on this issue—36 per cent in all—the development of a humanitarian substitute can often be detected. . . .

The majority of veterans not only reported a need for religion in their own lives, but as a rule gave evidence of tolerance and sympathy for the religious yearning in others. Often, however, there were thrusts at institutional religion and its representatives. Only one veteran had a favorable remark to make regarding the chaplain of his unit. Many more were critical. These few spontaneous judgments, of course, are no indication of the general effectiveness of the chaplains' devoted services. . . .

The principal complaints leveled against the clergy have to do with the veterans' feeling that they are inept in handling human relationships. Some advocate a wider training in psychological counseling and administrative techniques for the clergy. This admonition is in line with our observation that unpleasant experiences during the war with maladroit personnel officers of all types has enhanced the veteran's interest in the improvement of techniques in social relations.

We turn finally to the veteran in combat. By his own report he stands revealed as a praying animal (in times of stress). Since no direct question on this matter was included in our instrument we cannot quantify the phenomenon. Among the free answers (266 in number) we were struck by the high frequency with which the subject of prayer was mentioned. . . .

The individual who reaches the limits of his adaptive capacity adds to its natural powers a spiritual counterpart that seems to him reasonable and necessary. In some people this sense of complementation occurs only in times of crisis; in others, it apparently exists under circumstances of everyday living as well.

* * *

Many . . . comments show that the "survival value" of prayer, that is, its efficacy for personal protection, was an issue that worried many men. "My closest friend and myself never prayed," writes one veteran, "and were never even wounded. I saw one boy praying and killed during his prayer by a German 88 shell." Such experiences put a fatal strain on lingering childhood conceptions of prayer as a talisman.

We conclude: (a) War experiences were sufficiently traumatic to eradicate many juvenile conceptions of religion (especially of prayer). This fact would readily explain the 10 to 15 per cent lower religiosity in the formal and institutional sense showed by veterans in comparison with non-veterans. (b) Nearly two-thirds of all veterans still feel the need for religion in their lives. (c) War experience sharpened interest in the problems with which religion seeks to deal. (d) Taking these facts together it is apparent that the war speeded up the maturing of the veteran's personality in respect to his religious outlook—as it did no doubt in all departments of his life-activity.

* * *

ATTITUDE INVENTORY: ASPECTS OF RELIGIOUS BELIEF

Instructions: This Inventory does not ask you to give your name. It is strictly anonymous.

At the same time, its successful use in research imposes two requirements: (1) It should not be answered too hastily. Some questions will require reflection. Authentic and well-considered statements, without influence from outside, are wanted. So, please take your time, and ponder the questions adequately before answering them. (2) In order not to bias the sample, *all papers must be returned.*

1. Age ———
2. Are you married? ——— yes; ——— no
3. Do you feel that you require some form of religious orientation or belief in order to achieve a fully mature philosophy of life?

    ——— yes
    ——— no
    ——— doubtful

    a) *If yes,* do you think that *on the whole* the tradition and literature of some great religious system now existing satisfactorily meets your own religious needs, or do you think a substantially new type of religion is required?

        The following religious system strikes me on the whole as adequate:
        ——— Roman Catholicism
        ——— Anglo-Catholicism or Eastern Orthodoxy
        ——— Protestant Christianity
        ——— Liberalized Protestantism (e.g., Unitarianism, Universalism)
        ——— Ethical but not theological Christianity (e.g., humanism, ethical culture)
        ——— some form of Judaism
        ——— other: (specify)
    or ——— a substantially new type of religion is required

4. To what degree has religion been an influence in your upbringing?

      ——— very marked

      ——— moderate

      ——— slight

      ——— none at all

  a) What was the character of this influence (if there was any at all)?

      ——— Roman Catholicism

      ——— Anglo-Catholicism or Eastern Orthodoxy

      ——— Protestant Christianity

      ——— Liberalized Protestantism (e.g., Unitarianism, Universalism)

      ——— Ethical but not theological Christianity (e.g., humanism, ethical culture)

      ——— some form of Judaism

      ——— other: (specify)

5. If you were brought up under some religious influence, has there been a period in which you have reacted either partially or wholly against the beliefs taught?

      ——— yes

      ——— no

      ——— doubtful

  a) If you reacted against the beliefs taught did the doubt start

      ——— before age 10

      ——— 10-12

      ——— 12-15

      ——— 15-20

      ——— after 20

  b) If you have reacted against the beliefs taught, would you say that at the present time you

      ——— are in substantial agreement with the beliefs taught

      ——— partially agree with them

      ——— wholly disagree with them

6. If at any time you have felt yourself to be religious, which factors in the following list do you consciously recognize to have been contributing reasons? Check as many as apply.

      ——— parental influence

      ——— conformity with tradition

      ——— personal influence of people other than parents

      ——— fear or insecurity

      ——— sorrow or bereavement

      ——— gratitude

      ——— sex turmoil

      ——— a mystical experience (perhaps not fully understood)

      ——— studies in school or college

——— reading outside of school and college
——— church teachings
——— aesthetic appeal

7. Generally speaking, religion in childhood is marked by its external character; it is simply "there," to be believed along with the traditions and codes of the family and culture. This situation often changes so that at some time there is an *inner* experience which makes religion a distinctly subjective and personal matter. Does this statement characterize your own development?

——— yes
——— no

If yes,

a) At what age did the subjective awareness come?

——— before age 10
——— 10-12
——— 12-15
——— 15-20
——— after 20

b) One investigator defined three types of subjective religious awakening. Kindly check the type that best includes your own case.

1. *Definite crisis.* "A real crisis is reached and passed in which a definite change of attitude seems to have taken place." This type corresponds to what is commonly considered a distinct religious conversion. ———

2. *Emotional stimulus awakening.* Here the emotional upheaval is much reduced in intensity, or even entirely absent, but the subject looks back to some event which served as a stimulus to awaken the religious consciousness. ———

3. *Gradual awakening.* Here there are no single or specifiable occasions that are as decisive as those defined above. The religious sentiment has developed gradually. ———

8. a) How, in general, does the firmness of your belief in religion compare with your mother's belief?

——— more firm
——— less firm
——— about the same
——— don't know

b) with your father's belief?

——— more firm
——— less firm
——— about the same
——— don't know

9. How would you say that your own religious sentiments and needs compare with those of other young people of your own age?

    ——— stronger than average

    ——— about average

    ——— less strong than average

10. Do you feel that your views regarding religion, no matter what they are, in any way mark you off from your contemporaries, so that you sometimes feel embarrassed or isolated because of these views?

    ——— yes

    ——— no

    ——— doubtful

11. Check the one statement which most nearly describes your conduct:

    a) During the past six months I have gone to church

        ——— about once a week

        ——— about every other week

        ——— on an average once a month

        ——— once or twice only

        ——— not at all

    b) During the past six months I have prayed

        ——— daily

        ——— fairly frequently

        ——— occasionally

        ——— rarely

        ——— never

    c) During the past six months I have experienced a feeling of reverence, devotion, or dependence upon a Supreme Being.

        ——— daily

        ——— frequently

        ——— occasionally

        ——— rarely

        ——— never

12. How do you feel about the frequently mentioned conflict between the findings of science and the principal (basic) contentions of religion?

    ——— To my mind religion and science clearly support one another

    ——— The conflict is negligible (i.e., more apparent than real)

    ——— The conflict is considerable, but probably not irreconcilable

    ——— The conflict is very considerable, perhaps irreconcilable

    ——— The conflict is definitely irreconcilable

    Explain your answer briefly:

13. The Church (check the view that best corresponds to your own attitude):

    ——— 1. The Church is the one sure and infallible foundation of civilized life. Every member of society ought to be educated in it and required to support it.

——— 2. On the whole the Church stands for the best in human life, although certain minor shortcomings and errors are necessarily apparent in it, as in all human institutions.

——— 3. There is certain doubt concerning the nature of the total influence of the Church. It is possible that the Church may do a good deal of harm.

——— 4. While the intentions of most individual church members are no doubt good, the total influence of the Church may be on the whole harmful.

——— 5. The Church is a stronghold of much that is unwholesome and dangerous to human welfare. It fosters intolerance, bigotry and ignorance.

——— 6. Insufficient familiarity with the problem.

——— 7. A different attitude, as follows:

14. The Deity (check the one statement which most nearly expresses your belief):

——— 1. There is an infinitely wise, omnipotent Creator of the universe and of natural laws, whose protection and favor may be supplicated through worship and prayer. God is a personal God.

——— 2. There is an infinitely intelligent and friendly Being, working according to natural laws through which He expresses His power and goodness. There is the possibility of communication with this Deity in the sense that prayer may at least affect our moral attitude toward nature and toward our own place in the scheme of things.

——— 3. There is a vast, impersonal, spiritual source or principle throughout nature and working in man, incapable of being swayed or communicated with through prayer.

——— 4. Because of our necessary ignorance in this matter, I neither believe nor disbelieve in a God.

——— 5. The only power is natural law. There is neither a personal creator nor an infinite intelligent Being. Nature is wholly indifferent to man. Natural law may be spoken of as "spiritual force," but this in no way adds to or changes its character.

——— 6. The universe is merely a machine. Man and nature are creatures of cause and effect. All notions of a Deity as intelligent Being or as "spiritual force" are fictions, and prayer is a useless superstition.

——— 7. None of these alternatives sufficiently resembles my views to justify a choice between them.

15. The Person of Christ (check the position that best corresponds to your own view):

——— 1. Christ, as the Gospels state should be regarded as divine —as the human incarnation of God.

——— 2. Christ should be regarded merely as a great prophet or teacher, much as the Mohammedans accept Mahomet, or as the Chinese accept Confucius.

——— 3. In all probability Christ never lived at all, but is a purely mythical figure.

——— 4. None of these positions expresses my views well enough to justify a choice.

16. Immortality (check the position that best corresponds to your own view):

——— 1. I believe in personal immortality, i.e., the continued existence of the soul as an individual and separate entity.

——— 2. I believe in reincarnation—the continued existence of the soul in another body.

——— 3. I believe in the continued existence of the soul merely as a part of a universal spiritual principle.

——— 4. I believe that a person's immortality resides merely in his influence upon his children and upon social institutions.

——— 5. I disbelieve in immortality in any of these senses.

——— 6. None of the alternatives sufficiently resembles my views to justify a choice between them; or I have no view at all about this matter.

17. Please mark the extent of your agreement with each of the following statements:

a) If religion is to play a useful rôle in life, it should be regarded entirely as a natural human function. It should have nothing whatever to do with supernatural notions.

——— on the whole I tend to agree

——— on the whole I tend to disagree

——— no opinion

b) Denominational distinctions, at least within Protestant Christianity, are out of date, and may as well be eliminated as rapidly as possible.

——— on the whole I tend to agree

——— on the whole I tend to disagree

——— no opinion

c) Religion, as Karl Marx said, is the opiate of the people. People must claim what is rightfully theirs without the reactionary handicap of religious faith. Therefore, active resistance to organized religious forces is needed.

——— on the whole I tend to agree

———— on the whole I tend to disagree

———— no opinion

18. *Veterans only:*

Kindly check the ways in which your experiences *during the war* seem to have affected you.

———— on the whole made me more religious

———— on the whole made me less religious

———— no effect in this regard

———— on the whole made me more interested in the problems religion seeks to answer

———— on the whole made me less interested in the problems religion seeks to answer

———— no effect in this regard

Please state in your own words the principal type of effect war experience had (if any at all) upon your religious views:

CHAPTER SEVENTEEN

Ideals and Values

51

CHILDREN'S CONCEPT OF JUSTICE: A FURTHER COMPARISON WITH THE PIAGET DATA

by Dolores Durkin

In the following investigation Dolores Durkin of Teachers College, Columbia University explores the identification of possible developmental trends in children's concepts of justice and compares the findings with Piaget's theory of moral judgment. The function of intelligence in moral-judgment development is also examined. [From *Journal of Educational Research,* 1959, *52,* 252-257. Reprinted by permission of the author and Dembar Publications.]

This study is a second attempt to evaluate and extend Piaget's (1932) investigation of children's concepts of justice. Like the first attempt (Durkin, 1959), it is specifically concerned with children's judgments about the restoration of right order in instances of physical aggression; like the first, too, it examines the relationship between the intelligence of children and the kinds of judgments they make.

In the Piaget investigation, children ranging in age from six to twelve, and "from the poorer parts of Geneva," were questioned about certain problematical situations and, on the basis of their responses a theory was proposed concerning "the existence of three great periods in the development of the sense of justice" (Piaget, 1932, p. 314). During the first period, one defined in terms of a CA of about 7-8 years, justice is sought in the authority person. In a second period, covering the years 8-11, it is found in reciprocity. By 11-12 years, and the upper limits of this third period are never set by Piaget, justice continues to be sought in reciprocity but there also emerges, at this time, consideration of "equity"; that is, concern for the particular circumstances of the situation being judged.

For the purpose of evaluating the general applicability of this theory, the present writer, in an earlier study (Durkin, 1959), questioned 101 middle-class American children about what should be done in a situation wherein one child is physically aggressive toward another. Responses were analyzed for a threefold purpose: (1) to see whether a child's understanding of what is just undergoes, with age, the kinds of changes suggested by Piaget; (2) to see whether consideration of "equity" increases with age; and (3) to see whether Piaget, in his emphasis on chronological age, has minimized intelligence as a factor in the development of particular kinds of justice-concepts.

Findings in the study showed that acceptance of reciprocity as a justice-principle increased between grades two and five, but decreased significantly between grades five and eight. Eighth graders, like the second graders, tended to seek justice in the authority person. Eighth graders, too, more frequently than either second or fifth graders, showed consideration of "equity"; that is, they showed, through the questions they asked, greater overt concern for the particulars of the situation they were judging.

The role of intelligence was left undefined in the study. Using the 5 per cent level as the criterion of significance, the hypothesis of no relationship between kind of justice-concept and level of intelligence remained tenable for grades two and eight; for grade five, however, and again when all three grades were combined, the hypothesis could be rejected.

These various findings, coupled with those of Piaget, suggest further questions:

1. If children from a low socioeconomic stratum were chosen as subjects, would their responses tend to be more like those of Piaget's poor Swiss children, or like those of the middle-class American children interrogated by the present writer?

2. What would be the responses of older children; that is, children beyond the eighth-grade level?

3. With a different group of subjects, would the role of intelligence in moral judgment development come to be more exactly and consistently defined?

The present study is designed to consider each of these questions.

PROCEDURE

Subjects

The subjects are 119 boys and girls almost equally divided among grades two, five, eight and eleven. Subjects in grades two and five attend the same elementary school. Subjects in grade eight attend a junior high school; those in grade eleven, a senior high school. All three schools are located in decidedly low socioeconomic areas in a large West Coast city.

Two factors served as criteria for the selection of subjects within the chosen grade-levels and schools: (1) IQ scores above 69, and (2) American-born parents. The second factor frequently necessitated eliminating Caucasian children, and the result was that 88 of the total group of 119 subjects were Negroes. Sharing a common socioeconomic background, however, the two racial groups could be expected to have similar attitudes toward physical aggression (Davis and Havighurst, 1947).

Other descriptive data concerning the subjects are summarized in Table 1.

Instrument

As in the writer's first study, children's concepts of justice regarding one's person were arrived at through their responses to questions about story-situations depicting possible violations of justice.

The following was presented to male subjects:

A. One day when they were out at recess Bennett hit Van. What should Van do? Why?[1]

To those subjects who, in their responses to situation A, appeared to subscribe to reciprocity, the following situation and question were also presented:

B. What if Van hit Bennett back and gave him a push besides? What would you think of that? Why?

Situation B was included for the purpose of evaluating Piaget's finding that for children who accept reciprocity "the ideal aimed at is not to give more than one has received, but to mete out its mathematical equivalent" (Piaget, 1932, p. 295).

Since the specific content of the behavior described in situation

[1] Piaget questioned his subjects about what should be done "if someone punches you."

TABLE 1

RANGE, MEAN, AND STANDARD DEVIATION OF CA IN YEARS,
AND OF IQ SCORES IN THE FOUR GRADES

Grade	Range	Mean	S. D.
Two			
CA	7.0– 9.1	7.9	0.6
IQ Scores	72–113	98.9	9.5
Five			
CA	10.1–11.9	10.7	0.6
IQ Scores	70–113	91.9	11.6
Eight			
CA	12.6–14.9	13.4	0.7
IQ Scores	79–118	97.9	9.6
Eleven			
CA	15.3–17.8	16.1	0.8
IQ Scores	71–115	95.3	11.6

A (hitting) might, at least for some subjects, overshadow its general characteristic (physical aggression) as a criterion of evaluation, the following "what if" question was also posed:

C. If, instead of hitting him, Bennett had kicked Van, what should Van have done then? Why?[2]

Identical story situations, but now involving girls ("Adla" and "Hannah"), were presented to female subjects.

Interviews

As in the first study, subjects' oral responses were obtained in individual, tape-recorded interviews. At the beginning of each interview the investigator explained that she was interested in finding out what boys and girls really thought about certain kinds of things. She promised that nothing of what was said would be told to parents, teacher, or principal; and she also explained that respondents would remain anonymous.

Because of the intentionally brief form of the story situations, it was anticipated that some of the subjects would ask questions in response to the interviewer's. To be expected, for example, would be such questions as "How hard did he hit him?", or "Did he have a reason for hitting him?" If and when such questions were posed, the interviewer's standard responses were "Would that make a difference?" and "Why?"

[2] This question was not included in the writer's first study.

FINDINGS

Responses and Grade-Level

Kinds of responses given to the problem of what a child should do if another child hits him, and the number of subjects at each grade-level giving these responses, are summarized in Table 2. Testing the hypothesis of no relationship between age, as defined by grade-level, and kind of response, a Chi Square value of 20.24 was obtained (p<. 01).

TABLE 2

KIND AND FREQUENCY OF RESPONSES AT EACH GRADE LEVEL

Kind of Response	Grade			
	2	5	8	11
Tell authority person	19	25	17	17
Return aggression	6	4	10	2
Other				
Walk away	2	1	2	3
Forgive aggressor	1			
Try to be friendly			1	
Try to avoid aggressor			1	
Find out reason for aggression				7
Tell aggressor to stop				1

Among the total group of 22 subjects who, in response to situation A, showed approval of reciprocity, 19 disapproved of returning "a push besides" (situation B). Two of the subjects who did not object to returning more aggression than had been received were in grade eleven; one was in grade eight. This group of three explained their position in terms of:

Maybe her hit was hard or something, and she thought she'd better get in an extra lick.

That's OK. He started it, so give him a little more.

That's OK. Next time he won't mess with him.

Subjects asked a total of 24 questions about the particulars of situation A. Eleventh graders questioned the motive for the aggression (N = 12), the deliberativeness (N = 3), and the severity (N = 1) of the aggression. Eighth graders questioned the motive (N = 3) and the deliberativeness (N = 4). One subject in grade five asked about the motive. Testing the hypothesis of no relationship between age, as defined by grade-level, and this overt concern for particular circumstances ("equity") a Chi Square value of 27.0 was obtained (p< .01).

To situation C, a situation included for the purpose of examining specificity of attitudes toward different kinds of aggression, 14 subjects gave responses that were different from their responses to situation A. While at each grade-level the alterations in response could be chance occurrences, it was noted that their frequency increased as grade-level increased; that is, one subject in grade two changed his response, two subjects in grade five, four in grade eight, and seven in grade eleven. Each in this total group of fourteen evaluated the matter of kicking another as being more serious than hitting another, and nine out of the 14 changed their response from one classified as "other" to one classified as "tell."

Responses and IQ Level

Table 3 shows the number of subjects at two different IQ levels giving the various kinds of responses to situation A. It also lists the value of Chi Square and the level of significance obtained when hypotheses of no relationship between kind of response and IQ level were tested.

TABLE 3

KINDS OF RESPONSES AND NUMBER OF SUBJECTS AT TWO
DIFFERENT IQ LEVELS GIVING THEM

IQ Level	Kind of Response			Chi Square	
	Tell	Hit Back	Other	Value	p
Grade II (N = 28)				4.98	>.05
Above Median	7	4	3		
Below Median	12	2	0		
Grade V (N = 30)				2.04	>.30
Above Median	13	1	1		
Below Median	12	3	0		
Grade VIII (N = 31)				7.66	>.02
Above Median	9	2	4		
Below Median	8	8	0		
Grade XI				0.15	>.90
Above Median	9	1	5		
Below Median	8	1	6		
Grades II, V, VIII, XI				2.10	>.30
Above Median	38	9	12		
Below Median	40	13	7		

A Chi Square of 0.17 was obtained when the hypothesis of no relationship between IQ level and concern for particular circumstances ("equity") was tested (p> .50). Testing the hypothesis of no relationship between IQ level and change in response, the value of Chi Square was 0.00 (p> .99).

DISCUSSION

When findings in the present study are compared with those in the writer's earlier investigation (Durkin, 1959), both similarities and differences become apparent. Closest similarity is to be found in the emergence of "equity." In both studies, as Piaget's theory would suggest, it increases with age; in both studies, too, it does not appear to be related to intelligence.

A second kind of similarity lies in the inability of the studies to define with consistency the role of intelligence in the development of particular kinds of justice-concepts. In this study, as in the first, intelligence is significantly related to kinds of justice-concepts at one grade level, but is not significantly related at other grade levels.[3] In both studies, however, there is a trend toward no relationship.

One other kind of similarity in the studies lies in the fact that neither shows a trend in kinds of responses that bears resemblance to the one suggested by Piaget; for in neither do "children maintain with a conviction that grows with their years that it is strictly fair to give back the blows one has received" (Piaget, 1932; p. 301). Actually, at least at this verbal level, subjects in the present study, though some are older and all are from a lower socioeconomic stratum, accept such reciprocity with even less frequency than did subjects in the earlier investigation. In this very difference, it seems, lies evidence which lends support to one aspect of Piaget's theory, but which refutes another.

Piaget's (1932) theory, as outlined in *The Moral Judgment of the Child*, proposes that acceptance of reciprocity as a justice-principle is a function of the child's liberation from adult constraint. If it can be assumed that lower-class children attending middle-class oriented schools are more, or at least *feel* more constrained than

---

[3] In both studies it was decided, prior to statistical analysis, that a division of IQ scores on the basis of quartiles would result in theoretical frequencies that would be too small for the Chi Square tests. When quartile deviations are used, however, data in the two studies show, both within and between grade-levels, no significant relationship between IQ level and kind of justice-concept held.

do middle-class children, then it can be maintained that findings in the present study support this aspect of Piaget's theory.

However, another element in his theory proposes that this liberation from adult constraint necessarily increases with chronological age because, with age, child-adult social relationships tend to reflect more mutual respect and less unilateral respect. This age-relationship is hardly substantiated in the present study, or in the writer's first study. What is substantiated, rather, is that older children, at least on the basis of the reasons they give for their responses, are more experientially aware of what happens when the adult's admonition "Don't fight" is ignored; and, therefore, they are willing, at least at this verbal level, to seek justice in the authority person. If Piaget had questioned subjects older than 12 years, he too might have found similar reactions. And he might also have found, as did the present writer, that among older subjects who are "liberated" and who do propose reciprocity, there is no unanimous demand that it represent the "mathematical equivalent" of what was received.

Perhaps all of this is to say, as others have already said,[4] that Piaget's generalizations about children are based on samples that are too small and on a theoretical position that minimizes too much the influence of experience on development.

SUMMARY AND CONCLUSIONS

Subjects from a low socioeconomic stratum, and from grades two, five, eight and eleven were questioned about the just restoration of right order in instances of physical aggression between children. Their responses were examined in order to identify possible developmental trends in kinds of solutions proposed and, further, to compare these trends with those described by Piaget as being basic to the evolution of a sense of justice in the child. The function of intelligence in this evolutionary process was also examined.

Findings show that:

1. The oldest of the children, as well as the younger ones, tend to seek justice in the authority person. This does not support Piaget's contention that acceptance of reciprocity as a justice-principle increases with age.

2. Older children who do accept reciprocity do not unanimously demand, in turn, that it represent the "mathematical equivalent" of what was received. This also fails to duplicate a Piaget finding.

[4] Bruce, 1941; Deutsche, 1937; Grigsby, 1932; Hazlett, 1930; Harrower, 1934.

3. Older children tend to show greater overt concern for possible mitigating factors in the situation being judged. This bears out Piaget's findings concerning the emergence of "equity" with age.

4. Although not always statistically significant, there is a trend toward no relationship between a child's particular concept of what is just and his level of intelligence.

·············· **52** ··············

EXPRESSED STANDARDS OF BEHAVIOR OF HIGH SCHOOL STUDENTS, TEACHERS, AND PARENTS

by Laurence Siegel, Herbert L. Coon, Harold B. Pepinsky, and Stanley Rubin[1]

COMMENTS

Irwin A. Berg

High school students, teachers, and parents agree rather closely on how students should and should not act in seven different school situations. There is, however, a definite disagreement between students and adults about the specific means of attaining these standards of behavior. These are the general conclusions of the following selection by Laurence Siegel of Miami University, Herbert L. Coon and Harold B. Pepinsky of Ohio State University, and Stanley Rubin of Cleveland Vocational Guidance and Rehabilitation Service. Irwin A. Berg of Louisiana State University assesses the implications of the study. [From *Personnel and Guidance Journal*, 1956, *34*, 261-267. Reprinted by permission of the authors and the American Personnel and Guidance Association.]

The present study is one phase of a long-range research inquiry into the emotional health of school children (Coon and Pepinsky, 1955). As the research progressed, it appeared that information about students' reference group identifications could provide a better understanding of how they behaved. An individual's *reference group* was defined as the group from which he derived his conceptions of how to act, and against which he evaluated his own

[1] Undertaken jointly by the Ohio State University School and the research division of the Occupational Opportunities Service, and financed, in part, by the Ohio State University Development Fund.

behavior (Kelley, 1952). For a student, such reference groups might consist of fellow pupils, teachers, or parents. In a given situation, however, these three groups might be sufficiently congruent to provide a general and undifferentiated set of standards for the student to follow. Consequently, the purpose of this investigation was to determine the extent of agreement among pupils, parents, and teachers in a particular school setting, on describing how students should and should not act in a variety of typical school situations.

METHOD

The subjects in this investigation were obtained from three different groups. One group consisted of 225 students (all in attendance on the day the information was gathered) enrolled in the seventh through twelfth grades at the Ohio State University School. A second group consisted of a majority ($N = 19$) of the high school teachers in the school. The third group was comprised of a small number ($N = 18$) of parents who had children enrolled in the University School.

Each student was given a seven-item open-ended questionnaire to complete in class and to return at the end of the period to his counselor (core teacher). Inclusion of the name of the respondent was optional; the only positive identification of each subject was in terms of sex and grade. Similar questionnaires, differing only in identification of type of respondent, were given to parents and teachers. One-half of these subjects was given the following instructions: "In each of the following situations think of a student who acts the way *you* feel he *should*. Keep him (her) in mind as you write a few sentences or a short paragraph describing his actions." The words "should not" were substituted for "should" on the questionnaires distributed to the other half of the subjects.

Respondents were asked to describe "should" or "should not" behavior in the following situations:
1. In the classroom
2. Playing on a school team
3. On class trips or money-making projects
4. In the hallways between classes
5. Watching a school athletic event
6. On a public bus
7. Others (such as dining room, library, free time)
The responses to the questionnaire were analyzed independentl

ınd then jointly by research personnel, for the purpose of establishing behavioral categories for both desirable and undesirable behavior, as indicated by the subjects' responses. The behavioral
categories derived from inspection of the questionnaire responses are
cited in Table 1. Only the *desirable* categories (elicited from the
"should" form of the questionnaire) are listed. Each statement of
behavior in categories *A* through *G*, however, had an *undesirable*
counterpart (elicited from the "should not" form). Thus, *A-1:* "not
a storyteller" was paralleled by "storytelling"; the counterpart of
A-2: "mature conduct" was "childish conduct," etc. It is interesting
to note that statements in categories *H* and *I* were elicited only on
the positive form of the questionnaire.

TABLE 1

CATEGORIES FOR CODING "DESIRABLE" STUDENT BEHAVIORS

A. *Unobtrusive*
    1. Not a storyteller
    2. Mature conduct
    3. Does not show off
    4. No profanity to peers
    5. Does not make a fool of oneself or fool around
    6. Does not smoke, drink, or chew
    7. Is not a "know-it-all" or big shot
    8. Does not over- or underdress
    9. Not pseudo-sophisticated
    10. Does not neck publicly or flirt
    11. Modest
    12. Does not talk too much
    13. Generally unobtrusive
B. *Not Ordering Others*
    1. Does not force others
    2. Not domineering
C. *Not Tearing Down Others*
    1. Does not gossip
    2. Does not tear down others
    3. Kind
    4. Does not tease
    5. Does not embarrass others
    6. Is not overcritical
    7. Is not sarcastic—sassy, outspoken
D. *Skilled, Impressive*
    1. Skillful—on the ball—careful
    2. Alive, alert
    3. Neat—good manners

      4. Liked

      5. Sense of humor

      6. Can make decisions

E. *Respectful, Polite, etc.*

      1. Does not talk back to elders

      2. Is not a vandal, paper thrower

      3. Polite and courteous

      4. Not rude; is respectful

      5. Does not distract others

      6. Kind

      7. Does not tease

      8. Is not profane to elders

      9. Is not loud or noisy; does not yell

    10. Considerate

    11. Does not fight

    12. Good sportsmanship

    13. Does not embarrass others

    14. Not aggressive

    15. Does not talk out of turn

    16. Does not run around—walks quietly

    17. Orderly; not a rowdy

    18. Does not push or shove

    19. Obeys

    20. Attentive

    21. Does not argue

F. *Identification with Group*

      1. Unselfish, helpful

      2. Responsible

      3. Not cliquish

      4. Friendly

      5. Liberal and sharing

      6. Good school spirit

      7. Does not "steal the show"

      8. Cooperates

      9. Participates

G. *Miscellaneous*

      1. Efficient

      2. Content

      3. Not wasteful (including time)

      4. Truthful

      5. Not a trouble-maker

      6. Not submissive or shy

      7. Prompt

      8. Sets a good example; is a good leader

      9. Good reputation—as a person in general and pertaining to school

    10. Does not ask obvious questions—asks pertinent questions

    11. Honest

    12. Not impatient
    13. Not fidgety
    14. Takes interest in things
H. *Constructive and Creative*
    1. Suggests things; contributes
    2. Conscientious; tries his best
    3. Open-minded
    4. Stimulating; interesting; smart
    5. Constructive and creative
    6. Good student; studies and asks questions
    7. Independent thinker
    8. Alert and interested
    9. Good at sports
    10. Takes part in things
I. *Maturity*
    1. Self-control
    2. "Stick-to-it-iveness"
    3. Reliable
    4. Well-organized
    5. Self-awareness
    6. Good judgment; knows what to do
    7. Good personality
    8. Respected
    9. Knows how to have a good time
    10. Sensitivity to underlying goals

The key outlined in Table 1 was used to score all of the completed questionnaires. The scoring consisted simply of counting the number of *A-1, A-2 . . . I-10* responses made by each subject. Data from the two forms of the questionnaire were combined for subsequent analysis.

Two cautions should be observed in interpreting the results of our analyses. Group differences in responses to the questionnaire are differences only in expressed standards of conduct; we cannot expect that persons will conform in other aspects of their behavior to their verbalized standards of action. Furthermore, much of the discussion to follow assumes that we have adequately categorized these reported standards. This is particularly true of the analysis by major category, wherein specific kinds of behavior were grouped into general classes of behavior. Although the authors feel that these categories were suggested by the data, it is possible for such "factorization by inspection" to be misleading.[2]

[2] At a later stage of this investigation, a representative group of items from this study was "Q-sorted" by students, teachers, and parents. An actual factor-analysis of the items was made, and will be reported in a subsequent paper.

RESULTS

The data permitted three types of comparisons: (1) of students at each grade level, (2) of male and female students, and (3) of students, parents, and teachers.

These three comparisons were made separately for each of the nine major categories (A through I), which can be considered to represent general classes of behavior. In addition, responses to the specific sub-categories, kinds of behavior denoted in Table 1 by arabic numerals, were compared for male and female pupils, and for students vs. parents vs. teachers.

MAJOR CATEGORY

The responses of the various groups to all major categories are summarized in Table 2. The percentages cited for each category were computed by the formula:

$$\frac{\text{Number of responses in the category}}{\text{Total number of responses}}$$

Thus, parents made 466 scorable responses, of which 9.9 per cent were classified in category A, 0.4 per cent in category B, etc.

The comparison of these percentages on a grade level basis yields several patterns of response supported by significant t-ratios. These patterns did not always conform to our prior expectations. One of the original hypotheses involved the notion of a developmental sequence. Presumably such a sequence would manifest itself in a continuum of increasing or decreasing emphasis on certain kinds of behavior by pupils in progressively higher grades. This sequence was clearly apparent for Category A: Unobtrusive behavior; t-ratios between percentage of response for the twelfth grade with every other grade are significant at the 0.01 level of probability.

A somewhat similar sequence occurred in the case of Category C: Not Tearing Down Others. Although the seventh grade made no scorable responses, the eighth grade emphasized this category to a greater extent than did the subsequent grades; t-ratios are significant at less than the 0.05 probability level for comparisons of 8th with 9th, 10th and 12th grades, and at less than the 0.01 level for comparison of 8th and 11th grades.

Such a sequence was apparent again in the case of Category F: Identification with the Group, which tended to be emphasized by the upper grades in general. The 11th grade gave significantly more

TABLE 2

ALLOCATION OF RESPONSES TO MAJOR CATEGORIES OF BEHAVIOR BY

STUDENTS, TEACHERS, AND PARENTS

	Students Grade						Sex		Total	Teachers	Parents
	7	8	9	10	11	12	Boys	Girls			
Number of respondents	48	29	33	36	43	36	115	110	225	19	18
Number of responses	712	564	539	694	712	652	1802	2072	3873	446	466
% in A: Unobtrusive	8.0	8.0	8.0	8.0	8.0	15.0	11.0	8.0	9.0	6.5	9.9
% in B: Not Ordering Others	1.0	1.0	1.0	1.0	1.0	1.0	1.0	1.0	1.0	2.0	0.4
% in C: Not Tearing Down Others	0.0	4.0	2.0	2.0	1.0	2.0	2.0	2.0	2.0	2.9	3.4
% in D: Skilled, Impressive	4.0	3.0	4.0	3.0	1.0	3.0	3.0	3.0	3.0	3.1	4.5
% in E: Respectful, Polite, etc.	63.0	64.0	55.0	62.0	61.0	52.0	57.0	62.0	60.0	49.8	51.5
% in F: Identification with Group	11.0	9.0	11.0	13.0	15.0	12.0	12.0	13.0	13.0	15.5	13.5
% in G: Miscellaneous	5.0	5.0	7.0	5.0	6.0	6.0	7.0	5.0	6.0	8.1	6.7
% in H: Constructive and Creative	7.0	5.0	6.0	4.0	3.0	6.0	6.0	4.0	5.0	7.2	4.7
% in I: Maturity	2.0	1.0	4.0	2.0	4.0	3.0	2.0	3.0	3.0	4.9	5.4

responses of this type than did Grades 7 (t has a probability of less than 0.05), 8 (probability less than 0.01), and 9 (probability less than 0.05). Differences among the three upper grades are not statistically significant.

The last such sequence appears in the data for analysis of responses in Category *I: Maturity*. Students in the 7th grade made significantly fewer *I* responses than did pupils in the 9th and 11th grades (t has a probability of less than 0.05); those in the 8th grade made fewer *I* responses than those in the 9th, 11th, and 12th grades (probability of t less than 0.02). Although the relatively low frequency of responses to this category by 10th grade pupils seems to reverse the trend, it is felt that the general response pattern for the "maturity" category suggests a developmental influence.

Thus we have four patterns of behavior which might be attributed to developmental factors: unobtrusiveness, not tearing others down, identification with the group, and maturity. However, we must look elsewhere for an explanation of the fact that *D: Skilled and Impressive* was de-emphasized particularly by the 11th grade (probabilities less than 0.02); and *E: Respectful, Polite* was de-emphasized by both the 9th grade (probabilities generally less than 0.01) and the 12th grade (probabilities generally less than 0.01). Perhaps these differences resulted from specific teacher effects or other influences which are not yet clear.

Comparison of the responses of boys and girls yielded two differences which might be explained by their notions of acceptable behavior within the larger cultural setting. Thus girls more often emphasized *E: Respectful, Polite* (t probability of less than 0.01) and boys more often emphasized *H: Constructive and Creative* (probability of t less than 0.01). Furthermore, boys made significantly more *A:* Unobtrusive responses than did girls (probability less than 0.01).

The finding that parents are more concerned than students with Category *I: Maturity* (t probability of less than 0.05) is not surprising. However, the fact that students gave significantly more *E: Respectful, Polite* responses than either parents (probability of t less than 0.01) or teachers (probability less than 0.01) requires explanation! Is it possible that adults have learned to be satisfied with platitudes, whereas the students can be guided only by the concrete instances of what adults teach them?

Responses from parents and teachers exhibited a general high level of agreement with one exception. Teachers gave more Category *B: Not Ordering Others* responses (t probability of less than 0.02). Perhaps the teachers' emphasis upon this type of behavior is a reflection of their attempts to socialize simultaneously a rather large and heterogeneous group of youngsters.

The discussion up to this point has been concerned with what might be termed "within-category emphases." The findings suggest that intra-student group differences (*i.e.,* between grades and between sexes) are more noticeable than inter-group (students *vs.* teachers *vs.* parents) differences. All subjects, however, appear to respond similarly when the between-category frequencies are tabulated and analyzed. The greatest proportion of scorable responses consistently occurred in *E: Respectful, Polite,* the second greatest proportion in *F: Identification with the Group,* etc.[3] Conversion of the percentages to ranks yields a between-categories *rho* for students *vs.* teachers of 0.95; students *vs.* parents of 0.88; and teachers *vs.* parents of 0.96. Thus there appears to be a general frame of refer-

---

[3] Note that the proportions for categories *H* and *I* cannot be interpreted literally in this framework because they were elicited only on the *should* form of the questionnaire distributed to half the subjects.

ence that characterizes the responses of all subjects, apart from their particular group memberships.

An important characteristic of this frame of reference is that it is *essentially negative.* An inspection of the categories and sub-categories of Table 1 shows that students, teachers, and parents are prone to describe how students *should* behave by pointing at undesirable activities that they should not engage in. It appears that these persons, like so many in our society, are much better oriented to the avoidance of pathology than they are to the achievement of health (Coon and Pepinsky, 1955).

SPECIFIC BEHAVIORS

Disregarding the differences in emphases between general categories of behavior, we now inquire: "To what extent did the groups of subjects agree in their emphasis upon specific sub-categories?" A

TABLE 3

ALLOCATION OF RESPONSES TO SUB-CATEGORIES: SUMMARY OF SIGNIFICANT DIFFERENCES BETWEEN GROUPS

Sub-Category	Boys vs. Girls*	Students vs. Parents*	Students vs. Teachers*	Parents vs. Teachers*
A. 2. Mature conduct	..	Parents‡	Teachers‡	..
5. Does not make a fool of himself	..	..	Students†	Parents‡
7. Is not a "know-it-all"	Boys†	Students‡	Students†	..
B. 1. Does not force others	..	..	Students†	..
2. Not domineering	..	..	Teachers†	..
C. 6. Is not overcritical	..	..	Teachers†	..
D. 3. Neat—good manners	..	..	Students†	Parents‡
E. 9. Is not loud or noisy	..	Students‡	Students‡	..
10. Considerate	Girls†	Parents†	Teachers‡	..
F. 2. Responsible	..	..	Teachers‡	..
4. Friendly	..	Students‡	..	..
G. 1. Efficient	..	Students‡	..	..
7. Prompt	..	Students†	..	..
H. 1. Suggests things; Contributes	Girls†	..	..	..
6. Good student; studies and asks questions	..	Students‡	Students†	..
I. 1. Self-control	..	..	Students†	..
6. Good judgment	..	..	..	Teachers†
7. Good personality	Girls†	Students†	Students‡	..
9. Knows how to have a good time	Boys‡	..	Students†	..
10. Sensitivity to underlying goals	..	Parents†	Teachers†	..

* Group indicated in column has higher percentage of responses.
† t-ratio of percentage differences in the two groups is significant at less than the 0.05 level of probability.
‡ t-ratio significant at less than the 0.01 level of probability.

summary of the results of this more detailed analysis is presented in Table 3. This table summarizes the significant t-ratios between percentages computed by the formula:

$$\frac{\text{Number of responses in sub-category}}{\text{Number of responses in the major category}}$$

Thus the entry in the column labeled *"Boys vs. Girls,"* Row A-7, indicates that boys allocated significantly more of their category *A* responses to sub-category A-7 than did girls.

Relatively few differences in emphasis were found between parents and teachers. This evidence lends further support to the previous finding that these two groups seem to constitute a relatively homogeneous adult group. It is apparent, however, that students tended to differ from both their teachers and from the parent group in the importance students attached to a substantial number of specific kinds of behaviors. Thus, we may conclude that, although students share with teachers and parents a general set of conduct standards, students do differ from the parent and teacher groups in their conceptions of the specific devices by which such standards are to be achieved. It may be that students differ in, or have not yet learned, adult notions of the specific rules of procedure by which general patterns of behavior are rewarded and punished in an adult society.

SUMMARY

This study was designed to investigate the extent of agreement among students, teachers, and parents in describing how students should or should not act in a variety of school situations. The subjects consisted of 225 students representing Grades 7 through 12, 19 teachers representing these same grades, and 18 parents whose children were attending the Ohio State University School. One-half of the subjects filled out a questionnaire in which they were asked to describe how students *should* act in seven different school situations. Another questionnaire distributed to the remaining half of the subjects asked them to describe how students *should not* act in these same situations. Major categories and sub-categories of behavior were developed from the subjects' responses.

It is concluded that intra-student group differences in expressed (or stated) behavior are more noticeable than inter-group differences (students *vs.* teachers *vs.* parents). The changing frame of reference from grade to grade may be attributed, in part, to developmental factors. Although students, parents, and teachers agree rather closely upon general standards of desirable behavior, there is a noticeable cleavage between students and adults with respect to statements about the specific strategies whereby these standards are to be achieved. All persons sampled, however, seem better oriented to the avoidance of maladjustment than to the attainment of health.

COMMENTS

This study may be looked at from several aspects. One can look at it, for example, as an investigation of a minuscule fragment of human behavior, namely, verbal expressions concerning certain standards of conduct among teachers, students, and parents in a certain Ohio high school. Viewed in this way, the study is competently executed and with never a dash ahead of the data nor any unsupported generalizations. In this sense it is scientifically well-bred; for the authors caution us that only one school is sampled and also remind us that expressions concerning certain conduct are not identical with the conduct itself. The writers go on to remind us of possible imperfections in their categorizing of the verbal statements which constituted their data, and they are careful to emphasize the level of statistical significance for each difference obtained. Regarded as a thing in itself, when one takes into account the nature of the behavior under investigation, the study is workmanlike in design and execution—and like a thousand others.

But viewed in a much broader reference frame, the study is quite exciting because of what it implies. By the very nature of its particular subject matter, this study has implications which go far beyond a mere peep at student-teacher-parent-verbalizations concerning conduct. It is one first small step toward scientific understanding of one of the *Alice in Wonderland* facets of our culture. Riffling through a random selection of back issues of any newsmagazine provides abundant concrete illustrations of the problem. Here is a member of the United States Congress, for example, who solemnly swore to serve his government and the people he represented. But he went to prison, convicted of stealing from that same government and those same citizens. How could he *say* one thing and *do* another? The fact that his theft was on a grand scale is no answer; for here is a policeman, jailed for taking a ten-dollar bribe to circumvent the laws he swore to uphold. Conversely, why should a Chicago cop make headlines when he arrests law violators, whether judges or junkmen, without fear or favor as his oath said he must do? To understand this puzzle, we need to understand what the standards of conduct in verbal and performance terms are at different age levels as well as how these standards were acquired. The present study is a definite start, for it tells us of certain developmental differences in expressions of conduct standards. It suggests that adults learn to be satisfied with a platitude while children are influenced more by concrete and overt behavior. Finally, it uncovers an emphasis on the avoidance of pathology, as opposed to the achievement of health, which was inherent in most of the descriptions supplied by the subjects in the study. Perhaps this latter is really a kind of set for avoidance-of-trouble. That is, in expressed standards of conduct, we point out what gets one in trouble more often than what one should do in positive actions. Or putting it another way, perhaps we accept a platitude such as "be honest and true" and in the same breath recommend avoidance of trouble by some specific standards as "take your payoff only in cash."

The authors have studied only the expressed standards so far and not the accompanying behavior. But they have made a significant first step. Perhaps they did not intend originally to wrestle with a problem that pervades the heart and every niche and nook of our culture. They probably intended a sonnet which now looks like an ode and could be an epic. One is reminded of Herbart, who asserted that mental functions like learning and intelligence could never be measured, only to have investigators like Ebbinghaus and Binet prove him wrong. Similarly, there are those who hold that a *science* of ethics is a contradiction in terms. However, if from the foot one may deduce Hercules, one may also from this small research deduce a science of standards of conduct. It is a gigantic undertaking, but from the sample submitted, authors Siegel, Coon, Pepinsky, and Rubin should be able to do it.

•••••••••••••••••••••••••••••• 53 ••••••••••••••••••••••••••••••

THE DEVELOPMENT OF THE IDEAL SELF
IN CHILDHOOD AND ADOLESCENCE

by Robert J. Havighurst, Myra Z. Robinson,
and Mildred Dorr

Ideals develop from experiences with people and events and from reflections on these experiences. Ideals are important in directing be-

havior, especially when major decisions are involved. Robert J. Havighurst of the University of Chicago, Myra Z. Robinson of the Gary,
Ind., public schools, and Mildred Dorr, of New Paltz State Teachers
College, have studied the development of the ideal self of young
people from ages eight to eighteen who wrote essays on the persons
they would like to be like when they grow up. The results of their
study are described in the article that follows. [From *Journal of Educational Research*, 1946, *40*, 241-257. Reprinted by permission of the
authors and Dembar Publications, Inc.]

The purpose of this article is to describe the development of the
ideal self, or the ego-ideal, as this is revealed by self-reports during
childhood and adolescence. The data were obtained by asking boys
and girls to write a brief essay on the subject "The Person I Would
Like To Be Like."

The concept of an ego-ideal or an ideal self has been found useful
by the Freudian psychologists and by the social psychologists in
studying the development of personality and character. But there
is very little factual information on which to base an extensive use
of this concept.

The Freudians explain the origin of the ego-ideal as due to *identification* with people whom the child loves or admires or fears.
Through the process of identification the child comes to imitate the
values and attitudes of other people. The parents are the first and
most important objects of identification. It is not stated clearly by
the Freudians how important the later objects of identification are
—such as teachers, youth group leaders, heroes of adventure and romance, and attractive age-mates. However, these writers generally
attribute some importance to the people who follow the parents as
objects of identification, believing that the ego-ideal of the adult
is a composite of all the identifications the individual has made,
with the figures of the parents still holding the most prominent
place.

The social psychologists think of the ideal self as a name for the
integrated set of *roles* and *aspirations* which direct the individual's
life. These roles and attitudes they believe are taken on by the individual from parents, and from a variety of others, such as siblings,
playmates, teachers, preachers, and others with prestige, and historical and fictional heroes, and worked over into his own thought and
action.

While it is generally agreed that the ideal self or ego-ideal is important in the development of character and personality, and much attention has been given to the problem of its origin in the early years of life, very little work has been done on its development during childhood and adolescence.

PROCEDURE

The procedure in this study was to ask children to write a brief essay on the topic "The Person I Would Like To Be Like" . . . . We have used the following directions with boys and girls in the age-range 8 to 18:

> Describe in a page or less the person you would most like to be like when you grow up. This may be a real person, or an imaginary person. He or she may be a combination of several people. Tell something about this person's age, character, appearance, occupation, and recreations. If he is a real person, say so. You need not give his real name if you do not want to.

These directions give some very definite leads to the subject. This seems desirable, for many children would not know how to begin unless they were given some suggestion. Furthermore, this insures a degree of comparability in the essays, which makes it possible to rate them for the quality of the ideals expressed, something that has proved useful, though it is not reported in this paper.

It will be noted that the directions prevent the child from telling about his own age-mates as sources of his ideals, for he is asked to tell about the person he would like to be like *when he grows up.* This is an important limitation on the procedure, and prevents us from getting data on the relative importance of age-mates and of adults in the formation of the ego-ideal. Yet some children ignore the directions and describe an age-mate. This happens most often with children aged about fourteen. . . .

RESULTS

Analysis of the responses in several sets of papers led to the use of the following categories.

I P	Parents and other relatives of the parental or grand-parental generation.
II S	Parent-surrogates: teachers, neighbors of the parental generation.
III G	Glamorous adults: people with a romantic or ephemeral fame.

| | due to the more superficial qualities of appearance and behavior —e.g., movie stars, military figures, athletes. *Note:* characters in comic strips or radio dramas are included here, though they may be imaginary—e.g., Superman, Dick Tracy. |

IV H Heroes, people with a substantial claim to fame, usually tested by time—e.g., Florence Nightingale and Abraham Lincoln. However, certain living persons are placed in this category— e.g., Madame Chiang Kai-shek, the President, General Mac-Arthur.

V A Attractive and successful young adults within the individual's range of observation: these are usually young people who live in the community, or go to a local college, or lead a scout group, or are related to the subject—elder siblings, cousins, young uncles and aunts. They can be observed by the subject in three dimensions, as it were—going about their daily work, making moral decisions, getting along with family and friends, preparing for an occupation.

VI C Composite or imaginary characters: these are abstractions of a number of people. Sometimes they appear to be wholly imaginary, other times they are clearly a coalescence of qualities of two or three real persons.

VII M Age-mates or youths, only two or three years older than the subject. While the directions sought to prevent the naming of these people, some were named.

VIII NC Miscellaneous responses, not classifiable among those mentioned above. A fairly frequent response in this category is "myself."

* * *

Essays from several groups of subjects have been classified, with results shown in Table 1. The age of the group increases from left to right in the table. Groups *A* and *I* came from the same community, as did groups *C* and *E*. Changes with age should show most clearly in a study of these two pairs of groups. From inspection of the table it is at once evident that there is much apparently random variation from group to group, which is not explainable as due to change with age. This kind of variability from group to group may be explained as due to any or all of the following possible causes: (1) unreliability of the instrument, either in the responses of the subjects or in the categorization of the responses; (2) accidents of sampling, since the numbers in several of the groups are small; (3) differences in the social environments of the various groups. No doubt some of the variability is due to the sampling factor, but a considerable part is due to the other two factors, as will be shown later.

Several general conclusions may be drawn from Table 1. One conclusion is that the responses fall mainly into four categories, those of parents, glamorous adults, attractive and visible young adults, and composite, imaginary characters. Parent-surrogates such as teachers and older adults are seldom named, and heroes are very seldom named.

TABLE 1

CLASSIFICATION OF PERSONS DESCRIBED AS THE IDEAL SELF
PERCENTAGE DISTRIBUTION

BOYS

Group*	A	B	C	D	E	F	G	H	I
No. of Papers	60	26	89		94	85	106	31	48
Category									
I P	7	23	11		16	7	16	3	6
II S	0	0	0		0	2	2	0	11
III G	12	32	47		23	37	40	22	6
IV H	3	6	11		10	5	3	13	2
V A	53	30	23		21	15	24	9	25
VI C	25	6	8		28	28	15	19	48
VII M	0	0	0		2	1	0	13	2
VIII NC	0	3	0		0	5	0	19	0

GIRLS

Group*	A	B	C	D	E	F	G	H	I
No. of Papers	100	36	105	17	114	70	80		86
Category									
I P	6	32	14	6	11	7	20		3
II S	2	0	2	0	4	12	9		1
III G	16	17	27	23	21	37	21		1
IV H	2	3	3	6	1	7	7		4
V A	36	13	25	18	25	18	23		28
VI C	33	22	23	29	35	18	15		61
VII M	3	8	6	12	3	1	5		2
VIII NC	0	5	0	6	0	0	0		0

* Description of groups:
  A. Ten-, eleven-, and twelve-year-olds in a typical small midwestern community.
  B. Sixth-graders (age 11-12) in an industrial section of Chicago.
  C. Fifth- and sixth-graders (age 11-12) in a war industry community.
  D. Girls at a Chicago Settlement House (ages 11-14), mostly Italian.
  E. Seventh- and eighth-graders (age 13-14) in a war industry community.
  F. Middle-class Negro children (age 12-14) in Baltimore.
  G. Ninth-graders (age 14-15) in a lower-middle-class suburb of Chicago.
  H. Boys (age 16-17) in a Vocational High School in Chicago.
  I. Sixteen- and seventeen-year-olds in a typical small midwestern community.

A second conclusion is that an age sequence exists, moving outward from the family circle, becoming more abstract, and culminating in the composite, imaginary person. This is by no means a rigid sequence. Some steps are omitted by some children. Yet a comparison of groups *A* and *I* and *C* and *E* gives evidence of the reality of the age sequence when the subjects of different ages are drawn from the same social environment.

The following hypothesis appears to account for the observed age trends. The child from the age of six to about eight generally chooses a parent or some other family member. Most children then move on to a choice either of a glamorous person or an attractive, visible young adult. The age for choosing a glamorous person is about eight to sixteen. The choice of an attractive, visible young adult may start at eight or ten and continue all through adolescence, or it may give way to a more abstract ego-ideal in the form of a composite imaginary person. The final and mature stage of the ego-ideal is the composite of desirable characteristics, drawn from all of the persons with whom the individual has identified himself during his childhood and adolescence.

A third conclusion is that social environment affects the choice of the ideal self. This is to be expected, since different social environments expose children to different kinds of people who may serve as objects of identification, and teach different values and aspirations. The effect of social environment is seen by comparing the frequencies of response in the glamorous person and composite person categories for various groups. Children from families of lower socio-economic status name a higher proportion of glamorous persons. This is seen by comparing groups *A, B,* and *C,* in Table 1, the members of which are all about the same age. The average socio-economic status of the members of group *A* is higher than that of the members of groups *B* and *C.* Carroll (1945) compared a Negro middle-class with a Negro lower-class group (ages 12-14) and found that three-quarters of the lower-class responses fell into the category of glamorous adults, while only about half as many of the middle-class responses fell into this category.

A further influence of the social setting is to be found in the occasional presence of one or more unusually attractive adults in the environment of the group that is being tested. For example, one fifth-grade group happened to have a very attractive teacher, and the children mentioned this teacher frequently in their essays, although teachers generally are not mentioned very often.

The school program also has an influence on the responses of children in their essays. Sister Mary Phelan (1936) reports that for children in Catholic parochial schools the frequency of mention of religious persons increased after several months of teaching about ideals. Even such an event as a Washington's Birthday celebration will stimulate more mention than usual of George Washington.

Table 2 shows the age of the persons mentioned in the essays.

TABLE 2

AGES OF PERSONS DESCRIBED AS THE IDEAL SELF—PERCENTAGE DISTRIBUTION

Age of Persons Mentioned*	A	B	C and E	F	G	I
Under 20	16	18	23	14	13	6
20-29	72	33	35	49	36	65
30-39	9	29	29	27	51	16
40-49	3	16	10	4	(30 and	9
Over 50	0	4	3	6	over)	4

*Note: Ten to forty per cent of the papers did not give ages. The age was often omitted when parents were mentioned. For description of groups, see Table 1.

While there is again a good deal of variation among the groups, this variation does not appear to be related to the age of the children. Most of them think of their ideal selves as being in the twenties or thirties.

RELIABILITY OF THE CATEGORIES AND CONSISTENCY OF RESPONSE

Before we can proceed with any assurance to draw conclusions from the data in Tables 1 and 2 we must find out, first, whether our analysis of the papers is reliable, and second, whether the children give consistent responses—whether they give the same type of response upon repeating the essay.

The reliability of the analysis was tested by computing the percentage of agreement among two or more judges who assigned the papers to the categories. In comparing the work of several people we found that the percentage of agreement between two judges is 85 to 90 per cent. Occasionally the agreement is less, with a new judge or an unusual set of papers. Seldom is the agreement greater than 90 per cent, unless the judges work out some conventions together beforehand. The differences between judges usually are due to the following uncertainties:

Whether to place a paper in the "attractive, visible adult" category or in the "composite, imaginary character" category when the paper seems to be describing a real person but does not say so explicitly.

Whether to place a paper in the "composite" category when it names two or three definite people, such as the father and a military person, without much attempt at integration of their characteristics into a new, composite character.

Whether to place a paper in the "parent-surrogate" category or the "attractive, visible adult" category when the person mentioned is neither clearly a young adult nor definitely of the parental generation.

To get an answer to the question of the consistency of children's responses, we used the test—retest method, comparing the responses of a group with another set of responses from the same group after a ten-week interval. This experiment was carried out by one of us (M. Z. R.) on group G of Table 1. This was a ninth-grade group, aged 14-15, in the high school of a lower-middle-class suburb of Chicago. This group was 3 per cent Mexican, 5 per cent Polish, 8 per cent Italian, 17 per cent Negro, and 67 per cent old American largely of German and Scandinavian origin. Family incomes ranged from $100 to $400 per month (in 1943), with most of them about $200 per month.

Ten weeks after the first assignment, it was repeated with the following additional instructions:

Write on the subject "The Person I Would Like to be Like." You will probably remember that you were asked to write on this same subject some time ago. Just write anything you like, and do the best you can.

A few pupils inquired whether it was all right to repeat what they had said; and some asked whether they might change. Whichever question arose, pupils were told it was "all right" and both possibilities were stressed equally.

The pupil's choice of an ideal self may be said to be stable or consistent if it remains unchanged with respect to the following:

1. The person or the type of person described.
2. The traits of character and personality ascribed to this person.
3. The age ascribed to this person.

The essays were analyzed to find out the degree of consistency of response according to these three criteria.

Stability in the type of person mentioned was measured in two ways. The first way, called the "group method," consisted in counting the number of persons in a given category—for example, "parents"—on the first administration of the essay, and comparing this number with the number of responses in the same category on the second administration. Thus, as is shown in Table 3, the girls made seven mentions of parents on the first administration, and nine on the second. As a group, then, they gave seven consistent choices. The extra choices of two parents on the second administration are not counted as inconsistent because they mean two less choices in some other categories, and will be counted at these points.

The second way of measuring stability of choice, called the "individual method," consisted in finding out how many individuals made choices in the same category both times. For example, although seven girls chose parents the first time and nine the second time, only six individuals chose parents both times. Therefore, by the individual method, there were six consistent choices and one inconsistent choice (the seventh girl, who changed from a parent to a person in another category). The individual method gives a more rigorous test of stability than does the group method.

Stability of traits of character and personality mentioned was also measured by the group and individual methods. Here the amount of stability observed will depend partly upon the number and breadth of the categories used. If many highly specialized categories are used, the observed stability will tend to be lower than when a few broad categories are used. The number of categories chosen was seven, which allows for a considerable degree of differentiation of characteristics mentioned, and makes the test fairly rigorous. The items within a category were put together for two reasons: first, they tend to belong together psychologically (e.g., "honest, responsible, industrious"); and second, they tend to appear together in the essays (e.g., "friendly, courteous, polite, can take a joke").

Stability in the age ascribed to a person was measured by the same two methods, with ages thrown into three categories.

The results of this analysis are summarized in Tables 3, 4, and 5. They indicate that the degree of consistency is about 90 per cent when measured by the group method and 80 per cent when measured by the individual method. The girls were slightly more consistent than the boys.

We conclude that the reliability of the analysis and the consistency of responses are high enough to permit comparisons of groups of different ages and social backgrounds and to allow generalizations about the influence of these factors on the development of the ideal self.

TABLE 3

KINDS OF PEOPLE CHOSEN

	Number, first essay	Number, second essay	Number of consistent choices (Treated as a group)	Number of inconsistent choices (Treated as a group)	Number of consistent choices (Individual treatment)	Number of inconsistent choices (Individual treatment)	Average per cent in each category
BOYS							
Parents	11	6	6	5	5	6	16
Parent Surrogates	1	1	1	0	1	0	2
Glamorous adults	22	20	20	2	18	4	40
Heroes	3	0	0	3	0	3	3
Attractive young adults	11	15	11	0	10	1	24
Composite, abstract characters	7	9	7	0	6	1	15
Age mates	0	0	0	0	0	0	0
Totals	55	51	45	10	40	15	—
GIRLS							
Parents	7	9	7	0	6	1	20
Parent Surrogates	3	4	3	0	3	0	9
Glamorous adults	9	8	8	1	7	2	21
Heroes	4	2	2	2	2	2	7
Attractive young adults	8	10	8	0	7	1	23
Composite, abstract characters	6	6	6	0	5	1	15
Age mates	2	2	2	0	2	0	5
Totals	39	41	36	3	32	7	—

TABLE 4

CHARACTER AND PERSONALITY TRAITS MENTIONED

	Number, first essay	Number, second essay	Number of consistent choices (Treated as a group)	Number of inconsistent choices	Number of consistent choices (Individual treatment)	Number of inconsistent choices	Average per cent in each category
BOYS							
Material values—money, clothes, property	15	19	15	0	15	0	21
Good looks, good appearance, neat, clean	9	12	9	0	8	1	13
Good personality, stereotypes, popular	11	10	10	1	7	4	13
Friendly, lots of friends, courteous, polite, can take a joke	16	15	15	1	10	6	20
Honest, responsible, industrious, church-goer, kind	23	19	19	4	17	6	27
Cooperative, helpful, patient	3	2	2	1	1	2	3
Self-sacrificing, working for social justice, human brotherhood, altruism	3	1	1	2	1	2	3
Totals	80	78	71	9	59	21	—
GIRLS							
Material values—money, clothes, property	1	2	1	0	1	0	2
Good looks, good appearance, neat, clean	24	27	24	0	22	2	30
Good personality, stereotypes, popular	10	10	10	0	9	1	12
Friendly, lots of friends, courteous, polite, can take a joke	11	11	11	0	8	3	13
Honest, responsible, industrious, church-goer, kind	26	25	25	1	24	2	30
Cooperative, helpful, patient	10	8	8	2	8	2	11
Self-sacrificing, working for social justice, human brotherhood, altruism	2	1	1	1	1	1	2
Totals	84	84	80	4	73	11	—

TABLE 5

CONSISTENCY OF RESPONSE IN PERCENTAGES

	BOYS		GIRLS	
	Treated as a group	*Treated as individuals*	*Treated as a group*	*Treated as individuals*
Choices of people	83	73	92	82
Choices of character and personality traits	89	74	95	88
Choices in respect to age	96	84	95	84

The earlier studies made with a somewhat similar assignment are not strictly comparable with this one for two reasons. First, the directions were different. The assignment given in an early study, by Darrah (1898) was,

What person of whom you have heard or read would you most like to resemble? Why?

Hill (1930) gave a similar direction.

Of all persons whom you have heard, or read about, or seen, whom would you most care to be like or resemble? Why?

Sister Mary Phelan (1936) gave the pupil more latitude by asking,

Who is your ideal? Why have you chosen this ideal?

The directions given by Darrah and by Hill asked the child to name a person, whereas our direction explicitly told the child he could name a real person or an imaginary person. Sister Mary Phelan's direction falls between in the strength of its suggestion that a real person be mentioned.

In view of these differences in the assignment, we should expect that our study would get more frequent mentions of composite and imaginary characters; and this did happen. However, in the studies by Hill and Sister Mary Phelan a number of boys and girls insisted in spite of the directions, on describing abstract or composite characters, and their papers were thrown into a "Miscellaneous" category.

The second reason that our study is not strictly comparable with the earlier studies is that we have used a different scheme of analysis of the persons mentioned. We used this new scheme because it served to test our hypothesis concerning the development of the ideal self.

The earlier studies divided the persons mentioned on the essays

into two broad groups, one belonging to the immediate environment and the other to the remote environment. The persons in
the immediate environment were further divided into the categories
of parents, teachers, and other acquaintances; those from the remote
environment were separated into the categories of historical and
contemporary, literary, and religious characters.

No single one of our categories is identical with one of those used
in the earlier studies. The one which is most similar, our category
I P, consists not only of parents but also of other relatives of the
parental or grandparental generation. Consequently we shall not
attempt to make detailed comparisons.

There is one difference between our results and those of earlier
studies, however, which stands out quite clearly. We found very few
mentions of "heroes" or great people of history or literature, while
in the earlier studies the frequency of such characters was high. Sister Mary Phelan found over sixty per cent of the responses at ages
from 11 to 18 to be either religious or historical or contemporary
public figures. Hill got about the same over-all results from public
school children, although the number of religious characters was
much less than in the parochial school papers.

These figures are to be contrasted with our own finding of less
than ten per cent of the responses in the category of "heroes." However, to make our data more nearly comparable with those of Hill
and Phelan, we should add the "glamorous adults" to the "heroes";
for a movie star or a prize-fighter, if mentioned in one of Hill's or
Phelan's papers, was counted in the category of "historical and
contemporary characters." The examples given by these writers show
that the counterparts of present-day "glamorous adults" were mentioned in the earlier studies, including: Clara Bow, Billie Dove,
Babe Ruth, Douglas Fairbanks, Mary Pickford, Dizzy Dean, Jack
Oakie, Eddie Cantor, The Arkansas Woodchopper, Shirley Temple,
and Jackie Coogan.

It appears, however, that the "glamorous adult" was mentioned
somewhat less frequently and the "hero" somewhat more frequently
in the studies made ten, twenty, and fifty years ago.

CONCLUSIONS

This study shows a developmental trend in the ideal self of the
following nature. The ideal self commences in childhood as an
identification with a parental figure, moves during middle child-

hood and early adolescence through a stage of romanticism and glamour, and culminates in late adolescence as a composite of desirable characteristics which may be symbolized by an attractive, visible young adult, or may be simply an imaginary figure.

Parents or members of the parental generation play a declining role in the ideal self as it is described by children after the age of eight or ten. "Glamorous" adults have their day in the child's ego-ideal between the ages of ten and fifteen. Anyone older than fifteen who reports a "glamorous" person as his ego-ideal is probably immature, by standards of development as found in most young people. It is not certain whether the stage of greatest maturity is that represented by our category of the attractive, visible adult or that represented by our category of the composite, imaginary character. Evidence from adults might settle this point.

The environment of the child has a great effect on his ideal self. Children and young people from families of lower socio-economic status as a group lag behind those of middle socio-economic status in progressing through the stage of selection of a glamorous adult as the ideal. Individuals in the child's environment influence his ideal self, especially if they are young adults. Thus an especially attractive teacher or youth group leader may symbolize the ego-ideal during the age period usually dominated by the glamorous person. Furthermore, the teaching of the school, especially if it is aimed at inculcating ideals through teaching about the lives of great people, certainly influences the child's report concerning his ideal self.

The high susceptibility of the child's response about his ideal self to rather short-term and superficial teaching influences raises some doubts about the validity of our method of securing information. It seems probable that the individual's core values and attitudes do not change as rapidly and easily as might be suggested by his changing, for example, from a movie star to a solid, successful young man in the local community for the symbol of his ideal self. Probably very few children or adolescents have enough insight into their own personalities to give a full report on their ego-ideals. Some individuals may even have a good deal of unconscious resistance to recognizing the nature of the ideal self. This may be the case with a number of boys and a few girls who insist, in a defensive tone, that they want to be like themselves and no one else.

Nevertheless, we may be sure that an individual will not report an ideal which is repugnant to him, nor will he report a set of ideals which he has not thought about at all. There is nothing for the individual to gain in the essay-writing situation by giving false witness about himself. If there has been no coaching of the child to name certain kinds of people when asked questions about his ideal self, the results represent something genuine and deep down in his personality.

The set of categories we have used to classify the persons mentioned seems to us to be useful in testing hypotheses about *development* of the ideal self. However, it leaves something to be desired as a measure of increasing maturity of personality. We were forced to choose between categories of persons and categories of qualities of persons. Categories based upon qualities might serve as a better indicator of maturity. . . .

There is a great deal of evidence that the ideal self is deeply influenced by association with people who are in positions of prestige because they are older, more powerful, and better able to get the desirable things of life than the child or adolescent who observes them. Our study adds to this evidence. A boy or girl combines qualities of parents with qualities of attractive, successful young adults into a composite ego-ideal. The inference is clear that schools, churches and youth-serving agencies influence the ideals of youth as much or more through the presence and behavior of teachers, clergy, and youth-group leaders as through their verbal teachings.

·············· **54** ··············

THE MORAL BELIEFS OF SIXTEEN-YEAR-OLDS

by Hilda Taba

In this selection Hilda Taba, of San Francisco State College, gives us some understanding of the adolescents' code of morals with respect to qualities of friendliness, honesty, loyalty, moral courage, and responsibility. It is found that young people sixteen years of age are underdeveloped in the ability to apply moral beliefs to their daily experiences and tend to resolve their conflicts by using stereotyped slogans rather than value judgments. The selection is taken from a cooperative investigation that aims to study the character and personality of the sixteen-year-olds in a midwestern American community. [From *Adolescent Character and Personality*, by Robert J.

Havighurst and Hilda Taba, New York: John Wiley and Sons, Inc., 1949, pp. 83-87. Reprinted by permission of the authors and John Wiley and Sons, Inc.]

FRIENDLINESS

The prevailing concept of friendliness is that of being amiable and accommodating to all people, being popular, and having many friends. For example, 75 per cent of the students believe in not saying unkind things, in taking time to cheer up unhappy persons, in making strangers feel at home at a party, and in having many friends.

Whenever there is a conflict between personal friendship and attending to lessons, being honest, or just being busy, attention to friends is usually subordinated. Expressions of common politeness, such as paying attention to people neglected at parties, are accepted more frequently than acts of friendship involving sacrifice of personal values. Few subjects, for example, agreed with such statements as "When you haven't the time to keep up with your lessons and your friends, it is better to neglect your lessons than your friends," or "Keeping friends is so important that it would be foolish not to tell a little fib to accomplish that."

Loyalty to personal friends figures none too strongly and is usually subordinated to other values. Rarely is a boy or girl willing to defend the wrongdoing of a personal friend. On the surface this fact seems to contradict common observations as well as evidence from studies of adolescent gang loyalties. However, considered in the framework of this test and in the context of the community, it seems natural for these students to give precedence to character values other than friendliness—at least intellectually.

HONESTY

Of the five traits, standards of honesty are the most widely and unquestioningly accepted. Positive scores in this area are the highest, and negative scores are low.

The concept of honesty is dominated by ideas about the use of property and telling the truth. Such acts as borrowing things without permission and using small sums of the family's money without permission are highly disapproved. Telling the truth to employers, teachers, and parents is uniformly and rigorously accepted. Compromises occur only when telling the truth involves betraying another student, thus suggesting tattling. Usually, also, some compromise is attempted when protecting friends conflicts with being honest and truthful towards school authorities. Rigorous and even extreme standards are used in judging other people's honesty.

Only with reference to responsibility can one detect a similarly strict pattern of moral beliefs.

LOYALTY

Beliefs in this area seem to be confused and uncertain. . . .

Loyalty to personal friends is often subordinated to other values. Apparently for Prairie City subjects there is a code of not betraying friends outright, but not a similarly strong code of pleasing or cherishing friends.

Loyalty to school seems to be limited to obeying school rules—attending school parties and school activities is not taken very seriously. A somewhat more positive attitude is expressed in connection with the problem situations. These suggest willingness to contribute to school welfare, willingness to carry on certain activities in spite of the razzing of immediate friends, and willingness to stand up for worth-while causes against the criticism of peers. This suggests that loyalty to school is seen in terms of obvious, concrete actions but that a generalized concept of loyalty to school as an institution is lacking.

Loyalty to leaders is qualified by an unwillingness to support them if one disagrees with them.

The least-developed aspect is loyalty to ideas, principles, and values. A high degree of uncertainty characterizes reactions to all issues involving conflict of several loyalties or conflict of loyalty with other values, such as defending the family against criticism or dropping a friendship if one's reputation is endangered.

MORAL COURAGE

The strongest aspect of moral courage is that of defending and protecting one's own rights and those of others. There is practically a unanimous feeling that one must defend anyone against gossip. Yet doubt and fear are expressed about any opinion or action, no matter how right, which is likely to arouse the displeasure of any person in authority or jeopardize one's popularity with peers. There is hesitancy in raising questions of rightness and wrongness in criticizing peers, for fear of being regarded a prig. Subjects also show unwillingness to undertake action which may be needed for the benefit of a group or project, if that action suggests direct or implied criticism of other students. They seem inclined to leave others' business alone, even though other values may be sacrificed. Following the group, even into wrongdoing, is rather highly approved.

On the whole, rebels show more moral courage than do students who are generally amenable to accepted standards. This suggests that rebels and negatively disposed individuals have greater opportunity to develop moral courage because their personal make-up predisposes them to act in ways which are conducive to moral courage. Individuals with positive moral values, but more submissive dispositions, have fewer opportunities for defending their positive and desirable values.

RESPONSIBILITY

Standards of responsibility are highly developed, and they are applied under a variety of circumstances. Duties toward school, home, and employment are taken seriously. Punctuality in attending meetings, completing accepted jobs, and aiding the family financially stand high on the list of approved items. Especially rigorous standards are set up for other people, and lenience toward athletes or talented or forgetful people is highly disapproved.

There is a great assurance that the first duty of a student is toward his own success, whether in earning grades or in preparing for life work. Very few of our subjects consider it wise to sacrifice this value to any demands that might be made by the general school welfare. On the whole responsibility toward work outside school is taken more seriously than responsibility toward school work or school activities.

Uncertainties occur most frequently in the case of conflicts between family loyalty, school responsibilities, and friends.

SOME COMMON CHARACTERISTICS

Accepting familiar stereotypes is one outstanding characteristic of these beliefs. High agreement usually occurs on statements which express the obvious middle-class codes of conduct in stereotyped language requiring little thought or analysis. Thus, politeness characterizes the concept of friendship. Punctuality and completing accepted jobs characterize the concept of responsibility. Such general slogans as "One has to sacrifice fun for honesty in life" or "It is always a good policy to be nice to people" are among the most frequently marked items, as are such repeatedly emphasized verities as the necessity of obeying school rules no matter what they are, and doing boring jobs if the school needs them, in order to be a good citizen. These slogans are accepted in a general way without question; but exceptions and inconsistencies appear when these values are represented in specific situations.

Individual positions deviating from the generally accepted code are feared and shunned. This is shown by hesitancy in expressing opinions contrary to common beliefs and by approving wrong behavior if most of one's associates are involved in the act. There is a marked tendency to subordinate individually held positions and beliefs to both adult and peer-group opinion, even when one's own positions are considered morally right. Exceptions to this submissiveness to peer-group opinion occur only in cases of conflict between peer opinion and some higher authority, such as the church, parents, or the community code. Peer censure is often subordinated to parental censure.

A third common characteristic is the lack of readiness to face conflicts of choices. The predominant reaction to conflict situations is uncertainty or an attempt at a compromise solution. For example, there is hesitancy in taking positions when loyalty to friends and school work conflict, or when loyalty to family and loyalty to friends are opposed to each other. On the whole, uncertainties or negative responses are frequent on items expressing a conflict of values, whereas positive responses predominate on items stating a straightforward position.

CHAPTER EIGHTEEN

Social Attitudes and Opinions

55

TEENAGE ATTITUDES

by H. H. Remmers and D. H. Radler

What are the beliefs, problems, and desires of Americans of high-school age? The answer is sought through polls of about 3,000 high-school students in all parts of the United States. The "tendency to conformity among our younger generation . . . is the most striking and most consistent fact that has emerged from our polls through the 17 years." This is the general conclusion of the following selection by H. H. Remmers and D. H. Radler of Purdue University. [From *Scientific American*, June 1958, *198*, 25-29. Reprinted by permission of the authors and *Scientific American*.]

What is today's younger generation really like? What it its prevailing attitude; what is it thinking; how is it likely to handle its own and the world's problems when it grows up? These are perennial questions to which past ages have never had any dependable answer. Nowadays, thanks to the development of public-opinion polling, we can look into the matter in a systematic way and arrive at rather reliable conclusions. Of course generalizations are always open to question. The teenagers of the U. S. are a heterogeneous group, with all sorts of opinions and attitudes. Paraphrasing Edmund Burke, we must grant that we do not know a method of drawing up a description of a whole generation. Nevertheless on a statistical basis

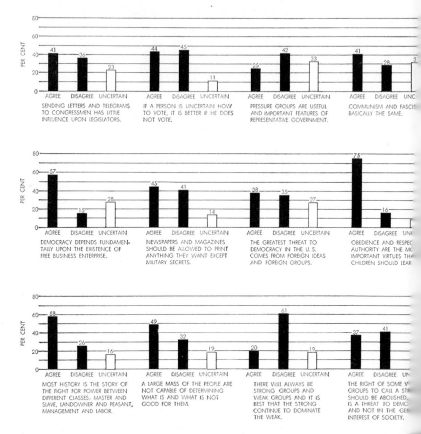

CHART 1. Social attitudes of teenagers are reflected by the bars in these charts. ▮
University. Each bar represents the percentage of the teenagers polled who indicate▮
school grades, various sections of the country, cities *v.* rural areas, and family

we can paint something like a portrait of "the typical teenager."
Scientific surveys of the nation's young people have made clear that
their problems, beliefs and desires follow a characteristic pattern.

One of the authors (Remmers) started this study of adolescents in
1941. During the past 17 years his group at Purdue University has
carried out more than 50 polls of samples of the U. S. teenage population. Last year we published a summary and interpretation of
the results of the first 45 polls in the book *The American Teenager*
Remmers and Radler (1957). This article not only brings the polling
results up to date but also gives us an opportunity to re-examine our
conclusions and to clarify the interpretations set forth in the book.

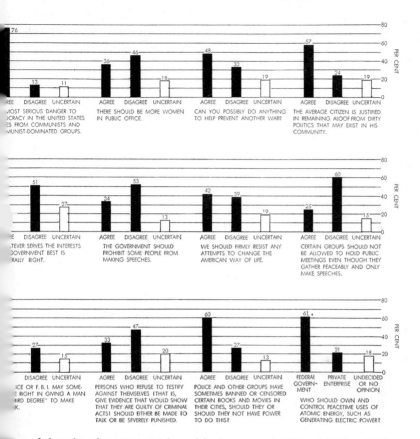

set of three bars is a statement framed by Remmers and his associates at Purdue
nse to the statement. The 3,000 teenagers polled were chosen to represent all high-
ds. Only a few of the many statements tested in the poll are shown in the charts.

Our samples of the younger generation have been drawn from the
nation's high schools, which since the early 1940s have enrolled
virtually all of the country's teenagers. Each sample consists of about
3,000 students, chosen to represent accurately all the high-school
grades, the various sections of the country, rural and city dwellers
and roughly the various family backgrounds. Aside from giving the
correct statistical representation to these groupings, the samples are
completely random. The poll questions are tested beforehand to
make sure that they really ask what we want them to ask and that
they will elicit uninfluenced answers; that is, the questions are made
as semantically "clean" as possible. The subjects' responses are re-

corded anonymously. They are put on punch cards and tabulated and analyzed by computers.

The most significant place to start our examination of the results of these polls is to look at what U. S. teenagers list as their most common problems [see Chart 3]. At the head of the list is the wistful plea: "Want people to like me more." And most of the things that 25 per cent or more of the teenagers list as problems express, in one form or another, the same sentiment. A majority of teenagers want to gain or lose weight or otherwise improve their appearance; they want more dates, more friends, more popularity; they get stage fright before a group, worry about their lack of self-confidence. Their overriding concern emerges again when they are asked direct questions about their feelings with respect to approval by others. More than half admit that they try very hard to do everything that will please their friends; 38 per cent declare that the worst of all calamities is to be considered an "oddball."

Naturally these feelings carry over into behavior. Nearly all the teenagers say they disapprove of high-school students drinking— but a quarter of them admit that they drink. More than three quarters disapprove of smoking—but 38 per cent smoke. The whole matter is summed up in the comment of a teenage girl: "It's hard for a teenager to say 'I don't care to when all the rest of the gang are saying, 'Ah, come on.' "

It is hardly necessary to point out that all this has a bearing on the problem of juvenile delinquency. In the high-delinquency slums of our big cities the *average* child is delinquent, according to police reports. Probably one of the most important factors making for delinquency is the need to be accepted as one of the gang: the "bad boy" may become that way because he wants to be "a good guy" in the eyes of his peers, particularly of the leader who sets the standards of acceptance as the head of the neighborhood gang.

But what should concern us much more is how the passion for popularity translates itself into an almost universal tendency to conformity among our younger generation. It runs through all social classes. American teenagers show substantial class differences in many aspects of their behavior, problems and aspirations, but in their desire for popularity and their conformist attitude they are as one: low-income or high-income, their highest concern is to be liked.

This is the most striking and most consistent fact that has emerged from our polls through the 17 years. Poll after poll among our youngsters has given statistical confirmation of the phenomenon o

American life which David Riesman (1950), in his book *The Lonely Crowd*, named "other-direction"—extreme sensitivity to the opinions of others, with a concomitant conformity. As a nation we seem to have a syndrome characterized by atrophy of the will, hypertrophy of the ego and dystrophy of the intellectual musculature.

This rather unpleasant portrait is an inescapable conclusion from the mass of data on the attitudes of the younger generation. More than half of our teenagers believe that censorship of books, magazines, newspapers, radio and television is all right. More than half believe that the Federal Bureau of Investigation and local police should be allowed to use wiretapping at will, that the police should be permitted to use the "third degree," that people who refuse to testify against themselves should be forced to do so. About half of our teenagers assert that most people aren't capable of deciding what's best for themselves; fully 75 per cent declare that obedience and respect for authority are the most important habits for children to learn. On practically all questions of social policy the youngsters lean strongly to stereotyped views [*see Chart 1*].

Such answers may represent either unthinking responses or convinced and deliberate acceptance of an authoritarian point of view. In either case the picture is equally unhappy. The road to totalitarianism is the same length whether we walk down it consciously or merely drift down it. Unthinking conformity provides a setting which makes it possible for a demagogue to lead a nation into slavery.

As individuals our nation's young people consistently value others' opinions above their own. Fewer than half claim that they think things out for themselves and act on their own decisions. Only one fourth report that they often disagree with the group's opinion. No more than 18 per cent are willing to say that their tastes are quite different from those of their friends. Yet in spite of these admissions most teenagers declare that their freedom is not too limited.

Such soundings of the younger generation's attitudes uncover some of the roots of anti-intellectualism in the U. S. Almost three quarters of the high-school students believe that the most important thing they can learn in school is "how to get along with people." Only 14 per cent place academic learning first. In a recent poll of a representative sample of college students we found that the same attitude prevails at the university level: 60 per cent would rather be popular than brilliant; 51 per cent believe that students with low grades are more likely to be popular than those who get good marks; 72 per cent believe that development of a well-rounded per-

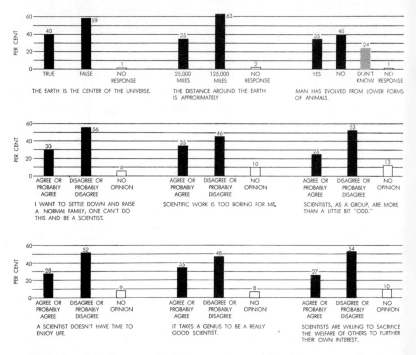

CHART 2. Attitudes toward science are suggested by the statements in these charts. Another response not indicated in the charts: When asked in October of last year whether they would like to be scientists, 68 per cent of the teenagers polled said that they would not.

sonality is the main purpose of education; 71 per cent feel that personality counts more than grades when it comes to looking for a job.

The disdain for learning shows up most sharply and most dismayingly in the attitude of teenagers toward science and scientists [see Chart 2]. Forty per cent of high-school students think that the earth is the center of the universe, and 63 per cent believe the earth's circumference is 125,000 miles! More than a third find scientific work boring; 25 per cent think scientists as a group are "more than a little bit odd"; about 30 per cent believe that a scientist cannot enjoy life or raise a normal family. In a poll in October, 1957—the month of Sputnik I—68 per cent of the teenagers said they would not like to be scientists. A majority asserted that scientists are likely to be radical, that they take no thought of the consequences of their work, that science should be restricted to physics and chemistry, that it is impossible to formulate scientific laws of human behavior. Most disquieting is the fact that views of this kind are just as common among students of high scientific aptitude as among those who have no interest in science. The climate of popular opinion among the nation's youth undoubtedly is keeping many able boys and girls out of science.

The current attempts to sell science on the basis of the benefits that flow from it seem to have sold the benefits but not the science from which they stem. Fully 90 per cent of the high-school youngsters agree that science has produced great practical fruits for mankind, but to most of them science has no appeal as an intellectual adventure. This attitude may well stem from the fact that the presentation of science by our schools and our press constantly plays "the one-note siren song of utility."

A need and craving to be liked, drifting with the crowd, conformity, a kind of passive anti-intellectualism—these seem to be outstanding characteristics of the present-day younger generation as it has expressed itself in our polls. Many of the youngsters themselves make this comment. One teenager observed: "High-school children think too much about what the crowd does or thinks rather than what they actually feel inside themselves. They seem to feel that if they go along with the crowd, they will be more popular. . . . We need to worry more about the person we live with all the time, our own self, rather than to worry so much about others."

The present conformist spirit—demonstrably not confined to the younger generation—seems to us something new in American life. It reverses our history and the American ideal, which has been, above all, individualistic. The American tradition suggests that we have not been in the past a people who passively accepted dictation by the crowd or surrender the exercise of our freedoms.

We shall not attempt to analyze the causes of this shift; that is a task for historians and philosophers. But we can venture some comments on the aspects of our culture reflected in the polls of the teenagers. Their attitude derives in large part, of course, from their parents. Riesman asserts that "today's parents make children feel guilty not so much about violations of inner standards as about failure to be popular," i.e., failure to get along with other children. He adds that the pressures of the home and school are re-enforced by our mass media. Vance Packard's (1957) book *The Hidden Persuaders* points out that modern advertising, dedicated to increasing mass consumption, deliberately bases its appeal primarily upon our need for identification with the vast majority. It inveigles us to purchase the products which are most popular—the most widely

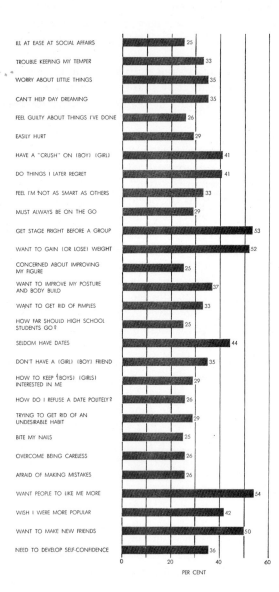

ILL AT EASE AT SOCIAL AFFAIRS — 25

TROUBLE KEEPING MY TEMPER — 33

WORRY ABOUT LITTLE THINGS — 35

CAN'T HELP DAY DREAMING — 35

FEEL GUILTY ABOUT THINGS I'VE DONE — 26

EASILY HURT — 29

HAVE A "CRUSH" ON (BOY) (GIRL) — 41

DO THINGS I LATER REGRET — 41

FEEL I'M NOT AS SMART AS OTHERS — 33

MUST ALWAYS BE ON THE GO — 29

GET STAGE FRIGHT BEFORE A GROUP — 53

WANT TO GAIN (OR LOSE) WEIGHT — 52

CONCERNED ABOUT IMPROVING MY FIGURE — 25

WANT TO IMPROVE MY POSTURE AND BODY BUILD — 37

WANT TO GET RID OF PIMPLES — 33

HOW FAR SHOULD HIGH SCHOOL STUDENTS GO? — 25

SELDOM HAVE DATES — 44

DON'T HAVE A (GIRL) (BOY) FRIEND — 35

HOW TO KEEP (BOYS) (GIRLS) INTERESTED IN ME — 29

HOW DO I REFUSE A DATE POLITELY? — 26

TRYING TO GET RID OF AN UNDESIRABLE HABIT — 29

BITE MY NAILS — 25

OVERCOME BEING CARELESS — 26

AFRAID OF MAKING MISTAKES — 26

WANT PEOPLE TO LIKE ME MORE — 54

WISH I WERE MORE POPULAR — 42

WANT TO MAKE NEW FRIENDS — 50

NEED TO DEVELOP SELF-CONFIDENCE — 36

0   20   40   60

PER CENT

CHART 3. Problems and desires which most concern teenagers were explored by sentences such as those in this chart. Each bar indicates percentage of teenagers polled who responded.

smoked or fastest-growing cigarette, the largest-selling automobile. Our economy, our uninsulated mode of life and our mass communications conspire to keep us under constant social pressure in our daily lives.

In recent decades we have seen the individual steadily depreciated even in intellectual pursuits. There is a rising admiration for "the power of the group mind." We have team research in science and "brainstorming" in industry. In every sphere group decision is replacing individual initiative.

In this light we must take a serious view of the tendency to conformity exhibited by the younger generation. In any circumstances it is always difficult for an adolescent to find himself. The teens are at time of transition, demanding adjustments to profound biological, emotional and social changes. Probably most parents today would testify from personal experience that the teenagers of our day are having an extraordinarily difficult time of growing up and finding themselves.

Ralph Waldo Emerson pointed out that the price of group agreement is descent to the least common denominator. As T. V. Smith and Eduard C. Lindeman (1959) remarked in their book *The Democratic Way of Life,* a democracy cannot afford to devalue "the finality of the individual," from whom "all things flow." In our view, the future of our democracy is not promising unless we restore a social climate which will reward independent thinking, personal morality and truly enlightened cooperation in place of going along with the crowd.

···················· 56 ····················

CHILDREN'S ATTITUDES TOWARD PEERS
AND PARENTS AS REVEALED BY
SENTENCE COMPLETIONS

by Dale B. Harris and Sing Chu Tseng

Using a promising projective approach, sentence completions, this selection reveals that boy–girl antipathies of the intermediate grades are primarily the result of the girls' attitudes toward boys, and that girls more than boys express greater negative attitudes toward their own sex with increasing age. Sex and developmental differences in attitudes toward parents are also noted. The authors are Dale B. Harris of Pennsylvania State University and his collaborator.[1] [From *Child Development*, 1957, 28, 401-411. Reprinted by permission of the authors and the Society for Research in Child Development.]

Students of child behavior generally believe that a child builds attachments to his parents as a result of their ministrations to him, and that he builds favorable attachments to other children in terms of pleasant and reinforcing experiences had with them. Observational studies of social behavior have sketched some detail within this general picture. Young children play together freely and select best friends regardless of sex. As children grow older there arises an increasing tendency to regard with favor one's own sex peers and with disdain, if not enmity, members of the opposite sex. This trend breaks down only during adolescence when both biological drives and the social setting favor heterosexuality. This period of increasing interest in and association with members of the opposite sex merges with the period of courtship and mate selection which society has institutionalized in various ways.

Along with the growing interest in the peer group and as the child develops skills and independence, there is a waning of interest in the parent figures. This is said to be particularly noticeable in early adolescence, when a period of antagonism or, indeed, outright conflict with parents occurs. This conflict is resolved by parents readjusting their expectations of the children and according more freedom. Evidence from various studies asking children to name their preferred parent or best friend has been used to support these trends. Such methodology has been criticized as too direct, yielding only socially approved results.

Theoretically, these phenomena have been explained by psychoanalysis in terms of cathection of the libido, and by learning theorists in terms of secondary drives built upon physiological appetites and extended by a process of conditioning to many persons in the environment. By modification of this latter viewpoint, changes in

[1] This investigation was supported in part by a research grant (M–690) from the National Institute of Mental Health, U.S. Public Health Service, and in part from funds supplied by the Institute of Child Welfare, University of Minnesota. Dr. Tseng, a Junior Scientist on this project staff, analyzed the data on the sentence completion test and originally suggested the project set forth in this paper.

pattern of the child's affective attachments to others are represented as a complex process, in which the child's "role" as perceived by himself and by others modifies with his increasing maturity. Consequently his attachments to others reflect this changing "role." Data accumulated by a sentence completion test given to some 3000 children from the third grade through high school[2] yield some interesting observations on this general picture of social development.

PROCEDURE

From a series of 32 sentences first developed by Wilson (1949), some 10 sentences were selected by an empirical procedure for inclusion in a battery of instruments designed to assess general adjustment (Anderson, *et al.*, 1953). These sentences were "scored" by the simple expedient of evaluating the completions in terms of the positive, negative, or neutral affect of the response. Using a guide list of typical responses, scores independently classifying responses attained the agreement expressed by correlation coefficients of $+.89$ to $+.96$ in several check samples.

Four sentences evoked attitudes toward parents and toward other children. These sentences were "Most boys _____," "Most girls _____," "My father _____," and "My mother _____."

This method of analysis makes no particular "projective" assumptions about hidden affect in sentence completions. Rather, the manifest affect as conveyed by the vernacular is taken as the basis for inferring "positive," "negative," or "neutral" attitudes. However, the technique is indirect; the sentences do not expressly call for an attitude toward parents or toward peers. These sentences, furthermore, are embedded among other sentences referring to school and to other common childhood experiences.

The items "Most boys _____," and "Most girls _____," can be treated as follows: A child may answer both items positively; an example would be "Most boys are nice," and "Most girls are pretty." He might answer both items negatively, as "Most boys are mean," and "Most girls are dumb." He can answer the items in such a way

---

[2] The total school population, public and parochial, in grades 3 through 12 of a county seat town of 8000 in rural Minnesota is included in this analysis. Grade groups ranged in size from 221 in the fourth grade to 123 in the tenth grade and were about evenly divided as to sex. The test was given as one item in a comprehensive program which included 12 instruments.

as to be neutral in both: "Most boys are tall," and "Most girls go to school." A child may answer an item positively for boys, but neutrally for girls, such as "Most boys are nice," and "Most girls are small." For any child there are nine possibilities with respect to completing the two sentences.

A child may answer the item referring to parents positively for both, for example: "My mother is the best mother in the world," and "My father is the best father in the world." He may answer them negatively, as "My mother yells at me," "My father is mean." A child may answer both items neutrally, as "My mother is a housewife," "My father is a farmer." He may answer neutrally for his mother but positively for father, "My mother is a teacher," "My father is a wonderful man." His responses may be negative for mother but positive for father, as: "My mother scolds me," and "My father is a nice guy" and so on for the nine various combinations of the three grades of responses to both sentences. It is clear that for a particular child a so-called "neutral" response might have positive or negative affect; we are limiting our interpretation to the usual semantic value of the words used.

RESULTS

By combining percentages of boys and girls in each school grade who give responses of a particular affect classification, it is possible to draw curves expressing certain trends in attitude change. Figure 1 depicts boys' attitudes toward other boys and girls. In this figure are plotted the percentage of responses positive or "favorable" to other boys and to girls,[3] smoothed by the three-point moving average method. Similar data are plotted for neutral attitudes. Curves showing negative or "unfavorable" responses are omitted because their plots complicate the graph visually, and their character is fully determined by the data shown in the favorable and neutral curves. Figure 2 shows girls' attitudes toward other girls and boys.

[3] To the percentage of boys giving favorable responses to both boys and girls are added the percentage of boys giving favorable responses to boys but neutral responses to girls, plus the percentage giving favorable responses to boys but unfavorable to girls. Data for the curve, "Neutral responses to boys" were obtained by combining the percentage of boys giving a neutral response to both boys and girls with the percentage giving a neutral response to boys but unfavorable to girls, and the percentage giving a neutral response to boys but favorable to girls. Similar combinations of percentages were made for Figures 2, 3, and 4.

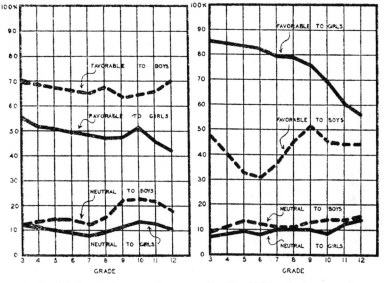

FIG. 1. Boys' attitudes toward peers.   FIG. 2. Girls' attitudes toward peers.

Figure 3 reports curves redrawn from Figures 1 and 2 to compare like-sex attitudes. Boys' positive responses toward boys are compared with girls' positive responses toward girls. On this chart negative responses are also plotted, neutral responses being omitted for sake of simplicity. Similarly, Figure 4 depicts cross-sex attitudes by plotting boys' *positive* responses toward girls and girls' *positive* responses toward boys. Negative responses are not plotted because the points would fall close to the percentage points for favorable categories and would complicate the diagram.

The figures speak for themselves but a few comments may be in order. Approximately 65 to 70 per cent of the boys give positive responses to other boys at all grade levels. Boys are more positive to boys than to girls in all grades. In general, taking into account the proportion of neutral attitudes, boys in the intermediate grades are more favorably than unfavorably disposed to girls, judged by the affect tone of their sentence completions. By grade 8, about the same proportion of boys give favorable as give unfavorable responses to girls. Indeed, this general decline in favorable or positive attitude toward girls is counteracted only slightly in the tenth grade, and continues noticeably thereafter. This finding does not bear out the

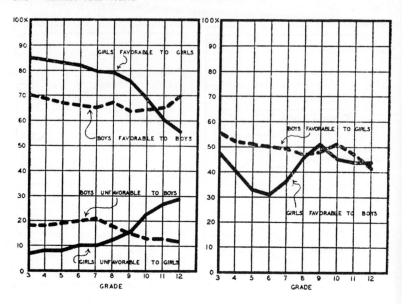

FIG. 3. Attitudes toward peers of like sex.   FIG. 4a. Attitudes toward opposite sex.

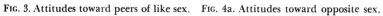

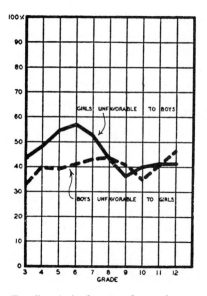

FIG. 4b.   Attitudes toward opposite sex.

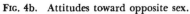

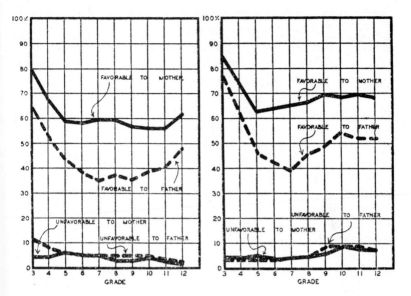

FIG. 5. Boys' attitudes toward parents.　　FIG. 6. Girls' attitudes toward parents.

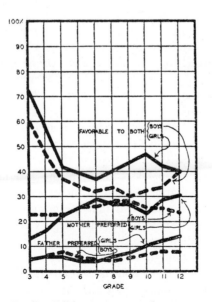

FIG. 7.　Children's parent preferences.

general expectation of boys' heterosexual attitudes in adolescence. It may be that, for older adolescent boys, a positive attitude toward girls is limited to *particular* girls. At any rate, there appears to be a fair proportion of boys throughout adolescence who give a negative completion to the general stimulus "Most girls _____."

A noteworthy trend in girls' attitudes is the noticeable increase in negative responses to other girls following the ninth grade. Perhaps this change expresses an increased competitiveness among females in the adolescent years! Paralleling this trend is the slight but noticeable increase in number of boys showing neutral attitudes toward other boys in the high school years. Perhaps girls personalize their feelings more toward their own sex in adolescence, while boys shift more toward neutrality, and do not move into negative feelings.

In general, there is a falling off in favorable responses extended peers as children grow older; this trend is partly accounted for by an increase in neutral responses. Only in girls is there evidence for an increase of negative response, and these are directed toward their own sex.

Both boys and girls give a large number of favorable responses to their own sex, with girls being more favorable to girls in general than boys are to boys, except in the late high school years. In general, both unfavorable and neutral responses given to the same sex are small, never exceeding 30 per cent, and involving usually between 10 and 20 per cent of children in all grade groups. Below grade 9 boys give noticeably more negative responses to other boys than girls give negative responses to other girls. Possibly the rough and tumble to which boys of this age are prone is not enjoyed by a fair portion of the group. Or possibly a percentage have "interiorized" the social disapproval often visited on the social behavior of boys in this age group.

When cross-sex attitudes are compared, it is interesting to note that more boys are favorable to girls in the intermediate grades than the proportion of girls which express themselves as favorable to boys. This difference increases through the intermediate grades, reaching a maximum around grade 6; then the curves tend to come back together. The suggestion is that the boy-girl antipathy in the intermediate grades is more a product of girls changing their attitudes toward boys than it is of boys changing their attitudes toward girls. The impatience of girls aged 10 to 12 with the boisterous conduct of boys is a familiar phenomenon in any family or school room.

These data strongly suggest that girls, in general, are more "emotional" in their attitudes toward peers than are boys. Despite their changing attitudes, girls generally give more positive responses than boys. Generally speaking, boys extend more neutral attitudes than girls. Both sexes give more negative responses to opposite sex than to own sex, and the difference is particularly noticeable in girls. The proportions of negative responses given by either sex to other children (boys and girls combined) are approximately the same. These percentages tend to be under 10 or 15 per cent.

There are not many other studies of peer attitudes which are comparable. Studies of friendships cast little light on children's favorableness or unfavorableness toward other children in general. Koch's (1944) study, which obtained preference choices by the paired-comparison method from each child in a number of grades, comes closest to giving comparable material. By limiting her analyses to frequency of preference choice in opposite sex pairs of names which did not include the judge but compared all other children in his room, Koch found that the members of each sex in all grades and usually even at the high school level were inclined to show a preference for their own sex. This "distance between the sexes" tended to increase with grade or age and then to decrease, the trend being conspicuous in high school. Her data also suggest that girls' preference for girls in the lower grades exceeds boys' preference for boys, but that this relative position is decreased and even reversed in the tenth and twelfth grades where boys are more likely to prefer boys than girls are to prefer girls.

All these findings are substantially in agreement with our own evidence, obtained by a very different method. In commenting on the decline in girls' preference for girls in bi-sex pairs of names in high school, Koch wonders whether older boys and men ultimately reduce their bias in favor of their own sex, as women do. The data of this study, using a quite different method, suggest that this "reduction of bias toward own sex" actually may be characterized in girls as an increase in negative attitude rather than as an increase in neutral attitude. This study, of course, sheds no light on Koch's speculation concerning men. Koch also suggests from indirect evidence in her data that there may be "more hostility to boys in the sex bias of girls than loyalty to girls." Our method, which evaluates the elicited affect toward the other sex in general, supports this conjecture, insofar as attitudes toward boys are concerned. Although Koch believes "girls reject boys more than girls prefer girls," our data do not show that the percentage of girls showing unfavorable affect toward boys ever approximates the proportion expressing favorable attitudes to other girls.

Campbell's (1939) study of social-sex attitudes in children was based on observations of same-sex and cross-sex contact in a coeducational club program. Actual contacts were not counted; rather, the character and quality of contacts were described in a systematic, but general manner for each child participating. Her descriptions of typical patterns of behavior support the general finding of like-sex preference in the grades, with girls showing a shift toward greater interest in boys by mid-teens, somewhat sooner than a comparable shift occurs in boys. She notes no behavior which would reflect the sharp increase we found in girls' unfavorable attitudes toward boys in the fifth, sixth, and seventh grades, nor the decline in favorable attitudes toward other girls in the high school years. Campbell records no behavior in boys which is inconsistent with the data of this study. Of the 14- to 17-year-old boy, she states that he "shys away from girls in a group but may be less shy when only one girl is to be considered." This observation is perhaps not incompatible with the data in Figure 1.

The data of our study are congruent with other findings, though not perhaps with the impression that boys go through an anti-girl phase in the elementary grades, followed by an increasing interest in girls in general in high school. This cycle of events does appear to characterize girls. Boys change their affect less as they grow older and incline more than girls to neutral attitudes in peer relationships. In general, children are cordial rather than antipathetic or neutral in their attitudes toward peers.

Figure 5 depicts boys' positively toned responses toward mother and father. Negatively toned responses are also plotted, but not "neutral" responses, which constitute a generous proportion. Figure 6 gives similar data for girls' attitudes toward mothers and fathers. Figure 7 shows the percentage of children expressing preference for mother, or liking parents equally well.[4]

---

[4] The percentage of children preferring the father was obtained in each grade group by combining the percentage giving a neutral response to mother but a favorable response to father with the percentage giving an unfavorable response to mother, but a neutral response to father, and with the percentage giving an unfavorable response to mother, but a favorable response to father. In every case the affect tone of the completion to the stimulus "My father——" was relatively more favorable than the affect tone given by the completion of the stimulus "My mother ——." The percentage "Like equally well" is found in Figure 7 by plotting only those giving a *favorable response to both*. The small percentage of children giving an unfavorable response to both parents (never over 4 per cent in any grade group) is omitted, as well as the fairly high percentage of responses which are neutral to both parents (this runs roughly between 25 and 35 per cent for most grade groups), even though both of these groups in a sense may be said to like their parents "equally well."

Young boys are more favorable to their mothers than to their fathers, and the sharp drop in favorableness to both parents between grades 3 and 5 is noteworthy. Neutral attitudes toward both father and mother rise sharply from grades 3 to 4 and remain largely unchanged until late high school years, when there is some shift back toward positive attitudes. Unfavorable attitudes toward parents remain close to 5 per cent in all samples. Young girls also show a sharp drop in favorable responses toward both parents between grades 3 and 5, with a corresponding rise in neutral attitudes. In both boys and girls there appears to be a shift away from the young child's uncritical fondness for parents to a more objective judgment which expresses itself in the greater proportion of neutrally toned, matter-of-fact completions. Unfavorable responses for girls, as for boys, constitute about 5 per cent or less for both father and mother, but girls' unfavorable responses, unlike boys', tend to rise slightly after about grade 8.

When we infer attitudes from sentence completions, we find no evidence for hostility to parents in early or mid-adolescence. Such feeling, if it occurs in many young people, either does not find expression in sentence completions or is so variously placed in the teen years and of such short duration that it cannot appear in cross-sectional data. The percentages of boys and girls giving negative responses to either parent are very similar and uniformly small. In these, as in the previous figures, the greater "neutrality" of the male appears.

Figure 7 shows that, in general, boys and girls in about the same proportion prefer the mother, between 20 and 30 per cent of preference choices being given to her. There is, perhaps, a slight increase in girls' preference for mother from grades 3 to 7, but no particular change in boys' preference for her. About the same proportions of boys and of girls prefer the father, the values tending to remain under 10 per cent at all grade levels. There is a very slight trend for more girls in the adolescent years to express a preference for fathers.

More girls than boys report equally favorable attitudes toward both parents at all ages except the twelfth grade, but the differences are certainly not striking. The sharp decline from the third to the fifth grade is of some interest. This study begins at the third grade, apparently toward the end of a period in which children give equally to both parents general, undiscriminating and positive attitudes. This trend coincides with and expresses the movement toward a greater proportion of neutrally toned responses noted in Figures 5 and 6.

These findings agree in general with results of other studies. Using a combination of the picture-story method, questions about preferential treatment at home, and a direct question about whom the child liked best at home, Simpson (1935) concluded that between ages five and nine, boys and girls alike show a decreasing preference for their fathers, with a very slight increase in the percentage favoring mothers. There was a pronounced increase up to age nine in the proportion of children stating that they "prefer both," which may be compared with the decreasing proportion reporting positive attitudes to both parents in the present study. Anderson (1936) in the White House Conference report of 1936 showed that by the mothers' report a majority of children expressed no preference between their parents, and that of those who did, the larger group favored the mother. The percentages for these attitudes changed very little with age. Likewise, Meltzer (1935), Stogdill (1937), and Mott (1937) found mothers more likely than fathers to be designated the favorite parent at all ages. None of these studies showed any trend comparable to the upswing in positive attitude toward parents during mid-adolescence which appears, particularly for boys, in the present study. These data offer a picture of increasing objectivity in later childhood, in part expressed by the increased proportion of children (particularly of boys) who use neutral expressions in their sentence completions, both towards peers and parents.

SUMMARY

A sentence completion technique, used to infer attitudes toward peers and parents, leads to the following conclusions:

1. Boys and girls are predominantly favorable to their peers, and at every age positive attitudes to own sex peers exceed those to opposite sex peers.

2. Boys somewhat more than girls express neutral attitudes. Girls clearly express more negative attitudes to their own sex as they grow older.

3. The so-called boy-girl antipathy of the intermediate grades is more a product of girls changing their attitudes toward boys than vice-versa. Boys show a slight over-all decrease in favorable attitudes toward girls, even in the later high school years.

4. Toward both mother and father, boys and girls extend more favorable than unfavorable attitudes, though there is a noticeable increase in neutral affect in the intermediate grades. Both sexes extend positive attitudes more frequently to mother than to father.

5. Boys in high school years show a slight rise in positive attitudes toward each parent; girls show a more pronounced increase in positive attitude toward father than toward mother in these same years.

6. The small proportions of boys showing negative attitudes toward mother and/or father decrease steadily through childhood and adolescence. The correspondingly small proportions of girls showing negative attitudes increase steadily through childhood and adolescence.

7. When a difference exists in the attitudes a boy or girl extends to his parents, he or she more often prefers the mother than the father. A larger group, however, extends similar (and positive) attitudes to both parents. There is a slight rise in girls' preference for father during the high school years.

57

CHILDREN'S CONCEPTS AND ATTITUDES ABOUT MINORITY AND MAJORITY AMERICAN GROUPS

by Marian Radke-Yarrow and Jean Sutherland Miller

What meanings do adolescents attach to such groups as Americans, Jews, Negroes? What are the sources of their concepts? Marian Radke-

Yarrow of the National Institute of Mental Health and her collaborator seek answers to these questions in their study of school children
from grades five through twelve, the results of which are reported in
the following article. [From *Journal of Educational Psychology*, 1949,
40, 449-468. Reprinted by permission of the authors and Warwick
and York, Inc.]

Early in their lives children learn to use the word 'American'
and, in time, to identify themselves as 'American.' It is a crucial
identification, for it is eventually bound up with the individual's behavior and attitudes in many areas of social living. He views the
world as an American; he has certain rights and duties and loyalties
as an American; his attitudes toward himself and others are partly a
matter of being an American. But 'American' is a concept applied
liberally and easily, and even a casual study of children's conversation reveals that it includes many confused and erroneous ideas.

The problem of this research is to study the meaning of 'American' to children of school age, and to discover, if possible, some of
the sources from which their concepts of American develop. The specific questions raised in the study are: (*a*) In what dimensions is
American perceived? (*b*) What values or attitudes are linked with
American? (*c*) What group differentiations are made, i.e., from
what groups is American differentiated? Which subgroups are included in American and which preclude being American? Can children conceive of subgroups which are different from themselves but
which belong to the same inclusive American group?

To obtain data on these problems, children were questioned concerning their own inclusive American group and two American
minority groups to which the children do not belong, Jewish and
Negro. A written questionnaire was used which asked for the meaning of each group and for explanations or rationalizations for the
meanings given.

SUBJECTS

Two hundred and seventy-five children of grades five through
twelve were studied. This number constituted the entire public
school population of these grades in a small midwestern town. The
town of several thousand inhabitants is like many midwestern communities—strikingly homogeneous in cultural background and social mores. There is an air of prosperity about it. The several

industries and small businesses furnish moderate, comfortable incomes for the residents. Though outside easy commuting distance, it lies within the orbit of several large urban centers. The majority of the population is German-American of the second, third and fourth generations, with a small percentage of the population of English, Scandanavian and Southern European descent. The community is predominantly Protestant. There is a recognizable Catholic minority. There is only one childless Jewish family. There are no Negroes in the town.

The children studied are similar in social and cultural backgrounds. They have had a minimum of personal experience with the two minority groups, fairly similar kinds of religious training, and the same school experience.

QUESTIONNAIRE

The questionnaire was administered in school to each class by the teacher. The instructions given by the teacher were:

Our school has been asked to help in a study of what school children (high-school students) think about various groups of American people. To do this, we are asked to answer some questions.

You will not be graded on these papers. You will not put your name on these papers. Your answers will not be read by the teachers. Your answers will be added to the answers of other children (students).

These are the questions about several groups of American people:
(1) What do you think Americans are like?
     What makes you think so?
(2) What do you think Negroes are like?
     What makes you think so?
(3) What do you think Jews are like?
     What makes you think so?

Write what you know and think about each question. Don't make up answers if you don't know. Give your own ideas. You will have twenty-five minutes to answer the questions.

The questions were phrased "What are Americans like?" rather than "What are Americans?" because it was found in preliminary questioning that the first form brought out, in addition to cognitive structure, many more value statements and comparisons of one group with another. This form of question has several advantages over a check-list of words from which the subject selects those words which he considers most appropriate for describing a group. The child must draw completely on his own ideas and formulate the description himself. In his formulation, his level of understanding and his feelings are often clearly revealed.

In asking "What makes you think so?" it was not expected that the children could supply the actual sources of their information and attitudes (except occasionally), but that in attempting to support their statements an indication would be given of the kind of justifications and experiences which accompany various kinds of concepts and attitudes.

Responses were analyzed by breaking down each answer into its component ideas. The frequency of the separate items and of the various patterns of items appearing in the responses are reported. In each case the percentages represent the percentage of children who answered in the given category.

RESPONSES TO THE QUESTION: "WHAT ARE AMERICANS LIKE?"

Responses to the question "What are Americans like" fall into four general categories:

(1) Democratic ideology and patriotism—"They are democratic and have the best form of government." "They have freedom of worship and speech." "I think they should be all treated alike."

(2) Kinds of people—in racial or cultural terms—"They are many people of different nationalities." "Americans belong to the white race." "People are classified in different groups—some wealthy and stuck-up, they look down on poor people. Some wealthy help poorer people along."

(3) A comparison of Americans with other peoples—"I think Americans are just as good as any other people in other countries." "Americans are or rather think they are superior than most other people." "They are becoming the leader of the world."

(4) Personal characteristics—"They are honest and well educated—they are clean." "They are stingy and only think of themselves." "They are kind to one another and to their neighbors."

The reliability of this method of categorizing responses to all the questions was measured by the percentage of agreement of two independent codings of eighty-five questions. The results are as follows:

"What are Americans (Negroes, Jews) like?"   92.8 per cent
"What makes you think so?"   89.4 per cent

Table 1 presents the responses to the question on the meaning of American. There is a striking lack of ideological content here. While there are many stereotypes which concern the individual behavior of Americans ("They're rugged," "They're go-getters,"

TABLE

"WHAT ARE AMERICANS LIKE?"

	PERCENTAGE OF CHILDREN Grades			
Response	5–6 (N=50)	7–8 (N=68)	9–10 (N=95)	11–12 (N=62)
Democratic ideology, patriotism				
Have many freedoms	12	22	24	10
Government by people	4	3	1	3
People loyal to government	14	36	13	11
Kinds of people				
Mixed nationalities	2	7	8	8
White people	6	2	1	0
Rich and poor	4	3	1	3
Comparison with other peoples				
Like others	28	25	7	13
Different from others	0	2	1	2
Better than others	4	12	12	16
A powerful nation	2	3	3	8
Personal characteristics				
Ambitious, energetic, achieving	20	19	31	46
Kind, honest, friendly	64	65	41	31
Clean	4	4	5	0
Educated, intelligent	4	12	14	19
Carefree	0	2	4	16
Religious	0	6	1	0
Value money, material possessions	4	6	11	13
Criticism of personal characteristics	6	16	15	21

"They are ambitious"), there are few group goals or values in evidence. The comments on American ideals or democratic government are mainly clichés such as: "Americans are in a land for the free and the brave" or "Americans are loyal." Freedom as an aspect of American life has a variety of meanings which are often imbedded in the daily experiences of the children ("Americans are free to choose the friends they want") as well in the more remote areas of their lives ("They have freedom of press"). The variety of meanings attached to freedom are listed below:

	Frequency
to value and appreciate freedoms	12
to do as they please	10
to fight to keep free	9
to hate dictators, don't like to be ordered around	4
to have many freedoms other countries don't have	3
to have freedom of speech and press	3
the right to own religious beliefs	3
the right to choose friends	1
the right to eat what you want	1
Negroes want to be free	1

When Americans are compared with other peoples, the other groups are usually unspecified, and Americans are perceived as different from, on a par with, or better than others. A decreasing proportion of children make statements of equality (twenty-eight per cent, twenty-five per cent, seven per cent, thirteen per cent) from the fifth and sixth to the eleventh and twelfth grades. Increasing with age are feelings about the superiority of Americans over other people (four per cent, twelve per cent, twelve per cent, sixteen per cent). Examples of this chauvinism at the younger and older age levels are quoted below:

"I think Americans are smart. They know more than the Negroes" (sixth grade).

"Americans are the best people of the races, they are Democrats and have the best form of government. They are easy-going, make friends easily, and are the most prized people in foreign nations" (twelfth grade).

The greatest number of responses are about personal characteristics. There are two clusters of traits: One is the bland and admirable qualities of nice, kind, friendly, honest, generous—which are found especially at the younger age levels (sixty-four per cent at grades five and six, and thirty-one per cent at grades eleven and twelve). The second group of traits which increases in frequency with age (from twenty per cent to forty-six per cent) has in common certain aggressive qualities—energetic, ambitious. Descriptions of Americans as educated people and as having material values appear more frequently in the older children than in the younger. Few personal descriptions are derogatory or critical; however, criticisms increase with age. They are of the following variety:

Americans are—	*Frequency*
conceited and selfish	11
lawless and criminal	13
wasteful and extravagant	5
unfriendly and uncooperative	6
prejudiced against different races	3
bad morally	2
take democracy for granted	2

Compared with the frequency and intensity of derogatory and rejective responses toward Negro and Jewish American minorities, the infrequency and scatter of criticisms on American stand in sharp contrast.

The descriptions of American do not reveal a highly structured group concept; stereotypes are varied but with the predominance of the "ambitious individualist"; the affect toward American is generally positive with little real criticism involved; and rarely is American differentiated from other groups of people. However, when the limits of the children's concepts of American are tested by asking for descriptions of minority groups . . . it becomes apparent that the ideals of freedom and the personal qualities of ambition, etc., are meant to apply to a restricted population.

RESPONSES TO THE QUESTIONS: "WHAT ARE NEGROES LIKE?" "WHAT ARE JEWS LIKE?"

Descriptions of Negroes and Jews have been categorized as follows:

(1) Group seen in terms of social problem—"They should be put in their place or where they came from. We do not want them nor did we bring them." "They have been chased around so much. They haven't had a chance." "They are picked on by the whites."

(2) Group described by a comparison of peoples—"I think Jews are just another part of the American race." "I think Negroes are just like any other people except for their color." "They are not as progressive as Americans."

(3) An effective reaction expressed toward the group—"I don't like Jews at all." "I think a good Negro is a dead Negro." "Jews are OK."

(4) Historical or cultural facts given—"They came from Africa originally and are now in the U.S." "They have a different religion."

(5) Personal or group characteristics ascribed to group—"Cheaters." "Negroes are dirty, not colert." "Selfish, hard, to get along with."

The instructions preceding the questionnaire presented all groups as Americans, although the form of the questionnaire tends to weaken this structuring. With these conditions of questioning, category 2 is significant. (see Table 2).

TABLE 2

"WHAT ARE NEGROES LIKE?" "WHAT ARE JEWS LIKE?"

PERCENTAGE OF CHILDREN

Descriptions in terms of:	NEGROES Grades				JEWS Grades			
	5–6	7–8	9–10	11–12	5–6	7–8	9–10	11–12
Social Problem								
Support discrimination	0	3	14	19	2	7	15	11
"Oppose" discrimination, but keep group "in its place"	0	0	1	3	0	0	1	0
Aware of discrimination (attitude not expressed)	0	7	7	14	4	6	7	13
Oppose discrimination	12	39	19	23	4	13	4	11
Comparison with other People								
Americans too	10	15	6	6	10	7	2	6
Like everyone else except skin color or religion	28	36	20	23	18	16	12	13
Different from Americans but as good	16	10	5	6	4	4	2	2
Different from Americans	4	4	11	11	6	0	2	0
Different from Americans and not as good	0	2	3	11	2	0	3	2
Affect toward Group								
"I like them; they're all right"	2	4	13	8	2	2	5	6
"I don't like them"	0	3	5	10	6	4	7	13
"I hate them; eliminate them"	0	0	1	5	0	6	3	6
Historical Events or Facts	6	9	1	2	2	7	3	5
Personal or Group Characteristics	76	83	87	91	84	80	80	85

Slightly more than half the children describe Negroes in comparative terms, and about one third, Jews in these terms. About ten per cent of the children describe Negroes as Americans, and between five per cent and ten per cent describe Jews as Americans too.

"He is a colored man or woman that came from Africa and is now an American" (eleventh grade).
"I think Jews are just another part of the American race. I think they

are all right even though I don't agree with their religion, but that is their own business" (tenth grade).

Another twenty-five per cent to thirty per cent perceive Negroes as "like anyone else" except for color of skin; and about fifteen per cent perceive Jews like anyone else.

"I think Negroes are just like any other people except the color of their skins and the way they work. I also think they would make better citizens if they were treated right" (tenth grade).
"Jews are just like any other race or class . . ." (tenth grade).

There is a small steady rise with age in the proportion of children who say that Negroes are not Americans (four per cent in the fifth and sixth grades, to eleven per cent in the eleventh and twelfth grades); or are not as good as Americans (zero per cent in the fifth and sixth grades to eleven per cent in the eleventh and twelfth grades). The corresponding categories appear infrequently in descriptions of Jews (about two per cent in each category).

It is significant that many of the children in describing Jews and Negroes are unable to do so for either group without first putting on record their own feeling toward them. The feeling is then "justified" by the addition of various undesirable characteristics as if to prove the right for disliking or discriminating.

"I don't like Jews. In one way they are smart—this is in making money. Many Jews are now running America. I don't think they should be allowed to do this, later they will want to run the whole world" (tenth grade).
"Jews are a kind of people I do not like. You find them owning all the large business or selling rags. Never doing real manual labor" (twelfth grade).

If the effect is positive, the supporting reason is more often in terms of standards of respect for all persons or democratic ideology. Thus:

"Jews are just like anyone else. All men are created equal" (seventh grade).

Statements of dislike increase with age for both minority groups. Statements showing accepting attitudes, however, show no consistent age trend. The frequency of negative attitudes within any one age compared with the frequency of positive attitudes reveals that negative expressions occur more often than positive expressions toward the Negro group at the highest grades, and toward the Jewish group at all ages.

Some of the most violent reactions of dislike are quoted below. They appear exclusively above the sixth grade. More statements of this kind are made concerning Jews than Negroes.

"Negroes are a people who think nothing of the whites' rights. Negroes are the worst type of people there are, especially when it comes to sex offenses, crime, etc. Get rid of them" (twelfth grade).

"The Jew, well there's no room for them and me in this country; either they're kicked out or I'm willing to go shoot 'em all" (twelfth grade).

"I think a dead Negro is a good Negro" (twelfth grade).

"Jews are the worst people on earth. Money-hoggers. Worst people in America. I'd like to wring their necks" (ninth grade).

"They're (Jews) cheaters, they can cheat you out of one-cent things. There are lots of other things I think about them that I could not write on this piece of paper" (seventh grade).

"I think everyone of them (Jews) ought to be shot or else tarred and feathered and ridden out of this country on a rail" (twelfth grade).

The responses of acceptance or rejection of either group are sometimes made with consciousness of the social import of various kinds of group relations. Awareness of a social problem requires more maturity than a simple statement of "I like" or "I don't like," and one would expect responses of this order more frequently in the older than the younger age levels. This is borne out in Table 2 in the responses under the category "Social Problem."

Recognition of a social problem does not preclude prejudiced attitudes. There is explicit support of discrimination against minority Americans, which increases with age. None of the children in the lowest grades support discrimination against Negroes; two per cent support discrimination against Jews. At the highest grades the corresponding percentages are twenty-two per cent for Negroes and eleven per cent for Jews. A child whose response falls in this category is:

"The Jews are different from Negroes. The Jews are breaking down our government and therefore they should be put in their place or where they came from. If possible give them Germany. . . . They are not American and this country is for Americans" (ninth grade).

When the other side of the coin is examined—how many children explicitly oppose discrimination—the age trends are unsteady, though also increasing with age. The percentage of children opposing discrimination rises from twelve per cent in grades five and six to twenty-three per cent in grades eleven and twelve in responses concerning Negroes, and from four per cent to eleven per cent in the same grades in responses concerning Jews. Examples of this point of view are:

"The Negroes to me are people just like I am only subjected to a crueller society by the white race. I want the Negroes to have the same advantages that I enjoy in social and economic life. I do not want to see him rise above me in government for some day at their birth rate they would control a country which belongs to the whites" (eleventh grade). "Negroes are like any other person and should be treated that way" (seventh grade).

Most of the children ascribe personal or group traits to the minority groups. There are favorable characteristics ("fine," "good," "intelligent" people), such as the traits ascribed to American, but there are many more which are derogatory in nature. The distribution of traits ascribed to Negroes and Jews by children of each grade is given below.

Characteristic	Ascribed to Negroes (Per cent)				Ascribed to Jews (Per cent)			
	5–6	7–8	9–10	11–12	5–6	7–8	9–10	11–12
Favorable	34	36	27	21	20	13	13	16
Inferior	26	41	39	67	4	4	3	8
Bad	0	18	23	27	50	45	69	80
Peculiar, unique	22	10	12	25	22	21	7	5

Inferior traits are most frequently ascribed to the Negro. This tendency increases with age. Similarly "bad" traits assigned to the Negro increase in frequency with age. Jews are most often described in terms of "bad" characteristics, and again there is an increase with age. Descriptions of Jews seldom imply inferiority.

The traits in each of the categories are itemized in Table 3. Between one-third and one-fourth of the subjects give some favorable quality in their descriptions, such as Negroes "are fine" or "good citizens." With minor exceptions, the remaining traits are uncomplimentary. Patronizing statements are made (Negroes are "gentle," "obedient," "polite") by seventeen per cent and eleven per cent of the younger and older children, respectively. Negro "inferiority" to white appears especially in the responses of the older children (twenty-nine per cent). The stereotypes of behavior ascribed to Negroes resemble closely the common stereotypes of the Negro in the adult white population (Katz and Braly, 1933). Descriptions of the group as slow, lazy, unambitious, and as tough, insolent, hostile, predominate. While the frequencies of the other traits are low, the list includes the familiar prejudiced descriptions: dirty, unintelligent, bad morals.

TABLE 3

CHARACTERISTICS ASCRIBED TO THE MINORITY GROUPS

PERCENTAGE OF CHILDREN

Characteristic	ASCRIBED TO NEGROES Grades		ASCRIBED TO JEWS Grades	
	5–8	9–12	5–8	9–12
Fine, respected, intelligent	36	24	16	14
(Patronizing)—polite, gentle	17	11	0	0
Inferior to whites (non-Jews)	10	29	4	5
Look different	13	4	0	1
Need to be controlled	0	8	3	8
Revengeful, prejudiced against whites	2	6	0	0
Slow, lazy, unambitious	4	20	2	5
Hostile, tough, unfriendly	5	10	0	0
To be feared	2	14	10	15
Stupid, superstitious	4	9	0	0
Bad morals, criminals	3	3	0	0
Sneaky, sly, dishonest	0	3	12	9
Money-making, money-grabbing	0	0	23	44
Greedy, miserly, stingy	0	0	8	11
Aggressive	0	0	5	4
Dirty	3	8	3	1
Like slaves, savages	0	3	0	0
Can endure hard work	2	6	0	0
Sell junk	0	0	10	1
Different speech, manners	1	1	3	1
Lack education, opportunities	10	10	0	0
Disloyal to America	0	0	4	2
Musical	0	3	0	0
Religious	0	5	3	1
Not religious	1	0	2	3

There is somewhat less variation in the traits assigned to Jews. A large proportion (thirty-one per cent and fifty-five per cent of the younger and older children, respectively) appear in the area of dishonest, greedy practices with regard to money. The remaining characteristics are again similar to the stereotypes of the adult anti-Semite—stereotypes of aggressiveness, disloyalty, domination of the country. Religion is mentioned infrequently. Favorable description are given much less frequently than for the Negro, by ten per cent and fifteen per cent of the younger and older children, respectively. A peculiar stereotype which occurs is that Jews "sell rags and junk" (fourteen per cent, seven per cent, zero per cent, three per cent for the grade, respectively). This idea probably goes along with the stereotype of "money"—a picture of bargaining, cheating, dealing in money and goods.

It appears that before a group of people has reality to the child, the group label has long been used as an adjective, an emotionally-toned word, or synonymous with a specific action or state of affairs: you "jew them down"; "there's junk for the Jew"; you get "dirty like a nigger." These are the experiences in the young child's life out of which a group attitude grows. "Jewish group" is an abstraction. When it is first met as an abstraction or in the form of a person so labeled there are already feelings for the label. Similarly for the Negro group. With this kind of beginning for the concepts, it is easy to see how the groups are perceived as "not American" by virtue of their "badness."

A small proportion of the subjects express fear of either groups. This fear is of one sort when it appears with regard to the Jewish group; namely, fear that Jews are dominating the government and business. When fear is expressed about Negroes it concerns the possibility of their trying to get "revenge" on the whites, or it is again fear of governmental domination, but not identical with this fear expressed in regard to Jews. The difference appears in the following quotations:

> "Jews think they can run the country."
> "They'd like to rule the earth."
> "They control business in the United States."
> "They're too powerful."

> "Negroes are trying to rise above us in government."
> "They'd like to run people."
> "They can't be trusted."
> "They can't be trusted to act and talk civilized."
> "They'll try for revenge."
> "They think nothing of whites' rights."
> "The South has a hard time controlling them and their bad habits."

The great number of derogatory descriptions occurring with reference to Negroes and Jews contrasts markedly with the number of criticisms of Americans. The three groups are compared below in the ratio of negative statements to neutral or positive statements expressed about each group. These ratios show not only the preponderance of positive statements for American and the slim margin of positive statements for both minorities, but also the tendency for the positive margin to decrease with age.

RATIOS OF NEGATIVE TO POSITIVE STATEMENTS

Grades	American	Negro	Jew
5-6	1:31	1:39	1:1
7-8	1:15	1:5	1:1
9-10	1:8	1:3	1:6
11-12	1:10	1:2	1:6

PATTERNS OF RESPONSES REGARDING NEGROES AND JEWS

The majority of children gave more than one idea in response to each group. The several ideas expressed by the child about a given group present sometimes a consistent attitude and sometimes a mixture or contradiction of feelings and opinions. Each child's answer was rated on the total of his ideas about each minority: whether he expresses wholly positive, neutral, or negative attitudes or a mixture of positive and negative feelings (Table 4). The patterns re-

TABLE 4

PATTERNS OF RESPONSES TOWARD MINORITY GROUPS

PERCENTAGE OF CHILDREN

Response	TOWARD NEGROES Grades				TOWARD JEWS Grades			
	5–6	7–8	9–10	11–12	5–6	7–8	9–10	11–12
Positive	66	50	40	36	40	43	18	27
Neutral	6	3	6	5	12	4	9	5
Inferior	26	16	20	18	0	0	2	0
Bad and inferior	0	4	14	21	0	0	0	0
Bad	0	0	0	0	32	25	34	39
Conflict: good, bad, inferior	0	22	13	18	12	12	26	19
Don't know and omits	2	4	7	3	4	16	11	10

veal the following data: Children give completely positive descriptions more frequently at the younger than at the older ages, and more frequently for Negroes than for Jews. Many of the responses in the positive pattern are rather nondescript—"They are kind" and "They are clean." They are not as positive in accepting the group as the negative categories are condemnatory.

Patterns of responses which describe Negroes as inferior occur often. Both patterns of inferior and "bad," for the Negro increase through the grades. The pattern of "bad" traits ascribed to Jews holds a fairly steady one-third proportion at all grades.

Although answers reflecting conflict might be expected to show an increase through the grades, there is no consistent trend. Conflict responses in most cases are better designated as contradictions, for the child does not seem aware of or disturbed by the contradictory points of view he expresses, thus—

"Because some are very poor. Can't find work because they are a Jew. Some practically run some whole cities. I think if the government doesn't watch them pretty soon they'll be running the whole country" (ninth grade).

The truly "conflict" responses, such as the following, occur infrequently. (This response has in it evidences of guilt over the incompatible views expressed):

"America was founded for the reason of peace. Until some thought that they could take it out on this peace-loving nation by bringing in different races and people who are not wanted in other countries, although America was founded for this reason" (tenth grade).

Patterns of responses on the questionnaires were evaluated also with attention to the correspondence among attitudes expressed toward the three groups by each child. If a child expresses prejudice against one minority group, is he likely to show a similar attitude toward the other? The following percentages of children give negative responses to one or both minority groups:

> 46 per cent at grades 5-6
> 53 per cent at grades 7-8
> 68 per cent at grades 9-10
> 68 per cent at grades 11-12

Of these children, the following percentages reject both minority groups:

> 17 per cent at grades 5-6
> 33 per cent at grades 7-8
> 48 per cent at grades 9-10
> 60 per cent at grades 11-12

Thus, there is an increase in age not only in the percentage of children who describe one or the other minority group in negative terms, but also in the percentage of children expressing dislike who do so for both groups.

Responses on American and accompanying reactions to minorities were studied. Responses to American were classed in four categories: boastful chauvinistic attitudes, descriptions of pride and good feeling, description of superficial and trivial aspects of American, and mainly critical responses. No relationships were found between these variations and descriptions of Negro and Jewish groups. The children for whom Americans are "the best that ever was" hold attitudes toward the minorities which are sometimes wholly condemnatory and sometimes completely accepting. Conversely, and it should be of especial importance in education, the child can express the philosophy of democracy and freedom in their concept of American and yet not apply these principles to American minority groups.

"Americans are a people that want to be free and independent and have a democracy for a form of government . . . so the common people have something to say.

"Negroes are black people. They seem funny when you see them. I always get the idea that I don't like them very well.

"I always thought they were a people that sometimes cheat people" (tenth grade).

The generalization of democracy, well spoken, is no guarantee of its application to persons or groups who deviate from the child's own in-group.

SOURCES FOR RESPONSES ON GROUPS

The subjects found it difficult to explain or justify the basis of their concepts or attitudes. When asked "What makes you think so," their replies are often vague and non-specific (Table 5). Most frequently they reply with further elaborations of the ideas they have given or with statements such as "because I know," thus:

"I think so because I am an American and have and do almost the same things as above" (sixth grade).

"My cerebrum" (seventh grade).

"I am one, I ought to know" (eleventh grade).

TABLE 5

SOURCES FOR CONCEPTS AND ATTITUDES ON MAJORITY
AND MINORITY GROUPS

PERCENTAGE OF CHILDREN

Source	AMERICANS Grades				NEGROES Grades				JEWS Grades			
	5-6	7-8	9-10	11-12	5-6	7-8	9-10	11-12	5-6	7-8	9-10	11-12
No source, only further elaboration	52	27	29	11	56	31	38	32	64	40	19	34
"I know it to be true"	18	27	27	35	14	15	18	24	4	9	12	**18**
Historical data, statistics	20	29	31	33	22	16	16	8	4	5	20	2
Personal experience	2	3	8	3	2	6	8	5	8	3	6	5
"People say"	0	2	0	0	0	2	3	3	6	2	4	3
Democratic principles	2	0	1	0	4	10	2	3	0	7	0	0
Parents	2	0	0	3	0	0	0	0	0	2	0	0
School	2	2	0	8	2	0	0	15	0	0	2	3
Books, papers	0	9	7	8	4	32	9	8	0	2	10	3
Movies, radio	0	2	2	3	4	0	1	3	2	0	0	0
Famous persons	0	0	0	0	0	4	2	0	0	2	0	2
Church	0	0	0	0	0	0	0	0	2	0	1	0
"I have no evidence"	0	0	0	0	0	0	1	3	0	0	11	5
Don't know	6	15	3	6	0	0	2	0	0	2	4	0
Omit	0	0	0	0	4	16	13	18	14	34	16	27

A very few children cite personal experience to support their opinions; many cite current happenings or events of history:

"I think that way because the men that brought Negroes over to the country were bringing men and womans to this country just like some people adopt children" (sixth grade).

"Because last year there have been quite a few Negro riots in Detroit and other cities" (tenth grade).

Rarely is a democratic principle given to support a point of view. In cases where a democratic principle is given as a source, the concepts or attitudes toward the minority group are usually accepting one. Only five children cite the church as a source. In each case the attitude is a positive one:

"Jews are not so bad. I have heard where they give great sums of money to the church." (What makes you think so?) "I think so because I have heard our pastor talk about it" (ninth grade).

The children who cite home, school, readings, and movies as sources describe constructive and negative influences.

"The Negroes present a great race problem in the United States. The South has a hard time controlling the Negroes and their poor habits." (Source) "I studied them in social studies" (twelfth grade).

"Jews are being treated the worst of any race in Europe. They are often accused of controlling all the big business in the United States but this is not really true because the ratio in business is about the same as the population, about 1/10." (Source) "Reading about Jewish problems and oppression and also studying about this in the topic of racial problems in social problems" (twelfth grade).

"Negroes are sometimes dishonest and unliked. They are a dirty race and I don't like them." (Source) "You can read in the papers about all the killings that have occurred from Negroes" (ninth grade).

"Jews get too much of the income of the United States people. They live in joy and comfort." (Source) "I think this because it tells it in books and I believe in books" (ninth grade).

"I don't know but I wouldn't misjudge them (Jews). I know they're some of our finest business men and are as talented as many of our own race." (Source) "I've debated it a lot—with myself. You can't with teachers, it doesn't pay!!!!!" (eleventh grade).

The difficulty which the children had in telling the bases for their concepts and attitudes suggests the 'unconscious' learning which takes place. It is not likely that concept or attitude is built upon a single vivid learning experience, but rather upon reactions from many sources, in many different settings in the child's daily life— heresay, opinions of others, expressions of derogation, the portrayal of group characteristics in history, fiction, current events, etc.

Implications for education would seem to lie in the direction of examining the content of education where cultural diversities can and do play a rôle, in order to ascertain the nature of influences in this part of the children's experiences.

SUMMARY AND DISCUSSION

Responses were obtained from two hundred seventy-five school children on the meaning of various American groups. The data reveal a relatively low level of understanding of cultural similarities and differences among people, except in a small proportion of the children. The responses do not indicate either the development of an identification with American or with democracy in which idealism or goals of human welfare play a significant rôle; or the development of social concepts and attitudes which coincide with the "official" or constitutional principles of an American group composed of diverse groups with equal rights and opportunities. These children have assimilated anti-minority prejudices through learning which is not based on personal experience with either minority group. The hostile reactions of some of the older children against Negroes and Jews ("kill them all," "the only good one is a dead one") could not be more violently expressed by the youth of totalitarian indoctrination.

If this sample represents a fair picture of the children of a small town in Midwestern United States, there are many implications for these schools and communities, if their youth is to be made ready and able to live together in a world composed of differences. The children studied show little evidence of constructive teaching from school or church or community which serves to counteract group prejudices. The mere absence of the derogated groups in the community makes teaching of democratic attitudes with respect to them no less necessary. Also, the concept of American leaves much to be desired. If it is to serve as a source of personal and group security or as a source of values upon which to build better human relations, it requires a deeper and more significant meaning than "Americans are rugged individualists."

58

THEY SAW A GAME: A CASE STUDY

by Albert H. Hastorf and Hadley Cantril

This "real life" study of a Dartmouth–Princeton football game shows how our identifications and loyalties to groups influence our perceptions and judgments. The authors are Albert H. Hastorf of Dartmouth College and Hadley Cantril of The Institute for International Social Research. [From *Journal of Abnormal and Social Psychology*, 1954, *49*, 129-134. Reprinted by permission of the authors and the American Psychological Association.]

On a brisk Saturday afternoon, November 23, 1951, the Dartmouth football team played Princeton in Princeton's Palmer

Stadium. It was the last game of the season for both teams and of rather special significance because the Princeton team had won all its games so far and one of its players, Kazmaier, was receiving All-American mention and had just appeared as the cover man on *Time* magazine, and was playing his last game.

A few minutes after the opening kick-off, it became apparent that the game was going to be a rough one. The referees were kept busy blowing their whistles and penalizing both sides. In the second quarter, Princeton's star left the game with a broken nose. In the third quarter, a Dartmouth player was taken off the field with a broken leg. Tempers flared both during and after the game. The official statistics of the game, which Princeton won, showed that Dartmouth was penalized 70 yards, Princeton 25, not counting more than a few plays in which both sides were penalized.

Needless to say, accusations soon began to fly. The game immediately became a matter of concern to players, students, coaches, and the administrative officials of the two institutions, as well as to alumni and the general public who had not seen the game but had become sensitive to the problem of big-time football through the recent exposures of subsidized players, commercialism, etc. Discussion of the game continued for several weeks.

One of the contributing factors to the extended discussion of the game was the extensive space given to it by both campus and metropolitan newspapers. An indication of the fervor with which the discussions were carried on is shown by a few excerpts from the campus dailies.

For example, on November 27 (four days after the game), the *Daily Princetonian* (Princeton's student newspaper) said:

> This observer has never seen quite such a disgusting exhibition of so-called "sport." Both teams were guilty but the blame must be laid primarily on Dartmouth's doorstep. Princeton, obviously the better team, had no reason to rough up Dartmouth. Looking at the situation rationally, we don't see why the Indians should make a deliberate attempt to cripple Dick Kazmaier or any other Princeton player. The Dartmouth psychology, however, is not rational itself.

The November 30th edition of the *Princeton Alumni Weekly* said:

> But certain memories of what occurred will not be easily erased. Into the record books will go in indelible fashion the fact that the last game of Dick Kazmaier's career was cut short by more than half when he was forced out with a broken nose and a mild concussion, sustained from a tackle that came well after he had thrown a pass.

This second-period development was followed by a third quarter out-break of roughness that was climaxed when a Dartmouth player deliberately kicked Brad Glass in the ribs while the latter was on his back. Throughout the often unpleasant afternoon, there was undeniable evidence that the losers' tactics were the result of an actual style of play, and reports on other games they have played this season substantiate this.

Dartmouth students were "seeing" an entirely different version of the game through the editorial eyes of the *Dartmouth* (Dart-mouth's undergraduate newspaper). For example, on November 27 the *Dartmouth* said:

> However, the Dartmouth-Princeton game set the stage for the other type of dirty football. A type which may be termed as an unjustifiable accusation.
> Dick Kazmaier was injured early in the game. Kazmaier was the star, an All-American. Other stars have been injured before, but Kazmaier had been built to represent a Princeton idol. When an idol is hurt there is only one recourse—the tag of dirty football. So what did the Tiger Coach Charley Caldwell do? He announced to the world that the Big Green had been out to extinguish the Princeton star. His purpose was achieved.
> After this incident, Caldwell instilled the old see-what-they-did-go-get-them attitude into his players. His talk got results. Gene Howard and Jim Miller were both injured. Both had dropped back to pass, had passed, and were standing unprotected in the backfield. Result: one bad leg and one leg broken.
> The game was rough and did get a bit out of hand in the third quarter. Yet most of the roughing penalties were called against Princeton while Dartmouth received more of the illegal-use-of-the-hands variety.

On November 28 the *Dartmouth* said:

> Dick Kazmaier of Princeton admittedly is an unusually able football player. Many Dartmouth men traveled to Princeton, not expecting to win—only hoping to see an All-American in action. Dick Kazmaier was hurt in the second period, and played only a token part in the remainder of the game. For this, spectators were sorry.
> But there were no such feelings for Dick Kazmaier's health. Medical authorities have confirmed that as a relatively unprotected passing and running star in a contact sport, he is quite liable to injury. Also, his par-ticular injuries—a broken nose and slight concussion—were no more serious than is experienced almost any day in any football practice, where there is no more serious stake than playing the following Saturday. Up to the Princeton game, Dartmouth players suffered about 10 known nose fractures and face injuries, not to mention several slight concussions.
> Did Princeton players feel so badly about losing their star? They shouldn't have. During the past undefeated campaign they stopped several individual stars by a concentrated effort, including such mainstays as Frank

TABLE 1

DATA FROM FIRST QUESTIONNAIRE

Question	Dartmouth Students (N = 163) %	Princeton Students (N = 161) %
1. Did you happen to see the actual game between Dartmouth and Princeton in Palmer Stadium this year?		
Yes	33	71
No	67	29
2. Have you seen a movie of the game or seen it on television?		
Yes, movie	33	2
Yes, television	0	1
No, neither	67	97
3. (Asked of those who answered "yes" to either or both of above questions.) From your observations of what went on at the game, do you believe the game was clean and fairly played, or that it was unnecessarily rough and dirty?		
Clean and fair	6	0
Rough and dirty	24	69
Rough and fair*	25	2
No answer	45	29
4. (Asked of those who answered "no" on both of the first questions.) From what you have heard and read about the game, do you feel it was clean and fairly played, or that it was unnecessarily rough and dirty?		
Clean and fair	7	0
Rough and dirty	18	24
Rough and fair*	14	1
Don't know	6	4
No answer	55	71
(Combined answers to questions 3 and 4 above)		
Clean and fair	13	0
Rough and dirty	42	93
Rough and fair*	39	3
Don't know	6	4

TABLE 1—(*Continued*)

Question	Dart-mouth Students ($N = 163$) %	Prince-ton Students ($N = 161$) %
5. From what you saw in the game or the movies, or from what you have read, which team do you feel started the rough play?		
Dartmouth started it	36	86
Princeton started it	2	0
Both started it	53	11
Neither	6	1
No answer	3	2
6. What is your understanding of the charges being made?**		
Dartmouth tried to get Kazmaier	71	47
Dartmouth intentionally dirty	52	44
Dartmouth unnecessarily rough	8	35
7. Do you feel there is any truth to these charges?		
Yes	10	55
No	57	4
Partly	29	35
Don't know	4	6
8. Why do you think the charges were made?		
Injury to Princeton star	70	23
To prevent repetition	2	46
No answer	28	31

* This answer was not included on the checklist but was written in by the percentage of students indicated.
** Replies do not add to 100% since more than one charge could be given.

Hauff of Navy, Glenn Adams of Pennsylvania and Rocco Calvo of Cornell.
In other words, the same brand of football condemned by the *Prince*—that of stopping the big man—is practiced quite successfully by the Tigers.

Basically, then, there was disagreement as to what had happened during the "game." Hence we took the opportunity presented by the occasion to make a "real life" study of a perceptual problem.[1]

[1] We are not concerned here with the problem of guilt or responsibility for infractions, and nothing here implies any judgment as to who was to blame.

PROCEDURE

Two steps were involved in gathering data. The first consisted of answers to a questionnaire designed to get reactions to the game and to learn something of the climate of opinion in each institution. This questionnaire was administered a week after the game to both Dartmouth and Princeton undergraduates who were taking introductory and intermediate psychology courses.

The second step consisted of showing the same motion picture of the game to a sample of undergraduates in each school and having them check on another questionnaire, as they watched the film, any infraction of the rules they saw and whether these infractions were "mild" or "flagrant."[2] At Dartmouth, members of two fraternities were asked to view the film on December 7; at Princeton, members of two undergraduate clubs saw the film early in January.

The answers to both questionnaires were carefully coded and transferred to punch cards.[3]

RESULTS

Table 1 shows the questions which received different replies from the two student populations on the first questionnaire.

Questions asking if the students had friends on the team, if they had ever played football themselves, if they felt they knew the rules of the game well, etc. showed no differences in either school and no relation to answers given to other questions. This is not surprising since the students in both schools come from essentially the same type of educational, economic, and ethnic background.

Summarizing the data of Tables 1 and 2, we find a marked contrast between the two student groups.

Nearly all *Princeton* students judged the game as "rough and dirty"—not one of them thought it "clean and fair." And almost nine-tenths of them thought the other side started the rough play.

[2] The film shown was kindly loaned for the purpose of the experiment by the Dartmouth College Athletic Council. It should be pointed out that a movie of a football game follows the ball, is thus selective, and omits a good deal of the total action on the field. Also, of course, in viewing only a film of a game, the possibilities of participation as spectator are greatly limited.

[3] We gratefully acknowledge the assistance of Virginia Zerega, Office of Public Opinion Research, and J. L. McCandless, Princeton University, and E. S. Horton, Dartmouth College, in the gathering and collation of the data.

TABLE 2

DATA FROM SECOND QUESTIONNAIRE CHECKED WHILE SEEING FILM

| | | Total Number of Infractions Checked Against | | | |
| | | Dartmouth Team | | Princeton Team | |
Group	N	Mean	SD	Mean	SD
Dartmouth students	48	4.3*	2.7	4.4	2.8
Princeton students	49	9.8*	5.7	4.2	3.5

* Significant at the .01 level.

By and large they felt that the charges they understood were being made were true; most of them felt the charges were made in order to avoid similar situations in the future.

When Princeton students looked at the movie of the game, they saw the Dartmouth team make over twice as many infractions as their own team made. And they saw the Dartmouth team make over twice as many infractions as were seen by Dartmouth students. When Princeton students judged these infractions as "flagrant" or "mild," the ratio was about two "flagrant" to one "mild" on the Dartmouth team, and about one "flagrant" to three "mild" on the Princeton team.

As for the *Dartmouth* students, while the plurality of answers fell in the "rough and dirty" category, over one-tenth thought the game was "clean and fair" and over a third introduced their own category of "rough and fair" to describe the action. Although a third of the Dartmouth students felt that Dartmouth was to blame for starting the rough play, the majority of Dartmouth students thought both sides were to blame. By and large, Dartmouth men felt that the charges they understood were being made were not true, and most of them thought the reason for the charges was Princeton's concern for its football star.

When Dartmouth students looked at the movie of the game they saw both teams make about the same number of infractions. And they saw their own team make only half the number of infractions the Princeton students saw them make. The ratio of "flagrant" to "mild" infractions was about one to one when Dartmouth students judged the Dartmouth team, and about one "flagrant" to two "mild" when Dartmouth students judged infractions made by the Princeton team.

It should be noted that Dartmouth and Princeton students were thinking of different charges in judging their validity and in assigning reasons as to why the charges were made. It should also be noted that whether or not students were spectators of the game in the stadium made little difference in their responses.

INTERPRETATION: THE NATURE OF A SOCIAL EVENT[4]

It seems clear that the "game" actually was many different games and that each version of the events that transpired was just as "real" to a particular person as other versions were to other people. A consideration of the experiential phenomena that constitute a "football game" for the spectator may help us both to account for the results obtained and illustrate something of the nature of any social event.

Like any other complex social occurrence, a "football game" consists of a whole host of happenings. Many different events are occurring simultaneously. Furthermore, each happening is a link in a chain of happenings, so that one follows another in sequence. The "football game," as well as other complex social situations, consists of a whole matrix of events. In the game situation, this matrix of events consists of the actions of all the players, together with the behavior of the referees and linesmen, the action on the sidelines, in the grandstands, over the loud-speaker, etc.

Of crucial importance is the fact that an "occurrence" on the football field or in any other social situation does not become an experiential "event" unless and until some significance is given to it: an "occurrence" becomes an "event" only when the happening has significance. And a happening generally has significance only if it reactivates learned significances already registered in what we have called a person's assumptive form-world (Cantril, 1950).

Hence the particular occurrences that different people experienced in the football game were a limited series of events from the total matrix of events *potentially* available to them. People experienced those occurrences that reactivated significances they brought to the occasion; they failed to experience those occurrences which did not reactivate past significances. We do not need to introduce "attention" as an "intervening third" (to paraphrase James on memory) to account for the selectivity of the experiential process.

[4] The interpretation of the nature of a social event sketched here is in part based on discussions with Adelbert Ames, Jr., and is being elaborated in more detail elsewhere.

In this particular study, one of the most interesting examples of this phenomenon was a telegram sent to an officer of Dartmouth College by a member of a Dartmouth alumni group in the Midwest. He had viewed the film which had been shipped to his alumni group from Princeton after its use with Princeton students, who saw, as we noted, an average of over nine infractions by Dartmouth players during the game. The alumnus, who couldn't see the infractions he had heard publicized, wired:

> Preview of Princeton movies indicates considerable cutting of important part please wire explanation and possible air mail missing part before showing scheduled for January 25 we have splicing equipment.

The "same" sensory impingements emanating from the football field, transmitted through the visual mechanism to the brain, also obviously gave rise to different experiences in different people. The significances assumed by different happenings for different people depend in large part on the purposes people bring to the occasion and the assumptions they have of the purposes and probable behavior of other people involved. This was amusingly pointed out by the New York *Herald Tribune's* sports columnist, Red Smith, in describing a prize fight between Chico Vejar and Carmine Fiore in his column of December 21, 1951. Among other things, he wrote:

> You see, Steve Ellis is the proprietor of Chico Vejar, who is a highly desirable tract of Stamford, Conn., welterweight. Steve is also a radio announcer. Ordinarily there is no conflict between Ellis the Brain and Ellis the Voice because Steve is an uncommonly substantial lump of meat who can support both halves of a split personality and give away weight on each end without missing it.
>
> This time, though, the two Ellises met head-on, with a sickening, rending crash. Steve the Manager sat at ringside in the guise of Steve the Announcer broadcasting a dispassionate, unbiased, objective report of Chico's adventures in the ring. . . .
>
> Clear as mountain water, his words came through, winning big for Chico. Winning? Hell, Steve was slaughtering poor Fiore.
>
> Watching and listening, you could see what a valiant effort the reporter was making to remain cool and detached. At the same time you had an illustration of the old, established truth that when anybody with a preference watches a fight, he sees only what he prefers to see.
>
> That is always so. That is why, after any fight that doesn't end in a clean knockout, there always are at least a few hoots when the decision is announced. A guy from, say, Billy Graham's neighborhood goes to see Billy fight and he watches Graham all the time. He sees all the punches Billy throws, and hardly any of the punches Billy catches. So it was with Steve.

"Fiore feints with a left," he would say, honestly believing that Fiore hadn't caught Chico full on the chops. "Fiore's knees buckle," he said, "and Chico backs away." Steve didn't see the hook that had driven Chico back. . . .

In brief, the data here indicate that there is no such "thing" as a "game" existing "out there" in its own right which people merely "observe." The "game" "exists" for a person and is experienced by him only in so far as certain happenings have significances in terms of his purpose. Out of all the occurrences going on in the environment, a person selects those that have some significance for him from his own egocentric position in the total matrix.

Obviously in the case of a football game, the value of the experience of watching the game is enhanced if the purpose of "your" team is accomplished, that is, if the happening of the desired consequence is experienced—i.e., if your team wins. But the value attribute of the experience can, of course, be spoiled if the desire to win crowds out behavior we value and have come to call sportsmanlike.

The sharing of significances provides the links except for which a "social" event would not be experienced and would not exist for anyone.

A "football game" would be impossible except for the rules of the game which we bring to the situation and which enable us to share with others the significances of various happenings. These rules make possible a certain repeatability of events such as first downs, touchdowns, etc. If a person is unfamiliar with the rules of the game, the behavior he sees lacks repeatability and consistent significance and hence "doesn't make sense."

And only because there is the possibility of repetition is there the possibility that a happening has a significance. For example, the balls used in games are designed to give a high degree of repeatability. While a football is about the only ball used in games which is not a sphere, the shape of the modern football has apparently evolved in order to achieve a higher degree of accuracy and speed in forward passing than would be obtained with a spherical ball, thus increasing the repeatability of an important phase of the game.

The rules of a football game, like laws, rituals, customs, and mores, are registered and preserved forms of sequential significances enabling people to share the significances of occurrences. The sharing of sequential significances which have value for us provides the links that operationally make social events possible. They are analogous to the forces of attraction that hold parts of an atom together, keeping each part from following its individual, independent course.

From this point of view it is inaccurate and misleading to say that different people have different "attitudes" concerning the same "thing." For the "thing" simply is *not* the same for different people whether the "thing" is a football game, a presidential candidate, Communism, or spinach. We do not simply "react to" a happening or to some impingement from the environment in a determined way (except in behavior that has become reflective or habitual). We behave according to what we bring to the occasion, and what each of us brings to the occasion is more or less unique. And except for these significances which we bring to the occasion, the happenings around us would be meaningless occurrences, would be "inconsequential."

From the transactional view, an attitude is not a predisposition to react in a certain way to an occurrence or stimulus "out there" that exists in its own right with certain fixed characteristics which we "color" according to our predisposition (Kilpatrick, 1952). That is, a subject does not simply "react to" an "object." An attitude would rather seem to be a complex of registered significances reactivated by some stimulus which assumes its own particular significance for us in terms of our purposes. That is, the object as experienced would not exist for us except for the reactivated aspects of the form-world which provide particular significance to the hieroglyphics of sensory impingements.

CHAPTER NINETEEN

Persistence and Change

of Attitudes

59

THE STABILITY OF THE SELF-CONCEPT

IN ADOLESCENCE[1]

by Mary Engel[2]

This two-year longitudinal study of the self-regarding attitudes of a group of high-school pupils examines the interrelationship between stability of the self-concept, quality of the self-concept, and three indices of adjustment (peer ratings, teacher ratings, and Minnesota Multiphasic Personality Inventory—MMPI—measures). Appended to the selection written by Mary Engel of the Michael Reese Hospital, Chicago, are the Self-Concept Q-Sort items, Peer Rating Scale, and Teachers' Forced Choice Test. [From *Journal of Abnormal and Social Psychology*, 1959, *58*, 211-215. Reprinted by permission of the author and the American Psychological Association.]

Recent theory and research point to the importance of the self-concept in understanding and predicting constancies as well as

[1] Based upon a dissertation submitted in partial fulfillment of the requirements for the Ph.D. degree, George Peabody College. The writer wishes to express her gratitude to Nicholas Hobbs and Julius Seeman for their guidance. She is also indebted to the Vanderbilt-Peabody Self Concept Research Group for helpful suggestions and comments.

[2] Written while USPHS postdoctoral clinical research fellow at the Menninger Foundation (MF–6502–C).

changes in behavior (Brownfain, 1952; Rogers & Dymond, 1954; Taylor, 1955). It is generally believed that an individual's concept of himself achieves a rather high degree of organization during the course of development and comes to resist change once self-differentiation and self-definition have taken place (Lecky, 1945). As yet it is not known by what age the process of self-definition reaches stability. While we know that the concept of self remains relatively stable, even over extended periods of time, in young adults (Taylor, 1955), and while there are a number of theoretical and partially supported statements in the literature about the storms and stresses of certain aspects of adolescent development (Hall, 1904; Kuhlen, 1948), the fate of the self-concept in adolescence is still a matter for speculation. The studies that examine individual differences in the self-concepts of adolescents from a number of vantage points and in several settings (Balester, 1955; Blodgett, 1953; De Lisle, 1953), represent an inroad into the area of self-concept development. However, it is the longitudinal approach that is most appropriate when seeking answers to questions of development.

The primary purpose of the present study was to investigate the stability of the self-concept in adolescence over a two-year period. It was also its purpose to examine the relationship between whatever stability is found and the quality of the self-concept. The interrelationship between self-concept stability, quality of the self-concept, and several indices of adjustment was also examined.

METHOD

The data were obtained by testing and retesting 172 public school students, 104 of whom were in the eighth grade and 68 of whom

TABLE 1

SEX DISTRIBUTION OF SUBJECTS

	8th–10th Grade	10th–12th Grade
Boys	48	28
Girls	56	40
Total	104	68
Grand Total	172	

were in the tenth grade at the time of the first testing. The same students served as subjects in 1954 and in 1956.[3] Table 1 presents the grade and sex distribution of Ss in the two-year study. An analysis of the fathers' occupations revealed that the Ss were mostly of lower-middle and middle-class background.

The hypotheses were formulated in 1954. Their testing required the use of the following measures:

1. Self-concept Q sort, paper and pencil form, consisting of items relevant to adolescent concerns.[4]

2. Verbal Subscale of the Differential Aptitude Test, as an estimate of intelligence.

3. Scales D, Pd, and K of the Minnesota Multiphasic Personality Inventory (MMPI), as measures of adjustment and "defensiveness."

4. Peer Rating Scale, as a sociometric assessment of adjustment, based on the model provided by Tuddenham (1952).

5. Teachers' Forced Choice Test as another independent measure of adjustment, developed by Ullman (1952).

The set of Q-sort items for the assessment of the self-concept in

TABLE 2

THE STABILITY OF THE SELF-CONCEPT OVER A TWO-YEAR PERIOD
ITEM-BY-ITEM CORRELATIONS OF Q SORTS IN 1954 AND 1956

Group	N	Mean z	s_z	r Corresponding to Mean z Scores
Girls				
8th–10th grade	45	.6107	.2059	.54
10th–12th grade	37	.6794	.2204	.59
Boys				
8th–10th grade	44	.4775	.2636	.45
10th–12th grade	23	.6004	.2222	.54
Mean		.5919		.53

adolescents was developed along lines largely in conformity with the principles put forth by Stephenson (1935). Briefly, a large pool of

[3] There were 243 Ss in 1954; the discrepancy between the 1954 and 1956 N can be accounted for by attrition during the two-year period. Detailed analysis of data from the attrition group will be presented elsewhere. Whereas the over-all N of the longitudinal sample was 172, an N of approximately 149 was available for the testing of certain hypotheses, due to the absence of some Ss on some of the testing days in 1956.

[4] Copyright applied for. A complete list of Q-sort items is included in University Microfilms Publication: Mic 57-2914. Send $2.25 to University Microfilms, 313 No. First Street, Ann Arbor, Michigan.

items was gathered covering areas of adolescent self-concern as empirically defined by Jersild (1952). The pooled judgments as psychologists, nonprofessional adults, and adolescents were used to reduce and refine the original set, 100 Q-sort items being retained. Judges could agree with demonstrable certainty that these items represent either positively or negatively toned self-referent attitudes. Examples are: "I can take criticism without resentment." "I see little about myself that's outstanding."

In responding, Ss had to distribute the 50 positively and 50 negatively toned items into 11 categories, ranging from "most like me" to "least like me." The frequency distribution of items was as follows:

Number of items
4   7   9   11   12   14   12   11   9   7   4
Category
1   2   3   4   5   6   7   8   9   10   11

Paper and pencil administration incurs some errors of measurement, probably not pertaining to item-sampling, that are not involved when the usual card sorting procedure is used. The test-retest reliability of the instrument was .68 over a ten-day period with an N of 23 (tenth grade students). This reliability figure was obtained by correlating the values assigned to each item, by each S, on two occasions and represents the mean of 23 correlations (z transformations were used in computing the mean r). It is slightly lower than similar statistics obtained by others, using the card sort (Taylor, 1955).

The maximum positiveness score that can be obtained on the Q sort used in this study is 600. A score of this magnitude would result from placing every one of the 50 positive items in the "most like me" end of the continuum. Placing an equal number of positive and negative items on the upper and the lower end of the continuum would give rise to a score of 300, the point of ambivalence. Customarily, the negative self-concept is defined as a positiveness score falling below the point of ambivalence, where as the positive self-concept is usually defined as a positiveness score above the point of ambivalence.

In responding to the Peer Rating Scale, each member of a class writes down one to three names of others who seem to suit some brief behavioral descriptions, for example: "Who is the good sport, the person who always plays fair?" "Who gets mad easily and loses his or her temper often?" These descriptions can be roughly ordered along an adjustment-maladjustment continuum. Each S receives a score that reflects the extent to which his peers see him as well functioning in the school situation. The reliability of the Peer Rating Scale was established by test-retest of 2 Ss (ninth graders) over a one-week interval. The resulting value of .96 indicates that the adjustment scores derived from ratings of any one subject by the group as a whole are highly reliable.

RESULTS AND DISCUSSION

Stability of Self-Concept

Analysis of the data obtained in 1954 from Ss who subsequently dropped out of school indicates that certain important personality differences may have existed between those who left and those who remained in the school.[5] Because of the strong possibility of selective attrition, caution is indicated when generalizing from the results of the present study.

It was expected that the Ss would form three groups with regard to the self-concept: those maintaining positive self-regarding attitudes, those with negative self-regarding attitudes, and those with defensively positive self-concepts. Hypotheses were formulated on the basis of this expectation. All predictions were made in 1954 and were tested in 1956.

It was hypothesized that the self-concept of adolescents would be relatively stable over the two-year period. This hypothesis implies that the stability, internal organization, and crystallization of the self-concept is achieved earlier in development. Stability was defined by relatively high correlations between self-concept Q sorts in 1954 and 1956. Relevant data are presented in Table 2. The over-all mean correlation of .53, for all Ss, indicates the extent of stability of the self-concept of adolescents over a two-year period, between grades eight and ten, and ten and twelve. Corrected for attenuation, the over-all mean correlation between the self-concept in 1954 and 1956 is .78.

It was also predicted that the self-concept of Ss with a positive attitude toward themselves in 1954 would be significantly more stable over the two-year period than the self-concept of Ss with a negative or defensive-positive self-concept. Results bearing on this prediction are presented in Table 3, in which the negative self-

[5] Analysis of personality differences between Ss in the longitudinal sample and the attrition group will be presented elsewhere.

concept is defined by scores falling in the lower 20% of the distribution of self-concept scores, and positive self-concept by scores in the upper 80%. Where the self-concept was positive, and S also obtained a K score greater than 17 (measure of "defensiveness" derived from the MMPI), S was classified as manifesting a defensive-positive self-concept.

To test the hypothesis, correlations between Q sorts were converted into z scores as measures of stability. An over-all F test of differences in stability between self-concept groups resulted in an F ratio of 28.12, greatly exceeding the ratio of 5.30 needed for significance at $p = .05$. Individual t tests between groups support the conclusions that (a) Ss whose self-concept was positive in 1954 were significantly more stable over the two-year period than Ss who had negative self-concepts in 1954; (b) Ss whose self-concept was defensive-positive in 1954 were significantly more stable than those who had negative self-concepts; (c) Ss whose self-concept was positive in 1954 did not differ significantly in stability from those whose self-concept was defensive-positive in 1954.

The prediction that older and younger Ss would not differ significantly in stability of self-concept over the two-year period was supported. Age group differences in magnitude of Q sort correlations (self-concept stability) resulted in a t ratio of .60.

It was also expected that stability of the self-concept would be

TABLE 3

COMPARISON OF SELF-CONCEPT STABILITY BETWEEN POSITIVE, NEGATIVE, AND DEFENSIVE-POSITIVE SELF-CONCEPT GROUPS OVER THE TWO-YEAR PERIOD

Groups	N^a	Per Cent of Total N (172)	Mean Stability[b]	s	t
Positive Self-concept	106	62	.6928	.2060	7.61*
Negative Self-concept	34	20	.3383	.1977	6.99*
Defensive-Positive Self-concept	32	18	.6379	.2138	
Defensive-Positive Self-concept and Positive Self-concept	—	—	—		1.30

* Significant beyond the .05 level.
a Classification on basis of 1954 data.
b Based on 1954 and 1956 data, total N for this column 149.

TABLE 4
POSITIVENESS OF THE SELF-CONCEPT IN 1954 AND IN 1956

	1954			1956		
	N	M	s	N	M	s
Girls						
8th–10th grade	56	359.98	32.01	45	362.76	29.41
10th–12th grade	40	358.40	36.82	37	365.59	38.44
Boys						
8th–10th grade	48	351.29	34.68	45	352.25	37.15
10th–12th grade	27	360.81	23.03	24	369.75	25.72

statistically unrelated to intelligence. Testing this prediction required correlating verbal intelligence scores (DAT) with self-concept stability scores. Correlations were nonsignificant, lending support to the hypothesis, except in the case of the tenth-twelfth grade girls, where an r of .36 was found between these two variables, which, with an N of 35, was significant beyond the .05 level.

On the assumption that cultural ambiguities concerning sex roles should be more likely to affect girls than boys, it was hypothesized that the self-concept of boys would be significantly more stable, over the two-year period; than that of girls. This hypothesis was not upheld. The comparison of the mean stability between boys and girls resulted in a t ratio of .76.

In comparing the mean positiveness scores of the Ss in 1954 and in 1956 (Table 4) we found an unpredicted increase in mean positiveness. With the sexes combined, both grades shifted in a positive direction, the mean shift being significant beyond the .05 level in case of the older group ($t = -2.44$).

Stability of Self-Concept and Adjustment

The relationship between the stability of the self-concept and three measures of adjustment (teacher ratings, peer ratings, and MMPI measures) was explored through the following prediction: Ss who persist in a positive self-regarding attitude should be better adjusted, in terms of the MMPI, teacher ratings, and peer ratings, than those who persist in negative or defensive-positive self-concepts. Table 5 summarizes the "fate" of the quality of the self-concept for all Ss over the two-year period.[6] More detailed analysis revealed that most of the shift in self-concept quality occurred in the negative

[6] The method of categorization used is too detailed for presentation here but is described in detail elsewhere (Engel, 1956).

self-concept group. Ss who were classified as having negative self-concepts in 1954 more closely approached the mean by 1956. Such shift could be attributed to regression, except that no such shifting toward the mean took place in the case of Ss originally giving evidence of a positive self-concept.

In applying analyses of variance to adjustment indices between groups, 1956 adjustment measures were used. Table 6 shows that F ratios on MMPI scores were significant, whereas F ratios based on other adjustment measures were not.

Differences in MMPI measures were further examined by individual t tests applied to the column means. MMPI adjustment measures showed the group maintaining negative self-concepts to

TABLE 5

THE DISTRIBUTION OF ALL SUBJECTS IN THE LONGITUDINAL SAMPLE WITH
REGARD TO THE CHANGES AND CONSTANCIES OF THE
SELF-CONCEPT AS SEEN IN 1956

Changes and Constancies of the Self-Concept Between 1954 and 1956	Number	Per Cent of Number Subjects
Maintained positive self-concept	76	44
Maintained negative self-concept	14	8
Maintained defensive-positive self-concept	11	6
Was defensive-positive in 1954 but did not maintain either defensiveness or positiveness of self-concept	16	9
Was positive but shifted to negative self-concept by more than 20 points	15	9
Was negative but shifted to positive by more than 20 points	17	10
Absent on more than one testing session in 1956 (unclassified)	23	13
Total	172	99

be significantly less well adjusted (scoring higher on D and Pd) in 1956 than others, partially upholding the hypothesis.

Concomitance of Change in Self-Concept and in Adjustment

It was predicted that a change in self-concept in the positive direction would be related to improved adjustment, and a change in self-concept in the negative direction would be related to impaired adjustment. For the purpose of testing this hypothesis Ss were re-grouped and considered either "positive shifters" or "negative shift-ers" depending on a change of 20 points away from their original positive self-concept score either in the positive or negative direc-tion. Only Ss on whom full sets of adjustment scores were available were included in this analysis. Adjustment scores for 1956 were subtracted from 1954 adjustment scores and t tests were applied to the mean difference scores. Table 7 presents the results bearing on this hypothesis, and supports the conclusion that "negative shifters" obtained significantly higher Pd and D scores in 1956 as predicted; however, "positive shifters" became more "defensive" in that they obtained significantly higher K scores in 1956 than in 1954; "posi-tive shifters" were seen as significantly more well adjusted by their peers in 1956 than in 1954. Changes in teacher ratings did not dif-ferentiate between groups. Thus, this final hypothesis was only partially confirmed.

It should be borne in mind that this study explored mainly one aspect of the self-concept, the conscious self-concept. It may well be that in spite of the consistencies found in adolescents over a two-year period, considerable changes took place in aspects of the concept of self that are less readily admissible into awareness. The exploration of self-concept consistency and its concomitants on a deeper level of personality would require a clinical approach which was pre-cluded by the use of a fairly large number of Ss in the present study.

SUMMARY

A study of the stability of the self-concept over two years in ado-lescence resulted in the following conclusions:

1. Relative stability of the self-concept was demonstrated by an over-all item-by-item correlation of .53 between Q sorts obtained in 1954 and in 1956, with an instrument of which the ten-day test-retest reliability was .68.

2. Subjects whose self-concept was negative at the first testing were significantly less stable in self-concept than subjects whose self-concept was positive.

3. Subjects who persisted in a negative self-concept over the two-year period gave evidence of significantly more maladjustment than subjects who persisted in a positive self-concept, when maladjust-

TABLE 6
COLUMN MEANS AND F RATIOS FOR THREE SELF-CONCEPT GROUPS ON
MEASURES OF ADJUSTMENT (1956 MEASURES USED)

Measures	Maintaining Positive Self-Concept		Maintaining Negative Self-Concept		Maintaining Positive Defensive Self-Concept		
	N	M	N	M	N	M	F
Pd	73	13.51	12	20.17	11	13.64	15.27*
D	73	14.90	12	22.25	11	15.18	21.20*
Peer rating	71	232.62	12	175.17	10	268.70	2.77
Teacher rating	72	22.00	14	18.86	10	23.00	2.18

* Significant beyond the .05 level.

ment is measured by high scores of scales *Pd* and *D* of the MMPI.

4. Subjects who showed less regard for themselves on the *Q* sort on retest, also shifted toward significantly more maladjustment on scales *Pd* and *D* of the MMPI.

5. Subjects who showed more regard for themselves on the *Q* sort on retest, also shifted toward significantly more adjustment on peer ratings.

6. The positive self-concept scores increased significantly between

TABLE 7
CHANGES IN ADJUSTMENT MEASURES CONCOMITANT WITH SHIFTS IN SELF-CONCEPT
(BASED ON DIFFERENCE SCORES; 1956 SCORES SUBTRACTED FROM 1954 MEASURES)

Adjustment Measures	"Positive Shifters"				"Negative Shifters"			
	N	M	s	t	N	M	s	t
Pd (MMPI)	30	−.47	3.83	.67	13	−3.15	3.53	−3.22**
D (MMPI)	35	−.60	4.89	.73	15	−3.80	4.75	−3.10**
K (MMPI)	35	−2.94	4.41	−3.95*	22	.23	4.85	.22
Teacher rating	40	.83	7.33	.02	22	.23	4.85	.23
Peer rating	37	−25.97	66.55	−2.37**	17	15.53	93.24	−.69

* Significant beyond the .05 level and in the direction opposite from the predicted one.
** Significant beyond the .05 level and in the predicted direction.

the two testings for the tenth-twelfth grade subjects, an increase which could not be attributed entirely to the effect of regression.

SELF-CONCEPT Q SORT

Directions

Here you will find 100 statements, things that people say about themselves.

First: Read all of them carefully. Then place a "+" in front of the ones that you think are like you, and a "−" in front of the ones that are not like you.

Second: Turn to the sheet with the rows of boxes on it. Of the statements you marked + (like you), pick out four that are *most like you*. Put the numbers of these into the four boxes in row 11. *Cross over these four statements so you won't be recording them again.*

Third: Pick out seven statements that are next most like you. Put their numbers into the boxes in row 10. Cross them out too. Now pick out nine statements that are next most like you. Put their numbers into row 9. Cross them out. Continue in this manner *until the first five rows are filled with numbers.* (Rows 11-7.)

Now: Pick out four statements of the ones you marked—and that are *least like you.* Put their numbers into the boxes in row 1. *Cross them out.* Pick out seven that are next least like you. Put the numbers into the boxes in row 2. Cross them out. Do this until rows 1-5 are filled with numbers.

You will have 14 statements left. These will probably be neutral to you. Put their numbers into row 6.

RAISE YOUR HAND IF YOU HAVE MORE OR LESS THAN 14 STATEMENTS LEFT. If you want to make any changes, you may erase.

1. I think I will be successful in life.
2. I should love my parents more than I do.
3. I am too darned selfish.
4. I think of myself as a person good in sports and athletics.
5. I worry about everything, even when I have no reason to worry.
6. I am happy.
7. I can be of little use to others.
8. It looks as if I am making a failure out of life.
9. I am always wondering what others think about me.
10. I never have trouble getting a date.
11. I am childish in many ways.
12. I am easy to get along with.
13. Most of the time I feel alone.
14. My feelings are easily hurt.
15. I am somewhat moody.

16. I am probably the best student in my class.
17. I feel unable to solve my problems.
18. I do things without thinking about them first.
19. I am a good dancer.
20. I have quite a few talents.
21. I have only a few problems in life.
22. I think of myself as a good "school citizen."
23. At home, I am a general bother.
24. I make a bad impression on people.
25. I have many friends.
26. I feel that I am in on family decisions.
27. It bothers me little when I have to recite in front of a group.
28. Usually, I wonder if I am any good at all.
29. I have an excellent sense of humor.
30. Usually I feel that I have little ability to measure up.
31. I always know for sure what the right thing to do is.
32. I am a happy-go-lucky kind of person.
33. I am the most popular boy (or girl) in the school.
34. I see little about myself that's outstanding.
35. I have fewer friends than most boys and girls.
36. I see the world as a mean, ugly place.
37. I get real pleasure out of making things with my hands.
38. I am confused most of the time.
39. Most people try to avoid me.
40. I have a great deal of confidence in myself.
41. I am really out of place at picnics and parties.
42. When I have a job to do, I get it done.
43. I wouldn't trade places with anybody else in the world.
44. When I want something, I just sit and wish I had it, instead of going out and getting it.
45. I seldom worry, usually taking things as they come.
46. I am a pretty unattractive looking person.
47. I carry grudges.
48. I generally look on the bright side of things.
49. My teachers like me.
50. I am at ease with other people.
51. I know I will live up to the things people expect of me.
52. I think I am above average in most respects.
53. I am a pretty stupid person.
54. Too often I let others make up my mind for me.
55. I am usually a leader in clubs.
56. I can contribute little to team work.
57. I am real useful to have around.
58. My personality is uninteresting.

59. I usually reach my goals.
60. At home, I co-operate with my parents and feel that I am a help to them.
61. I am fairly popular.
62. At picnics and parties I enjoy myself more than most people.
63. I am able to do many things well.
64. I "lose my head" easily.
65. Most of the time I am angry with myself.
66. I am a decent sort of person.
67. I have little confidence in myself.
68. I know I can always take care of myself.
69. I feel inferior to most people I know.
70. The world is a decent place for me.
71. I feel at home wherever I am.
72. I think of myself as a person with no special talents.
73. I am only afraid of things when I have good reason to be afraid.
74. I am pretty smart.
75. I lack self-control.
76. I will go to a good deal of trouble to help someone else.
77. I think I have disappointed my parents in many ways.
78. I try to understand people and why they do things.
79. I can usually stick to my work until I have finished it.
80. I am even-tempered.
81. I am pleased with the way my life is going.
82. Only some teachers like me.
83. I am a bundle of nerves.
84. I think I am a person with little sense of humor.
85. I have no talent in sports and games.
86. I am so far from perfect, it's not even funny.
87. I am a poor student.
88. I can't get any farther than I do because I have a terrific inferiority complex.
89. The world would be better off without me.
90. I make it hard for people to be friendly with me.
91. The opposite sex finds me a bore.
92. I have a lot of self-control.
93. I have little trouble getting started on the things I have to do.
94. I think I understand myself pretty well.
95. I am able to make decisions.
96. I am always afraid someone is going to make fun of me.
97. I am easily discouraged.
98. I am a coward.
99. I can take criticism without resentment.
100. I am not the person I would like to be.

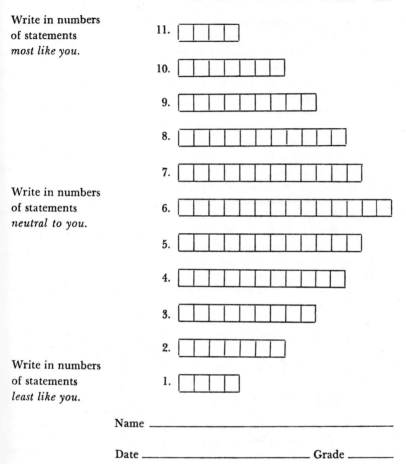

Write in numbers
of statements
most like you.

11.

10.

9.

8.

7.

Write in numbers
of statements
neutral to you.

6.

5.

4.

3.

2.

Write in numbers
of statements
least like you.

1.

Name _____

Date _____ Grade _____

PEER RATING SCALE

Here are some questions about the things people do or the way they
feel. Write after each question the names of one, two or three people *in
this class,* boys or girls, who may fit the description. You may name yourself.
Just be sure you name at least one person for each description.

1. Who finds it hard to sit still in class, moves around in his or her seat,
   or gets up and walks around?
2. Who can really concentrate on work, can study and work quietly without moving around too much?
3. Whom does everybody like?
4. Whom does nobody like?
5. Who is always smiling and laughing and is full of fun?
6. Who does not smile much and is sad and serious?

7. Who is always ready to take a chance at things that are new and unusual?

8. Who won't take a chance when something unexpected or unusual happens?

9. Who is not a very good sport, a poor loser?

10. Who is the good sport, the person who always plays fair?

11. Who is always ready to talk to visitors, even to those he does not know very well? Sometimes he or she does the talking for others in the class who will not speak for themselves.

12. Who is shy with people he does not know, and gets someone else to do the talking for him?

13. Who is full of enthusiasm when playing games and sports?

14. Who always prefers to sit quietly when others are playing, and does not enter into active games and sports?

15. Who gets mad easily and loses his temper often?

16. Who hardly ever gets mad and loses his or her temper seldom?

17. Who is always trying to get others to watch what he can do, or to listen to him talk about the things he can do?

18. Who does not seem to mind when people make him (or her) the center of attention, yet does not seem always to want to be the center of attention?

19. Who always knows how to start something interesting to do, so others like to join in?

20. Who always waits for somebody else to think of something to do and will rather follow the suggestion of others than think of something interesting to do himself?

21. Who is very friendly, has a lot of friends and is nice to everyone?

22. Who does not care to make friends, or is bashful about being friendly?

23. Who can laugh at a joke on himself or herself?

24. Who can never take a joke on himself or herself and just gets mad or hurt about it?

25. Who is your best friend?

Your name

Date

TEACHERS' FORCED CHOICE TEST

Below you will find 18 sets of descriptive statements. Each set contains 4-6 statements. Out of each set pick out one statement that fits the child most aptly. Place the letter of that description in the proper column on the record sheet, beside the child's name, under the number that corresponds to the set. When you are finished, there should be 18 entries for each pupil on the record sheet.

Do not be concerned when the description does not apply exactly, and do not dwell too long on your decision. Just pick out the statement in each set which comes closest—the one which the pupil is "most like."

1. A. Sees the bright or funny side of things.
   B. Likes to be praised.
   C. Obedient.
   D. Participates actively in school functions.
2. A. Pitches in when things are to be done.
   B. Requires corrections.
   C. Needs much extra help.
   D. Respects rules.
3. A. Is easily excited.
   B. Dislikes criticism.
   C. Works better when praised.
   D. Popular, has many friends.
4. A. Talkative.
   B. Is happy and easy to get along with.
   C. Is conscientious.
   D. Will always manage to get along.
5. A. Carries through an undertaking about as well as others of his age.
   B. Figures out things for himself.
   C. Requires encouragement and praise.
   D. Omits optional assignments.
6. A. Would answer truthfully if asked a question but would not volunteer any information harmful to himself.
   B. Recognizes his own shortcomings.
   C. Shows emotions in a restrained way.
   D. Helps others who are having difficulty.
7. A. Other children are eager to be near him or on his side.
   B. Sensitive.
   C. Enjoys just being a part of the group without taking the lead.
   D. A scattered thinker.
8. A. Is easily irritated, flustered or upset.
   B. Talks about self, what he has done, how he feels, etc.
   C. Has trouble getting along.
   D. Quiet.
9. A. Resentful.
   B. Puts up a good front.
   C. Gives up a habit which is annoying to others when it is called to his attention.
   D. A typical child for his years.
10. A. Will work hard at a task only when he has chosen it himself.
    B. Is easily upset.
    C. Is more apt to give in than continue a quarrel.
    D. Rubs people the wrong way.

11. A. Does not seem to profit by experience.
    B. Criticizes other people.
    C. Is easily confused.
    D. Quiet.
12. A. Other children regard this child as a pest.
    B. Is always thinking up alibis.
    C. In group work, often insists that his way is better.
    D. When something goes wrong, is more apt to blame himself than the other fellow.
13. A. Never gives up, regardless of how difficult the job.
    B. Is self-confident.
    C. Resents it when people hurt his feelings.
    D. Repeats mistakes.
14. A. Is rarely asked for his opinions by other students.
    B. Considers the welfare of his class, team, club or school as his own personal interest.
    C. Maintains a calm appearance and behavior even when emotionally disturbed.
    D. Lacks confidence in himself.
15. A. Can become absorbed in his own interests.
    B. Gets along well in school activities.
    C. Is alert, interested.
    D. Laughs at children who clown.
    E. An active child.
    F. Can be depended upon by an adult leader of a group to do his share.
16. A. Needs much prodding.
    B. Expresses his annoyance when provoked.
    C. Makes sensible, practical plans.
    D. Is popular with all his classmates.
    E. Pretty honest, on the whole, though he may occasionally "slip."
    F. Assertive.
17. A. Others come to him for help.
    B. Reports those who break the rules.
    C. Sometimes disturbs others by laughing and talking, but stops at once when reminded.
    D. Continually is on the defensive.
    E. Is forgetful.
    F. Show-off, attention getter.
18. A. When assigned work in school, does only part of it.
    B. Others cannot work with him.
    C. Will not give in even when proven wrong.
    D. Likes to daydream, but can bring himself back to reality when there is work to be done.

E. Is tense or ill-at-ease when reciting.

F. Although he does not show enthusiasm for group activities, he co-operates when assigned a task.

·························· 60 ··························

MODIFICATION OF AN EMOTIONALLY HELD

ATTITUDE THROUGH ROLE PLAYING[1]

by Frances M. Culbertson

The findings of the following selection give us further understanding of persistence and change in social attitudes: (1) A role-playing experience can change an emotionally held attitude such as a specific attitude toward Negro integration in housing or a general attitude toward the Negro. (2) Participants in a role-playing session are more likely to change in attitude than observers. (3) Subjects high in "authoritarianism" are significantly less likely to be influenced in their attitude toward housing integration than subjects low in "authoritarianism." The nature of the mediating process induced by the role-playing experience is also explored by Frances M. Culbertson of Arlington, Virginia. [From *Journal of Abnormal and Social Psychology*, 1957, *54*, 230-233. Reprinted by permission of the author and the American Psychological Association.]

Despite the wide use of role playing in therapy and training, and the existence of a voluminous literature on the subject, there are few experimental studies concerning its effects, and none dealing with its ability to change an emotionally loaded attitude. This study is intended to contribute to the filling of this gap.

It is generally agreed that attitudes toward minority groups are difficult to change. Weltfish (1945) noted that: "It seems probable

[1] This paper is based upon a thesis submitted to the Department of Psychology of the University of Michigan in partial fulfillment of the requirements for the degree of Doctor of Philosophy. The writer wishes to express her appreciation to Dr. Daniel Katz for his generous advice and assistance in connection with the study.

from evidence to date that many individuals must go through what amounts to a therapeutic experience rather than the more typical conception of an educational procedure before ego-anchored prejudices can be yielded up for new sources of satisfaction." Lewin's (1947) concept of "social habit" also embodies the factor of resistance to change. He observed: "To overcome this inner resistance, an additional force seems to be required, a force sufficient to 'break the habit,' to 'unfreeze' the custom." This experiment attempted to explore the reversal of roles in role playing as such an influence on one kind of "social habit," the attitude of white people toward the Negro.

Psychodramatic literature indicates that the dynamic elements that differentiate role playing through role reversal from other learning situations are three: (a) role reversal, the taking on of attitudes, feelings, and behaviors that differ from one's own; (b) projection of needs and feelings, Moreno's (1953) "s" factor; and (c) development of self-insight. These dynamic factors should affect the experiencing individual's life space, including his attitudes. However, the potency of these forces for shifting "customs" would seem to depend upon the specific nature of the psychodramatic experience. Pearl Rosenberg (1951) and Janis and King (1954) have called attention to one variable that may be significant in this respect, the element of role position. Their findings indicate that the closer a person is to a role—for example, as a participant rather than an observer—the more likely are his cognitive and motivational dispositions to be affected by the experience.

Another variable that may limit and modify the effectiveness of a psychodramatic session in changing attitudes toward a minority group is the "authoritarian personality" syndrome as measured by the F scale (Adorno, et al., 1950). "Authoritarianism" so defined should be related both to role-playing ability and to attitudes toward the Negro. Individuals high in authoritarianism should be relatively unable to expose themselves to the unstructured experiences of psychodrama, which jeopardize their defenses against repressed impulses; their minority group prejudice should therefore be relatively little affected by the psychodramatic experience.

Three hypotheses were therefore formulated for investigation: (a) A role-playing experience involving favorable attitudes toward integration of Negro and white housing results in favorable modification of the pertinent specific attitude, and to a lesser degree, in more favorable generalized attitude toward the Negro; (b) the de gree of favorable change resulting from the psychodrama is greater among participants than among observers; and (c) the degree of favorable change in attitude toward housing integration is greater among low "authoritarian" Ss than among high "authoritarian" Ss.

METHOD

To test these hypotheses the traditional three-stage design was used: (a) a pretest of Ss' specific and generalized attitudes toward the Negro, (b) a psychodramatic procedure directed at changing attitudes, and (c) a posttest of the specific and generalized attitudes. A control group was employed.

Subjects

Ninety-five students, 20 in an evening course on marriage and the family, and 75 in three separate classes in introductory sociology at a junior college in an east central state, were the experimental Ss. Twenty students in an introductory psychology course, who participated only in the pretest and posttest, were the control Ss. All of the data were gathered during the spring semester of 1954.

Attitude Measures

The first measurements were made during a regular class period by the instructor of the class. The Ss were told that the purpose of the scales was to establish norms for some groups in the area. The specific attitude measured was that toward allowing Negroes to move into neighborhoods that had previously been occupied only by whites. The six alternatives presented for choice ran from "I am completely opposed . . ." to "I am completely in favor of allowing Negroes to move into white neighborhoods." Each S was required to rank the statements in the order in which they represented the person's own choices. His attitude position was obtained by coding his first three rankings. Using only transitive rankings, the three ranks gave a 16-point scale. For example, on the pretest, with statement a the most favorable, b the next, etc., the ranking abc was assigned position 1, the most favorable attitude toward Negro integration in housing; bac was assigned position 2, and so on to position 16, fed. The discrepancy in scale position between pretest and posttest yielded an index of change in the specific attitude. Posttest alternatives were presented in the opposite order from pretest ones.

The measure of change in generalized attitude toward the Negro consisted of the discrepancy between total pretest and posttest scores on Likert's 1932 scale. Since question 10 on this scale concerns attitude toward Negro integration in housing, Ss whose change in total score was due to this item alone were considered as not having changed.

The Ss at the favorable extreme on the specific attitude and on the Likert scale were excluded from the analysis, since they could not show change in the direction of the roles played or observed. There remained for analysis 87 Ss with respect to the specific attitude, of whom 45 were role players and 42 were observers, and 90 for the Likert scale, of whom 46 were role players and 44 role observers. Code numbers were used throughout the study to maintain Ss' anonymity.

Role-Playing Procedure

The role playing was conducted by E two weeks after the pretest measures had been obtained, in the guise of a laboratory session on human relations. The problem of the psychodrama was this: A considerable increase in the number of Negroes in the community was expected because of movement into the area of a defense plant. It was agreed that there would not be segregation, as there had not been any in the past. There was, however, concern about the possible development of tensions and antagonisms during the adjustment period. To minimize this danger, an educational program was planned by the local government. What should be the major theme of this educational program? Each of the three roles of the psychodrama involved the presentation of and advocacy of a specific theme for the educational program. Each of the themes was completely in favor of integration of the Negroes.

The Ss were divided randomly into groups of six, each group consisting of three participants and three observers, with each observer instructed to associate himself with an assigned role player. Members of each group were arranged in a circle. In order to facilitate group discussion, the role players were instructed to arrange themselves in alphabetical order according to the names of the roles they were to play. This arrangement permitted them to call one another by name and also permitted each observer to remember who had the par ticular role with which he had been instructed to associate. Before the role playing began, all Ss were given three minutes to consider how they would act the given role. At the end of this time, the 15 minutes of role playing began.

The posttest measures were administered seven to ten days later as a class exercise. A number of questions were added to determine whether Ss knew the purpose of the study, and whether their ideas on this had influenced their responses.

RESULTS AND DISCUSSION

Analysis of the data was in terms of chi-square comparisons of frequencies of positive change. Since the study centered on directional hypotheses a one-tailed test was used in chi-square tests for one degree of freedom. Differences at the .05 level and below were accepted as significant. The results of the study are summarized in Table 1.

TABLE 1

FREQUENCY OF POSITIVE CHANGES

	N	Number Showing Positive Change	Comparisons, χ^2 and p values
Integration in Housing			
Control Group	18	2	χ^2 18.2
Role Players	45	30	$p < .0005$
Control Group	18	2	χ^2 7.2
Role Observers	42	18	$p < .0045$
Role Players	45	30	χ^2 5.99
Role Observers	42	18	$p < .008$
F Scale—above median	48	20	χ^2 9.16
F Scale—below median	39	28	$p < .0023$
Generalized Attitude			
Control Group	19	4	χ^2 19.3
Role Players	46	35	$p < .0005$
Control Group	19	4	χ^2 8.3
Role Observers	44	25	$p < .0035$
Role Players	46	35	χ^2 4.67
Role Observers	44	25	$p < .018$

The first objective was to test whether a psychodramatic experience can change an emotionally held attitude. In regard to the specific attitude toward Negro integration in housing, a chi-square value of 18.2 ($p < .0005$) was obtained in the comparison between role players and control group, and a chi-square value of 7.2 ($p < .0045$) for role observers and control group. In regard to general attitude toward the Negro, corresponding chi squares were obtained of 19.3 ($p < .0005$) for the comparison of role players and control group, and 8.3 ($p < .0035$) for the comparison of role observers and control group. Changes of the sort hypothesized were clearly produced by the psychodrama, and persisted 7-10 days until the time of the posttest.

The second aim was to investigate whether positions in a psychodrama as participant and as observer result in different degrees of attitude change. The findings are positive and significant here also. Participants to a greater degree than observers shifted in the direction of the role experience. They changed more in the specific attitude toward Negro integration in housing, as indicated by a chi square of 5.99 ($p < .008$), as well as in attitude toward the Negro in general, as indicated by the chi-square value of 4.67 ($p < .018$) on the Likert scale.

The third objective was to explore the relationship between "authoritarianism" and attitude change through psychodrama. The data show that high-F Ss, those above the median, are significantly less likely to be influenced by role playing in their attitude toward housing integration than low-F Ss, those below the median, chi square being 9.16 ($p < .0023$). A next step suggested by these findings would be to investigate with resistant Ss the separate and combined effectiveness of role playing and role observing.

Differences in Motivation and Involvement

The confirmation of the hypotheses underlying this study leaves open the nature of the mediating processes induced by the psychodrama. The difference in results between role players and role observers indicates—since both had the same information—that factors other than information were influential in reducing prejudice. Also, since high-F Ss would be expected to exhibit high degrees of conformity, the fact that low-F Ss changed in attitude to a greater degree than high-F Ss suggests that the diminishing of Negro prejudice was not merely a result of conformity pressures in the experimental situation. To what, then, can the change be attributed?

The theory underlying this investigation assumed that projection of feelings and self-insight were modifying forces. Supplementary data obtained from a questionnaire given immediately after the psychodrama showed that role players were more highly self-involved in the drama than observers, as evidenced by their emotions, perceptions, and judgments regarding the role experience. The following factors were all present to a greater degree—significant beyond the .05 level—for participants than for observers: (a) degree of association with assigned role, (b) time during which attention was paid to a given role, (c) emotional involvement with the role, (d) perception of the drama in terms of feelings, thoughts and emotions rather than in terms of the situation and actions of the characters, (e) positive rather than negative solutions regarding the role problem, and (f) noncritical rather than critical judgment regarding the role behavior and role session. Thus role participation appears to have led to greater degrees of motivation and involvement in the drama than role observation. The part played by projection and self-insight in these effects, however, remains to be explored.

SUMMARY

This experiment investigated (a) whether role playing can change an emotionally loaded attitude, (b) whether a participant position in a role-playing session is more likely to result in a change in attitude than an observer position, and (c) whether Ss high in "authoritarianism" are less affected than Ss low in "authoritarianism."

Ninety-five experimental Ss responded to questionnaires before and after a role-playing experience: (a) a measure of attitude toward "allowing Negroes to move into White neighborhoods," the specific attitude associated with the role session, and (b) the Likert scale measuring the generalized attitude toward the Negro. Twenty control Ss took similar measures, without exposure to the psychodrama. The attitude change procedure was a 15-minute role-playing session in which Ss were randomly assigned either to be participants or observers with particular roles. All roles were completely in favor of Negro integration in housing.

The findings were significant and in the predicted direction. Experimental Ss shifted their attitude toward Negro integration in housing as well as their general attitude toward the Negro in the direction of the role experience. Role players shifted to a greater degree than observers in a favorable direction. Those Ss below the

median on the F scale changed more in a favorable direction in
attitude toward Negro integration in housing than those above the
median on the F scale. Findings on degree of self-involvement indicate that role players were more motivated and more involved in the
drama experience than role observers.

····························· 61 ····························

DOES HIGHER EDUCATION INFLUENCE

STUDENT VALUES?

by Philip E. Jacob

SOME REACTIONS FROM . . .

W. C. H. Prentice, Irwin Abrams, James S. Coles

In this summary of his book (Jacob, 1957) Philip E. Jacob of the
University of Pennsylvania concludes, "A study of what happens to
the values of American students of today shows that their college
experience barely touches their standards of behavior, quality of
judgment, sense of social responsibility, perspicacity of understanding,
and guiding beliefs." Following the article are comments by W. C. H.
Prentice of Swarthmore College, Irwin Abrams of Antioch College,
and James S. Coles of Bowdoin College. [From *National Education
Association Journal*, 1958, *47*, 35-38. Reprinted by permission of the
authors and the National Education Association.]

Colleges and universities must face a hard fact about their present
accomplishment before they can plan realistically for their role in
the not-too-distant future. For the most part, they seem to lack the
capacity to influence students, or maybe today's students are incapa
ble of being influenced by higher education.

In any case, a study of what happens to the values of American
students of today shows that their college experience barely touches
their standards of behavior, quality of judgment, sense of social
responsibility, perspicacity of understanding, and guiding beliefs.

This means that if institutions of higher learning are expected to fulfil the historic humanistic mission of what we have called liberal education, they will have to learn how to do it. They are *not* doing it now with most of their students.

This conclusion stems from an analysis of three main types of data, which social scientists obtained from over 100 institutions: studies of student attitudes conducted during the last 15 years, recent evaluations of the outcomes of general education and other courses and of various methods of teaching, and a number of comprehensive self studies by particular institutions. [A detailed inventory and analysis of this material is available in a report prepared by Dr. Jacob for the Edward W. Hazen Foundation: *Changing Values in College*. Harper. 1957.]

Fortunately, not all evidence is negative. There are some institutions in which students' values seem to develop, some teachers whose influence penetrates and stays, and some educational techniques which help open the sensibilities as well as the intellectual perceptions of some students. But the prevailing situation concerning the influence of college on contemporary student values is as follows:

1. The values of American college students are remarkably homogeneous, considering the variety of their backgrounds and their relatively unrestricted opportunities for freedom of thought and personal development.

A dominant characteristic of the current student generation is that the students are gloriously contented, both in regard to their present day-to-day activity and their outlook for the future.

The great majority of students appear unabashedly self-centered. They aspire to material gratifications for themselves and their families. They intend to look out for themselves first and expect others to do likewise.

Social harmony, with an easy tolerance of the dissident and the different, also pervades the student environment. Conformists themselves, the American students do not expect others to conform to the socially accepted standard. They are, for the most part, ready to live in a mobile society without racial, ethnic, or income barriers. But they do not intend to crusade for nondiscrimination, merely to accept it as it comes.

Although most students value the traditional code of moral virtues, they are not inclined to censure those who choose to depart from it. Nor do they feel personally bound to unvarying conformity to the code, especially when a lapse is socially sanctioned. For instance, systematic academic cheating is the custom at many major institutions.

Students normally express a need for religion and often attend church on Sundays, but their religion does not carry over into the secular world. The majority appear to believe that God's place is in church or home, not in business or community.

American students are also only dutifully responsive toward government. They expect to obey its laws and pay its taxes—without complaint but without enthusiasm. Except for voting, however, they are politically irresponsible and politically illiterate.

They have contradictory attitudes toward international affairs. They predict another major war within a dozen years, yet indicate that during the immediate future they expect to give little personal attention to international problems.

Students by and large set great stock by college in general and their own college in particular. Only a minority, however, seem to value their college education for its intellectual contribution or for its nurturing of personal character. Vocational preparation and skill and experience in social "adjustment" head the rewards which students expect from college.

The available data indicate that the profile just given may broadly characterize 75 or 80% of the students. To the remainder, some or most of the generalizations are not applicable. Also, on some issues, such as how much government the country needs, students have no common mind. But the dominant impression is a nation-wide norm of values pervading the campus.

*2. **The main effect of higher education upon student values is to bring about general acceptance of a body of standards and attitudes characteristic of college-bred men and women in America.***

There tends to be more homogeneity and greater consistency of values among college seniors than among freshmen, indicating that the senior has ironed out serious conflicts of values or at least achieved a workable compromise. Throughout college, changes are rarely drastic or sudden. Such changes as do occur tend to emerge on the periphery of the student's character rather than to affect his core of values.

The values of college graduates do differ in some ways from the rest of society. They are more concerned with status, achievement, and prestige. As a whole, they tend to be more self-important, more conservative, more tolerant, and less superstitious and prejudiced than those without college.

It seems reasonable to credit these differences to college, partly to its positive influence in bringing students' outlook into line with a "standard," partly to a subtle selective process which tends to eliminate those not sufficiently adaptive to acquire the value-patterns of the college graduate.

But to call this process a liberalization of student values is to use a misnomer. The impact of college rather is to socialize the individual, to refine or shape up his values so that he can fit into his society more congenially.

3. For the most part, students' values do not vary greatly whether they have pursued a conventional liberal-arts program, an integrated general-education curriculum, or a professional-vocational opinion.

The more liberally educated students may take a somewhat more active interest in community responsibilities and keep better informed about public affairs. But the distinction is not striking, and it does not occur consistently. It does not justify the conclusion that a student acquires a greater maturity of judgment on issues of social policy or a more sensitive regard for human values because he has had more liberal education.

There is also no solid evidence of a delayed reaction. The college alumnus exhibits no unusual trademark identifying his undergraduate curriculum.

The same negative conclusion applies to the general effect of social-science courses. Although many students testify that such courses have increased their understanding of world affairs or interest in politics, the values actually expressed by social-science students—either verbally or in action—are little different from those of others. There is little evidence, for instance, that actual participation in public life has increased as a result of students' taking social science.

4. Quality of teaching has little effect upon the value-outcomes of students' general education.

Students have demonstrated an uncanny capacity to evaluate the performance of instructors according to objective criteria. Yet, by and large, the impact of the teacher they consider good is indistinguishable from that of the poor one—at least in terms of his influence upon the students' values.

Some teachers, however, do exert a profound influence on *some* students, even to the point of causing particular individuals to adopt new and usually more socially responsible vocational goals. It is perhaps significant that faculty members having this power are likely to be those whose own value-commitments are openly expressed and who are outgoing and warm in their student relationships.

5. *The method of instruction seems to have only a minor influence on students' value judgments.*

Under special circumstances, "student-centered" teaching reportedly has resulted in a more satisfactory student adjustment and a more congenial learning situation. But the weight of evidence gives little indication that different teaching methods—say the lecture system versus recitation, conference, discussion, or tutorial methods—greatly alter students' beliefs or behavior.

However, individual students are often deeply affected by participation in experiences which vividly confront them with value issues, and possibly demand decisions on their part whose consequences they can witness.

But the practical difficulties of working such activities into the educational process are very great, especially in the general part of the curriculum in which large numbers of students are involved. For the essence of a potent laboratory practice in citizenship, a creative work camp, a meaningful experiment in international living, a stimulating work-study curriculum, or even a well-conceived field study is this: Each student personally engages in the action.

Vicarious experience does not deliver the same punch, even though role-playing techniques in the classroom and the analysis of challenging case studies and problem situations do arouse more interest.

6. *Similar as the patterns of student values appear on a mass view, the intellectual, cultural, or moral climate of some institutions stands out as having a peculiar potency.*

The response of students to education within these institutions is strikingly different from the national pattern.

Such colleges and universities do not fit any institutional type. However, they seem to have in common a high level of expectancy of their students. *What* is expected is not the same.

For instance, the institution may primarily stress intellectual initiative, profound respect for the worth of work, world-mindedness, or a dedication to humanitarian service. But everyone is conscious of the mission to which the institution stands dedicated, though this is not necessarily loudly trumpeted at every convocation, nor elaborated in the college or university bulletin.

In these colleges, students seem drawn to live up to the college standard, even if it means a wrench from their previous ways of thought.

With a distinctive quality of this kind, an institution evokes a deep loyalty from students, alumni, and staff. A community of values is created which persists long after graduation and often influences the choice of college by the next generation.

7. Recent research has identified certain personality characteristics of students which filter their educational experiences.

Some students have a set of mind so rigid, an outlook on human relations so stereotyped, and a reliance on authority so compulsive, that they are incapable of understanding, much less accepting, new ideas. Such students quail in the presence of conflict and uncertainty. They crave "right answers," recoil from creative discussion.

Under most conditions of general education, where content and teaching method have been more or less standardized to suit the average student, the personalities just described become dead wood. A few institutions, however, are exploring special approaches to general education for this type of student, with promising results.

These students rarely achieve the autonomy of those whose personality is freer to start with. But they have shown striking gains in critical thinking and developed more responsible and sensitive social values when their general education in social science, for instance, has been tailored to their particular needs. Because the number of students with such personality characteristics is large and growing, this type of experimentation seems unusually important.

The points presented here imply that no specific curricular pattern of liberal education, no pedigree of instructor, and no wizardry of instructional method should be patented for its impact on students' values. Indeed, the impact of American higher education as a whole upon the value patterns of college youth as a whole seems negligible.

The values of some students do change in college. But even with these, the impetus to change does not come primarily from the formal educational process. It comes from the distinctive climate of a few institutions, the individual and personal magnetism of a sensitive teacher with strong values, or the value-laden personal experiences which students occasionally undergo during college.

In short, college can contribute to the growth of a student's values only when it penetrates the core of his life and confronts him with fresh and often disturbing implications, which are different from those which he and his society have taken for granted. This can hardly occur as a by-product of a curricular assembly line. It requires a highly personal relationship between the college community and the individual student—a relationship that is warm and considerate, but at the same time mutually aggravating.

SOME REACTIONS FROM . . .

W. C. H. Prentice

When Dr. Jacob says that students are "contented" or "self-centered," to whom is he comparing them? To themselves in high school? To earlier college generations? To college-age students who are not attending college? Or to some ideal? He never makes it clear what the standard of reference is, and the investigations themselves are notable for their lack of useful control groups.

If it should turn out to be true that college students are remarkably like their noncollege compatriots, would that mean that the colleges are failing in their job? Or merely that values of the kind studied are formed early and by influences with similar impacts on college and noncollege people?

Indeed, what are the real or implied alternatives? It is said that students are self-centered. Would we have them government-centered? Church-centered? It is said that students are "gloriously contented." Would we have them discontented? It is said that students accept the business culture of our society. Would we have them reject it? It is said that students expect their futures to depend on their own actions. Would we make them fatalists? Each charge against contemporary student values implies that they are worse than some other alternative.

Is the research adequate to demonstrate what real alternatives may exist, given the constraints of our kind of society? Even if we assume the situation is about as painted, can we be sure that there are better possibilities about the reasonable alternatives? The report shows measurable changes from freshman to senior year in a number of dimensions that are highly acceptable to many college teachers and administrators. However, these are given little prominence or are dismissed as mere conformity to college norms.

What measures could ever discriminate such conformity from genuine convergent changes resulting from common experience—the very thing that the report seems to hope for and claims not to find?

Finally, suppose that, all other doubts satisfied, we accepted the most extreme interpretations of the report. Could we change the situation without risking a much worse moral climate and without jeopardizing our major purposes?

Are there values on which all colleges (or at least a working majority of people within each college) can agree? After trying to get educators to agree on a set of goals in this area, I think not.

If, theoretically, we could settle on such values, would we know how to teach them? Could we teach them without interfering with traditional educational goals? Would we know how to recognize success?

The report sometimes seems to imply that college students should agree on values that are not accepted by noncollege people.

A clear dichotomy of that sort is improbable on many grounds. Is it in any way desirable? What other criterion of success would be acceptable?

The central purpose of liberal education is to impart those values concerned with the life of the mind.

The student should learn to put a high value on ideas, on the dispassionate examination of evidence, on philosophic and artistic contemplation, on humility about his conclusions, pride in the use of his creative and analytic gifts, and respect for the rights and dignity of others who are making their own way along the intellectual road. A college that tries to do more or other than this will endanger its primary goals.

Certainly not all institutions are succeeding in this task; probably none is attaining its ideal. We need careful research to measure our achievement.

Irwin Abrams

As Dr. Jacob states, some colleges do appear to have a definite influence upon student values. They are, for the most part, small liberal-arts institutions where the students sense that a devotion to certain values is expected of them.

There is also evidence that values can be affected when a college course sets out to involve the student in a real-life situation of social or political action. Certain laboratory experiences in citizenship courses have left students more actively concerned with political issues. Also, such off-campus experiences as work camps and foreign study profoundly affect student values.

Are there indications here for educational planning? What would happen, for example, if the philosophy course were coordinated with student experience in helping formulate and maintain the college code of conduct?

What about the extracurricular activities in which the great majority of students invest so much of their emotional lives? Are not the highest loyalties more likely to be exercised in the stadium and fraternity house rather than the classroom?

Perhaps the corollary of the Jacob report would be a study of those influences on the campus that sustain the student's disposition to go along unthinkingly with the crowd and that stunt the growth of idealism.

No one has to worry that colleges are producing radicals, but there is cause for grave concern if what they are actually producing are herds of materialistic, self-centered conformists. For the college can remain faithful to its mission of preserving and carrying forward a great intellectual and spiritual heritage only when it is giving its students a liberal education. If this means the freeing of the mind and spirit of the student to realize his highest potentialities, then educators are faced today with an unprecedented challenge to make liberal education worthy of its name.

James S. Coles

In provocative style, Professor Jacob achieves with his readers that "relation which is warm and considerate, but at the same time mutually aggravating." His report, a product of much study and sincere concern, if taken at face value is a heavy indictment of our colleges. As such, it cannot be cavalierly dismissed.

However, in evaluating the Jacob study, certain essential factors must be considered. The study is a secondary collation based upon the work of numerous others, some dating back almost two decades. The results of objective-type or multiple-answer questionnaires are generally recognized to be markedly influenced by the manner in which the questionnaires are drawn; some of those involved are open to criticism. Further, these studies are dependent upon the *verbalization* of deep-seated social, religious, and moral attitudes and values—a verbalization difficult even among professionals devoted to such considerations.

Assuming for the moment, validity of the data presented, the inferences derived must be carefully examined. In the opinion of many, the derivations are not uniformly sound. For example, the report states that religion does not appear to be a vital concern of most students. This inference is apparently based upon multiple-choice selections in response to the question: "What three things or activities in your life do you expect to give you the most satisfaction?"

According to the choices made by the students examined, in terms of *giving satisfaction,* religion rates poorly relative to career, family relationships, or leisure activities. But is the primary role of religion to "give satisfaction"? With equal objectivity one should examine the basis for conclusions of the report concerning material gratifications and other factors.

Tolerance has been successfully taught in our schools and churches for a generation. Even though we may not like it, the same tolerant attitude could well carry over to what Professor Jacob describes as "morality—with elbow room"; there is no distinction between areas where tolerance is desired and where it is to be avoided.

Although some may take issue with parts of Professor Jacob's report, we are indebted to him for focusing upon vital problems of our age his dedicated concern. The inculcation of proper values is obviously important, and to the extent this is not accomplished in the home, the church, and the school, or is nullified by the social mores, colleges and universities will have to fill the void. Without question American students tend far too much to conformity and need a sense of greater dedication. And if any society is to advance, its values must continually be improved.

.... **62** ....

CHANGES IN ATTITUDES DURING COLLEGE

by Harold Webster

This report by Harold Webster of the University of California (Berkeley) is part of a large-scale study conducted at Vassar College which aims to increase our understanding of the processes of learning and personality development during the college years. On the basis of an attitude "developmental scale" and interview data it is found that Vassar College seniors are less authoritarian, less conventional, and more tolerant than when they were freshmen. Problems arising in evaluating test-retest attitude-measurement data for college students are discussed. [From *Journal of Educational Psychology*, 1958, *49*, 109-117. Reprinted with the permission of the author and the American Psychological Association.]

For several years, the Mary Conover Mellon Foundation has supported a research program, the main purpose of which is to increase our understanding of the processes of learning and personality development in undergraduates who attend a women's liberal arts college.[1] The research has made use of a variety of information concerning both students and alumnae (Sanford, 1956; Sanford, Webster, and Freedman, 1957; Webster, 1957). Data have been collected by means of interviews, testing, and general observation.

The present paper reports some results of the personality testing program. Although at the research level there is always some confusion in distinguishing between attitudes, interests, values, and the like, it seems reasonable to regard most personality inventory responses as expressions of attitudes, including attitudes about the self. The test items to be discussed concern human feelings and experiences which are quite general; for some purposes they are probably superior to the more specific kinds of items found in interest inventories (Dressel, 1954; Matteson, 1955).

Students undergo changes in attitudes, in widely varying degrees, while attending college (Arsenian, 1943; Hunter, 1942; Jones, 1938; Kuhlen, 1941; Matteson, 1955; Newcomb, 1943; Sanford, 1956). It is difficult, however, to relate such changes directly to college education; during late adolescence some variations in attitudes undoubtedly have little to do with formal educational experience. Intellectual maturation continues well into the college years (Flory, 1940; McConnell, 1934), but its effect on attitudes at this age level is largely unknown.

Methods for measuring longitudinal change involve some serious problems. Corey (1936) pointed out the error in equating observed differences between classes with changes which might have been found by later retesting the same students. True change may also be obscured, however, in retesting the same persons, either because it is confounded with measurement error (Lord, 1956), or because its sources have not been identified experimentally. If the internal

[1] During the present study, research staff members included John Bushnell, Mervin Freedman, Richard Jung, Nevitt Sanford, coordinator, and the writer. Donald Brown, Department of Psychology, Bryn Mawr College, has devoted five summers to work on the project.

consistency of the measures is low, longitudinal comparisons for individuals may not be meaningful, for true changes occurring simultaneously in more than one kind of attitude may then go undetected. This is the case even if "comparable forms" are employed for the testing. In the present paper "reliability" will always refer to internal consistency (test homogeneity).

CONSTRUCTION OF A DEVELOPMENTAL SCALE

The initial selection of items and scales for an experimental battery was necessarily diverse because the aims of the research were quite general. The first battery, administered in 1952 by Nevitt San-ford (1956), contained many verbal and nonverbal personality items, which, together with certain college entrance data, made possible comprehensive descriptions of students. Subsequently, a revision, which contained 677 verbal items, was administered to freshman and senior classes for four consecutive years. The battery was eventually revised a second time so that several new scales, including the one to be described, could be scored from it (Webster, 1957).

From studies of both interview and test data, it was evident early in the research that more could be learned by studying *changes* in students, rather than by focusing on relatively permanent aspects of personality. This approach was also believed more likely to lead directly to facts of importance for educators who are primarily concerned with inducing special kinds of change. It appeared that much personality development and reorganization was taking place in freshman subjects. As a result we began to study test material to which freshman responded differently from older students.

The Developmental Scale therefore contains personality inventory items found to discriminate graduating seniors from entering freshmen. As previously reported (Sanford, 1956; Webster, 1957) the scale was made up of items selected by comparing concurrent classes of seniors and freshmen. The present paper presents items which functioned best in single tests, and identifies those remaining after further cross-validation using a sample of 274 students twice, first as freshmen and later as seniors. Items which have survived both kinds of validation are likely to be of general interest. The procedures used will be described only briefly.

For the first sample (1953), 220 of the 677 items discriminated the classes (441 freshmen and 237 seniors) at the .05 level of significance, the majority of them also reaching the .001 level. Of these, 197 items with means in the range .09 to .91, inclusive, were retained for the test. In a second sample (1954, 225 freshmen and 192 seniors, selected randomly) 123 of the 197 items were still functioning, according to the same criteria.

At this point in the research two kinds of evidence suggested that items validated by using scores for the same persons would not differ markedly from items already selected using data from concurrent classes: Mervin Freedman in an unpublished study reported no significant differences in performance on the items between those who remained and those who withdrew from college; and the variances for senior total scale scores (based on the 123 items) were significantly larger than the variances for freshmen, an effect opposite to that which would be observed if there were increased homogeneity due to withdrawals from college.

Subsequently most of the 1953 freshmen became seniors and were retested with the same battery shortly before graduation in 1957. The test-retest data ($N = 274$) show that most of the items also function satisfactorily for the same persons.

An approximate statistical test for correlated frequencies based on an exact test by McNemar (1955, p. 56), was used for identifying items, responses to which differed significantly in the same sample for the two occasions.

THE SCALE ITEMS

Of the 123 items, 79 are listed in Table 1. Some data on misclassification proportions and homogeneity appear elsewhere (Sanford, 1956). The Kuder-Richardson formula 21 reliability (KR 21) in an independent sample of 130 Vassar freshmen and 81 seniors is .84 for the first 31 items and .88 for the first 72. The reliability for all 123 items was only .84 for this sample, and it was also substantially below that of the 72-item scale in some other samples. Items in Table 1 which did *not* discriminate the same persons as freshmen and seniors at the .01 level of significance are preceded by an asterisk; the final seven items could be substituted for these starred items, probably with little effect on total scale reliability.

RESULTS AND DISCUSSION

The staff studied the content of the items, classifying them under such rubrics as freedom from compulsiveness, flexibility and toler-

TABLE 1

THE DEVELOPMENTAL SCALE[a]

I would rather be a steady and dependable worker than a brilliant but unstable one. (F, 31–55)

In school I always looked far ahead in planning what courses to take. (F, 44–62)

Straightforward reasoning appeals to me more than metaphors and the search for analogies. (F, 30–49)

I have never done anything dangerous for the thrill of it. (F, 55–70)

I would disapprove of anyone's drinking to the point of intoxication at a party. (F, 30–65)

I set a high standard for myself and I feel others should do the same. (F, 31–44)

No man of character would ask his fiancée to have sexual intercourse with him before marriage. (F, 35–64)

I would be ashamed not to use my privilege of voting. (F, 19–29)

Lawbreakers are almost always caught and punished. (F, 47–66)

Every family owes it to the city to keep their sidewalks cleared in the winter and their lawn mowed in the summer. (F, 30–44)

I have very few quarrels with members of my family. (F, 32–42)

It is a pretty callous person who does not feel love and gratitude towards his parents. (F, 32–56)

One of my aims in life is to accomplish something that would make my mother proud of me. (F, 30–48)

Sometimes I used to feel that I would like to leave home. (T, 37–50)

My home life was always happy. (F, 28–45)

I have often gone against my parents' wishes. (T, 16–26)

In the final analysis, parents generally turn out to be right about things. (F, 15–44)

I have often either broken rules (school, club, etc.) or inwardly rebelled against them. (T, 28–41)

Only a fool would try to change our American way of life. (F, 50–76)

I go to church almost every week. (F, 50–72)

I pray several times every week. (F, 36–57)

I believe in a life hereafter. (F, 39–53)

In religious matters, I believe I would have to be called an agnostic. (T, 16–35)

I should like to belong to several clubs or lodges. (F, 38–68)

I used to steal sometimes when I was a youngster. (T, 23–35)

I like to talk about sex. (T, 38–65)

I do not always tell the truth. (T, 49–62)

People would be happier if sex experience before marriage were taken for granted in both men and women. (T, 18–32)

I dislike women who disregard the usual social or moral conventions. (F, 39–69)

[a] Responses, T for true, F for false, are those used more often by high-scorers, that is, by seniors. Figures are percentages of the same group of 274 individuals as freshmen and as seniors, respectively, who responded in the direction indicated.

THE DEVELOPMENTAL SCALE—*Continued*

I believe women ought to have as much sexual freedom as men. (T, 24–47)

*The history of mankind is a record of continual progress, and there is no reason to believe that it will not continue. (F, 25–27)

I have had periods of days, weeks, or months when I couldn't take care of things because I couldn't "get going." (T, 21–32)

*I do not like to see people carelessly dressed. (F, 32–41)

It is annoying to listen to a lecturer who cannot seem to make up his mind what he really believes. (F, 16–37)

A strong person will be able to make up his mind even on the most difficult questions. (F, 52–63)

I don't like to work on a problem unless there is the possibility of coming out with a clear-cut and unambiguous answer. (F, 60–78)

For most questions there is just one right answer, once a person is able to get all the facts. (F, 65–93)

I think I am stricter about right and wrong than most people. (F, 58–70)

I always tried to make the best school grades that I could. (F, 29–51)

A large number of people are guilty of bad sexual conduct. (F, 49–69)

The trouble with many people is that they don't take things seriously enough. (F, 50–71)

At times I have been so entertained by the cleverness of a crook that I have hoped he would get by with it. (T, 34–56)

A person who doesn't vote is not a good citizen. (F, 27–43)

Some of my family have habits that bother and annoy me very much. (T, 46–61)

*My parents have often disapproved of my friends. (T, 12–15)

*Army life is a good influence on most young men. (F, 35–41)

Disobedience to the government is never justified. (F, 65–83)

If I were confronted with the necessity of betraying either my country or my best friend, I would prefer to betray my country. (T, 11–24)

Communism is the most hateful thing in the world today. (F, 67–87)

I believe in the second coming of Christ. (F, 75–84)

Everything is turning out just like the prophets of the Bible said it would. (F, 78–91)

I believe there is a God. (F, 10–25)

Human passions cause most of the evil in the world. (F, 30–50)

The best theory is the one that has the best applications. (F, 31–55)

In illegitimate pregnancies, abortion is in many cases the most reasonable alternative. (T, 22–37)

I have used alcohol excessively. (T, 05–17)

I have never done any heavy drinking. (F, 13–43)

If I could get into a movie without paying and be sure I was not seen I would probably do it. (T, 22–46)

I have never indulged in any unusual sex practices. (F, 06–17)

My sex life is satisfactory. (F, 16–26)

*I often do whatever makes me feel cheerful here and now, even at

THE DEVELOPMENTAL SCALE—*Continued*

the cost of some distant goal. (T, 39–41)

I would be uncomfortable if I accidentally went to a formal party in street clothes. (F, 24–41)

*Some of my friends think that my ideas are impractical, if not a bit wild. (T, 23–26)

Kindness and generosity are the most important qualities for a wife to have. (F, 47–60)

I believe we are made better by the trials and hardships of life. (F, 12–38)

Any man who is able and willing to work hard has a good chance of succeeding. (F, 07–24)

I am an important person. (T, 16–31)

I hardly ever tell people what I think of them when they do something I dislike. (F, 35–59)

I have never felt better in my life than I do now. (F, 37–53)

At periods my mind seems to work more slowly than usual. (T, 53–66)

My daily life is full of things that keep me interested. (F, 04–15)

*Sometimes I feel that I am about to go to pieces. (T, 26–28)

I don't like modern art. (F, 62–81)

Our thinking would be a lot better off if we would just forget about words like "probably," "approximately," and "perhaps." (F, 81–94)

It is a good rule to accept nothing as certain or proved. (T, 23–44)

Every citizen should take the time to find out about national affairs, even if it means giving up some personal pleasure. (F, 10–20)

People have a real duty to take care of their aged parents, even if it means making some pretty big sacrifices. (F, 15–28)

I would like to hear a great singer in an opera. (T, 76–92)

It is very important for my feeling of security that people about me like me personally. (F, 13–25)

ance for ambiguity, impunitive attitudes, critical attitudes toward authority (including parents or family, the state, religion, rules, etc.), intraception, mature interests, unconventionality or nonconformity, rejection of traditional feminine roles, freedom from cynicism about others, realism, and so on; such clusters have not been studied statistically. A factor method (Wherrey, Perloff, and Campbell, 1951) was applied which produced the scales consisting of the first 31 and the first 72 items in Table 1. The general factor of either scale was called "Rebellious Independence," a name which seems adequate only if "independence" is interpreted broadly enough; for example, it should include an attitude of tolerance toward human weaknesses.

Some statistics for the 72-item scale appear in Table 2. The cooperation of Dr. Pergrouhi Najarian, of the Beirut College for Women, in obtaining the Arab data, and of Dr. Margaret Luszki, of the National Institute of Mental Health, in providing the Paine College data for Southern Negroes, is greatly appreciated. For use with

TABLE 2

COMPARISON OF VARIOUS GROUPS ON THE SHORT FORM $(N = 72)$

DEVELOPMENTAL SCALE

Sex	Classes	College	N	X	S	r_{TT}[a]
F	Freshmen	Vassar	321	23.567	9.229	.825
F	Freshmen	Beirut	28	24.929	5.769	.518
F	Freshmen	Paine	58	16.603	6.011	.656
M	Freshmen	Paine	30	19.867	7.008	.717
F	Sophomores	Paine	44	17.841	5.604	.581
M	Sophomores	Paine	18	18.889	6.999	.726
F	Juniors	Paine	28	21.571	6.310	.629
M	Juniors	Paine	14	24.357	3.518	.000
F	Seniors	Paine	26	19.000	6.765	.704
M	Seniors	Paine	21	23.286	6.057	.578
F	Seniors	Vassar	197	34.700	11.010	.864
F	Seniors	Beirut	33	25.667	5.988	.547
F	1930–35	Vassar	50	31.060	8.675	.776
F	1904	Vassar	82	17.780	7.295	.759
F	Total	Paine	156	18.244	6.340	.670
M	Total	Paine	83	21.277	6.658	.671

[a] Reliabilities estimated by Kuder-Richardson Formula 21.

diverse groups KR 21 is known to be the most logical reliability measure (Lord, 1955), even though it is slightly smaller on the average than any kind of split-half coefficient. The values for KR 21 in Table 2 are cause for some skepticism regarding the meaning for other cultural groups of the 72-item scale. Beirut and Paine students had more than average difficulty in understanding some items, which probably decreased reliability. It is likely, however, that "Rebellious Independence" would have been expressed somewhat differently if scales had been constructed primarily for use with either Arab girls or Southern Negroes. The same argument applies, with less force, for Vassar alumnae; as expected, however, there is less decrease in reliability for alumnae samples. Also, low reliability often accompanies reductions in variance—and smaller variances in Table 2 for alumnae, in comparison with Vassar seniors, would be expected for reasons discussed below. If the scale were to be used for comparing individuals, reliability could be improved by presenting the items with multiple response alternatives.

The difference between standard deviations of the scores for the concurrent classes of Vassar seniors and freshmen in Table 2 is significant, as it also is for the test-retest group of Table 5. Variability on a majority of the other personality scales has also been observed to be larger for Vassar seniors than for freshmen, either for the same or different students. Whatever the cause of this effect, it is strong enough to more than compensate for increased homogeneity due to withdrawals from college. For the four classes of Paine women students of Table 2, however, the differences among standard deviations are not large and would be expected by chance alone as often as 16% of the time.

It may be that with more reliable and general measures, the effect of increasing variances with increasing age will hold more generally, at least up to a certain age, after which a decrease would be expected. Matteson (1955) found support for his hypothesis that interests of college students increased with actual experience, and Strong (1943) has noted an increased diversification of interests for males between ages 15 and 25. To the extent that this process of diversification was uneven, or entailed earlier changes in some subjects than in others, variances would at first increase with age. A number of studies of personality development, for example, those of White (1952), have emphasized the unevenness of the processes involved in attaining greater maturity. Some data of Corey's (1936), on attitude items show larger variances for student groups at later ages. In agreement with this theory, standard deviations of Vassar age groups in Table 2 vary significantly, rising and falling for freshmen, seniors, middle-aged alumnae, and older alumnae.

If Vassar seniors are more diverse than their elders on the trait, Rebellious Independence, at the same time possessing on the average more of it (see Table 2), then they may also have become more aware of, or more sensitized to, the immediate problems of social conformity, Jacob (1957).[2] Interview data indicate that this is undoubtedly the case for the majority of these young women at this time in their lives. There is little evidence, however, that this increased awareness of, or concern with, conformity is actually accompanied by increasingly homogeneous attitudes, or, for that matter, by increasingly conforming behavior within college classes. On the contrary, seniors appear generally to be less homogeneous and less conforming than freshmen. The one exception, which agrees with a general observation by Jacob (1957), is that seniors, paradoxically perhaps, express more uniformly than freshmen a greater degree of *tolerance* for nonconforming ideas and behavior. Among dozens of personality scales, those measuring authoritarianism, lack of tolerance, etc. are among the few for which obtained variances for seniors

[2] [For a summary of this book see selection 61 in this volume. Ed.]

are usually slightly less than those for freshmen; of course the mean tolerance scores are much higher for seniors, in either concurrent or test-retest comparisons (Sanford, 1956).

The freshman-senior mean differences for institutions in Table 2 are in the expected direction, even though the one for the Beirut sample is not significant, and that for Paine females reaches only the 12% level. The test ratio for Paine women is significant if pairs of extreme classes are grouped ($t = 3.06$, homogeneous variances), and the four means vary significantly ($F = 4.28$). There are also large differences among Vassar age-group means; the low mean for the oldest alumnae group may reflect decline in vigor rather than lack of desire for independence. The higher Beirut freshman mean may be due to selectivity from a culture in which only very exceptional women attend college.

The large mean differences between Vassar and Paine women students are difficult to interpret without more information about the latter. Social situation, including status within the general age group, may be involved. A trend downward for Paine senior women

TABLE 3

CORRELATIONS OF DEVELOPMENTAL SCALE SCORES WITH
MEAN TRAIT RATINGS OF 50 ALUMNAE BY
5 ASSESSMENT STAFF RATERS[a]

Trait	Correlation
Authoritarianism	−.31
Esthetic appreciation	.31
Capacity for further growth	.39
Intraception	.30
Complexity	.48
Independence of judgment	.36
General ability	.50
Appreciation of intellectual activities	.41
Originality	.36
Emotional interference	−.35
Self-insight	.34
Sensuality	.33
Likeableness	.35
Anxiety about fulfilling own aspirations	.32
Anxiety about behaving in accordance with own standards	−.37
Breadth of psychological awareness	.34

[a] Trait ratings for which the correlation was less extreme than ±.30, of which there were 16, have been omitted.

TABLE 4

CORRELATIONS OF DEVELOPMENTAL SCALE SCORES WITH
OTHER PERSONALITY SCALE SCORES FOR 50 ALUMNAE

Scale	Correlation
Authoritarianism, F Scale	—.36
Ethnocentrism, E Scale	—.44
Authoritarianism, derived scale	—.57
Developmental Scale, long form: 123 items	.94
Impulse Expression	.70
Masculinity-Femininity subscales	
MF I, Conventionality	—.44
MF II, Passivity	—.56
MF III, Intraception	.32
MMPI Scales	
L, Validity	—.37
F, Validity	.49
D, Depression	.31
Pd, Psychopathic Deviate	.54
Pt, Psychasthenia	.35
Sc, Schizophrenia	.41
Terman Concept Mastery—Form B	.05

might be related to anticipated re-entry into a larger culture which will demand conservative or submissive behavior from them. The Paine college sex difference is significant ($t = 3.45$), and although there is little known concerning the meaning of the scale for men, this agrees with a preliminary finding reported by Lisa Alfert on differences between German university men and women. The scale undoubtedly reflects some attitudes which are culturally more acceptable when expressed by men rather than by women. Correlations of the scale with a reliable suppression measure (Webster, 1957) were uniformly low for the samples of Table 2, except for Paine freshmen women for whom it was —.54.

Some validity studies, using college major groups and interview data, are discussed elsewhere (Sanford, 1956). Tables 3 and 4 summarize additional validation material for the assessment sample[3] of 50 Vassar alumnae, which also appears in Table 2. The correlation with intelligence, as measured by the Terman Concept Mastery test, is negligible. Otherwise the correlations in Tables 3 and 4

---

[3] In addition to staff members listed in the first footnote, the following also took part in the assessment project: Frank Barron, Jack Block, and Richard Crutchfield of the University of California; Dwight Chapman and Robert Nixon of Vassar College; and Eugenia Hanfman of Brandeis University.

differ significantly from zero in the expected directions, despite attenuation by unreliability. Correlations in Table 3 are in agreement with some adjectives checked significantly often by assessment staff members to describe the 50 alumnae. The adjectives describing high-scorers included complex, individualistic, interesting, sophisticated, frank, rebellious, and the like, while low-scorers were described as conforming, conventional, conservative, dutiful, mild, etc.

The correlations in Table 4 with Impulse Expression and measures of authoritarianism are of the magnitudes found for contemporary students; it was previously reported that seniors, when compared with freshmen, were more aware of impulses and emotional needs, but at the same time were less authoritarian (Sanford, 1956; Sanford, Webster, and Freedman, 1957). This is probably also the case for high-scoring alumnae, in comparison with low scorers. The other correlations in Table 4 are also similar in magnitude to those obtained for students. The fact that high scorers tend to be low on authoritarianism and ethnocentrism is consistent with the idea that the scale measures an aspect of social maturity. Increases in maturity are accompanied by more independence and hence by more freedom to criticize, more resentment of formalized authority, and better understanding of the kinds of adaptation which are necessary in complex situations; but the energy and aggression required for such independence is not directed either toward the self or toward others who are misperceived as entirely different from the self.

The test-retest correlation of .671 was used in computing the test ratios for both differences in Table 5. Sampling bias could not

TABLE 5

DEVELOPMENTAL SCALE FRESHMAN-SENIOR TEST–RETEST DATA
FOR 274 VASSAR STUDENTS

	Freshman	Senior	Difference Test Ratio[a]
Mean	22.737	35.628	26.06
Variance	81.749	120.993	4.39
Standard Deviation	9.041	11.000	....
Reliability	.821	.863	....

[a] Both values of t, calculated with allowance for the correlation (McNemar, 1955), are significant at the .001 level.

have affected the results in Table 5 very much: of 288 freshmen, only one did not take the test; of the 287 who took the test as freshmen, 13 either failed to appear, or else did not complete the test, at the end of the senior year.

SUMMARY

Problems arising in evaluating test-retest data for college students, especially in the area of attitude measurement, are discussed. A scale is presented which was derived by selecting attitude items which discriminated seniors from freshmen, both for concurrent classes and for 274 freshmen retested near the end of their senior year. New reliability and validity data for the scale are summarized. It would be advantageous to have a more reliable instrument for purposes of cross-cultural research. Also scores of the present scale may not be very valid indicators of the maturity of attitudes for subjects from other populations, for example, elderly subjects or persons from radically different cultures.

Data support some previous findings that there are substantial changes in attitudes during college, and that the attitudes expressed will vary with age, sex and culture. The variations occur not only in means, but also in variances, a fact attributable to differential maturation rates: rates of change toward greater amounts of Rebellious Independence, the first factor in the scale, differ enough among Vassar college students to more than compensate for increasing homogeneity due to withdrawals from college.

Results are interpreted as supporting those personality theories which emphasize increasing complexity, differentiation, ability and independence during late adolescence; they do not support the view that college students become more alike in their general attitudes while attending college.

.... 63 ....

ATTITUDE DEVELOPMENT AS A FUNCTION OF
REFERENCE GROUPS: THE BENNINGTON STUDY

by Theodore M. Newcomb

What changes in attitudes on public issues occur in a group over a period of years? To answer this question Theodore M. Newcomb of the University of Michigan studied a series of entering Bennington College freshmen through their senior year. It was found that although the majority of the girls became more liberal during their successive years of attendance at the college some showed no change from their earlier conservatism and a few actively resisted the "liberalism" of the local atmosphere. An explanation is offered for these differences—namely, that although all the girls had membership in the college group, the attitude development of each girl was a result not only of the way she related to the college membership group but also of her identification with off-campus reference groups which provided support for her conservative attitudes. The selection is a partial summary of the author's *Personality and Social Change* (1943). [From Maccoby, E. E., Newcomb, T. M., and Hartley, E. L., Editors, *Readings in Social Psychology*, Third Edition, Holt, 1958, pp. 265-275. Reprinted by permission of the author and Henry Holt and Company.]

Membership in established groups usually involves the taking on of whole patterns of interrelated behavior and attitudes. This was one of the hypotheses pursued in the study which is reported here in part. The group selected for study consisted of the entire student body at Bennington College—more than 600 individuals—between the years 1935 and 1939. One of the problems to be investigated was that of the manner in which the patterning of behavior and attitudes varied with different degrees of assimulation into the community.

Not all of the attitudes and behaviors that are likely to be taken on by new members, as they become absorbed into a community can be investigated in a single study. A single, though rather inclu sive, area of adaptation to the college community was therefore selected for special study, namely, *attitudes toward public affairs.* There were two reasons for this selection: (1) methods of attitude measurement were readily available; and (2) there was an unusually high degree of concern, in this community at this time, over a rather wide range of public issues. This latter fact resulted partly from the fact that the college opened its doors during the darkest days of the depression of the 1930's, and its formative period occurred in the period of social change characterized by the phrase "the New Deal." This was also the period of gathering war clouds in Europe. Underlying both of these circumstances, however, was the conviction on the part of the faculty that one of the foremost duties of the college was to acquaint its somewhat oversheltered students with the nature of their contemporary social world.

In a membership group in which certain attitudes are approved (i.e., held by majorities, and conspicuously so by leaders), individuals acquire the approved attitudes to the extent that the membership group (particularly as symbolized by leaders and dominant subgroups) serves as a positive point of reference. The findings of the Bennington study seem to be better understood in terms of this thesis than any other. The distinction between membership group and reference group is a crucial one, in fact, although the original report did not make explicit use of it.

The above statement does not imply that no reference groups other than the membership group are involved in attitude formation; as we shall see, this is distinctly not the case. Neither does it imply that the use of the membership group as reference group necessarily results in adoption of the approved attitudes. It may also result in their rejection; hence the word *positive* in the initial statement. It is precisely these variations in degree and manner of relationship between reference group and membership group which must be known in order to explain individual variations in attitude formation, as reported in this study.

The essential facts about the Bennington membership group are as follows: (1) It was small enough (about 250 women students) so that data could be obtained from every member. (2) It was in most respects self-sufficient; college facilities provided not only the necessities of living and studying, but also a cooperative store, post office and Western Union office, beauty parlor, gasoline station, and a wide range of recreational opportunities. The average student visited the four-mile-distant village once a week and spent one week end a month away from the college. (3) It was self-conscious and enthusiastic, in large part because it was new (the study was begun during the first year in which there was a senior class) and because of the novelty and attractiveness of the college's educational plan. (4) It was unusually active and concerned about public issues, largely because the faculty felt that its educational duties included the familiarizing of an oversheltered student body with the implications of a depression-torn America and a war-threatened world. (5) It was relatively homogeneous in respect to home background: tuition was very high, and the large majority of students came from urban, economically privileged families whose social attitudes were conservative.

Most individuals in this total membership group went through rather marked changes in attitudes toward public issues, as noted below. In most cases the total membership group served as the reference group for the changing attitudes. But some individuals changed little or not at all in attitudes during the four years of the study; attitude persistence was in some of these cases a function of the membership group as reference group and in some cases it was not. Among those who did change, moreover, the total membership group sometimes served as reference group but sometimes it did not. An oversimple theory of "assimilation into the community" thus leaves out of account some of those whose attitudes did and some of those whose attitudes did not change; they remain unexplained exceptions. A theory which traces the impact of other reference groups as well as the effect of the membership group seems to account for all cases without exception.

The general trend of attitude change for the total group is from freshman conservatism to senior nonconservatism (as the term was commonly applied to the issues toward which attitudes were measured). During the 1936 presidential election, for example, 62 per cent of the freshmen and only 14 per cent of the juniors and seniors "voted" for the Republican candidate, 29 per cent of freshmen and 54 per cent of juniors and seniors for Roosevelt, and 9 per cent of freshmen as compared with 30 per cent of juniors and seniors for the Socialist or Communist candidates. Attitudes toward nine specific issues were measured during the four years of the study, and seniors were less conservative in all of them than freshmen; six of the nine differences are statistically reliable. These differences are best shown by a Likert-type scale labeled Political and Economic Progressivism (PEP) which dealt with such issues as unemployment, public relief, and the rights of organized labor, which were made prominent by the New Deal. Its odd-even reliability was about .9, and it was given once or more during each of the four years of the study to virtually all students. The critical ratios of the differences between freshmen and juniors-seniors in four successive years ranged between 3.9 and 6.5; the difference between the average freshman and senior scores of 44 individuals (the entire class that graduated in 1939) gives a critical ratio of 4.3.

As might be anticipated in such a community, *individual prestige was associated with nonconservatism.* Frequency of choice as one of five students "most worthy to represent the College" at an intercollegiate gathering was used as a measure of prestige. Nominations were submitted in sealed envelopes by 99 per cent of all students in two successive years, with almost identical results. The nonconservatism of those with high prestige is not merely the result of the fact that juniors and seniors are characterized by both high prestige and nonconservatism; in each class those who have most prestige are least conservative. For example, ten freshmen receiving 2 to 4 choices had an average PEP score of 64.6 as compared with 72.8 for freshmen not chosen at all (high scores are conservative); eight sophomores chosen 12 or more times had an average score of 63.6 as compared with 71.3 for those not chosen; the mean PEP score of five juniors and seniors chosen 40 or more times was 50.4 and of the fifteen chosen 12 to 39 times, 57.6, as compared with 69.0 for those not chosen. In each class, those intermediate in prestige are also intermediate in average PEP score.

Such were the attitudinal characteristics of the total membership group, expressed in terms of average scores. Some individuals, however, showed these characteristics in heightened form and others failed to show them at all. An examination of the various reference groups in relation to which attitude change did or did not occur, and of the ways in which they were brought to bear, will account for a large part of such attitude variance.

Information concerning reference groups was obtained both directly, from the subjects themselves, and indirectly, from other students and from teachers. Chief among the indirect procedures was the obtaining of indexes of "community citizenship" by a guess-who technique. Each of twenty-four students, carefully selected to represent every cross section and grouping of importance within the community, named three individuals from each of three classes who were reputedly most extreme in each of twenty-eight characteristics related to community citizenship. The relationship between reputation for community identification and nonconservatism is a close one, in spite of the fact that no reference was made to the latter characteristic when the judges made their ratings. A reputation index was computed, based upon the frequency with which individuals were named in five items dealing with identification with the community, minus the number of times they were named in five other items dealing with negative community attitude. Examples of the former items are: "absorbed in college community affairs," and "influenced by community expectations regarding codes, standards, etc."; examples of the latter are: "indifferent to activities of student committees," and "resistant to community expectations regarding codes, standards, etc." The mean senior PEP score of fifteen individuals whose index was +15 or more was 54.4; of sixty-three whose index was +4 to −4, 65.3; and of ten whose index was −15 or less, 68.2.

To have the reputation of identifying oneself with the community is not the same thing, however, as to identify the community as a reference group for a specific purpose—e.g., in this case, as a point of reference for attitudes toward public issues. In short, the reputation index is informative as to degree and direction of tendency to use the total membership group as a *general* reference group, but not necessarily as a group to which social attitudes are referred. For this purpose information was obtained directly from students.

Informal investigation had shown that whereas most students were aware of the marked freshman-to-senior trend away from conservatism, a few (particularly among the conservatives) had little or no awareness of it. Obviously, those not aware of the dominant community trend could not be using the community as a reference group for an attitude. (It does not follow, of course, that all those who are aware of it are necessarily using the community as reference group.) A simple measure of awareness was therefore devised. Subjects were asked to respond in two ways to a number of attitude statements taken from the PEP scale: first, to indicate agreement or disagreement (for example, with the statement: "The budget should be balanced before the government spends any money on social security"); and second, to estimate what percentage of freshmen, juniors and seniors, and faculty would agree with the statement. From these responses was computed an index of divergence (of own attitude) from the estimated majority of juniors and seniors. Thus a positive index on the part of a senior indicates the degree to which her own responses are more conservative than those of her classmates, and a negative index the degree to which they are less conservative. Those seniors whose divergence index more or less faithfully reflects the true difference between own and class attitude may (or may not) be using the class as an attitude reference group; those whose divergence indexes represent an exaggerated or minimized version of the true relationship between own and class attitude are clearly not using the class as an attitude reference group, or if so, only in a fictitious sense. (For present purposes the junior-senior group may be taken as representative of the entire student body, since it is the group which "sets the tone" of the total membership group.)

These data were supplemented by direct information obtained in interviews with seniors in three consecutive classes, just prior to graduation. Questions were asked about resemblance between own attitudes and those of class majorities and leaders, about parents' attitudes and own resemblance to them, about any alleged "social pressure to become liberal," about probable reaction if the dominant college influence had been conservative instead of liberal, etc. Abundant information was also available from the college personnel office and from the college psychiatrist. It was not possible to combine all of these sources of information into intensive studies of each individual, but complete data were assembled for (roughly) the most conservative and least conservative sixths of three consecutive graduating classes. The twenty-four nonconservative and nineteen conservative seniors thus selected for intensive study were classified according to their indexes of conservative divergence and of community reputation. Thus eight sets of seniors were identified, all individuals within each set having in common similar attitude scores, similar reputations for community identification, and similar degrees of awareness (based upon divergence index) of own attitude position relative to classmates. The following descriptions of these eight sets of seniors will show that there was a characteristic pattern of relationship between membership group and reference group within each of the sets.

1. *Conservatives, reputedly negativistic, aware of their own relative conservatism.* Four of the five are considered stubborn or resistant by teachers (all five, by student judges). Three have prestige scores of 0, scores of the other two being about average for their class. Four of the five are considered by teachers or psychiatrist, or by both, to be overdependent upon one or both parents. All of the four who were interviewed described *their major hopes,* on entering college, *in terms of social rather than academic prestige;* all four felt

that they had been defeated in this aim. The following verbatim quotations are illustrative:

E2:   "Probably the feeling that (my instructors) didn't accept me led me to reject their opinions." (She estimates classmates as being only moderately less conservative than herself, but faculty as much less so.)

G32:   "I wouldn't care to be intimate with those so-called 'liberal' student leaders." *(She claims to be satisfied with a small group of friends.* She is chosen as friend, in a sociometric questionnaire responded to by all students, only twice, and reciprocates both choices; both are conservative students.)

F22:   "I wanted to disagree with all the noisy liberals, but I was afraid and I couldn't. *So I built up a wall inside me against what they said. I found I couldn't compete, so I decided to stick to my father's ideas. For at least two years I've been insulated against all college influences.*" (She is chosen but once as a friend, and does not reciprocate that choice.)

Q10:   (who rather early concluded that she had no chance of social success in college) "It hurt me at first, but now I don't give a damn. *The things I really care about are mostly outside the college.* I think radicalism symbolizes the college for me more than anything else." (Needless to say, she has no use for radicals.)

For these four individuals (and probably for the fifth also) the community serves as reference group in a *negative* sense, and the home-and-family group in a positive sense. Thus their conservatism is dually reinforced.

2. *Conservatives, reputedly negativistic, unaware of their own relative conservatism.* All five are described by teachers, as well as by guess-who judges, to be stubborn or resistant. Four have prestige scores of 0, and the fifth a less than average score. Each reciprocated just one friendship choice. Four are considered insecure in social relationships, and all five are regarded as extremely dependent upon parents. In interviews four describe with considerable intensity, and the fifth with more moderation, precollege experiences of rebuff, ostracism, or isolation, and all describe their hopes, on entering college, in terms of making friends or avoiding rebuff rather than in terms of seeking prestige. All five felt that their (rather modest) aims had met with good success. Each of the five denies building up any resistance to the acceptance of liberal opinions (but two add that they would have resented any such pressure, if felt). Three believe that only small, special groups in the college have such opinions, while the other two describe themselves as just going their

own way, *paying no attention to anything but their own little circles and their college work.* Typical quotations follow:

Q47: "I'm a perfect middle-of-the-roader, neither enthusiast nor critic. I'd accept anything if they just let me alone. . . . I've made all the friends I want." (Only one of her friendship choices is reciprocated.)

Q19: "*In high school I was always thought of as my parents' daughter.* I never felt really accepted for myself. . . . I wanted to make my own way here, socially, but independence from my family has never asserted itself in other ways." (According to guess-who ratings, she is highly resistant to faculty authority.)

L12: "What I most wanted was to get over being a scared bunny. . . . I always resent doing the respectable thing just because it's the thing to do, but I didn't realize I was so different, politically, from my classmates. At least I agreed with the few people I ever talk to about such matters." (Sociometric responses place her in a small, conservative group.)

Q81: "I hated practically all my school life before coming here. I had the perfect inferiority complex, and I pulled out of school social life—out of fear. I didn't intend to repeat that mistake here. . . . I've just begun to be successful in winning friendships, and I've been blissfully happy here." (She is described by teachers as "pathologically belligerent"; she receives more than the average number of friendship choices, but reciprocates only one of them.)

For these five individuals, who are negativistic in the sense of being near-isolates rather than rebels, the community does not serve as reference group for public attitudes. To some extent, their small friendship groups serve in this capacity, but in the main they still refer such areas of their lives to the home-and-family group. They are too absorbed in their own pursuits to use the total membership group as a reference group for most other purposes, too.

3. *Conservatives, not reputedly negativistic, aware of their own relative conservatism.* Three of the five are described by teachers as "cooperative" and "eager," and none as stubborn or resistant. Four are above average in prestige. Four are considered by teachers or by guess-who raters, or both, to retain very close parental ties. All four who were interviewed had more or less definite ambitions for leadership on coming to college, and all felt that they had been relatively successful—though, in the words of one of them, none ever attained the "really top-notch positions." All four are aware of conflict between parents and college community in respect to public attitudes, and all quite consciously decided to "string along" with parents, feeling self-confident of holding their own in college in

spite of being atypical in this respect. Sample quotations follow:

Q73: *"I'm all my mother has in the world. It's considered intellectually superior here to be liberal or radical. This puts me on the defensive,* as I refuse to consider my mother beneath me intellectually, as so many other students do. Apart from this, I have loved every aspect of college life." (A popular girl, many of whose friends are among the nonconservative college leaders.)

Q78: *"I've come to realize how much my mother's happiness depends on me, and the best way I can help her is to do things with her at home as often as I can.* This has resulted in my not getting the feel of the college in certain ways, and I know my general conservatism is one of those ways. But it has not been important enough to me to make me feel particularly left out. If you're genuine and inoffensive about your opinions, no one really minds here if you remain conservative." (Another popular girl, whose friends were found among many groups.)

F32: *"Family against faculty has been my struggle here.* As soon as I felt really secure here I decided not to let the college atmosphere affect me too much. Every time I've tried to rebel against my family I've found out how terribly wrong I am, and so I've naturally kept to my parents' attitudes." (While not particularly popular, she shows no bitterness and considerable satisfaction over her college experience.)

Q35: "I've been aware of a protective shell against radical ideas. When I found several of my best friends getting that way, I either had to go along or just shut out that area entirely. I couldn't respect myself if I had changed my opinions just for that reason, and so I almost deliberately lost interest—really, *it was out of fear of losing my friends."* (A very popular girl, with no trace of bitterness, who is not considered too dependent upon parents.)

For these five the total membership group does not serve as reference group in respect to public attitudes, but does so serve for most other purposes. At some stage in their college careers the conflict between college community and home and family as reference group for public attitudes was resolved in favor of the latter.

4. *Conservatives, not reputedly negativistic, not aware of their own relative conservatism.* All four are consistently described by teachers as conscientious and cooperative; three are considered over-docile and uncritical of authority. All are characterized by feelings of inferiority. All are low in prestige, two receiving scores of 0; all are low in friendship choices, but reciprocate most of these few choices. Two are described as in conflict about parental authority, and two as dependent and contented. All four recall considerable anxiety as to whether they would fit into the college community; all

feel that they have succeeded better than they had expected. Sample statements from interviews follow:

D22: "I'd like to think like the college leaders, but I'm not bold enough and I don't know enough. So the college trends means little to me; I didn't even realize how much more conservative I am than the others. *I guess my family influence has been strong enough to counterbalance the college influence.*" (This girl was given to severe emotional upsets, and according to personnel records, felt "alone and helpless except when with her parents.")

M12: "It isn't that I've been resisting any pressure to become liberal. The influences here didn't matter enough to resist, I guess. *All that's really important that has happened to me occurred outside of college,* and so I never became very susceptible to college influences." *(Following her engagement to be married, in her second year, she had "practically retired" from community life.)*

Q68: "If I'd had more time here I'd probably have caught on to the liberal drift here. But I've been horribly busy making money and trying to keep my college work up. *Politics and that sort of thing I've always associated with home .instead of with the college.*" (A "town girl" of working-class parentage.)

Q70. "Most juniors and seniors, if they really *get excited about their work, forget about such community enthusiasms as sending telegrams to Congressmen.* It was so important to me to be accepted, I mean intellectually, *that I naturally came to identify myself in every way with the group which gave me this sort of intellectual satisfaction.*" (One of a small group of science majors, nearly all conservative, who professed no interests other than science and who were highly self-sufficient socially.)

For none of the four was the total membership group a reference group for public attitudes. Unlike the nonnegativistic conservatives who are aware of their relative conservatism, they refer to the total membership group for few if any other purposes. Like the negativistic conservatives who are unaware of their relative conservatism, their reference groups for public attitudes are almost exclusively those related to home and family.

5. *Nonconservatives, reputedly community-identified, aware of their relative nonconservatism.* Each of the seven is considered highly independent by teachers, particularly in intellectual activities; all but one are referred to as meticulous, perfectionist, or overconscientious. Four are very high in prestige, two high, and one average; all are "good group members," and all but one a "leader." None is considered overdependent upon parents. All have come to an under-

standing with parents concerning their "liberal" views; five have "agreed to differ," and the other two describe one or both parents as "very liberal." All take their public attitudes seriously, in most cases expressing the feeling that they have bled and died to achieve them. Interview excerpts follow:

B72: *"I bend in the direction of community expectation*—almost more than I want to. I constantly have to check myself to be sure it's real self-conviction and not just social respect." (An outstanding and deeply respected leader.)

M42: "My family has always been liberal, but the influences here made me go further, and for a while I was pretty far left. Now I'm pretty much in agreement with my family again, but it's my own and it means a lot. It wouldn't be easy for me to have friends who are very conservative." (Her friendship choices are exclusively given to nonconservatives.)

E72: "I had been allowed so much independence by my parents that I needed desperately to identify myself with an institution with which I could conform conscientiously. Bennington was perfect. I drank up everything the college had to offer, including social attitudes, though not uncritically. I've become active in radical groups and constructively critical of them." (Both during and after college she worked with C.I.O. unions.)

H32: "I accepted liberal attitudes here because *I had always secretly felt that my family was narrow and intolerant, and because such attitudes had prestige value.* It was all part of my generally expanding personality—*I had never really been part of anything before.* I don't accept things without examining things, however, and I was sure I meant it before I changed." (One of those who has "agreed to differ" with parents.)

Q43: "It didn't take me long to see that liberal attitudes had prestige value. But all the time I felt inwardly superior to persons who want public acclaim. Once I had arrived at a feeling of personal security, I could see that it wasn't important—it wasn't enough. *So many people have no security at all. I became liberal at first because of its prestige value.* I remain so because the problems around which my liberalism centers are important. What I want now is to be effective in solving the problems." (Another conspicuous leader, active in and out of college in liberal movements.)

The total membership clearly serves as reference group for these individuals' changing attitudes, but by no means as the only one. For those whose parents are conservative, parents represent a negative reference group, from whom emancipation was gained via liberal attitudes. And for several of them the college community served as a bridge to outside liberal groups as points of reference.

6. *Nonconservatives, reputedly community-identified, not aware of their own relative nonconservatism.* The word *enthusiastic* appears constantly in the records of each of these six. All are considered eager, ambitious, hard-working, and anxious to please. Four are very high in prestige, the other two about average. None is considered overdependent upon parents, and only two are known to have suffered any particular conflict in achieving emancipation. Each one came to college with ambitions for leadership, and each professes extreme satisfaction with her college experience. Sample quotations follow:

Qx: "Every influence I felt tended to push me in the liberal direction: my underdog complex, *my need to be independent of my parents, and my anxiousness to be a leader here.*"

Q61: "I met a whole body of new information here; I took a deep breath and plunged. When I talked about it at home my family began to treat me as if I had an adult mind. *Then too, my new opinions gave me the reputation here of being open-minded and capable of change.* I think I could have got really radical but I found it wasn't the way to get prestige here." (She judges most of her classmates to be as nonconservative as herself.)

Q72: "I take everything hard, and so of course I reacted hard to all the attitudes I found here. I'm 100-percent enthusiastic about Bennington, and that includes liberalism (but not radicalism, though I used to think so). Now I know that you can't be an *extremist if you're really devoted to an institution,* whether it's a labor union or a college." (A conspicuous leader who, like most of the others in this set of six, *judges classmates to be only slightly more conservative than herself.*)

Q63: "*I came to college to get away from my family,* who never had any respect for my mind. Becoming a radical meant thinking for myself and, figuratively, thumbing my nose at my family. *It also meant intellectual identification with the faculty and students that I most wanted to be like.*" (She has always felt oppressed by parental respectability and sibling achievements.)

Q57: "It's very simple. *I was so anxious to be accepted that I accepted the political complexion of the community here.* I just couldn't stand out against the crowd unless I had many friends and strong support." (Not a leader, but many close friends among leaders and nonconservatives.)

For these six, like the preceding seven, the membership group serves as reference group for public affairs. They differ from the preceding seven chiefly in that they are less sure of themselves and are careful 'not to go too far." Hence they tend to repudiate "radicalism," and to judge classmates as only slightly less conservative than themselves.

7. *Nonconservatives, not reputedly community-identified, aware of own relative nonconservatism.* Each of the six is described as highly independent and critical-minded. Four are consistently reported as intellectually outstanding, and the other two occasionally so. All describe their ambitions on coming to college in intellectual rather than in social terms. Four of the five who were interviewed stated that in a conservative college they would be "even more radical than here." Two are slightly above average in prestige, two below average, and two have 0 scores. Three have gone through rather severe battles in the process of casting off what they regard as parental shackles; none is considered overdependent upon parents. Sample interview excerpts follow:

Q7: *"All my life I've resented the protection of governesses and parents.* What I most wanted here was the intellectual approval of teachers and the more advanced students. Then I found you can't be reactionary and be intellectually respectable." (Her traits of independence became more marked as she achieved academic distinction.)

Q21: "I simply got filled with new ideas here, and the only possible formulation of all of them was to adopt a radical approach. *I can't see my own position in the world in any other terms. The easy superficiality with which so many prestige-hounds here get 'liberal' only forced me to think it out more intensely."* (A highly gifted girl, considered rather aloof.)

C32: *"I started rebelling against my pretty stuffy family before I came to college.* I felt apart from freshmen here, because I was older. Then I caught on to faculty attempts to undermine prejudice. I took sides with the faculty immediately, against the immature freshmen. I crusaded about it. *It provided just what I needed by way of family rebellion,* and bolstered up my self-confidence, too." (A very bright girl, regarded as sharp tongued and a bit haughty.)

J24: *"I'm easily influenced by people whom I respect,* and the people who rescued me when I was down and out, intellectually, gave me a radical intellectual approach; they included both teachers and advanced students. *I'm not rebelling against anything.* I'm just doing what I had to do to stand on my own feet intellectually." (Her academic work was poor as a freshman, but gradually became outstanding.)

For these six students it is not the total membership group, but dominant subgroups (faculty, advanced students) which at first served as positive reference groups, and for many of them the home group served as a negative point of reference. Later, they developed extra-college reference groups (left-wing writers, etc.). In a secondary sense, however, the total membership group served as a negative point of reference—i.e., they regarded their nonconservatism as a mark of personal superiority.

8. *Nonconservatives, not reputedly community-identified, not aware of own relative nonconservatism.* Each of the five is considered hard-working, eager, and enthusiastic but (especially during the first year or two) unsure of herself and too dependent upon instructors. They are "good citizens," but in a distinctly retiring way. Two are above average in prestige, and the other three much below average. None of the five is considered overdependent upon parents; two are known to have experienced a good deal of conflict in emancipating themselves. All regard themselves as "pretty average persons," with strong desire to conform; they describe their ambitions in terms of social acceptance instead of social or intellectual prestige. Sample excerpts follow:

E22: *"Social security is the focus of it all with me.* I became steadily less conservative as long as I was *needing to gain in personal security, both with students and with faculty.* I developed some resentment against a few extreme radicals who don't really represent the college viewpoint, and that's why I changed my attitudes so far and no further." (A girl with a small personal following, otherwise not especially popular.)

D52: *"Of course there's social pressure here to give up your conservatism.* I'm glad of it, because for me this became the *vehicle for achieving independence from my family.* So changing my attitudes has gone hand in hand with two *very important things: establishing my own independence and at the same time becoming a part of the college organism."* (She attributes the fact that her social attitudes changed, while those of her younger sister, also at the college, did not, to the fact that she had greater need both of family independence and of group support.)

Q6: "I was ripe for developing liberal or even radical opinions because so many of my friends at home were doing the same thing. So it was really wonderful that I could agree with all the people I respected here and the same time move in the direction that my home friends were going." (A girl characterized by considerable personal instability at first, but showing marked improvement.)

Qy: "I think my change of opinions has given me *intellectual and social self-respect at the same time.* I used to be too timid for words, and I never had an idea of my own. As I gradually became more successful in my work and made more friends, I came to feel that it didn't matter so much whether I agreed with my parents. It's all part of the feeling that I really belong here." (Much other evidence confirms this; she was lonely and pathetic at first, but really belonged later.)

These five provide the example *par excellence* of individuals who came to identify themselves with "the community" and whose attitudes change *pari passu* with the growing sense of identity. Home-and-family groups served as supplementary points of reference, either positive or negative. To varying degrees, subgroups within the community served as focal points of reference. But, because of *their need to be accepted, it was primarily the membership group as such which served as reference group for these five.*

SUMMARY

In this community, as presumably in most others, all individuals belong to the total membership group, but such membership is not necessarily a point of reference for every form of social adaptation, e.g., for acquiring attitudes toward public issues. *Such attitudes, however, are not acquired in a social vacuum. Their acquisition is a function of relating oneself to some group or groups, positively or negatively.* In many cases (perhaps in all) the referring of social attitudes to one group negatively leads to referring them to another group positively, or vice versa, so that the attitudes are dually reinforced.

An individual is, of course, "typical" in respect to attitudes if the total membership group serves as a positive point of reference for that purpose, but "typicality" may also result from the use of other reference groups. It does not follow from the fact that an individual is "atypical" that the membership group does not serve for reference purposes; it may serve as negative reference group. Even if the membership group does not serve as reference group at all (as in the case of conservatives in this community who are unaware of the general freshman-to-senior trend), it cannot be concluded that attitude development is not a function of belonging to the total membership group. The unawareness of such individuals is itself a resultant adaptation of particular individuals to a particular membership group. The fact that such individuals continue to refer attitude toward public issues primarily to home-and-family groups is, in part at least, a result of the kind of community in which they have membership.

In short, the Bennington findings seem to support the thesis that, in a community characterized by certain approved attitudes, the individual's attitude development is a function of the way in which he relates himself both to the total membership group and to one or more reference groups.

Part Six

....

UNDERSTANDING AND
HELPING THE ADOLESCENT

CHAPTER TWENTY

Individual Approaches

.... 64 ....

THE CASE OF PAUL

by the Bureau of Educational Research, Michigan State University

The case history of a person is a description of his development and behavior and of the influences in his environment which have shaped his personality. *The Case of Paul* provides many of the aspects and considerations which must be taken into account when studying an individual. The test questions which accompany the data are designed more to promote discussion than to serve as a measure of achievement. [From *The Case of Paul*, Professional Series Bulletin No. 16, Bureau of Educational Research, College of Educational, Michigan State University, 1956. Reprinted by permission of Michigan State University.]

IDENTIFYING DATA

Paul is 18 years of age and an 11th grade student. He has come to see you, a teacher-counselor, because he says that he is dissatisfied with his marks. He states that perhaps you can help him by suggesting some study techniques. A full-time, trained counselor is available in the school.

HOME AND FAMILY BACKGROUND

Paul and his family moved into Silver City two years ago. His father is a traveling salesman for a manufacturing concern. Neither of his parents completed high school. He has an older brother (age 21) who is attending the state university and majoring in engineering. Paul's parents were separated for a short time since moving into Silver City. There is neighborhood gossip that another separation is imminent. They are living together at the present time. Paul and his mother attend events in the community together. The father rarely accompanies them. According to the mother, the older brother is on the college honor roll and will be graduating from college in June.

PREVIOUS SCHOOL EXPERIENCE AND PRESENT SCHOOL RECORD

Paul attended elementary and junior high school in a small town. He entered his present school in the 10th grade. The students in the school he is now attending have high average scholastic ability. His class has an average I.Q. of 112 in a group intelligence test administered in the 10th grade.

Records from the previous schools reveal marks of about a "B" average: English—B; Mathematics—B; Social Studies—B; Industrial Arts—A.

Records also indicate that Paul was a "model" student while in the former school. While in Silver City High School he has been somewhat of a disciplinary problem. He has been reprimanded for smoking on the school grounds and taking part in unauthorized hazing of freshmen students. His marks in the Silver City High School have been as follows:

Grade 10	Grade 11
English—C	English—C
Geometry—C	U. S. History—B
Biology—C	Geometry—C
World History—C	Science—C

Paul has been a member of the History and Travel clubs and is now in the Speech club. He has served on numerous school committees. His teachers report that he has not always fulfilled his duties on these committees. Teachers also report that Paul has a tendency to stutter when reciting before the class.

There are a number of anecdotal records in his personnel folder. They contain such statements as: "Paul is extremely lazy in preparing his lessons," "Paul is always starting fights," "Paul is always seeking attention," "Paul recently had a fight with Jim, a classmate of his." During the course of a conversation with his teacher-counselor, Paul stated that he and some other boys skipped school a short time ago and wrote their own excuses.

TEST DATA

	I.Q.
Kuhlman-Anderson Intelligence Test—5th grade	101
Otis Self-Administering Test of Mental Ability,	
Higher Form—9th grade	115

Iowa Tests of Educational Development—10th grade   Percentile
(Silver City High School Norms)

Understanding of Basic Social Concepts	72
Background in Natural Science	41
Correctness in Writing	28
Ability in Quantitative Thinking	56
Ability to Interpret Reading Materials	
in the Social Studies	58
Ability to Interpret Reading Materials	
in the Natural Sciences	53
Ability to Interpret Literary Materials	40
General Vocabulary	46
Use of Sources of Information	18

Kuder Preference Record—11th grade—percentile scores
(national norms)

Mechanical	88	Computational	16	Scientific	89
Persuasive	93	Artistic	44	Literary	65
Musical	50	Social Service	31	Clerical	10

Bell Adjustment Inventory—11th grade
Home Adjustment—average
Health Adjustment—good
Social Adjustment—aggressive
Emotional Adjustment—unsatisfactory

HEALTH AND SOCIAL

Paul is 5'11" tall and weighs 160 pounds. He has been absent from school for what his mother describes as sinus headaches. Glasses were worn while in the earlier grades, but not since attending Silver City

High School. Paul's mother also reports that lately Paul has been crying himself to sleep while sucking his thumb.

Since shortly after the beginning of this semester, Paul has been going "steady" with a girl of non-Protestant faith. Paul's mother has not approved since Paul is Protestant.

Paul has stated that he used to attend church and take an active part in church activities. Lately, Paul's church attendance has been infrequent.

GOALS

Paul has indicated that he desires to study mechanical engineering. In the 9th grade Paul had prepared a career book in which he studied baseball as a career. Also, in the 10th grade a lawyer spoke to his class and Paul changed his goal from baseball to law. Since his brother has been in college Paul has changed his choice to engineering.

DISCUSSION QUESTIONS

The following questions require application of information contained in the case study of Paul. Read all questions carefully. Refer to the case study if necessary. There is only *one* best answer for each question.

1. As a teacher-counselor, your first job when beginning to counsel with Paul would be to:
   A. administer tests to determine the area of difficulty.
   B. establish a good working relationship.
   C. determine if there is a need for a conference.
   D. have Paul write out his problem for clarification.
   E. call Paul's parents so they will be aware of proceedings.
2. As a teacher-counselor, to whom Paul has come for help, one of your first steps would be to:
   A. send Paul to the school counselor as he has had more training in counseling with students.
   B. give Paul an assignment so that you may study his work habits.
   C. conduct your study from the present as every student deserves a fresh start.
   D. administer a standardized achievement test to be sure his grades are justified.

E. examine his past records for indications of difficulty and strength.

3. When Paul first came to your office you should have:
   A. assumed that achieving better grades is the main problem.
   B. taken steps to obtain help in remedial reading since low reading ability is a common cause of poor grades.
   C. been alert for any evidence of problems other than grades.
   D. called the parents for a conference or made a home visit.
   E. asked the school counselor to come in for a joint conference.

4. In view of the apparent family conflict, it would probably be best for you to:
   A. talk to the parents and try to keep Paul from being the victim of a broken home.
   B. try to arrange for Paul to live with his father as he needs the association of another man.
   C. persuade the mother to move from the city with Paul so as to leave unpleasant associations behind.
   D. take no direct action in attempting a reconciliation of the parents.
   E. talk to the father and try to get him to change his ways.

5. When Paul told you that he skipped school and signed his own excuse you should have:
   A. notified the principal or superintendent so that they may take administrative action.
   B. called the other boys to be certain they were guilty.
   C. kept the confidence.
   D. notified the parents.
   E. told Paul that he must admit this to all concerned.

6. You have evidence on Paul's intelligence to indicate that:
   A. there is probably no serious discrepancy between his subject-matter achievement and intelligence level.
   B. Paul is above the average intelligence in his class.
   C. Paul's intelligence is improving.
   D. Paul should be doing better work in school.
   E. Paul has been receiving unjustified grades.

7. The difference in the two I.Q. scores:
   A. probably is an indication that Paul's intelligence is increasing.
   B. is of no significance.
   C. is evidence that when administering a second intelligence test it should be by the same author as the first.
   D. indicates that the Otis was better administered than the Kuhlmann-Anderson.
   E. may be an indication that Paul's reading ability has improved.

8. Considering the information available on Paul's intelligence it would be advisable to:
   A. administer another intelligence test to define more clearly his intelligence.

B. administer another intelligence test and then average all three scores.

C. ignore the information as the discrepancy in scores makes the tests valueless.

D. ignore the first test and consider only the more recent one.

E. administer another intelligence test to see if his reading ability is still improving.

9. The information on the achievement tests indicate that:

A. Paul should be set back at least one grade so that he may catch up with the other students.

B. Paul needs remedial work in some areas.

C. Paul's school grades have been too high.

D. either the intelligence test scores or the achievement test scores are incorrect.

E. Paul is weak in nearly all areas.

10. A study of the Kuder scores indicates that:

A. 10 per cent of a group are more interested in clerical duties than Paul.

B. Paul answered 65 per cent of the questions concerning literary interests.

C. Paul is more interested in mechanical duties than 12 per cent of his fellow students.

D. Paul is in the second quartile in artistic interests.

E. Paul has more aptitude for social service work than clerical work.

11. The results of the Kuder Preference Record also indicate that:

A. Paul has some aptitude for mechanical work.

B. Paul wouldn't be very interested in many of the activities performed by an office clerk.

C. Paul is twice as interested in mechanical work as he is in artistic work.

D. Paul would do well in debate.

E. Paul would probably make a good salesman.

12. Considering the information available in the Bell Adjustment Inventory, you should:

A. inform the parents of the results so that they will realize there is a serious problem.

B. obtain the scores for the areas tested and average his total adjustment.

C. examine the individual items so as to identify further the problem areas.

D. establish the validity of Paul's responses.

E. go over the scores with Paul.

13. The available evidence indicates that Paul at present is probably:

A. an underachiever.

B. an overachiever.

C. achieving up to his level of ability.

D. working only in areas of his interests.

E. achieving only in the easier subjects.

14. In using the test data available, it would be best to:

    A. have the parents look over the scores so that any interpretation will be their responsibility.

    B. explain to Paul that he is above average intelligence for his group.

    C. have the parents see Paul's high scores first.

    D. present your interpretation of the data to Paul and his parents.

    E. have the parents look over Paul's responses on the Bell Adjustment Inventory so that they can see where they have failed as parents.

15. The total information indicates that:

    A. Paul is in need of special help in all areas of his school work.

    B. special remedial work is unnecessary.

    C. Paul is a poor reader for his group.

    D. Paul's grades are too low for his ability.

    E. Paul needs special help with work in certain areas.

16. As a teacher dealing with Paul's stuttering in the classroom it would be best for you to:

    A. have Paul recite only when he desired.

    B. insist that Paul recite often so that he will get over his nervousness.

    C. explain to Paul that there is no reason for him to stutter as he should not be nervous.

    D. treat his stuttering by having him repeat sentences.

    E. have Paul's mother treat his difficulty in the more natural home surroundings.

17. There is evidence that Paul:

    A. is abnormally unstable in the selection of a vocation.

    B. would fit into many different occupations.

    C. is following a normal pattern of job selection for adolescents.

    D. should listen to speakers representing many occupations.

    E. needs someone else to diagnose his capabilities and decide for him his best choice of occupations.

18. A reliability coefficient of .92 is reported for the Otis Self-Administering test of Mental Ability; this means that:

    A. 92 per cent of the items test mental ability.

    B. 92 per cent of those taking the test receive valid scores.

    C. that we can predict the success in intellectual pursuits of 92 per cent of the people who take the test.

    D. there is evidence that the test measures consistently.

    E. the test is a good measure of intelligence.

19. Considering the "thumb sucking and crying himself to sleep," you have evidence that:

    A. Paul is trying to get attention from his father.

    B. Paul's intelligence is lower than the intelligence tests indicate.

    C. Paul's early childhood was probably his unhappiest period.

    D. Paul is insecure.

    E. Paul is adjusting through the mechanism of pseudofeeble-mindedness.

20. Paul's "model" behavior in the former school can most likely be attributed to:

    A. higher status among the students at that school.

    B. his better grades and the resulting less frustration.

    C. a curriculum that met his needs better.

    D. different standards of behavior in the two schools.

    E. less emotional stress at that period.

21. Probably the least serious bit of evidence we have is:

    A. his aggressive behavior in class.

    B. the "thumb sucking and crying himself to sleep."

    C. the lower grades he has received in Silver City High School.

    D. his stuttering in class.

    E. his skipping school.

22. Of the following, the most serious bit of evidence is probably:

    A. the hazing of the freshmen.

    B. the lower grades in Silver City High School.

    C. his aggressive behavior in class.

    D. absence from school because of repeated headaches.

    E. his "thumbsucking and crying himself to sleep."

23. In the instance when Paul and Jim were fighting, it would have been best to:

    A. stop the fight and talk to them later.

    B. send them down to the gymnasium to put on the gloves.

    C. send them to the principal who should handle serious discipline problems.

    D. insist that Paul apologize for starting the fight.

    E. settle the issue immediately.

24. An acceptable procedure in overcoming Paul's refusal to recite in class would be to:

    A. impress upon Paul's parents the importance of reciting in class.

    B. ask some of Paul's friends to show approval whenever Paul does recite.

    C. read off the names of those who have not recited.

    D. build his confidence by recognition of work he has done.

    E. make an agreement with Paul to ask him only easy questions.

25. Considering the type of anecdotal records that is available, you, as a teacher-counselor, should:

    A. consider the anecdotal records valuable since the other teachers have determined the basis for some of Paul's main problems.

B. present Paul with these statements so as to hear his side of the story.
C. question the value of the anecdotal records as evidence of his present status.
D. consider them as your best objective evidence.
E. present the parents with the records.

26. If Paul's parents were consulted, it would be most desirable to say:
A. "We find that students' problems in school frequently stem from the home."
B. "I can help Paul with your cooperation."
C. "I would like to settle this since Paul is holding back the rest of the class."
D. "I am interested in helping Paul."
E. "Our tests indicate that Paul needs help."

27. Which of the following is the safest prognosis of Paul's academic success in college?
A. It is quite likely that Paul would not succeed.
B. Success would depend to a considerable degree upon emotional adjustment.
C. Going to college would motivate him to do better work.
D. He would probably be successful, but not in engineering.
E. Success would depend upon the extent of his social and extra-curricular activities.

28. As a teacher-counselor, which of the following would be best for you to consider as a part of a program to help Paul?
A. Help Paul to improve his grades to his previous level of accomplishment.
B. Attempt to reconcile the parental differences.
C. Reduce the apparent emotional tension.
D. Try to get Paul's brother to take an active interest in him.
E. Help Paul to recognize and accept the incompatability of his parents.

ANSWERS

1. B	5. C	9. B	13. C	17. C	21. C	25. C
2. E	6. A	10. D	14. D	18. D	22. E	26. D
3. C	7. E	11. B	15. E	19. D	23. A	27. B
4. D	8. A	12. C	16. A	20. E	24. D	28. C

THE PERSONALITY OF JOSEPH KIDD:

PSYCHOLOGICAL APPRAISAL AT EIGHTEEN

AND A HALF YEARS

by Robert W. White

The psychological appraisal of the personality of an eighteen-year-old male college student is presented in the following selection by Robert W. White of Harvard University. Using a number of tests and many interviews, the report depicts the interplay between Kidd's constitutional endowments and environmental factors that led to the crisis in the development of his ego-structure. Kidd was studied again eleven years later, and the complete account of his life history forms part of a book (White, 1952). [From *Character and Personality*, 1943, *11*, 318-338. Reprinted by permission of the author and of Duke University Press.]

In the first [part of this report] (White, 1943) we described in some detail the life history of Joseph Kidd up to the middle of his nineteenth year. It was possible to show that certain characteristics of the environment, especially the attitudes of his parents, encouraged a number of tendencies that finally brought him to grief. Many recent studies have called attention to the disastrous effects of parental rejection, but Kidd's troubles had their origin in just the opposite condition: an excess of praise and gratuitous benefits. By being made a center of admiring attention, he was encouraged in self-consciousness and a tendency to value himself in accordance with the expressed valuation of others. By being showered with love and praise, he was encouraged to expect a very high esteem-income. By being given what he wanted and helped with his difficulties, and by having the constant support of a vigorous older brother, he was encouraged to rely on borrowed strength rather than his own energetic resources. Thus the forces of his immediate environment pressed him to become affectionate, passive, submissive, succorant, and keenly self-conscious. These attitudes carried him successfully enough through childhood but left him unequipped to meet the sterner demands of adolescence and manhood, so that eighteen and a half years found him all but destitute of esteem-income and all but shattered in his ego-structure.

It is impossible, however, to rest content with a purely historical account of personality. In the interaction between person and environment the person is anything but a *tabula rasa;* he is endowed with his own peculiar pattern of temperamental traits, capabilities, and limitations, which share with outside forces the power to determine his destinies. At various points, moreover, the life history gives a feeling of incompleteness, of sequences not fully explained by visible factors, of effects badly out of proportion to their causes. So far we have photographed the environmental banks between which flow the currents of behavior, but we have taken no soundings to determine the shoals and deep places, the material and contours of the river bed. We shall now complete our survey by conducting a psychological appraisal of Joseph Kidd, calling to our assistance a considerable array of tests and interviews. This will prepare us to work out the contribution of constitutional factors and of unconscious tendencies to the development of his personality.

For brevity's sake we shall not describe separately the results of each examination. Our appraisal will be arranged according to a convenient outline which brings together the main findings regardless of their source. The complete list of examinations runs as follows:

1. Measure of Somatotype
2. Wechsler-Bellevue Adult Intelligence Test
3. Wells Modified Alpha Intelligence Test
4. Atwell-Wells Multiple Choice Vocabulary Test
5. Scholastic Aptitude Test (College Entrance Examination Board)
6. O'Connor Finger Dexterity and Tweezer Dexterity Tests
7. Self-Ratings and Interview on Abilities
8. Rorschach Test
9. Self-Ratings on Needs and Traits (Murray, 1938)
10. Bernreuter Personality Inventory
11. Interview on Emotions and their Control
12. Interview on Temperament
13. Hypnotic Susceptibility
14. Hull Postural Sway Test of Suggestibility
15. Allport-Vernon Study of Values
16. Self-Rating on Sentiments (Murray, 1938)

PHYSIQUE

The standard photographs of Joseph Kidd, made according to the method recently developed by Sheldon, Stevens and Tucker (1940), reveal a somatotype of 4-5-1½ (endomorphy 4, mesomorphy 5, ectomorphy 1½), a solid, strong physique well adapted for energetic and strenuous living yet entirely free from strain and tenseness. The shoulders and chest are broad, the hips narrow, and the muscles of the arms and legs large and well-developed. Considering the social value attached to strength and energy in childhood, Kidd seems to have had a fortunate physical endowment. We have seen that he won the greater part of his fights, and he tells us that his arm muscles were always especially good so that he was "able to beat the best of fellows in wrist contests." He has taken part successfully in numerous sports: football, baseball, hockey, tennis, and cross-country running. Kidd's physique is such as to be felt as an asset and reason for self-respect, the more so because his face and coloring caused him to be esteemed first as a pretty child and later as a good-looking young man.

In spite of his excellent build, however, Kidd speaks of a "sluggish, lethargic" feeling and pronounces himself less inclined toward athletics than the others of his school group. Such a feeling is certainly not characteristic of his somatotype, described by Sheldon as "usually of tremendous energy," so that we must look elsewhere for its explanation. It is possible that the energy and assertiveness that would seem to be inherent in his physique may be somewhat softened by a moderate bisexual or gynandromorphic tendency. His strong arms, broad shoulders, and narrow hips argue against a very high rating on gynandromorphy, but there is a little more softness in his face and shoulders, smallness in his features and fullness in his lower trunk than would be found in the most masculine specimens of his somatotype. On the other hand, Kidd may have misjudged his energy by comparing himself mostly with older playfellows, especially his brother, who even at the present time is a little taller, leaner, and more rugged. A third possibility lies in the sphere of motivation: as the youngest of his group he could rarely excel in games, yet as an erstwhile center of attention he craved prominence and lost interest when it was denied him. It is consistent with the last two possibilities that he was more assertive, even belligerent, before his double promotion in school.

MENTAL ENDOWMENTS

At home Kidd was considered very intelligent and at school he was looked upon as a promising pupil. Since puberty, however, he has shown so little interest in studies that he has barely made passing grades. Since he aspires to graduate from college, and even entertains plans of going to medical school, he will find himself frustrated unless his intellectual abilities are of a high order.

In the Wechsler-Bellevue Adult Intelligence Test, Kidd scored an I.Q. of 118, putting him in the 90 percentile of the general population. He was much better on the verbal scale (I.Q. 126, 97 percentile) than on the performance tests (I.Q. 107, 68 percentile). Weighted scores on the subtests run as follows:

Comprehension	12	Picture arrangement	11
Information	15	Picture completion	12
Digit span	16	Object assembly	9
Arithmetical reasoning	12	Block design	14
Similarities	13	Digit-symbol substitution	10
Vocabulary	14		
Verbal test average	15	*Performance tests average*	11

Immediate recall seems to be particularly good, and he speaks of good retention in everyday life, saying that "any situation is vividly pictured" even when he is not concentrating upon it. Although he loved arithmetic in grammar school and was successful with geometry in high school, the tests show no great signs of mathematical ability. Reasoning and associative thinking are comparatively poor, a finding that is fortified by the low W and Z scores on the Rorschach test and by his complete inability to discuss general ideas clearly. He claims deep thinking on philosophical subjects, believing that he could "stay in an argument with any priest" on the theme that man is only an animal, but from his exposition of this theme one gets the impression of a ruminating pictorial mind rather than one that makes its way actively to clear concepts and rational synthesis.

The Rorschach test gives further evidence of intellectual limita tion. Kidd adopts a peculiar manner of approach: whole responses occur only twice, while tiny details are chosen for interpretation eleven times and white spaces twenty-six. For some reason his attention is drawn to the edges of the ink-blots where in the tiny details and especially the white spaces he looks for human profiles and animal heads. This preference may arise from a natural tendency of mind toward limited, fragmented perceptions, but it is also likely that Kidd, in an attempt to perform well on the test, suggested to himself, perhaps from experience with newspaper puzzles, that the finding of faces and profiles in obscure places is a mark of excellence. This interpretation is supported by another sign of misguided ambition, the extraordinarily large total of responses (R98). Apparently he made an extreme effort to be original and clever, but in doing so he only revealed the essential shortcomings of his natural ability.

A brighter picture of his intellectual ability is yielded by the modified Alpha Examination (Wells) where the score of 173 on the verbal part puts him at the 99 percentile and 165 in the numerical part at 98, both higher than the average for Harvard College students. On the Atwell-Wells Multiple Choice Vocabulary Test he makes a score of 84, just at the average for the junior class, but low in comparison with his Alpha, probably on account of his poor cultural background. On the other hand, he fell far below his collegemates on the Scholastic Aptitude Test of the College Entrance Examination Board, so low that there was at first some question whether he would be able to succeed with college work. Events have proved that he can usually earn a passing grade by working hard at the last moment, thus utilizing to the fullest his good immediate recall. His college record, however, has been a dreary succession of just-passing and just-not-passing grades, so that he has been on probation most of the time.

Taken as a whole, the tests give a picture of intellectual endowments scarcely sufficient for successful college work. A mind such as Joseph Kidd's is flattered by intelligence tests with their highly disjunctive mental operations. Such a mind, quick and retentive, makes its best impression in the early school years, but progressively reveals its limitations as the scope of its activity expands. The Scholastic Aptitude Test, with its emphasis on comprehending the contents of a paragraph and grasping the ideas set forth, affords a better prophecy of Kidd's academic career. He has a good sentence-mind, a weaker paragraph-mind, and a very poor chapter-mind; he can learn his lessons, but the significance of general ideas escapes him. Students thus endowed sometimes get through college by dint of unceasing labor. Their effort is the more heroic because the burden is not lightened by the rise of spontaneous scholarly interests. Kidd, however, does not have a pattern of motives sufficiently strong to overcome the limitations of his endowment.

Although Kidd is badly restricted in his grasp of general ideas and abstractions, he is not without gifts of imagination. He produces four movement responses to the Rorschach ink-blots and tells stories of better than average originality in the thematic apperception test. His use of language is frequently crude and awkward, but narrative seems to bring out his best power of organization, as is shown by his reasonably conjunctive stories and especially by his account of his own life where the motive for understanding was intense. Such organization, however, is the spontaneous product of passive brooding rather than an active mastery of experience. Kidd rates himself as less than average logical and coherent in his thinking and admits that he has spent little time trying to formulate his ideas clearly for communication. Outside of college work his reading is limited to newspapers and weekly news magazines.

GENERAL ABILITIES

Kidd stands fairly high in *manual dexterity*. The O'Connor Finger Dexterity Test finds him at the 90 percentile, while in Tweezer Dexterity he falls at 70. In the matter of fine motor coordination he claims unusual excellence. According to his own account he made the best dissection of the dogfish brain that his instructor in biology had ever seen. Another manifestation of this skill is his ability at picking locks; at camp, he opened four trunks, the owners of which had forgotten their keys. Although he disclaims *mechanical insight,* he has a good record in the rapid mastery of such skills as driving a car and running a motor boat. Good *practical sagacity* is indicated by his success at making money. He thinks of "ways to make money a little easier," such as getting two jobs and farming one out to a girl of his acquaintance for half the proceeds. For an undergraduate he has achieved an unusually good income and has contributed a share toward his college expenses even though he loves to spend money in order to impress people. There are several respects in which Kidd can claim unusual competence; unfortunately, they do not help him much with his college career.

Questioned about his *leading and governing* ability, Kidd almost desperately disclaims it. "I can't have anyone depending on me to show them," he says, "I really can't, and I can't take the initiative at a supper table." Similarly he disclaims *social ability,* the ability to make friends easily, get on with people, be liked and trusted, and sustain loyal enduring friendships. Influenced perhaps by unfavorable comparisons with a very affiliative acquaintance, Kidd finds himself "not really interested" in friends, "not very dependable or trustworthy," and quite unable to keep confidences. He seems to have, however, a few friendships of rather long standing. He rates himself quite low on *artistic sensitivity and creativity,* a judgment from which we cannot dissent in view of his remarks.

I don't know one color from another. I can't tell a good piece of poetry from a bad. I can't see yet why they rave over Shakespeare. As for painting, I just see whether a picture looks natural. I have a good understanding of music: classical, probably something soft and mellow.

Although we may assume that he would be strongly inclined to exaggerate his *erotic ability,* there seems to be no doubt that he is in demand as an erotic partner. Many of his girl friends take active steps to see him, and he is usually the one to terminate any relation. Behind his competence in this sphere lies considerable strength in the realm of *feeling*: he is capable of real sympathy, real love, and some measure of power to evoke love. In the thematic apperception test his stories show unusual insight into certain kinds of feeling, and in his deeper affections he is extremely persistent and tenacious. Badly mixed up as he is with his own feelings, he appears to have distinct potentialities in the sphere of human relations.

PATTERN OF MANIFEST NEEDS

The strongest manifest strivings in Joseph Kidd are *sex, acquisition, succorance, abasement, and exhibition.* That he expends much energy searching for the goals of *sex* and *acquisition* requires no further evidence. The high self-rating that Kidd gives himself in *succorance* can be taken very much at its face value since no young man of college age is particularly eager to confess such a tendency. Kidd indicates that he often feels neglected and unloved, that he greatly desires sympathy when sick or depressed, and that he considers his lot in life a hard one. He marks himself very high on those items under *nurturance* which describe an emphatic feeling for the sorrows of other people, but his nurturing tendencies rarely extend to action in behalf of the unfortunate. This kind of nurturance, stronger in feeling than in action, probably arises out of his succorant need which sensitizes him to the troubles of others. He considers himself unusually gentle and protective in his relations with women, and finds himself readily drawn to women who are sympathetic.

When we turn to *abasement* and *aggression*, needs which display themselves chiefly in his relations with men, we find him badly self-deceived. Although on individual items he admits that he sometimes acts the coward, cannot always hold up his end in a fight, and typically feels nervous and anxious in the presence of superiors, he gives himself a low average on *abasement* as a whole, and he puts *aggression* among his strongest tendencies. The consistency of his answers on aggression suggests that his contemporaries often find him irritable and impulsively critical; he indicates that his friends do not consider him compliant and that he likes to argue and carry on a verbal battle to the bitter end. In the autobiography he makes it plain that in critical situations he is far more abasive than aggressive. In his self-ratings he shows us how he tries to counteract this unwelcome tendency by a bold argumentative verbal front.

In view of the prominent place occupied by *exhibition* in his early memories, it is of interest to scrutinize the pattern of Kidd's present self-ratings on this need. He gives himself high marks on all items that have to do with saying humorous things, acting the clown, talking about himself, boasting, showing off, and telling tales with dramatic exaggeration. These marks seem to refer to what he does in congenial and familiar surroundings; under more exacting circumstances, especially when he is called upon to perform before a group, his behavior receives a much lower rating and he never takes the lead in enlivening a dull evening. He very much likes to have people watch him do something that he does well, but with equal vehemence he dislikes to feel that they are just looking at him or that their eyes are upon him. The need for *exhibition* appears to be exceedingly strong, but it is associated with such a low frustration-tolerance that he does not always dare to express it openly. Deep preoccupation with the impression made on others is indicated by his maximal self-ratings on the following five items:

I often think about how I look and what impression I am making upon others; my feelings are easily hurt by ridicule or by the slighting remarks of others; when I enter a room I often become self-conscious and feel that the eyes of others are upon me; I often interpret the remarks of others in a personal way; I pay a good deal of attention to my appearance: clothes, hats, shoes, neckties.

Certain common tendencies are unusually weak in Joseph Kidd. He shows little *counteraction, order,* or *striving* for *achievement,* and still less of *dominance, autonomy,* and *construction.* The whole pattern can best be shown in the following summary of our markings on manifest needs, rated on a six-point (0-5) scale:

n Abasement	5	n Infavoidance	3	n Order	1
n Sex	5	n Play	3	n Rejection	1
n Succorance	5	n Affiliation	2	n Retention	1
n Acquisition	4	n Aggression	2	n Sentience	1
n Exhibition	4	n Nurturance	2	n Autonomy	0
n Blamavoidance	3	n Understanding	2	n Construction	0
n Defendance	3	n Achievement	1	n Dominance	0
n Deference	3	n Counteraction	1		

His self-ratings on the Bernreuter Personality Inventory class him as "emotionally unstable" (95 percentile on neurotic tendency) but not, strictly speaking, neurotic, and his Rorschach record does not fall into any of the mental disease patterns.

PATTERN OF LATENT STRIVINGS

Our chief source of information about the pattern of Kidd's latent strivings, aside from inferences that can be made from his behavior and his remarks about himself, is the Thematic Apperception Test. This test, introduced by Morgan and Murray (1935), is based on the hypothesis that imaginative productions point the way to important tendencies in personality. The subject is asked to make up stories, prompted by a series of pictures usually susceptible to several interpretations. In performing such a task the story-teller draws on whatever resources he may possess, including stories he has heard and events in his own life, but the special value of the methods lies in its power to reveal tendencies which are barely or not at all conscious and which could not otherwise be discovered except by long and searching analysis. A noticeable repetition of themes in the stories usually indicates some persistent emotional problem in the teller, and further inferences can be drawn from the behavior and competence of his heroes, the attitudes displayed toward parent-figures and love-objects, and the way the plots are brought to an outcome.

Three themes appear so insistently in Kidd's fantasies that we can accept them as clues to important latent strivings. The first theme centers around the longing and loneliness engendered by loss of a loved person. There are five occurrences of this situation in the course of the twenty stories. Given a picture of an elderly woman peering from the threshold of a half-opened door, Kidd relates the following unusual story:

This picture, to me, depicts an old woman, about seventy years old, peering with longing in her eyes. She is alone in this house in which she lives and has been alone there for the past ten years since her husband left—died, I mean. They were a devoted couple and loved each other dearly. His death shocked her and since they were childless, she was left positively alone. The past ten years haven't at all worn off his absence. At times the sense of loneliness so greatly overcomes her that she begins searching the house for him believing he is still there, sitting and reading. This idea which she holds, that he is still alive and present in the house so overwhelms her as years go on, that eventually, one night, she imagines seeing him in a chair and goes over and speaks to him. The next morning some neighbors, missing her, search the house and find her seated in a chair very comfortably opposite an empty chair. She had died of a heart attack during the night.

In another story a young husband "by his constant nagging, jealousy, and sureness of himself" kills his wife's love and drives her to leave him and marry again. He soon discovers, however, that he cannot bear her loss; he becomes "an outcast because of his eccentricities" and finally commits suicide. Here it is recognized that the hero, if such he may be called, by his selfishness sacrificed the treasure of love, but the value of this treasure in the storyteller's estimation seems all the greater from the tragic events that follow.

These stories, a sufficient sample of the five that turn on lost love and longing, give evidence that Kidd has experienced a deep feeling of bereavement. Since the chief characters in his life history are all still alive, this feeling probably comes from the steady decline of his esteem-income, especially the gradual moderation of his parents' love and the growing indifference of Mildred. It is important that he several times makes his heroes to blame for injuring a love relation, just as he blames himself for having alienated Mildred's affections. In any event, the repetition of this theme in the stories gives evidence of an unusually intense craving for love, a craving that seems to be strongly mingled with succorance. Kidd is still longing for a golden age which passed when he ceased to be a child.

The second outstanding theme occurs virtually unchanged in three of the twenty stories and with variations in four more. Perhaps the clearest expression is given in response to a picture which shows a gray-haired man looking at a young man who is sullenly staring into space. The younger man, according to Kidd, is a surgeon whose wealthy upbringing has given him an inhuman attitude.

His operations were rash and sometimes without sympathy. Rather than spend precious time mending a mangled member he would take the easy way out and amputate. He sometimes unnecessarily operated because it was always quicker to learn the trouble that way than slowly studying the symptoms and this caused many of his patients to die. His career was on the brink of downfall when a kind old physician took him in hand, and for a whole year showed him the other side of life with its millions of people; its poverty; its sorrows; its love. The surgeon explained not from a lecture hall, but from an intimate standpoint, his duties toward these people. What arms or legs meant to them and what life and death meant to them, which must be included in our education towards profession. This, of course, caused this young doctor to realize he was dealing with people and not running a business, and then with this advice he succeeded.

The young man in this story is spoiled, thoughtless, cruel, and, judged from the phrase "running a business," greedy. These traits begin to spell disaster for his career, but he is taken in hand by an older man who is obviously interested in his success and who forwards it by educating him in kindness. The underlying theme of this story can be expressed as follows: *transformation of cruelty and greed by the sympathetic interest of an older man.* This theme occurs in another story with much less help from the picture, which shows only the silhouette of a man's figure against a bright window. Kidd tells of a poet who has a grudge against the world and writes spiteful poetry which nobody buys. When he is on the brink of starvation an old man who has read all his work tells him to climb a certain tower and find great wealth. Expecting to find money, he obeys, but instead he encounters a vision of light and human happiness which sets him on a successful literary career. The third occurrence of the theme is in response to a picture showing the dejected form of a boy huddled against a couch. Kidd sees a lad who has become vengeful "against his religion and his people" because of the death of his father. A priest, however, realizes his frame of mind and comforts him so that he "braces up and goes ahead." All three of these stories make it clear that the principal character (the identification figure) is activated by hate, and two mention greed. The kindly intervention of the older man is completely successful in effecting a reformation and in setting the hero's feet on the road to success.

By variations on the theme we mean stories in which the hero is impelled by the same destructive motives but in which no older man comes to the rescue. In one such story aggression and acquisition reign unchecked so that the chief character commits what amounts to murder and is left in an agony of fear and horror before a punishment that fits the crime. In another, an inventor uses his ingenuity to get rich from the sale of explosive chemicals; he reforms and devotes himself to medical science only after an accidental explosion has killed his beloved wife. From such stories we can infer that Kidd feels a profound helplessness to control the forces in himself. His villainous heroes, the victims of circumstance, are pushed on by destructive impulses only to be severely punished for the consequences. Insofar as these stories reflect subjective experience, they tell us of a weak ego unable to cope with the id and superego or to resolve their conflict advantageously. Only once does the hero try to change himself, influenced by love for a beautiful girl, and here he "finds the struggle hard" and is "tortured constantly by evil temptations," although he conquers in the end. In the main, Kidd does not borrow much strength from women. Perhaps they are too closely bound up with his aggressive problem to save him from it: two women are killed and a third alienated in his stories. His formula for ego-strength is the affectionate interest of an older man, who alone has the power to transform and socialize his impulses and save him from feelings of remorse. We learn from this how highly Kidd has valued his father's love and how deep a loss he has sustained by its withdrawal just as he reached an age when independence was expected of him and when father-substitutes were not easy to find.

The two themes so far discussed do not put us in possession of entirely new information. To say that Kidd longs for love and succorance, that he feels helpless to control his impulses, and that he craves the affectionate interest and guidance of older men, is not to point out wholly unsuspected latent strivings; indeed, Kidd shows all of these tendencies in his manifest behavior. But the repetition of such themes in fantasy is not without great significance. Fantasy is a realm of freedom where wishes are horses and beggars may ride. Kidd, however, proves quite unable to use this freedom to create a better world where love and succor are provided and where heroes lay hold of their destinies, conquer their weaknesses, and claim the captaincy of their souls. From this we discern no new qualities, but we discover that certain strivings are backed by very large reserves of energy, so large that they repeatedly polarize the field of fantasy.

Kidd's third theme, on the other hand, points to tendencies that are not overtly expressed. There are unmistakable signs that he enjoys the contemplation of cruelty. His inventor is gripped by a "lust for money and power" which includes a willingness to blow up most of mankind and which actually results in the death of his wife. His young surgeon uses the scalpel with callous brutality. A boy with a stolen car runs down the mother of seven children and is thereupon forced to view the mangled body. Most striking is a story about "the cruelest man in the Roman Empire" who constantly thought up new tortures for enemies of the state and who "loved to see them squirm, plead for mercy, and then slowly, very slowly, die in the worst possible way." From such reveling in aggressive scenes we conclude that there is somewhere in Kidd a sadistic and masochistic striving, using these terms in their original sense to denote a fusion of erotic and aggressive tendencies. The masochistic aspect is to be found in the suffering experienced by the heroes; even the cruelest Roman ends at the scaffold, vainly pleading for his life. We recall at this point that several of Kidd's early memories suggested a latent masochism: the boys being given the rattan by the teacher, the fight that he lost, and the occasion when he dropped his pencil three times and got nine slaps.

In view of the progressive deprivation of esteem that Kidd has suffered since childhood, we can surmise that he has had occasion for much resentment. That so little of this resentment comes to expression may be explained by his dependence on his parents and the strong feelings of guilt described in the autobiography. Aggression, in all probability, though finding outlets on the playground, was always well suppressed in the family circle, and this led to its persistence in a rather primitive form. At what point and in what manner it became connected with erotic pleasure our material does not tell. It is not difficult to believe that Kidd's early childhood relation to his older brother, who cannot have enjoyed his less-favored position, accounted for the masochistic turn of events, and that the remembered lost fight, which began with bold assertiveness but ended with being put "on his back," to use a phrase of his own choosing, stands as a symbol for many scuffles which even in their unsuccessful outcome were toned with pleasurable sensations.

Plausible hypotheses might be developed around the relation to the father, who was a doting yet authoritative parent. All this, however, is conjecture; we know only that Kidd's stories are overloaded with somewhat primitive sadistic and masochistic images and that he seems to enjoy enlarging on scenes of cruelty. We can only add that if he has been influenced by a latent masochistic striving of uncommon strength it is easier to understand the stubborn persistence and compulsive character of his submissive attitude in the presence of men and boys.

FUNDAMENTAL TRAITS

In a study of two hundred college men Sheldon and Stevens (1942) have worked out the chief functional or behavioral traits associated with his three first-order variables of physique. The degree of association is naturally less than perfect, but the correlations were found to be in the neighborhood of $+.8$. Kidd fulfills some of Sheldon's expectations, but in other respects he diverges widely from the pattern of traits usually associated with his somatotype. It is noteworthy that this divergence occurs mainly on traits which have to do with human relations, characteristics which are therefore most subject to influence by unusual forces in the human environment. In the matter of general relaxation, love of comfort, quiet tempo, and a certain softness which Sheldon calls the "untempered" characteristic he runs true to his 4 in *endomorphy;* the traits are moderately represented, but by no means outstanding. Similarly he has the eating habits, the liking for exercise, and the rather low sensitivity, though not, as it happens, the overmaturity of appearance, which go with a 5 in *mesomorphy,* and he properly lacks all signs of the tenseness, vigilance, sensitiveness, and physiological over-irritability which accompany *ectomorphy.* It is in the more socially colored traits that he shows marked divergence. Sheldon has found that endomorphy is generally associated with interest in people, friendly feeling toward them, and desire for their approval, affection, and support in time of trouble. Mesomorphy, in contrast, is associated with an assertive, competitive, dominant relation to others, while ectomorphy generally goes with an unsociable, seclusive attitude often marked by shyness and apprehensiveness. It is at once clear that Kidd does not fit this part of the pattern. To be sure, he seems to have fitted it better in his belligerent younger school days, but at the present time he shows all too little assertive ness, disclaims any ability or desire to lead and direct others, **with-draws and daydreams considerably, and is extremely uneasy in the presence of people.** Moreover, when it comes to a greed for affection and approval, a trait generally associated with endomorphy, he must be assigned the highest rank in the scale rather than the moderate 4 that characterizes his physique. When asked about his very quiet normal speaking voice, the exact opposite of what is expected in predominantly mesomorphic physiques, he explained, "I don't raise my voice because when I do it goes high and sounds like a soprano, not masculine."

These findings strongly suggest that Joseph Kidd's social attitudes have been injured or deflected from their natural channels by events taking place in the course of his history. Sheldon's scheme must no doubt still be regarded as somewhat tentative, but the present findings nonetheless illustrate the great practical convenience arising from ready methods of estimating the strength of constitutional factors: if we know how a person "ought" to behave, in the sense of what is natural for his constitutional make-up, we can more quickly discern those places where environmental deformation has occurred.

In an interview on the various emotions and their control Kidd placed himself far on the *impulsive* side. "I lose my temper easily," he said, "and do nothing to stop it." Arguing and being angry he finds pleasant, but control of temper proves almost impossible. Likewise he exerts little control over his sex drive; indeed, it seems that he has almost no power of control and cannot stop impulses unless he is afraid of the consequences. He declares that his feelings are easily aroused, that he gives them full vent when he is stirred, and that he generally acts on the spur of the moment without stopping to think. Consistent with this are his decisively low self-ratings on *sameness* and *conjunctivity*, where he reveals himself as a highly changeable and disorganized person, unstable in his cathexes and sentiments, erratic in his habits and in the pursuit of his goals. He gives himself a high rating on the statement, "I find that my likes and dislikes change quite frequently," but he drops to a low mark when it comes to the item, "I find that a well-ordered mode of life with regular hours and established routine is congenial to my temperament." For the statement, "I am on time for my appointments," he selects the lowest rating, a fair warning, one might say, of the long series of tardily kept or entirely forgotten appointments which marked his relation to the Clinic. He also denies himself any efficiency in the matter of studying or in the matter of making his daily life run smoothly. All in all, he professes a degree of disorganization that seriously interferes with adaptation to the college world.

Pursuing the same pattern, Kidd gives himself a low rating on *superego integration* and a high one on *superego conflict*. These two variables indicate the way in which a person has dealt with the ideals and prohibitions arising out of parental discipline in infancy and childhood. If these ideals and prohibitions have been incorporated into the ego so that they function effectively and silently to control behavior, superego integration is said to have occurred. If, on the other hand, behavior is not successfully controlled, but instead the person is visited by feelings of guilt and remorse for what he does, then ego and superego are said to be in conflict. Kidd leans strongly to the second condition. The residues of parental discipline do not keep him from occasional untruthfulness and dishonesty nor do they block his active erotic career, but he is not spared feelings of shame after these acts. Impulse generally has its way, but the superego exacts an uncomfortable tribute.

Perhaps the most inclusive generalization that can be applied to Kidd is to say that he is wide open to influences outside the ego and has no counterbalancing forces within that region. We have seen that he lacks the power to order his daily life and to control his impulses. In personal relations he is dependent and submissive; even when he tries to take a preconceived role he cannot sustain it against the slightest frustration of his need to be loved. It appears, moreover, that he has not elaborated enduring structures within the ego: he is guided less by ideals of his own than by what the world expects of him, and he is constrained not so much by his own moral code as by a still infantile superego. The Rorschach test, to be sure, shows an even experience-balance (M: sum $C = 4:3.5$), but an index considered more fundamental by Klopfer and Kelley (1942), the proportion of responses to colored cards, puts him well on the extratensive side (46 per cent). Kidd proves to be very readily susceptible to hypnotic suggestion, passing quickly into the hypnotic state though not reaching the deepest possible trance. In the Hull (1933) postural sway experiment he was markedly responsive to heterosuggestion, but when given the chance to initiate the suggestions by his own spoken words he swayed only one-seventh as far. This imbalance between heterosuggestion and autosuggestion stands as a perfect example of the state which seems to be characteristic of Kidd in all aspects of his life. He is at the mercy of forces outside the ego, whether they be his own impulses his guilt feelings, or suggestions and expectations arising from other people. Even his mental endowments fall into the same pattern: he is much better at observing, registering, reproducing, and passive brooding than at organizing his experience and carrying on independent thought. The ubiquity of this trait suggests that we are confronting a basic constitutional endowment. The chief manifestations are Kidd's failure to organize his daily life, to control impulses, to check his weakness for daydreaming, to resist suggestion, to achieve stable attitudes in personal relations, to develop interests of his own, to elaborate independent ideas and plans, and to effectuate the ideals and standards adopted from others. It is difficult to think of this behavior as a pure consequence of experience. However much his environment may have encouraged passivity, dependence, and an expectation that somebody would always provide for him, there are numerous signs that his temperament eagerly ratified every such proposal. He was a peculiarly spoilable child because he was responsive to whatever pressures the environment offered. Under different pressures he might have led a happy, friendly, vigorous, assertive life, though scarcely a consistent and constructive one; his temperament would have been quite as ready to ratify this plan. In short, the trait we have in mind can be distinguished from the passivity, dependence, and submissiveness that Kidd's environment printed on his personality. It made him take the imprint readily, but of itself it by no means required what he in fact became. Let us provisionally call this trait an *innate lack of ego-strength* and conceive it as a relative feebleness in the ego-region of personality. . . .

VALUES AND SENTIMENTS

Love in its broadest sense—the *social value* of Spranger and the Allport-Vernon test—is the highest value in Kidd's life. Human relations are paramount in his hierarchy of cathexes, and their disturbance is the chief cause of his present unhappiness. If he were rich, Kidd says on the test blank, he would rather endow a hospital than support a church, forward scientific research, or stimulate industrial development; if at leisure, he would prefer to establish a mental hygiene clinic than go into banking, make a collection of fine paintings, or launch a political career. At the theater he prefers a play with a theme of human suffering and love;

next to this, a play that treats the life of a great man; problem plays he puts in third place and ballet at the bottom. The *political value* is second on his list, indicating a greater interest in power than he shows in everyday life. It may be suspected from this that fantasies of personal power and influence enjoy a considerable if covert development in Kidd's mind, sharpening his inner resentment at the submissive role which he so often is forced to play. Least meaningful for him are the realms of aesthetic and religious experience.

Kidd's life values are but weakly implemented by appropriate concrete sentiments. Not deeply interested in religion, he nevertheless trots out with approval all the conventional moral and religious precepts of his devout parents. He even gives vehement assent to severe legal restrictions on the sexual behavior of unmarried people and opposes teaching the use of contraceptives, thus lending verbal support to standards he has found it easy in practice to evade. His valuation of *love* is but dimly reflected in sentiments applying to human relations and the social order, for neither he nor his family take an interest in politics. Like many college students, Kidd is still working out his problems in a personal sphere and is unprepared to transform felt values into useful lines of conduct, the more so because his mind abhors general ideas and critical thinking. Although he claims in an interview that he has departed widely from his parents' views, it turns out in fact that parents and son share strictly conservative religious sentiments and mildly liberal views on the social order. Whether Kidd can free himself from imposed verbal standards sufficiently to apprehend his own values and effectuate them in a way of life is one of the urgent problems of his immediate future. It is of interest to notice that the parents, in spite of business success and an obvious desire to push their children upward on the ladder of social status, have not relaxed their religious faith nor abandoned their liberal political sentiments. They have not taken on the folklore of capitalism even though they would like to see their children clad in the garments of wealth.

RETROSPECT ON THE LIFE HISTORY: THE CONVERGENCE OF FACTORS

Now that we are better acquainted with our subject we can profitably look back over his life history and find out what part was played in it by constitutional endowments and by latent strivings. At the very outset we observe a perfect example of convergence between constitutional and environmental factors. Kidd was a beautiful, bright, responsive child; his native endowment served to set him off from his less attractive older brother and later from his next younger brother. Such natural gratuities, however, do not of themselves determine any particular pattern of personality nor require that a child shall become a center of attention. It was the attitude of the parents, their warm-hearted love, their naïve pride, and their social ambition that intensified to momentous strength what might otherwise have remained a moderate feature of Kidd's psychological situation. An instructive comparison can be made with Chatwell, another subject from our records who was endowed with great personal attractiveness in childhood. Parental emotions were more restrained in the Chatwell family, the child being praised only for real accomplishments and urged to take care of himself. Curiously enough, one of his earliest memories finds him, like Kidd, on a tricycle, but he remembers what he was *achieving*—pulling a string of sleds—rather than what he *looked like*. Even so, Chatwell's need for exhibition remained strong; in both subjects, one consequence of personal attractiveness persisted through different environments.

In Kidd's case it seems almost certain that the tendencies which resulted from being a center of attention—dependence, passivity, and self-consciousness—received substantial encouragement from his fundamental traits. We may well regret the insufficiency of our knowledge about constitution, but we cannot deny an impressive weight of evidence which suggests that Kidd was naturally low in ego-strength, preponderantly open to his human environment, with little capacity to combat obstacles, to amuse himself, or to develop sustained interests of his own. Acting on such a nature, the praise of his parents produced a loving but helpless child, an effect that could hardly have been worked on a boy richly endowed with capacity for spontaneous interests, curious about his world and adventurous in his explorations. It was not difficult, moreover, to effect a suppressing of aggression; Kidd found few attractive alternatives to the affectionate attention of his parents. Lastly, it was easy for him to develop a dependent relation to his older brother, a relation which strengthened submissiveness and even added, as we have seen reason to surmise, a distinctly masochistic coloring. A differently constituted child could not have tolerated this relation, much less enjoyed it.

Kidd's mental endowments made a decidedly good impression in his family and in the public school. He studied faithfully and learned his lessons quickly. This led to his double promotion, but this important event again illustrates the principle of convergence: it must be attributed not only to his ability but to his mother's zeal in the cause of rapid advancement. The chief effect of the double promotion was to strengthen his submissive tendencies and fixate the social roles of "clown" and "stooge." We observe again that such a result is not compulsory; it received silent consent from his need to be loved and from his lack of ability to develop interests away from the group, if not also from the assumed latent masochistic striving. From this point onward, Kidd's innate limitations began to play a decisive part in his career. The time came when the shortcomings of his mental endowment overbalanced his quickness and retentiveness. With greater intellectual resources he might have taken the path of the good scholar who wins the respect of his teachers and dispenses with that of his athletic friends. With slightly more athletic ability than he possessed he might have achieved the respect of his comrades on the playground. With greater internal resources he might have built up some interests of his own, so that in the face of social difficulties he could have turned to something more constructive than daydreaming, masturbating, and listening to the radio. One of his assets, manual dexterity, fell by the wayside for lack of encouragement at school. With none of these resources at his disposal he was helpless to meet the new social demands of adolescence or to initiate effective substitute strivings. However strongly this dilemma was encouraged by his previous experience, his constitutional limitations cast a number of decisive ballots.

At some point in high school Kidd began to be unable to meet the educational aspirations of his parents. One teacher advised him not to attempt college, but the lure of a degree with its social implications was too strong for his parents to resist. Kidd came to college without intellectual interests, without capacity to develop them, without motivation to slave at his books, an obedient actor in his parents' fantasy. He brought with him no group of friends, no experience in how to make the kind of friends he would find at college, and no inclination to risk being rejected. What happened to his personality under these circumstances we have already described. Our account now stands complete up to the middle of his nineteenth year.

What must happen to Joseph Kidd if he is to emerge success

lly from his present vicissitudes? It seemed to us at the time that
he following developments would have to take place. (1) Kidd
needs to scale down his vocational aspirations. Medical school is
clearly beyond his reach, there being even some doubt as to whether
he can graduate from college. He will have to arrive at an occupation which is within his intellectual powers, which does not make
too great demands on initiative and self-sustained action, and which
at the same time does not shatter his claim to superior social status.
(2) Not unrelated to the matter of vocational hopes is the establishment of greater independence from the desires and expectations of his parents. Kidd will have to learn, either with encouragement from outsiders or, better still, by his own efforts, to decide
for himself what he is going to do and how he is going to lead his
life even when these decisions run counter to his parents' wishes.
(3) He will have to break down the barriers between sex and love
so that he can bring to love some of the confidence and assertiveness that he has developed exclusively in the sphere of promiscuous
sex. Since he has deep desires and distinct capacities for love, he
needs to rescue this motive from strangulation by succorance. (4)
Finally, he will have to achieve a more stable social role, shifting
from the now compelling submissiveness to a true affiliation free
from fears and subsequent regrets. Only by accomplishing these
developments can he escape from his limitations, use his capacities with satisfaction, and build up reasons for self-respect. Kidd
has the possibility to make a successful solution of all these problems. His major liability in doing so is his dependence on outside
forces: finding the right job, running into the right counselors and
friends, meeting the right girls, arriving in the right social milieu.
He depends on a certain amount of luck, having little capacity to
shape his own destiny. What befell him during the next three years
will be the subject of [another communication] (White, 1943a).

.... 66 ....

CASE STUDY OF A THIRTEEN-YEAR-OLD

FIRE-SETTER. A CATALYST IN THE GROWING

PAINS OF A RESIDENTIAL TREATMENT UNIT[1]

by Leonard Siegel, M.D.

This report of fire-setter Freddy, age thirteen, undergoing treatment in a residential hospital, shows the tendency of the child and his mother to re-create their earlier relationships and describes the meaning of the child's antisocial acting out within this relationship. The data suggest the hypothesis that the mother herself had unconscious urges toward antisocial acting out, overtly told Freddy to "act good" but covertly encouraged him to act otherwise as had her father encouraged her. Leonard Siegel of New York City also depicts how Freddy and his mother influenced the development of the residential treatment unit. [From *American Journal of Orthopsychiatry*, 1957, *27*, 396-410. Reprinted by permission of the author and the American Orthopsychiatric Association.]

This case report is a companion paper to the one by Dr. Gordon and myself (1957) describing the evolution of the Program of Psychotherapy on the Children's Unit of the National Institute of Mental Health. In that paper, we mentioned some of the problems in clinical management of our "first patient group," which was with us during our second four months of operation. In the present paper, I should like to describe these problems in greater detail by focusing on one of the boys, Freddy, who was a member of this first patient group. This group of patients had been admitted for a period of diagnostic evaluation in a residential setting.

As was our usual practice for this group, I was assigned, primarily as diagnostician, without specified therapeutic goals, to both the patient and his family. I shall try to show how, on the one hand, in this case, the practice of one psychiatrist working with both

[1] This material was prepared within the Laboratory of Child Research, National Institute of Health, as part of a larger research program under the direction of Fritz Redl.

patient and parent dramatically exposed the nature of the relationship between Freddy and his mother; and how, on the other hand,
it hampered my effectiveness in relating to each of them.

Using the clinical data recorded by the counselors, teachers, administrative staff, and myself, I shall try to demonstrate how the kind
of relationship which had developed between Freddy and his mother
resulted in the type of problems he manifested, and shall touch
briefly on how the overriding needs and provocative behavior of
both the patient and his mother influenced the course of our own
development as a therapeutic team.

Some four months before he came to us, Freddy, 13, had been
picked up by the police for setting fires. He toured the neighborhood
with the fire marshals and with little reluctance pointed out the
places where he had set several dozen small fires. The mother, weakly
supported by the father, fought every step in the subsequent legal
preliminaries to residential treatment of the child. The lengthy
court trials with cross-examinations of the psychiatrists in the presence of the child and his parents, a prolonged stay in the overcrowded detention home, and a period of observation on the adult
ward of a psychiatric hospital seemed to aid in cementing the bonds
of the pre-existent ambivalent alliance between the patient and his
mother. The data available on admission indicated that fire-setting
was only one aspect of a broad spectrum of disturbed behavior: a life
history of soiling, several episodes of running away, difficulties in
school, truancy, nightmares, and temper tantrums.

DEVELOPMENT OF RELATIONSHIP WITH MOTHER

During the first week of Freddy's hospitalization I saw the mother
for three hours and the father for one hour. The father seemed to
be disinterested in further contact—a disinterest which was covertly
encouraged by his wife. During the first month I continued to see
the mother weekly.

Initially the mother contended that Freddy's confession to setting
fires had been forced out of him by the authorities. She was angry
with the court for having committed him to residential care, denied
that he had any problems, insisted that he was a normal boy, and
repetitively demanded that he be released to her. She depicted herself as a self-sacrificing and loving mother, her husband as a devoted
father, and the whole family as a respectable and God-fearing little
group. The history she gave was slanted in such a way as to cor-

roborate the impression she was trying to make. Her version of th
situation, initially confirmed by Freddy's conforming behavior o
the ward, was at first rather convincing. Despite her attempt t
maintain the validity of her position, however, it soon became ap
parent that she was an angry, seductive, and manipulative woman

One pivotal point in her essentially paranoid position was th
massive load of guilt over her tendency to exploit Freddy for her ow
ends. This guilt was usually projected onto the other person, whom
she perceived as destructively accusing her of being a "bad mother"
and a "bad person." She retaliated to this perceived attack by blam
ing others, particularly those who had played a parental role towar
Freddy, for all her own and Freddy's difficulties; by a barrage o
techniques for evoking guilt and anxiety in others; and by a multi
plicity of exploitative-manipulative operations.

As it gradually became apparent to her that she was not makin
headway in her attempts to persuade me to release Freddy home t
her, she began to cancel appointments and tried, unsuccessfully, to tal
the ward administrator into seeing her on a regular basis. Three
weeks later (after Freddy had been here for seven weeks) she mad
a complete about-face in her interviews with me, and unburdene
herself of a detailed and relatively uncensored confession which
included the past history of the whole family, events she felt guilt
about and ashamed of, and current pressing dilemmas. What wer
some of the determinants of this remarkable change in attitude?

Since we had not yet told her definitely what we would recom
mend as to further disposition for Freddy, she probably felt ther
was still hope of having him home and that her confession an
appeal for help might move us to make a "favorable" recommen
dation.

In preparing the mother and father for Freddy's first visit home
the Chief of the Laboratory, in his only interview with them, ha
described in some detail Freddy's temper tantrums on the hospita
ward. To the mother, this meant that Freddy had "let the cat ou
of the bag" and that her former pose was untenable.

There had been suggestions even during the early part of m
relationship with the mother that underlying her bitter disappoint
ment with me for not releasing Freddy to her, and for not reportin
to her the details of my interviews with Freddy, there was a dee
current of very impelling dependency strivings directed toward me
Her confession, with its implicit cry for help, was, I feel, an expres
sion of these strivings.

When she learned that I was no longer seeing Freddy in regularl scheduled interviews (as I shall describe later), and she felt reassured that she was maintaining her wedge in the relationship between Freddy and me, she could then risk beginning her own relationship with me.

This phase spanned the second and third months of Freddy's stay with us. In the beginning of the fourth month, I told her that our recommendation to the agency responsible for Freddy would be that he should have further residential treatment, and that the agency would soon apply for Freddy's admission to a suitable treatment center. This center happened to be at some distance from the family home.

This statement precipitated an overtly psychotic episode in a woman who had managed previously to conceal the explosive severity of her illness. In this interview she said:

. . . You're destroying me. You're making me crazy. . . . You've decided to take him away from me only because I told you he was illegitimate. . . . You don't think I'm fit to be his mother. . . . But I'll hurt you where it'll hurt the most. I know where you live and I know when I can find your wife at home. . . . And I don't want to listen to a lot of talk about what kind of treatment he needs, either. . . . If you're going to take him away from me, I don't care what happens to him. . . . I know you've got a hidden microphone in this room and they're all listening in and laughing. . . . As soon as I leave this office, I'll run to the nearest phone, and I'll call Freddy, and I'll tell him that you're going to send him to a reformatory and that you're against him and that he should set fire to the hospital.

I managed to block her attempt to tell Freddy this, but she did lurk around the corridors of the hospital for several hours and did make threatening phone calls to the child care staff. During the subsequent several weeks, in the course of her frantic involvement of the ward administrator, her husband, her lawyer, the agency caseworker, and several members of the community, her psychotic tantrum abated and she returned to her former precarious adjustment.

HISTORY

In her "confessions," the mother painted a lurid picture of her past history. In a highly dramatized way, she described a poverty-ridden home with punitive and alcoholic parents. She reported that long before her first sexual experience, her father frequently accused her of sexual promiscuity and an alcoholic uncle made fumbling attempts to seduce her. She said that her mother was emotionally cold and neglected her children. Four died in infancy and child-hood; of the surviving five, mother was the oldest and was prematurely forced into the role of nursemaid, housekeeper and bread-winner. She said the first kindness she had ever known came from her first boy friend, who was ultimately driven away by her father.

Embittered by these experiences, she began the pattern of acting out which was to be repeated in her son: she began running away from home, she had her own experience in a state institution for adolescent girls, and she entered a clandestine relationship with an older man. Like her father he was alcoholic, explosive, and punitive; and he was basically passive and amenable to manipulation. He had a wife and children and repeatedly tried to escape from mother. She repeatedly dragged him back by a variety of manipulative operations: After she found out he had a family, she had her first sexual experience with him and eventually became pregnant, thus fulfilling her father's prophecies. Of this pregnancy, she had herself aborted. If he did not telephone her, she badgered him at work and threatened to tell his wife about their illicit relationship. When this did not hold him, she again became pregnant by him. This child, Freddy, she registered under his father's name. When Freddy's father again drifted away, she married another man, only to divorce him abruptly when Freddy's father reappeared. Finally, his wife divorced him; and when Freddy was three years old, his mother and father were married. The mother quickly became dissatisfied with her husband, and their marriage was punctuated by a series of angry separations.

During her "confessions," the mother began a discussion of her current pressing conflicts, which included her conflict as to whether or not she should divorce her husband and should tell Freddy he was born out of wedlock. This discussion was terminated by her angry withdrawal from me after I told her Freddy would be transferred to another institution.

In late adolescence, Freddy's mother had met an older couple, the Smiths, who turned out to be parental surrogates for her and alternate parents for Freddy. She frequently left Freddy with them for long periods of time. They were not only intimidated by Freddy's tyrannical behavior but their authority was repeatedly undermined by the mother, who insisted on maintaining the favored position in the child's eyes.

Freddy's father was disgusted with his wife for being so indulgent with Freddy and for favoring Freddy over her stepsons; he was likewise appalled at Mrs. Smith for catering to the child. Freddy's mother was infuriated at her husband's inattentiveness and strictness with the boy. Mrs. Smith was dismayed at the mother's corrupting influence on Freddy.

Freddy, in effect, had two sets of parents. This he rather neatly symbolized in a dream (which he reported to me during his hospitalization) wherein he saw double images of several people, including a former "girl friend" and Mr. Smith. There were thus four parents, all involved in some form of disagreement with each other, whom he could play off one against the other in various combinations as the situation demanded. The multangular formations thus created in this group of parents, substitute parents, and stepbrothers, proved to be the prototype for similar kinds of multangular relationships abortively restaged on our unit at the National Institutes of Health.

When Freddy was unable to get what he wanted or genuinely needed from one set of parents, he would run away to the other set, who would initially console him and then finally send him back.

The Smiths could be relied on to live permanently in one place and to welcome him and be willing to keep him. His parents, however, repeatedly changed their place of residence, either looking for jobs or escaping from each other or from Freddy.

BEHAVIOR IN THE HOSPITAL

We found Freddy, on admission, to be a soft-looking pubertal boy, a little on the pudgy side, and somewhat bruised, both emotionally and physically, from his fights with the other boys in the detention home. He was polite, conforming, and enthusiastically curious about everything. He was productive in arts and crafts, showed initiative and skill in a variety of activities, and advertised a scholarly interest in many school subjects, including a special interest in plant and animal ecology. He played up to the adults and presented them with small gifts he had made. His behavior, in this respect, gradually assumed a busy and driven character.

It soon emerged that Freddy was no small-time operator as a procurer of special privileges. He tried to wangle from us privileges, toys, and equipment we did not even know we had. He began platforming for unlimited use of the phone, for frequent visits home, for frequent visits from his mother, for privileges to leave the hospital unattended, and for permission to use typewriters, dictaphones, microscopes, and wheel chairs.

Freddy was relentlessly driven, as we came to understand, by intense feelings of helplessness and emptiness. The full spectrum of his defensive manipulative and revengeful operations rather quickly unfolded. Of these, the following were striking in their intensity:

Playing one adult off against another; e.g., when the counselor would not give in to him on some demand, he would tell her his doctor had said that it was all right for him to do it.

Trying to outwit the adult; e.g., when his request to be present during my interviews with his mother was refused, he would ask the counselor to take him to the arts and crafts room, which just happened to be near my office.

Trying to make an alliance with one adult by derogating another; e.g., if he was trying to soften up counselor A so she would let him watch television at a certain time, he would describe to her how mean and nasty counselor B had been to him.

Holding out on one issue in an attempt to blackmail the adult into bribing him with what he really wanted; e.g., on an outing he might say, "I won't go back to the unit with you unless you give me a cigarette."

Exploiting another child's illness for his own ends; e.g., he would provoke Jimmy into a full-blown temper tantrum and then refuse to go to school on the grounds that Jimmy did not have to go to school.

Playing on the adult's sense of fair play; e.g., by saying, "You don't trust me" or "It ain't fair, you let Jacky do it."

Exploiting the adult's indecisiveness as to whether or not a certain type of behavior should be permitted; threatening to get the adult into trouble with higher authorities; needling and goading the adult into retaliation and then evoking guilt by demonstrating how shabbily he had been treated.

Intimidating, either by direct threats or by long-range strategy. He would start out by rather deliberately attacking the adult or by destroying property, without really being out of control or in a genuine temper tantrum. After the adult had experienced a few of these attacks he would tend, if not aware of the meaning of the behavior, to succumb to Freddy's demands in order to avoid its repetition.

In many instances, these maneuvers would temporarily unnerve certain members of the staff. This would threaten Freddy because it invalidated the source of parental firmness and dedication he so much needed. At other times the staff was competent—and increasingly so—in handling the manipulative aspects of his power operations and was successful in relating to Freddy's underlying needs. This also was threatening to the neurotic structure of his personality and he would feel powerless and defenseless, and even more revengeful. It was then that his outbursts of rage escaped from his control and became genuine temper tantrums. His "good little boy" pose and his scholarly interests evaporated. His behavior in the schoolroom and on the unit took on a more regressive character; and his demandingness, an infantile wheedling quality. His attention span was shortened. He went feverishly from one exploitative sally to another. There were several episodes of soiling, especially during this period of regression and open aggressiveness. One episode of soiling occurred just before he set a small fire on the unit.

In his relationships with the other boys, he was unable to form anything approaching a genuine chumship. The closest he could get to this would be to form an alliance with another boy against the adults or against the other boys. He would characteristically maintain his front of innocence while seducing the weaker, more suggestible boys into acting out for him. His capacity for influencing these boys was striking and was exemplified by his almost magical ability to bring one of them out of a temper tantrum—for his own ends—long before adult attempts at intervention might succeed. He would try to incite the whole group of boys into sit-down strikes or anti-adult riots. It was clear, on the other hand, that he felt helpless in defending himself against the other boys after he had finally provoked their attack. Indeed in other institutions, with a tougher group of boys and with less adult protection, his boastful and overbearing manner, his attempts to buy himself into their good graces, and his inner fearfulness eventuated in his being relentlessly made the scapegoat. In these instances, he would run away from the institution in a state of helpless despair.

COURSE OF DOCTOR-PATIENT RELATIONSHIP

The course of my relationship with Freddy was remarkably like that of my relationship with his mother. Indeed it left me with an eerie feeling to talk to one of them on one day; and on the very next day, to hear some of the same words from the other, even though I knew there had been no direct communication between them in the interim.

As was our practice at the time, I began to see Freddy three times a week in adult-type verbal interviews in my office. Although these interviews were primarily aimed at making a diagnostic evaluation, I was also personally interested in exploring the possibility of doing some form of brief insight-therapy with Freddy and with my other patient in the group. During the first several weeks, when he and his mother were trying to make a "good impression," he came to the office readily. After a spontaneous recitation of his fire-setting which sounded like the report he had given in court, he became bored and restless and increasingly resentful of my interest in his relationships with his parents, stepsiblings, peers, and with me.

During the next several weeks, he manifested increasing resistance to coming to the office and filled the sessions with demands for special privileges. After it became clear to him that there would be no immediate discharge from the hospital, and no subsequent punishment, he flatly refused to come to the office. This sequence was synchronous with parallel phases in my relationship with the mother. Dr. Gordon and I have described (1957), in reference to all of the boys in Freddy's group, some of the determinants of this resistance, such as the effects of the "defrosting process," the difficulties of the boys in verbal communication of their thoughts and feelings, the boys' need for play activities as a vehicle for relating, their insecurity as to how long they would stay in the hospital, our difficulties in making a firm interview schedule and synchronizing it with the daily activity program, and the confusing effect on the boys of the multiple role-functions of the therapists. The following are some other factors which determined Freddy's increasing resistance:

The fact that I was a psychiatrist fed into the tendency of Freddy and his mother to view me as a member of the "enemy camp," which included for them the court psychiatrists. He was extremely litiginous and referred to me at times as the "chief prosecutor."

The mother was convinced that any relationship I might form with Freddy was bound to be one which would turn him against her and therefore, as she put it, "take him away" from her. This she could not tolerate and she bent her efforts toward undermining the relationship between Freddy and me. She did this by rather subtly devaluating me to Freddy and by "demonstrating" to him that I was against both of them. She would notify him beforehand of her appointments with me and would indirectly encourage him to get over to my office while I was seeing her. When his schemes to get to my office were foiled, he would become enraged at me.

His poker-faced denial of all problems, his casual rejection of any offer of help, and his consistent maintenance of interpersonal distance by operating in the relationship as if it were exclusively a battle of wits, all left me with a feeling of helplessness and discouragement in my attempts to relate meaningfully to this boy. The apparent invulnerability of his character armor, plus the anticipated brevity of his stay in the hospital, tended to goad me into making premature confrontations and interpretations in reference to his power operations and his self-defeating allegiance to his mother. He could not accept this entrance into the psychological inner sanctum of his life as being of any potential help to him. He could perceive this as but a hostile invasion of the only *status quo* he had ever known, and became progressively more provocative and openly hostile in an attempt to evoke counteraggression in me and to drive me away from him.

For a period of several weeks, there occurred a process of mutual withdrawal in which there were no office interviews and only infrequent contacts on the unit. We have described in some detail the meaning and determining factors of this mutual withdrawal as it applied generally to all the therapists and patients in this group (Gordon and Siegel, 1957). Perhaps most specifically characteristic of my relationship with Freddy was that he had used manipulative techniques to such an extent that I began to suspect that his orientation toward me was purely exploitative and I became unable to relate effectively to the constructive needs underlying his behavior. The mutual distrust thereby generated had reached such proportions that any attempt to push the relationship further would actually have been destructive. After I had gained some perspective on these factors, I renewed my visits to Freddy on the ward, and he seemed less resistant to seeing me.

During the latter part of his hospitalization, I had the feeling that Freddy was torn between his ambivalent allegiance toward his mother and his growing hopes, as they arose in his relationships with all of us, that he could obtain some satisfaction and security in relating to others.

In the beginning of his fourth and last month in the hospital, I told Freddy that he was to be returned to the detention home, where he would await transfer to another residential treatment home. He became extremely angry with me and threatened to destroy us or to run away. In this he was encouraged by his mother when, after her psychotic tantrum, we allowed her to phone him again. Along with this he made suicidal gestures and suffered from what we felt were periods of real depression. In contradiction to his protestations of a desire to go home to his mother, his behavior during this period actually communicated, in its nightmarish vividness, the message that he was a seriously disturbed child and unconsciously wanted further treatment.

At the very end of his stay with us, the period of panic, which had had the appearance of an eternal temper tantrum, subsided. There was a truce in his warfare with us and a terminal lull in his threats to destroy us or to run away. This seemed to me to be more than a truce and more than a simple restitution in preparation for his return to the detention home. It seemed as if he allowed a momentary sober and meaningful exchange between us. It meant to me that he had perhaps "heard" a good deal of what had been "said" to him during his stay here, including my interpretations, even though his surface behavior had indicated otherwise.

FORMULATION OF DYNAMICS

Amongst the hypotheses I have used to structure the case material is that of Johnson and Szurek (1952), who report: "The parents find vicarious gratification of their own poorly-integrated forbidden impulses in the acting-out of the child, through their unconscious permissiveness or inconsistency toward the child in these spheres of behavior." In reference to their dynamic schema, the data are suggestive of the hypothesis that the mother herself had unconscious urges toward antisocial acting out, including setting fires, and that she unwittingly encouraged Freddy to act out these urges. From the evidence at hand, the type of interpersonal process described by these authors had repeated itself over the course of at least two generations.

Just as Freddy's mother had overtly told him to "act good" and had covertly encouraged him to be otherwise, so had her father done toward her. On the one hand, he exhorted her to remain "pure." On the other hand, his predictions that she would become a "tramp," his coldness and punitiveness, his jealous rejection of her boy friends, and his unconscious sexual seductiveness toward her eventuated in her sexual acting out and her greedy exploitations of others.

Robbed of her childhood and bereft of parental tenderness, the mother sought frantically for some kind of fulfillment in her husband. Having, however, compulsively picked a man who was basically so much like her father, and being encumbered by characterological traits which tended to integrate exploitative and hate-ridden kinds of relationships, she found no fulfillment in her husband.

She turned therefore to her newborn child. With him she did

find a blissful kind of gratification and fulfillment in which she could give to herself through the child the kind of tenderness she so much craved.

When, however, he began to manifest tendencies to grow and to separate himself from her, she was as sorely threatened as she was later when he was taken away from her by court action. In order to sustain her own precarious balance, the mother was compelled to perpetuate the child's symbiotic dependence on her. To do this, she had to prevent him from relating on a meaningful and satisfying basis to anyone else, including his father:

She inculcated in the child the illusion that he was significantly different from and superior to all others and devaluated those with whom he tried to make a relationship.

She would bribe him with tempting kinds of gratifications. This not only bound him to her but led him to expect and to demand gratification from others which it would have been entirely inappropriate and unreasonable for them to fulfill. When they refused him, the child would become enraged and, as his mother had wanted, would return to her.

The mother rendered him ineffective in relating to his peers by preventing him from fighting back physically. As each of them reported to me, she exhorted him never to fight and would beat him whenever he got into a fight. This left him with a feeling of powerlessness and a loss of self-esteem in dealing with his peer group.

When he would manifest his genuine dependent needs for growth, for tenderness, and for rational limits, she would become anxious and menacing; he would thereupon become extremely uncomfortable. So "conditioned," he would incorrectly "see" the same reactions in others and would perceive them as ungiving and destructive. She subtly taught him her own view that people are universally malevolent and that one must attack first or else be destroyed.

These actions and attitudes of the mother toward Freddy left him with a severely disturbed motivational and perceptual system. He was motivated by the infantile hunger for dependency gratification which his mother had been unable to satisfy and which had been both whetted and twisted in his relationship with her; and by the hostility attendant on his distorted perception of others as ungiving and hating persons. Both of these motivational vectors operated at all times in Freddy's behavior but each varied in its relative strength in any particular behavioral pattern. With this in mind, his behavior with us might be listed on the following spectrum, from relatively more dependency-motivated to relatively more hostility-motivated: a rather charming form of approval-seeking, a more overt form of flattery to ingratiate himself, excessive requests for special privileges, more aggressive demandingness, manipulative exploitation of others, provocative needling and goading, hostile sexual advances toward female and some male counsellors, and severe bursts of rage with assaultiveness and destruction of property. The soiling during his period of hospitalization seemed to be related both temporally and psychodynamically to the bursts of destructive urges in general and to the urges toward fire-setting in particular.

At times, Freddy had a precociously grown-up quality. He was able to charm some adults, particularly women, into becoming very dedicated to him, and even, in a sense, somewhat dependent on him. I feel that this quality had developed in Freddy in response to his mother's infantile needs for a fatherly and husbandly person. Furthermore, with this quality Freddy was trying to bind the other person to him, in the hope of obtaining some genuine love and also in order to perpetuate with the other person the type of predominantly sadomasochistic integration which characterized his relationship with his mother.

Buried within his characteristic demandingness toward us was his infantile hunger for dependency gratification and its distorted derivatives. Since he was convinced he could not obtain satisfaction by open admission of his needs, he unwittingly denied and disguised the needs, and tried to obtain satisfaction by coercion and shrewd manipulation. The usually negative reaction of others to these techniques for obtaining satisfaction in turn confirmed his hopelessness.

Integrated in Freddy's manipulative exploitation of others and his provocativeness were the components of the sadomasochistic feud with his mother. It is conceivable that if Freddy had completely dissociated his needs for independent growth and his nascent capacity to relate to others, the relationship with his mother might have remained placidly symbiotic. Mixed in with his rebellious attempts to break out of the symbiotic stranglehold and to assert his own needs would be a provocative playback of her manipulations of him. At times he was temporarily successful in exploiting her for his own ends. Most of the time, on the other hand, she would balk and he would become more openly provocative; at this point he might be victorious in demoralizing her and then his provocations would boomerang: she would ragefully counterattack. When he made it too uncomfortable for her, she would abandon him to the Smiths. In his experiences with his mother and spreading into his experiences with other adults, he discovered that when he defeated, demoralized, or outwitted the adult—as he also felt he was doing with his fire-setting, retaliatory practical jokes, and running away —he had the neurotic satisfaction of revengeful triumph over the perceived enemy (which now unconsciously included his mother) and some reassurance that he was not completely helpless and insignificant. When the adults caring for him were provoked into anger and retaliation, this confirmed Freddy's misperception that all adults without exception were enemies.

Even if his mother had been hundreds of miles away from the hospital when he was with us, it is my feeling that Freddy would have perceived us, at least for many months, as ungiving and hating, and that he would have behaved accordingly. Indeed, he was, in a sense, trying to prove that his mother was "right" about our hating him when he tried to provoke angry and retaliatory feelings in us. As it was, his mother was in town, and she telephoned him daily and visited him weekly—as we allowed parents to do at that time —and we learned from our own observation how she encouraged him in his angry demands and revengeful operations. In this way, she could safely express through the child her own hostile-destructive and revengeful impulses and could derive the reassurance that he loved only her. His response to her orders, to the extent that it was inappropriate to the reality of the situation, seemed to us to have very much the quality of the hypnotic subject "blindly" carrying out posthypnotic suggestions.

Freddy's mother was unconsciously sexually seductive toward him, as manifested most strikingly in certain games they played at bedtime. In his sexual advances toward the female counselors Freddy was not only manifesting his emergent pubertal sexual drives but was also unconsciously striving to re-enact overtly the relatively more covert mutual seduction between himself and his mother. These sexual advances toward the counselors were hostile in quality, and he was thus, through displacement, avenging himself on his mother for the destructive effects of her seduction of him.

On the one hand, Freddy and his mother perceived the intervention of society, as exemplified by his hospitalization by us, as a disruptive threat to their relationship; and their angry and frantic behavior toward us was, to a significant extent, a response to this threat. On the other hand, the difficulties in school, the lying and stealing, the truancy, and certain episodes of fire-setting and running away, represented, in part, a decompensation of the symbiotic system and manifested Freddy's desperate and misguided efforts to break out of the relationship. These efforts were supercharged by the impending necessity for him, at the time of puberty, to make a choice between his mother and others. When he could no longer tolerate the self-destructive and malevolent integration with his mother, he had himself caught by the police and bodily removed from her. It is my impression that he cherished the inner hope that he would find in the institution the "Good Mother" he so much needed.

Furthermore, I feel that although Freddy's father had sensed the destructiveness in his wife's relationship with their son, he was so preoccupied with his own needs, so deeply withdrawn and depressed over his ineffectiveness in his job and in his two marriages, that he was unable to rescue the child from the mother. In reference to Freddy's strivings toward adult men, including the male members of our staff—for example, his invoking the protection of the fire marshals and the police, his frantic attempts to get himself, his mother, and me together in one room, and his characteristic pattern of trying to make an alliance with the man in top authority— implicit in this behavior was his search for the strong father who could either exclude or effectively contain and tame the mother, and allow and help Freddy to grow.

Some of Freddy's conflicts are manifested in a dream he had during his eighth week in the hospital. On the day of the dream, Freddy told a counselor, "I don't like Len Siegel. I don't like his looks. He looks like my father." He was especially hostile to the female counselors. He described to another counselor how he could blow up the whole building. The next morning, while he was still half-asleep, he told me the following dream.

I was with a lot of men. . . . We were in an airplane flying down a road in Germany. In the airplane there was the pilot and his wife. His wife had a kitchen knife and a pitchfork and she was sharpening them. We went into a prison camp. There were a lot of people there and everybody was trying to escape. And then I was in a big boat and there were millions of people on the boat and everybody was running around all confused.

In the dream, the male (including Freddy and his father) is doomed to psychological imprisonment and impotence because the woman (mother) holds all the domestic weapons. Even though Freddy wishes that his father and/or his doctor would steer a constructive life course for him (as, in the dream, he placed the male pilot at the controls), the people outside of the family are enemies (Germany) and the road inevitably leads to imprisonment and fina panic. The mother is depicted as purely destructive and castrating and there is no trace of Freddy's conscious allegiance to her. The prison-camp scene might represent both Freddy's conscious perception of the locked ward and his unconscious perception of his own psychological imprisonment; it would thus depict his frantic attempts to escape from what he unconsciously perceived as an insoluble dilemma. The panic-like confusion of the voyagers might represent Freddy's own panic and confusion, his feeling of "being at sea"; his fear of drowning, either within the confines of his mother's personality or in his attempt to escape from his mother (as she is perhaps more heavily disguised in the boat symbol); and his confusion as to where he would escape to even if he could get away from her.

DISCUSSION

The data that we have collected on this mother and child are of interest to us in many areas: (1) the dramatic illustration of an intensely symbiotic relationship between the patient and his mother, in disequilibrium, and the meaning of his antisocial acting out within that context; (2) the striking ability of the mother to stymie therapy by maintaining the son's quasi-delusional expectation of malintent by the therapeutic community; (3) the tendency of the mother and child to re-create in the hospital the kinds of multangular relationships which had characterized an earlier epoch in their lives.

A fourth area of interest, which I have only touched on thus far, is the way in which the pressing needs of the patient and his mother influenced the course of our own development as a residential treatment unit:

The excessive demands of Freddy and his mother for special privileges revealed to us that we had not yet developed sufficiently well-formulated policies on such privileges—privileges on visiting, on the use of certain equipment, etc.—and stimulated us to develop more explicit policies.

The deeply buried, extreme hunger, in both the patient and his mother, for meaningful relatedness eventuated in a bitter rivalry between them which made it extremely difficult for me to deal with both at the same time. The suspiciousness of each toward anyone working with the other was a part of this difficulty. This difficulty was one factor, among others, which influenced the development of our current practice in which the patient and his parents are seen collaboratively by different staff members.

The three-month interim between the time Freddy was admitted and the time he and his mother were told our final recommendations for further treatment played into Freddy's underlying insecurity as to what would become of him, and increased his mother's frantic attempts to get him back. This plus other determinants resulted in the desperate and confused behavior which manifested the underlying ambivalence of both the patient and his mother toward treatment. Neither could tolerate anything less than an explicit, tangible, and rigidly scheduled plan of action. In retrospect, I feel it would have been preferable to have told them at the outset that Freddy would be in the hospital for a period of time and would then be returned to the detention home, following which the responsible agency would make final disposition. Our current policy is to be as explicit as possible with the patient and his parents as to our over-all plan of treatment.

Because of the crucial effect on Freddy of the processes of extreme inconsistency, rivalry, and disagreement between the significant people in his past life, he had developed, as a survival measure, a hypersensitivity to these processes in the people in his life space, was constantly vigilant for their appearance, and tended to expose them wherever he could find them. The impact of this hypersensitivity on us, as it was brought into operation on our unit, affected the course of our own felt need to reduce as much as we could any form of inconsistency, rivalry, and covert disagreement between the members of the therapeutic team; to refine our methods for up-to-the-minute intrastaff communication; and to develop and make explicit to the entire staff the details of our guiding policies on what behavior is sanctioned, what is tolerated, and what is stopped.

The adults in Freddy's life had repeatedly shifted from reward-giving to punitive positions. This left him with an inability to differentiate between constructive and destructive motives. My operating in several administrative and nonadministrative roles was confusing to him and reinforced his suspicious hypersensitivity to me as an adult in a position of authority. The clear emergence of this process was one factor which accelerated our work in defining the differential aspects of the roles of ward administrator and individual therapist (Bloch and Silber, 1957).

Freddy's distrust of anyone interested in his problems in living, his difficulty in verbal communication of such problems, his use of other boys and other adults to dilute his relationship with hi psychiatrist, and his need for manual and physical activities and play media as a vehicle for relating and as a means of expressing his conflicts, along with similar problems and needs in the other boys of his group, played a significant role in the eventual development of our current program of playroom psychotherapy (Gordon and Siegel, 1957).

·································· 67 ··································

THE MEANING OF EXTERNAL CONTROL TO A

SCHIZOPHRENIC ADOLESCENT GIRL[1]

by Ann Wilkins Appelbaum, M.D.

The process of individual psychotherapy with fourteen-year-old Laura is described in this selection by Ann Wilkins Appelbaum of The Menninger Foundation. The course of treatment involves physical restraint to control aggressive behavior and to relieve anxiety. The selection analyzes how the physical control of destructive behavior takes on different meanings both for the patient and the therapist. [From *Bulletin of the Menninger Clinic,* 1957, *21,* 140-151. Reprinted by permission of the author and The Menninger Foundation.]

The need of the adolescent for external controls, during a period of maturation when the rapid burgeoning of instinctual life renders the ego relatively weak, has been recognized by many authors.[2] In attempting to work with disturbed adolescents, the therapist must function as an auxiliary ego from which the youngster can borrow strength when his inner controls are failing (Hamilton, 1947). While we are accustomed to thinking of ourselves as being on the side of the healthy ego, we may not feel quite at home in the role of an auxiliary superego (Wexler, 1951). Yet the adolescent sorely needs buttressing of a superego from which his ego has alienated itself in the attempt to achieve independence from the incorporated parental

---

[1] Written to meet a requirement of the Scientific Writing Course in the Menninger School of Psychiatry.
[2] Gitelson and Falstein, 1942; Hacker and Geleerd, 1945; Josselyn, 1951; Knight, 1946; Redl and Wineman, 1952.

figures (Hacker and Geleerd, 1945; Josselyn, 1951). Thus the therapist, at least in the beginning of treatment, may have to take a stand that is firmly on the side of authority, and against the gratification of instinctual demands, until the patient can be helped to cope with his impulses and to find acceptable modes of gratification.

Ordinarily we think of "taking sides" in psychotherapy only in the sense of making certain kinds of interpretations, or expressing attitudes and opinions, or, at the most, directly forbidding certain kinds of behavior. But when such means of providing controls are inadequate to stem erupting impulses, what then? Here we enter a more controversial area, which is rendered still more difficult by the position of the adolescent patient, somewhere between infancy and adulthood, and changing from day to day or even from moment to moment his level of functioning. When the conventional modes of providing external controls fail, we can invoke rules and systems of punishment and reward, or depend upon locked doors and the firm support of auxiliary personnel to help us prevent the patient from behaving in a dangerous or destructive way. But what about those times during therapy sessions when the therapist himself must demonstrate to the angry, assaultive patient that he can protect the youngster against the bad impulses, and prevent their damaging the patient, the therapist, and the treatment situation? At such times, one scarcely resembles a tower of strength if one calls for help, or beats a retreat with the honest but unreassuring explanation, "I can't help you when you are behaving in this way."

Upon beginning the treatment of patients, most traditionally trained psychiatrists have certain attitudes, including some taboos, that they are reluctant to give up. In medical training they overcame fears about handling the bodies of other persons, then they learned that the psychotherapist is generally wiser to avoid touching the patient. After such a process of learning, unlearning, and then relearning a taboo that has immense emotional implications, one departs from it with great reluctance. Not for the sophisticated psychotherapist is that rough-and-tumble method of establishing rapport, so often carried out successfully in motion pictures, in which the probation officer first demonstrates his strength by knocking the belligerent young delinquent down and is then immediately accepted as protector and friend. We hope to establish ourselves as auxiliary egos by more subtle and less violent means.

Thus when I found myself in what can only be described as free-for-alls with an adolescent girl, I wondered what these battles meant to the patient, and whether recovery could take place under such conditions. In an effort to clarify the changing meanings of these struggles in terms of the development of the relationship between patient and therapist, I shall describe my year's experience with 14 year old Laura, now that we have emerged battle-scarred but intact to enter upon a more conventional and peaceful phase of our work together.

Since Laura was so disturbed at first that there was doubt as to whether she was treatable at all, therapy was entirely empirical, the therapist responding *ad hoc* to whatever vicissitudes arose. The goal was to establish a trusting relationship with the patient, but there could scarcely be a plan for doing this. It was only upon reviewing the process of treatment that certain sequences of events formed a clear pattern in what had been experienced as a chaotic series of encounters.

HISTORY

Laura was the product of a love affair between an ignorant, lonely young woman and an irresponsible man who later showed the characteristics of an antisocial personality. Abandoned by her lover, the mother placed the newborn child in an orphanage, and took a job there. At the age of three, Laura spent two weeks in a foster home, where she was punished for minor misdeeds by being locked for hours in a closet. Because of this, her mother sent her to another foster home where she got along well for the next three years. Although she was visited frequently by her mother during this time, Laura was not sure who her real mother was.

Six years after Laura's birth, her father's brother learned of the child's existence and offered to marry the mother in whom he had been interested in his adolescence. Informing Laura that he was her real father, her uncle and mother attempted to provide a home for her. It was never a dependable one. Both parents were emotionally unstable; economic vicissitudes arising from the parents' social inadequacies forced them to move from one community to another over the next six years. Repeatedly uprooted from school and friends, the child did poor academic work, and was never able to establish lasting relationships with others.

An older boy attempted to rape her when she was eleven, and Laura had a period of panic and confusion lasting about a week after this episode. The following year she was informed by her parents of the circumstances of her birth, and learned that her stepfather was not her real father. During the next year she was involved in many minor delinquencies as a member of a gang of pre-adolescent children.

She had her first menstrual period at age 12. Shortly before the second menses, she experienced an episode of dissociation, wandered about for several hours and was eventually found by a searching party. After this incident, her parents noticed a change in her personality. She became increasingly hostile toward them. One day she turned on them in a fury and had to be physically restrained until she was admitted to the state hospital the next day.

In the hospital she remained excited and hostile, tore up her mattress and clothing, talked about hating the whole world, and rebuffed all attempts to approach her. She was started on insulin coma therapy, but she went into prolonged coma early in the treatment, and it was discontinued. Although Laura was a little more accessible while on insulin, she soon reverted to her previous state. She had to be kept in seclusion, and was almost constantly in restraints or cold wet sheet packs for the next five months, required spoon feeding, and made incessant assaults upon her surroundings.

During her next six months in the hospital, she was seen by a volunteer worker for an hour each day. Laura used the allotted time to express her thoughts and feelings. She improved to the extent of not requiring continuous control. But after this friendly figure left the hospital, Laura became depressed for awhile, then reverted to her destructive, unapproachable behavior.

After nearly a year in the hospital she improved to the extent of being able to attend classes in the Children's Unit. She was the most disturbed child in the group. She looked like a little savage, with her long, unkempt, black hair almost hiding her face which had the drawn look of an old woman's. She walked with one leg twisted almost backward. She had outbursts of rage, during which she fought bitterly whomever tried to control her, needing often as many as five adults to hold her. She was distractible and over active, able to sit still only a few minutes at a time. She chose for friends the most disturbed patients, and showered the personnel with obscene abuse. Nevertheless, there was something appealing about the youngster. Her whimsical bravado had in it a pathos that drew the nursing staff to her and prevented them from reacting with anger or rejection to her curses. They sensed an underlying long-ing for companionship, and a kind of rugged honorableness in Laura that made them want to help her.

She ran away from the hospital twice, each time contriving to ge herself returned to the hospital. On one occasion she cut her hand severely with glass upon being brought back to the Unit. Two years after admission she started in group psychotherapy. She continued to make a gradual improvement, and began visiting her parents on week ends. She seldom required seclusion and was able to share a dormitory room with two other girls.

THE COURSE OF PSYCHOTHERAPY

First Phase: The Struggle Against Wishes for Dependency

Two and one half years after her admission to the hospital, Laura started in individual psychotherapy, one hour a week. Her appearance had changed considerably. A pale, thin girl, dressed in jeans, she kept her hair cut short and slicked back like a boy's. She walked with a slouching swagger, stuck out her chin, and expressed with her entire body the warning, "Don't try to get close to me!" Yet there was a touch of humor in her swagger, and of warmth in her insults.

In the first three hours of therapy she betrayed her fears about beginning the new relationship. She talked about how doctors kill their patients and, metaphorically, about her terror of getting into deep water and drowning. Between herself and the therapist she built a cardboard fence behind which she talked bravely of having been in gangs that beat their enemies with chains, and fiercely protected their members against rival gangs and the police.

In the fourth hour she told about the friendly volunteer who had left her. At once she entered into a period of mounting anger, as though she were already being abandoned once again. At first this manifested itself in the form of mild assaults upon various objects in the office. This behavior was not checked. She asked, "Will you quit giving me therapy if I act so bad that they put me in seclusion?" I replied that in that event I would see her in her room.

Striving to avoid any hint of rejection, I sat quietly for several sessions while she tore up and took apart whatever objects she could find. In a short time, Laura was amply confirming Dr. Frieda Fromm-Reichmann's (1952) observation that, "Silent acceptance of violence in word or action is inadvisable, not only in self-defense, but also in pursuit of the respect due to patients, and in protection of their self-respect." The "inadvisability" of my permissiveness became apparent as Laura's assaults moved toward my person, first in the form of smashing my package of cigarettes, then of tossing cigarette butts and bits of dirt into my lap, threatening to burn my hands with the cigarette lighter, and "to beat you up so you won't ever come back again!" Finally she began to talk about the other doctors who were leaving soon, and I told her that I would neither leave her nor permit her to hurt me.

The next four sessions were relatively tranquil. She controlled her hostile impulses by leaving the office from time to time and talking to me from the corridor. She continued to be preoccupied with whether I would leave her. But after having thus openly expressed her fears of being abandoned, she redoubled her efforts to persuade me to do just that, hurling invective at me, along with showers of cigarette butts, ashes, and dead moths. An hour became too long for me to tolerate this steady bombardment, and I began meeting with her twice a week for half an hour at a time.

I continued to interpret her behavior as an expression of her fear that I would get angry with her and leave. I took no steps to control her aggressive behavior until the fourteenth session when she was on the verge of throwing the telephone at me. I told her firmly that she could not do that. She promptly set the telephone down and then spent the most profitable hour in weeks in a verbal interchange uninterrupted by aggressive outbursts. In fact, when the firm "no" checked the motor expression of anxiety, her words poured out in a torrent, as if literally a new channel for her impulses had been forced open by the pressure of her thoughts.

In the ensuing sessions she acted out her conflicting desires to damage and destroy and to restore and heal—throwing water on the desk, then mopping it up; moving furniture about the room, then replacing it, meanwhile making verbal threats to injure me. In a teasing, experimental way, she scratched my arm lightly with a paper clip then scratched her own, asking, "Does that hurt?" trying to find out if it felt the same to me as it did to her, and if my skin would produce a red line as hers did.

At last, fairly exhausted by the tension her behavior was evoking, I told her that I would try not to let her hurt me, but that if she had to act in this way I would have to leave before the time was up. After I had told her, in effect, "I cannot control you: thus I will have to desert you," Laura became highly excited. Her hate and rage poured forth without interruption over the next two sessions. It became clear that I had either to interrupt the treatment until the patient established better controls, or to protect myself against her violence. My permissiveness seemed to kindle her hate. What was wrong? Why didn't it work, this effort to "make up for the tremendous deficit of love experienced in the patient's life?" (Rosen, 1953).

My state of mind during the past few sessions revealed the answer: "It isn't love, but fear, and sometimes hatred, which makes us abandon the child (and the patient) to his own emotional devices. You must sometimes hold the baby, and hold it tight, or it will be too much frightened by the rage and lust inside" (Wexler, 1951). It was true: probably no one can submit for long a barrage of missiles and blows without developing a real resentment against the assailant, no matter how sick and frightened and obviously in need of love he may be. Trying to conceal such objective hate instead of facing it with the patient does not help him to test reality (Winnicott, 1949). Furthermore, Laura needed at this point not love so much as care and protection (Bettleheim, 1950).

It seemed that "accepting" her violence must convey to the patient not kindness but fear. And there were excellent internal and external reasons for fear at this point: to stop the assault meant a battle, which could only be frightening to both patient and therapist. Until I was fully aware of how useless, indeed, how terrifying my "loving" attitude was to the patient, I could not see how much more truly an expression of love would be the firm control of the behavior that was threatening to wreck her treatment. I decided to hold Laura until she could "hold" her own impulses.

The first attempt at this was unsuccessful. I was tentative and half-hearted about breaking the taboo against physical contact with a patient, and therefore Laura managed to inflict a number of blows before I could immobilize her. But during the next hour a remarkable thing happened: In mid-assault she told me, "Don't you dare cross my arms and hold me that way, because then I can't get loose!" Gratefully I followed this suggestion, and found that I could hold her firmly. It was exhausting to pinion her this way for twenty minutes, while repeating to her as calmly as possible that her fear of being left was making her try to drive me away. Yet it was not nearly as uncomfortable as had been the preceding sessions, with their gradually mounting resentment and anxiety. Furthermore, Laura was "participating" in therapy for the first time, by helping me to control her.

The following session was the most peaceful and productive one in weeks. She then renewed her attack, prefacing it with the announcement that some of the doctors had left that morning, thus hinting at her fears of being deserted by the therapist. During the ensuing struggle, Laura expressed her ambivalence about our relationship: on the one hand, she tried to pummel me, saying she hated me and wanted to stop treatment; on the other hand, she kept her back against the door and said, "I won't let you leave!" Then I noticed that she was hanging on tightly to my hands, and I let them relax in hers. We stood in this way for a long time—Laura was holding me, not the other way round. As she clung to my hands, she told me about how doctors are afraid to be locked up alone with their patients, preferring to be able "to leave you whenever they feel like it."

In subsequent sessions Laura gave me further instructions in methods of holding her so that neither of us could be hurt, always giving them as an injunction *not* to do this or that. At the same time, she fantasied that I was trained in *jujitsu* and had superhuman strength. It is interesting to speculate here on the concept of "lending" ego strength to the patient. Who was "borrowing" from whom, in the case of Laura and myself? It turned out to be a mutual affair (as I suspect it always is[3]), the patient unconsciously "lending" to the therapist the capacity to provide the control that was so desperately needed, while "borrowing" the strength to master her anxiety.

Gradually Laura's defenses against closeness and friendliness softened. She was helped by a physical illness to acknowledge her dependent needs without so much guilt (Searles, 1955). While sick in bed, she could accept kindness without her usual frightened retaliation. Characteristically, right after an unusually frank expression of her wish for a personal and close relationship, she experienced a recoil from the dangerous intimacy. Battering me, she cried that she would wear me out, until I finally gave up trying to treat her. In this struggle, she scratched my finger which bled a little. Seeing this she sprang away and, with a look of terror, raked her own forearm with a pencil. This sort of behavior persisted with mounting intensity over a period of two weeks. During these violent periods there seemed to be no healthy ego to which one might appeal—only a seething bundle of hate and flying fists.

Yet, at last, she was able to give freer expression to her dependent longings than ever before. For nearly two months the assaults stopped. During this time I met her on the ward rather than in the office, where the "seduction of gadgets" (Redl and Wineman, 1952) and the relative isolation from the friendly support of the ward

---

[3] Eric Erikson (1954) states this as a general principle when he writes, "A family can bring up a baby only by being brought up by him. His growth consists in a series of challenges to them to serve his newly developing potentialities for social interaction."

personnel made her unduly anxious. Simply knowing about the proximity of the nursing staff was of considerable help to her, making it less necessary for her to relieve her anxiety by trying to arouse fear in me.

Second Phase: Accepting the Oral Needs

During this two month period, which she spent mostly in seclusion, Laura was able for the first time to accept candy from me. She asked to have her therapy sessions lengthened to an hour twice a week, and even had me called in for extra sessions when she felt especially lonely and afraid.

Her general behavior improved, and gradually she was given more freedom on the ward and spent less time in seclusion. As the external controls loosened, her anxiety increased. Following her first visit home in several months, she assaulted the aides and had to be returned to her locked room. Two weeks later, after a visit from her mother, she ran in front of a car and injured her hand. During the ensuing period of semi-invalidism, she talked more freely about her loneliness, her suffering in the orphanage, and her feeling of having been rejected by her real father "because I wasn't a boy." She talked a good deal about women being raped, about men who had tried to have sexual relations with her, about the dangers of going about city streets at night. She demonstrated an extreme prudery about sexual matters in general, but had particular difficulty in uttering the word "breast."

When the controls of the ward were again relaxed, she began a new kind of assault upon the therapist. She clung childishly to my clothing ("Let me have the pretty button!") and when she struck out, invariably aimed the blows at the breasts. Her movements were playful and poorly coordinated, like those of a young infant. Sessions like this alternated with peaceful, friendly ones, in which she began to "give" me cigarettes. This "giving" dramatized her perception of giving as a hostile, forcing act. She literally shoved the gift at me, shouting, "Here, take it, you bitch!" This alternating pattern of giving to the therapist and then attacking the breast, with increasingly infantile motor behavior, was associated with a marked improvement in her behavior outside of therapy.

At last, during an hour when her playful assaults had made it necessary for me to hold her, she relaxed against me, laid her head on my shoulder, and became drowsy and comfortable. Holding her gently, I told her that she had needed to be held in this way as a

little baby, and that the reason she had been fighting with me was
that she still longed to be held on mother's lap so that she would
not feel so lonely and frightened. In a dreamy way, Laura talked
about being a little baby in the orphanage, and not having any
mother: "I don't believe my mother is my real mother. Anyone
might be my mother—even you."

Third Phase: Accepting the Phallic Needs

Immediately after revealing her fantasy of the therapist as the
real mother, Laura began exchanging love letters with one of the
boys in her Unit—her first display of heterosexual interest since
entering the hospital. She began going to hospital dances, and holding hands with her boy friend.

But she reacted to the threat of her surrender to the pleasant
regression to babyhood by attacking me like a prize fighter the next
time I saw her (session number 93). The flabby, uncoordinated infant of the previous week was suddenly a hard-as-nails, bitter killer.
It was impossible to hold her. But I felt that I could now tell her
frankly that her behavior was too hard for me to handle, without
rekindling her fears of being abandoned. I told her I would have
to wait until she calmed down, and then I left.

In subsequent sessions she told of her disappointment in her "love
affair" with the boy, and of the ensuing upsurge of homosexual
thoughts about one of the girls. She said, "Help me control these
feelings." While openly asking for help, she carried on a teasing
attack during each session, forcing me to hold her. As soon as she
was firmly pinned down, she relaxed, obviously enjoying being held
the moment she was released she renewed her provocative behavior
She talked about wanting to "hold on" to the object of her consciou
homosexual strivings by engaging with the other girl in mutua
masturbation. Her provocative play with the therapist was inter
preted to her as an attempt to "hold on" to me, by forcing me t
control her.

After this interpretation of her erotic impulses toward the the
apist, Laura injured her foot. "Now I can't do anything bad," sh
said. She talked freely of the injury as both a punishment for th
"bad" wishes, and a preventive against acting upon them. Afterwar
her assaultive behavior ceased. She continued to walk with a gr
tesque limp long after the injury healed. She had found a neurot
defense against her hostile and erotic impulses, and no longer neede
external control from the therapist. Her "injury" did not hamp

her in everyday activities; but she occasionally reminded me, "I couldn't run away from you because of my foot—you could easily catch me!"

Her appearance and general behavior on the ward became more feminine—sometimes even seductive—although she always donned her old jeans and T shirt for therapy sessions. She chose friends among the less severely disturbed patients. Her swearing became milder and less frequent. She was no longer seen by the ward personnel as "the sickest girl in the Unit," but rather as one with a good chance for further improvement.

DISCUSSION

We may review the course of treatment thus far in terms of the meaning of Laura's assaultive behavior at various levels of the transference: what it meant to both patient and therapist, and how the patient experienced the way in which the therapist responded to her aggressive onslaughts.

First Phase

In the beginning, the motive for attack was chiefly the wish to maintain the *status quo:* painful as her loneliness and isolation were, she was "used to it—and I like what I'm used to." Entering into a relationship meant running the risk of being deserted. The best solution she could find was to drive the therapist away before it was too late.

The therapist's acceptance of the initial, mild aggression frightened Laura, since the therapist thus became identified with the instinctual demands against which the patient so sorely needed an ally (Blos, 1953). By the time control was provided, the patient's anxiety was so great that it could not be relieved by interpretations, nor even by firmly forbidding the destructive behavior. The ego was swamped by rage and fear, and was available neither to interpretations or commands (Redl and Wineman, 1952). Nothing but physical restraint could stem the anger and relieve the overwhelming anxiety.

In addition to fending off a potentially dependent relationship and preserving the *status quo,* the early assaults had a reality-testing function: "How strong is the therapist? Strong enough to grapple with the hate and destructiveness in me? How reliable is she? Will she run away as soon as I show her how bad I am?" (Rall, 1947). Laura could verbalize all this. But on a more primitive level, she had to find out if the therapist was real: "Where does my body leave off and hers begin? Does she feel it when I scratch myself? Does she react to pain in the same way that I do?" Like an infant, she had to find these ego boundaries by punching and prodding and trying to take apart the vague "other," learning its responses to such investigations over a long period of time, until she could finally feel fairly sure that we were distinct, and yet similar.

But all this injured the therapist, and that aroused Laura's guilt and necessitated severe self-punishment. She had to exact talion punishment, symbolically sacrificing a part of her body in order to save the whole (Menninger, 1940) from the avenging, primitive superego that she had projected onto the therapist.

Her infantile erotic wish for tactile contact mobilized anxiety, since contact and fusion were synonymous for her: she had to struggle to maintain her individuality, to remain distinct from the other person who was arousing deep needs for dependency and amalgamation (Searles, 1955). She fought against this wish for fusion by trying to injure the therapist. Such a vicious circle could be broken only by holding her so firmly that neither the outwardly hostile nor the self-punishing impulses could be acted upon, until her fear of losing either the therapist or her own identity could be mastered.

While we were dealing with her fears of being "drowned" (losing her body image), abandoned, or killed if she permitted expression of her need for love and care (to express the need meant to recognize its inevitable frustration), being held by the therapist meant to Laura: "I will not leave you. I will not destroy you. I will not let your bad impulses destroy us. You do not need to be afraid, because I am not afraid to be all alone with you and your murderous rage." Laura, struggling to master these fears, wanted all this to be true. Therefore she not only "taught" the therapist how to control her, but developed a reinforcing fantasy of the therapist as a powerful woman and an expert at *jujitsu*. At the same time, being held was a partial gratification of the very needs for closeness and trusting helplessness that the patient had to deny so strenuously.

Throughout this long period of almost unabated expression of hate, a strong negative transference was in operation. Whatever positive feelings the patient had toward the therapist were displaced to other female figures, and were acted out in the form of open expressions of worshipful love. She selected for this purpose individuals who were known transients in her life—for instance, the ward doctor who would remain in the Unit for only six months. Laura could love the ward doctor without too much anxiety because the ultimate desertion was predetermined, and thus could not take her by surprise. So threatening were her positive feelings for the therapist that if she could not have acted them out with other figures, her anxiety might have blocked the therapeutic process.

Laura had to see the therapist as hostile and rejecting because she had projected onto the therapist her own brutal, primitive superego, that forbade gratification and exacted the death penalty for misdeeds. Moreover, she projected upon the therapist the hostility that was aroused when her unfulfilled dependent needs—and their unavoidable frustration—came close to consciousness. This hostility led to guilt, which could be relieved by finding justification for her hate through perceiving the therapist as evil (Searles, 1955).

It subsequently became clear that neither the negative transference nor the therapist's forceful response to the patient's aggression destroyed rapport. The negative feelings were easier for the patient to face than the positive ones, against which her hate served a defensive purpose. It was the therapist, not the patient, who was the more disturbed about the negative feelings, and therefore found it difficult to hear the cries for help behind the violent attacks. With so many narcissistic and physical injuries to cope with, the therapist was hampered in understanding and recognizing the dependent needs. Only when control was established, and no one had to be afraid of getting hurt, could the therapist really listen.

Second Phase

When at last it became relatively safe to be close to the therapist, Laura could enjoy being held and could provoke this response without having to inflict real injury. As a result she experienced less guilt and perceived the therapist's control of her as an expression of motherly tenderness. She could now permit herself the fantasy of the therapist as the "good" mother—the real mother. She could accept oral gratification from the therapist in the form of candy. This suggested that her fear that her dependent needs would cause her to take in something harmful was diminishing: she did not need the paranoid defense against the wish to eat up and destroy the outer world (Searles, 1955) since her needs for being taken care of and protected were being recognized and partially gratified.

Only after Laura perceived the therapist-mother as a "giving" mother in the oral sense was it possible for her to see the therapist as a "giving" mother in the phallic sense: giving permission to enjoy sexual pleasure. Not until the dependency problems had been partly solved was there energy available for Laura to invest in homosexual and heterosexual relationships.

Third Phase

So long as Laura was dominated by the "bad" mother of the archaic superego, heterosexuality was prohibited. The cruel superego had been externalized, projected upon the therapist, hated and rebelled against: but also feared, so much that Laura could not express any heterosexual wishes. She spoke of men only to condemn them as rapacious, dangerous creatures. Although certain of her experiences confirmed such a viewpoint, it was also true that she had to investigate the therapist's attitudes toward sexuality while maintaining on her own part a safely moralistic attitude. Only when Laura had completed a long process of revision of the image of the therapist could she recognize some of her erotic fantasies and venture a little way into maturity. Even so, she had to keep her boy friend a secret from the therapist until after he had rejected her.

She reacted to the rejection by entering into a fantasied homosexual relationship, verbally expressing her feelings about her girl friend while attacking the therapist in such a way as to force her to hold the patient once again. As soon as the meaning of these assaults had been clarified ("You want me to hold you to help you control your sexual feelings. By making me do this, you hold on to me, so that I won't leave you now when you need help so badly."), Laura could give up her aggressive behavior. During this phase, being held was experienced by the patient both as a protection against direct expression of erotic fantasies and as partial gratification of her wishes.

SUMMARY AND CONCLUSIONS

In the psychotherapy of disturbed adolescents, physical force applied by the therapist to control aggressive behavior does not necessarily destroy the therapeutic relationship, but may sometimes be the only way to make such a relationship possible. By forcing the therapist to restrain him, the patient demonstrates his need for the powerful ally against threatening instinctual impulses. At the same time, the patient may express his unconscious wish for external control by facilitating in subtle ways its application.

Like any other consistent pattern of behavior on the part of the therapist, physical control of destructive behavior takes on different meanings for the patient at different levels of the transference. This can be interpreted with beneficial effect. Physical contact with the patient has meaning for the therapist and arouses his fear and anxiety, which reduce effectiveness unless they can be understood and mastered. The therapist's anxiety about the use of force may be a greater hindrance to treatment than either the patient's anxiety about it or the method of control itself.

Great as the need of the patient for control may be, physical force may not often be necessary or appropriate in the treatment of adolescents. When it is, some workers may prefer to have other people apply the control. Nevertheless, in certain cases it may be of great value to the patient to find the therapist, himself, capable of supporting the healthy ego against impulses that threaten to destroy patient, therapist, and treatment.

················· **68** ·······················

MUST COUNSELING BE INDIVIDUAL?

by Clifford P. Froehlich[1]

This selection reveals no difference in the effectiveness of individual and multiple counseling as judged by agreement between self-rating and test scores on the Differential Aptitude Tests. Clifford P. Froehlich (1914-1959) late of the University of California concludes, ". . . the findings do not support the claim that counseling must be individual." [From *Educational and Psychological Measurement*, 1958, *18*, 681-689. Reprinted by permission of the author and Dr. G. Frederic Kuder.]

Traditionally, definitions of counseling have stated or implied that the individual interview was THE *modus operandi* of counseling. This position has been challenged by the writer and others who, from their own experience, have felt that the group approach was a potentially effective avenue to counseling objectives. The writer coined the term "multiple counseling" to designate a procedure in which a counselor works simultaneously with several counselees manifesting symptoms of at least one problem in common. The details of the multiple counseling approach have been reported elsewhere (Froehlich, no date; Hoppock, 1950). To date, the relative effectiveness of multiple and individual counseling has been largely a matter of conjecture. Bilovsky (1953), reported a comparison of individual and group counseling, but the data were

---

[1] The writer is indebted to Mr. Shepard Insel, Director, Student Personnel Services and Research, Sequoia Senior High School District, California, for his assistance in gathering data for this study.

not reported in a manner which yielded clearcut evidence of counseling effectiveness. Driver (1952), and Peres (1947), also presented research on the effectiveness of multiple counseling, but they did not compare it with individual counseling. It is the purpose of this study to do so.

The most difficult task confronting the person who wishes to evaluate counseling is the selection of a criterion, because there is none about which it is feasible to collect data and which has been widely accepted by counselors. The major criterion in this study, therefore, was not selected because of its general acceptance; rather, it was chosen because, from the writer's orientation, it reflects a logical outcome of counseling, and because it is being used in a series of studies of which this is one.

The criterion was agreement between self-rating and test scores. Both pre-counseling and post-counseling ratings are compared with test scores. Application of the criterion assumes that a person should learn about himself during counseling. If he does, presumably his self ratings should be in closer agreement with his tested abilities after counseling than before.

The students used as subjects in this study were seniors in a large California high school. The problem they had in common was an indicated desire for more information about themselves in order to make post-high-school plans. The students participated in the testing and counseling program voluntarily; part of the testing was done outside of school hours. The decision regarding which students were provided with individual counseling and which had multiple counseling was made arbitrarily and was influenced primarily by practical consideration of scheduling. Seventeen students were counseled individually, and 25 were counseled in small groups of four to six students.

In this study, self-ratings were obtained by asking students to rate themselves before counseling and again after counseling. Each subject rated himself on a five point scale in each of the areas measured by the *Differential Aptitude Tests*; these areas are listed in Table 2. In order to facilitate statistical treatment of the data, each step on the rating scale was assigned a numerical value from one through five; the highest rating was assigned five; the next highest, four; and so on. Because the extreme steps contained so few cases, they were combined with adjacent steps when the data were processed. That is, ratings of one were combined with ratings of two, and ratings of five were combined with ratings of four. Hence, for each subject there were eight pre-counseling ratings and eight post-counseling ratings distributed on a three-step scale: the first step which was given a value of two included ratings of one and two, the next step with a value of three contained only ratings of three, and the last step with a value of four included ratings of four and five.

In addition to rating himself before and after counseling, each student completed the *Differential Aptitude Test* battery. The scores on this test were converted to centile ranks and were then assigned numerical values of two, three, or four in a manner similar to the assignment of numerical values to the rating scale steps. Centile ranks of 76 or above were assigned a value of four, ranks from 25 through 75 were given the value of three, and ranks below 25 were classified as two. As a result, each student had a rated-test-score value of two, three, or four for each of the eight areas of the *Differential Aptitude Test*. Throughout the remainder of this report, the phrase "test score" is used to refer to rated-test-score value obtained in the manner just described.

THE FINDINGS

The data in Table 1 summarize the agreement between ratings and test scores for all eight areas taken together. The first category indicates the total number of ratings that were the same as the corresponding test score both before and after counseling. In other words, the rating was correct before counseling. Hence, no change in rating was required to bring it into agreement with the corresponding test score. The post-counseling rating was the same as the pre-counseling rating; therefore, it also agreed with the test score. Of the 336 ratings available, 126, or 38 per cent required no change. The counseling objective in this case was merely one of confirming the counselee's original rating.

The second category of Table 1 contains those pre-counseling ratings which were not in agreement with test scores before counseling but the corresponding post-counseling ratings were in agreement. Such a change in ratings reflects a desired outcome of counseling if it is assumed that correctness of ratings is related in a meaningful way to self-concept and this in turn to choices which might be made by the counselee. Sixty-five, or 19 per cent of all ratings were of this type.

In the third classification are those post-counseling ratings which were the same as corresponding pre-counseling ratings neither of which agreed with its test-score counterpart. These were 80 such ratings, 24 per cent of the total. Essentially, counseling in this instance was ineffective.

The final category contains cases in which the first rating was not the same as the second rating and neither the first nor second rating agreed with the rated test score. Persons whose ratings fell into this category may be considered counseling failures according to the criterion applied in this study. There were 65 ratings of this type, 19 per cent of the total.

The distributions of agreement of ratings and test scores by categories for individual and multiple counseling reported in Table 1

TABLE 1

AGREEMENT OF RATINGS AND TEST SCORES BEFORE AND AFTER
COUNSELING BY TWO METHODS OF COUNSELING

Categories of Agreement	Individual counseling	Multiple counseling	Total by category
Pre- and post-counseling ratings both agree with test score (no change, none required)	48	78	126
Pre-counseling rating not in agreement with test, but post-counseling rating agreed (correct change)	27	38	65
Pre- and post-counseling ratings agreed with each other, but not with test score (no change, one required)	29	51	80
Pre- and post-counseling do not agree with each other; the post-counseling rating does not agree with test score (incorrect change)	32	33	65
Total ratings (8 times number of subjects)	136	200	xxx

were tested by chi-square to see if the hypothesis that they came from the same population was tenable. It must be remembered that for chi-square to be an appropriate test in this instance the independence of the entries in the cells of Table 1 had to be assumed (Lewis and Burke, 1949; Peters, 1950). On this assumption chi-square was found to be 3.032, which is not statistically significant. Hence, it was concluded that no difference in the effectiveness of counseling methods as judged by the agreement criterion used in this study was revealed by the data in Table 1. This finding is negative in the sense that the superiority of either individual or multiple counseling is not demonstrated. Because it was believed that the assumption or method of treating the data may have not revealed differences further analyses were made.

The criterion was applied to the data in another manner. This was done by comparing the number of ratings which agreed with test scores before counseling with the number which agreed after counseling. The results of this comparison are reported in percentage form in Table 2. The first row of this table indicates that 59 per

TABLE 2

PERCENTAGE OF RATINGS IN AGREEMENT WITH TEST SCORE

D.A.T. Area	Individual Counseling		Multiple Counseling	
	Pre- counseling rating	Post- counseling rating	Pre- counseling rating	Post- counseling rating
Verbal reasoning	59	71	64	68
Numerical reasoning	53	53	48	76
Abstract reasoning	59	76	60	56
Space relations	47	59	36	52
Mechanical reasoning	59	35	48	72
Clerical speed and accuracy	47	47	44	48
Spelling	41	47	60	76
Sentences	35	65	52	60

cent of the pre-counseling ratings of verbal reasoning agreed with test scores and 71 per cent of the post-counseling ratings agreed. Comparable figures for multiple counseling are 64 and 68, respectively. Succeeding rows in this table, with few exceptions, reveal substantially the same picture, a slightly higher percentage of agreement for post-counseling ratings than for pre-counseling ratings. Albeit, when a test of significance was applied, none of the differences between the pre- and post-counseling percentage of agreement was statistically significant.

The number of agreements upon which the percentage in Table 2 are based, were summed for all areas of the test. The resulting totals and corresponding percentages are presented in Table 3.

The significance of the difference between the percentage of ratings in agreement with tests before individual counseling and the percentage after counseling was found to be at .10 level. In contrast, the comparable difference for the multiple counseled group was significant at the .008 level. After multiple counseling the subjects

TABLE 3

AGREEMENT BETWEEN TEST SCORES AND ALL RATINGS FOR

INDIVIDUAL AND MULTIPLE COUNSELED GROUP

	Individual		Multiple	
	Number	Per cent[a]	Number	Per cent[b]
Pre-counseling rating	68	50	103	52
Post-counseling rating	77	57	127	64

[a] Based on N = 136 ratings, 8 for each of 17 individuals before and after counseling.

[b] Based on N = 200 ratings, 8 for each of 25 individuals before and after counseling.

in this study apparently brought their ratings into closer agreement with their scores than before counseling. Individual counseling appears not to have influenced self rating in a significant way.

Another approach to evaluation of the data was made through the use of an index number which reflected relative agreement between an individual's test score and his rating. Preliminary to computing this index, a numerical value was assigned to each rating and test score in the manner previously described. The pre-counseling-agreement index was computed by subtracting the test-score value from the pre-counseling-rating value and adding a constant of five to eliminate negative numbers and summing these figures for the eight areas for each individual. The process is illustrated by the following data concerning one student:

	D.A.T. Areas							
	1	2	3	4	5	6	7	8
Pre-counseling-rating value	3	4	2	3	4	3	4	2
Test-score value	2	3	3	3	4	3	2	2
Rating value less score value plus constant of five	6	6	4	5	5	5	7	5

In the first column the result of the subtraction of the test-score value from the pre-counseling-rating value and the addition of a constant of five or six, shown in the last row. When all of the eight figures in the last row were added, the total was found to be 43, his pre-counseling-agreement index. The post-counseling-agreement index was computed in a similar manner except that post-counseling ratings were used. The mean and standard deviation for pre-counseling and for post-counseling indices for the individual counseled group and for the multiple counseled group were computed,

TABLE 4

MEANS, STANDARD DEVIATIONS, AND T-RATIOS BETWEEN
MEANS OF TOTAL AGREEMENT INDICES

	Individual Counseled		Multiple Counseled		t between means in same row
	Mean	Standard deviation	Mean	Standard deviation	
Pre-counseling index	39.8	3.18	41.2	2.72	1.44
Post-counseling index	40.7	3.84	41.0	2.79	.27
t between means in same column	1.10		.29		

the resulting statistics are reported in Table 4. When the significance of the differences between the means in Table 4 was evaluated by the t-ratio, none was found to be significant. The conclusions based on this method of analysis must be stated in negative terms: neither individual nor multiple counseling appeared to affect the means of the agreement indices. Likewise, the means of the individual and multiple groups are essentially the same.

The agreement index has a definite shortcoming in that the effect of ratings which were too high in terms of corresponding test score could be cancelled out by low ratings. The net result is an obliteration of the individual's variability of agreement between his ratings and score. Cronbach and Gleser (1953) have discussed a method of profile analysis which overcomes this limitation. The method defines similarity between profiles in terms of the linear distance between the respective points on the profiles being compared. The eight pre-counseling ratings were treated as one profile, the post-counseling ratings as another, and the test scores as the third. A pre-counseling profile-agreement score was computed by the formula (rating value-score value).[2] The method of computation is illustrated by the data for the student who was used to illustrate the computation of the agreement index.

	D.A.T. Areas							
	1	2	3	4	5	6	7	8
Pre-counseling rating value	3	4	2	3	4	3	4	2
Test-score-value	2	3	3	3	4	3	2	2
Rating-value minus score value	1	1	−1	0	0	0	2	0
(Rating value minus score value)[2]	1	1	1	0	0	0	4	0

In the first column, the test-score value has been subtracted from the pre-counseling-rating value, the difference was one, the square of this was one, as shown in the third and fourth rows, respectively. The figures in the last row were added, their total, seven, is the pre-counseling-profile-agreement score. In a like manner, the post-counseling-profile-agreement scores were computed. The mean and standard deviation of the pre- and post-counseling-profile-agreement scores for the individual counseled group and for the multiple counseled group were obtained and are shown in Table 5. The difference between

TABLE 5

MEANS, STANDARD DEVIATIONS, AND T-RATIOS BETWEEN
MEANS OF PROFILE-AGREEMENT SCORES

	Individual counseled (N = 17)		Multiple counseled (N = 25)		t-ratio between means in same row
	Mean	S.D.	Mean	S.D.	
Pre-counseling-profile score	2.176	.859	2.284	.514	.452
Post-counseling-profile score	2.146	.992	1.992	.338	.592
t-ratio between means in same column	.136		2.584		

the mean of the pre-counseling-profile-agreement scores and the mean of the post-counseling-profile-agreement scores for the multiple counseled group is significant at the .05 level, no other difference between the means in Table 5 is significant. This analysis of the data appears to favor the conclusion that multiple counseling is more effective in terms of the criterion than is individual counseling. These data also point out that the individual and multiple counseled were very similar both before and after counseling.

In addition to the criterion described, a supplementary criterion based on counselee rating of counselor helpfulness was also used. Counselees rated on a five-point scale the amount of help they thought they had received from the counselor. This criterion was used to determine if the counselees would be more favorably impressed by an individual interview than by the group situation. Some counselors believe that because a counselee gets individual attention in a private interview a situation is created in which he feels comfortable and is helped thereby to move toward counseling objectives. On the other hand, these counselors view the group situation as threatening and productive of negative attitudes toward the process. After the ratings were converted to numerical values in the manner previously described, the mean of the individual counseled group was found to be 4.06 and the standard deviation equaled .56. The multiple counseled group was found to have a mean of 3.94, the standard deviation was .68. A t-test of the difference between means revealed that it was not statistically significant. The subjects in both groups were apparently not different in their evaluation of their counselor's helpfulness.

DISCUSSION

Of course, like other studies of counseling effectiveness the criteria used in this study may be questioned because they do not indicate what actions the counselee took as a result of counseling. But if self-knowledge is a necessary prelude to intelligent planning and doing, then the self-rating criterion has the endorsement of a logical approach.

The writer recognizes the limitations imposed upon the conclusions by the smallness of the sample, the use of a single test, and similar shortcomings. Nevertheless, the data presented in this report point to one major conclusion: Insofar as the criteria used in this study reflect desirable counseling outcomes, the findings do not support the claim that counseling must be individual.

.... 69 ....

AN EXPERIMENTAL SOCIOGRAPHIC STUDY OF A STRATIFIED TENTH-GRADE CLASS

by Lloyd Allen Cook

One method of learning more about the relationships between members of a group is by social mapping, or sociometry. The map, or sociogram, is constructed on the basis of the choices of one group member by another. In the following two year study, Lloyd Allen Cook of Wayne University shows, by means of sociograms, the extent to which individual counseling procedures and group activity projects change the friendship structure and further the social adjustment of a group of high-school pupils. [From *American Sociological Review*, 1945, *10*, 250-261. Reprinted by permission of the author and the American Sociological Society. Some of the footnotes have been omitted.]

A year ago, we described a projected study of a 10th grade high school class, indicating some initial finding (Cook, 1943). In June, 1944, this work was concluded and the present paper is an overall report. Though similar studies are now in process, we shall confine discussion to the Crestview project. The viewpoint is that of an educational sociologist, interested in understanding child groups and peer cultures, and the work was done under a number of very practical limitations.

I

At a state educational conference in September, 1942, the writer spoke on the use of sociographic methods. Among the school people expressing interest were two former graduate students, one a social studies teacher, the other the personnel officer, at the Crestview High School. As the study project shaped up, these persons, along with the principal and the writer, became the planning group, making decisions over the two year period.

The group selected was a 10th grade social studies class. It enrolled at the outset 44 pupils, all but seven of the eligible 15 year olds in the school. The course was a flexible "core type" course, with students accustomed to planning units of study, making class trips and the like. No changes were made except that the teacher was to go with the class into its 11th year.

Objectives for the first year of study were three. We wanted to determine, by sociographic test, the friendship structure of the group, comparing first and second semester sociograms for changes and stabilities. We wanted also to stratify these 44 adolescents by use of the Warner technic of social class analysis, and thirdly, to see what light these status data would throw on "best friend" choices. With these base lines known, the second year experimental program could be started. Its general aim was "to improve the learning situation by democratizing pupil attitudes and behaviors."

For the first semester, the approach was to be via individual guidance, for the second group management, with effects in either case to be noted in group and individual sociograms.

As a community, Crestview cannot be exactly typed. Though a kind of residential suburb, it has a thriving socioeconomic life of its own. It is a small midwestern town of about 4,500, not far from a large city. Three fourths of its people are native white of native parentage with the remainder about equally foreign born and Negro. Since mid-1942, over a third of its wage workers have been employed in city war plants. Close to a hundred family heads own their own business or are in professions. Over half of these are active members of the "old crowd," in distinction to the "new crowd," two thirds of whom have lived in Crestview for five years or more. At least three fifths of all families are said to "own" their own homes, with property values ranging from $3,500 to over $25,000. Wealth is concentrated in the "old crowd," with five or six kin groups reported as "running the town." A sense of "old family," while much less evident than in New England or the South, is distinctly present. There are some but not many exclusive cliques and clubs.

As participants in civic affairs, through home visits and other contacts as supplemented by small but pointed school-made surveys, we had hoped to stratify large segments of the adult population, even to construct skeletal sociograms. Both of these tasks proved too much for us, though some work was done. Without concretizing, we were satisfied after three months of observation as to the very probable existence of a three level class system. We judged that three fifths of all families were middle class, about 70 families were identified as upper or near upper class, with the remainder low class. Rough though these estimates were, we believed them to be satisfactory for our purpose.

II

Since we would need a number of sociograms of the same high school group, it seemed best to make an indirect approach. We drew up a one page blank on "extracurricular activities," giving it with minor changes each semester to various classroom groups. Students were told that their reactions, for example fewer assemblies, more dances, would be passed on to the student council, a promise on which we always made good. Midway on the blank were the two sociometric questions. One asked for the names of best friends in school, "one, two, three or more as you like," and the other for the names of boys and girls "about your own age, whom you don't like so well, don't care to associate with." We thought these questions would be overshadowed by extra curricular concerns which, on repeated check, proved to be the case. The task of stratifying these youngsters was not solved to our satisfaction. We had Warner and Lunt's (1941) book, in addition to the writer's contacts with this group. We used in all three kinds of data, the first relating to *pupil home backgrounds*. Starting with 30 odd items, we tested and came to use ten: location of home, number of rooms, length of residence, number of servants, parental educational status, father's occupation, approximate annual income, mother's sociocivic clubs, family magazine subscriptions, and family's social prominence. On the latter item, each home was rated by five or more adults who knew the family well, usually of the same social class level.

Our second set of data defined the *pupil's reputation among his peers*. By use of a two-page form, followed as needed in the school's continuous "guidance checkups," we secured reactions to an array of "guess who," "show me" and social distance items. For instance, "who always thinks about keeping very clean, well dressed and tidy," or the reverse. Or on the "show me" test, after describing an out-of-class incident calling for pupil leadership, we asked for leader names. Our general hypothesis was that each adult social class instills into children its own norms and values, its ways of living. The intent was not to measure these subcultures but to sample child expressions of them, to get pupil ratings on such items as dress, grooming, language usages, moral ideals, and boy-girl conduct. Thus a child named as dirty, or "smart aleck," or "real leader," might or might not be so, yet he must make his adjustment to the group in terms of his reputation.

Since these tests sought only reputational ratings, they would not appear to need validation in the sense of comparison with external criteria. On internal consistency as judged by several of our colleagues and on inter-test comparisons, they came well up to expectations. Their reliability, as inferred from similar studies, was rather high. For instance, Tryon (1943, p. 548) reports test-retest correlations on the "guess-who" for 7th grade boys and girls .76 and .80. Newsletter (1938, p. 36), studying summer camp groups in successive weeks by the Moreno test, found an average .5. Zeleny (1939, p. 804), using the same test with college students, .8 and .95; and Jennings (1943, p. 31), in a retest of a cottage unit of girls, .96 for positive choices and .93 for negative.

Our third type of data, in some ways the most revealing, came from observations as to *who ran with whom* as an equal and an intimate. We simply kept a record of these associations at school, in school affairs, student hangouts, etc., placing each 10th grader in reference to associates of a known high, middle or low prestige rank. Marginal cases were left as marginal, a practice followed throughout the study.

In using these several kinds of data to bracket children in class levels, we did not proceed in any mechanical fashion. In every case, we used our combined best judgment in assigning a prestige rating, thus introducing a subjective element but one that was known, hence under some control.

III

The two group sociograms, Figures 1 and 2, were the major products of our initial year of work. They hold two points of general interest. The first point, as seen in Figure 1, is the basic structure of this 'teen age group. Here are the usual sociographic patterns—the *isolate,* W, Will, B, Bob, etc. not chosen as a friend by any classmate; the *pair,* U-V, Una and Violet a mutual choice; the *chain,* R-Ro-M, Ralph *et al.,* a series of one way choices; and the "cluster" with its "star." This "cluster" we shall call a *clique* and there are two types. The H or H-T grouping, Howie and Tom, is an open clique with leader role constant but members shifting and authority shared, whereas the G, George, clique is closed. Leadership is centered and autocratic and members are unchanging. There is also in the sociogram the *all-group leader,* notably L, Lois, although no *factions* as Whyte (1943) described them in street corner gangs are evident.

The above interpersonal and subgroupal network is, in general, about what we are coming to expect in 'teen age classrooms in primary communities. Almost three fourths of all positive choices, in sum 96, fell within the 10th grade, and all within the school. A majority were within own sex, own status level, with *out choices* being most common in boy-girl attractions, *up choices* most frequent in claims on high ranking "stars" by middle class children. Negative choices, while not depicted in any of our published sociograms, were more or less the reverse of these trends.

Questionnaire data show that upper class children received far more than their fair share of choices on every positive reputational item, for example best dressed, best liked, most fun, and real leader. At the opposite extreme, low class children were seldom mentioned except by other low class children. In negative ratings, these latter pupils were named with great frequency by upper and middle levels as "not liked," "dirty, smelly," "fights a lot" and

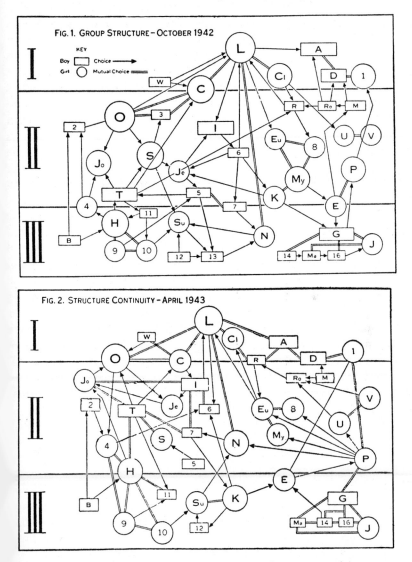

FIG. 1. GROUP STRUCTURE – OCTOBER 1942

FIG. 2. STRUCTURE CONTINUITY – APRIL 1943

"dumb." Middle class children cast as a rule more positive votes for top level friends than for their own rank order, viewing both levels as "sharp," "rugged" or "solid," in contrast to bottom level "drips" and "jerks." The phrase most often used by the latter in referring to most upper level children was "the sissies," the "sissy crowd."

The second point of interest in the sociograms is the relative stability of the classroom structure over six months of time. This is seen by comparing Figures 1 and 2. For example, Lois is still the pert little queen, though Olive is in better position to contest her leadership. Bob, a crippled boy, names the same two friends but is still unnamed by anyone. The George clique, while a bit more unified, is much the same. All in all, *stabilities in contrast to changes are about five times as numerous.* R, Ralph, has moved to, or into, top status ranking, the children whom three out of each five middle class mothers want their own youngsters to have as friends. T, Tom, star athlete and social extrovert, is a fine example of middle class talent mobility, E, Eloise, a quasi-member of the rowdy George clique, has lost status, due chiefly to a newly acquired reputation as a "bad girl."

Enough has been said, perhaps, about these sociograms to show that we are dealing with a structured universe, a network of "attractions and repulsions" that underlies the official organization of the class. Each child must live in these twin worlds, informal and formal, where behavioral norms are not readily, if at all transferable. Each has a position to maintain, a role to play, a status to advance, although the question of how this is done is beyond the scope of the paper. In general, the classroom system is a three way product—a creation of the children, an imposition of adult status values, and a result of teacher middle-class rewards and punishments. It seeks of course, like every social system, to preserve itself, or concretely to assimilate teacher rule, deflect or defeat it. Though frozen for the moment, it is anything but static. It is an ever shifting equilibrium, a struggle process, a competitive effort to better one's self in peer ratings.

IV

It was from thinking of this sort that we set up the second year work. The aim, as was said, was to create a better learning situation, a more democratic atmosphere, by use first of *individual guidance.* Our discussions of democracy, good teaching and the like, can be omitted. By guidance, we came to mean "adjusting the individual to the group," a phrase whose operational content can be sensed by noting its application to cases. It was agreed that we must work, not only on individuals, but through individuals, else guidance could not be distinguished from group management, for the latter also envisioned personality changes. Thus the variables under test were technics not assumptions, purposes, etc., the one set psychological, the other sociological, keeping the two as separate as possible.

Assuming that no teacher could do much with forty odd students, we began to spot experimental cases. B, Bob, and J, Julie, were to be "integrated into the group." The George clique was to be "broken up." N, Nancy, P, Pat, and J, Jan, were fairly obvious "sex problems." U-V, Una and Violet, a tightly woven "crush relation," were in need of a wider circle of friends. L, Lois, we felt should be "dethroned" and taught a more honest and pervasive concern for her classmates. O, Olive, was to be guided toward increasing responsibility as a group leader. It was here, about half way through our cases, that unanimity ended. This is, no doubt, a way of saying that our problems changed character. They were no longer commonsense and behavioral but deeply internal and attitudinal. For example, T, Tom, and K, Katie, were both well-liked middle class children extremely sociable and upwardly mobile. And yet, as we cannot show here, each was a prime personality problem. Tom revealed a "rigid or conscientious" character structure, Katie a "temperamental or scattered" structure and both were in need of help.

In all, 15 subjects were selected, marked in Figure 3 with a bar. Six were boys, 9 were girls; 3 upper class, 7 middle and 5 lower. Age range was from 15 to 17 years; IQ, 90 to 115, with two cases above normal grade placement and two below. Three were social isolates, one an aggressive clique leader, three were sex problems, one a domineering class leader, three talented potential leaders, two in an unhealthy pair relation, and the remainder subjective personality problems. We did not regard these adolescents then, nor do we now, as anything other than a minerun sample of almost any high school class.

Our aim was not to force changes on any child. We did not, however, try to set up an honestly "permissive environment" (Allen, 1943, Chap. 3), if such is ever possible, or to engage in "nondirective therapy." Our task was to guide these children—to give direction, meaning and support to the changes *they willed* to make. Our technic was almost wholly the private conference, a guided interchange of ideas; adaptive, emotionalized and suggestive but not, we believe, too insistently so. From five to ten sessions were held with each child, each lasting from 15 to 30 minutes or over. No child was told that he had been singled out for study, and we had a perfect cover in the recurring "guidance checkups" for all students.

It was with George, the clique leader, that we scored our great failure, and a fragment of an interview will suggest our general procedure. Rough and tough and happy in his role, George remained negative to the last, until in fact the Army took him over.

Guidance Conference: A Segment

G. Here comes George, bad old George. I'll flop here. (Pulls a chair to window, sits with his back to the teacher.)

T. Hello, George, you know I like to talk with you. Do you like to come here?

G. Ok, Ok, I guess. No need to. Not a need. . . .

T. Well, I've been thinking about this. What are you going to do when you finish school?

G. (No reply. Picks up a magazine and thumbs pages.)

T. Tom says he's going to war. He is going to be . . . .

G. (Interrupting.) I don't care what . . . I got my eye on something. A bomber pilot. . . .

T. Then you'd have a crew, wouldn't you. I read a story about that. The pilot and crew were a team.

G. (Finds picture of Fortress. Studies it.)

T. It was in England. . . . The crew liked that pilot. He got along with everybody. . . . They would do anything for him. Once, over Bremen . . . . That took courage, didn't it, courage and teamwork?

G. Yeh. He had what it takes. He ran his gang. He told 'em what. Nobody argued back.

T. There was a big dance one night at the base. Lots of girls were there . . . Everybody liked the pilot. He was friendly and got along with everybody.

G. I can take care of myself. I run my gang. Let the rest of them (the class) go hang.

T. I didn't tell you all about that pilot. He had a problem, a tough one. . . . He wasn't afraid to talk things over. It takes courage to do that.

G. Who's afraid? I ain't afraid. I'm stubborn, that's what. I'm stubborn.

T. That pilot was stubborn when the flak hit. Remember? That wasn't bad, was it?

G. Naw, hold on. Hold on and fight, fight, fight.

T. Should one change his course sometimes, like the pilot did? You know, be a little different, a better leader?

G. The sissies (referring to his own classmates).

T. Tom likes you. Others like you. I would make a bet that . . . .
G. (Rises; kicks at chair. With an "I'll be seein' ya," he starts toward the door.)

This is a segment of the sixth interview, each a little more direct. It can be argued that we did not know how to deal with George, which is quite correct. In all fairness, George was no easy boy to affect. Out of one scrap into another, his clique broke into an unoccupied house just after this conference. They drew crude sex symbols on the walls, carried away removable fixtures, and built a fire on an upstairs hardwood floor. They made a pallet out of old blankets and, with Jan, engaged in sex intimacies. A name on a piece of paper gave the thing away. George's father, as did other dads, professed complete surprise. His most revealing remark was: "I didn't know the kid was doin' nothin'. I'm gonna lick h--l outa him twice a week, reg'lar."

We failed with George but how and why are still conjectural. In our opinion, we worked on a false premise. The boy was a star in every sport, a school hero of first rank importance. Having great prestige in the school at large, he could be indifferent to, or aggressive toward, classmates and teacher. Neither class nor teacher had anything to offer him that he wanted, no way to motivate status strivings, to shake his supreme self confidence, hence the learning (or integrative) process could not get started. Our mistake was not to recognize his solid anchorage in the school and to work from this angle.

V

What can be said, in general, about our success or failure in using individual guidance? It will be evident, in comparing Figures 3 and 2, that Lois is less popular, less in position to swing the class as she likes. Olive has advanced in best friend choices into a place of all-class leadership, an effect we worked for. Bob, the isolate, has made one mutual friend and been named by one classmate. Julie and Dan, also isolates, have done less well, yet some outreaching is apparent. Tom and Ikie have won acceptance from higher ranking peers, with the Jewish boy the major link between the nascent Olive and Lois factions. Lois has dropped Nancy, a newcomer to the community and a distant relative, to check her own imminent downward movement, and Nancy has begun to make middle class friends. Elizabeth has broken with the George clique and Katie also seems to be leaving bottom level associates.

Of equal interest are the changes we did not make, the attractions and repulsions too strong for us. The George clique is better integrated than before, with one new member. While Jan is on the way out, Pat or Nancy is likely to take her place. Pat, in particular, is in an insecure position. Her individual sociogram, for instance, shows that she names 13 classmates as best friends and rejects 5, whereas no one, except George and Nancy, names or rejects her. Such a gap between self conceptions and group acceptance, is not uncommon (Jennings, 1943, pp. 166-169), but in this case it is, at least in part, an effect of guidance, an overstress on friend making. Una and Violet remain inseparable, with only the latter showing any effect of our efforts.

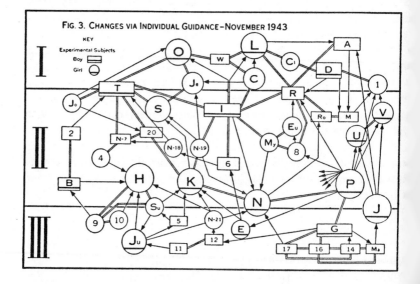

FIG. 3. CHANGES VIA INDIVIDUAL GUIDANCE—NOVEMBER 1943

Changes of another type should be mentioned, alterations not intended and over which we had no control. For example, Josephine, a confidant of Olive, has moved inside a four-way upper status grouping, a cluster of leaders united against, more or less, the Lois faction. In this faction, Ralph has assumed a key position, a mediator role between lesser units on both sides, a part as our case materials show that he plays to perfection. Arthur, the young *H. M. Pulham, Esq.* of Crestview's youthful elite society, cannot quite make up his mind to become a real fellow, to make and keep friends below his station in life. The fact that he is named by Jan, the *Kitty Foyle* of the group, is more than we can explain

VI

We shall turn now to what is, perhaps, the most interesting part of the experiment, the *group management approach*. While an eye was kept on changes in process, our target was in truth the whole group. The aim was to teach what someone called "the spirit of willing cooperation," an ideal running counter to dominant core values in our culture, hence not easy of achievement (Cook, 1940).

Assuming that these attitudes and skills could not be taught, or well taught, by teacher talk, or by sitting and listening, we planned to start "activity projects" in which all pupils would want to participate. A large measure of power, the power of decision, was to be lodged within the group, and the group guided in using this power in the interest of all class members. We believed, with Slavson (1943, Chap. 6), that a child group could learn how to control its members, yet we could not go all the way with him in creating a "permissive environment." Our concept of teacher role was patterned closely on Lippitt's (1940), "democratic group leader," though it varied somewhat with the situation. End results were to be pictured in sociograms and, as usual, explanatory data collected via questionnaire, case studies and group observation.

During this last semester, we made use of three types of projects. The first consisted of *fun parties* of which there were seven, such as after-game hayrides and stunt nights. Each was organized by the class with only incidental help from the teacher. The second type of project comprised war service activities, of which there were three, and the third two rather stumbling attempts at "role practice" (Zander and Lippitt, 1944).

War service projects can be illustrated by a two weeks "scrap hunt." The teacher had "wondered" at two class meetings if the group "could help more" in current war activities. The idea of collecting scrap—paper, tinfoil, razor blades, rubber, etc., arose the next class meeting. It was proposed by Howie and supported once by Olive and Tom. Seeing that it stood to win a following, the writer began to make rough notes. While a flow chart of this sort fills several pages, excerpts from it will help to define the group process.

A SCRAP DRIVE: SEGMENTS OF GROUP PROCESS

Defining the situation (2nd session)

Lois: Each one bring stuff. (Superior air; unenthused.)

Howie: No, not that way. Bring lots and lots of stuff to help win the war. Everybody.

Lois: You can, all you want. Bring what you want.

Teacher: Is the idea to make a real drive, an all-out drive?

Class: Yes, yes. (Nods; no opposition.)

Olive: Oh, I would like that. It would be fun. Can we?

Howie: Sure, like I said. Let's get going.

Tom: What we need is organization, like on a team.

Pat: Go every place and ask everybody in town. . . .

Tom: But first we need organization. Got to have that. . . .

Lois: Who will be president to run it?

Nancy: Ask Miss E——— (teacher). Who, Miss E———?

Teacher: Well, in our country we vote our choices. We elect our leaders.

Sue: Yes, we elect. I nominate Tom.

Ralph: I nominate Lois.

Tom: I nominate Olive.

(Others named. First ballot: Tom 12; Lois 14; Olive 10. Second ballot: Tom 22; Lois 14.)

Organizing the group (3rd session)

Tom: Let's get going. I guess we need some committees. (Goes to blackboard.) What gangs do we want?

Dan: Committee on junk.

Tom: Let's break that up. One on waste paper, that's one. (Four areas are defined. Lois, then Olive, chooses a committee and these fill up.)

Tom: Wait a minute. There's two other committees. . . .

Pat: I could take the one on tinfoil and stuff.

Tom: You be on it. Let each team elect its captain.

Teacher: Will we need a group on transportation and one on publicity?

Tom. Sure. Katie you be on publicity? Who'll see about trucking the stuff? You, George?

George: Thanks, pal. That's work.

Ikie: Dad's got two trucks. Guess he'd loan 'em to us.

Tom: OK. (Writes Ikie's name down.) Now what else?

Maintaining morale (6th session)

Tom: Now we'll have committee reports. Ikie.

Ikie: All set for Saturday. Got two trucks and need four more loaders.

Tom: Who can go along? (Two volunteers.) Dan? Howie?

Dan: No can do. Sorry.

Tom: Well, we can't flop now. Got the stuff and we gotta get it in. Dad said it's the best thing the school has ever done for the town. . . .

Howie: I'll go if you'll go, Tom.

Teacher: Tom works Saturdays (at a store). Is there anybody who will go with Howie?

Sue: Will said he'd go.

Will: Sure. You come on too, Sue?

Sue: I'll go.

Tom: Good work, gang, good work. Now for another committee.

Julie: People don't know about fats. . . . Mom didn't.

Pat: Our committee seen everybody, most everybody. (Committee on fats.)

Julie: Not mom, I know.

Teacher: Do you have a list of places where you've been?

Pat: No, we didn't make any. We tried to do a good job.

Tom: Ok, Pat, you've done ok. Let's check where your gang has been. . . .

Evaluating results (9th session)

Tom: Quiet down, quiet down. This is our last meeting unless you want to go on. Lots of scrap to get in.

Sue: I'm for going on. . . .

Lois: Let's do something exciting. Have some fun.

Nancy: Ask teacher what. What, Miss E———?

Teacher: I've been amazed at the work you've all done.

Tom: Work and sweat, like the guy said.

Teacher: Has it all been worth doing? I wonder if it has.

Katie: Look at the stuff we've got. (At Tom's prompting, reads amounts collected.)

Olive: Fine, Katie, fine. It looks good to me. Let's go on.

Nancy: I like this better'n studying. You learn more.

Teacher: More of what, would you say?

Bob: Getting stuff in. Doing your part. Being ok.

Tom: Like a team, I'd say. We put it over. The town can count on us.

Teacher: Yes, it was a big job and all of you put it over. Every team-mate did his part.

George: Old razzle dazzle. I don't go for that.

Dan: Dad said it's ok. We oughta go on and finish up.

Howie: I move we go on. (A chorus of seconds.)

George: Ok, suckers. Include me out.

Such work stands in sharp contrast to formalistic, or parliamentary, efforts at teaching group action as observed in many classrooms, and on the other hand, to the several kinds of make-believe play games so lacking in reality. While member roles invite detailed comment, we shall simply state the general theory. Our aim was to teach the class how to manage the group process, *to work together as a self directing team with a job to do*. The teacher's role was, in the main, to lead the leaders, to see them face choices and make "mistakes," at least to the point where the total project was endangered (Cook, 1941). And then, in terms of our theory, intervention was necessary. Education was to be guided so that more education could go on. Thus a group of this sort is not unlike democracy itself—always falling apart and always, we hope, being saved in the nick of time.

Our third approach to group management was via *role practice.* Hendry's (1944) work is fully descriptive of our less mature efforts. We started with a persistent gripe, the ever present "youth problem." Why does Crestview have youth problems? Why doesn't somebody do something? After a little warming up, student ideas came as fast as they could be written down. These wants, wishes, tensions, etc., formed the basis for a series of character parts, or roles, each with a central emphasis. Students built them up out of their own experiences and a listing will suggest something of their essential nature.

Some Character Parts: The Youth Problem

Father, no interest	Father Crestview, go slow
Mother, chronic worry	Aver. boy, "nothing to do"
Minister, bad morals	Aver. girl, "nowhere
Business man, costs	to go"
Farmer, work, work	Youth leader, modern
Police, "whatya up to"	ideas, a youth program
Sch. supt., discipline	

We cannot overstress the realism with which these roles were enacted in two experimental sessions. There was no rehearsal, no coaching, the flow of conversation being impromptu. In these discussions, the leader took no part until, at last, he stopped the session for a role analysis. In this appraisal the class, forewarned, joined with the participants in judging character parts as to representativeness, consistency and the like with the teacher guiding their analyses and projections. What might have been done over time with this approach, we were never to know at Crestview, due to our own bad judgment. Impressed with our second session, the principal invited the group to "put on the show" in assembly. The thing fell flat. Students either made long-winded speeches or else sat speechless, and all of us lost interest in the sociodrama. We have since profited by this mistake.

VII

The combined effect of these three approaches to group integration is seen in Figure 4. This sociogram is very different from any other. It differs, first of all, in that the class is now definitely *factionalized.* We had not intended this effect, in fact foresaw it and tried to guard against it. While interpretations of its meaning will differ, we do not believe that this structure is undemocratic. It is, for instance, quite like American communities, with special interests, large and small pressure groupings. Its opposite would be, in one form, an unorganized, amorphous mass, quite incapable of concerted action.

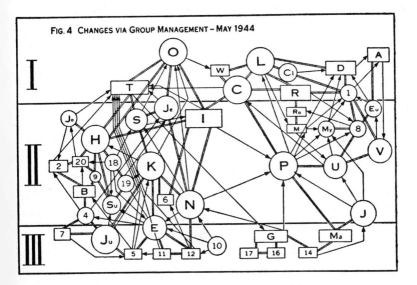

FIG. 4 CHANGES VIA GROUP MANAGEMENT – MAY 1944

Another striking feature of the sociogram is the *increased volume of social interaction*. This can be seen best by reference to Table 1. From October 1942 to May 1944 the average number of best

TABLE 1

AVERAGE NUMBER OF TIMES BY SOCIAL CLASS LEVEL THAT CRESTVIEW 10TH GRADE STUDENTS CHOOSE AND ARE CHOSEN AS BEST FRIENDS OVER A TWO YEAR PERIOD.

Social class	October 1942		April 1943		November 1943		May 1944		Average	
	Chooses	Chosen	Chooses	Chosen	Chooses	Chosen	Chooses	Chosen	Chooses	Chosen
Upper	2.57	3.43	2.55	3.77	3.45	4.27	3.81	4.81	3.18	4.13
Middle	2.21	2.08	2.80	3.05	4.00	4.30	5.10	5.04	3.54	3.60
Lower	2.64	2.42	3.23	2.00	3.28	2.21	3.91	3.25	3.24	2.45
Average	2.40	2.40	2.80	2.80	3.64	3.64	4.51	4.51	—	—

friend choices increased from 2.40 to 2.80, 3.64 and 4.51.[1] Thus the trend toward greater contact is clear, and the last two averages in particular are significant. Even more revealing are comparative totals for the two school years. For the first year, 1942-43, when

[1]Again, for lack of space, the September 1943 average, 2.24, has been omitted. In all respects, and as to be expected, September data approximate those for October 1942.

no experimentation was attempted, friendship choices averaged 2.64; for the second year, 4.80. That this increase was due pretty largely to individual guidance and group management is, we believe, a reasonable conclusion. It could hardly be due to a carryover from the first year, for these same youngsters have lived and played and gone to school together most of their life.

Table 1 is of interest for still other reasons. While these high school juniors did not vary greatly or uniformly, by social level in the number of choices made, the same cannot be said for direction of choice. At every sampling period over the two years, upper class children were "over chosen," whereas lower class boys and girls were "under chosen." Put otherwise, *the trend in friend making is upward,* not outward or downward. This phenomenon, with all that it implies, is a basic feature of the adult class system, thus the school group parallels the environing social order.

Figure 4 shows various *positional changes* which we shall not take the time to analyze out. The George clique, for example, is disintegrating. After resisting a host of pressures for the two years, it is splitting up from within. While it may be incorrect to claim credit for this effect, an activity program such as the one described, does churn up a group. It sets going new currents and cross-currents of influence, enforcing new adjustments. And yet, to repeat an earlier inference, the impressive thing is not the changes in but the stability of group structure.

VIII

With schools moving steadily toward social learning, a study of this sort has practical values. Dare one claim to have taught co-operation, to have democratized a classroom, without pre- and end-test measures? Sociograms, with or without status level research, provide a simple indicator of changes, a base line from which to plan individual and group guidance. Moreover, they will bring our all too often chaotic "activity programs" under some kind of control, an imperative if we are to get anywhere in any sort of directive teaching.

Aside from its practical nature, the Crestview study has implications for the growing field of child socialization. Admitting the need for better methods, we believe none the less that *our data support the hypothesis of class level stratification among 'teen age children.* So far this idea, when advanced at all, has rested on fragmental case studies which have been made, in turn, the basis for rather sweeping generalizations. Quantification, along with clearer conceptual definition, are on the way and greatly needed. In comparison with what is known about individual personality variants, we know little about the simplest subgroupal structures, for example pairs, chains, cliques and factions. This is, we believe, a fertile field for the educational sociologist.

•••••••••••••••••••••••••••••• **70** ••••••••••••••••••••••••••••••

AN EVALUATION OF GROUP AND INDIVIDUAL

PROGRAMS IN VOCATIONAL GUIDANCE

by Donald P. Hoyt

How effective is a group vocational guidance program as compared with an individual program? On the basis of four criteria of success, Donald P. Hoyt of Kansas State College finds no differences between the effectiveness of the individual counseling program and the group program. The practicality of instituting group programs in vocational guidance is discussed. [From *Journal of Applied Psychology*, 1955, *39*, 26-30. Reprinted by permission of the author and the American Psychological Association.]

Counselors seldom complain about a shortage of clients. Rather, appointment books are usually filled for a week, two weeks, or even a month in advance. Probably this state of affairs underestimates the demand, and if more time could be found, the number of applicants for counseling would increase rapidly.

But a realistic look at the situation reveals that hopes of alleviating this pressure through an increased staff are small because of both the lack of trained counselors and necessary budget restrictions. One solution that suggests itself is dealing with clients in groups.

Stone (1948) and Richardson and Borow (1952) have demonstrated the usefulness of group procedures in preparing clients for individual vocational counseling. Although a few experiential and theoretical reports have appeared in the literature (e.g., Baer, 1947; Lasoff, 1952), little experimentation with the use of groups in vocational and educational planning has been done.

A recent report of such an experiment (Bilovsky, *et al.*, 1953)

showed that high school seniors who participated in a group vocational guidance program made just as realistic vocational choices
as did those who had individual counseling. Unfortunately, a control group was not provided, so that these results could be attributed
to an equal *ineffectiveness* of both procedures. An unpublished study
by Nissenson (1948) investigated the effects of a group vocation
guidance program with high school boys. The study was well controlled, and the major findings indicated that the program was
effective in fulfilling the following objectives: (a) an increased awareness on the part of the subjects (Ss) of the need for help in career
planning; (b) an increased use of individual counseling services;
(c) an increased reading of occupational literature; and (d) an
increased understanding of the occupations tentatively chosen.

Such studies provide us with justifications for looking further into
the matter of working in groups with vocationally undecided students. The present study is a step in that direction.

OBJECTIVES OF THE GROUP PROGRAM

A committee of the University of Minnesota Student Counseling
Bureau counselors[1] met to consider the question of objectives for a
group vocational guidance program. It was decided that if we hope
to make use of groups as economical substitutes for individual vocational counseling, the objectives should be similar in both types of
programs. Four objectives were designated: These were to increase:
(a) satisfaction with vocational choice, (b) certainty of vocational
choice, (c) realism of vocational choice, and (d) the appropriateness
of certainty in terms of realism.

The latter objective was included because it was felt that if an
individual merely became more certain of an unrealistic choice
after counseling, the counseling was not effective. Therefore, we fel
that (a) for realistic choices, certainty should increase, and (b) for
unrealistic choices, certainty should decrease.

HYPOTHESES

The major hypothesis of the study was that participation in

[1] The author wishes to express his appreciation to Dr. Ralph Berdie and th
entire Student Counseling Bureau staff for their cooperation in planning an
carrying out this research.

group vocational guidance program is associated with achievement of the four objectives listed above.

A second hypothesis was that participation in an individual vocational counseling program is associated with achievement of the four objectives.

Thirdly, it was hypothesized that students participating in groups would not differ from students participating in individual counseling in the achievement of the four objectives.

METHOD

Sample

Names of freshman men who had indicated that they were undecided about their vocational plans at the beginning of the school year were obtained from a student information sheet collected by the Office of the Dean of Students. These students were invited to participate in the group program which had been planned. Students who were interested returned a post card on which they indicated what their tentative vocational choice was, how certain they felt of it, and how satisfied they were with this choice. A total of 191 returns were obtained.

Those students who were unable to attend at the scheduled times were eliminated from the sample and invited to make individual counseling appointments. In addition, records in the Student Counseling Bureau were checked, and students who had been counseled there earlier in the year or who had incomplete test records were also eliminated from the sample. The remaining 60 students composed the sample.

Procedure

These 60 students were divided into three groups: 30 Group Experimentals, who were to participate in the groups; 15 Individual Experimentals, who were to receive the typical individual vocational counseling provided at the Student Counseling Bureau; and 15 Controls, who were to participate in neither the group nor individual program during the experimental period. Assignments to these groups were made by a random method.

The Individual Experimentals and the Controls were individually contacted by telephone, and it was explained that the requests to participate in the group program had exceeded our expectations and that the groups were already full. Individual Experimentals were invited to take advantage of the individual counseling facilities of the Counseling Bureau and appointments were made for them. An apology was offered to the Controls, and a promise to include them in the next quarter's program was made (and subsequently kept).

The experimental treatment for the Individual Experimentals consisted of the typical counseling methods of the Student Counseling Bureau (Williamson, 1950). Fourteen of the 15 students kept the first appointment,[2] and the average number of appointments was 2.6. Thus, about 39 counseling hours were used on this group.

For the Group Experimentals, the procedure was as follows: The students first attended an introductory lecture of about 30 minutes in which the general problem of choosing a vocation was discussed. Brief mention was made of the importance of a knowledge of one's own abilities, interests, values, and personality characteristics, as well as a knowledge of jobs. Pitfalls in self-analysis were pointed out, and the values of group discussion and of the give and take within a group were stressed.

Then small discussion groups of from five to seven students were formed, and individual counselors acted as group leaders. Each student was provided with a copy of his Strong Vocational Interest test results, and frequently this provided the stimulus material for discussion. Just as frequently a short questionnaire the students had filled out prior to the group lecture stimulated the discussion. After about 30 minutes the students were told that the time for the meeting had ended, and arrangements were made for further group meetings for those who were interested.

Twelve groups were formed. A total of 79 students participated in these groups. Fifty-four of these students were not included in the experiment for one or more of the reasons cited earlier; the other 25 were originally selected as Group Experimentals.[3] The 12 groups met an average of 2.3 times after the first meeting with a range of from one to six hours, so that about 34 hours of counselor time were involved in dealing with these 79 students.

Six weeks after the last meeting of any group, all 60 experimental

---

[2] The one student who failed to keep his appointment was retained in the experimental sample in order to keep motivation for counseling equal for control and experimental groups.

[3] Five students originally selected as Group Experimentals attended no meetings but they were included as part of the sample in order to keep motivation for counseling constant for control and experimental groups.

Ss were again contacted and asked to fill out another card indicating their current vocational choice, how certain they were of it, and how satisfied they were with it. A 100 per cent return was obtained. In order to avoid as much as possible the "hello-goodbye" effect (Hathaway, 1948), the students were told that this was a study of the development of vocational choices during the freshman year. No mention was made of the experiment except that the students were reminded that information concerning their vocational choices had been collected earlier for a different purpose.

Measuring Instruments

Changes in certainty and satisfaction could readily be analyzed since the student himself provided a quantitative rating on an 11-point scale. Realism of vocational choice was not so easily measured. The clinical judgment of experienced vocational counselors was used.[4] The data provided to these judges were as follows: (a) scores on the Strong Vocational Interest test; (b) scores on the 1947 edition of the ACE psychological examination; (c) the student's high school rank; (d) scores on the Cooperative English test, Form S; (e) grades earned during the first year in college; (f) special aptitude tests, including the General Aptitude Test Battery for 21 students, the Ohio Psychological for 24 students, and engineering aptitude tests for 13 students; (g) a biographical data sheet, which included a summary of work experiences, hobbies, family background, and extracurricular participations; and (h) the two vocational choices made by the student. Naturally the judges did not know if they were judging an experimental or a control S; neither did they know which choice represented the pretest and which represented the posttest.

A realistic choice was defined as one in which the probability was high that the student could complete the necessary training, could find employment in the chosen job, and would succeed and remain in this work over a period of years. The judges were asked to rate each choice as to whether or not it was realistic. Then they were asked to indicate how certain they were of this rating on an 11-point certainty scale. If a choice was rated as "unrealistic" and the counselor making the rating was "very certain," the choice was given a score of —11. If the choice was rated as "realistic" and the judge was

[4] Special thanks are due to Miss Alice Christian, Dr. Theda Hagenah, Dr. Vivian Hewer, Mr. James Lyon, Dr. Mabel Powers, and Dr. Cornelia Williams for contributing their time to this part of the project.

TABLE 1
MEANS AND STANDARD DEVIATIONS OF PRE- AND POSTTEST SCORES ON
FOUR CRITERIA OF SUCCESS IN VOCATIONAL GUIDANCE

Criteria		Control (N = 15)		Individual Experimentals (N = 15)		Group Experimentals (N = 30)	
		Pretest	Posttest	Pretest	Posttest	Pretest	Posttest
Certainty	M	5.40	5.33	5.80	7.60	4.93	6.50
	SD	2.3	2.4	2.1	1.8	2.7	2.0
Satisfaction	M	6.93	6.13	6.67	8.20	6.70	7.77
	SD	2.6	1.9	2.4	1.5	2.9	1.7
Realism*	M	17.50	16.36	19.57	24.07	16.23	21.92
	SD	16.0	15.8	15.7	14.4	13.8	15.2
Appropriateness of certainty in terms of realism*	M	8.71	9.43	8.86	10.79	8.92	11.38
	SD	6.1	6.1	6.5	8.0	6.0	6.7

* The N's for these variables were 14, 14, and 26, respectively (see text).

"very certain," the choice was given a score of +11. Two judges rated every choice, and the score for a given choice was the sum of the two ratings. The agreement between the judges was reasonably high ($r = .72$). Of the 85 choices rated, the judges disagreed as to whether or not a choice was realistic 15 times, or 17.6 per cent of the time. In cases of disagreement, a choice was called realistic if the sum of the ratings was positive, and unrealistic if the sum of the ratings was negative.

Appropriateness of certainty in terms of realism was measured as follows: If the choice was originally realistic and was changed to an unrealistic choice, or if both choices were unrealistic, any increase

TABLE 2
NUMBER AND PERCENTAGE OF STUDENTS MAKING REALISTIC VOCATIONAL
CHOICE BEFORE AND AFTER EXPERIMENTAL PERIOD

Group	Before		After	
	No.	%	No.	%
Control (N = 14)	5	35.7	5	35.7
Individual experimentals (N = 14)	6	42.9	8	57.1
Group experimentals (N = 26)	9	34.6	15	57.7

in certainty was scored negatively, and any decrease was scored positively. If the choice was originally unrealistic and was changed to a realistic one, or if both choices were realistic, increases in certainty were scored positively and decreases were scored negatively.

Six students (1 Individual Experimental, 1 Control, and 4 Group Experimental) were unable to specify even a tentative vocational choice at the beginning of the experiment. They were arbitrarily given a rating of 1 on certainty and satisfaction, but were not included in the analysis of the other two variables.

RESULTS

Table 1 summarizes the changes found on the four variables. It is apparent from the table that mean scores on all four variables *increase* for both the Individual and Group Experimentals. There were slight *decreases* in the mean certainty, satisfaction, and realism scores for the Controls, and a slight increase in the mean score on appropriateness of certainty in terms of realism.

The significance of these trends was tested by the analysis of covariance. Posttest scores for each experimental group were compared with posttest scores for the Controls, with pretest scores held constant.

When the Group Experimentals are compared with the Controls, differences significant beyond the .01 level are found on both certainty and satisfaction. The difference on realism was significant between the .05 and .01 level. On appropriateness of certainty in terms of realism no significant difference was found ($p > .10$). These data as a whole corroborate the first hypothesis.

Similar results were obtained in comparing the Individual Experimentals with the Controls. Thus, differences favoring the experimental group were significant beyond the .01 level on both certainty and satisfaction. The difference on realism was significant between the .10 and .05 level of probability. Again, no significant difference existed on appropriateness of certainty in terms of realism ($p > .10$). The second hypothesis appears to be generally corroborated.

When the two groups of experimental Ss are compared with each other, no significant differences were found. Thus, the final hypothesis is also corroborated.

Changes on the realism criterion are presented in a different way in Table 2. Here the number of Ss making realistic and unrealistic choices before and after the experimental period is presented. For the Control group, the percentage of realistic choices is 35.7 on both occasions. This figure is 42.9 before counseling and 57.1 after counseling for the Individual Experimentals. The Group Experimentals show a change in the percentage of realistic choices from 34.6 to 57.7. This difference, while not statistically significant, is certainly in the expected direction.

DISCUSSION

The findings reported above indicate that vocational guidance by either the individual or group method is effective in producing positive changes on relevant criteria. More important, however, is the finding that there were no differences between the two methods of dealing with vocationally undecided students. According to the criteria adopted for this study, as effective work was accomplished using group procedures as by the more traditional individual approach.

In view of the amount of time required for the group approach as contrasted with the individual approach, this research would seem to provide a strong endorsement for group programs in vocational guidance.

Certain limiting restrictions on this generalization are required. It should be remembered that the experimental population was artificially restricted by limitations on college class, sex, motivation for group participation, lack of previous counseling contacts, and the completeness of psychometric records. As a consequence, the conclusions apply strictly to only a very limited segment of the total potential population. A second limitation is that our results apply only to those programs in vocational guidance where the objectives are similar to our objectives. To generalize to other types of guidance programs, or to all counseling, is certainly unwarranted.

However, the results are encouraging enough to suggest further studies of the group approach in more generalized populations and in different types of counseling programs.

SUMMARY AND CONCLUSIONS

The heavy demand for professional services to vocationally undecided students makes the search for more economical ways of dealing with such students imperative. This study investigates the effectiveness of a group method in vocational guidance, and compares its effectiveness with that of individual counseling.

Sixty freshman males who volunteered to participate in a group vocational guidance program composed the sample. Each student was assigned, by a random method, to one of three groups: (a) Individual Experimentals who received individual counseling: (b) Group Experimentals who participated in the group program; or (c) Controls who were not exposed to either treatment until after the experimental period.

All 60 Ss indicated their tentative vocational choices, how certain they were of them, and how satisfied they were with them both before and after the experimental period. Skilled counselors rated each choice as to its realism.

Using the analysis of covariance, the results led to the following conclusion:

1. With original status held constant, the Group Experiments are significantly more certain of their vocational choices ($p < .01$), more satisfied with these choices ($p < .01$), and more realistic in them ($p < .05$) than the Controls.

2. With original scores held constant, the Individual Experimentals are significantly more certain of their vocational choices ($p < .01$), more satisfied with these choices ($p < .01$), and probably more realistic in them ($p < .10$) than the Controls.

3. No differences were found between the effectiveness of the individual counseling program and the group program.

4. No differences were found in appropriateness of certainty in terms of realism, probably because the Controls appropriately became less certain, and the Experimentals appropriately became more certain.

5. The time-saving quality of the group program, together with its demonstrated effectiveness, argues for the institution of group programs in vocational guidance.

6. A strong recommendation to this effect cannot be made until further studies have defined the limits of the generalization.

.... 71 ....

THE LATER CAREERS OF BOYS WHO WERE

EARLY- OR LATE-MATURING

by Mary Cover Jones

Early- or late-maturing may have a considerable bearing upon the social life and personal adustment of some adolescents.[1] Perhaps of greater importance is the inquiry as to long-term effects of relationships in adult life. In the following systematic follow-up study of early- and late-maturing adolescents who are now in their early thirties, Mary Cover Jones of the University of California (Berkeley) finds that group differences in physique have practically disappeared; however, young adults who had been physically retarded adolescents differ from those who had been accelerated in several important psychological characteristics. [From *Child Development*, 1957, *28*, 113–128. Reprinted by permission of the author and Society for Research in Child Development, Inc.]

A previous study (Jones and Bayley, 1950)[2] compared two groups of boys who had been classified as physically accelerated or retarded, in terms of skeletal age. These groups represented approximately the 20 per cent at each extreme of a normal public school sample.

[1] See selections 13 and 14 in this volume.
[2] Selection 13 in this book.

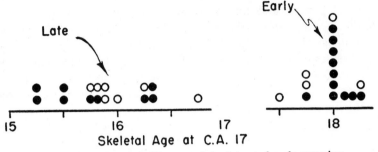
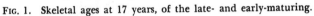

Fig. 1. Skeletal ages at 17 years, of the late- and early-maturing.

The comparison showed differences in physical growth, sexual maturing, and in a number of psychological measures, and led to the conclusion that "... those who are physically accelerated are usually accepted and treated by adults and other children as more mature. They appear to have relatively little need to strive for status. From their ranks come the outstanding student body leaders in senior high school. In contrast, the physically retarded boys exhibit many forms of relatively immature behavior: this may be in part because others tend to treat them as the little boys they appear to be. Furthermore, a fair proportion of these give evidence of needing to counteract their physical disadvantages in some way—usually by greater activity and striving for attention, although in some cases by withdrawal" (p. 146).

It is clear that early- or late-maturing may have a considerable bearing upon the social life and personal adjustment of some individuals during the middle years of their adolescence. Perhaps of greater importance, however, is the inquiry as to longer-term effects or relationships in adult life, and on this point no evidence has previously been offered.

The subjects who participated in the original study are now in their early thirties. Contacts have been maintained with many of the group during the intervening years; in a systematic follow-up study[3] beginning in 1954 current data have been obtained for 20 of the early- and late-maturing boys, out of an original sample of 32.

ADOLESCENT DIFFERENCES

Figures 1 to 7 present data from the adolescent period for the

[3] Acknowledgments are due to the U.S. Public Health Service for a grant in support of this study. The follow-up study was a joint project of the Institute of Child Welfare and the Donner Laboratory.

original groups, and for the subsamples available in the present study. Figure 1 shows the distribution of skeletal ages (at around chronological age 17) for the early- and late-maturing. Each circle represents an individual case: the black circles those included in the follow-up and the open circles those who have dropped out.[4] It can be seen that the new selection has not substantially altered the maturity differential of the two groups.

Figures 2 and 3 present cumulative records for height and weight in terms of standard scores at ages 12 to 17. Standard scores (in which 50 is taken as the mean and 10 as the SD) are indicated on the left vertical axis, and percentiles on the right. In these and the following figures, the points on connecting lines represent averages for the follow-up group, consisting of 11 early- and 9 late-maturing individuals. The adjacent points denote averages for the original 16 early- and 16 late-maturing.

The early-maturing tend to fall at the 75 percentile or above, and the late-maturing at the 25 percentile or below, with differences which are at a maximum at around 14 years, when the early-maturing are on the average approximately 8 inches taller and 34 pounds heavier.

In these physical measures the adolescent data for the follow-up sample are similar to those of the original sample, and this is also shown in Figure 4, based on a measure of static dynamometer strength (right grip).

Other physical comparisons included Greulich's (1942) 5-point standards of maturity (rated by physicians from pubic hair and external genitalia) and Bayley and Bayer's (1946) ratings of androgeny. On the Greulich scale the late-maturing boys at age 14 averaged only 2.0, well below the norm; while the early-maturing average 4.5, or close to the scale maximum. In the androgeny assessments, the early-maturing were nearly all in the "masculine" or "hyper-masculine" zone, while approximately half of the late-maturing were classified as "asexual," "bisexual," "hypo-bisexual," or physically "disharmonious." In these as in other respects the follow-up samples yielded distributions similar to those of the original study.

With such marked adolescent differences in size, strength, masculine conformation, and associated athletic abilities, we might also predict, in our culture, average differences in reputational status

[4] Skeletal age was assessed from X-rays of the hand and knee, using Todd standards. Of the 12 cases lost from the original sample, three have died, one has not been located, one is non-cooperative, three have been scheduled but not yet seen in the follow-up and the remaining four have moved away and are for the time being unavailable because of residence abroad, or in other states.

HEIGHT : BOYS

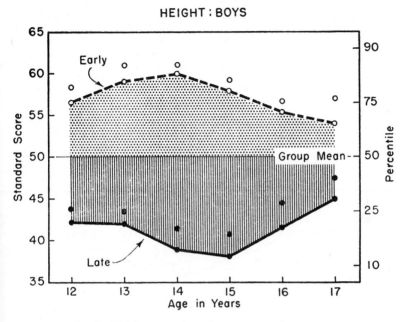

FIG. 2.   Height comparisons for two contrasting groups.

WEIGHT : BOYS

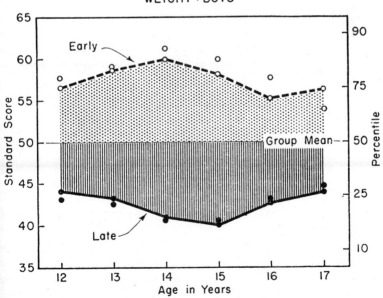

FIG. 3.   Weight comparisons.

RIGHT GRIP : BOYS

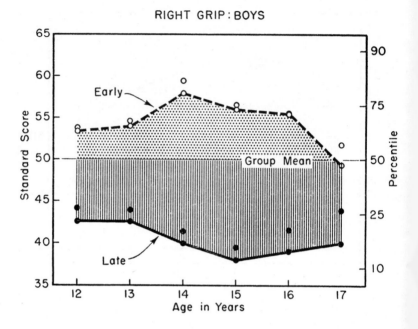

FIG. 4.   Strength comparisons.

and in some aspects of self-acceptance. In the original study comparisons were presented, at an average age of 16, for a series of ratings made in "free play" situations. The early-maturing were judged to be more attractive in physique and as showing more attention to grooming. They tended to be more relaxed, more matter-of-fact and less affected in their behavior. Differences were significant at the .05 level for each of these traits; for a number of other characteristics, such as interest in the opposite sex, and "good-naturedness," quite consistent differences were obtained over nine semesters of observation. The late-maturing were significantly more expressive, but their small-boy eagerness was also associated with greater tenseness and more affected attention-seeking mannerisms.

Figure 5 represents average measures for attractiveness of physique, based on independent ratings by three staff members. Figure 6 gives similar cumulative records for an illustrative aspect of expressive behavior (eagerness). The early-maturing are centered close to the average in this characteristic while the late-maturing are judged to be more juvenile and less poised in their expressiveness, especially in the middle years of adolescence. Similar results were

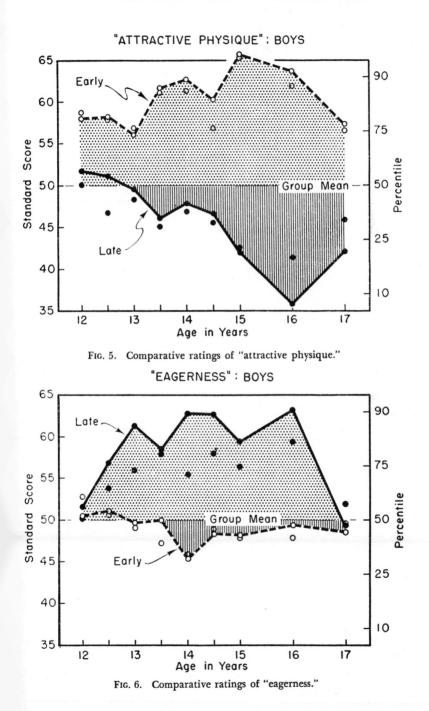

FIG. 5. Comparative ratings of "attractive physique."

FIG. 6. Comparative ratings of "eagerness."

found for such characteristics as "animated," "talkative," and "un-inhibited."

On behavior items suggesting a large component of self-acceptance (being relaxed, unaffected and matter-of-fact) the early-maturing were rated higher at the end of the study, with the late-maturing becoming increasingly "tense" and "affected" in the high school years.[5] Figure 7 illustrates this for the characteristic which we have

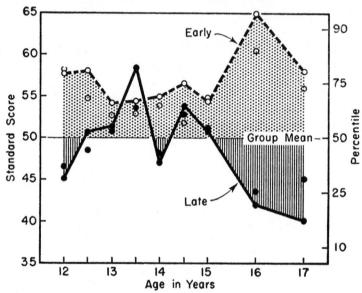

Fig. 7. Comparative ratings of "matter-of-factness."

called "matter-of-fact." Both groups fluctuate around the average in this trait until age 16 when they separate noticeably, the early-maturing falling on the favorable or well-adjusted side, and the late-maturing on the attention-seeking or show-off side of the scale. Similar wide separation at ages 16 and 17 has been found for the trait "unaffected-affected" and for "relaxed-tense." In these, as in other relevant psychological measures, the follow-up groups had adolescent records similar to those of the original study; the loss of cases has not substantially changed the selection.

[5] A study of the Thematic Apperception Test responses at age 17 suggests that early-maturing boys tend to be more self-accepting and to feel less threatened than late-maturing. [The study is selection 14 in this book. Ed.]

ADULT DIFFERENCES

We may now consider the adult characteristics of the early- and late-maturing, as observed at an average age of 33 years. As was predicted at age 17, the differences in gross size tend to disappear. The early-maturing average only half an inch taller, at 5 feet 10 inches; and 7 pounds heavier, at 172 pounds. These differences are not significant. In body build, the prediction is that the early-maturing would be more mesomorphic. The tendency is in this direction, but the differences are not significant. The chief thing to note is the wide range of physiques within each group (both in adolescence and in adulthood) and the marked consistency over the years. A slight change is apparent in the direction of greater mesomorphy in eight of the nine late-maturing and they now present a somewhat more developed and sturdy appearance.

Some differences would be expected in constitutional indices of masculinity. Among the late-maturing, the majority of the original study and of those included in the follow-up were rated as having a deficiency in masculine development, at age 17. At age 33, how-ever, Sheldon (1940) ratings of gynandromorphy in the two groups showed considerable overlap and only a small and nonsignificant difference in favor of the early-maturing.

Personality differences in adult life have been examined with reference to a number of criteria. Two sources of data to be considered here are Gough's (1951) California Psychological Inventory and the Edwards (1954) Personal Preference Schedule. The first of these, the C. P. I., attempts to appraise aspects of character and temperament which are significant for social living and interpersonal behavior and which are related to personal maturity and creative achievement. Eighteen scales are available which describe individuals in terms of social responsibility, tolerance, flexibility, academic motivation, self-control[6] and the like.

Most of the above scales did not show significant differences between the groups. One outstanding exception is the scale entitled "good impression," (interest in, and capacity for, creating a "good impression" on others) (Gough, 1952). Differences here favored the early-maturing with a significance at the .006 level.

Some of the interpretative phrases associated with high scores on this scale include: "is turned to for advice and reassurance; fatherly; is concerned with making a good impression; is persistent in working toward his goal." High scorers on this "Gi" scale are also desig-

---

[6] "Self-control" is indicated by a low score on the impulsivity scale.

nated as responsible, cooperative, enterprising, sociable and warm. In our groups the early-maturing tend in addition to obtain higher scores on the C. P. I. scales for socialization, dominance, self-control and responsibility. Although none of these shows differences at a significance level better than .07, it is true that the early-maturing have high average scores and present a consistently favorable personality picture with regard to these important social variables.

The phrases and adjectives associated with high scores on these five scales (good impression, socialization, dominance, self-control, and responsibility) remind us strikingly of the social behavior and personal traits attributed, by their peers and by adults, to the early-maturing boys in adolescence. For the total group of 43 boys thus far included in the follow-up, a correlation of .50 (significant at the .01 level) was found between the "good impression" score on the C. P. I., and their level of skeletal maturity 18 years earlier. The corresponding Pearson r for the socialization[7] score at age 33, and skeletal maturity at age 15, was .40, significant at the .01 level. For these correlations skeletal quotients were computed (skeletal age over chronological age), to make allowance for slight differences in the age at which the skeletal X-rays were obtained.

One other scale yields an interesting difference, significant at the .05 level. This is the scale for what has been termed "flexibility." Those who score high on this scale are described by Gough as tending to be rebellious, touchy, impulsive, self-indulgent, assertive, and also insightful. Low scorers are described as deliberate, methodical, industrious, rigid, mannerly, overly-controlling of impulses, compliant. In these terms, the late-maturers tend to be more "flexible" than the early-maturers.

We might hazard the guess that some of the little boy behavior —the impulsiveness, playfulness and also the "touchiness" repeatedly noted in late-maturing adolescents is mirrored in the description of high scorers on this scale. We might speculate further that in the course of having to adapt to difficult status problems, the late-maturers have gained some insights and are indeed more flexible, while the early-maturing, capitalizing on their ability to make a good impression, may have clung to their earlier success pattern to the extent of becoming somewhat rigid or over-controlled.

[7] This "socialization" scale was first presented by Gough (1954) and described as a scale for "delinquency." It is now scored in the opposite direction so as to emphasize the "socialization" side of a socialization-asocialization continuum. In a validation study lowest scores were obtained by those nominated as high school "best citizens"; highest scores by delinquents.

The Edwards (1954) Personal Preference test shows relatively few significant differences between the two groups. This is a self-report device which measures 15 variables named from Murray's list of needs.

On the Edwards test, two of the scales are discriminating for our groups at the 4 and 5 per cent levels respectively. The early-maturing group scores high on the *dominance* scale: "to be a leader, persuade, argue for a point of view," while the late-maturing score high in *succorance*: "to seek encouragement, to be helped by others, to have a fuss made over one when hurt." For the total group of 40 who took the Edwards test at around age 33, skeletal maturing at age 17 correlated .40 with dominance, and —.48 with succorance

TABLE 1

SUMMARY OF STATISTICAL FINDINGS FOR THE FOLLOW-UP COMPARISONS

Physical Measures: Means

	Early		Late	
	Age 14	*Age 33*	*Age 14*	*Age 33*
Height	5 ft. 8 in.	5 ft. 10 in.	5 ft.	5 ft. 9½ in.
Weight	126.9 lb.	172 lb.	93.2 lb.	165 lb.
Endomorphy*	2.6	3.1	3.1	3.3
Mesomorphy*	4.5	4.6	3.9	4.3
Ectomorphy*	3.4	3.4	3.7	3.7

Psychological Scales

	Means		Signif. of		Signif.
	Early	Late	Difference†	r‡	Level
California Psychological Inventory					
Good Impression	25.6	15.7	.006	.50	<.01
Flexibility	9.7	13.8	.05	—.23	
Delinquency§	13.9	20.3	.07	—.40	<.01
Impulsivity	17.1	23.4	.13	—.31	<.05
Dominance	31.7	27.4	.17	.26	
Responsibility	32.9	30.0	.19	.35	<.05
Edwards Personal Preference Schedule					
Dominance	19.4	12.6	.04	.40	<.01
Succorance	7.1	12.4	.05	—.48	<.01

* Rating on 7-point scale; 7 is high.
† Significance level, Wilcoxon Rank Test.
‡ Pearson product-moment correlation with skeletal age/chronological age, at 15 years.
§ A low score indicates "socialization."

(both significant at the .01 level). Table 1 summarizes the statistical findings for the follow-up comparisons.[8]

To those of us who have known these young men for over 20 years, some of the most interesting questions remain to be answered. What have been their successes and failures in achieving occupational and personal goals? All are married, and in each group the present number of children averages 2.3. Socioeconomic ratings, based on homes and neighborhoods, show no differences for the two groups. There are no significant differences in average educational level, although a slightly higher proportion of the later-maturing have college degrees and the only college teacher is in this group.[9]

There is some indication that more of the early-maturing have attained vocational goals which are satisfying and status-conferring. Among this group five are in professional careers; four are executives; one is a skilled mechanic and one in a clerical position. Of the executives, three are in positions of somewhat impressive status.

Among the late-maturing, four are in professions, two are still university students, two are salesmen, and one is a carpenter. None has attained an important managerial position and several, by their own account and the nature of their work, seem somewhat precariously unsettled.

In the former study descriptive pictures were given of late-maturing boys who illustrated contrasting behavior patterns of attention-seeking activity and of withdrawal. It may be appropriate here to summarize individual records for several of those at the early- and late-maturing extremes.

Tom, a late-maturing boy as described in a previous article (Jones and Bayley, 1950),[10] was at the age of 13 a chubby small boy, very rosy of cheek, sparkling-eyed, laughing and dimpled. He was gay, active, good-humored, emotionally volatile. Even as a senior in high school he was still a "little boy." His voice had not changed. At a time when most of his classmates were paying careful attention to cleanliness and grooming he often came to school with dirty hands and in misfit clothes. He was likely to get into childish scuffles; physically, however, he was not able to cope with his classmates, and

[8] Statistical analysis of the data was completed under a research grant from the Department of Education, University of California.

[9] The writer is indebted to Mr. Read Tuddenham who secured much of the interview material through a grant from the Office of Naval Research.

[10] [This article is selection 13 in this volume. Ed.]

would sometimes break down and cry when things went badly.

Unlike most of the physiologically retarded group, he seemed not to be anxious about his immaturity. Growth continued during his college years, when he added four inches to his height, and 20 pounds to his weight. As a graduate student Tom began to play baseball on an intramural team and for the first time, according to his own report, was able to hold up his end of the game. So impressed was he with his own physical gains (there had never been any doubt about his mental abilities) that he raised his sights in regard to vocational goals, achieved a graduate degree and joined the academic ranks as a college teacher.

The interviewer who saw him most recently at the age of 33 described him as: "A genial smiling young man, well integrated, mature, observant, well satisfied with his life situation." He is making excellent progress professionally, and achieving recognition among his colleagues. We now feel that we were justified in the impression gained during his high school years, that Tom was able to cope with the problems of late-maturing without permitting these to create a basic feeling of handicap.

Lonnie, on the other hand, was a late-maturing boy whose physical deficiencies in size and athletic prowess were a persistent source of tension and anxiety. His activity pattern was expressed in excessive verbalizations which became more aggressive and compulsive as he progressed through adolescence.

Excerpts from a staff group conference after a camping trip illustrate this point:

(W.J.C.) Lonnie was by far the most talkative in this very talkative crowd. ... Saturday night after most of the boys had gone to sleep Lonnie turned to a question which had to do with the history of religion. He pursued the subject with vehemence.

(M.C.J.) On Sunday morning when we were just finishing breakfast, Mr. G. mentioned a friend who had been working with a growth-promoting hormone. He had hardly uttered a sentence when Lonnie, who had been at the next table, suddenly appeared by his side.

(J.C.) This led to further discussion throughout the day and on Monday, at school. ... He was again on the subject of the hormone. He wanted to offer himself as a subject because he had always been small and underweight, "skinny." ...

(T.C.) Lonnie talks with ceaseless energy, with a good deal of ego at stake ... "I know a fellow who is a grandson of a Senator. But when we argue I can beat him everytime with cold facts—statistics."

In a current interview many of the same characteristics of restless energy emerged. The interviewer commented that he was hard to rate because of tendencies which were superficially in contradiction to each other. He seemed self-centered, self-sufficient, and with a strong drive for autonomy, but was also dependent on his wife and "socially-minded" in the sense of having abstract interests in groups, social issues, etc. "He seems to have achieved a fairly stabilized adjustment—if not a conventional one. Seems able to work toward long term goals because he has considerable personal freedom. He is tense, rebellious, intellectual, too bent on satisfying his own needs in relationships to relate well to groups either as a member or a leader."

When asked what he would do differently if he had the last 15 years to live over again, Lonnie replied that he would have gone ahead as fast as possible with academic work. "As it was, I was out for Adventure with a capital A and Experience with a capital E— a hollow sort of goal which doesn't satisfy. I travelled a lot but could have done as much living just around the corner."

Late-maturing was merely one of Lonnie's problems, but it led to an impaired status which was an immediate source of frustration, and of rebellious compensatory strivings. These patterns are still apparent in his adult life, although he now seems to take a more realistic view of the roles which are possible for him.

A third late-maturing boy, with a very different set of behavior patterns, was *Charles*—one of the two brothers described in the earlier publication as socially inconspicuous, extremely quiet and self-contained. Although not especially noticed or approved by his peer group, he had a variety of substantial individual interests, and congenial family ties.

Charles is described as "Frank and open in expression, individualistic, and outspoken, primarily an introvert. Though somewhat odd, he is probably fairly well liked by his associates. He seems relatively insecure, requiring support and reassurance. He expresses both hostility and dependence in relation to authority figures. . . . He is mildly self-centered, somewhat imperceptive of others' feelings."

In his own description of current activities, he observed, "My job requires relatively little contact with people. I like it this way. . . My wife is not overly fond of people. . . . My wife and I are very congenial, we talk over everything together."

Charles, who used to be so shy about girls, so retiring and quietly accepting of his own physical deficiencies, now seems to have established a way of life similar to that of his parents, and one which meets his needs with reasonable adequacy.

Howard was early-maturing. In the eyes of adult observers an classmates, he was advantaged in this respect as well as in family background and personal endowment. He was the younger of two boys from a home well above average in financial security, community status, and interpersonal compatibility.

He was well-liked by both boys and girls but although Howard had the same best friend for many years he seemed less dependent upon social ties than was the case with most youngsters of his age. "The girls would like him to take more interest in them," wrote one observer in the ninth grade. He learned to dance in the eighth grade but was a little shy at first with girls.

By the ninth grade he had lost his shyness, but led too busy a life with his own individual projects and his family's activities to be more than casually interested in girls or to accept more than a few of the many party invitations which he received. "He is a grand-looking boy and the girls feel it a great loss that he is not more interested in them."

Even in his senior year at high school when one girl seemed to be steadfastly claiming his attention, he was described as follows at a staff conference after a party which involved both swimming and dancing: "In his customary manner, Howard left Clare to her own devices and went to join the boys in the pool. He enjoys athletic activities even more than devotion to his lady love. . . . I have a feeling that any girl who goes with Howard will have to stand for that arrangement . . ."

Referring to his social development 15 years later he said, "My interest in girls was not any problem in high school."

Throughout the years of the study, descriptions of Howard stressed his maturity in relation to the group: "Has always been one of the largest and best looking. . . . His prestige among boys is quite marked, with no striving on his part (age 14.4). . . . Howard, like several of his friends this semester, seemed to have reached the stage of 'putting away the childish.' They sat and talked after lunch while the other boys played ball. He has unquestioned prestige, though he seems unaware of it . . ." (14.9).

"Howard is large, seems much more mature than almost any of our group (15.9). . . . Considerable maturity of manner, talked at length to H. E. J., and as an equal, about cameras and photographic equipment" (16.0). A student assistant in the physiology laboratory, impressed with Howard as a 16-year-old said: "He doesn't attempt to make a show of himself or his accomplishments although he now holds the record for vital capacity of 6.40 liters and of 3 minutes 37 seconds for holding his breath."

In spite of the fact that others recognized his accelerated maturity from the time he was in elementary school, Howard, in retrospect, described his own development as physically retarded.

A possible clue to this erroneous belief comes from his position in the family, as the younger boy. His father was past middle age when Howard was born and according to his own analysis of the situation, it was the older brother who had received the understanding and attention of a young, vigorous, active father. Howard missed this when he was growing up. It was his older brother who, in turn, furnished the active, interested companionship in which Howard may have felt a fatherly, as well as a brotherly quality. He certainly compared himself to this older brother and may have, growing up in the shadow of this comparison, thought of himself as inadequate in many ways, including rate of maturing. An interpretation of his response to the Murray pictures suggests that this is so:

Age 17: Howard's conflict seems to lie in his inability to reconcile his position as an individual with his position as a member of his family. . . . He tells of his fear that he is inadequate as a family member. His relationship to his older brother is basic to his difficulty. He is impressed with his older brother's superiority. Howard is far from the inadequate person he imagines himself to be in comparison with his brother. It seems likely that he does not feel inadequate except when measuring himself against his exaggerated notion of his brother's accomplishment.

In other circumstances, while his demands on himself are high, he appears to be able to meet them. In his struggle to emulate his brother he has developed qualities basic to superior performance. He shows determination and persistence, a high level of energy, and the capacity to direct and maintain effort toward the goal he sets for himself. In the stories, he exaggerates his weakness but he indicates, as well, his strength.

As an adult in his early thirties, Howard seems to have come to realize his potentialities. "I've developed a good deal more self-confidence. . . . I feel I have had enough education and experience to tackle a job that I have some feel for, so I'm optimistic. In my work, I'm in a dominant position and you build up self-confidence. In college, fraternity life and athletics helped, too."

The interviewer summarizes: "Mr. F. has strong needs for acquisition and mastery. He is dominant, active, a leader and autonomous. It would be hard to keep him down."

Bob provides another example of the socially advantaged early maturing boy. An only son in a prosperous upper-middle-class family, Bob had a pattern cut out for him to follow. He was expected to enter his father's business. His mother knew exactly how sh wanted him to grow toward manhood and what course to pursue in fulfilling this goal. "I will not have a dirty boy," she said on one occasion. But this meant that he had to wash up after strenuous play, not that activity was prohibited. She understood that boys like to ride bicycles, build boats, and later, drive cars; that they are happy when playing with neighborhood boys in the backyard as pre-adolescents, and that as adolescents their social interests include girls, dancing, parties. Creditable scholarship and practice in leadership were encouraged in school.

All of these goals were easily attained. Bob was slightly above the average of our group in intelligence and achievement tests. He was rated consistently on the favorable side, in a wide range of social and personal characteristics. Class-mates placed him very high in leadership and popularity. In self-report, he was consistently on the well adjusted side—above the eightieth percentile for the group in all categories, which implied family, social, school and personal satisfactions.

After 15 years, Bob has achieved the realization of his own and his family's goals: "I enjoy my work very much . . . it's a business of my father's that I've always been interested in going into." To the question about how he might live his last 15 years over again he responded: "I'd do them about the same."

Two interviewers, a man and a woman, reveal their own somewhat different biases when summing up their impressions of Bob: The male psychologist wrote: "Mr. A is a tanned, dark-haired, immaculately dressed business man, self-assertive, confident in general bearing but not quite at ease during the interview. He is satisfied with himself and the mores of his business milieu . . . a rigid personality with little insight, little ability to relax and enjoy himself. He puts business first. He has no conflict since he faces no difficult external problems."

The woman who interviewed Bob reacted as follows: "Mr. A fits happily into the 'ideal' stereotype of a successful upper-middle-class business man with no strain and with none of the unfavorable connotations. Although he has social ambitions not yet attained and lets work invade leisure time to a minor extent, he does not seem under pressure about his work. His range of interests are not wide or differentiated . . . he accepts the stereotype of upper-middle-class without much thought . . . his interests are social (in the sense of personal enjoyment) rather than directed along power lines . . . he exhibits more freedom from anxiety than any subject I have seen so far."

Unlike the two preceding cases, Rod was an early-maturing boy with persistent difficulties in social adjustment. These stemmed in part from a family background which was a handicap in a school where acceptable behavior followed upper-middle-class standards.

In our first records (at 10.5 years) he was described as tall and thin, talkative and outgoing with adults, friendly with strange boys whom he was meeting for the first time. These characteristics were continued during the period of the study.

But from the classroom and the playground came reports of difficulties. While some of the attributes ascribed to him by classmates were socially desirable—"a leader, daring, active in games, happy and enthusiastic," he was also said to be a fighter, lacking in a sense of humor about himself, inclined to be extremely bossy, and attention-seeking. His friendship relations must have been unsatisfactory also, in the early adolescent years, since he mentioned five boys as best friends but was mentioned by none of them in return. He was quarrelsome in games.

During a period of exceptionally rapid growth, in the seventh and eighth grades, this rough and quarrelsome behavior seemed to increase. Rod's superior size and strength provided an easy means of dominating others. "Rod seems driven by an urge to tease; the other boys do not like him very well but cannot dispute his attacks since none of the group approaches his size." Although recognized as a stormy adolescent, often using physical aggression as a defense against his feelings of social inadequacy, he gradually learned to channel his energies in more acceptable directions. He was active in games, and gained some prestige as an athlete. As the other boys caught up with him in size and strength, he was less tempted to draw them into situations involving bullying or fighting. He became more popular, and although still considered "bossy," he was less of a show-off and more considerate of others.

Usually the physical build and stature of early-maturing boys is attractive. During the middle years of adolescence this was not the case with Rod, whose growth in weight did not keep up with his growth in height. He was embarrassed rather than pleased by his height; he worried about it, and seemed to slump as he sat and to stoop as he walked.

In the later years of high school he gained better proportions and began to be rated as "good-looking." He became an expert dancer and although still preferring athletics he was now frequently included in mixed parties. His classmates rated him as a leader, and as having a good sense of humor.

Thus we see that a boy from "across the tracks" at first used the physical competence accompanying early-maturing as a means of asserting himself in an environment in which he felt ill at ease. He was disliked for his undisciplined behavior, and his physical power was a liability rather than an asset.

By the end of adolescence, however, he had learned more effective social techniques. His size and strength were not to be disregarded, and his classmates began to perceive him in a more favorable light.

After high school Rod saw service in the Pacific—a handsome, swashbuckling soldier who wrote of his adventures to various members of the study staff. He is now settled down as a business man. Interviewers describe him as devoted to his wife and three children, hard-working, ambitious. He impressed an interviewer as not being very perceptive about or concerned with other people's opinions, except as having a general wish to make a good impression. "Interests in others' motivations and his own are relatively superficial. He expresses his feelings impulsively without much anxiety; seems to be able to disregard the needs of others but is probably warm to those close to him. Perhaps he is too self-centered to care much about group activity and does not seem to care for the kind of prestige which he would get from exploiting a group."

Though friendly he was thought to be a little defensive about having no recreational or cultural interests to report. He said, "I have three main interests: the family, the business, and sports." But an account of his daily living revealed that the business got most of his attention. He was able to report fair financial success as the result of his devotion to work. He described with some pride the house which he owns: "It is supposed to be elite. I lived on the wrong side of the tracks too long. But now where I live each house has its own patio and there are lots of swimming pools in the subdivision."

SUMMARY AND CONCLUSION

Boys who had been classified as physically accelerated or retarded in terms of skeletal age during adolescence were compared as young adults at age 33, to determine the long-term effects of rate of maturing upon personality.

Although some cases were lost from the original sample, the data for the follow-up group as reconstituted showed no substantial alteration in the adolescent differentials of the early- and late-maturing.

For the original sample and for the subsample available in the present study, analysis of ratings by adults and classmates indicated that the early-maturing boys were significantly more attractive in physique, more relaxed, poised and matter-of-fact. Consistent differences in other characteristics, such as interest in the opposite sex and "good-naturedness," were obtained over nine semesters of observation. Late-maturing boys were described as more expressive, active, talkative, eager, attention-getting.

The physical differences noted for these boys at adolescence have tended to disappear in adulthood. Personality characteristics as appraised by the California Psychological Inventory and the Edwards Personal Preference Schedule have shown a number of significant differences on the various scales for which the tests are scored (e.g., higher scores for the early-maturing on measures of "good impression" and "socialization.") Where such differences were found, they tended to describe the young adults much as they had been described in adolescence.

No differences were found between the early- and late-maturing in present marital status, family size or educational level. A few of the early-maturing have made exceptionally rapid progress as junior executives and a few of the late-maturing are still somewhat unsettled, vocationally.

The foregoing presentation of data and the case summaries remind us again of the conclusions to the original study which stressed individual differences within each group, resulting from the complex interplay of factors. During the adolescent period late-maturing is a handicap for many boys and can rarely be found to offer special advantages. Early-maturing carries both advantages and disadvantages. In our culture it frequently gives competitive status, but sometimes also involves handicaps in the necessity for rapid readjustments and in requiring the adolescent to meet adult expectations which are more appropriate to size and appearance than to other aspects of maturing. The adolescent handicaps and advantages associated with late- or early-maturing appear to carry over into adulthood to some extent, and perhaps to a greater extent in psychological than in physical characteristics.

.... 72 ....

THE GIFTED GROUP AT MID-LIFE:
FULFILLMENT OF PROMISE

by Lewis M. Terman and Melita H. Oden

The following selection summarizes thirty-five years' follow-up of nearly 1,500 gifted children who were first studied in 1921 when most were about eleven years old. Lewis M. Terman (1877-1956) and Melita H. Oden of Stanford University answer the following questions: Have these gifted individuals maintained their intellectual ability? What use have they made of their intellectual superiority? Are they successful in their vocations? Have their accomplishments been recognized? In short, have these mentally endowed men and women in mid-life fulfilled the promise of their youth? [Reprinted from *The Gifted Group at Mid-Life*, pp. 143-152, by Lewis M. Terman and Melita H. Oden with the permission of the publishers, Stanford University Press. Copyright 1959 by the Board of Trustees of Leland Stanford Junior University.]

In the past 35 years we have watched the gifted child advance through adolescence and youth into young manhood and womanhood and on into the fuller maturity of mid-life. The follow-up for three and one-half decades has shown that the superior child, with few exceptions, becomes the able adult, superior in nearly every aspect to the generality. But, as in childhood, this superiority is not equally great in all areas.

The superiority of the group is greatest in intellectual ability, in scholastic accomplishment, and in vocational achievements. Physically the gifted subjects continue to be above average as shown in their lower mortality record and in the health ratings. While personal adjustment and emotional stability are more difficult to evaluate, the indications are that the group does not differ greatly from the generality in the extent of personality and adjustment problems as shown by mental breakdowns, suicide, and marital failures. The incidence of such other problems as excessive use of liquor (alcoholism) and homosexuality is below that found in the total population, and the delinquency rate is but a small fraction of that in the generality. Clearly, desirable traits tend to go together. No negative correlations were found between intelligence and size, strength, physical well-being, or emotional stability. Rather, where correlations occur, they tend to be positive.

THE MAINTENANCE OF INTELLECTUAL ABILITY

But if gifted children are not prone to die young or, as they advance in years, to become invalids or to suffer to any extent from serious personality or behavior difficulties, there remains the question of the degree to which their intellectual superiority is maintained. The evidence on this score is conclusive. Test scores of 1927-28, 1939-40, and 1950-52 showed the majority of the subjects close to the 99th percentile of the generality in mental ability. This is true even of those whose careers have not been particularly notable. It was especially interesting to find that the average Concept Mastery test score in 1950-52 of the subjects who did not go beyond high school was exactly the same as that of a group of candidates for advanced degrees (Ph.D. or M.D.) at a leading university. Of additional interest are the results of a comparison of Concept Mastery test scores of 1939-40 and 1950-52 of the same individuals. The test-retest comparisons showed a reliable gain in the 11-to-12-year interval with increases occurring at all educational and occupational levels, in all grades of ability, and at all ages. The data indicate that not only do the mentally superior hold their own but that they actually increase in intellectual stature as measured by the Concept Mastery test.

APPRAISAL OF ACHIEVEMENT

From a practical and utilitarian point of view the real test of the significance and value of this high degree of mental ability is the use that is made of such gifts. The record points to the conclusion that capacity to achieve far beyond the average can be detected early in life through tests of general intelligence. Such tests do not, however, enable us to predict what direction the achievement will take, and least of all do they tell us what personality factors or what accidents of fortune will affect the fruition of exceptional ability. The appraisal of achievement of our gifted subjects will be concerned with their educational attainments, their vocational records, their contributions to knowledge and culture, and the recognitions that have been won.

The educational record is a distinguished one. More than 85 per cent of the group entered college and almost 70 per cent graduated. The latter figure is about ten times as high as for a random group of comparable age. Graduation honors and elections to Phi Beta Kappa and Sigma Xi were at least three times as numerous as in the typical senior-college class, with better than 35 per cent of the graduates winning one or more of these distinctions. Of the college graduates, two-thirds of the men and nearly three-fifths of the women continued for graduate study. The Ph.D. or comparable doctorate was taken by 80 men and 17 women, or about 14 per cent of men and 4 per cent of women graduates. The proportion of the generality of college graduates of corresponding age who have taken a doctorate is less than 3 per cent.

The occupations and occupational status of the men and women of the gifted group have been evaluated separately since the pattern in this regard has been so different. The careers of women are often determined by extraneous circumstances rather than by training, talent, or vocational interest. Whether women choose to work and the occupations they enter are influenced both by their own attitudes and by the attitudes of society toward the role of women. These attitudinal factors also influence the opportunities for employment and for advancement. But in spite of the fact that American women on the average occupy positions of lesser responsibility, opportunity, and remuneration than do men, the gifted women have a number of notable achievements to their credit, some of which have been described in Chapter VII. That 7 women should be listed in *American Men of Science*, 2 in the *Directory of American Scholars*, and 2 in *Who's Who in America*, all before reaching the age of 43, is certainly many times the expectation from a random group of around 700 women. Publications of the gifted women include 5 novels; 5 volumes of poetry and some 70 poems that have appeared in both literary and popular journals; 32 technical, professional, or scholarly books; around 50 short stories; 4 plays; more than 150 essays, critiques, and articles; and more than 200 scientific papers. At least 5 patents have been taken out by gifted women. These figures do not include the writings of reporters and editors, nor a variety of miscellaneous contributions.

Our gifted women in the main, however, are housewives, and many who also work outside the home do so more to relieve the monotony of household duties or to supplement the family income rather than through a desire for a serious career. There are many intangible kinds of accomplishment and success open to the housewife, and it is debatable whether the fact that a majority of gifted women prefer housewifery to more intellectual pursuits represents a net waste of brain-power. Although it is possible by means of rating scales to measure with fair accuracy the achievement of a scientist or a professional or business man, no one has yet devised a way to measure the contribution of a woman who makes her marriage a success, inspires her husband, and sends forth well-trained children into the world.

As for the men, close to three and a half decades after their selection solely on the ability to score in the top 1 per cent of the school population in an intelligence test, we find 86 per cent in the two highest occupational categories: I, the professions, and II, the semiprofessions and higher business. Eleven per cent are in smaller retail business, clerical, and skilled occupations. Farming and related occupations account for nearly 2 per cent and the remaining 1 per cent are in semiskilled work. The representation in the two highest groups is many times their proportionate share, with a corresponding shortage of gifted representation in the middle-occupational levels. No gifted men are classified in the lowest levels of the occupational hierarchy (service workers and slightly skilled or unskilled laborers), whereas 13 per cent of the total urban population are in these categories.

A number of men have made substantial contributions to the physical, biological, and social sciences. These include members of university faculties as well as scientists in various fields who are engaged in research either in industry or in privately endowed or government-sponsored research laboratories.[1] Listings in *American Men of Science* include 70 gifted men, of whom 39 are in the physical sciences, 22 in the biological sciences, and 9 in the social sciences. These listings are several times as numerous as would be found for unselected college graduates. An even greater distinction has been won by the three men who have been elected to the National Academy of Sciences, one of the highest honors accorded American scientists. Not all the notable achievements have been in the sciences;

[1] A detailed study of the vocational correlates and distinguishing characteristics of scientists and nonscientists among the gifted men was made in 1952 under the sponsorship of the Office of Naval Research and has been published in a separate monograph (Terman, 1954) and also appeared in an abbreviated version as an article in the *Scientific American* (Terman, 1955).

many examples of distinguished accomplishment are found in nearly all fields of endeavor.

Some idea of the distinction and versatility of the group may be found in biographical listings. In addition to the 70 men listed in *American Men of Science,* 10 others appear in the *Directory of American Scholars,* a companion volume of biographies of persons with notable accomplishment in the humanities. In both of these volumes, listings depend on the amount of attention the individual's work has attracted from others in his field. Listings in *Who's Who in America,* on the other hand, are of persons who, by reasons of outstanding achievement, are subjects of extensive and general interest. The 31 men (about 4 per cent) who appear in *Who's Who* provide striking evidence of the range of talent to be found in this group. Of these, 13 are members of college faculties representing the sciences, arts and humanities; 8 are top-ranking executives in business or industry; and 3 are diplomats. The others in *Who's Who* include a physicist who heads one of the foremost laboratories for research in nuclear energy; an engineer who is a director of research in an aeronautical laboratory; a landscape architect; and a writer and editor. Still others are a farmer who is also a government official serving in the Department of Agriculture; a brigadier general in the United States Army; and a vice-president and director of one of the largest philanthropic foundations.

Several of the college faculty members listed in *Who's Who* hold important administrative positions. These include an internationally known scientist who is provost of a leading university, and a distinguished scholar in the field of literature who is a vice-chancellor at one of the country's largest universities. Another, holding a doctorate in theology, is president of a small denominational college. Others among the college faculty include one of the world's foremost oceanographers and head of a well-known institute of oceanography; a dean of a leading medical school; and a physiologist who is director of an internationally known laboratory and is himself famous both in this country and abroad for his studies in nutrition and related fields.

The background of the eight businessmen listed in *Who's Who* is interesting. Only three prepared for a career in business. These include the president of a food distributing firm of national scope; the controller of one of the leading steel companies in the country; and a vice-president of one of the largest oil companies in the United States. Of the other five business executives, two were trained in the sciences (both hold Ph.D.'s) and one in engineering; the remaining two were both lawyers who specialized in corporation law and are now high-ranking executives. The three men in the diplomatic services are career diplomats in foreign service.

Additional evidence of the productivity and versatility of the men is found in their publications and patents. Nearly 2000 scientific and technical papers and articles and some 60 books and monographs in the sciences, literature, arts, and humanities have been published. Patents granted amount to at least 230. Other writings include 33 novels, about 375 short stories, novelettes, and plays; 60 or more essays, critiques, and sketches; and 265 miscellaneous articles on a variety of subjects. The figures on publications do not include the hundreds of publications by journalists that classify as news stories, editorials, or newspaper columns, nor do they include the hundreds, if not thousands, of radio, television, or motion picture scripts. Neither does the list include the contributions of editors or members of editorial boards of scientific, professional, or literary magazines. There have also been a sizeable number of scientific documents reporting studies in connection with government research which are restricted publications. We do not have information on the exact number or content of these.

The foregoing are only a few illustrations of conspicuous achievement and could be multiplied many times. They by no means represent all of the areas or types of success for there is scarcely a line of creditable endeavor in which some member of the group has not achieved outstanding success. There are men in nearly every field who have won national prominence and 8 or 10 who have achieved an international reputation. The latter include several physical scientists, at least one biological scientist, one or two social scientists, two or three members of the United States State Department, and a motion picture director. The majority, though not all so outstanding as those mentioned, have been highly successful vocationally from the standpoint of professional and business accomplishment as measured by responsibility and importance of position, prestige, and income.

There is, however, another side to the picture. There are various criteria of success, but we are concerned here with vocational achievement, and success has been defined as the extent to which the subject has made use of his intellectual ability. This calls for a very high level of accomplishment since the intellectual level is so high and not all have measured up to it vocationally. Although not more than three or possibly four men (again women are not included) could be considered failures in relation to the rest of the group there are 80 or 90 men whose vocational achievements fall considerably short of the standard set by the group as a whole. Since the less successful subjects do not differ to any extent in intelligence as measured by tests, it is clear that notable achievement calls for more than a high order of intelligence. After the 1940 follow-up a detailed analysis was made of the life histories of the 150 most successful and 150 least successful men among the gifted subjects in an attempt to identify some of the nonintellectual factors that affect life success. The results of this study indicated that personality factors are extremely important determiners of achievement. The correlation between success and such variables as mental health, emotional stability, and social adjustment is consistently positive rather than negative. In this respect the data run directly counter to the conclusions reached by Lange-Eichbaum (1932) in his study of historical geniuses. A number of interesting differences between the two sub-groups were brought out but the four traits on which they differed most widely were "persistence in the accomplishment of ends," "integration toward goals," "self-confidence," and "freedom from inferiority feelings." In the total picture the greatest contrast between the two groups was in all-around emotional and social adjustment, and in drive to achieve. This study is fully reported in *The Gifted Child Grows Up* (Terman and Oden, 1947).

OUTLOOK FOR FUTURE ACHIEVEMENT

The careers of the gifted subjects, now in their mid-forties, are pretty well set in their present courses. In a very few cases, there are no higher rungs on the particular professional or executive ladder they have climbed. But for most of the group, advances to greater levels of achievement and more important roles can be looked for. Lehman (1953) has shown that the median age at which positions of leadership are reached has greatly increased in the last 150 years. In field after field the increase has amounted to 8, 10, or even 12 years and numerous positions of high-ranking leadership are most likely to be acquired and retained from fifty to seventy years of age. Lehman has also shown that in nearly all fields of intellectual achievement the most creative period is between thirty and forty-five years. But here Lehman is concerned with *quality* of achievement. Productivity as measured by quantity is often greater after forty than before. And regardless of the merit of one's work, the peak of recognitions, honors, and earned income is usually not reached until the fifties.

On the basis of Lehman's data as well as on the evidence from their own records, the peak of achievement for this group is not yet reached. More than half were still under age 45 in 1955 and there was little evidence of any slackening of pace. Whether the rise in the next 10 years will be as steep as that between 1945 and 1955 is doubtful, principally for the reason that they are so much nearer the top. The group has made tremendous strides in the past ten or fifteen years. This is true in every field and in every walk of life. There is almost no one who has not improved his status, even though he may still be well below the average of the group in terms of realizing his intellectual potential in his vocational accomplishments.

We said some years ago (Terman and Oden, 1947) that only a professed seer would venture a statistical forecast of the future achievements of the group. However, we did venture some predictions on the basis of the data to 1945, among which were the following:

The peak of *recognition* for achievement will come much later, probably not before another fifteen or twenty years have elapsed. Listings in *American Men of Science* may well be doubled by 1960, and listings in *Who's Who* may be trebled or quadrupled by 1970. In the decade 1960 to 1970 there should be several times as many holding positions of high responsibility as in 1945, and several times as many of national or international reputation in their special fields of accomplishment (Terman and Oden, 1947, p. 369).

These were indeed conservative estimates. Instead of the doubling of the listings in *American Men of Science* which was thought might take place by 1960, the number has quadrupled, with 77 names (70 men and 7 women) compared to the 19 men and no women to 1945. The list in *Who's Who in America* has grown from 5 names (all men) to 33 (31 men and 2 women), an increase of more than six times rather than the trebling or quadrupling cautiously predicted for the still-distant 1970.

In 1945 probably not more than a half-dozen had a national reputation, and perhaps one was internationally known. By 1955 several dozen at least have become national figures and 8 or 10 are known internationally. Moreover, the group now includes three men who have been elected to the National Academy of Sciences as compared with only one at the earlier date.

It is hard to say in which fields the greatest advances will take place in the next five or ten years. Business will certainly be one, and law another. The scientists are probably nearer their peak than are the rest of the group but even here there are a number of younger scientists with great promise. Regardless of the degree of productivity yet to be attained, the number of those winning special honors and distinctions will increase. This is true because of the time lag between achievement and recognition. Although *American Men of Science* listings are probably now close to their maximum, at least one and possibly two scientists are so outstanding that eventual election to the National Academy of Sciences can be predicted for them. There will undoubtedly be a considerable increase in the number of *Who's Who* biographies but we hesitate to estimate the ultimate number.

There are, however, a few fields, all dependent on special talent, in which there has been a lack of outstanding accomplishment. These are the fine arts, music and, to a lesser extent, literature. The group has produced no great musical composer[2] and no great creative artist. Several possessing superior talent in music or art are heading university departments in these fields and have produced some excellent original work, but none seems likely to achieve a truly great piece of creative work. There are a number of competent and highly successful writers among the subjects but not more than three or four with a high order of literary creativity. Perhaps it is not surprising, in view of the relatively small size of our group, that no great creative genius in the arts has appeared, for such genius is indeed rare. In any case these are the only major fields in which the achievement of our group is limited.

[2] An exception in the case of musical composer should be noted. This is a man of rare creative genius who was not included in the statistics of this report because his intelligence level was not definitely established in childhood. He is several years older than anyone included in the group, and when he was a child no satisfactory IQ test had been devised. However, the senior author has followed his development since 1910, when he was 13 years old, and has known him about as intimately as any gifted subject under observation. He is an eminent musician who has produced hundreds of musical compositions, authored two books and scores of articles on musical theory; invented new musical techniques, given recitals throughout the United States and Europe; lectured in leading American Universities; founded and edited a musical magazine, and won recognition as an authority on musicology and primitive music. His compositions cover a wide range with respect to type, theme, and technique. Many of his productions have been recorded; several of his orchestral selections are played by leading conductors; and some of his briefer compositions are famous among musicians because of their originality (Terman and Oden, 1947).

SOME COMMENTS ON SUCCESS

Our discussion so far has been concerned with achievement of eminence, professional status, and recognized position in the world of human affairs. But these are goals for which many intelligent men and women do not consciously strive. Greatness of achievement is relative both to the prevailing patterns of culture and the individual's personal philosophy of life; there neither exists nor can be devised a universal yardstick for its measure. The criterion of success used in this study reflects both the present-day social ideology and an avowed bias in favor of achievement that calls for the use of intelligence. It is concerned with vocational accomplishment rather than with the attainment of personal happiness. And the record shows that the gifted subjects, in overwhelming numbers, have fulfilled the promise of their youth in their later-life achievements.

There are other criteria of success and other goals and satisfactions in life, however, and in the biographical data blank the gifted men and women have expressed their own opinions on what constitutes life success. The final question in the blank was worded as follows: *From your point of view, what constitutes success in life?* There was a wide range of replies, often overlapping, and frequently a respondent gave more than one definition. The definitions most frequently given fall into five categories, each noted by from around 40 to 50 per cent of the group (with the exception of category c). None of the other definitions of success was mentioned by more than 15 per cent, and only two by more than 10 per cent of the subjects. The five most frequently mentioned definitions of life success are:

a. Realization of goals, vocational satisfaction, a sense of achievement;

b. A happy marriage and home life, bringing up a family satisfactorily;

c. Adequate income for comfortable living (but this was mentioned by only 20 per cent of women);

d. Contributing to knowledge or welfare of mankind; helping others, leaving the world a better place;

e. Peace of mind, well-adjusted personality, adaptability, emotional maturity.

We would agree with the subjects that vocational achievement is not the only—perhaps not even the most important—aspect of life success. To many, the most important achievement in life is happi-

References

[*Names and dates in parentheses in the text correspond to entries in this list.*]

Abernethy, E. M. 1936. Relationships between mental and physical growth. *Monograph of the Society for Research in Child Development*, Vol. 1, No. 7.

Achilles, P. S. 1923. *The effectiveness of certain social hygiene literature.* American Social Hygiene Association.

Adorno, T. W., *et al.* 1950. *The authoritarian personality.* Harper.

Allen, F. H. 1942. *Psychotherapy with children.* Norton.

Allport, G. W. 1937. *Personality: a psychological interpretation.* Holt.

Anderson, E. M. 1948. A study of leisure-time reading of pupils in junior high school. *Elementary School, 48,* 258-267.

Anderson, J. E. (ed.). 1936. *The young child in the home.* Appleton-Century-Crofts.

———. 1940. The prediction of terminal intelligence from infant and preschool tests. *Thirty-ninth Yearbook, National Society for the Study of Education,* Chap. 13, pp. 385-403. Univ. Chicago Press.

———, *et al.* 1953. Unpublished work accomplished in 1953 on the Nobles County Project, Institute of Child Welfare, Univ. Minn.

Anderson, V. V. 1929. *Psychiatry and Industry.* Harper.

Angyal, A. F. 1948. The diagnosis of neurotic traits by means of a new perceptual test. *J. Psychology, 25,* 105-135.

Arbuthnot, M. H. 1947. Children and the comics. *Elementary English, 24,* 183.

Arrieta, U. D. 1932. Menstrual biology of the Peruvian woman. *La Cronica Medica, 49,* 277-287.

Arsenian, S. 1943. Changes in evaluative attitudes during four years of college. *J. Applied Psychology, 27,* 338-349.

Ausubel, D. P. 1951. Prestige motivation of gifted children. *Psychological Monographs, 43,* 53-117.

———, and H. M. Schiff. 1955. A level of aspiration approach to the measurement of goal tenacity. *J. General Psychology, 52,* 97-110.

———, ———, and E. B. Gasser. 1952. A preliminary study of developmental trends in sociempathy: Accuracy of perception of own and others' sociometric status. *Child Development, 23,* 111-118.

———, ———, and M. Goldman. 1953. Qualitative characteristics in the learning process associated with anxiety. *J. Abnormal Social Psychology, 48,* 537-547.

———, ———, and M. P. Zeleny. 1953. "Real life" measures of level of academic and vocational aspiration in adolescents: Relation to laboratory measures and to adjustment. *Child Development, 24,* 155-168.

Baer, M. F. 1947. Vocational guidance in group activities: distinguishing values and principles. *Occupations, 26,* 530-554.

Baker, H. L. 1938. High-school teachers' knowledge of their pupils. *School Review, 46,* 175-190.

Bakke, E. W. 1934. *Unemployed man.* Dutton.

Bakwin, H. 1949. Emotional deprivation in infants. *J. Pediatrics, 35,* 512-529.

Baldwin, B. T. 1928. Determination of sex maturation in boys by laboratory method. *J. Comparative Psychology, 8,* 39-43.

Balester, R. S. 1955. The self-concept and juvenile delinquency. Unpublished doctoral dissertation. Vanderbilt Univ.

Bancker, J. 1951. *Digressive behavior in middle- and lower-class organized youth groups.* Unpublished master's thesis. Univ. Chicago Press.

Bayer, L. M. 1940. Weight and menses in adolescent girls, with special reference to build. *J. Pediatrics, 17,* 345-354.

——, and N. Bayley. 1947. Directions for measures and radiographs used in predicting height. *Child Development, 18,* 85-87.

Bayley, N. 1940. Factors influencing the growth of intelligence in young children. *39th Yearbook, National Society for the Study of Education,* Pt. 2, pp. 49-79. Univ. Chicago Press.

——. 1943. Size and body build of adolescents in relation to rate of skeletal maturing. *Child Development, 14,* 47-90.

——. 1946. Tables for predicting adult height from skeletal age and present height. *J. Pediatrics, 28,* 49-64.

——. 1949. Consistency and variability in the growth of intelligence from birth to eighteen years. *J. Genetic Psychology, 75,* 165-196.

——. 1951. Development and maturation. In H. Helson (ed.), *Theoretical foundations of psychology,* pp. 145-199. Van Nostrand.

——. 1955. On the growth of intelligence. *American Psychologist, 10,* 805-818.

——. 1957. Data on the growth of intelligence between 16 and 21 years as measured by the Wechsler-Bellevue Scale. *J. Genetic Psychology, 90,* 3-15.

——, and L. M. Bayer. 1946. The assessment of somatic androgyny. *American J. Physical Anthropology, 4,* 433-460.

——, and M. H. Oden. 1955. The maintenance of intellectual ability in gifted children. *J. Gerontology, 10,* 91-107.

Beaglehole, E. 1936. Hopi hunting and hunting ritual. *Yale University Publications in Anthropology, 4,* 1-26.

——, and P. Beaglehole. 1935. Hopi of the second mesa. *Memoirs of the American Anthropological Association, 44,* 1-65.

Beaglehole, P. 1935. Census data from two Hopi villages. *American Anthropologist, 37,* 41-54.

Beilin, H. 1955. The application of general developmental principles to the vocational area. *J. Counseling Psychology, 2,* 53-57.

Bell, H. M. 1938. *Youth tell their story.* American Council on Education.

Bellin, S., and F. Riessman. 1949. Education, culture, and the anarchic worker. *J. Social Issues, 5,* 24-32.

Bennett, J. W., and M. M. Tumin. 1948. *Social life: structure and function.* Knopf.

Berger, R. M., J. P. Guilford, and P. R. Christensen. 1957. A factor-analysis study of planning abilities. *Psychological Monographs,* Vol. 71, No. 6.

Berkson, I. B. 1943. *Education faces the future.* Harper.

Bernhardt, K. S., and R. Herbert. 1937. A further study of vitamin B deficiency and learning with rats. *J. Comparative Psychology, 24,* 263-267.

Bettelheim, B. 1950. *Love is not enough.* Free Press.

——, and M. Janowitz. 1950. *The dynamics of prejudice.* Harper.

Bilovsky, D., *et al.* 1953. Individual and group counseling. *Personnel Guidance J., 31,* 363-365.

Birdwhistell, R. 1944. *The Hopi life cycle.* Unpublished ms. Indian Education Research, Committee on Human Development. University of Chicago.

Blair, A. W., and W. H. Burton. 1951. *Growth and development of the preadolescent.* Appleton-Century-Crofts.

Blanton, S. M. 1919. Mental and nervous changes in children of Volkschule of Trier, Germany. *Mental Hygiene, 3,* 343-386.

Bloch, D. A., and E. Silber. 1957. The role of the administrator in relation to individual psychotherapy in a residential treatment setting. *American J. Orthopsychiatry, 27,* 69-74.

Blodgett, H. E. 1953. *An experimental approach to the measurement of self-evaluation among adolescent girls.* Unpublished doctoral dissertation. Univ. Minnesota.

Blos, P. 1941. *The adolescent personality: a study of individual behavior.* Appleton-Century-Crofts.

———. 1953. The contribution of psychoanalysis to the treatment of adolescents. In M. Heiman (ed.), *Psychoanalysis and social work,* pp. 210-241. International Universities.

Boas, F. 1928. Family traits as determined by heredity and environment. *Proceedings, National Academy of Science, 14,* 496-503.

———. 1932. Studies in growth. *Human Biology, 4,* 307-350.

Bonney, M. E. 1947. Sociometric study of agreement between teacher judgments and student choices. *Sociometry, 10,* 133-146.

Bordin, E. S. 1943. A theory of vocational interests as dynamic phenomena. *Educational Psychological Measurement, 3,* 49-65.

Bowlby, J. 1951. Maternal care and mental health. *World Health Organization, Technical Monograph Series,* No. 2.

Boynton, B. 1936. The physical growth of girls: a study of the rhythm of physical growth from anthropometric measurements on girls between birth and eighteen years. *University of Iowa Studies in Child Welfare,* Vol. 2, No. 4.

Brewer, J. 1927. Causes for discharge. *Personnel J., 6,* 171-172.

Bridges, K. M. B. 1930. A genetic theory of the emotions. *J. Genetic Psychology, 37,* 514-527.

———. 1931. *The social and emotional development of the preschool child.* Kegan Paul.

———. 1932. Emotional development in early infancy. *Child Development, 3,* 324-341.

Brissenden, P. F., and E. Frankel. 1922. *Labor turnover in industry.* Macmillan.

Bromley, D. D., and F. H. Britten. 1938. *Youth and sex: a study of 1300 college students.* Harper.

Browe, J. H., and H. B. Pierce. 1950. A survey of nutritional status among school children and their response to

nutrient therapy. *Milbank Memorial Fund Quarterly, 28,* 223-237.

Brown, D. G. 1956. Sex-role preference in young children. *Psychological Monographs, 70,* No. 14.

———. 1957. Masculinity-femininity development in children. *J. Consulting Psychology, 21,* 197-202.

———. 1958. Sex-role development in a changing culture. *Psychological Bulletin, 55,* 232-242.

———, and A. Tolor. 1957. Human figure drawings as indicators of sexual identification and inversion. *Perception Motor Skills, 7,* 199-211.

Brownfain, J. J. 1952. Stability of self-concept as a dimension of personality. *J. Abnormal Social Psychology, 47,* 597-606.

Bruce, M. 1941. Anamism vs. evolution of the concept "alive," *J. Psychology, 12,* 81-90.

Brush Foundation and Western Reserve University. 1930. *Proceedings of Conference on Adolescence: physical and mental adolescent growth.*

Buehler, C. 1933. *Der menschliche lebenslauf als psychologisches problem.* Hirzel.

Burt, C. 1955. The meaning and assessment of intelligence. *Eugenics Review, 47,* 81-91.

Butterfield, O. M. 1939. Love problems of adolescence. *Teachers College Contributions to Education,* No. 768. Teachers College, Columbia Univ.

Calvin, A. D., et al. 1955. A further investigation of the relationship between manifest anxiety and intelligence. *J. Consulting Psychology, 19,* 280-282.

Cambridge University, Department of Experimental Medicine. 1951. Studies of undernutrition, Wuppertal 1946-1949, *Medical Research Council Special Report Series,* No. 275. H. M. Stationery Office.

Campbell, E. H. 1939. The social-sex development of children. *Genetic Psychology Monographs, 21,* 461-552.

Campbell, J. D. 1952. *Subjective aspects of occupational status.* Unpublished doctoral dissertaion. Harvard Univ.

Cantril, H. 1950. *The "why" of man's experience.* Macmillan.

Carroll, R. E. 1945. Relation of social environment to the moral ideology and the personal aspirations of negro boys and girls. *School Review, 53*, 30-38.

Cattell, R. B., and L. G. Tiner. 1949. The varieties of structural rigidity. *J. Personality, 17*, 321-342.

Cava, E. L., and H. L. Raush. 1952. Identification and the adolescent boy's perception of his father. *J. Abnormal Social Psychology, 47*, 855-856.

Cavan, R. S., et al. 1949. *Personal adjustment in old age.* Science Research Associates.

Centers, R. 1950. Children of the new deal: social stratification and adolescent attitudes. *International J. Opinion Attitude Research, 4*, 315-335.

Chapple, E. D., and C. M. Arensberg. 1940. Measuring human relations: an introduction to the study of interaction of individuals. *Genetic psychology monographs, 22*, 5-147.

Chein, I. 1945. On the nature of intelligence. *J. Genetic Psychology, 32*, 111-126.

Chicago Area Project, no date. *Delinquency rates in the city of Chicago for males age 10-16, during the years 1945-1951.*

Child, I. L. 1954. Personality. *Annual Review Psychology, 5*, 149-170.

Christal, R. E. 1958. Factor analytic study of visual memory. *Psychological Monographs, 72*, No. 13.

Coch, L., and J. R. P. French, Jr. 1948. Overcoming resistance to change. *Human Relations, 1*, 512-532.

Coffin, T. E. 1949. Television's effects on leisure-time activities. *J. Applied Psychology, 32*, 550-558.

Cohen, A. R. 1953. *The effects of individual self-esteem and situational structure on threat-oriented reactions to power.* Unpublished doctoral dissertation. Univ. Michigan.

Cohen, L. D. 1949. *Level of aspiration behavior in certain psychosomatic disorders.* Unpublished doctoral dissertation. Duke Univ.

Cole, L. 1936. *Psychology of adolescence.* Rinehart.

Cook, L. A. 1940. Education for group unity and action. *Review of Educational Research, 13*, 48-59.

————. 1941. *Community action and the school.* Ohio State Univ. Press.

————. 1943. A sociographic study of a 10th grade class. In H. H. Remmers (ed.). *Studies in Higher Education,* No. 48. Purdue Univ.

Coon, H. L., and H. B. Pepinsky. 1955. Contributing toward a language of emotional health. *Educational Leadership, 12*, 476-479.

Corey, S. M. 1936. Attitude differences between college classes. *J. Educational Psychology, 27*, 321-330.

Corsini, R. J., and K. K. Fassett. 1953. Intelligence and aging. *J. Genetic Psychology, 83*, 249-264.

Counts, G. S. 1925. Social status of occupations. *Scholastic Review, 33*, 16-27.

Cowdry, E. V. (ed.). 1942. *Problems of aging: biological and medical aspects.* Williams & Wilkins.

Crespi, L. P., and G. S. Shapleigh. 1946. The veteran: a myth. *Public Opinion Quarterly, 10*, 361-372.

Cronbach, L. J. 1949. *Essentials of psychological testing.* Harper.

————, and G. C. Gleser. 1953. Assessing similarity between profiles. *Psychological Bulletin, 50*, 456-473.

————, and P. E. Meehl. 1955. Construct validity in psychological tests. *Psychological Bulletin, 52*, 281-302.

Culbertson, F. M. 1955. *The modification of emotionally held attitudes through role playing.* Unpublished doctoral dissertation. Univ. Michigan.

Dale, E. 1955. Quotable. *Nation's Schools, 56*, 34.

Darley, J. G., and T. Hagenah. 1955. *Vocational interest measurement.* Univ. Minnesota Press.

Darrah, E. M. 1898. A study of children's ideals. *Popular Science Monthly, 53*, 88-98.

Davenport, C. B. 1926. Human metamorphosis. *American J. of Physical Anthropology, 9*, 205-233.

————. 1930. Adolescent spurt in growth. In *The laws of life.* Prague Czechoslovakia.

Davidson, P. E., and H. D. Anderson. 1937. *Occupational mobility in an American community.* Stanford Univ. Press.

Davis, A. 1944. Socialization and adolescent personality. *43rd Yearbook, National Society for the Study of Education*, Pt. 1, pp. 198-216. Univ. Chicago Press.

———, and J. Dollard. 1940. *Children of bondage*. American Council on Education.

———, and R. J. Havighurst. 1946. Social class and color differences in child-rearing. *American Sociological Review, 11*, 698-710.

———, — ———. 1947. *Father of the man*. Houghton Mifflin.

Davis, K. B. 1929. *Factors in the sex life of twenty-two hundred women*. Harper.

Dearborn, W. F., and J. W. M. Rothney. 1941. *Predicting the child's development*. Sci-Art.

Deeg, M. E., and D. G. Paterson. 1947. Changes in social status of occupations. *Occupations, 25*, 205-208.

Deese, J., and R. S. Lazarus. 1952. The effects of psychological stress upon perceptual-motor performance. *USAF, Human Resources Research Center, Research Bulletin*, No. 53-19.

DeHaas, J. H., and J. H. Posthuma. 1946. Nederlandsche kinderen in Japensche interneerings kampen op Java. *Nederlands Tijdschrift voor Geneesk., 90*, 1530-1541.

DeLisle, F. H. 1953. *A study of the relationship of the self-concept to adjustment in a selected group of college women*. Unpublished doctoral dissertation. Michigan State Univ.

Dennis, W. 1940. *The Hopi child*. Appleton-Century-Crofts.

Deutsch, M. 1949. An experimental study of the effects of cooperation and competition upon group process. *Human Relations, 2*, 199-231.

———. 1949a. A theory of cooperation and competition. *Human Relations, 2*, 129-152.

Deutsche, J. M. 1937. The development of children's concepts of causal relations. *Institute of Child Welfare Monograph Series*, No. 13. Univ. Minnesota Press.

DiDonato, P. 1939. *Christ in concrete*. Bobbs-Merrill.

Dimock, H. S. 1935. Research in adolescence. I. Pubescence and physical growth. *Child Development, 6*, 177-195.

———. 1936. New light on adolescent religion. *Religious Education, 31*, 273-279.

———. 1937. *Rediscovering the adolescent: a study of personality development in adolescent boys*. Association.

Diven, J. 1923. Peculiarities of disease in childhood. In I. A. Abt (ed.), *Pediatrics*, Vol. II. Saunders.

Dodge, A. F. 1937. Social dominance of clerical and sales persons as measured by the Bernreuter Personality Inventory. *J. Educational Psychology, 28*, 71-73.

Dorfman, R. I., W. W. Greulich, and C. I. Solomon. 1937. Excretion of androgenic and estrogenic substances in urine of children. *Endocrinology, 21*, 741-743.

Douvan, E. 1957a. *Character processes in adolescence*. Paper read at the American Psychological Association.

Douvan, E. 1957b. Independence and identity in adolescence. *Children, 4*, 186-190.

Dreizen, S., *et al*. 1950. The effect of milk supplements on the growth of children with nutritive failure I: height and weight changes. *Growth, 14*, 189-211.

Dressel, P. L. 1954. Interests—stable or unstable. *J. Educational Research, 48*, 95-102.

Driver, H. I. 1952. Small group discussion. *Personnel Guidance J., 31*, 173-175.

Dudycha, G. J. 1933. Religious beliefs of college students. *J. Applied Psychology, 17*, 585-603.

Durkin, D. 1959. Children's concepts of justice: a comparison with the Piaget data. *Child Development, 30*, 59-67.

Ebert, E., and K. Simmons. 1943. The Brush Foundation study of child growth and development I: psychometric tests. *Monographs of the Society for Research in Child Development*, Vol. 8, No. 2.

Edwards, A. L. 1954. *Edwards Personal Preference Schedule*. Psychological Corp.

Eggan, F. 1933. *Social organization of the Western Pueblos*. Unpublished master's thesis. Univ. Chicago.

Ehrman, W. W. 1959. *Premarital dating behavior*. Holt.

Eichler, R. M. 1951. Experimental stress and alleged Rorschach indices of anxiety. *J. Abnormal Social Psychology, 46*, 344-355.

Elias, G. 1944. *A study of certain methods of attitude measurement and related variables*. Unpublished master's thesis. Purdue Univ.

Ellis, H. 1936. *Psychology of Sex*. Random House.

Ellis, R. W. B. 1945. Growth and health of Belgium children during and after the German occupation, 1940-1944. *Archives Diseases Childhood, 20*, 97-109.

Emmerich, W. in press. A study of parental identification in young children. *Genetic Psychology Monographs*.

Engel, M. 1956. *The stability of the self-concept in adolescence*. Unpublished doctoral dissertation. George Peabody Coll.

Engle, E. T., and M. C. Shelesnyak. 1934. First menstruation and subsequent menstrual cycles of pubertal girls. *Human Biology, 6*, 431-453.

Erikson, E. H. 1954. Growth and crises in the healthy personality. In C. Kluckhohn and H. A. Murray (eds.). *Personality in nature, society, and culture*, pp. 185-225. Knopf.

Espenschade, A. 1940. Motor performance in adolescence. *Monographs of the Society for Research in Child Development*, Vol. 5, No. 1.

Exner, M. J. 1915. *Problems and principles of sex instruction*. American Social Hygiene Association.

Farnham, M. L. 1951. *The adolescent*. Harper.

Fenichel, O. 1945. *The psychoanalytic theory of neurosis*. Norton.

Festinger, L., K. Back, and S. Schachter. 1950. *Social pressures in informal groups: a study of human factors in housing*. Harper.

Fink, H. J. 1953. *The relationship of time perspective to age, institutionalization and activity*. Unpublished doctoral dissertation. Michigan State Univ.

Fisher, R. A. 1938. *Statistical methods for research workers*. 7th ed. Oliver and Boyd.

———. 1946. *Statistical methods for research workers*. 10th ed. Oliver and Boyd.

———, and F. Yates. 1938. *Statistical tables for biological, agricultural, and medical research*. Oliver and Boyd.

Fisher, S. 1949. An overview of trends in research dealing with personality rigidity. *J. Personality, 17*, 342-352.

Florey, C. D. 1936. Osseous development in the hand as an index of skeletal development. *Monographs of the Society for Research in Child Development*. Vol. 1, No. 3.

———. 1940. The intellectual growth of college students. *J. Educational Research, 33*, 443-451.

Foulds, G. A., and J. C. Raven. 1948. Normal changes in the mental abilities of adults as age advances. *J. Mental Science, 94*, 133-142.

Frank, J. 1954. *Your child's reading today*. Doubleday.

Frank, L. K. 1928. The management of tensions. *American J. Sociology, 33*, 706-722.

———. 1941. General considerations: certain problems of puberty and adolescence. *J. Pediatrics, 19*, 294-301.

Franzblau, A. N. 1934. Religious beliefs and character among Jewish adolescents. *Teachers College Contributions to Education*, No. 634. Teachers College, Columbia Univ.

Fraser, R., et al. 1947. The incidence of neurosis among factory workers. *Medical Research Council, Industrial Health Research Board*, Report No. 90. His Majesty's Stationery Office.

Freeman, F. N., and C. D. Flory. 1937. Growth in intellectual ability as measured by repeated tests. *Monographs of the Society for Research in Child Development*, Vol. 2, No. 2.

Frenkel-Brunswik, E. 1948. A study of prejudice in children. *Human Relations, 1*, 295-306.

Friend, J. G., and E. H. Haggard. 1948. Work adjustment in relation to family background. *Applied Psychology Monographs*, No. 16. Stanford Univ. Press.

Froehlich, C. P., no date. *Multiple counseling—a research proposal*. Univ. California, Berkeley.

Fromm-Reichmann, F. 1952. Some aspects of psychoanalytic psychotherapy with schizophrenics. In E. B. Brody and F. C. Redlich (eds.), *Psychotherapy with schizophrenics*, pp. 89-111. International Universities.

Gallup, G. 1955 (June). *Gallup Poll*. Audience Research, Inc.

Garrett, H. E. 1946. A developmental theory of intelligence. *American Psychologist, 1*, 372-378.

Gesell, A., and H. Thompson. 1934. *Infant behavior: its genesis and growth*. McGraw-Hill.

Ginzberg, E., *et al*. 1951. *Occupational choice*. Columbia Univ. Press.

Gitelson, M., and E. I. Falstein. 1942. Direct psychotherapy in adolescence (symposium). *American J. Orthopsychiatry, 12*, 1-35.

Gordon, G., and L. Siegel. 1957. The evolution of a program of individual psychotherapy for children with aggressive acting-out disorders in a new residential treatment unit. *American J. Orthopsychiatry, 27*, 59-68.

Gough, H. G. 1948. A sociological theory of psychopathy. *American J. Sociology, 53*, 359-366.

———. 1949. A short social status inventory. *J. Educational Psychology, 40*, 52-56.

———. 1951. *The California Psychological Inventory*. Univ. California (Berkeley) Press.

———. 1952. On making a good impression. *J. Educational Research, 46*, 33-42.

———. 1954. Systematic validation of a test for delinquency. *American Psychologist, 9*, 381.

———. 1955. *Reference handbook for the Gough Adjective Checklist*. (Mimeo.) Univ. California (Berkeley).

———. 1957. *Manual for the California Psychological Inventory*. Consulting Psychologists Press.

———, and D. R. Peterson. 1952. The identification and measurement of predispositional factors in crime and delinquency. *J. Consulting Psychology, 5*, 207-212.

Gould, H. N., and M. R. Gould. 1932. Age of first menstruation in mothers and daughters. *J. American Medical Association, 98*, 1349-1352.

Gould, J. 1950. Pupils' time spent at TV rivals hours in classes. *New York Times*, March 6.

Grace, A. G. 1932. The relationship of mental ability to occupational choices of adults. *Vocational Guidance Magazine, 10*, 354-358.

Graham, A. W., E. A. Hines, and R. P. Gage. 1945. Blood pressures in children between ages of 5 and 16 years. *American J. Diseases Children, 69*, 203-207.

Gray, H., and J. G. Ayres. 1931. *Growth in private school children with averages and variabilities based on 3,110 measurings on boys, and 1,473 on girls from the ages of one to nineteen years*. Univ. Chicago Press.

Gray, S. W., and R. Klaus. 1956. The assessment of parental identification. *Genetic Psychology Monographs, 54*, 87-109.

Greulich, W. W., and S. I. Pyle. 1950. *Radiographic atlas of skeletal development of the hand and wrist*. Stanford Univ. Press.

———, and H. Thomas. 1944. Growth and development of pelvis of individual girls before, during and after puberty. *Yale J. Biology and Medicine, 17*, 91-97.

———, *et al*. 1938. A handbook of methods for the study of adolescent children. *Monographs of the Society for Research in Child Development*, Vol. 3, No. 2.

———, *et al*. 1942. Somatic and endocrine studies of puberal and adolescent boys. *Monographs of the Society for Research in Child Development*, Vol. 7, No. 3.

Grigsby, O. J. 1932. An experimental study of the development of concepts of relationship in preschool children as evidenced by their expressive ability. *J. Experimental Education, 1*, 144-162.

Grunes, W. F. 1954. *The American high school student looks at the world of occupations*. Unpublished doctoral dissertation. Univ. California (Berkeley).

———. 1956. On perception of occupations. *Personal Guidance J., 34*, 276-279.

Guetzkow, H., and J. Brozek. 1946.

Intellectual functions with restricted intakes of B complex vitamins. *American J. Psychology, 59,* 358-381.

Guilford, J. P. 1955. Les dimensions de l'intellect. In H. Laugier (ed.), *L'Analyse factorielle et ses applications,* pp. 55-77. Centre National de la Recherche Scientifique, Paris.

———. 1956. The structure of intellect. *Psychological Bulletin, 53,* 267-293.

———. 1957. A revised structure of intellect. *Reports from Psychological Laboratory,* No. 19. Univ. Southern California.

———. 1958. New frontiers of testing in the discovery and development of human talent. In *Seventh Annual Western Regional Conference on Testing Problems,* pp. 20-32. Educational Testing Service.

———. 1958a. A system of the psychomotor abilities. *American J. Psychology, 71,* 164-174.

———. 1959. *Personality.* McGraw-Hill.

Hacker, F. J., and E. R. Geleerd. 1945. Freedom and authority in adolescence. *American J. Orthopsychiatry, 15,* 621-630.

Haire, M., and W. F. Grunes. 1950. Perceptual defenses: processes protecting an organized perception of another person. *Human Relations, 3,* 403-412.

Hall, G. S. 1904. *Adolescence, Vol. 1.* Appleton-Century-Crofts.

———. 1922. *Senescence, the last half of life.* Appleton-Century-Crofts.

Haly, T. C. 1936. Survey of the schools of Euclid, Ohio. Ohio State University Studies. *Bureau Educational Research Monographs,* No. 22, pp. 139-142.

Hamilton, G. 1947. *Psychotherapy in Child Guidance.* Columbia Univ.

Hamilton, G. V. 1929. *A research in marriage.* Boni.

Harrell, R. F. 1943. Effect of added thiamine on learning. *Teachers College Contributions to Education,* No. 877. Teachers College, Columbia Univ.

———. 1946. Mental response to added thiamine. *J. Nutrition, 31,* 283-298.

Harrower, M. R. 1934. Social status and the moral development of the child. *British J. Educational Psychology, 4,* 75-95.

———, and M. E. Steiner. 1945. *Large scale Rorschach techniques: a manual for the group Rorschach and multiple-choice test.* Thomas.

Hartshorne, H., and M. A. May. 1928. *Studies in deceit, 1.* Studies in the nature of character. Macmillan.

———, ———, and J. B. Maller. 1929. *Studies in service and self-control, 2.* Studies in the nature of character. Macmillan.

———, ———, and F. K. Shuttleworth. 1930. *Studies in the organization of character, 3.* Studies in the nature of character. Macmillan.

Hathaway, S. R. 1948. Some considerations relative to nondirective counseling as therapy. *J. Clinical Psychology, 4,* 226-231.

———, and J. C. McKinley. 1943. *The Minnesota Multiphasic Personality Inventory.* Univ. Minnesota Press.

Hattendorf, K. W. 1932. A study of the questions of young children concerning sex. *J. Sociol Psychology, 3,* 37-65.

Havighurst, R. J. 1952. *Developmental tasks and education.* Longmans, Green.

———. 1953. *Human development and education.* Longmans, Green.

Hazard, P. 1947. *Books, children and men.* Horn.

Hazlitt, V. 1930. Children's thinking. *British J. Psychology, 20,* 354-361.

Heath, C. W., et al. 1945. *What people are: a study of normal young men.* Harvard Univ. Press.

Hendry, C. E. 1944. Role practice brings the community into the classroom. *Sociometry, 7,* 196-204.

———, R. Lippitt, and A. Zander. 1944. Reality practice as educational method. *Psychodrama Monographs,* No. 9.

Hersey, R. B. 1932. *Workers' emotions in shop and home.* Univ. Pennsylvania Press.

Hill, D. S. 1930. Personification of ideals by urban children. *J. Social Psychology, 1,* 379-393.

Hofstaetter, P. R. 1954. The changing composition of "intelligence":

study of *t*-technique. *J. Genetic Psychology, 85,* 159-164.

Hollingshead, A. B. 1949. *Elmtown's youth.* Wiley.

Honzik, M. P., J. W. MacFarlane, and L. Allen. 1948. The stability of mental test performance between two and eighteen years. *J. Experimental Education, 17,* 309-324.

Hoppock, R. 1950. *Group guidance: principles, techniques, and evaluation.* McGraw-Hill.

————. 1935. *Job satisfaction.* Harper.

————, and S. Spiegler. 1938. Job satisfaction: researches of 1935-1937. *Occupations, 16,* 636-643.

Horney, K. 1945. *Our inner conflicts.* Norton.

Horowitz, R. 1939. Racial aspects of self-identification in nursery school children. *J. Psychology, 7,* 91-99.

Hubert, M. A. G., and J. H. Britton. 1957. Attitudes and practices of mothers rearing their children from birth to the age of two years. *J. Home Economics, 49,* 208-223.

Hughes, W. 1926. Sex experiences of boyhood. *Social Hygiene, 12,* 262-273.

Hull, C. L. 1933. *Hypnosis and suggestibility: an experimental approach.* Appleton-Century-Crofts.

Hull, R. L., and A. Kolstad. 1942. Morale on the job. In G. Watson (ed.), *Civilian morale, Second Yearbook of the Society for the Psychological Study of Social Issues,* pp. 349-364. Reynal.

Hunter, E. C. 1942. Changes in general attitudes of women students during four years in college. *J. Social Psychology, 16,* 243-257.

Hutt, M. L. 1947. A clinical study of "consecutive" and "adaptive" testing with the revised Stanford-Binet. *J. Consulting Psychology, 11,* 93-103.

Jack, L. M. 1934. An experimental study of ascendant behavior in preschool children. *University of Iowa Studies in Child Welfare,* Vol. 9, No. 3, pp. 9-65.

Jacob, P. E. 1957. *Changing values in college.* Hazen Foundation.

Janis, I., and B. T. King. 1954. The influence of role playing on opinion change. *J. Abnormal Social Psychology, 9,* 211-218.

Jenkins, D. H. 1948. Feedback and group self-evaluation. *J. Social Issues, 4,* 50-60.

Jennings, H. H. 1943. *Leadership and isolation: a study of personality in interpersonal relations.* Longmans, Green.

Jennings, J. 1929. Leisure reading of junior high school boys and girls. *Peabody J. Education, 6,* 343-347.

Jensen, K. 1932. Differential reactions in new-born infants. *Genetic Psychology Monographs, 12,* 391-479.

Jersild, A. T. 1952. *In search of self.* Teachers College, Columbia Univ.

Johnson, A. M., and S. A. Szurek. 1952. Genesis of antisocial acting out in children and adults. *Psychoanalytic Quarterly, 21,* 323-343.

Jolles, I. 1952. A study of the validity of some hypotheses for the qualitative interpretation of the H-T-P for children of elementary school age: I. Sexual identification. *J. Clinical Psychology, 8,* 113-118.

Jones, H. E. 1940. Observational methods in the study of individual development. *J. Consulting Psychology, 4,* 234-238.

————. 1943. *Development in adolescence: approaches to the study of the individual.* Appleton-Century-Crofts.

———— (ed.). 1944. *43rd Yearbook, National Society for the Study of Education,* Pt. 1. Univ. Chicago Press.

————. 1946. Skeletal maturing as related to strength. *Child Development, 17,* 173-185.

————. 1949a. Adolescence in our society. In Anniversary Papers of the Community Service Society of New York, *The Family in a Democratic Society,* pp. 70-82. Columbia Univ. Press.

————. 1949b. *Motor performance and growth.* Univ. California Press.

————. 1955. Age changes in adult mental abilities. In Gerontological Congress, *Old age in the modern world,* pp. 267-274. Livingstone, London.

————. 1955a. Trends in mental abilities. *American Psychologist, 10,* 405.

————, and H. S. Conrad. 1933. The growth and decline of intelligence: a study of a homogeneous group between the ages of ten and sixty. *Genetic Psychology Monographs, 13,* 223-294.

Jones, M. C. 1957. The later careers of boys who were early- or late-maturing. *Child Development, 28,* 113-128.

———. 1959. A study of socialization patterns at the high school level. *J. Genetic Psychology, 93,* 87-111.

———, and N. Bayley. 1950. Physical maturing among boys as related to behavior. *J. Educational Psychology, 41,* 129-148.

Jones, V. A. 1938. Attitudes of college students and changes in such attitudes during years in college. *J. Educational Psychology, 29,* 14-35.

Jonxis, J. H. P. 1946. Nutritional status of Dutch children in war time. *Nutrition Reviews, 4,* 97-99.

Jordaan, J. P. 1949. *Socioeconomic status and the measured vocational interests of mechanically gifted boys.* Unpublished doctors dissertation. Teachers College, Columbia Univ.

Josselyn, I. M. 1951. Psychological problems of the adolescent, Part II. *Social Casework, 32,* 250-254.

Katz, D., and F. H. Allport. 1931. *Students' Attitudes.* Craftsman.

———, and K. Braly. 1933. Racial stereotypes of college students. *J. Abnormal & Social Psychology, 28,* 280-290.

———, and H. Hyman. 1947. Industrial morale and public opinion methods. *International J. Opinion Attitude Research, 1,* 13-30.

Kelley, H. H. 1952. Two functions of reference groups. In G. E. Swanson, T. M. Newcomb, and E. L. Hartley (eds.), *Readings in social psychology,* pp. 410-414. Holt.

Kelly, E. L., and D. W. Fiske. 1951. *The prediction of performance in clinical psychology.* Univ. Minnesota Press.

Kendall, M. G. 1948. *Rank correlation methods.* Griffin, London.

Kennard, E. A. 1937. Hopi reactions to death. *American Anthropologist, 39,* 491-496.

Kettner, N. W., J. P. Guilford, and P. R. Christensen. 1956. A factor-analytic investigation of the factor called general reasoning. *Educational Psychological Measurement, 16,* 438-453.

Keys, A. J., *et al.* 1950. *The biology of human starvation, 2 Vols.* Univ. Minnesota Press.

Kik, M. C., and R. R. Williams. 1945. The nutritional improvement of white rice. *National Research Council,* Bulletin No. 112. Washington, D. C.

Kilpatrick, F. P. (ed.). 1952. *Human behavior from the transactional point of view.* Institute for Associated Research.

Kinsey, A. D., W. B. Pomeroy, and C. E. Martin. 1948. *Sexual behavior in the human male.* Saunders.

———, *et al.* 1953. *Sexual behavior in the human female.* Saunders.

Kitay, P. M. 1940. A comparison of the sexes in their attitudes and beliefs about women: a study of prestige groups. *Sociometry, 3,* 399-407.

Klopfer, B., and D. M. Kelley. 1942, 1946. *The Rorschach technique.* World.

Knight, R. P. 1946. Psychotherapy of an adolescent catatonic schizophrenia with mutism. *Psychiatry, 9,* 323-339.

Knobloch, H., and B. Pasamanick. 1953. Further observations on the behavioral development of Negro children. *J. Genetic Psychology, 83,* 137-159

Koch, H. L. 1944. A study of some factors conditioning the social distance between the sexes. *J. Social Psychology 20,* 79-107.

Komorovsky, M. 1946. Cultural contradictions and sex roles. *American J Sociology, 52,* 184-189.

———. 1950. Functional analysis c sex roles. *American Sociological Re view, 15,* 508-516.

———. 1953. *Women in the moder world.* Little, Brown.

Kounin, K. 1941. Experiment studies of rigidity. *Character Perso ality, 9,* 231-282.

Krechevsky, I. 1932. Hypotheses rats. *Psychological Review, 6,* 516-53

Kuder, G. F. 1946. *Revised manu for the Kuder Preference Record.* S ence Research Associates.

Kuhlen, R. G. 1941. Changes in at tudes of students and relations of t responses to judgments of associat *School Society, 53,* 514-519.

———. 1948. Age trends in adju ment during adult years as reflec in happiness ratings. *American P chologist, 3,* 307.

Lasoff, B. 1952. *A definition of gro vocational guidance.* B'nai Brith.

Lazar, M. 1937. Reading interests, activities and opportunities of bright, average, and dull children. *Teachers College Contributions to Education*, No. 707. Teachers College, Columbia Univ.

Lazarus, R. S., J. Deese, and S. F. Osler. 1952. The effects of psychological stress upon performance. *Psychological Bulletin, 49,* 293-317.

Lazowick, L. M. 1955. On the nature of identification. *J. Abnormal Social Psychology, 51,* 175-183.

Lease, E. J. 1953. Corn meal enrichment. *American Dietetic Association J., 29,* 866-872.

Lecky, P. 1945. *Self-consistence: a theory of personality.* Island Press.

Lee, E. A., and L. P. Thorpe. 1946. *Occupational Interest Inventory, Advanced Form A.* California Test Bureau.

Leighton, G., and P. L. McKinlay. 1930. *Milk consumption and the growth of school children.* H. M. Stationery Office, London.

LeShan, L. L. 1952. Time orientation and social class. *J. Abnormal Social Psychology, 47,* 589-592.

Lewin, K. 1947. Group decision and social change. In T. M. Newcomb and E. L. Hartley (eds.), *Readings in social psychology,* pp. 330-344. Holt.

———. 1948. *Resolving social conflicts.* Harper.

Lewis, D., and C. J. Burke. 1949. The use and misuse of the chi-square test. *Psychological Bulletin, 46,* 433-489.

Lewis, O. 1951. *Life in a Mexican village: Tepoztlan restudied.* Univ. Illinois Press.

Lewis, W. D. 1941. A comparative study of the personalities, interests and home backgrounds of gifted children of superior and inferior educational achievement. *J. Genetic Psychology, 59,* 207-218.

Likert, R. 1932. A technique for the measurement of attitudes. *Archives Psychology,* No. 140.

Linton, R. 1936. *The study of man.* Appleton-Century-Crofts.

———. 1945. *The cultural background of personality.* Appleton-Century-Crofts.

Lippitt, R. 1940. An experimental study of the effect of democratic and authoritarian group atmospheres. *University of Iowa Studies in Child Welfare,* Vol. 16, No. 3, pp. 43-195.

———. 1949. *Training in community relations.* Harper.

———, and R. R. White. 1947. An experimental study of leadership and group life. In T. M. Newcomb and E. L. Hartley (eds.), *Readings in Social Psychology,* pp. 315-330. Holt. Also in G. E. Swanson, T. M. Newcomb, and E. L. Hartley (eds.), 1952. *Readings in Social Psychology,* pp. 340-355. Holt.

Lord, F. M. 1955. Sampling fluctuations resulting from the sampling of test items. *Psychometrika, 20,* 1-22.

———. 1956. The measurement of growth. *Educational Psychological Measurement, 16,* 421-437.

Lorge, I. 1945. Schooling makes a difference. *Teachers College Record, 46,* 483-492.

Lowrie, S. H. 1948. Dating: a neglected field of study. *Marriage and Family Living, 10,* 90-91, 95.

Lynd, R. S., and H. M. Lynd. 1937. *Middletown in transition.* Harcourt, Brace.

Lyness, P. I. 1951. Patterns in the mass communication tastes of the young audience. *J. Educational Psychology, 42,* 449-467.

Lynn, D. B. 1955 (Jan.) . Development and validation of a structured doll play test for children. Quarterly Bulletin, Indiana Univ. Medical Center.

———. 1957a. *Father-absence and personality development of children in Norwegian sailor families.* Paper read at the Midwestern Psychological Association.

———. 1957b. Structured doll play test manual. (Mimeo.) Indiana Univ. Medical School.

———, and R. Lynn. In press. The structured doll play test as a projective technique for use with children. *J. Projective Techniques.*

———, and W. L. Sawrey. In press. The effects of father-absence on Norwegian boys and girls. *J. Abnormal Social Psychology.*

Maas, H. S. 1950. Personal and group factors in leaders' social perception. *J. Abnormal and Social Psychology, 45,* 56-63.

————. 1951a. Some social class differences in the family systems and group relations of pre- and early adolescents. *Child Development, 22,* 145-152.

————. 1951b. A study of group life in human development. *Human Development Bulletin, 4,* 11-15.

McArthur, C. 1954. Long-term validity of the Strong interest test in two subcultures. *J. Applied Psychology, 38,* 346-353.

McClelland, D. C., et al. 1953. *The achievement motive.* Appleton-Century-Crofts.

McConnell, T. R. 1934. Changes in scores on the psychological examination of the American Council on Education from the freshman to the senior year. *J. Educational Psychology, 25,* 66-69.

MacDonald, M., C. McGuire, and R. J. Havighurst. 1949. Leisure activities and the socioeconomic status of children. *American J. Sociology, 54,* 505-519.

McEntire, D. 1952. *Leisure activities of youth in Berkeley, California.* Univ. California (Berkeley).

MacFarlane, J. W., L. Allen, and M. P. Honzik. 1954. A developmental study of the behavior problems of normal children between 21 months and 14 years. *Univ. California Publications Child Development,* Vol. 2. Univ. California (Berkeley).

McGranahan, D. V., and M. Janowitz. 1946. Studies of German youth. *J. Abnormal & Social Psychology, 41,* 3-14.

McKeachie, W. J. 1951. Anxiety in the college classroom. *J. Educational Research, 45,* 153-160.

————, D. Pollie, and J. Speisman. 1955. Relieving anxiety in classroom examinations. *J. Abnormal Social Psychology, 50,* 93-98.

McKee, J. P., and A. C. Sherriffs. 1957. The differential evaluation of males and females. *J. Personality, 25,* 356-371.

MacLean, A. N. 1930. Idea of God in Protestant religious education. *Teachers College Contributions to Education,* No. 410. Teachers College, Columbia Univ.

MacLeod, R. B. 1947. The phenomenological approach to social psychology. *Psychological Review, 54,* 193-210.

McNemar, Q. 1955. *Psychological statistics.* Wiley.

Maier, N. R. F. 1949. *Frustration.* McGraw-Hill.

Main, T., and M. Nyswander. 1949. *Some observations on the third national training laboratory in group development.* (Mimeo.) National Training Laboratory in Group Development.

Martin, W. E. 1954. Learning theory and identification: III. The development of values in children. *J. Genetic Psychology, 84,* 211-217.

Matteson, R. W. 1955. Experience-interest changes in students. *J. Counseling Psychology, 2,* 113-121.

Mead, M. 1928. *Coming of age in Samoa.* Morrow.

————. 1930. Social organization of Manua. *Bernice P. Bishop Museum Bulletin,* No. 76. Honolulu.

————. 1949. *Male and female.* Morrow.

Meltzer, H. 1935. Children's attitudes toward parents. *American J. Orthopsychiatry, 5,* 244-265.

Menninger, K. 1940. Psychoanalytic psychiatry: theory and practice. *Bulletin Menninger Clinic, 4,* 105-123.

Meredith, H. V. 1935. The rhythm of physical growth: a study of eighteen anthropometric measurements on Iowa City white males ranging in age between birth and eighteen years. *University of Iowa Studies in Child Welfare,* Vol. 11, No. 3.

————. 1939. Length of head and neck, trunk and lower extremities of Iowa City children aged seven to seventeen years. *Child Development, 10,* 129-144.

————. 1939a. Stature of Massachusetts children of North European and Italian ancestry. *American J. Physical Anthropology, 24,* 301-346.

————. 1949. Height and weight private school children in three successive decades. *School Society, 7,* 72-73.

————, and B. Boynton. 1937. Transverse growth of extremities: analysis girth measurements for arm, forearm thigh and leg taken on Iowa City white children. *Human Biology, 9,* 366-403.

Merton, R. K. 1940. Bureaucratic structure and personality. *Social Forces, 18,* 560-568.

Michelson, N. 1944. Studies in the physical development of Negroes: IV, onset of puberty. *American J. Physical Anthropology, 2,* 151-166.

Miles, W. B. 1942. Psychological aspects of aging. In E. V. Cowdry (ed.). *Problems of aging,* pp. 756-784. Williams & Wilkins.

Miller, D. C., and W. H. Form. 1951. *Industrial sociology.* Harper.

Mills, C. A. 1937. Geographic and time variations in body growth and age at menarche. *Human Biology, 9,* 43-56.

———. 1939. *Medical climatology.* Thomas.

———, and C. Ogle. 1936. Physiologic sterility of adolescence. *Human Biology, 8,* 607-615.

Mooney, R. L. 1942. Surveying high school students' problems by means of a problem check list. *Educational Research Bulletin, 21,* 57-69.

Moore, C. R. 1944. Sex endocrines in development and prepuberal life. *J. Clinical Endocrinology, 4,* 135-141.

Moreno, J. L. 1934, 1953. *Who shall survive?* Beacon House.

Morris, W. W. 1955. Ontogenetic changes in adolescence reflected in the Drawing-Human-Figures Techniques. *American J. Orthopsychiatry, 25,* 720-728.

Mott, S. M. 1937. Mother-father preference. *Character Personality, 5,* 302-304.

Mowrer, O. H. 1950. *Learning theory and personality dynamics.* Ronald.

———. 1953. *Psychotherapy: theory and research.* Ronald.

Munroe, R. L. 1945. Prediction of the adjustment and academic performance of college students by a modification of the Rorschach method. *Applied Psychology Monographs,* No. 7.

Murphy, G. 1947. *Personality: a biosocial approach to origins and structures.* Harper.

———, L. B. Murphy, and T. M. Newcomb. 1937. *Experimental social psychology.* Harper.

Murphy, L. B. 1937. *Social behavior and child personality: an exploratory study of some roots of sympathy.* Columbia Univ. Press.

Murray, H. A. 1938. *Explorations in personality.* Oxford.

Nathanson, I. T., R. B. Miller, L. E. Towne, and J. C. Aub. 1941. Close correlation of androgen and creatinine excretion in normal children. *Endocrinology, 28,* 866-870.

———, L. E. Towne, and J. C. Aub. 1941. Normal excretion of sex hormones in childhood. *Endocrinology, 28,* 851-865.

Neugarten, B. L. 1946. Social class and friendship among school children. *American J. Sociology, 51,* 305-313.

New York Department of Educational Nursing. 1948. *Aging—guide for public health nurses.* Pamphlet No. 8. Community Service Society.

Newcomb, T. M. 1943. *Personality and social change.* Holt-Dryden.

Newman, F. B. 1946. The adolescent in social groups. *Applied Psychology Monograph,* No. 9.

Newstetter, W. I., M. J. Feldstein, and T. M. Newcomb. 1938. *Group adjustment: a study in experimental sociology.* Western Reserve Univ. Press.

Nisbet, J. D. 1956. *Intelligence test and re-test after twenty years' interval.* Paper read at British Psychological Society.

Nissenson, N. 1948. *An evaluation of some aspects of a group vocational guidance program.* Unpublished master's thesis. Northwestern Univ.

Norvell, G. W. 1950. *The reading interests of young people.* Heath.

Nutrition Reviews. 1946. Mental response to thiamine supplement. *Nutrition Reviews, 4,* 343-345.

———. 1948. Effect of added thiamine on growth, vision and learning ability of children. *Nutrition Reviews, 6,* 174-175.

———. 1949. Thiamine supplementation and learning capacity. *Nutrition Reviews, 7,* 220-222.

———. 1951. Gluatmic acid and mental function. *Nutrition Reviews, 9,* 113-117.

———. 1953. Effect of glutamic acid

on intelligence. *Nutrition Reviews, 11,* 201-204.

Office of Strategic Services. 1948. *Assessment of men.* Rinehart.

Olson, V. E. 1951. *Hostile aggression in organized youth groups.* Unpublished doctoral dissertation. Univ. Chicago.

Orr, J. B., and J. L. Gilks. 1931. Studies of nutrition: the physique and health of two African tribes. *Medical Research Council, Special Report Series,* No. 155. H. M. Stationery Office, London.

Otis, A. S. 1950. *Otis self-administering tests of mental ability.* World.

Owens, W. A. 1953. Age and mental abilities: a longitudinal study. *Genetic Psychology Monographs, 48,* 3-54.

Packard, V. 1957. *The hidden persuaders.* McKay.

Palermo, D. S., A. Castenada, and B. McCandless. 1956. The relationship of anxiety in children to performance in a complex learning task. *Child Development, 27,* 333-337.

Parsons, E. C. 1925. A Pueblo Indian journal. *Memoirs of the American Anthropological Association, 32,* 1-123.

———. 1939. *Pueblo Indian religion.* 2 vol. Univ. Chicago Press.

Paterson, D. G., and J. G. Darley. 1936. *Men, women, and jobs.* Univ. Minnesota Press.

Payne, D. E., and P. H. Mussen. 1956. Parent-child relations and father identification among adolescent boys. *J. Abnormal Social Psychology, 52,* 358-362.

Peck, M. W., and F. L. Wells. 1923. On the psycho-sexuality of college graduate men. *Mental Hygiene, 7,* 697-714.

Peres, H. 1947. An investigation of nondirective group therapy. *J. Consulting Psychology, 11,* 159-172.

Peters, C. C. 1950. The misuse of chi-square—a reply to Lewis and Burke. *Psychological Bulletin, 47,* 331-337.

———, and W. R. Van Voorhis. 1940. *Statistical procedures and their mathematical bases.* McGraw-Hill.

Phelan, M. I. 1936. *An empirical study of the ideals of adolescent boys and girls.* Catholic Univ. America.

Phipard, E. F., and H. K. Stiebling.

1951. Adequacy of American diets. In *Handbook of nutrition: a symposium prepared under the auspices of the Council on Foods and Nutrition of the American Medical Association.* Blakiston.

Piaget, J. 1932. *The moral judgment of the child.* Harcourt, Brace.

Pilcher, J. D., and H. Tuchewicz. 1943. Premenstrual state in young girls. *American J. Diseases Children, 65,* 296-304.

Pintner, R. 1931. *Intelligence testing.* Holt.

Pollak, O. 1948. Social adjustment in old age. *Social Science Research Council Bulletin,* No. 59.

Pope, B. 1953. Prestige values in contrasting socioeconomic groups of children. *Psychiatry, 16,* 381-385.

Proctor, W. M. 1937. A 13-year follow-up of high school pupils. *Occupations, 15,* 306-310.

Pryor, H. B. 1936. Certain physical and physiologic aspects of adolescent development in girls. *J. Pediatrics, 8,* 52-62.

Pruette, L., and D. Fryer. 1923. Affective factors in vocational maladjustment. *Mental Hygiene, 7,* 102-118.

Rabban, M. 1950. Sex-role identification in young children in two diverse social groups. *Genetic Psychology Monographs, 42,* 81-158.

Rall, M. E. 1947. Dependency and the adolescent. *J. Social Casework, 28,* 123-130.

Rapaport, D. 1945. *Diagnostic psychological testing.* Yearbook Pub. Co.

Redl, F., and D. Wineman. 1952. *Controls from within.* Free Press.

Remmers, H. H., and W. A. Kerr. 1945. Home environment in American cities. *American J. Sociology, 51,* 233-237.

———, and D. H. Radler. 1957. *The American teenager.* Bobbs-Merrill.

Reuter, E. B. 1937. The sociology of adolescence. *American J. Sociology, 43,* 414-427.

Rheingold, H. L. 1956. The modification of social responsiveness in institutional babies. *Monographs of the Society for Research in Child Development,* Vol. 21, Series No. 63.

Ribble, M. 1944. Infantile experience in relation to personality development. In J. McV. Hunt (ed.), *Personality and the behavior disorders*, Vol. 2, pp. 621-651. Ronald.

Richards, T. W., and V. L. Nelson. 1939. Abilities of infants during the first eighteen months. *J. Genetic Psychology*, *55*, 299-318.

Richardson, H., and H. Borow. 1952. Evaluation of a technique of group orientation for vocational counseling. *Educational Psychological Measurement*, *12*, 587-597.

Richey, H. G. 1937. The relation of accelerated, normal and retarded puberty to the height and weight of school children. *Monograph of the Society for Research in Child Development*, Vol. 2, No. 1.

Riesman, D. 1950. *The lonely crowd*. Yale Univ. Press.

Robertson, E. C., et al. 1947. The effect of added thiamine on growth, vision, and learning, using identical twins. *J. Nutrition*, *34*, 691-700.

Roethlisberger, F. J., and W. J. Dickson. 1939. *Management and the worker*. Harvard Univ. Press.

Rogers, C. R., and R. F. Dymond (eds.). 1954. *Psychotherapy and personality change*. Univ. Chicago Press.

Rokeach, M. 1949. Rigidity and ethnocentrism: a rejoinder. *J. Personality*, *17*, 467-474.

Rosen, J. N. 1953. *Direct analysis*. Grune and Stratton.

Rosenberg, P. P. 1951. *An experimental analysis of psychodrama*. Unpublished doctoral dissertation. Harvard Univ.

Sanford, N. 1955. The dynamics of identification. *Psychological Review*, *62*, 106-118.

———— (ed.). 1956. Personality development during the college years. *J. Social Issues*, Vol. 12, No. 4.

————, H. Webster, and M. Freeman. 1957. Impulse expression as a variable of personality. *Psychological Monographs*, Vol. 71, No. 11.

Sarason, S. B., and G. Mandler. 1952. Some correlates of test anxiety. *J. Abnormal Social Psychology*, *47*, 810-817.

Sarbin, T. R. No date. *Personality word card*. Univ. California (Berkeley) Press.

————. 1952. A preface to a psychological analysis of the self. *Psychological Review*, *59*, 11-22.

————. 1954. Role theory. In G. Lindzey (ed.), *Handbook of social psychology*, pp. 223-258. Addison-Wesley.

Scammon, R. E. 1930. The measurement of the body in childhood. In J. A. Harris, et al. *The measurement of man*, pp. 173-216. Univ. Minnesota Press.

Schachter, S. 1950. *Deviation, rejection, communication*. Unpublished doctoral dissertation. Univ. Michigan.

Schaefer, E. S., R. Q. Bell, and N. Bayley. 1956. Quantification of maternal behavior and consistency of mother-child interaction. *American Psychologist*, *11*, 404.

Scheussler, K. E., and D. R. Cressey, 1950. Personality characteristics of criminals. *American J. Sociology*, *55*, 476-484.

Schiller, B. 1934. Verbal, numerical and spatial abilities of young children. *Arch. Psychology*, No. 161.

Schneck, M. R. 1929. The measurement of verbal and numerical abilities. *Arch. Psychology*, No. 107.

Schneider, L., and S. Lysgaard. 1953. The deferred gratification pattern: a preliminary study. *American Sociological Review*, *18*, 142-149.

Schonfeld, W. A. 1943. Primary and secondary sexual characteristics: study of their development in males from birth through maturity, with biometric study of penis and testes. *American J. Diseases Children*, *65*, 535-549.

Schuessler, K. E., and D. R. Cressey. 1950. Personality characteristics of criminals. *American J. Sociology*, *55*, 476-484.

Searles, H. F. 1955. Dependency processes in the psychotherapy of schizophrenia. *J. American Psychoanalytic Association*, *3*, 19-66.

Sears, P. S. 1953. Child-rearing factors related to playing of sex-typed roles. *American Psychologist*, *8*, 431.

Sears, R. R., E. E. Maccoby, and H. Levin. 1957. *Patterns of child rearing*. Row, Peterson.

————, M. H. Pintler, and P. S. Sears.

1946. Effect of father separation on preschool children's doll-play aggression. *Child Development, 17,* 219-243.

Sebrell, W. H. 1953. Enrichment: a public health approach to better nutrition. *Public Health Reports, 68,* 741-746.

——. 1953a. Nutrition—past and future. *Nutrition Review, 11,* 65-68.

Seward, G. H. 1946. *Sex and the social order.* McGraw-Hill.

Shakow, D., and S. Rosenzweig. 1937. Play technique in schizophrenia and other psychoses. *American J. Orthopsychiatry, 7,* 36-47.

Shaw, C. R. 1929. *Delinquency areas.* Univ. Chicago Press.

——, and H. D. McKay. 1931. *Report on the causes of crime.* National Commission Law Observance and Enforcement, Washington, D. C.

Sheldon, W. H., and S. S. Stevens. 1942. *The varieties of temperament.* Harper.

——, ——, and W. D. Tucker. 1940. *The varieties of human physique.* Harper.

Sherman, M., and T. R. Henry. 1933. *Hollow folk.* Crowell.

Sherriffs, A. C., and R. F. Jarrett. 1953. Sex differences in attitudes about sex differences. *J. Psychology, 35,* 161-168.

——, and P. P. McKee. 1957. Qualitative aspects of beliefs about men and women. *J. Personality, 25,* 451-464.

Sheviakov, G. V., and J. Friedberg. 1939. *Evaluation of personal and social adjustment. Evaluation in the eight-year study.* Progressive Education Association.

Shock, N. W. 1942. Standard values for basal oxygen consumption in adolescents. *American J. Diseases Children, 64,* 19-32.

——. 1943. The effect of menarche on basal physiological functions in girls. *American J. Physiology, 139,* 288-292.

——. 1944. Basal blood pressure and pulse rate in adolescents. *American J. Diseases Children, 68,* 16-22.

——. 1944a. Physiological changes in adolescence. *43rd Yearbook, National Society for the Study of Education,* Pt. 1, pp. 56-79. Univ. Chicago Press.

——, and M. H. Soley. 1939. Average values for basal respiratory functions in adolescents and adults. *J. Nutrition, 18,* 143-153.

Shorr, E. 1941. Endocrine problems in adolescence. *J. Pediatrics, 19,* 327-346.

Shuttleworth, F. K. 1937. Sexual maturation and the physical growth of girls age six to nineteen. *Monographs of the Society for Research in Child Development,* Vol. 2, No. 5.

——. 1938. The adolescent period: a graphic and pictorial atlas. *Monographs of the Society for Research in Child Development,* Vol. 3, No. 3.

——. 1938a. Sexual maturation and the skeletal growth of girls age six to nineteen. *Monographs of the Society for Research in Child Development,* Vol. 3, No. 5.

——. 1939. The physical and mental growth of girls and boys, age six to nineteen, in relation to age at maximum growth. *Monographs of the Society for Research in Child Development,* Vol. 4, No. 3.

Simmons, K. 1944. The Brush Foundation study of child growth and development. II. Physical growth and development. *Monographs of the Society for Research in Child Development,* Vol. 9, No. 1.

——, and W. W. Greulich. 1943. Menarcheal age and height, weight and skeletal age of girls age 7 to 17 years. *J. Pediatrics, 22,* 518-548.

Simpson, M. 1935. *Parent preferences of young children.* Teachers College, Columbia Univ.

Sinha, A. K. P. 1950. *Experimental induction of anxiety by conditions of uncertainty.* Unpublished doctoral dissertation. Univ. Michigan.

Smith, D. A., and M. F. A. Woodruff. 1951. Deficiency diseases in Japanese prison camps. *Medical Research Council Special Report Series,* No. 274. H. M. Stationery Office, London.

Smith, S. 1939. Age and sex differences in children's opinion concerning sex differences. *J. Genetic Psychology, 54,* 17-25.

Smith, T. V., and E. C. Lindeman. 1959. *The American way of life.* New American Library.

Sopchak, A. 1952. Parental "identification" and "tendency toward disorders" as measured by the MMPI. *J. Abnormal Social Psychology, 47,* 159-165.

Sparling, E. 1933. Do college students choose vocations wisely? *Teachers College Contributions to Education,* No. 561. Teachers College, Columbia Univ.

Spencer, D. M. 1939. The composition of the family as a factor in the behavior of children in Fijian society. *Sociometry, 2,* 47-55.

Spies, T. D., and S. Dreizen. 1949. The effect of milk supplements on the growth of children with nutritive failure: Wetzel grid findings. *J. Pediatrics, 34,* 393-413.

———, et al. 1943. Emotional disturbances in persons with pellagra, beri-beri and associated deficiency states. In *The role of nutritional deficiencies in nervous and mental diseases,* Chap. XI. Williams & Wilkins.

———, et al. 1952. Detection and treatment of nutritive failure in children. *J. American Medical Association, 148,* 1376-1382.

———, et al. 1953. Skeletal maturational progress of children with chronic nutritive failure. *American J. Diseases Children, 85,* 1-12.

Spitz, R. A. 1945. An inquiry into the genesis of psychiatric conditions in early childhood, I. hospitalization. *Psychoanalytic Study Child, 1,* 53-74.

Steinbeck, J. 1939. *The grapes of wrath.* Viking.

Stephen, A. M. 1936. Hopi journal. E. C. Parsons (ed.). *Columbia University Contributions to Anthropology, 38,* 1-2.

Stephenson, W. 1935. Correlating persons instead of tests. *Character Personality, 6,* 17-24.

Stewart, N. 1947. AGCT scores of army personnel grouped by occupations. *Occupations, 26,* 5-41.

Stiebling, H. K. 1950. Trends in family food consumption. *J. American Dietetics Association, 26,* 596-598.

Stogdill, R. M. 1937. Survey of experiments of children's attitudes toward parents: 1894-1936. *J. Genetic Psychology, 51,* 293-303.

Stoke, S. M. 1950. An inquiry into the concept of identification. *J. Genetic Psychology, 76,* 163-189.

Stolz, H. R., and L. M. Stolz. 1944. Adolescent problems related to somatic variations. In *43rd Yearbook of the National Society for the Study of Education,* Pt. 1, pp. 81-99. Univ. Chicago Press.

Stone, C. H. 1948. Are vocational orientation courses worth their salt? *Educational Psychological Measurement, 8,* 161-181.

Stone, C. P., and R. G. Barker. 1937. Aspects of personality and intelligence in postmenarcheal and premenarcheal girls of the same chronological ages. *J. Comparative Psychology, 23,* 439-455.

———, and ———. 1937a. On relationship between menarcheal age and certain measurements of physique in girls of ages 9 to 16 years. *Human Biology, 9,* 1-28.

———, and ———. 1939. The attitudes and interests of premenarcheal and postmenarcheal girls. *J. Genetic Psychology, 54,* 27-71.

Strang, R. 1934. *Personnel development and guidance in college and secondary school.* Harper.

Strong, E. K. 1943. *Vocational interests of men and women.* Stanford Univ. Press.

Stuart, H. C. 1944. Studies of the nutritional state of children in unoccupied France in the fall of 1942. *J. Pediatrics, 25,* 257-264.

Super, D. 1949. *Appraising vocational fitness.* Harper.

———. 1951. Vocational adjustment: implementing a self-concept. *Occupations, 30,* 88-92.

Sutherland, E. H. 1951. Critique of Sheldon's "Varieties of delinquent youth." *American Sociological Review, 16,* 10-13.

Sweetland, A., and H. Quay. 1953. A note on the K scale of the Minnesota Multiphasic Personality Inventory. *J. Consulting Psychology, 17,* 314-316.

Symonds, P. M. 1931. *Diagnosing personality and conduct.* Appleton-Century-Crofts.

———. 1936a. Life interests and problems of adolescents. *School Review, 44,* 506-518.

———. 1936b. Sex differences in the life problems and interests of adolescents. *School Society, 43,* 751-752.

Talbot, F. B., E. B. Wilson, and J. Worcester. 1937. Basal metabolism of girls: physiologic background and application of standards. *American J. Diseases Children, 53,* 273-347.

Talbot, N. B., *et al.* 1943. Excretion of 17-ketosteroids by normal and by abnormal children. *American J. Diseases Children, 65,* 364-375.

Taylor, D. M. 1955. Changes in the self concept without psychotherapy. *J. Consulting Psychology, 19,* 205-209.

Taylor, J. A. 1953. A personality scale of manifest anxiety. *J. Abnormal Social Psychology, 48,* 285-290.

———. 1955. The Taylor Manifest Anxiety Scale and intelligence. *J. Abnormal Social Psychology, 52,* 347.

Teevan, R., and W. McKeachie. 1954. Effects on performance of different instructions in multiple-choice examinations. *Michigan Academy Science, Arts Letters, 39,* 467-475.

Terman, L. M. 1938. Psychological factors in marital happiness. McGraw-Hill.

———. 1954. Scientists and non-scientists in a group of 800 gifted men. *Psychological Monographs, 68,* No. 7.

———. 1955. Are scientists different? *Scientific American.* 1955 (Jan.), *192,* 25-29.

———. 1956. *Concept Mastery Test.* Psychological Corp.

———, and M. H. Oden. 1947. The gifted child grows up: twenty-five year follow-up of a superior group. Vol. IV, *Genetic studies of genius.* Stanford Univ. Press.

———, *et al.* 1938. *Psychological factors in marital happiness.* McGraw-Hill.

Thelan, H. 1950. Human dynamics in the classroom. *J. Social Issues, 6,* 30-55.

Thibaut, J. 1949. *The relationship of group cohesiveness to intergroup status differences.* Unpublished doctoral dissertation. Massachusetts Institute of Technology.

Thorndike, R. L. 1948. Growth of intelligence during adolescence. *J. Genetic Psychology, 72,* 11-15.

Thrasher, F. M. 1927. *The gang.* Univ. Chicago Press.

Thurstone, L. L. 1938. Primary mental abilities. *Psychometric Monograph,* No. 1. Univ. Chicago Press.

Tiller, P. O. 1958. Father absence and personality development of children in sailor families. *Nordisk Psykologi's Monogr.,* Ser. No. 9.

Titiev, M. 1937. A Hopi salt expedition. *American Anthropologist, 39,* 244-258.

———. 1944. *Old Oraibi: a study of the Hopi Indians of third mesa.* Cambridge.

Todd, T. W. 1930. The roentgenographic appraisement of skeletal differentiation. *Child Development, 1,* 298-310.

———. 1937. *Atlas of skeletal maturation: hand.* Mosby.

Tolman, E. C. 1943. Identification and the post-war world. *J. Abnormal Social Psychology, 38,* 141-148.

Tolor, A., and B. Tolor. 1955. Judgment of children's popularity from their human figure drawings. *J. Projective Techniques, 19,* 170-176.

Toronto, Canada. 1942. *A height and weight survey of Toronto elementary school children.* Ottawa.

Trémolières, J., *et al.* 1950. Contribution à l'étude du phénomène de croissance et de stature en France de 1940 à 1948. *Rec. Trav. Inst. Nat. d'Hyg., 4*(1).

Tryon, C. M. 1939. Evaluations of adolescent personality by adolescents. *Monographs of the Society for Research in Child Development,* Vol. 4, No. 4.

———. 1943. Evaluations of adolescent personality by adolescents. In R. G. Barker, J. S. Kounin, H. F. Wright (eds.), *Child behavior and development,* pp. 545-566. McGraw-Hill.

———. 1944. The adolescent peer culture. In *43rd Yearbook of the National Society for the Study of Education,* Pt. 1, pp. 217-239. Univ. Chicago Press.

———, and J. W. Lilienthal, III. 1950. Developmental tasks: 1. The concept and its importance. 2. Discussion of specific tasks and implications. In C. Tryon (ed.), *Fostering mental health in our schools*, pp. 77-128, 1950 Year-book of Association of Supervision and Curriculum Development. National Education Association.

Tuddenham, R. D. 1952. Studies in reputation. *Psychological Monographs*, Vol. 66, No. 1.

Tyler, L. E. 1951. The relationship of interests to abilities and reputation among first-grade children. *Educational Psychological Measurement, 11*, 255-264.

Ullman, C. A. 1952. Identification of maladjusted school children. *U. S. Public Health Monographs*, No. 7.

U. S. Bureau Census. 1950. *Alphabetical index of occupations and industries.*

U. S. Bureau Employment Security. 1949. *Dictionary of occupational titles.*

Valaoras, V. G. 1946. Some effects of famine on the population of Greece. *Milbank Memorial Fund Quarterly, 24*, 215-234.

Wallin, P. 1950. Cultural contradictions and sex roles: a repeat study. *American Sociological Review, 15*, 288-293.

Warner, W. L. 1952. *Structure of American life*. Edinburgh Press.

———, and P. S. Lunt. 1941. *The social life of a modern community*. Yale Univ. Press.

———, M. Meeker, and K. Eells. 1949. *Social class in America: a manual of procedure for the measurement of social status*. Science Research Associates.

Watson, G., and J. M. Seidman. 1941. Dissatisfactions in work. *J. Social Psychology, 13*, 183-186.

Watson, J. B., and M. Pijoan. 1943. *A casual inquiry into Hopi foodways.* (Unpublished ms.) U.S. Office of Indian Affairs.

Webster, H. 1957. *Research manual for VC Attitude Inventory and VC Figure Preference Test*. Vassar College.

Wechsler, D. 1944. *The measurement of adult intelligence*. Williams & Wilkins.

———. 1956. Recent changes in rate of decline of intelligence test scores of the American adult. In *Primer Congreso Panamericano de Gerontologia.*

Ciudad Universitaria, Mexico.

Weider, A., and P. A. Noller. 1950. Objective studies of children's drawings of human figures. I. Sex awareness and socioeconomic level. *J. Clinical Psychology, 6*, 319-325.

———, ———. 1953. Objective studies of children's drawings of human figures. II. Sex, age, intelligence. *J. Clinical Psychology, 9*, 20-23.

Wells, F. L. 1944. A research focused upon the normal personality: a note. *Character and Personality, 12*, 299-301.

Weltfish, G. 1945. Racial and religious prejudices in everyday living. *J. Social Issues*, Vol. 1, No. 1.

West, E. D. 1936. Stage of ossification as a measure of growth and its relation to intelligence-test score. *Harvard Teachers Record, 6*, 162-168.

Wexler, M. 1951. The structural problems in schizophrenia: therapeutic implications. *International J. Psycho-Analysis, 32*, 157-166.

Wheeler, L. R. 1942. A comparative study of the intelligence of east Tennessee mountain children. *J. Educational Psychology, 33*, 321-333.

Wherry, R. J., R. Perloff, and J. T. Campbell. 1951. An empirical verification of the Wherry-Gaylord iterative factor analysis procedure. *Psychometrika, 16*, 67-74.

White, R. W. 1943. History of an adolescent crisis in the development of the ego-structure. *Character and Personality, 11*, 183-208.

———. 1943a. Three years of ego-reconstruction. *Character and Personality, 11*, 339-360.

———. 1952. *Lives in progress: a study of the natural growth of personality*. Holt-Dryden.

White House Conference on Child Health and Protection, 1932. *Growth and development of the child*. 4 vols. Century.

Whyte, W. F. 1943. *Street corner society: the social structure of an Italian slum*. Univ. Chicago Press.

Wilder, R. M., and R. R. Williams. 1944. Enrichment of flour and bread: a history of the movement. *National Research Council*, Bulletin No. 110. Washington, D. C.

Williamson, E. G. 1950. *Counseling adolescents.* McGraw-Hill.

Wilson, I. 1949. The use of a sentence completion test in differentiating between well-adjusted and maladjusted secondary school pupils. *J. Consulting Psychology, 13,* 400-403.

Winnicott, D. W. 1949. Hate in the countertransference. *International J. Psycho-Analysis, 30,* 69-74.

Wittenborn, J. R., *et al.* 1956. A study of adoptive children: III. relationships between some aspects of development and some aspects of environment for adoptive children. *Psychological Monographs,* Vol. 70, No. 3.

Woellner, M. H. B. 1949. Children's voluntary reading as an expression of individuality. *Teachers College Contributions to Education, No. 944.* Teachers College, Columbia Univ.

Young, G. 1950. Operation video. Clearing House, *24,* 156-157.

Zander, A. 1947. Within the bonds of freedom. *Childhood Education, 24,* 23-26.

———. 1950. Resistance to change: its analysis and prevention. *Advanced Management, 15,* 9-12.

———, and R. Lippitt. 1944. Reality practice as educational method. *Sociometry, 7,* 129-151.

Zeleny, L. D. 1939. Sociometry of morale. *American Sociological Review, 4,* 799-808.

Index